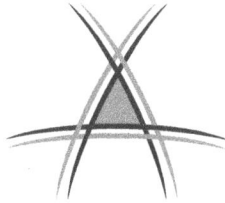

ASCENT®
CENTER FOR TECHNICAL KNOWLEDGE

I0131689

Autodesk® 3ds Max® 2017 (R1) Fundamentals

Student Guide
1st Edition

AUTODESK.
Authorized Publisher

CONTINUING EDUCATION

AIA®

ASCENT - Center for Technical Knowledge®
Autodesk® 3ds Max® 2017 (R1)
Fundamentals
1st Edition

Prepared and produced by:

ASCENT Center for Technical Knowledge
630 Peter Jefferson Parkway, Suite 175
Charlottesville, VA 22911

866-527-2368
www.ASCENTed.com

Lead Contributor: Renu Muthoo

ASCENT - Center for Technical Knowledge is a division of Rand Worldwide, Inc., providing custom developed knowledge products and services for leading engineering software applications. ASCENT is focused on specializing in the creation of education programs that incorporate the best of classroom learning and technology-based training offerings.

We welcome any comments you may have regarding this student guide, or any of our products. To contact us please email: feedback@ASCENTed.com.

AS-3DS1701-FND1NU-SG   //   IS-3DS1701-FND1NU-SG

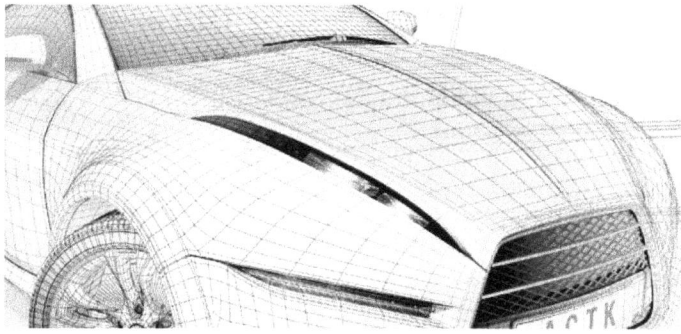

Contents

Preface

The *Autodesk® 3ds Max® 2017 (R1): Fundamentals* student guide provides a thorough introduction to the Autodesk 3ds Max 2017 (R1) software that will help new users make the most of this sophisticated application, as well as broaden the horizons of existing, self-taught users.

The practices in this student guide are primarily geared towards real-world tasks encountered by users of the Autodesk 3ds Max software in the Architecture, Interior Design, and Civil Engineering industries.

Advanced topics, such as character animation and rigging, are not covered in this student guide.

Topics Covered

- Introduction to Autodesk 3ds Max 2017 (R1)

- Autodesk 3ds Max Interface and Workflow

- Assembling Files by importing, linking, or merging

- 3D Modeling with Primitives and 2D Objects

- Using Modifiers to create and modify 3D objects

- Materials and Maps

- Autodesk 3ds Max Lighting

- Lighting and Rendering with mental ray

- Rendering and Cameras

- Animation for Visualization

Note on Software Setup

This student guide assumes a standard installation of the software using the default preferences during installation. Lectures and practices use the standard software templates and default options for the Content Libraries.

Students and Educators can Access Free Autodesk Software and Resources

Autodesk challenges you to get started with free educational licenses for professional software and creativity apps used by millions of architects, engineers, designers, and hobbyists today. Bring Autodesk software into your classroom, studio, or workshop to learn, teach, and explore real-world design challenges the way professionals do.

Get started today - register at the Autodesk Education Community and download one of the many Autodesk software applications available.

Visit www.autodesk.com/joinedu/

Note: Free products are subject to the terms and conditions of the end-user license and services agreement that accompanies the software. The software is for personal use for education purposes and is not intended for classroom or lab use.

Lead Contributor: Renu Muthoo

Renu uses her instructional design training to develop courseware for AutoCAD and AutoCAD vertical products, Autodesk 3ds Max, Autodesk Showcase and various other Autodesk software products. She has worked with Autodesk products for the past 20 years with a main focus on design visualization software.

Renu holds a bachelor's degree in Computer Engineering and started her career as a Instructional Designer/Author where she co-authored a number of Autodesk 3ds Max and AutoCAD books, some of which were translated into other languages for a wide audience reach. In her next role as a Technical Specialist at a 3D visualization company, Renu used 3ds Max in real-world scenarios on a daily basis. There, she developed customized 3D web planner solutions to create specialized 3D models with photorealistic texturing and lighting to produce high quality renderings.

Renu Muthoo has been the Lead Contributor for *Autodesk 3ds Max: Fundamentals* since 2010.

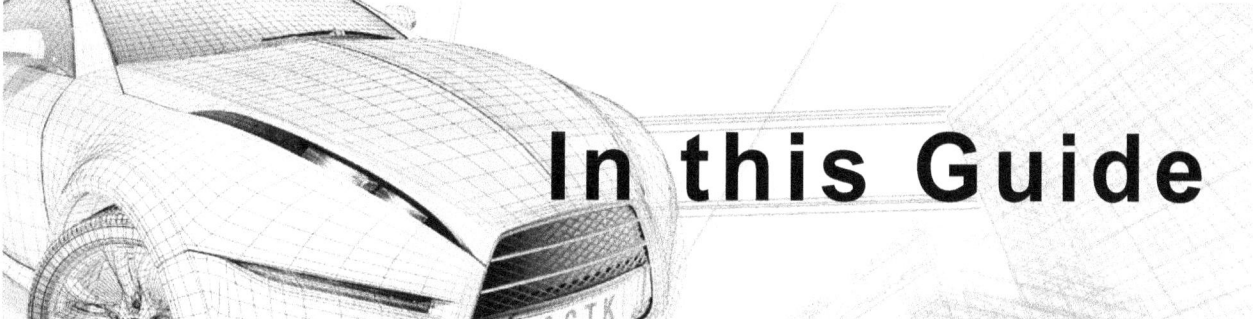

In this Guide

The following images highlight some of the features that can be found in this Student Guide.

Practice Files

To download the practice files for this student guide, use the following steps:

1. Type the URL shown below into the address bar of your Internet browser. The URL must be typed exactly as shown. If you are using an ASCENT ebook, you can click on the link to download the file.

   http://www.ASCENTed.com/getfile?id=xxxxxxxx — Address bar

2. Press <Enter> to download the ZIP file that contains the Practice Files.

3. Once the download is complete, unzip the file to a local folder. The unzipped file contains an EXE file.

4. Double-click on the EXE file and follow the instructions to automatically install the Practice Files on the C:\ drive of your computer.

   Do not change the location in which the Practice Files folder is installed. Doing so can cause errors when completing the practices in this student guide.

   http://www.ASCENTed.com/getfile?id=xxxxxxxx

Stay Informed!
Interested in receiving information about upcoming promotional offers, educational events, invitations to complimentary webcasts, and discounts? If so, please visit www.ASCENTed.com/updates/

Help us improve our product by completing the following survey: www.ASCENTed.com/feedback
You can also contact us at: feedback@ASCENTed.com

FTP link for practice files

Practice Files

The Practice Files page tells you how to download and install the practice files that are provided with this student guide.

Chapter 1

Getting Started

In this chapter you learn how to start the AutoCAD® software, become familiar with the basic layout of the AutoCAD screen, how to access commands, use your pointing device, and understand the AutoCAD Cartesian workspace. You also learn how to open an existing drawing, view a drawing by zooming and panning, and save your work in the AutoCAD software.

Learning Objectives in this Chapter

- Launch the AutoCAD software and complete a basic initial setup of the drawing environment.
- Identify the basic layout and features of AutoCAD interface including the Ribbon, Drawing Window, and Application Menu.
- Locate commands and launch them using the Ribbon, shortcut menus, Application Menu, and Quick Access Toolbar.
- Locate points in the AutoCAD Cartesian workspace.
- Open and close existing drawings and navigate to file locations.
- Move around a drawing using the mouse, the **Zoom** and **Pan** commands, and the Navigation Bar.
- Save drawings in various formats and set the automatic save options using the **Save** commands.

Learning Objectives for the chapter

Chapters

Each chapter begins with a brief introduction and a list of the chapter's Learning Objectives.

Instructional Content

Each chapter is split into a series of sections of instructional content on specific topics. These lectures include the descriptions, step-by-step procedures, figures, hints, and information you need to achieve the chapter's Learning Objectives.

Side notes

Side notes are hints or additional information for the current topic.

Practice Objectives

Practices

Practices enable you to use the software to perform a hands-on review of a topic.

Some practices require you to use prepared practice files, which can be downloaded from the link found on the Practice Files page.

Chapter Review Questions

Chapter review questions, located at the end of each chapter, enable you to review the key concepts and learning objectives of the chapter.

Command Summary

The Command Summary is located at the end of each chapter. It contains a list of the software commands that are used throughout the chapter, and provides information on where the command is found in the software.

Autodesk Certification Exam Appendix

This appendix includes a list of the topics and objectives for the Autodesk Certification exams, and the chapter and section in which the relevant content can be found.

Icons in this Student Guide

The following icons are used to help you quickly and easily find helpful information.

New in **2017**	Indicates items that are new in the Autodesk 3ds Max 2017 (R1) software.
Enhanced in **2017**	Indicates items that have been enhanced in the Autodesk 3ds Max 2017 (R1) software.

Practice Files

To download the practice files for this student guide, use the following steps:

1. Type the URL shown below into the address bar of your Internet browser. The URL must be typed **exactly as shown**. If you are using an ASCENT ebook, you can click on the link to download the file.

Address bar

http://www.ASCENTed.com/getfile?id=buteo

File   Edit   View   Favorites   Tools   Help

2. Press <Enter> to download the .ZIP file that contains the Practice Files.

3. Once the download is complete, unzip the file to a local folder. The unzipped file contains an .EXE file.

4. Double-click on the .EXE file and follow the instructions to automatically install the Practice Files on the C:\ drive of your computer.

   Do not change the location in which the Practice Files folder is installed. Doing so can cause errors when completing the practices in this student guide.

http://www.ASCENTed.com/getfile?id=buteo

Stay Informed!

Interested in receiving information about upcoming promotional offers, educational events, invitations to complimentary webcasts, and discounts? If so, please visit:

www.ASCENTed.com/updates/

Help us improve our product by completing the following survey:

www.ASCENTed.com/feedback

You can also contact us at: *feedback@ASCENTed.com*

Introduction to Autodesk 3ds Max

The Autodesk® 3ds Max® software is a modeling, rendering, and animation package used for the visualization and presentation of scenes. Projects can be created and modeled in the software or files from other software packages can be linked/imported for use in the software. A solid understanding of the interface, configuration settings, and the workflow used to create, render, and animate models enable you to visualize your models prior to building the final design.

Learning Objectives in this Chapter

- Identify the various data sources that can be imported into and then output from the Autodesk 3ds Max software.
- Understand the common workflow process to plan your visualization projects.
- Understand the various components of the interface.
- Set the preferences for the scene.
- Set the project folder to organize all of the files in the project.
- Set the path locations of reusable data files and reconfigurable items.
- Identify the display drivers available with the software.
- Identify the viewport display labels and the various options available in them.

1.1 Overview

The Autodesk® 3ds Max® software is a modeling, rendering, and animation package used for design visualization. It can be used to create high-quality 3D models, single-frame still renderings of virtually any size (including large-format presentation graphics), and desktop animations.

Input Into Autodesk 3ds Max

You can create geometry directly in the 3ds Max software or import it from multiple data sources, including the following:

- **AutoCAD® drawing files (.DWG, .DXF):** Including objects created in AutoCAD vertical applications, such as the AutoCAD® Architecture and AutoCAD® Civil 3D® software.

- **Autodesk® Revit® Architecture designs:** Linked into the Autodesk 3ds Max software using .RVT files or the exported .FBX or .DWG files. The Autodesk® Revit® Structure and Autodesk® Revit® MEP software can also be imported using .DWG.

- **AutoCAD® Civil 3D® (VSP3D):** Using **Autodesk Civil View**, you can import files from various civil design programs.

- **Autodesk® Inventor® files (.IPT, .IAM):** The Autodesk Inventor software must be installed on the same machine as the Autodesk 3ds Max software to import these files.

- **3D Studio Mesh format (.3DS):** A common data format used when transferring between 3D applications.

- Autodesk® Alias® .Wire files and the Autodesk® Showcase® .APF (Autodesk Packet File).

- LandXML and DEM data files.

- **Adobe Illustrator (.AI):** The Autodesk 3ds Max software only supports the Adobe Illustrator 88 software.

Vector Data

The input data formats are considered to be vector data. Graphics displayed from vector data formats are defined by point locations and mathematical formulas. Since their data is defined mathematically, vector graphics can be redrawn or regenerated at different scales or from different 3D viewpoints. The Autodesk 3ds Max software file format (.MAX file) is also a vector data file.

Output from Autodesk 3ds Max

Autodesk 3ds Max software stores its data in vector-based .MAX files, used to generate raster images as final products. These images, called *renderings*, can be configured as simple illustrations or fully realized photorealistic images. The most common Autodesk 3ds Max animations are created by combining a series of individually-rendered raster images into a desktop animation file (e.g., Windows .AVI or QuickTime .MOV).

Raster Data

Raster graphics consist of a grid of colored points called pixels Pixels are viewed at a resolution at which they cannot be identified individually, and instead are permitted to present a unified image, as shown in Figure 1–1.

Figure 1–1

The Autodesk 3ds Max software is also used to create raster images or raster based animations (Autodesk 3ds Max renderings). Raster image renderings must be recreated (re-rendered) if the point-of-view is animated or otherwise changed. Common raster file formats include .JPEG, Windows bitmap (.BMP), and .TIFF files. They can also be used as input into the Autodesk 3ds Max software to supplement the vector geometry as follows:

- Scanned or digital photographs of a proposed construction site can be used as a background image.

- Images that illustrate material texture, such as wall coverings, wood grain, or a scratched metal surface.

- Image files created in other computer graphic applications can be used as signs, posters, or company logos.

1.2 Visualization Workflow

Each visualization project can be very different from the next, but most follow a common general workflow. A suggested approach to plan your visualization project is as follows.

1. Setting Goals and Expectations

Every project should start with a clear understanding of the deliverables and expectations.

- Determine viewpoints, animation paths, lighting conditions, etc. before modeling.
- Sketch a mock-up storyboard to agree on the content and scope of an animation.
- Incorporate resolution time in your time estimates. Simple oversights and design problems are often found during the visualization process.

2. Scene Creation and Modeling

The next step is to gather data together into scenes (.MAX files).

- Create a project folder to store all of your data and source material, such as site photos, textures, drawings, scans, in the appropriate locations.
- Import or link 2D or 3D data into one or more scene files, when it is available from other design applications.
- Merge together or externally reference scene files when a project requires multiple scene files.
- Add modeled geometry at this stage. The **Graphite Modeling** tools have many new features for creating new geometry on the surfaces of imported files.

3. Material Design

Materials define how surfaces display and how light interacts with them. Often the next step is to configure the surface characteristics using the Material Editor. It is recommended that you consider the lighting and rendering as materials might need to be coordinated with renderers and lights.

- Detail materials to help simplify the geometry. For example, you do not need to model the grout along a brick wall. Material definitions, such as bump mapping, can add the appearance of depth.

- Fine-tune the material properties, as required, to make them realistic.
- Lighting and materials are often adjusted together, but it can be useful to have a first draft of your materials completed before adding lights.

4. Lighting Design

For realistic results, the 3D models need light sources to illuminate the objects.

- There are different approaches to lighting scenes in the Autodesk 3ds Max software, some are more straightforward and some are more technical.
- Most scenes might require lighting adjustments.

5. Configuring Rendered Views and Animations

Once your model, materials, and lights have been initially configured, you can focus on the final output.

- The length of any animations, their frame rate, and the required time display should be assigned first.
- Camera objects can then be positioned to set up both single-frame still renderings and animations.
- Objects are animated and animated details such as clouds blowing through the sky, pedestrians on the sidewalks, etc. can then be added.
- The rendering options should be configured at this stage.

6. Testing and Final Adjustments

Test the rendering and adjust the model, materials, and lights to achieve the required results. Note that computer processing of the renderings can be very time-consuming, especially for long animations or large still renderings.

7. Post Production

You can add details to your final renderings outside the Autodesk 3ds Max software using third-party image editing programs (Adobe Photoshop or Adobe AfterEffects) and other video post-production software (Autodesk Combustion). Usually, the finished animation segments are mixed with actual video footage, voice-over narration, background sound effects, and music in a different software (such as Apple's Final Cut Pro, or another video editing and assembly tool).

1.3 The Autodesk 3ds Max Interface

To launch the Autodesk 3ds Max software, use one of the following methods:

- Double-click on ▣ (3ds Max) on your desktop.

- Click **Start** in the Windows Task Bar and select **All Programs>Autodesk>Autodesk 3ds Max 2017> 3ds Max 2017**.

Welcome Screen

If you are opening the software for the first time, a Welcome screen displays, as shown in Figure 1–2. It contains three separate panels: Learn, Start, and Extend. This is a starting point for users as it provides access to help, information for learning the software and new and enhanced features, options for starting a new scene or opening a file. You can do the following:

- Clear the **Show this Welcome Screen at startup** option to prevent the Welcome Screen from displaying when you launch the Autodesk 3ds Max software.

- Close the dialog box by clicking ▣.

- Open the Welcome Screen any time during the current session by selecting **Welcome Screen** in the Help menu.

Learn

The Learn Panel (shown in Figure 1–2) contains:

- Startup videos, sample scenes, and online resources that help you to learn about the new features in the current release of the software.

- Learning movies on the Autodesk 3ds Max YouTube Channel, and additional resources on the web.

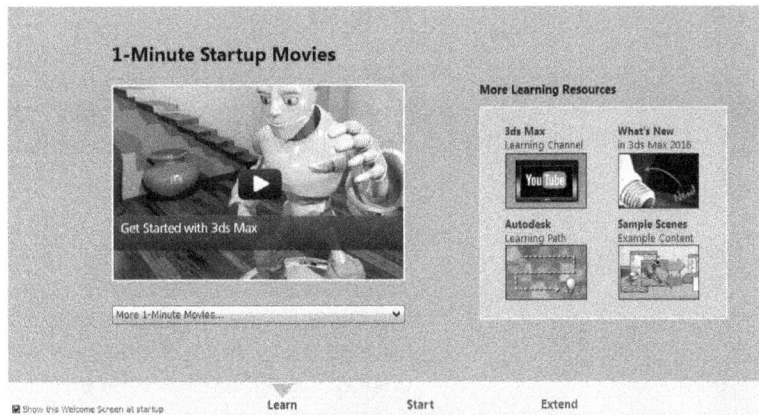

Figure 1–2

Start

The Start Panel contains:

*   Options for opening an already saved .MAX file (**Browse**) or opening a file from the list of recently opened files.

*   Five standard start-up templates (shown in Figure 1–3) are available for creating a new empty scene. These templates contain built-in settings (rendering, environment, lighting, units, etc.) optimum for that particular type of scene enabling you to quickly and easily create a new scene. Select a template and click **New Using Selected Template** to open a scene from a template.

*   The **Open Template Manager** options enable you to create new templates or modify the existing ones.

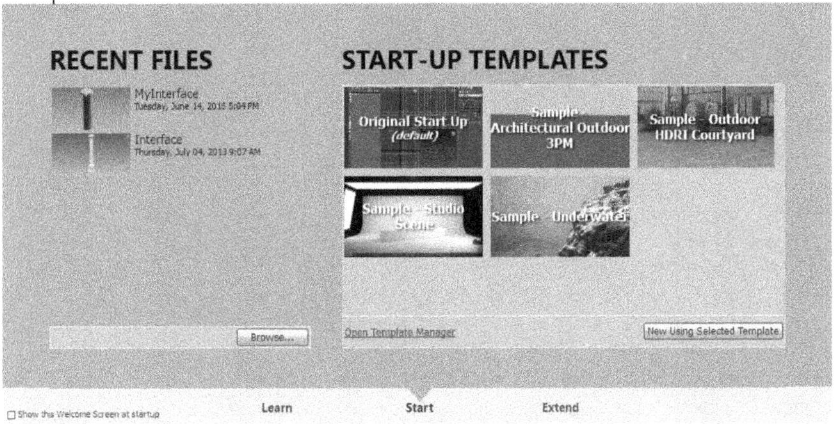

Figure 1–3

Extend

This page provides links to the Autodesk Exchange Apps center and Autodesk 360 to access online services. It enables you to connect to the online community of artists and forums such as Scriptspot and Area.

Interface

*For printing purposes, the UI color scheme used in the figures is **ame-light** (Menu bar: Customize>Custom UI and Defaults Switcher> UI schemes), and the Theme has been set to **Light** in the Customize User Interface dialog box>Colors tab.*

The Autodesk 3ds Max software consists of a main modeling window, called the *viewport*, which is surrounded by interface tools and panels. Figure 1–4 shows an example of a model created using various modifiers in the Command Panel, to display the different interface features.

- By default, the scene is set as one viewport/four equal viewports that display the model at different viewing angles.

- You can toggle between the four viewport displays or one maximized viewport (as shown in Figure 1–4), by clicking

  ![icon] (Maximize Viewport) or pressing <Alt>+<W>.

- The active viewport displays a yellow border. Clicking in empty space in a viewport makes it active.

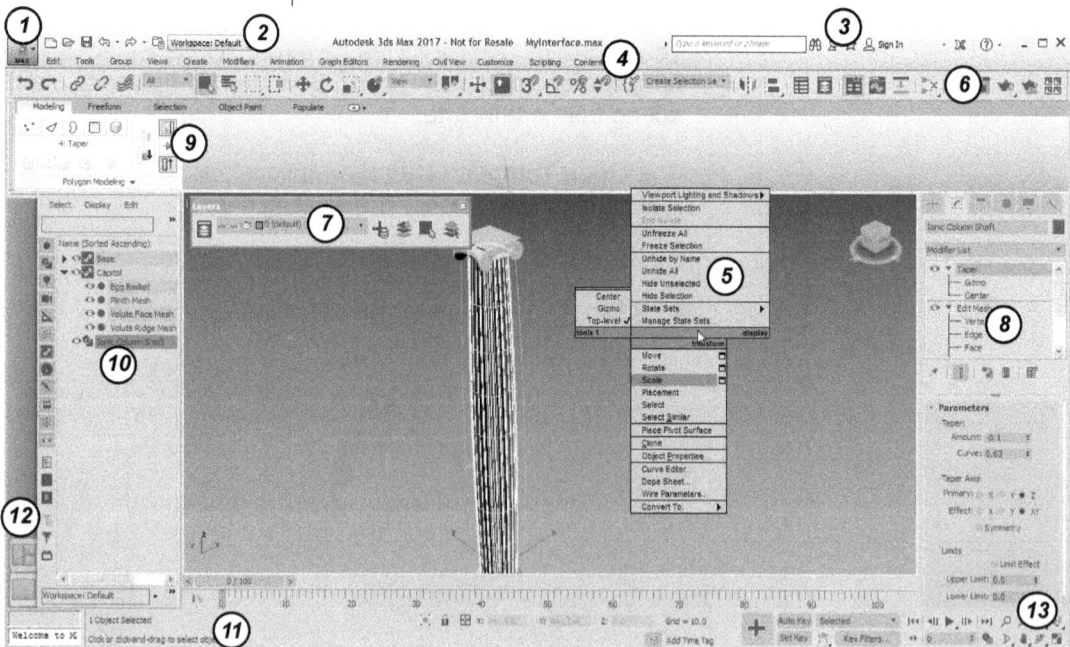

Figure 1–4

1. Application Menu

(Application Menu) provides access to the file commands, settings, and recently opened files, as shown in Figure 1–5. The Recent Documents can be sorted by date and pinned in the stack to prevent them from scrolling. Using [icon], the display can be customized to display them as icons or viewport thumbnails as shown in Figure 1–5.

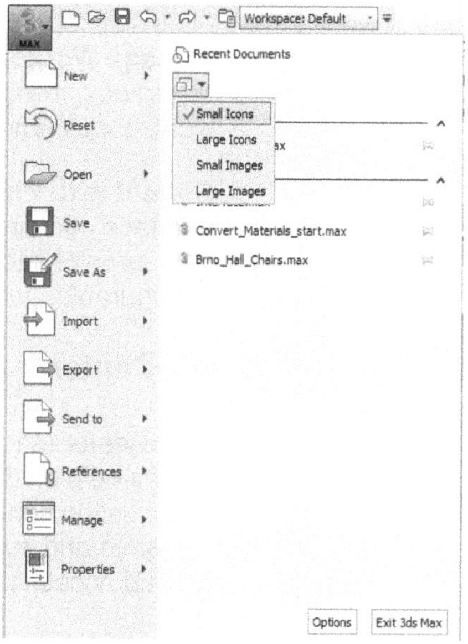

Figure 1–5

2. Quick Access Toolbar

The Quick Access Toolbar (shown in Figure 1–6) contains:

- One-click tools for saving, opening, or creating new scenes, using undo/redo, and setting the project folder.

- The Undo and Redo stack: Can be accessed using the drop-down arrows.

- ᵥ : Opens a drop-down list where you can select tools to create a custom quick access toolkit.

- The workspaces list (shown in Figure 1–6): Enables you to manage and switch between different interface setups. You can create a custom interface setup, containing commonly used toolbars, menus, quad menus, viewport layout settings, ribbon tools, and hotkeys for commands.

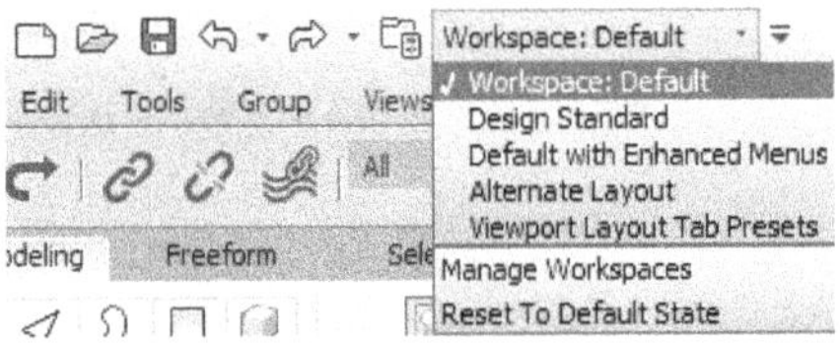

Figure 1–6

- **Manage Workspaces**: Opens the Manage Workspaces dialog box, in which you can add new workspaces, edit workspaces, and delete workspaces.

- **Default with Enhanced Menus:** Displays an enhanced interface containing additional menus in the menu bar, tooltips linking to relevant help topics, a display that is highly configurable, and a keyboard search for menu commands.

3. InfoCenter

The InfoCenter (shown in Figure 1–7) enables you to quickly search for help on the web, access the subscription services and communication center, open the Autodesk Exchange Apps center, save and access topics as favorites, sign into Autodesk A360, and access the Autodesk 3ds Max help.

Figure 1–7

4. Menu Bar

*The display of the menu bar can be controlled using the Quick Access Toolbar by clicking ▼ and selecting **Hide/Show Menu Bar** in the drop-down list.*

The Menu Bar contains working commands that are grouped together in the menu titles. There are two different menu bars: Standard and Enhanced. The menus in the Standard Menu Bar are described as follows:

Edit	Contains undo and redo functions, object selection options, copying (cloning), and delete functions.
Tools	Contains the **Mirror**, **Array**, **Align**, and **Measure Distance** options.
Group	Contains tools to create and edit Autodesk 3ds Max group objects. Groups function similar to AutoCAD groups.

Views	Contains features, such as preset viewport views, viewport display options, and ViewCube and SteeringWheel options.
Create	Contains options that enable you to create objects, such as 3D geometry, 2D shapes, cameras, and lights.
Modifiers	Contains sub-menus categorized by the available modifiers.
Animation	Contains common features used when creating animations.
Graph Editors	Contains several Track View features. Track View offers advanced controls for animations.
Rendering	Contains functions for rendering, such as setting up the scene environment, advanced lighting controls, and output image resolution.
Civil View	Contains features that can be used for displaying the contents of a scene created in a civil design program and to create visualizations of civil engineering projects. It offers support for various civil design programs, including the AutoCAD® Civil 3D® software. If you are opening Civil View for the first time, you need to initialize it and set the system units, country resource kit, and start mode.
Customize	Contains features for customizing the user interface, setting up the drawing units, and setting the overall Autodesk 3ds Max default options.
Scripting	Contains tools for working with the MAXScript programming language used by the Autodesk 3ds Max software.
Content	Links you to the Creative Market Store, which lists 3D and 2D assets . These assets can be licensed for use in your project. You can also launch the Autodesk Exchange App Store, where the Autodesk 3dx Max Asset Library is available for download along with various other apps.
Help	The **Help** menu connects you directly to the Autodesk 3ds Max Help documentation on the autodesk.com website. It contains features, such as Online Reference manuals, Tutorials, and Network-version license borrowing and return options.

Enhanced Menu Bar

The Enhanced Menu Bar can be displayed by selecting **Default with Enhanced Menus** in the Workspaces drop-down list in the Quick Access Toolbar. The Enhanced Menu Bar contains various menus: **Objects**, **Edit**, **Modifiers**, **Animation**, **Simulate**, **Materials**, **Lighting/Cameras**, **Rendering**, **Scene**, **Civil View**, **Lighting Analysis**, **Customize**, **Script**, **Content**, and **Help**.

- The commands and functions are organized as menu items, with submenus containing the relevant commands.

- Hovering the cursor over an item displays an information tooltip (as shown in Figure 1–8), and provides a link to the relevant help topic.

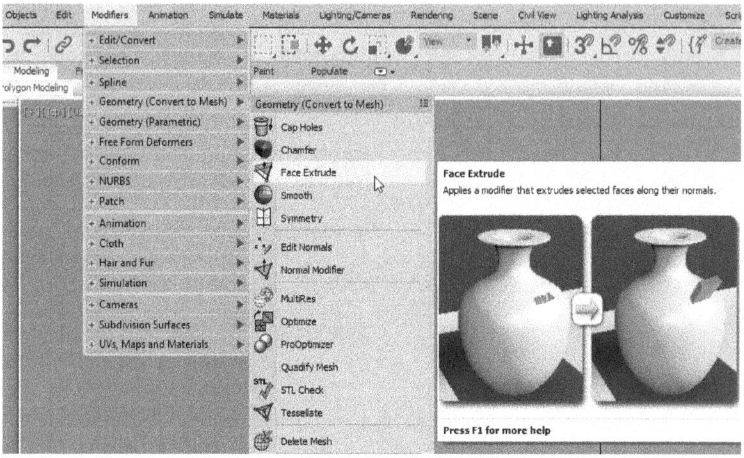

Figure 1–8

Hint: Global Menu Search

You can search for any menu command or action using the global menu search method. Press <X> to open the Search actions edit box at the cursor location and enter the name of the command or action that you want to use. As you enter the first letter of the command, a list of matching actions displays, as shown in Figure 1–9. Select an option in the list or enter another letter to display a more specific list of actions. To clear the search action, click the red **X** icon in the upper right corner of the *Search* edit box. Click in empty space or press <Esc> to exit the search feature.

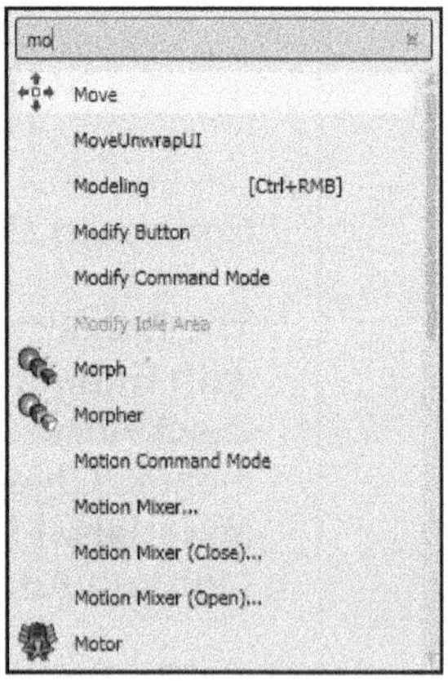

Figure 1–9

5. Quad Menu

The Quad Menus (shown in Figure 1–10) are a series of context-sensitive menus that open when selecting and right-clicking on one or more objects in the viewport. The commands are displayed in different quadrant areas and each quad menu can have a maximum of four quadrant areas, as shown in Figure 1–11.

- Quad menus also display when nothing is selected.

- Different quad menus display when <Ctrl>, <Alt>, or <Shift> are combined with right-clicking.

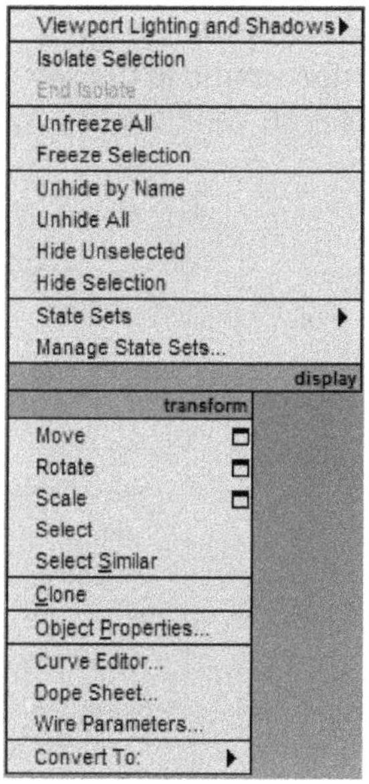

Figure 1–10

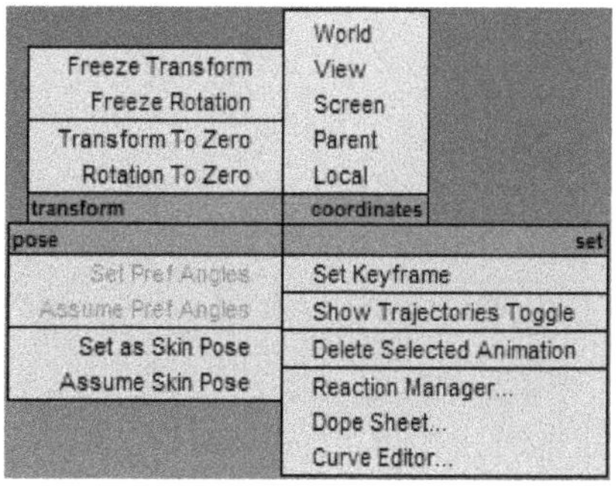

Figure 1–11

6. Main Toolbar

The Main Toolbar (shown in Figure 1–12), is visible by default and contains tools for some of the most commonly used options. These include the **Selection**, **Transforms**, **Snap**, and **Rendering** tools.

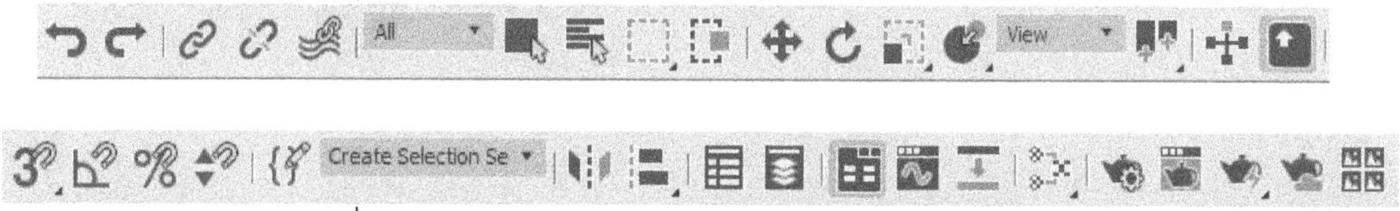

Figure 1–12

- The Main Toolbar can extend beyond the interface and some of the tools are not visible on the screen. To slide the buttons left or right, hover the cursor over the gray empty area until the cursor changes into a Pan cursor (hand icon), hold the left mouse button and drag.

- If the Main Toolbar is not visible, you can display it by selecting **Customize>Show UI>Show Main Toolbar**.

7. Toolbars

By default, the toolbars (except the Main Toolbar) are not displayed. Right-click on the title bar of an open toolbar or on the gray empty space of a docked toolbar to open the **Customize Display** menu (shown in Figure 1–13) where you can select the required toolbar name to display it. As with other interface components, you can float or dock the toolbars.

	Customize...
✓	Command Panel
✓	Ribbon
✓	Viewport Layout Tabs
	Brush Presets
✓	Main Toolbar
	Axis Constraints
	Layers
	State Sets
	Extras
	Render Shortcuts
	Snaps
	Animation Layers
	Containers
	MassFX Toolbar

Figure 1–13

8. Command Panel

The options in the lower portion of each panel are grouped into rollouts. You can expand and collapse the rollouts by clicking on the title bar of the rollout, or the +/- signs (or upward/downward facing double arrows).

The Command Panel enables you to efficiently create, edit, and manage the settings of 3D objects. It contains six different panels or tabs, each with a different appearance and function. Figure 1–14 shows the Object Type rollout in the Create panel (+).

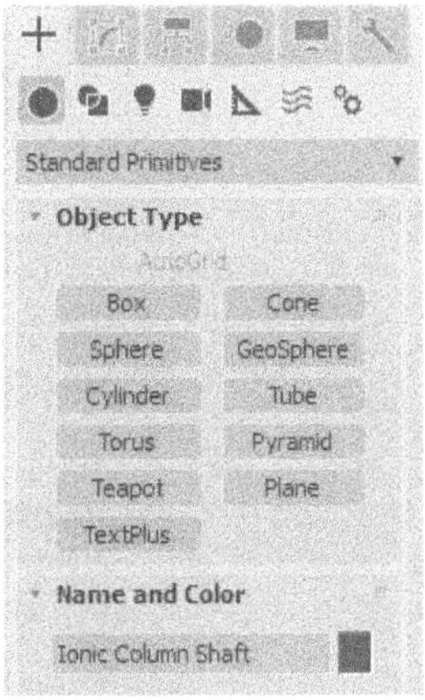

Figure 1–14

*   If the list of rollouts are extensive and extend beyond the bottom of the interface, pan the list up and down by holding and dragging the mouse button in the Command Panel.

*   By default, the Command Panel is docked along the right side of the viewport window. You can minimize the Command Panel by hovering the cursor over the top right edge of the Command Panel until the cursor displays as 🖱, then right-clicking and selecting **Minimize**. Once minimized, hover the cursor over the Command Panel title bar, (displayed vertically) to display it. To maximize it, right-click along the right edge of the Command Panel and select either **Dock>Right** or **Dock>Left**.

+ Create Panel

The Create panel enables you to interactively create objects in the Autodesk 3ds Max software and contains the following categories of object types:

●	**Geometry** is 3D objects.
	Shapes are 2D objects.
●	**Lights** are used to illuminate the scene.
■	**Cameras** are objects that provide scene views.
◢	**Helpers** are non-rendering tools that help with layout or work with other objects, such as a distance measuring tape object.
≋	**Space warps** are non-renderable objects that deform or otherwise influence the geometry of other objects. They are used to create ripples and waves, using forces such as wind and gravity.
°o	**Systems** contains the Sunlight and Daylight Systems, Biped, and the controls for some 3rd party plug-ins.

Modify Panel

The Modify panel shows the selected object's parameter values, a list of modifiers added to an object, and the parameters that apply to them.

- Modifiers are geometric modifications and additional property controls that can be added to objects, as required.

- Object and modifier parameters can be changed at any time after the object's creation, if the Modifier Stack remains intact.

- The **Modifier List** drop-down menu contains all of the modifiers that can be applied to the current selection.

- The Modifier Stack lists the modifiers that have been applied to an object. Figure 1–15 shows the Modifier Stack of a circle that was edited, extruded, and tapered into a 3D column shaft.

- The Modify panel is blank if no object is selected or if more than one object is selected.

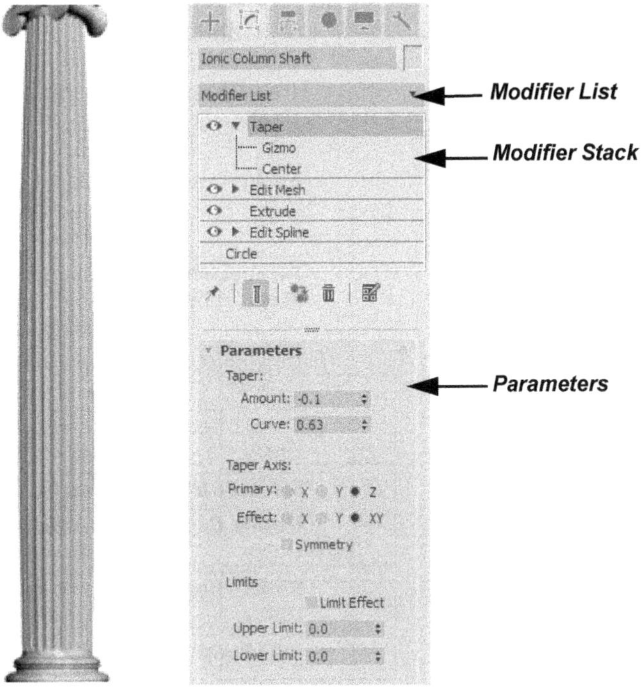

Figure 1–15

Hierarchy Panel

The Hierarchy panel contains controls for objects that are linked together into hierarchies, such as for mechanical equipment with interconnected parts.

Motion Panel

The Motion Panel contains sophisticated motion controls for animating.

Display Panel

The Display panel contains object-level visibility controls, enabling you to hide or unhide objects individually or by category, independent of the layer settings.

Utilities Panel

The Utilities panel contains a number of miscellaneous utilities as follows:

Asset Browser	Enables you to review and select content such as 3D objects or 2D bitmaps from your local drive or across the web.
Perspective Match Utility	Helps match the position and field of view of the camera in your 3D scene to the perspective photographic background image.
Collapse Utility	Removes the modifiers from an object's stack, turning the object into an editable mesh or poly.
Color Clipboard Utility	Stores color swatches for copying from one map or material to another.
Measure Utility	Lists the surface area and volume of objects.
Motion Capture Utility	Enables you to animate virtual objects with the real-time movement of the mouse or they input device.
Reset XForm Utility	Removes rotation and scale values of an object, applying them to the XForm modifier gizmo.
MAXScript	Accesses a scripting language that can be used to automate repetitive functions or build new tools and interfaces.
Flight Studio Utility	Enables you to open and manage the open Flight models.
More...	Provides access to a complete list of Utilities, including the controls for many 3rd party plug-in applications.

9. Modeling Ribbon

The Modeling ribbon (shown in Figure 1–16) provides easy access to polygon modeling tools, including the editing and modification tools used at sub-object level. The ribbon contains most of the commonly used tools that are also found in the Command Panel's Modify panel (at the Edit Poly sub-object level).

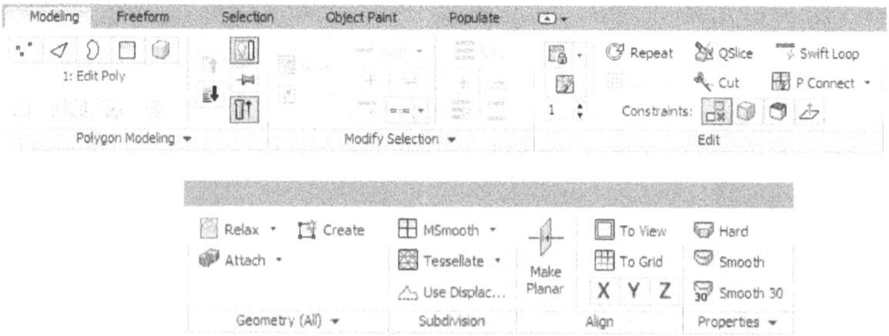

*If the ribbon is not displayed, in the menu bar, select **Customize> Show UI>Show Ribbon**. You can also click ▦ (Toggle Ribbon) in the Main Toolbar or select **Ribbon** in the Customize Display right-click menu.*

Figure 1–16

The ribbon contains five tabs: *Modeling*, *Freeform*, *Selection*, *Object Paint*, and *Populate* that are further subdivided into various panels that are context dependent. All of the tools are grouped based on context and are placed in separate panels.

- For example, the *Modeling* tab contains the tools used for modeling and are grouped in the Polygon Modeling panel, Modify Selection panel, Edit panel, etc. Each of the panels has a set of related tools and commands present for easy access. For example, the Polygon Modeling panel contains tools used for **Edit Poly** modifier, as shown in Figure 1–17.

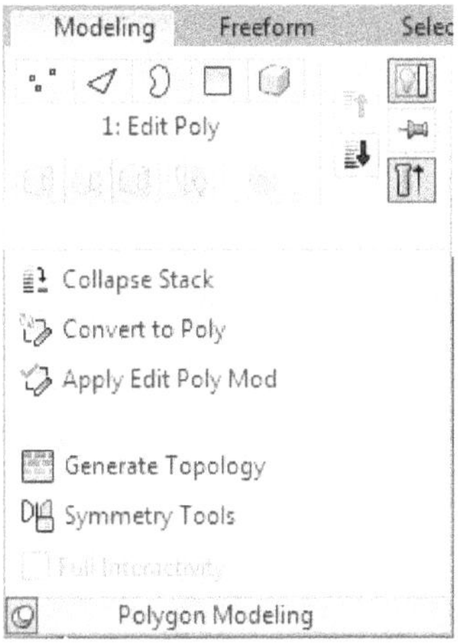

Figure 1–17

- The ribbon might be minimized to the panel tiles, and is docked under the Main Toolbar. Click ⊡ to maximize the ribbon.

- The display of the tabs and panels can be controlled by right-clicking on the ribbon and select the options in the menu, as shown in Figure 1–18.

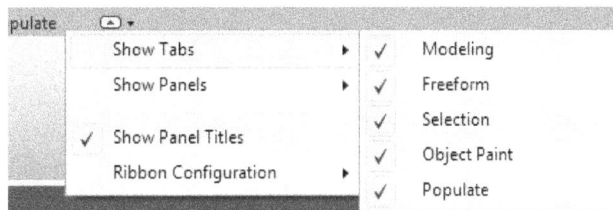

Figure 1–18

- If you are continuously using the options from a panel, you can click ⊨ in the expanded panel to lock it.

Hint: Caddy Display for Edit Poly Modifier

The caddy display (shown in Figure 1–19) enables you to enter values on the screen for various modifiers at the Edit Poly sub-object level. The modifications are dynamically updated and reflected in the model.

- The values can be typed in the edit boxes or you can hold and drag the spinner arrows for dynamical viewing and updating of the changes.

- Click ⊘ to accept the change ⊕ to accept the change and continue in the same modifier.

Figure 1–19

- The caddy interface can be accessed through:

  - **Modeling ribbon**: Hold <Shift> and select the sub-object level modifier tool or click the down arrow next to the modifier and select the setting, as shown for the Bevel modifier in Figure 1–20.

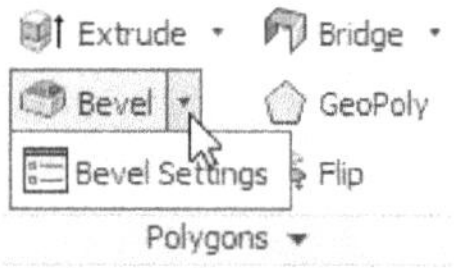

Figure 1–20

  - **Command Panel**: Click ▢ (Settings) next to the sub-object level modifier option. This enables you to enter the values while performing the operation.
  - The display of the caddy interface is controlled by the **Enable Caddy Controls** option in the Preference Settings dialog box>*General* tab>*UI Display* area. By default, the option is selected.

Hint: Design Workspace

The Design Workspace Ribbon contains the commonly used 3ds Max commands and features grouped together in tabs, as shown in Figure 1–21. It can be started by selecting **Design Standard** in the Workspaces drop-down list in the Quick Access Toolbar, or by opening a template, which uses a Design Standard workspace from the Welcome screen>Start panel.

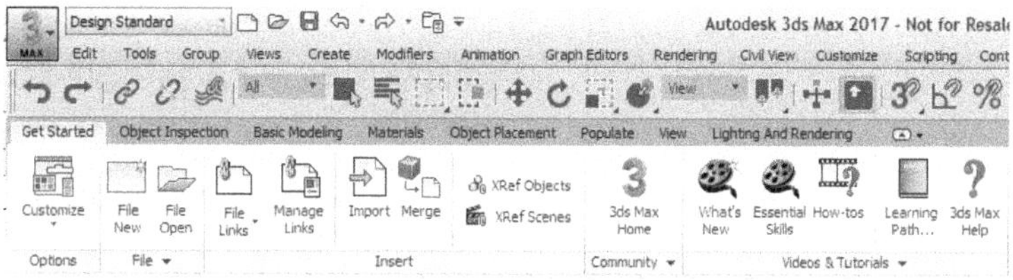

Figure 1–21

The various tabs included are:

- **Get Started**: Commands for starting a new scene, opening an already saved scene, and linking geometry and files from other 3D data software. It also contains commands for customizing the software and accessing to learning resources.

- **Object Inspection**: Commands used to control the display of objects in viewports and also explore the geometry in the scene.

- **Basic Modeling**: Tools for creating new geometry in the scene.

- **Materials**: Tools for creating, managing, and editing the materials.

- **Object Placement**: Tools for moving, placing and editing geometry. You can also open Civil View from this tab.

- **Populate**: Tools for adding animated or idle people to a scene.

- **View**: Commands to add cameras and control the viewport display.

- **Lighting and Rendering**: Tools for adding lights and creating renderings of the scene.

10. Scene Explorer

The Scene Explorer (shown in Figure 1–22) lists all of the objects that are present in a scene in the form of a tree structure, along with each object's properties displayed in a tabular form.

- By default, the Scene Explorer is docked along the left side of the viewport. You can float it or dock it to left/right by hovering the cursor over on the top or top left edge till the cursor displays as 🖰, then right-clicking and selecting the required option.

- It is a modeless dialog box that can remains open while you are working in the scene.

- You can open and manage the Scene Explorer from the Tools menu bar.

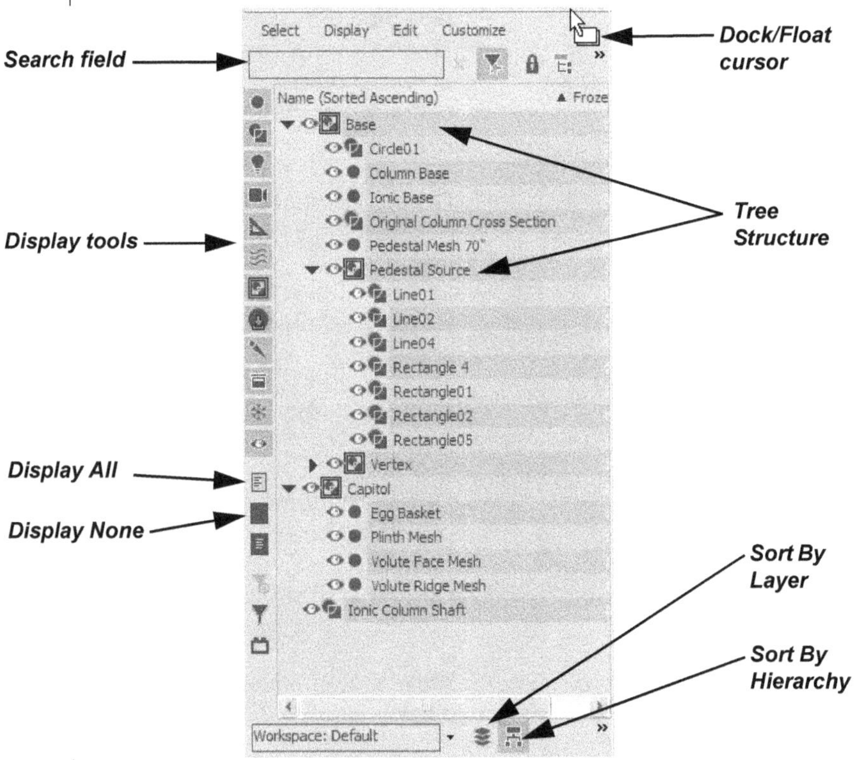

Figure 1–22

- A default Scene Explorer is included for each workspace and can be saved with a specific name with that workspace.

- The objects can be toggled to be displayed either as hierarchies (🔗) or as layers (≋).

- Objects and layers can be nested to any depth. Use the arrow next to the name to expand or collapse the group.

- You can perform actions and modifications such as sorting, filtering, selecting, renaming, hiding, and freezing objects, directly in the Scene Explorer.

- You can drag and drop objects and layers to reorganize the groups.

- A toolbar is provided along the left edge of the Scene Explorer that enables you to list only those objects that belong to a particular category. There are tools for various categories such as ⬤ (Display Geometry), ▥ (Display Cameras), 💡 (Display Lights), etc. When the tool for a category is active (i.e., displays with a yellow background), the objects belonging to that category are listed. The 📄 (Display All) tool lists all of the different categories of objects. To only list the objects belonging to the category that you need, use ▮ (Display None) to clear any existing selections, and then select the required display category.

- To easily find and select an item, use the *Search* field.

11. Status Bar

The Status Bar (shown in Figure 1–23) found along the bottom left and center of the interface contains the following elements:

| | None Selected | ▣ 🔒 ⊞ X: 402.605 | Y: 497.52 | Z: 0.0 | Grid = 100.0 |
| Welcome to M₁ | Loading... | | | 🕐 Add Time Tag |

Figure 1–23

MAXScript Mini-Listener	Enables you to enter commands and receive feedback (MaxScript commands)
Status Line	Identifies the number of objects selected
Prompt Line	Prompts for the next action or input that is required.
(Isolate Selection Toggle)	Zooms the current selection in the active viewport while temporarily hiding unselected objects in all viewports (except the **Camera** viewport). This enables you to work on the required object without the other objects getting in your way. You can also access this command by selecting Tools>Isolate Selection or pressing <Alt>+<Q>.
(Selection Lock Toggle)	Toggles a lock to prevent you from changing your current selection between options. Pressing the space bar toggles this on or off.
or (Absolute/Offset Transform Mode Toggle)	Enables you to toggle between Absolute mode (which sets the coordinates in the world space) and the Offset transform mode (which transforms the objects relative to its coordinates).
Transform Type In	Enables you to review and adjust transform values for the X, Y, and Z coordinates.
Grid Setting Display	Controls the distance between grid lines. Select Tools>Grids and Snaps>Grid and Snap Settings to open the dialog box. Use the *Home Grid* tab to adjust the spacing. To toggle the Grid on or off, press <G>.
(Adaptive Degradation Toggle)	Enables you to toggle adaptive degradation on or off. Right-click to open the Viewport Configuration dialog box in the *Display Performance* tab (the Adaptive Degradation tab is for legacy drivers). You can improve the viewport quality progressively and set the resolution for the texture display (for nitrous drivers). It also contains options for controlling adaptive degradation.
Time Tag	Enables you to add or edit time tags, which are labels describing specific points of an animation.

12. Viewport Layouts tab bar

The Viewport Layouts tab bar is a vertically, expandable bar containing a list of viewport layouts that can be selected to quickly change the layout of the viewports, as shown in Figure 1–24.

- For a new scene, a single layout tab is available. Once you have saved additional viewport layouts, they are listed along with the default one. The Viewport Layouts tab bar displays the default layout and three additional viewport layouts that were saved.

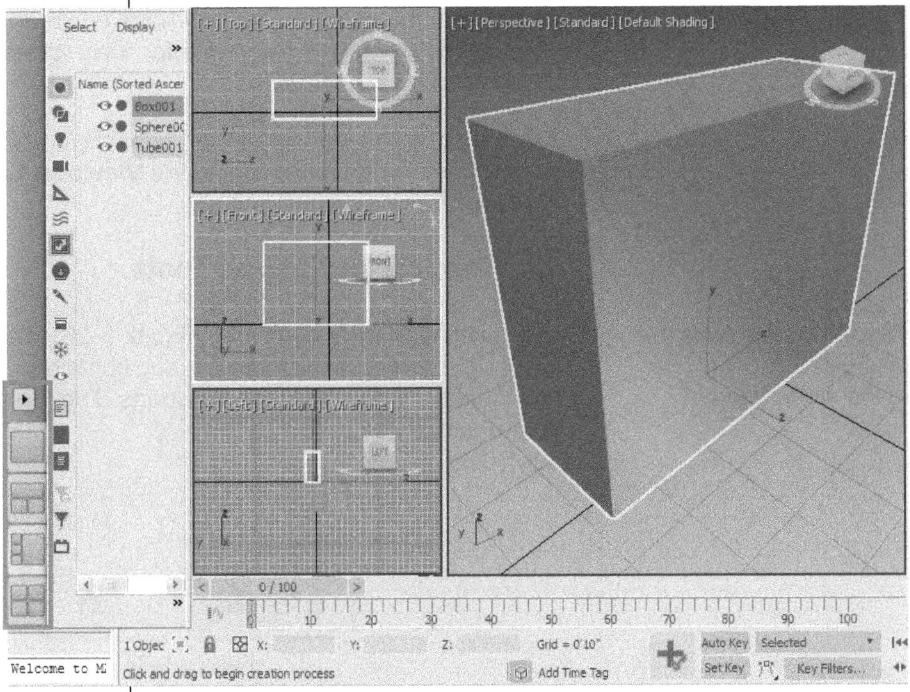

Figure 1–24

- Click ▶ (as shown in Figure 1–25), to open the available standard viewport layouts for selection and customization. Once you have selected a layout, it is listed in the tab bar with any previously saved layouts. The viewports are displayed as the new layout.

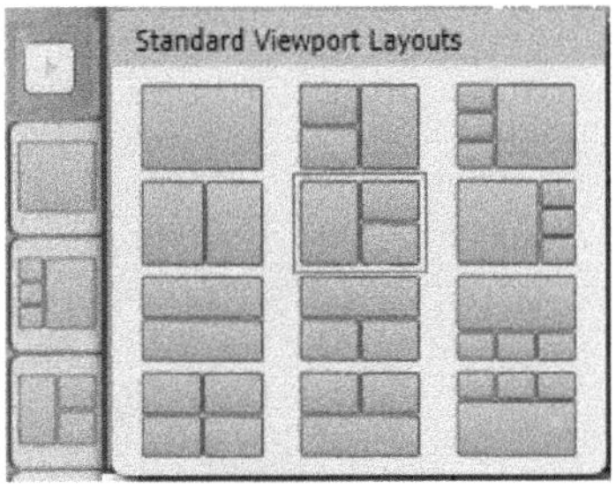

Figure 1–25

- To customize a preset layout, select it from the preset layouts, move the boundaries by clicking and dragging them to new positions, set the required Point of View and Shading modes, and then save the custom viewport layout. Save it by right-clicking on the newly custom tab and selecting **Save Configuration as Preset**. Set its name by entering a new name in the edit box. The newly saved viewport configuration is saved along with the scene for easy retrieval in a later session.

- To display or hide the tab bar, right-click in an empty area of the Main Toolbar, and toggle the **Viewport Layout Tabs** option.

13. Viewport Navigation Tools

The navigation tools are discussed in detail later in the student guide.

The navigation tools (shown in Figure 1–26), are located in the lower right corner of the interface and contain tools for navigating and displaying objects in the viewports. The tools are dependent on the active viewport.

Figure 1–26

1.4 Preferences

The Preference Settings dialog box (shown in Figure 1–27) contains tabs that control the display and operational settings at the program level. The dialog box is available through the **Application Menu>Options** or in the menu bar **Customize> Preferences**.

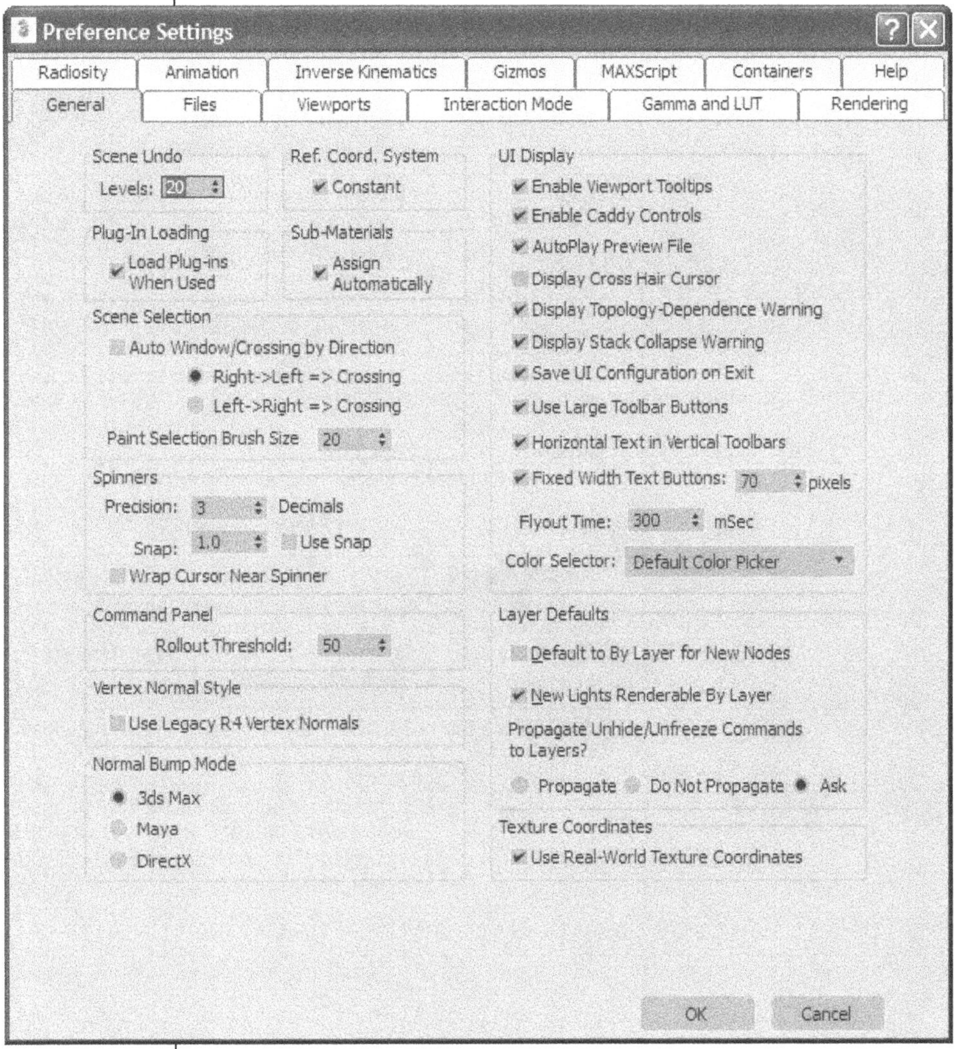

Figure 1–27

The various tabs are described as follows:

General tab	Controls the interface settings, such as Number of Scene Undo steps (levels) that are saved, settings for the transform center, user interface display options, etc.
Files tab	Contains options for file handling, such as Automatic backup save settings.
Viewports tab	Contains options for viewport settings, highlighting options for selection and preview, and setting the display drivers.
Interaction Mode tab	Sets how the mouse and keyboard shortcuts are going to behave. You can set the mouse shortcut behavior to match with earlier releases of 3ds Max or Maya.
Gamma and LUT tab	Sets the compatibility options with respect to other Autodesk programs for a consistent display of colors among various programs
Rendering tab	Controls the rendering settings, such as the ambient light default color settings.
Animation tab	Controls the various animation settings. You can assign the sound plug-ins and controller defaults.
Inverse kinematics tab	Sets the Applied IK (for accuracy) and Interactive IK (for real-time response) settings.
Gizmos tab	Sets the display and behavior of the Transform gizmos.
MAXScript tab	Sets the various features used for the MAXScript editor, such as what font and font size to use.
Radiosity tab	Controls the radiosity settings in viewports and if the light levels with radiosity are saved with a file or not.
Containers tab	Controls the Status and Update settings in viewports.
Help tab	Controls where help documentation is accessed from. By default, help is accessed through the Autodesk.com website. Alternatively, you can download the documentation locally and then specify its installation path in the *Help* tab.

Hint: Gamma and LUT Settings Mismatch

Gamma and LUT Settings are saved with the defaults for the current file based on the current UI. Opening or merging a scene, whose file gamma or LUT settings are different from the gamma and LUT settings of the system in which it is being opened, causes the Mismatch dialog box to open, as shown in Figure 1–28. It provides you with options to use the current settings or adopt the file settings.

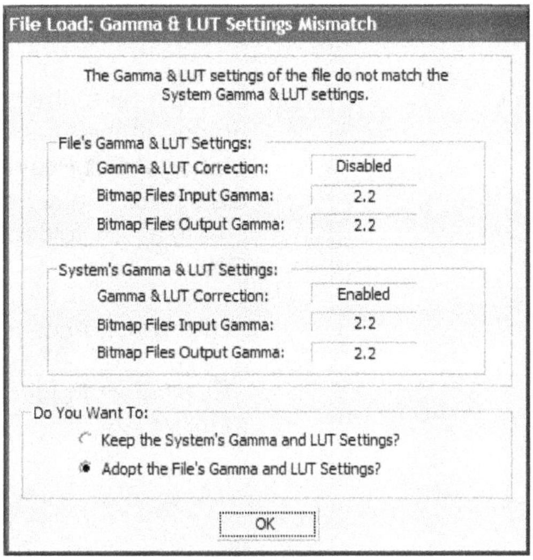

File Load: Gamma & LUT Settings Mismatch

The Gamma & LUT settings of the file do not match the System Gamma & LUT settings.

File's Gamma & LUT Settings:

Gamma & LUT Correction:	Disabled
Bitmap Files Input Gamma:	2.2
Bitmap Files Output Gamma:	2.2

System's Gamma & LUT Settings:

Gamma & LUT Correction:	Enabled
Bitmap Files Input Gamma:	2.2
Bitmap Files Output Gamma:	2.2

Do You Want To:

○ Keep the System's Gamma and LUT Settings?

◉ Adopt the File's Gamma and LUT Settings?

OK

Figure 1–28

1.5 Setting the Project Folder

Setting a project folder enables you to better organize all of the files for a project.

- By default, the project folder is set to your local /3dsmax folder. Once the project folder is created, a series of subfolders (e.g., scenes, render output) are generated. The project folder is maintained when the Autodesk 3ds Max software is restarted.

- You can reset the project folder by clicking 📁 (Project Folder) in the Quick Access Toolbar or **Application Menu> Manage>Set Project Folder** to open the Browse For Folder dialog box. Select a folder to be set as your project folder or create a new folder to be used as your project folder and click **OK**.

- In the Quick Access Toolbar, hover the cursor over 📁 (Project Folder) to display its name, as shown in Figure 1–29.

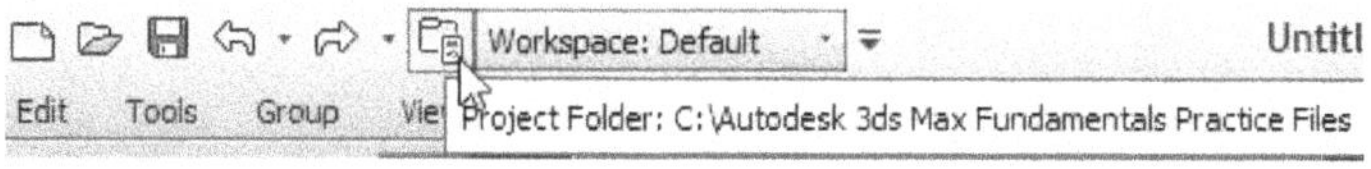

Figure 1–29

1.6 Configure Paths

Projects can use external files such as fonts, image maps for materials, IES (Illuminating Engineering Society) data files for lights, etc. The locations of these and other required data files are identified in the Configure System Paths and Configure User Paths dialog boxes. These dialog boxes can be opened by selecting **Customize>Configure System Paths/Configure User Paths**.

Configure System Paths

The Configure System Paths dialog box (shown in Figure 1–30) stores paths to data files and contains the following tabs:

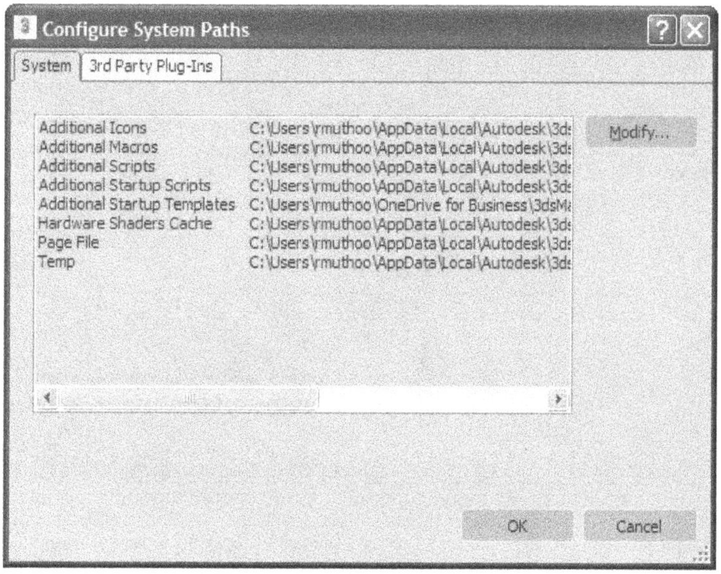

Figure 1–30

System	Paths used for additional buttons, macros, scripts and startup scripts, and temp files.
3rd Party Plug-Ins	Default paths to search for add-on application data (some standard functions and 3rd party products).

Configure User Paths

The Configure User Paths dialog box (shown in Figure 1–31) stores items that might be reconfigured for different users or for different projects. The User path settings can be saved as a path configuration (.MXP) file and later re-loaded as required. The dialog box has the following tabs:

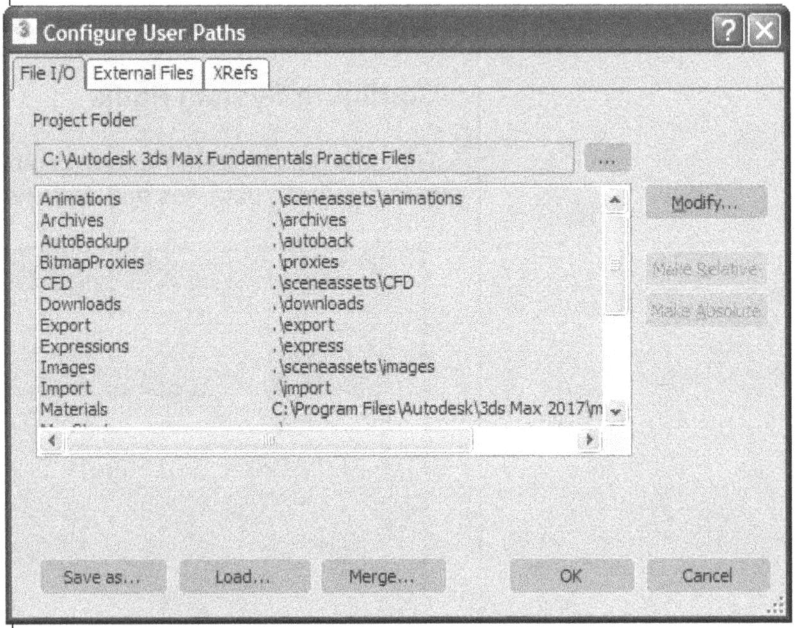

Figure 1–31

File I/O	Paths used to locate files for options such as open, save, export, etc.
External Files	Paths to external data files such as image maps, IES files, etc.
XRefs	Paths that are searched to find externally referenced objects and scene files.

- Since multiple workstations often make use of the same data files, it is often helpful to create shared network locations for these files (especially when network rendering).

- Relative paths are used to help prevent *missing external files* problems when sharing or moving files from one location to another. In the Configure User Paths, all of the paths are preceded with a dot and backslash (.\) indicating a relative path.

- You can use the Configure User Paths dialog box to change hard-coded absolute paths from earlier versions to Relative paths. Select the path and click Make Relative.

Hint: Asset Tracking

In the **Application Menu>References**, select **Asset Tracking** to change hard-coded absolute paths from earlier versions to relative paths. In the Asset Tracking dialog box, select *Paths* tab>**Make Path Relative to Project Folder**, as shown in Figure 1–32.

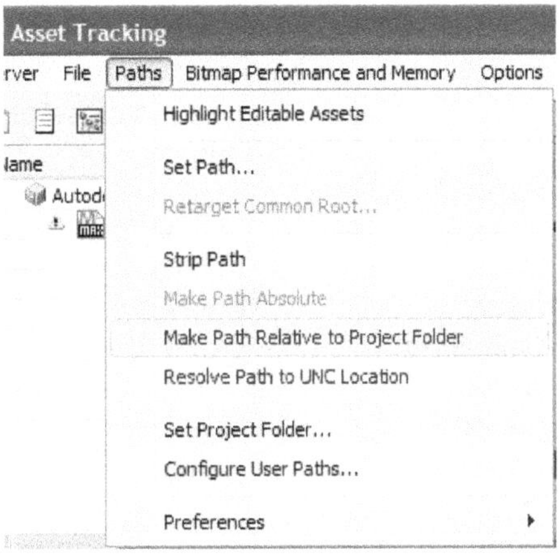

Figure 1–32

1.7 Display Drivers

The Nitrous Direct3D 11 driver is the default and recommended display driver, but you can change to the other Nitrous drivers or legacy drivers. Nitrous Direct3D 9 is set as the default driver if the graphics card or operating system on your system does not support Nitrous Direct3D 11.

To open the Preference Settings dialog box, select **Customize> Preferences** or **Application Menu>Options**. In the *Viewports* tab, and in the *Display Drivers* area, click **Choose Driver**. Then, select the required driver in the Display Driver Selection dialog box, as shown in Figure 1–33. If you change the display driver, you need to close and reopen the software for the changes to take effect.

*You can also change the graphics driver outside the software using the Windows Start menu. Select Windows **Start>All Programs> Autodesk>Autodesk 3ds Max 2017> Change Graphics Mode**. This launches the software and provides the option of selecting the display driver.*

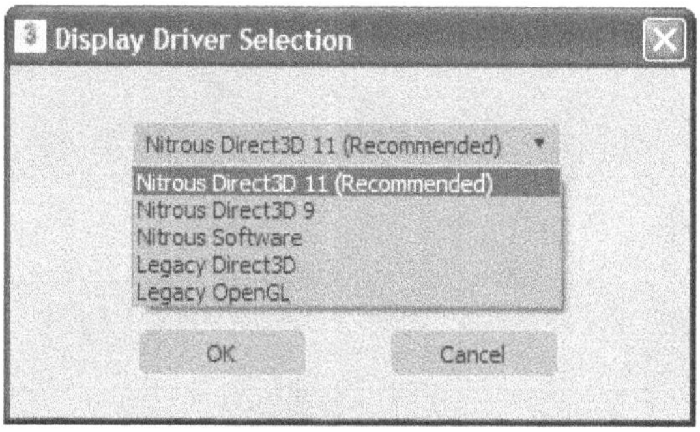

Figure 1–33

The following display drivers are available:

- **Nitrous Direct3D 11:** The Nitrous Direct 3D 11 driver requires Direct 3D 11.0. This driver takes advantage of video card features (when available), and provides high quality realistic viewport display options and faster rendering times. The visual display is render quality and supports unlimited lights, shadows, tone mapping, etc. The Nitrous driver also enables you to display your scenes in stylized images (pencil, acrylic, ink, etc.) in the viewports.

- **Nitrous Direct3D 9:** The Nitrous Direct 3D 9 driver requires Direct3D 9.0. It works in the same way as the Direct3D 11 driver.

*The **OpenGL** and **Direct3D** options are useful if your system supports those forms of hardware acceleration. Experiment with these options to determine the best option for your workstation.*

- **Nitrous Software:** The Nitrous Software driver has similar capabilities to the other nitrous drivers, but the hardware support is not required and it might be slower during rendering.

- **Legacy Direct3D:** The Direct3D driver supports data culling and works well for the high-color displays.

- **Legacy OpenGL:** The OpenGL driver works well for hardware acceleration, including geometry acceleration and rasterization acceleration. You cannot display shadows or ambient occlusion in viewports while using this driver.

1.8 Viewport Display and Labels

Enhanced
in 2017

Geometry opens in the software through one or more viewports, which can be configured to show objects from different viewing angles and with different viewport shading modes.

Three Viewport label menus (shown in Figure 1–34) display in the upper left corner of each viewport. Note that the four labels are only available for the Nitrous displays, while the legacy driver display shows only three labels.

[+] [Perspective] [User Defined] [Default Shading]

Figure 1–34

General Viewport

Click on **[+]** to open the **General Viewport** label menu, as shown in Figure 1–35. It includes the ability to display grids, the ViewCube, and the SteeringWheels. It also contains tools for the **xView** functionality, which enables you to show statistics and diagnose problems in polygonal geometry such as overlapping faces, unwelded vertices, or face normal orientation issues.

	Restore Viewport	Alt+W
	Active Viewport	▸
	Disable Viewport	D
✓	Show Grids	G
	ViewCube	▸
	SteeringWheels	▸
	xView	▸
	Create Preview	▸
	Configure Viewports...	
	2D Pan Zoom Mode	

Figure 1–35

Point Of View

The **Point of View** label displays the name of the view projection (i.e., Perspective, Orthographic) that is being shown in the viewport. Clicking on this Viewport label opens the **Point of View** label menu (shown in Figure 1–36), which enables you to change the view type.

The three most common view types are:

*You can also change the view using the shortcut keys that are listed next to the type in the label menu (e.g., <T> for **Top**, <B> for **Bottom**, etc.).*

- **Perspective View:** This view displays what is seen with human vision and uses vanishing points to make distant objects appear to recede from view. The most realistic output is shown through perspective views or the camera view, as shown in Figure 1–37.

[+] [Perspective] [User Defined] [Default Shading]

	Cameras	▶
	Lights	▶
✓	Perspective	P
	Orthographic	U
	Top	T
	Bottom	B
	Front	F
	Back	
	Left	L
	Right	
	Restore Active Perspective View	
	Save Active Perspective View	
	Extended Viewports	▶
	Show Safe Frames	Shift+F
	Viewport Clipping	
	Undo View Change	Shift+Z
	Redo View Change	Shift+Y

Figure 1–36

[+] [Camera - Lobby1] [Standard] [Edged Faces]

Figure 1–37

You might find Orthographic views easier to navigate (especially when zooming with a mouse wheel), but the rendered output often does not display as realistic as from a perspective view.

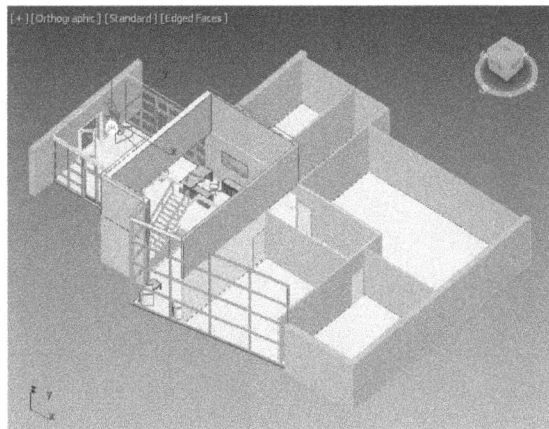

- **Orthographic (Axonometric Rotated) View:** Orthographic views (shown in Figure 1–38) do not use vanishing points or convergence; therefore objects do not seem to recede over distance. You can think of Orthographic views as being similar to Isometric views (Isometric views are special cases of Axonometric views where the axes are equally inclined to the screen).

[+] [Orthographic] [Standard] [Edged Faces]

Figure 1–38

- **Other Views:** The **Left**, **Right**, **Top**, **Bottom**, **Front**, and **Back** views are all types of predefined views, which show a 2D projection of the model.

Shading Viewport

The Shading Viewport label provides options to change the shading display methods used in the viewport, such as **High Quality**, **Standard**, **Performance**, **DX Mode**, and **User Defined** (as shown in Figure 1–39). In addition to shading, this menu contains tools for the **Lighting and Shadows**, and display of materials with textures and maps.

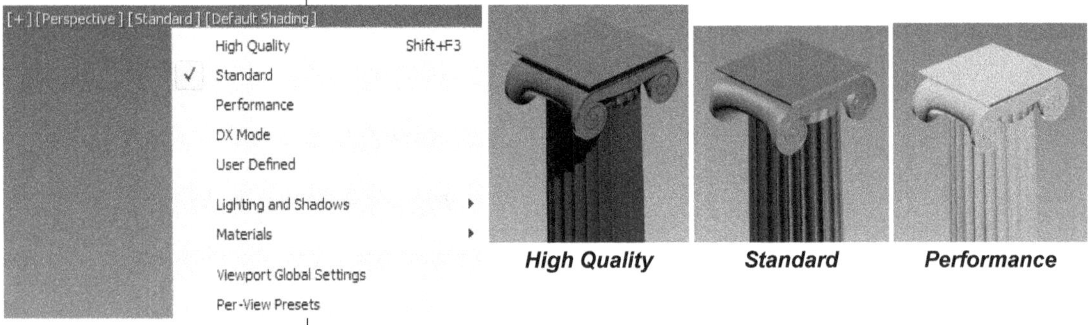

Figure 1–39

Per-View Preference

The Per-View Preference label menu (shown in Figure 1–40) displays the visual style methods for a view, such as **Default Shading**, **Facets**, **Bounding Box**, **Clay**, etc. You can select different edge modes and with the selected shading method. This menu also contains tools for various **Stylized** options, **Lighting and Shadows**, and **Viewport Background**. You can use the **Display Selected** options to control the display of selected geometry in shaded viewports.

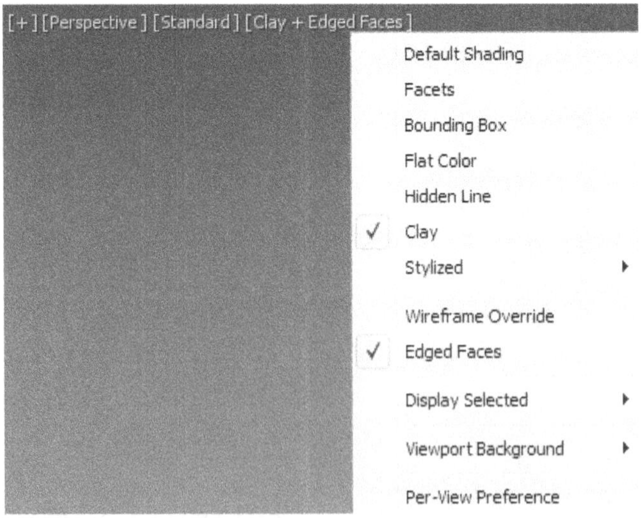

Figure 1–40

Some of the visual style modes (using the Standard shading viewport display) are shown in Figure 1–41.

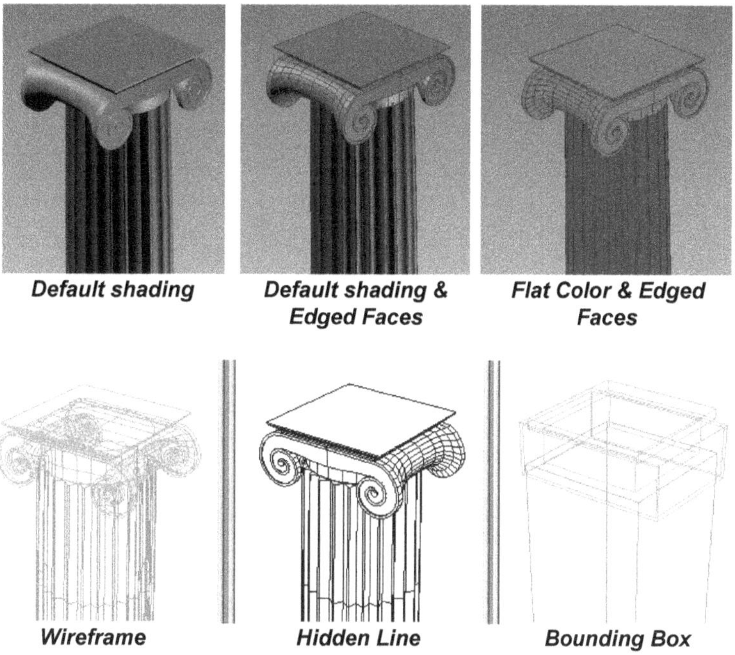

Default shading *Default shading & Edged Faces* *Flat Color & Edged Faces*

Wireframe *Hidden Line* *Bounding Box*

Figure 1–41

- The **Default Shading** mode displays the object as smooth with Phong shading being applied to it.

- In the **Flat Color** mode, lighting effects are disabled and the object is displayed with just the color.

- The **Edged Faces** option overlays a wireframe over any other visual style, such as Default shading, Facets, Clay, and others.

- The **Facets** option always displays the geometry as faceted even if the Smooth modifier or Smoothing have been applied to the object. This enables you to precisely locate the edges in the model and makes it easier to work with the geometry.

- The **Hidden Line** option improves the Wireframe display by hiding the lines that are on the backside of the objects.

- The **Bounding Box** option is useful when scenes are extremely complex and software performance is an issue. Alternatively, in this situation, individual objects can be set to view as bounding boxes through Object Properties.

- The **Clay** option displays the geometry in a terracotta color without any material or texture color.

- The **Stylized** menu options enables you to display objects with a variety of effects that are non-photorealistic, as shown in Figure 1–42.

| Graphite | Color Pencil | Pastel |

Figure 1–42

Hint: Legacy Driver Display Labels

The legacy driver display shows only three labels:

- The **General Viewport** label and the **Point of View** label contains the same menu options as for the nitrous drivers.

- The **Shading Viewport** label has menu options pertaining to the legacy drivers, as shown in Figure 1–43.

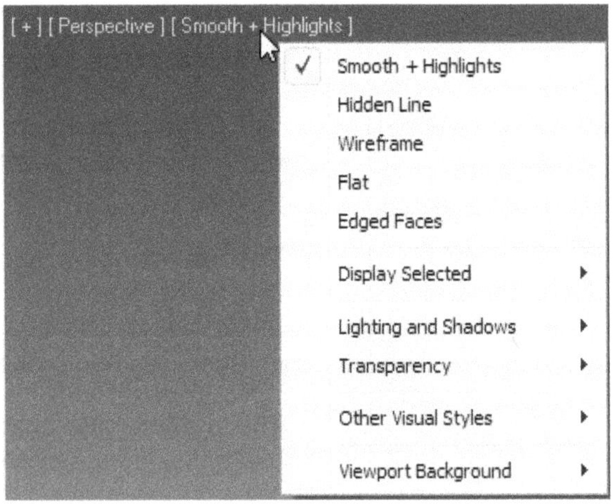

Figure 1–43

Practice 1a

Organizing Folders and Working with the Interface

Practice Objectives

- Set the project folder and configure User Paths.
- Create Viewport Layouts and navigate the graphic user interface
- Modify an object using the Command Panel and using the Scene Explorer.

Estimated time for completion: 20 minutes

In this practice you will work with the Autodesk 3ds Max software by setting the project folder to organize the files in the project. You will also configure the user paths to set the folders. You will then create different Viewport layouts by changing the viewing angles and different shading modes. You will also navigate the graphic user interface. To complete the practice you will open a file and modify the objects using different interface components.

For printing purposes, the UI color scheme used for this practice is **ame-light** (Menu bar: Customize>Custom UI and Defaults Switcher>ame-light in UI schemes list), and the *Theme* has been set to **Light** in the Customize User Interface dialog box.

Task 1 - Set the Project Folder.

1. Install the practice files by launching the self-extracting .EXE file. Ensure that the files are located in the *C:\Autodesk 3ds Max Fundamentals Practice Files* folder.

2. Launch the Autodesk 3ds Max 2017 (R1) software.

   - If a Welcome Screen is displayed, clear **Show this Welcome Screen at startup** and close the Welcome Screen.
   - If it is already running, reset the program by selecting **Reset** in the **Application Menu**. This closes the current file and opens a new blank file. If an unsaved scene is open, you might be required to save or discard the changes to the scene. Click **Don't Save**. Click **Yes** to reset the file.

3. In the Quick Access Toolbar, click (Project Folder).

4. In the Browse For Folder dialog box, navigate to C:\ and select the *Autodesk 3ds Max Fundamentals Practice Files* folder.

If an Invalid Path dialog box opens, click OK.

5. Click **OK**. You only have to set the project folder once.

6. In the Quick Access Toolbar, hover the cursor over

   (Project Folder) to display the set project folder. Ensure that it displays as C:*Autodesk 3ds Max Fundamentals Practice Files*, as shown in Figure 1–44.

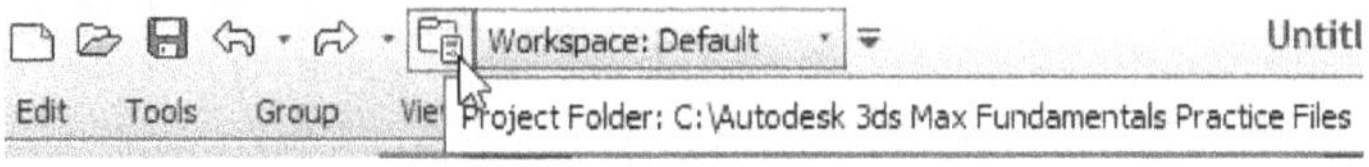

Figure 1–44

Task 2 - Setting Preferences.

*Alternatively, you can also select **Application Menu> Options**.*

1. In the menu bar, select **Customize>Preferences**. The Preference Settings dialog box opens.

2. In the *General* tab, in the *Ref. Coord. System* area, select **Constant**, as shown in Figure 1–45. This enables the Transform types to use the same Reference Coordinate System.

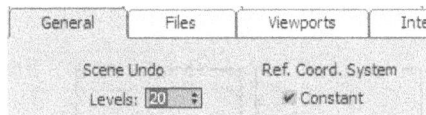

Figure 1–45

3. In the *Layer Defaults* area, clear **Default to By Layer for New Nodes**, if not already cleared, as shown in Figure 1–46. Click **OK**.

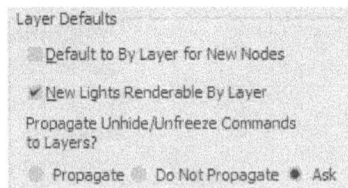

Figure 1–46

Task 3 - Configure the User Paths.

1. Select **Customize>Configure User Paths** to open the Configure User Paths dialog box.

2. Verify that the *File I/O* tab is selected. In the list, select **Materials** and click **Modify**. In the Choose Directory for Materials dialog box, browse to *C:\Program Files\Autodesk\ 3ds Max 2017\materiallibraries*. Click **Use Paths**. The path is displayed as shown in Figure 1–47.

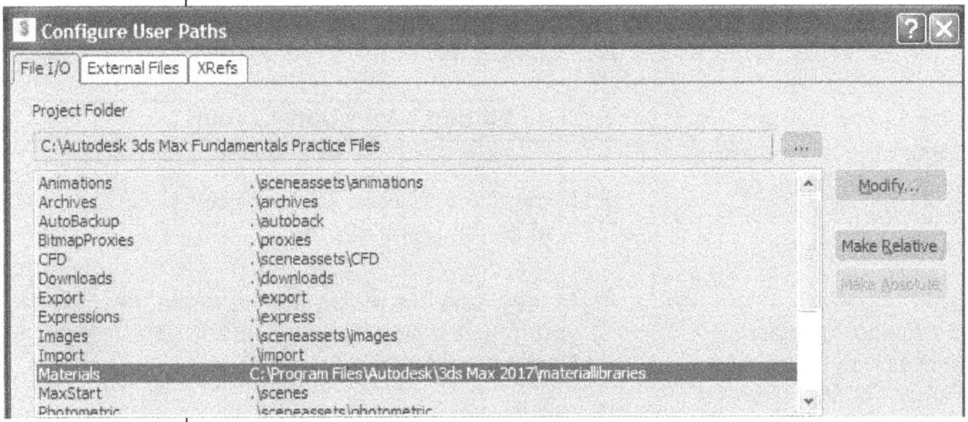

Figure 1–47

3. In the Configure User Paths dialog box, select the *External Files* tab and click **Add**.

*If you double-click on a folder, you are not required to click **Use Path**.*

4. In the Choose New External Files Path dialog box, navigate to *C:\Autodesk 3ds Max Fundamentals Practice Files* (select it but do not double-click). Click **Use Path**. Double-click on the *Maps* folder and click **Use Path**. Verify that you have returned to the Configure User Paths dialog box. This enables all of the folders under the main folder to be searched for missing external files.

The paths are searched in order from top to bottom, so moving a custom path to the top saves time when searching for files.

5. In the Configure User Paths dialog box, verify that the Maps new path is still selected and continue clicking **Move Up** until the new path is at the top of the list, as shown in Figure 1–48.

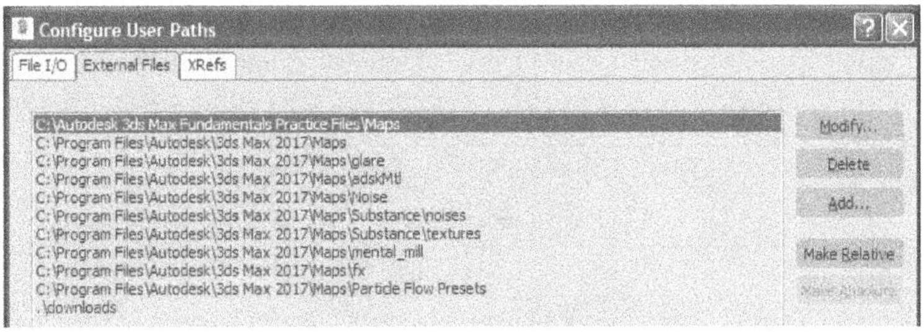

Figure 1–48

6. Select the *XRefs* tab and click **Add...**. In the Choose New XRef Path dialog box, navigate to your practice files folder (C:*Autodesk 3ds Max Fundamentals Practice Files)*, double-click on the *scenes* folder and click **Use Path**.

7. Click **OK** to exit the Configure User Paths dialog box. These settings are not specific to the scene file, so there is no need to save the file at this point.

Task 4 - Setting a Viewport Layout.

If you have created something in the current scene, you might be prompted to save or discard any changes.

1. In the Quick Access Toolbar, click 📂 (Open File) or use Application Menu>**Open**.

2. In the Open File dialog box note that the ...*scenes* folder in your practice files folder is already set, shown in Figure 1–49. Select the file **Interface.max** and click **Open**.

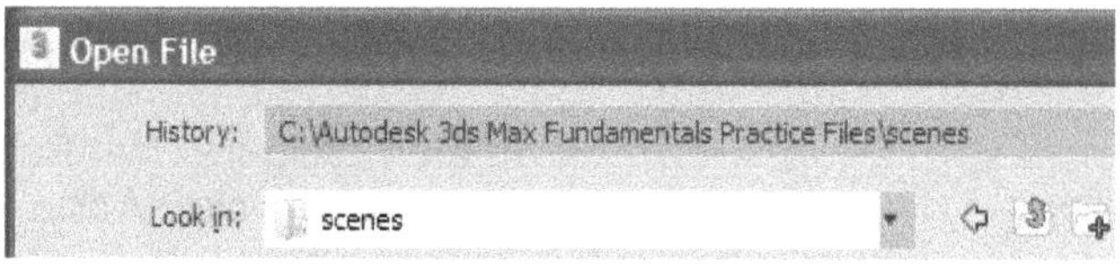

If a dialog box opens prompting you about a File Load: Mismatch for Gamma & LUT settings, click OK to accept the default values.

Open File

History: C:\Autodesk 3ds Max Fundamentals Practice Files\scenes

Look in: scenes

Figure 1–49

3. The model should display similar to that shown in Figure 1–50. Note that it opens in one maximized viewport layout, which was previously saved with the scene.

4. Verify that the Viewport Layout tab bar and the Scene Explorer are displayed and docked along the left side of the viewport.

If the ribbon is covering the top portion of your model, minimize it by clicking ⊡.

5. In the Scene Explorer toolbar, click ▇ (Display None) to clear all the categories. Note that the object list is empty.

6. Click ▤ (Display All) to activate all the different categories of objects. All of the selected tools have a blue background, indicating that they are active. Note the three main objects that make up the model are listed, as shown in Figure 1–50.

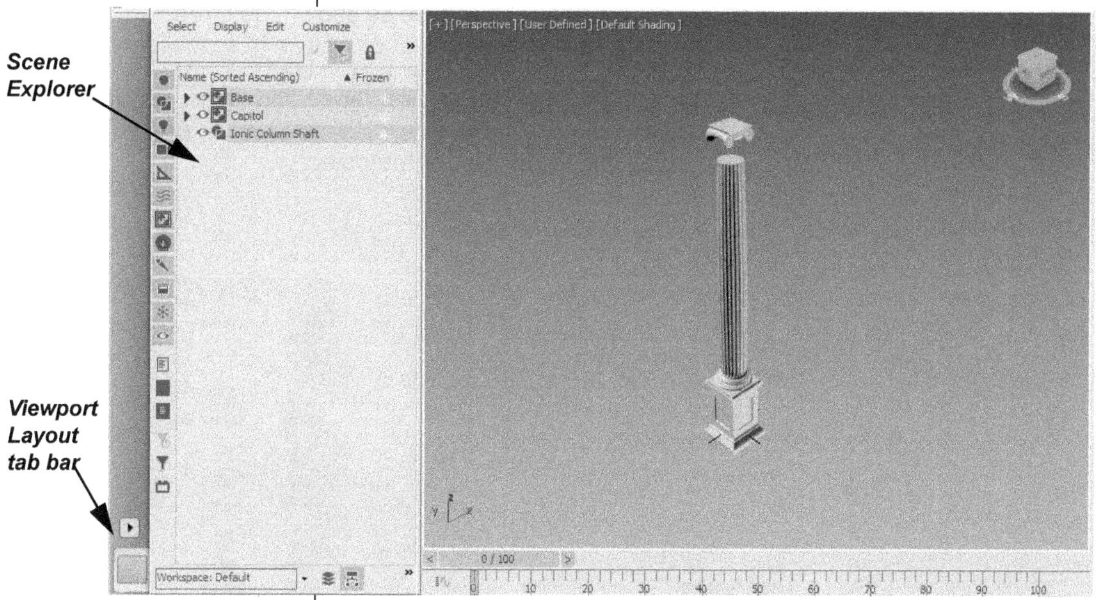

Scene
Explorer

Viewport
Layout
tab bar

Figure 1–50

- The file can be zoomed out by rolling the middle mouse button to display the complete model in the viewport.

7. In the Viewport Layouts tab bar, click [▶] to expand the Standard Viewport Layouts panel. Select the layout, as shown in Figure 1–51 (second row, second column).

- Note that the model displays in three viewport layouts and the newly selected layout is added to the tabs list, as shown in Figure 1–52.

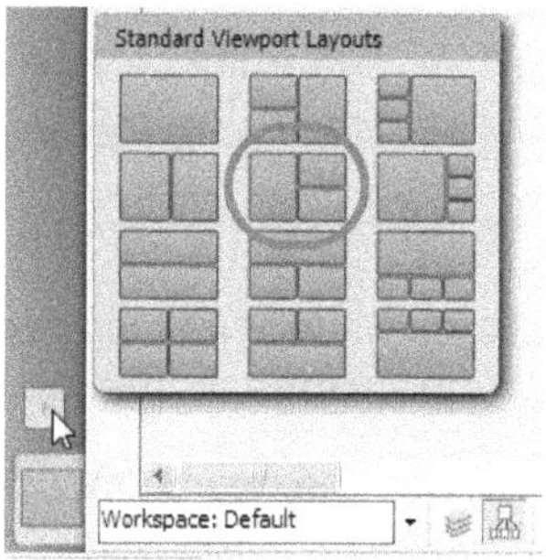

Figure 1–51

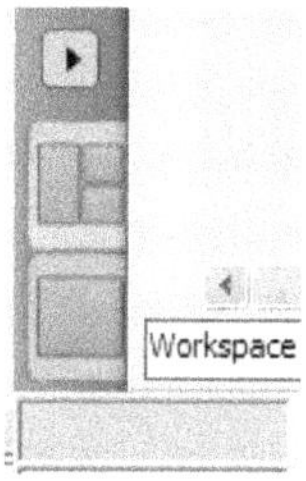

Figure 1–52

8. Note that a yellow border displays around the **Top** viewport, indicating that it is the active viewport. In this viewport, click on **[Wireframe]** (Per-View Preference label) to display the menu.

9. Select **Stylized>Graphite**, as shown in Figure 1–53. Note the change in the display of objects in this view only.

10. Click on **[Top]** (Point of View label) and select **Right**, as shown in Figure 1–54. Alternatively, you can press <R> to display the **Right** view of the object.

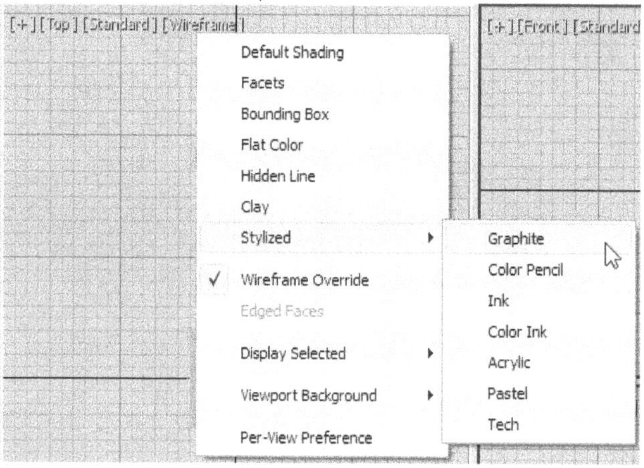

Figure 1–53

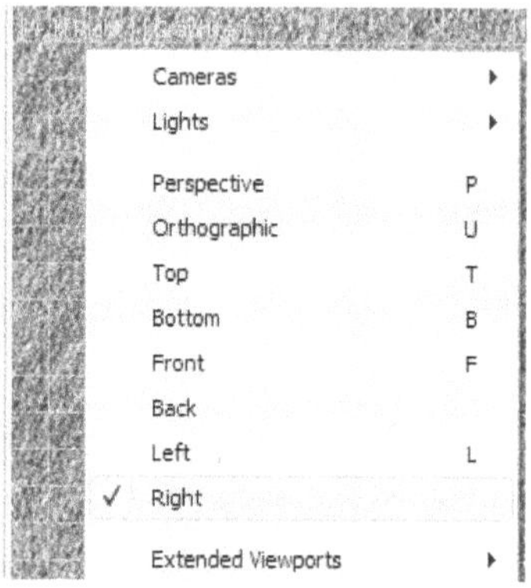

Figure 1–54

11. Use the mouse wheel to zoom out so that the complete model is displayed in this viewport. While holding the middle mouse button, drag the cursor to pan the objects so that they are centrally located in the viewport.

Click on [Left] (Point of View label) will be referred to set the Left Point of View label.

12. Click in empty space in the lower right viewport (**Left** view). Note that the yellow border now displays around this viewport, indicating that it is the active viewport. Set the following:

- *Left* Point of View label: **Perspective**
- *Wireframe* Per-View Preference: **Default Shading**

13. Press <Z> to zoom in to the objects in this viewport.

14. In the top right viewport, ensure that the *Point of View* is set to **Front** and change the *Wireframe* Visual Style to **Clay**.

15. Use the middle mouse button to pan and zoom to display the objects in this view.

- The objects and the viewport layout should look similar to those in Figure 1–55.

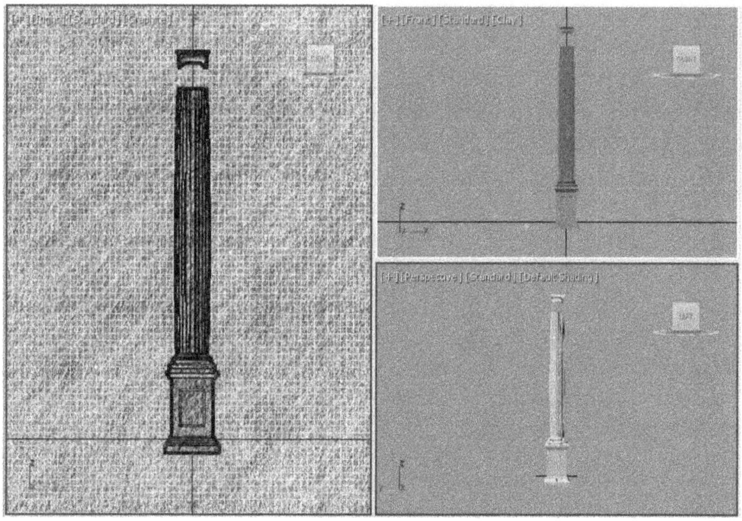

Figure 1–55

Task 5 - Modifying the objects using the Command Panel.

1. In the Viewport Layout tab bar, select the initial layout that existed with the scene, as shown in Figure 1–56. The objects display in a single viewport in the **Perspective** view with the **Default Shading** Visual Style.

2. In the Command Panel, select the Create panel ($+$), if required (active by default), as shown in Figure 1–57.

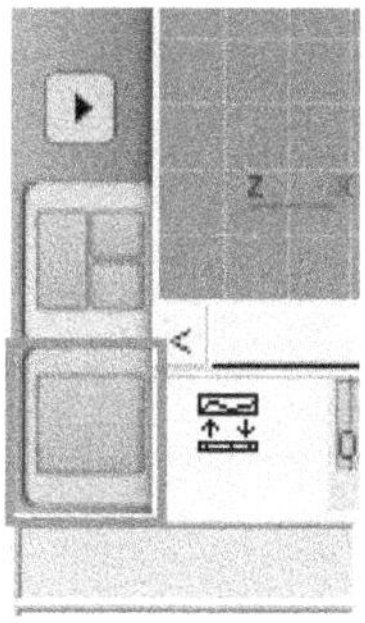

Figure 1–56

Figure 1–57

3. Select the *Geometry* category by clicking (Geometry), if required (active by default). The different types of geometry that you can create are listed here.

4. In the Command Panel, select the Modify panel (![icon]). The panel is empty as no objects are currently selected.

5. In the Main Toolbar, click ![icon] (Select Object), if required (active by default).

Names only display when the cursor is hovered over an unselected object. Once the object has been selected, its name is displayed in the Modifier Stack.

6. In the viewport, hover the cursor over the cyan (blue) object to display its name, **Ionic Column Shaft**. Click the object to select it. The **Ionic Column Shaft** is also highlighted in the Scene Explorer, indicating that it is selected. The name and modifiers that have been applied are displayed in the Command Panel. The Status Line at the bottom of the viewport, displays **1 Object Selected**, as shown in Figure 1–58.

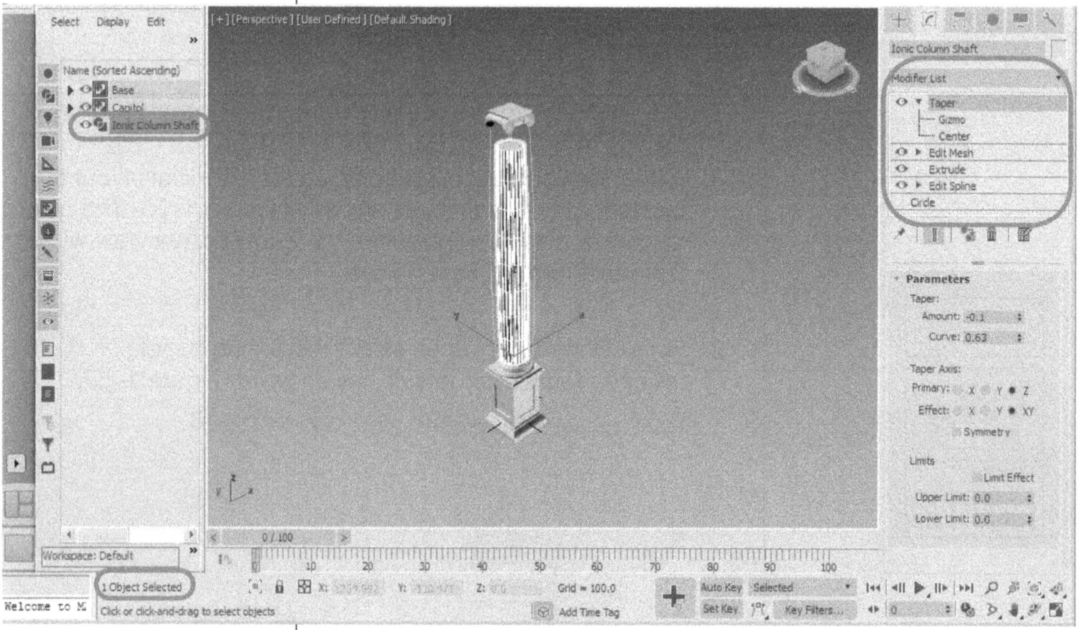

Figure 1–58

7. In the Command Panel, next to the object name **Ionic Column Shaft**, select the color swatch. Select a different color and click **OK** to change the color of the column shaft.

8. In the Modifier Stack, the list of modifiers that have been used on the column shaft are displayed, as shown in Figure 1–59.

    Click ![eye icon] (eye) next to the **Taper** modifier to toggle the taper off and then on again and note the effect on the object. Leave it on.

9. In the Modifier Stack, select the **Extrude** modifier. In the Warning dialog box, click **Hold/Yes** to continue.

10. The **Extrude** parameters are displayed in the rollouts. Note that the *Amount* displays the height of the shaft. Change it to **440.0** (as shown in Figure 1–60) and press <Enter>. The column shaft is extended and touches the top. The modifiers above the extrude are automatically reapplied to the object with its new height.

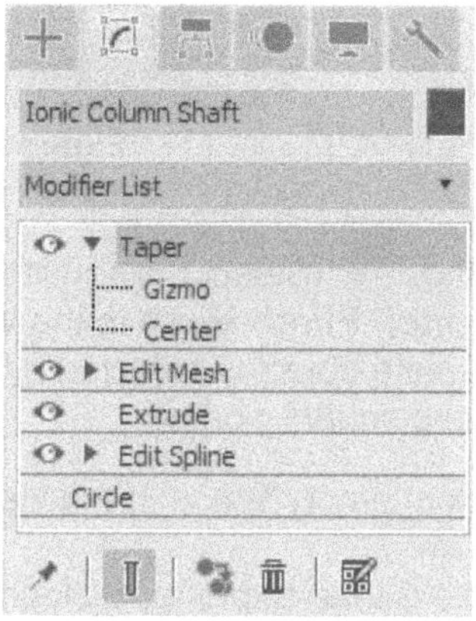

You can adjust parameters at any level of the Modifier Stack. To change the parameter, enter the value in the Amount edit box or use the spinners ⬍.

Figure 1–59

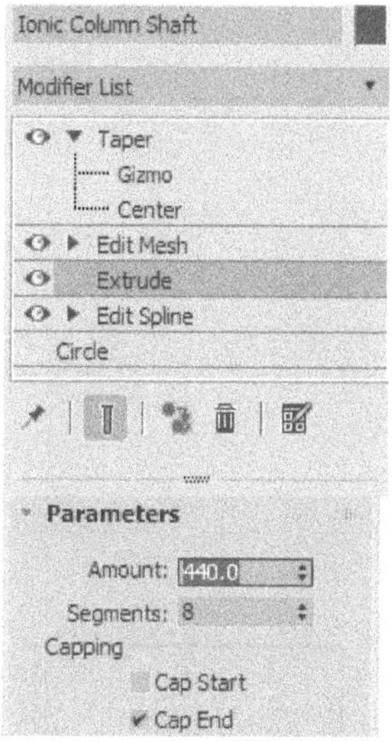

Figure 1–60

Task 6 - Using the Scene Explorer.

---

1. In the Scene Explorer, note an arrow besides the objects **Capitol** and **Base,** indicating that each have a group of objects inside it. Click on the arrow besides **Capitol** to expand the group and note the different objects sorted in a hierarchical fashion, as shown in Figure 1–61.

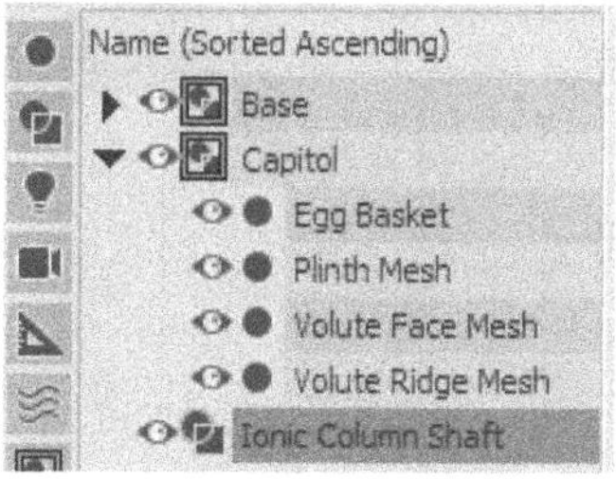

Figure 1–61

2. Click in empty space in the viewport to clear the selection. Note that the Command Panel is empty as there are no objects currently selected. Also note that nothing is highlighted in the Scene Explorer.

3. In the viewport, hover the cursor over the top gray square portion of the object. It displays the name as **[Capitol] Plinth Mesh**, as shown in Figure 1–62.

Figure 1–62

4. As the [icon] (Select Object) is already active, click on **[Capitol] Plinth Mesh** in the viewport to select it. The complete object is selected although, the Plinth Mesh is just the top square portion.

5. Click in empty space in the viewport to clear the selection.

6. In the Scene Explorer, click on [icon] for **Plinth Mesh** and note that only the top most square object of the Capitol is hidden in the viewport, as shown in Figure 1–63.

Figure 1–63

7. Similarly, in the Scene Explorer, click on 👁 for **Volute Face Mesh** and **Volute Ridge Mesh** and note that only the inner cylindrical object remains visible, as shown in Figure 1–64.

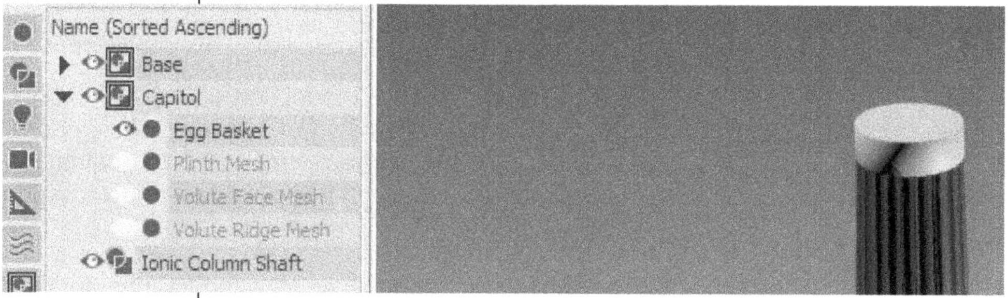

Figure 1–64

8. In the Scene Explorer, click on ▢ (grayed out eye) for the three hidden sub objects to make them visible again.

9. Select **Application Menu>Save As** and save your work as **MyInterface.max**.

- When you save a file, verify that it is being saved to the ...\scenes folder.

Clicking 💾 *(Save File) in the Quick Access Toolbar or selecting* **Save** *in the* **Application Menu**, *overwrites the existing file. If you are saving an unnamed file for the first time, these options work as* **Save As**.

Practice 1b

Autodesk 3ds Max Quickstart

Practice Objective

- Create primitive objects and apply basic animation to a primitive object.

Estimated time for completion: 15 minutes

In this practice, you will model and animate a teapot driving through a city of pyramids. This practice will introduce you to the Autodesk 3ds Max interface and workflow fundamentals. Many of the commands used in this practice are discussed later in the student guide.

Many of you will probably never need to animate a teapot driving through a city of pyramids. This practice is designed to introduce you to interactive 3D modeling and animation, and working with the interface.

Task 1 - Create Primitive Objects.

If an unsaved scene is open, you might be required to save or discard any changes to the scene.

1. Select **Application Menu>Reset** to start a new file. Click **Yes** in the confirmation dialog box.

2. In the Command Panel, verify that the Create panel (+)

   and ● (Geometry) are selected (active by default). Also, ensure that the *Standard Primitives* sub-category is displayed.

3. In the Object Type rollout, click **Pyramid** to activate it, as shown in Figure 1–65.

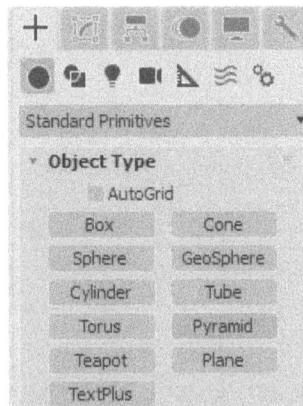

Figure 1–65

*If the Scene Explorer is not displayed, select **Tools>Scene Explorer** and then dock it.*

4. In the **Perspective** viewport (which is maximized), near the center of the grid, click and drag to create the base for a pyramid, as shown in Figure 1–66. Release the mouse button and continue to move the cursor up to set the height of the pyramid. When your pyramid displays correctly (similar to that shown in Figure 1–67), click to end the creation process. In the Scene Explorer, note that a highlighted geometry is listed with the name **Pyramid001,** indicating that it is selected.

| **Figure 1–66** | **Figure 1–67** |

To make any changes, the object should be selected.

5. In the Command Panel, click the **Color** swatch to the right of the pyramid name (**Pyramid001**), select a different color in the Object Color dialog box and verify that **Assign Random Colors** is selected. This enables you to create objects with different colors automatically. Click **OK**. Note that the color of the pyramid and the swatch change in the viewport.

6. In the Navigation toolbar, found in the lower right corner of the interface, click ▨ (Maximize Viewport) or use <Alt>+<W>. Note that the pyramid is displayed in four equal viewports with different viewing angles.

The transform tools are discussed in detail, later in the student guide.

7. You might need to move the pyramid to the upper left quadrant of the home grid. In the Main Toolbar, click

   ✛ (Select and Move). In the **Top** view (upper left viewport), right-click to make it active with the object still selected.

   • Clicking in a viewport makes it active, but loses the selection of objects. To maintain the selection of objects, right-click to activate the viewport.

8. Click and hold the yellow square (anywhere along the two outer edges when the cursor displays as a move cursor) of the Transform gizmo, as shown in Figure 1–68. While holding the object, drag it to the new location. Leave the gizmo once the object is at the correct location.

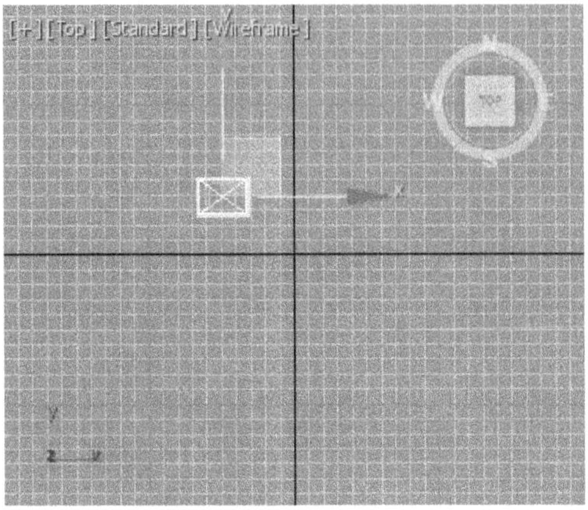

Figure 1–68

9. In the Object Type rollout, click **Pyramid** again. In the **Top** viewport, click and drag to create the base for another pyramid on the lower side of the main grid line, opposite to the first one. Release the mouse button and continue to move the cursor up to set the height of the pyramid. Because you are in the **Top** viewport, the height of the pyramid is not displayed. You can visually note the height in other three viewports in which the height is displayed. Once the pyramid displays as required, click to complete the command.

10. Similarly, create a number of pyramids on the home grid. Create a row of pyramids in one direction and a few others to create a street corner in the pyramid city, as shown in Figure 1–69. Try to keep all of the pyramids in the grid visible in the **Perspective** viewport.

You can create objects in any viewport, but the orientation of the objects depends on the viewport created. Note that their creation is also displayed interactively in other viewports.

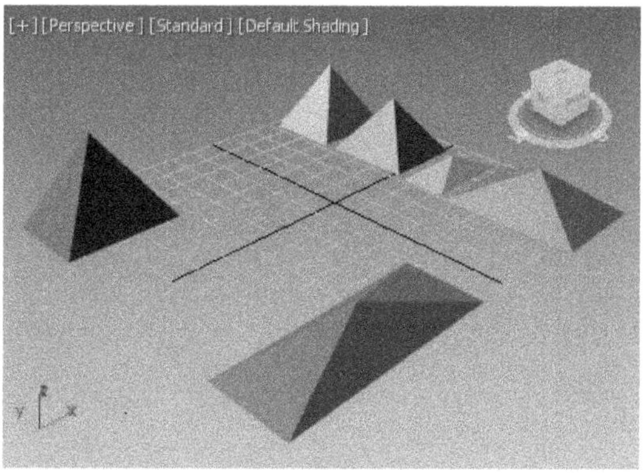

Figure 1–69

To display all of the pyramids in a viewport, use the middle mouse wheel to zoom in and out and press, hold, and drag it to pan.

11. Once the required number of pyramids have been created, right-click in empty space or press <Esc> to exit the **Pyramid** command.

12. Make the **Perspective** viewport active and maximize the

   viewport by clicking [image] (Maximize Viewport) or use <Alt>+<W>. You can click anywhere in empty space to clear a selected object and activate the viewport.

13. In the Create panel (+)> [image] (Geometry), in the Object Type rollout, click **Teapot** to activate it.

14. In the lower left area of the **Perspective** viewport, click and drag to create a teapot, as shown in Figure 1–70.

Figure 1–70

Task 2 - Add Basic Animation.

Animation controls are discussed in detail later in the student guide.

1. The Animation controls are next to the Status Bar at the bottom of the screen. Click **Auto Key**, as shown in Figure 1–71. Once you click it, the time slider bar and border around the active viewport (**Perspective** viewport) are highlighted in red.

Figure 1–71

2. Drag the time slider in the red slider bar until the frame indicator displays **30/100** (< 30 / 100 >), as shown in Figure 1–72.

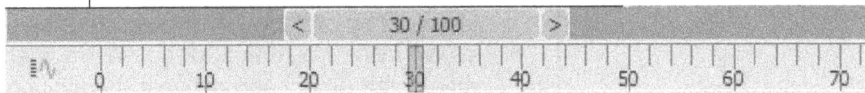

Figure 1–72

3. Click on the teapot, if not already selected, right-click and select **Move** in the **transform** quad menu, as shown in Figure 1–73. Alternatively, in the Main Toolbar, click

 (Select and Move) after selecting your teapot.

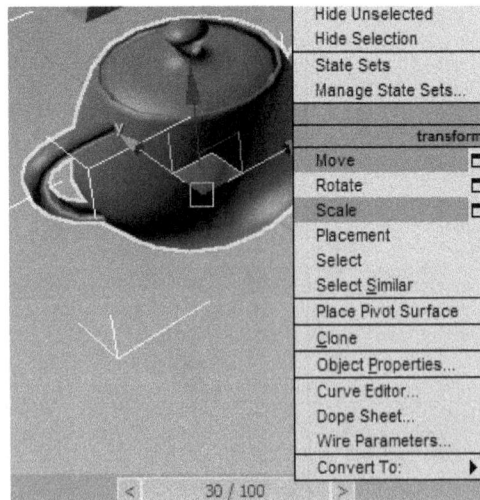

Figure 1–73

4. Move the cursor over the X axis (red arrow) of the teapot Move gizmo so that it displays in yellow. Hold and drag to move the teapot in the X direction, as shown in Figure 1–74. Move it to midway between the original position and the intersection of the home grid.

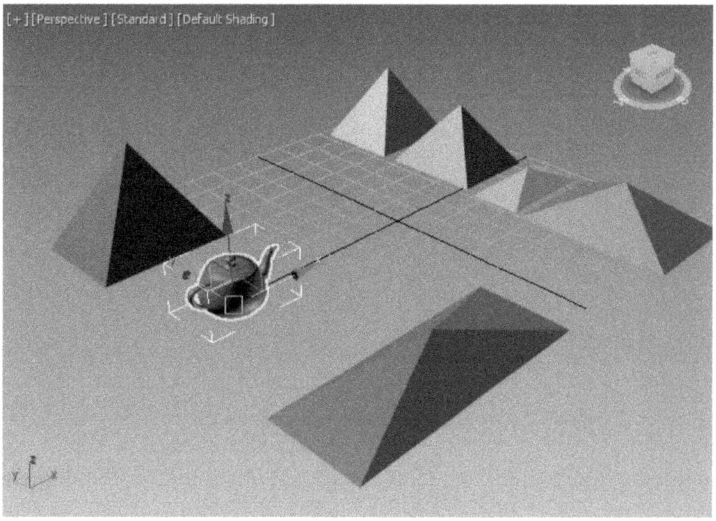

Figure 1–74

5. Move and drag the time slider again to read **60/100**.

6. Move the teapot in the X direction till it reaches the intersection of the horizontal street, as shown in Figure 1–75.

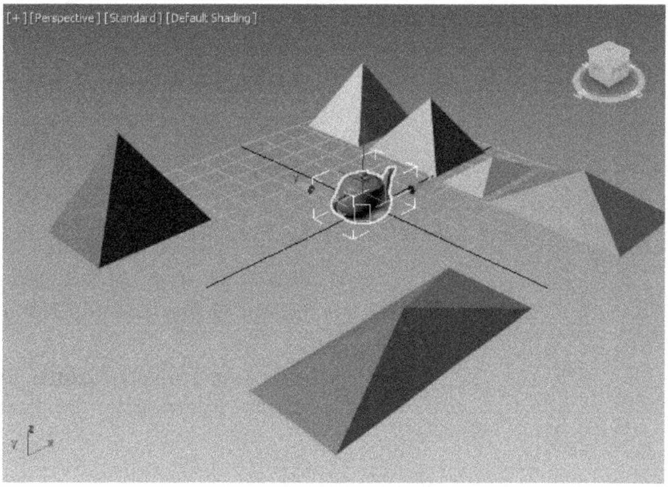

Figure 1–75

7. Move and drag the time slider to read **90/100**. Move the teapot in the Y direction (left, green arrow) till it reaches the end of the horizontal street, as shown in Figure 1–76.

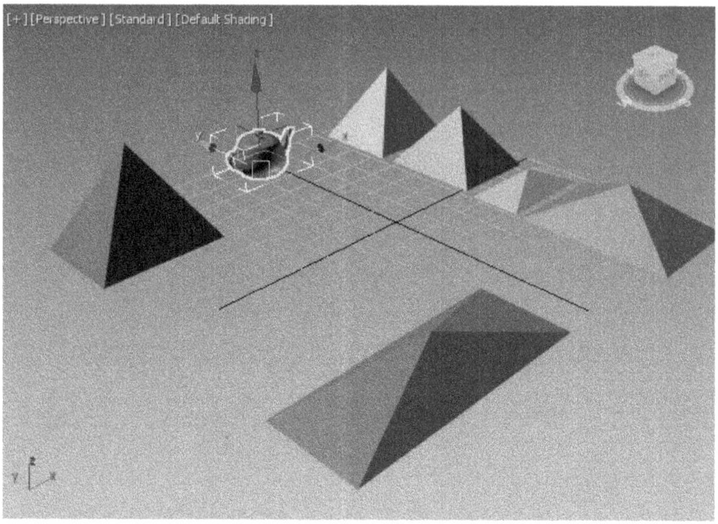

Figure 1–76

- The track bar below the time slider now has four red boxes indicating that the keyframes have been set at frames 0, 30, 60, and 90.

8. In the Animation Controls (|◄◄ ◄ⅠⅠ ▶Ⅰ ⅠⅠ▶ ▶▶Ⅰ) located near the bottom right of the screen, click ▶Ⅰ (Play). The teapot is now animated in the viewport, moving through the pyramid city. Click ⅠⅠ (Stop Animation) to stop the animation.

9. You can add a rotation to the teapot. Drag the time slider to frame **60**.

10. Click ◤ (Maximize Viewport) to change to four equal viewports. In all of the viewports, note that the teapot has moved to the grid intersection position. Right-click on the teapot and select **Rotate**. You can also click ↻ (Select and Rotate) in the Main Toolbar.

11. The Rotation Transform gizmo is displayed on the teapot. Move the cursor over the horizontal axis (yellow circle). Rotate the teapot counter-clockwise so that the spout is pointing to the left. The rotation angle is displayed in the viewport, as shown in Figure 1–77. The rotation angle is also displayed in the *Transform Type-in* fields in the Status Bar.

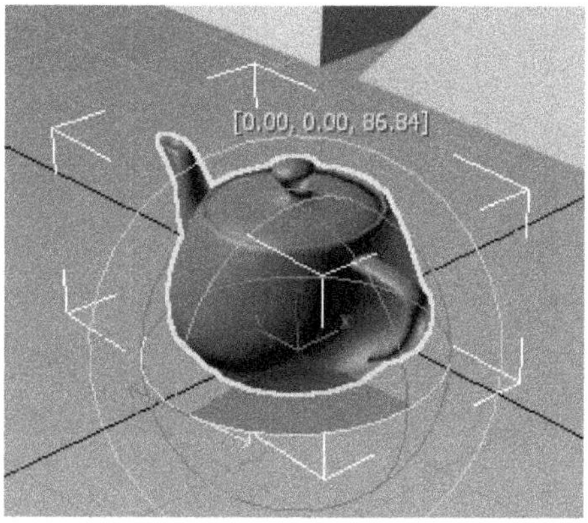

Figure 1–77

- At frame 60, the time slider now displays a red and green box indicating both rotation and position keys

12. Play the animation using ▶ (Play). Click ⏸ (Stop) to stop the animation. You can also view the animation by dragging the time slider back and forth. This is called *scrubbing* the time slider.

13. To only rotate the teapot after frame 45, add a keyframe rotation of **0** at frame 45. Play the animation to view the changes.

14. Toggle off **Auto Key** mode by clicking the red **Auto Key**.

15. Click in empty space to clear the object selection.

16. Select **Application Menu>Save As** and save your work as **MyPyramidCity.max**. Verify that it is being saved in the ...\scenes folder.

- You can also open **Pyramidcity.max** from your practices files folder to compare with a similar type file.

Chapter Review Questions

1. Which of the Autodesk 3ds Max interface components contains 🔒 (Selection Lock)?

   a. Modeling Ribbon

   b. Status Bar

   c. InfoCenter

   d. Quick Access Toolbar

2. Which of the following tabs are part of the Modeling ribbon? (Select all that apply.)

   a. Freeform

   b. Display

   c. Utilities

   d. Modeling

3. In the Configure User Paths dialog box, which tab stores the location of the files for open, save, export, etc.?

   a. *XRefs* tab

   b. *System* tab

   c. *External Files* tab

   d. *File I/O* tab

4. Which display driver does not require hardware support?

   a. Nitrous Direct3D 11

   b. Nitrous Direct3D 9

   c. Nitrous Software

5. Which of the following is not a **Stylized** menu option?

   a. **Color Pencil**

   b. **Graphite**

   c. **Shaded**

   d. **Pastel**

Command Summary

Button	Command	Location
+	Create panel	• **Command Panel**
📂	Open	• **Quick Access Toolbar** • **Application Menu:** Open>Open
📁	Project Folder	• **Quick Access Toolbar** • **Application Menu:** Manage
▦	Ribbon	• **Main Toolbar** • **Customize:** Show UI>Show Ribbon
N/A	Save As	• **Application Menu:** Save As
💾	Save File	• **Quick Access Toolbar** • **Application Menu:** Save
N/A	Scene Explorer	• **Tools:** Saved Scene Explorers>Workspace:Default

Autodesk 3ds Max Configuration

The Autodesk® 3ds Max® software layout and unique to other Autodesk products. Becoming familiar with its navigation tools, viewing the model in the viewport, and how to work with the model in the interface is an important step to efficiently create a visualization project.

Learning Objectives in this Chapter

- Move around in a scene using the various navigation tools.
- Set the layout and viewport configuration settings.
- Select objects using the object selection tools.
- Assign and change units in a scene.
- Group similar objects together in a layer and adjust layer properties.
- Modify the display settings of layers and objects.

2.1 Viewport Navigation

Navigation tools are used to change the point of view in viewports. Perspective, User, and Orthographic views (non-camera views such as Top, Front, etc.) share common viewport controls. The navigation tools are different in the non-camera and camera views.

Viewport Navigation Toolbar

The navigation tools (shown in Figure 2–1) are available in the lower right corner of the interface.

Figure 2–1

- When selected, the tool button is highlighted. Press <Esc> or select another tool to toggle a selected tool off.

- Several buttons contain an arrow symbol in the lower right corner, which you can hold to expand a flyout.

Zooming with the mouse wheel in a perspective view might not work in all scenes due to roundoff issues. If you are unable to zoom, click ☉ (Zoom Extents) and use ☌ (Zoom) instead of the mouse wheel.

☌	**Zoom:** When this tool is active, click, hold, and drag the cursor to zoom in or out of the active viewport.
☌	**Zoom All:** Activate and then click and drag to zoom in or out simultaneously in all viewports.
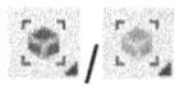 ☉/☉	**Zoom Extents/Zoom Extents Selected:** Zooms to the extents of all visible objects/selected objects only in the active viewport.
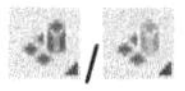 ☉/☉	**Zoom Extents All/Zoom Extents All Selected:** Zoom to the extents of all visible objects/selected objects only in all viewports.
☷	**Zoom Region** (zoom window) in the active viewport.
☌	**Field of View:** This is a flyout option in Zoom Region, available only in **Perspective** or **Camera** view. It adjusts the perspective of the view, similar to changing the focal length of a camera. Even small changes to the Field of View setting can cause large distortions. To reset, enter a default field of view value of **45 degrees** in the Viewport Configuration dialog box.
✋	**Pan View:** Hold in a viewport and drag to pan your objects. You can also hold and drag the middle mouse wheel to pan.

![icon]	**2D Pan Zoom mode:** A flyout option in Pan View, available in **Perspective** and **Camera** views only. It enables you to zoom/pan on objects in a viewport that are not located in the rendering frame. The camera remains unchanged when you are panning and zooming in the **Camera** viewport.
![icon]	**Walk Through:** A flyout option in Pan View, available in **Perspective** and **Camera** views only. Click and hold while moving the cursor to change where you are looking. Use the arrow keys to walk forward, back, and to the side. Move up or down by pressing <Shift>+<Up> or <Down>. To speed up a movement hold <]> (right bracket) while moving, and slow down movement by pressing <[> (left bracket).
![icon]	**Orbit**, **Orbit Selected,** and **Orbit SubObject**: Enables you to rotate the view by clicking and dragging inside or outside a trackball. Dragging inside the trackball causes the view to rotate around the scene, while dragging outside causes the view to twist in place. Click and drag on the boxes that display along the trackball to constrain the rotation to a single axis.
![icon]	**Orbit Point of Interest**: The point of interest is set as the point of rotation around which the view is rotated.
![icon]	**Maximize Viewport:** Toggles between the display of multiple viewports and the display of a single maximized viewport. Keyboard shortcut is <Alt>+<W>.

New 💡
in 2017

Hint: Switching Maximized Viewports

When you maximize a single viewport from a multi-viewport layout, you can switch to other viewports while in the current maximized viewport display. In the maximized viewport display, hold <Win> (the Windows logo key, which might also be <Start>) and then press <Shift> (do not hold <Shift>). An overlay opens displaying all of the available viewports and the currently maximized viewport highlighted with a yellow border, as shown in Figure 2–2. While holding <Win>, press <Shift> repeatedly to highlight the next viewport option and release <Win> to maximize the highlighted viewport.

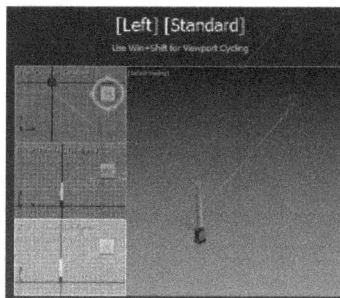

Figure 2–2

Viewport Navigation Toolbar (Camera Viewport)

Camera viewports show what is visible to the camera object based on its Field of View. Similar to other viewports, camera viewports can be directly navigated, but some of the controls are slightly different, as shown in Figure 2–3.

Figure 2–3

- Note that most of these controls actually move the camera or target object.

	Dolly Camera is similar to **Zoom**. The flyout contains options to dolly (move) the camera, the target, or both along the camera's directional axis.
	Perspective is a combination of **Field of View** and **Dolly** that attempts to maintain the same scene composition while changing the camera's Field of View.
	Roll Camera rotates a camera along the axis of its view.
	Orbit Camera rotates a camera around the target position similar to **Orbit**. The flyout option (**Pan Camera**) rotates the target around the camera instead.
	Truck Camera is similar to Pan when used in a **Camera** view.

Viewport Navigation using the ViewCube

The ViewCube (shown in Figure 2–4) is a navigation tool and by default, it displays in the top right corner of each viewport indicating the orientation of the scene. The ViewCube is activated by hovering the cursor over it in the active viewport.

- Selecting any of the ViewCube faces or edges, causes the viewport to immediately swing around to that view. You can also select the ViewCube and drag the mouse to quickly rotate the Viewport.

- When the ViewCube is active, the **Home** icon becomes visible near the top left corner. Clicking the **Home** icon resets the viewport.

Home

Menu button

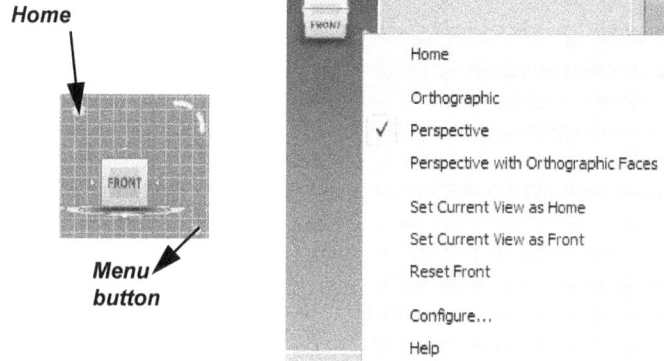
Figure 2–4

The ViewCube tool options can also be accessed in the **Views** menu.

• Clicking on the menu button or right-clicking on the ViewCube provides you with additional options (shown in Figure 2–4) that enable you to set the current view as Home, Orthographic, Configure etc.

• Selecting the **Configure** option, opens the Viewport Configuration dialog box in the *ViewCube* tab containing options to show or hide the ViewCube, control its size and display, control what happens when dragging on the ViewCube, and displaying the compass below the ViewCube.

Viewport Navigation using the SteeringWheel

The SteeringWheel (shown in Figure 2–5) is another navigation tool and it can be toggled on by pressing <Shift>+<W> where it gets attached to the cursor.

• It provides instant access to zoom/pan, orbit, etc. The **Rewind** feature is unique to this tool and provides a thumbnail of all of your previous views. It also enables you to visually select any of them to return to that view. Press <Shift>+<W> to toggle the SteeringWheel on and off. You can also press <Esc> to hide its display.

The Steering wheel tool options can also be accessed in the **Views** menu.

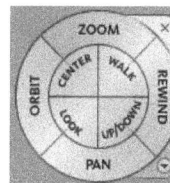
Figure 2–5

2.2 Viewport Configuration and Settings

Viewport Configuration

The layout and display settings of your viewports can be set through the Viewport Configuration dialog box. In the Viewport label, click [+] (General label) to display the label menu and select **Configure Viewports**, as shown in Figure 2–6. Alternatively, select the **Shading Viewport** label>**Viewport Global Settings**.

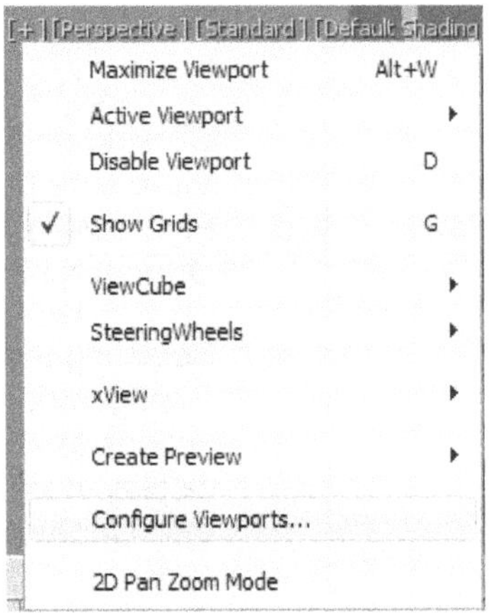

[+] [Perspective] [Standard] [Default Shading	
Maximize Viewport	Alt+W
Active Viewport	▶
Disable Viewport	D
✓ Show Grids	G
ViewCube	▶
SteeringWheels	▶
xView	▶
Create Preview	▶
Configure Viewports...	
2D Pan Zoom Mode	

Figure 2–6

If you have selected one of the legacy display drivers (Direct 3D or OpenGL), the Rendering Method tab displays.

The Viewport Configuration dialog box opens and contains tabs which differ based on the selected display driver. By default, the Viewport Configuration dialog box opens with the *Display Performance* tab active. Some of the tabs that are available in the Viewport Configuration dialog box are described in the following section. The remaining tabs are discussed throughout the student guide, as required.

Layout tab

The *Layout* tab in the Viewport Configuration dialog box (shown in Figure 2–7) enables you to set the size and shape of viewports and its view type. Select one of the preset viewport layouts to select a view type.

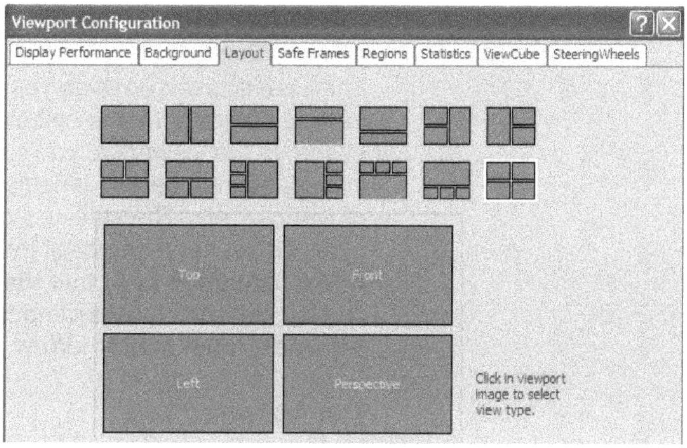

You can also set up multiple viewport layouts and switch between them by selecting the saved tabs in the Viewport Layouts tab bar.

Figure 2–7

SteeringWheels tab

The *SteeringWheels* tab (shown in Figure 2–8) enables you control the properties of the Steering Wheel such as displaying them as Big or Mini Wheels and setting their respective sizes and opacity. You can also set the options for tools, such as the **Zoom** tool and the **Orbit** tool.

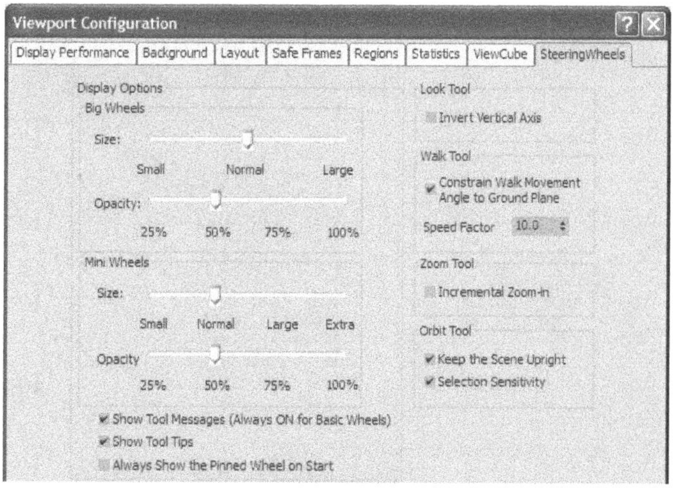

Figure 2–8

ViewCube tab

Similar to the *SteeringWheels* tab, the *ViewCube* tab has options for controlling the display of the ViewCube. You can control the size of the ViewCube, what the ViewCube displays when selected, and the position of the compass.

Statistics tab

The *Statistics* tab enables you to customize the display of various statistics for the selected geometry or the complete scene. In the viewports, you can display the number of polygons in a scene, number of triangular faces, number of edges, number of vertices, etc. The statistics can be displayed on the screen, near the left hand corner of the active viewport by selecting **Show Statistics in Active View** in the dialog box. You can also display statistics by selecting **Show Statistics** in the **General Viewport label menu>xView** or by pressing <7>.

Background tab

The *Background* tab (shown in Figure 2–9) enables you to set an image, environment map, or animation as the background of your active viewport or all viewports.

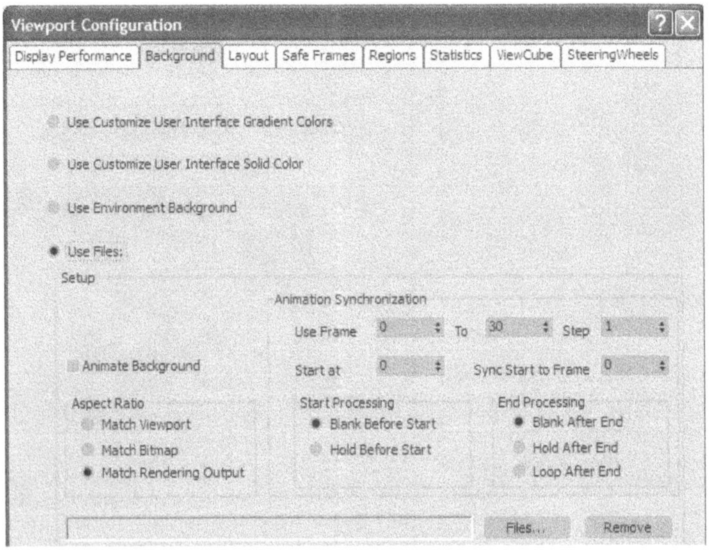

Figure 2–9

Viewport Setting and Preferences

New
in 2017

You can control the viewport display of the models in the Viewport Setting and Preference dialog box, as shown in Figure 2–10. To open the dialog box, in the viewport, click the **Shading Viewport** label and in the label menu select **Per-View Presets**, as shown in Figure 2–10. Alternatively, select **Per-View Preference>Per-View Preference**.

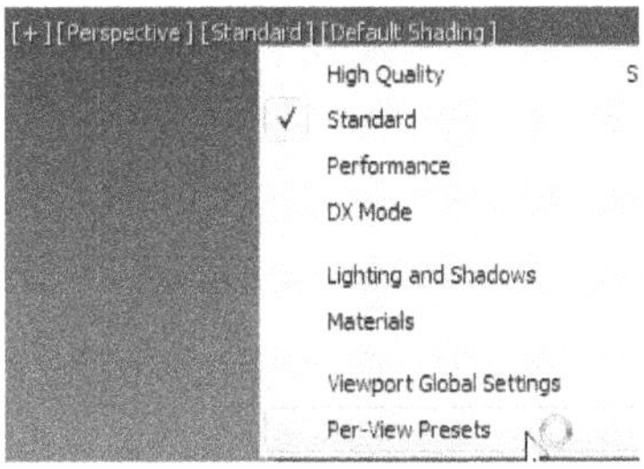

Figure 2–10

The Viewport Setting and Preference dialog box contains two tabs: *Per-View Presets* and *Per-View Preferences*. The *Per-View Presets* tab (shown in Figure 2–11), has the following options:

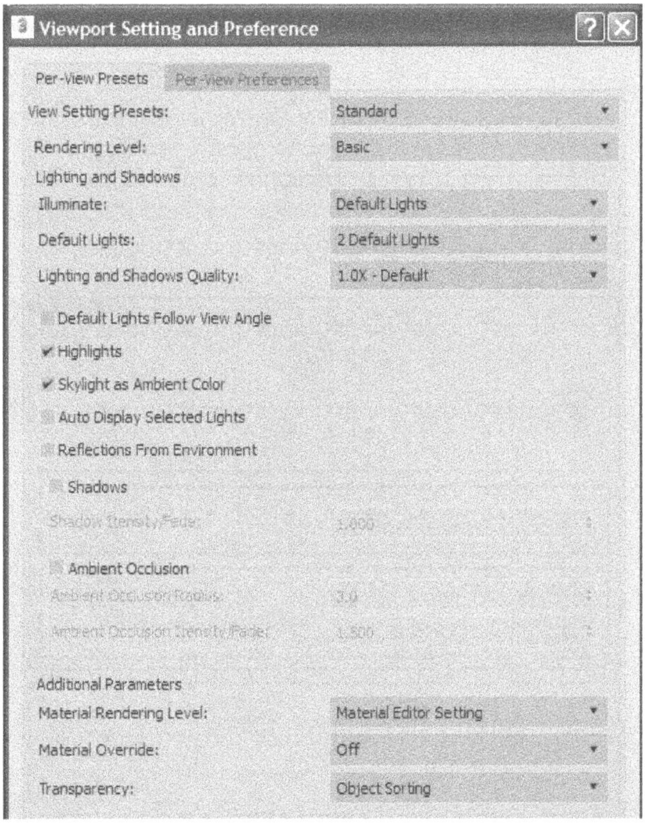

Figure 2–11

- You can create and add a user-defined view setting preset to the list of choices. Note, however, that you can have only one user-defined view setting, and you cannot change the four existing presets (i.e., High Quality, Standard, Performance or DX mode).

- The **Default Lights** are used to illuminate the viewports, providing even illumination. You can select **1 Default Light** or **2 Default Lights**.

- The **Default Lights Follow View Angle** option tracks changes to the position of the viewport using two default lights.

- The **Skylights as Ambient Color** option causes the skylights to emit ambient color and not cast shadows.

- The **Shadows** options renders the scene with shadows and the **Ambient Occlusion** helps improve the display of shadows.

- The *Additional Parameters* area contains settings for various material-related options, such as Material override and Transparency.

The *Per-View Preferences* tab (shown in Figure 2–12) enables you to control the display of selected objects in a specific viewport. You can set a selection to display using a selection bracket, or shade the selected faces/objects with or without edges.

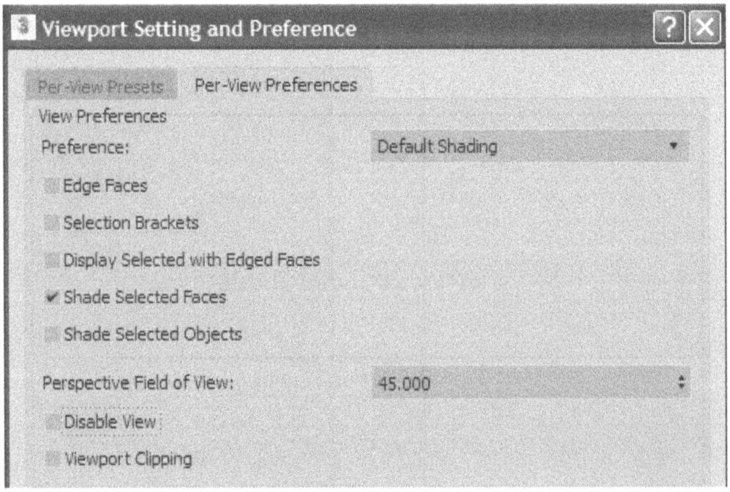

Figure 2–12

Practice 2a

Viewport Configuration and Navigation

Practice Objectives

- Set the configuration of the viewport.
- Move around a scene using different navigation tools.

Estimated time for completion: 5 minutes

In this practice, you will set various configuration option for an exiting viewport layout. You will then move around a scene and experiment with changing the camera position by using navigations tools such as **Zoom**, **Orbit**, **Pan View** and other **SE Camera** options.

1. In the Quick Access Toolbar, click 📂 (Open File) or click **Application Menu>Open>Open**, to open the Open File dialog box. If you were working in the software, you might be prompted to save or discard any changes to the scene.

    - In the Open file dialog box, note that the *C:\Autodesk 3ds Max Fundamentals Practice Files\scenes* folder is set, because you have already set the Project Folder. If you did not set the path to your practice files folder, return to **Chapter 1: Introduction to Autodesk 3ds Max** and complete Task 1 to Task 3 in **Practice 1a: Organizing Folders and Working with the Interface**. You are required to set the project folder only once.

*If a dialog box opens prompting you about a Mismatch, click **OK** to accept the default values.*

2. In the Open File dialog box, select **Navigation.max** and click **Open**.

    - If the Viewport Layout tab bar is not displayed, right-click in an empty space of the Main Toolbar, clear and select the **Viewport Layout Tabs** option, and then dock it. If the Scene Explorer is not displayed, select **Tools>Scene Explorer** and then dock it.

    - The file opens the objects in four equal sized viewports. Along the left edge of the interface, in the Viewport Layouts tab bar, note that the file has been saved with two viewport layouts.

Alternatively, select the required viewport layout in the Viewport Configuration dialog box>Layout tab.

3. To create another layout, in the Viewport Layouts tab bar, click ▶ to expand the Standard Viewport Layouts panel. Select the layout shown in Figure 2–13.

Figure 2–13

- The pillar objects display in the **3 X 1** viewport layout and another layout tab is added to the Layouts tab bar.

4. Note that the **Top** viewport is the active viewport (it displays a yellow border). In the Navigation toolbar, note the available navigation tools are for the **Orthographic** view, as shown in Figure 2–14.

Figure 2–14

5. The complete objects are not displayed in the viewports. In the Zoom Extents flyout, click ⚏ (Zoom Extents All) to zoom to the extents of all of the objects in all of the viewports.

6. Click on empty space in the **Front** viewport to activate it.

*If the Scene Explorer is not displayed, select **Tools>Scene Explorer** and then dock it.*

7. In the Scene Explorer, select **Base** to select the base objects in all the viewports, as shown in Figure 2–15.

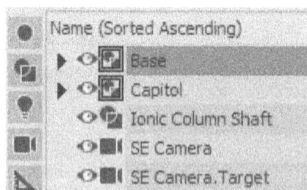

Figure 2–15

8. In the Zoom Extents All flyout, click ⚏ (Zoom Extents All Selected). Note that you are zoomed to the extents of the selected objects (Base) in all of the viewports.

9. With the Base still selected, click (Zoom Extents All). The camera zooms to the extents of all of the objects in all of the viewports.

10. Right-click in empty space in the **Left** viewport. Note that the **Left** viewport becomes active and the base object remains selected.

11. Click in empty space in the **Top** viewport to make it active. Note that this also clears the selection.

12. Hover the cursor over the left edge of the **Perspective** viewport. The cursor displays as a two-sided arrow. Click and drag the arrow horizontally to resize the viewports, as shown in Figure 2–16.

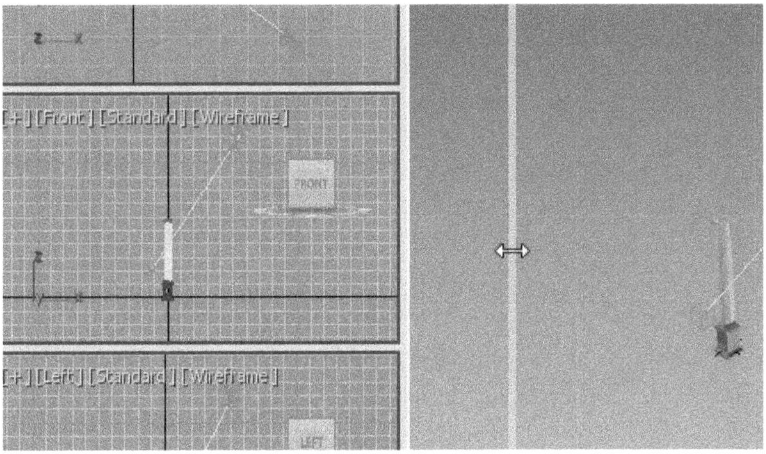

Figure 2–16

13. Click in the **Perspective** view to make it active. In the Viewport navigation tools, click (Maximize Viewport Toggle) to maximize the active viewport. Select the toggle again to return to the four viewport arrangement. Alternatively, press <Alt>+<W> to toggle between the maximized single viewport and multiple viewports. Leave the **Perspective** viewport maximized.

You must hold <Win> continuously for the overlay to display.

14. Hold <Win> (windows logo or the <Start> key) continuously and press <Shift> once. An overlay displays all of the available viewports in the layout, as shown in Figure 2–17. With <Win> still pressed, press <Shift> repeatedly to cycle through all of the viewports. When [Left] [Wireframe] is highlighted (as shown in Figure 2–17), release <Win> to maximize the viewport.

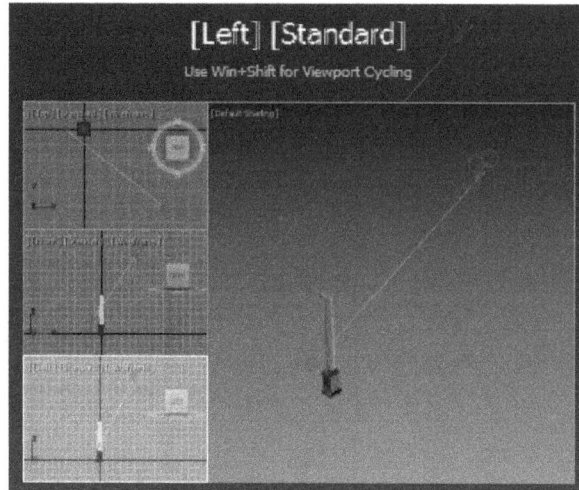

Figure 2–17

15. Select the **[Left]** Point of View label. In the label menu, select **Cameras>SE Camera**, as shown in Figure 2–18, to display the **Camera** view.

Figure 2–18

- Note that the navigation tools are different in a camera viewport, as shown in Figure 2–19.

Figure 2–19

16. Click (Maximize Viewport Toggle) to toggle to the four viewport display.

17. Click ![icon] (Zoom Extents All). Note that the **SE Camera** (lower left viewport) does not change because the non-camera navigation tools do not affect the camera views.

18. Click in the **Perspective** view to make it active and note how the navigation tools change.

19. Click in the **SE Camera** viewport to make it active.

20. Click ![icon] (Orbit Camera) and use it in the **SE Camera** viewport to orbit the camera. In the other viewports, note that the camera object is moving simultaneously as the pillar object moves in the camera viewport.

21. Experiment with changing the camera position using ![icon] (Roll Camera) and ![icon] (Dolly Camera).

You can use the mouse wheel to zoom in and out in a viewport and hold and drag the middle mouse button to pan.

22. In the **Perspective** viewport, practice navigating with the **Zoom**, **Zoom All**, **Orbit**, and **Pan View** options.

23. Close the file without saving.

2.3 Object Selection Methods

Working with modifiers and other functions requires you to select objects accurately, using various methods. The recommended method is to click on the required geometry in one of the

viewports to select it. It uses the ▨ (Select Object) tool in the Main Toolbar which is active by default.

Selection Preview

In the Nitrous viewports, hovering the cursor over an object displays a yellow outline for that object. This enables you to easily determine the object that is going to be selected. Once you click on an object a blue outline displays indicating the selection, as shown in Figure 2–20.

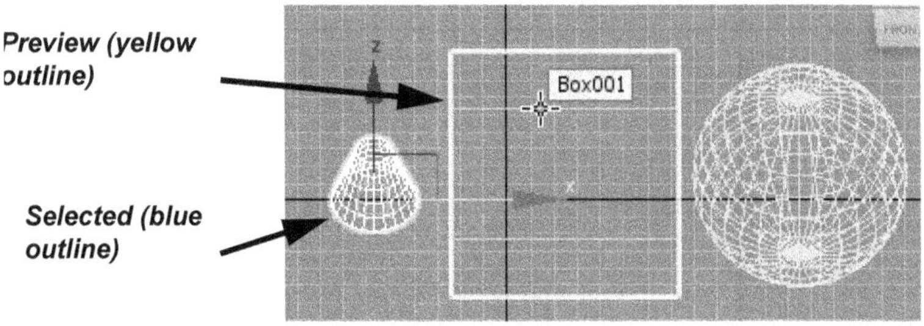

Preview (yellow outline)

Selected (blue outline)

Box001

Figure 2–20

The highlighting can be controlled in the Preference Settings dialog box>*Viewports* tab, as shown in Figure 2–21.

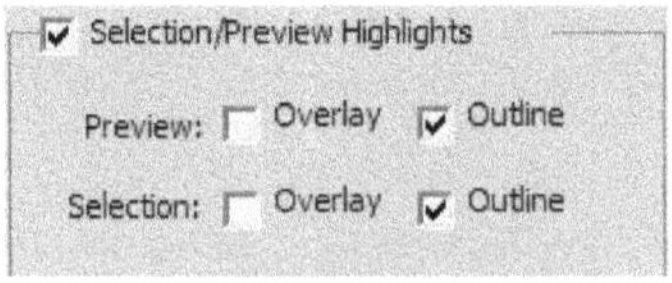

☑ Selection/Preview Highlights

Preview: ☐ Overlay ☑ Outline

Selection: ☐ Overlay ☑ Outline

Figure 2–21

Scene Explorer

If the Scene Explorer is not displayed, click

⊞ *(Scene Explorer) in the Min toolbar or select **Tools>Scene Explorer**. Dock the Scene Explorer.*

Being a modeless interface component, you can have the Scene Explorer open while working in the viewports.

- The Scene Explorer can be used to easily select objects. If you know the name of the object, locate it in the tree list and select it, as shown in Figure 2–22. It gets selected in the viewports interactively. Use <Ctrl> to click on multiple objects in the list to select them together.

Figure 2–22

- You can use the Scene Explorer toolbar to list only those objects that belong to the particular type and then select it.

  Use ■ (Display None) first to clear all the selected categories, and then select the tools for the required categories to list only the objects belonging to that category.

- To easily find and select an item you can use the *Find* field in the Scene Explorer. Enter the initial letters to select only the objects that begin with the entered letters

- In the **Display** menu, verify that the **Display Children**, **Display Influences**, and **Display Dependants** are cleared for all the objects to be displayed in the list.

Main Toolbar

A variety of selection tools are provided in the Main Toolbar, as shown in Figure 2–23.

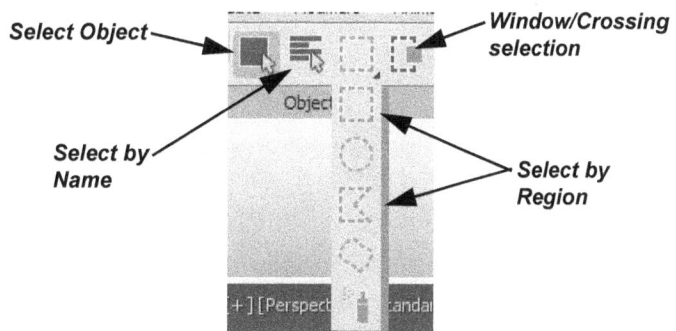

Figure 2–23

Select by Name tool

(Select by Name) opens the Select From Scene dialog box (shown in Figure 2–24), which enables you to select one or more objects. It is a modal version of the Scene Explorer, and therefore works the same way as the Scene Explorer. However, the only difference is that after selecting objects in the list of the dialog box, you must click **OK** to close the dialog box in order to continue working with the selection.

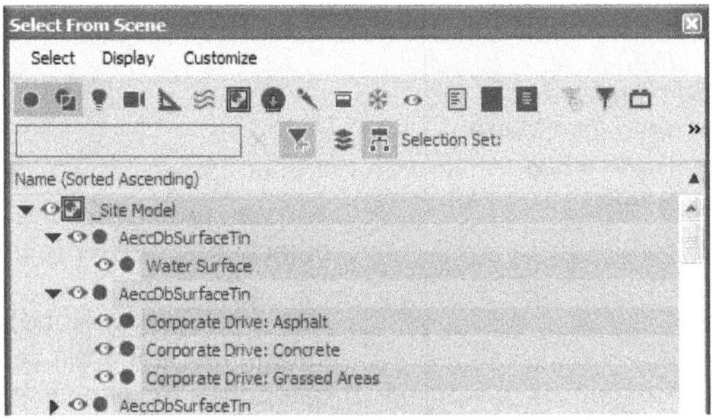

Figure 2–24

Select Object tool

(Select Object) enables you to select objects and to drag selection regions inside your viewports depending on the selected Region selection type.

* You can add to your current selection if you select or drag a region while holding <Ctrl>. You can remove items from the selection with <Alt>.

* You can also select with the **Move**, **Rotate**, **Scale**, and **Place** tools.

* You can access **Select** in the quad menu.

* If one of the **Transform** tools is active, you can click

   (Select Object) or press <Q> to activate select objects.

   If    (Select Object) is already active, press <Q> repeatedly to cycle through the various Region selection types.

Rectangular Selection Region

(Rectangular Selection Region) in the Main Toolbar enables you to draw the shape of your selection region. The default is a rectangular region. There are also flyout options for **Lasso**, **Paint**, **Circular**, and **Fence** selections, as shown in Figure 2–23. Paint selection is particularly useful when you have thousands of objects or vertices that need selecting.

Window/Crossing

/ (Window/Crossing) enables you to define the *Window Selection Region* (only objects completely within the region are selected), or the *Crossing Region* (objects within or crossing the boundary are selected) as the selection toggle.

Edit Menu

The **Edit** menu also has a number of important selection options including **Select All**, **Select None**, **Select Invert**, **Select Similar**, **Select Instances**, and **Select By** (e.g., **Color**). These options also work in Sub-object mode.

Layer Explorer

(Layer Explorer) (in the Main Toolbar) lists and select objects directly from the Layer Explorer.

Edit Named Selection Sets

(Edit Named Selection Sets) (in the Main Toolbar) enables you to create and edit named selection sets. Named Selection Sets are different than layers, in that an object can be in many different named selections. An object can only be on one layer, making Named Selection Sets more flexible.

Practice 2b Selection Methods

Practice Objective

- Select objects using **various** selection tools.

Estimated time for completion: 5 minutes

You must set the paths to locate the External files and Xrefs used in the practice. If you have not done this already, return to **Chapter 1: Introduction to Autodesk 3ds Max** and complete Task 1 to Task 3 in **Practice 1a: Organizing Folders and Working with the Interface**. You only have to set the user paths once.

In this practice you will select objects in a scene using the Window and Crossing selection tools. You will also use the Scene Explorer and Select from Scene dialog box to select objects.

*If prompted that there is a File Load: Mismatch, click **OK** to accept the default values.*

1. In the Quick Access Toolbar, click (Open File) to open the Open File dialog box. If you were working in the software, you might be prompted to save or discard any changes to the scene. Open **Selection Methods.max**.
2. Click in the **Perspective** viewport to make it active.
3. Maximize the **Perspective** viewport to fill your screen by clicking (Maximize Viewport Toggle) or by pressing <Alt>+<W>.

*Depending on how you rotate the viewing angle, it might be difficult to select a specific object. Setting the viewport shading to **Wireframe Override** can make it easier to select.*

4. In the viewport, click on one of the parking lot light poles. Note that it is selected as a blue outline that encloses the object and all the face edges of the geometry are highlighted as white, with white bounding brackets enclosing the geometry.

5. Hover the cursor on the other parking lot light poles and note that it is highlighted with a yellow outline indicating the selection preview as shown in Figure 2–25.

Figure 2–25

6. Click on the **[Edged Faces]** Per-View Preference viewport label and select **Per-View Preference** in the label menu. The Viewport Setting and Preferences dialog box>*Per-View Preferences* tab opens. Select the **Display Selected with Edged Faces** option, and then clear all of the other options, as shown in Figure 2–26. Ensure that **Apply to All Views** (near the bottom of the dialog box) is cleared. Click **OK**.

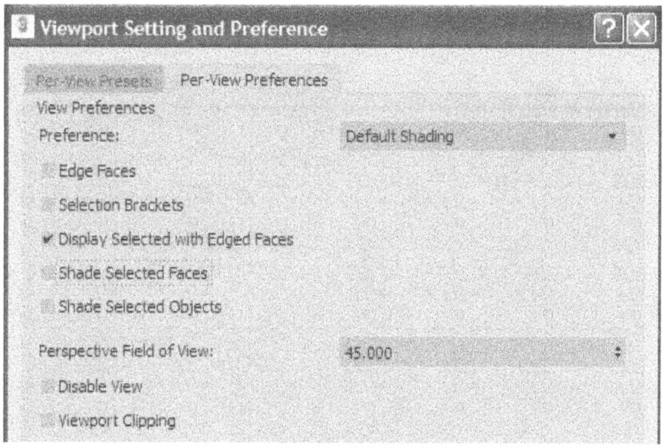

Figure 2–26

- In the viewport, note how the white bounding brackets are no longer displayed.

7. Open the Viewport Setting and Preferences dialog box. In the *Per-View Preferences* tab, select **Selection Brackets** and then click **OK**. The selection brackets are displayed.

8. Expand the **Edit** menu, and click **Select None** or click in empty space to clear your selection.

9. In the Main Toolbar, verify that the Window/Crossing toggle is set to [icon] (Crossing) and the Selection Region is set to [icon] (Rectangular). Starting in a blank area, near the top left corner of the parking lot light, click and drag the cursor diagonally down to create a rectangular crossing region around the light pole. The scene is complex and the crossing window will select several other objects in the background, in addition to the light pole.

   • In the Status Line, near the bottom left of the screen, note the number of objects selected.

10. Click in empty space to clear the selection.

11. Toggle the **Selection/Crossing** toggle from [icon] (Crossing) to [icon] (Window). Drag the selection region around the light pole completely.

   • In the Status Line, note that you selected fewer objects than before, but some additional objects are also selected.

If the Scene Explorer is not displayed, click

[icon] *(Scene Explorer) in the Main toolbar or select **Tools>Scene Explorer**.*

12. In the Scene Explorer toolbar, click [icon] (Display None). Note that the list is empty.

13. In the Scene Explorer toolbar, click [icon] (Display All). Note that the list of objects is very long as all the different categories of objects are listed.

14. In the Scene Explorer toolbar, click ■ (Display None) and then click ● (Display Geometry) to display all of the geometry objects in the scene. Note that some objects are highlighted (as shown in Figure 2–27), indicating that they are selected in the viewport.

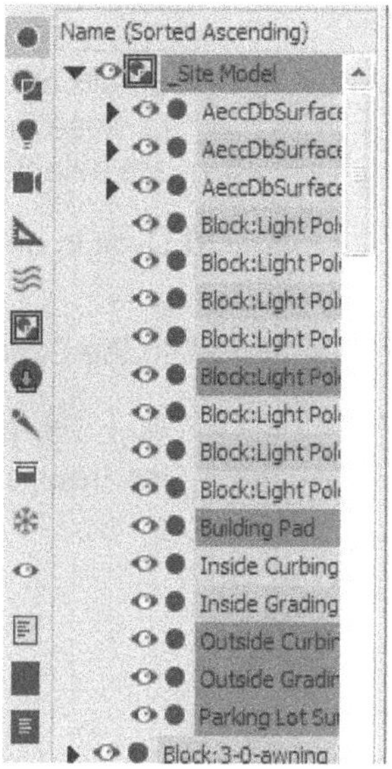

Figure 2–27

15. Click in empty space in the viewport to clear the selection.

16. In the Main Toolbar, click 📇 (Select by Name) to open the Select From Scene dialog box.

The Select From Scene dialog box is similar to the Scene Explorer.

17. The objects listed depend on the selection tools that are toggled on in the toolbar in the dialog box. In the toolbar, click

■ (Display None) to clear any selection group. Verify that

📇 (Sort by Hierarchy) is selected, as shown in Figure 2–28.

Figure 2–28

18. In the Select From Scene dialog box, click ![icon](Display Shapes), as shown in Figure 2–29. This enables you to filter the number of items listed in the dialog box so that you can easily select the required items.

Figure 2–29

19. Select all of the **Block:Light Pole- Single** shapes. Click **OK** to close the dialog box. Note that all of the Single light poles are selected.

20. Click in empty space in the viewport to clear the selection.

21. In the Scene Explorer toolbar, click ![icon](Display None) and click ![icon](Display Shapes) as shown in Figure 2–30. Expand the tree list, if required.

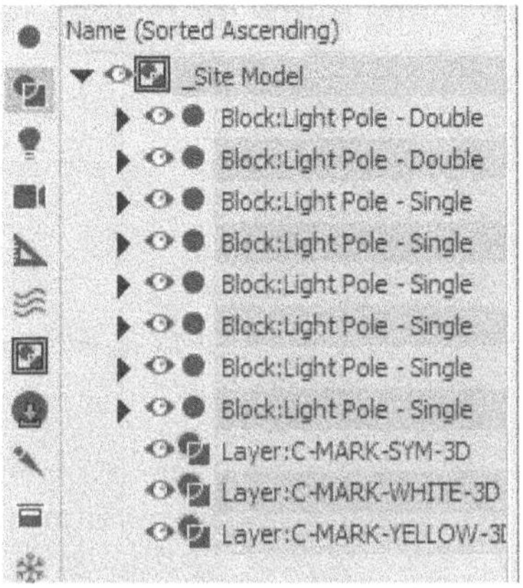

Figure 2–30

22. Select the first **Block:Light Pole - Single**. Note that it is not the light pole in the viewport because it is not selected.

23. Select the second **Block:Light Pole - Single** and keep on selecting the next ones. The third **Block:Light Pole - Single** selects the light pole in the view as shown in Figure 2–31.

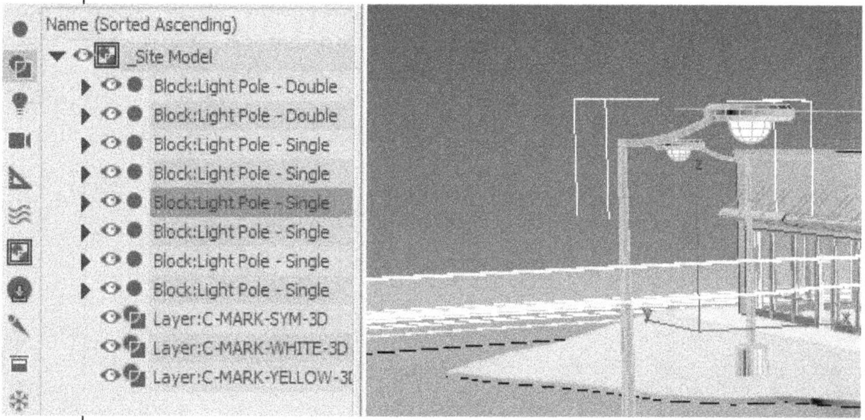

Figure 2–31

24. In the list, click again on the highlighted entry to convert it into an edit box and rename it to **Block:Light Pole - Front Left** and then click anywhere. Note that the newly-named entry moves above **Block:Light Pole - Single,** as shown in Figure 2–32, as the list is sorted in ascending order.

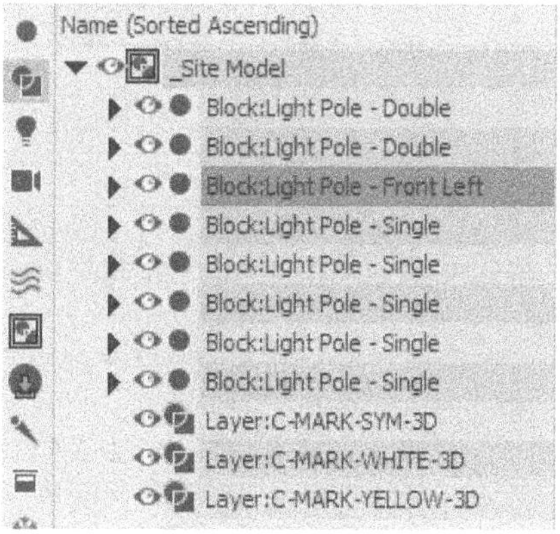

Figure 2–32

25. Select **Application Menu>Reset**. Click **Don't Save** and click **Yes** to close the current file without saving it.

2.4 Units Setup

Each scene file is based on a unit of measurement called the System Unit Scale. You can change and assign the units settings using the Units Setup dialog box. Select **Customize> Units Setup** to open the Units Setup dialog box, as shown in Figure 2–33. In the dialog box, click **System Unit Setup** to open the System Unit Setup dialog box, as shown in Figure 2–34.

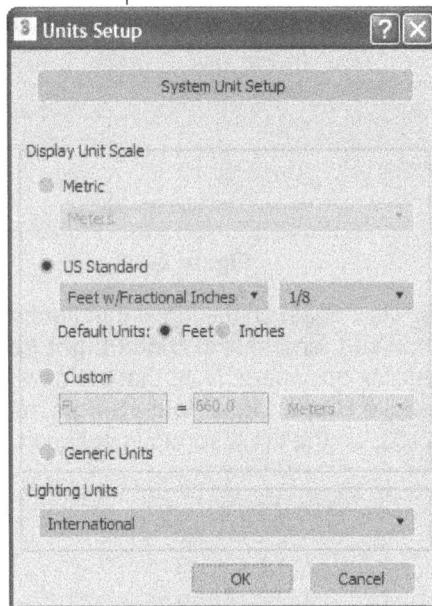

Figure 2–33

Figure 2–34

* For efficient viewport rendering, the Autodesk 3ds Max software might incur round off errors to very large and very small numerical values, as displayed by the slider bar in the System Unit Setup dialog box. These round off errors become problematic when the geometry is located further away from the center of the virtual universe.

* The Autodesk 3ds Max Help recommends that you center scene geometry close to the origin and not have any significant details smaller than one system unit. (For example, a unit scale of meters might not be appropriate for architectural work. Instead, you might consider using a **System Unit Scale** of inches, millimeters, or centimeters.) It is recommended not to make changes to the System Unit Scale unless there is a viewport problem due to very small or large models.

- Assign the unit scale before adding any geometry to the scene. Changing the System Unit Scale later does not rescale the existing objects. (To rescale objects, use the **Rescale World Units** utility in the Command Panel's Utilities panel ( ).

- Selecting **Respect System Units in Files** enables individual scene files that have different Unit Scales assigned to them to be scaled when merging them together.

The Display Unit Scale does not need to match the System Unit Scale.

- The *Display Unit Scale* area defines the units to be displayed by the interface when measuring coordinates and distances.

- When the Display Unit Scale is set to **Feet w/Fractional Inches** or **Feet w/Decimal Inches,** the **Default Units** option identifies how a distance is read if a value is entered without a unit designation (' or ").

- If the current System Unit Scale does not match that of a file that is opened, you are warned with the Units Mismatch dialog box, as shown in Figure 2–35. It is recommended to select **Adopt the File's Unit Scale**, unless you specifically want to change the Unit Scale of the file being opened.

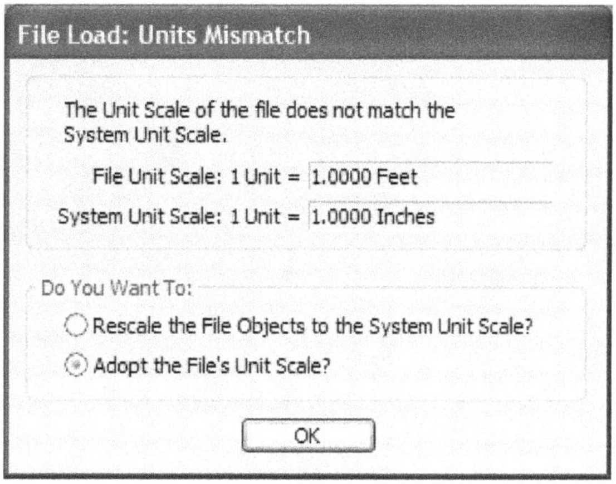

File Load: Units Mismatch

The Unit Scale of the file does not match the System Unit Scale.

File Unit Scale: 1 Unit = 1.0000 Feet

System Unit Scale: 1 Unit = 1.0000 Inches

Do You Want To:

○ Rescale the File Objects to the System Unit Scale?

◉ Adopt the File's Unit Scale?

OK

Figure 2–35

Practice 2c

Estimated time for completion: 5 minutes

If an unsaved scene is open, you might be required to save or discard the changes to the scene.

Working with Units Setup

Practice Objective

- Assign and set up units in a scene.

In this practice you will setup units for the projects.

1. Select **Application Menu>Reset** and click **Yes** in the confirmation dialog box.

2. Select **Customize>Units Setup** to open the Units Setup dialog box. Click **System Unit Setup**.

3. In the System Unit Setup dialog box, in the *System Unit Scale* area, verify that *1 Unit =* is set to **1.0** and to **Inches**. Click **OK**.

4. You are returned to Units Setup dialog box. Select **US Standard**, and then select **Feet w/Fractional Inches** and **1/8** in the respective drop-down lists, as shown in Figure 2–36.

5. Set the following, as shown in Figure 2–36:
   - *Default Units:* **Inches**
   - *Lighting Units:* **American**

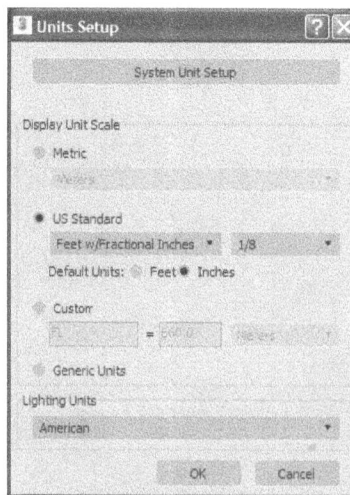

Figure 2–36

6. Click **OK** to close the Units Setup dialog box.

7. Select **Application Menu>Save As** to save your work as **MyUnits Setup.max**. Verify that it is being saved in the ...\scenes folder.

2.5 Layer and Object Properties

It is convenient to group similar objects into layers to modify these objects' properties and control their visibility together.

Layers Toolbar

By default, the Layers toolbar is not displayed. To display it, right-click anywhere on the blank space in the Main Toolbar and select **Layers**, as shown in Figure 2–37. The toolbar enables you to set an active layer by selecting it from the drop-down list. Additionally, it contains various tools.

Figure 2–37

	Opens the Layer Explorer.
	Creates a new layer.
	Adds selected objects to the current layer.
	Selects all objects in the current layer.
	Sets the current layer to the layer of a selected object.

Layer Explorer

Enhanced
in 2017

To open the Scene Explorer - Layer Explorer with ≋ (Sort by Layer) selected, click 📇 (Layer Explorer) either in the Main Toolbar or in the Layers toolbar, or select **Tools>Layer Explorer**. This version of Scene Explorer has tools and functions that are specific to layers, as shown in Figure 2–38.

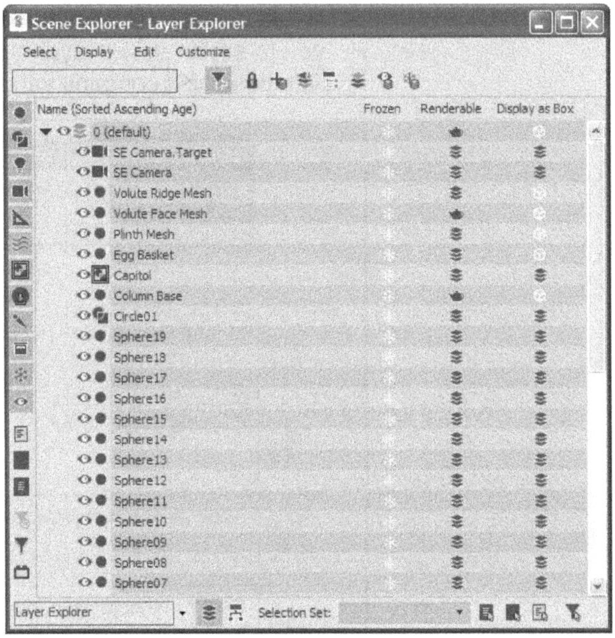

Figure 2–38

- View all of the objects on a layer by expanding the layer and clicking the arrow beside it, as shown in Figure 2–38. Right-clicking on an object in the list enables you to select and/or change its **Object Properties**.

- Click 📄 (gray layer icon) next to a layer to make the layer active. Active layers display the ≋ (blue layer icon).

Tools in the Layer Explorer

You can create and adjust layers using the tools in the Layer Explorer toolbar.

➕	Creates a new layer and makes it the active layer. Using this button in the Layer Explorer automatically moves selected objects to a new layer. If no objects are selected, an empty layer is created.

	Moves selected objects to the active layer.
	Selects all of the objects in the selected layer.
	Activates the selected layer.
	Hides or Unhides all of the layers. Hiding a layer makes those objects invisible in the viewports and in renderings.
	Freezes or Thaws all of the layers. You can freeze or thaw an individual object or layer by clicking ❄ in the *Frozen* column. Freezing a layer (or individual object) displays those objects, but makes them unselectable. Frozen objects display as gray in the viewports, but render normally.
	Toggles whether a layer is included when the scene is rendered.

- The **Layers** quad menu (shown in Figure 2–39) opens by right-clicking on the name of the layer in the Layer Explorer and enables you to view and adjust other layer properties.

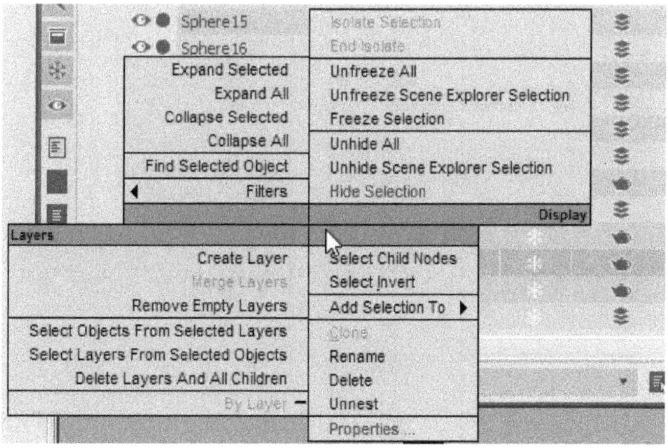

Figure 2–39

- You can also modify the display settings of one or more layers using the Layer Properties dialog box, that can be opened by selecting **Properties** in the **Layers** quad menu. Layer properties apply to all objects on that layer that do not have overrides set in their Object Properties.

Layer Properties

The Layer Properties dialog box (shown in Figure 2–40) contains two tabs:

- *General* tab: Used to set the display properties, hide and freeze options, or the rendering options of the layer.

- *Adv. Lighting* tab: Used to set the radiosity properties such as whether the layer objects can cast shadows and receive illumination.

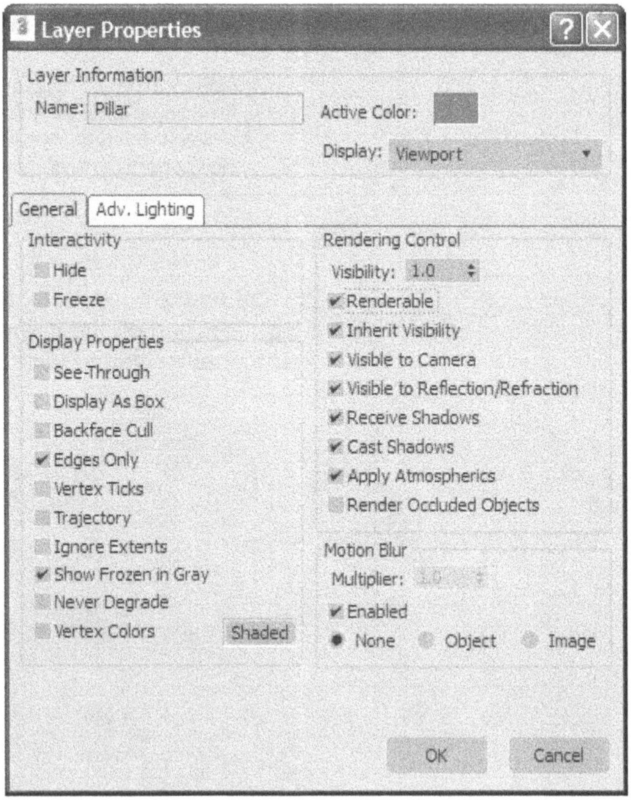

Figure 2–40

Object Properties

Right-clicking on an object in the Scene Explorer or Layer Explorer opens the quad menu for the object, as shown in Figure 2–41. In this menu, you can quickly edit or modify the properties of an object. Using the menu to edit the Display Properties is shown in Figure 2–41.

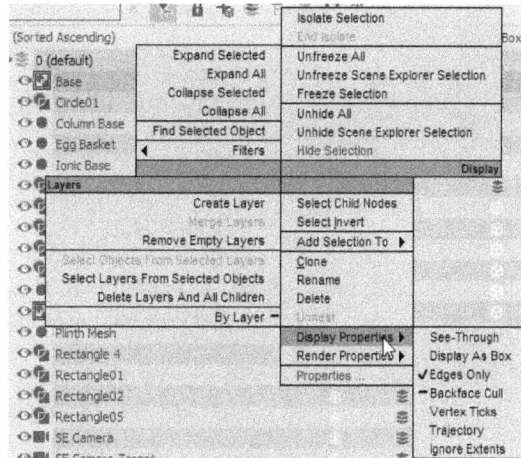

Figure 2–41

You can modify the detailed properties of an object in the Object Properties dialog box, as shown in Figure 2–42. The Object Properties dialog box is opened by selecting **Properties** in the quad menu. Alternatively, you can right-click on an object in a viewport and select **Object Properties**.

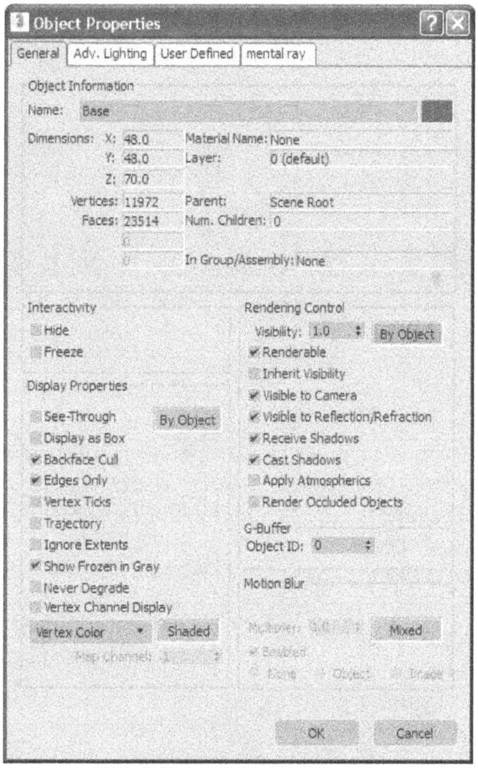

Figure 2–42

- It lists important information about an object, such as the name of the object, how many faces it consists of, the material assigned to it, whether its properties are controlled by layer or by object, etc.

- Changes made in the Object Properties dialog box override any layer settings for that object. The *Rendering Control* area in the Object Properties dialog box enables you to change setting for casting shadows on individual objects in a layer. This is useful when you do not want an object to cast shadows, while keeping the display of the other objects.

- To override the layer properties for an object, click the appropriate **By Layer** so that it changes to **By Object**.

Display Panel

The Command Panel's Display panel ( ) also contains controls for hiding and freezing objects, as shown in Figure 2–43.

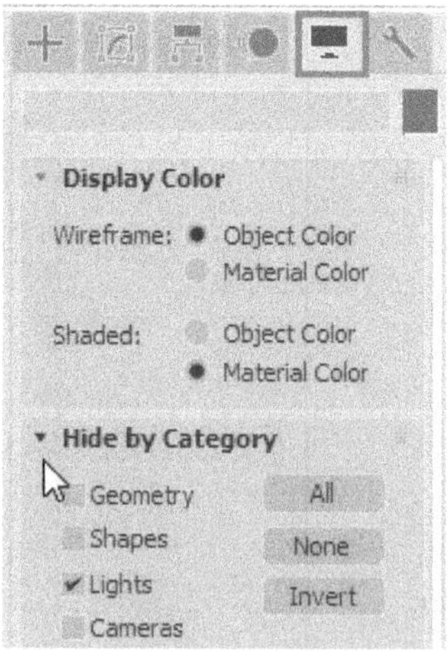

Figure 2–43

The Display panel enables you to:

- Hide all objects by category (all lights, all geometry, etc.).

- Hide or Freeze objects individually or by selecting them first.

- Unhide or Unfreeze all objects, or do so by object name. You can also freeze or hide by hit.

*A Display Floater is available in the **Tools** menu, where you can **Hide**, **Unhide**, **Freeze**, and **Unfreeze** objects.*

*You can also use the right-click on the **Display** quad menu.*

Practice 2d | Layer and Object Properties

Practice Objectives

- Create a new layer and move objects into a layer.
- Adjust properties of the layer and objects in the layer.

Estimated time for completion: 10 minutes

In this practice you will create a new layer and move several objects into it. You will also set and modify the properties of the layer and of an individual object using Layer Properties and Object Properties respectively.

You must set the paths to locate the External files and Xrefs used in the practice. If you have not done this already, return to **Chapter 1: Introduction to Autodesk 3ds Max** and complete Task 1 to Task 3 in **Practice 1a: Organizing Folders and Working with the Interface**. You only have to set the user paths once.

Task 1 - Practice Layer Management.

*Use 🗁 (Open File) in the Quick Access Toolbar or click **Application Menu > Open>Open**.*

*If a dialog box opens prompting you about a File Load: Mismatch, click **OK** to accept the default values.*

1. Open **Layers.max** from the ...*scenes* folder.

2. In the Main Toolbar, right-click anywhere on the blank space and select **Layers** to display the Layers toolbar. Click

    ▤ (Layer Explorer) in the Main Toolbar or in the Layers toolbar to open the Layer Explorer (Scene Explorer in the Layer mode).

3. In the Layer Explorer, next to layer **0 (default)** note the

    ≋ (blue layer icon) indicating that it is the active layer. Verify that the **Name (Sorted Ascending)** is displayed as the title heading to display the **0 (default)** at the top of the list. If it does not display as mentioned, keep on clicking on the title to cycle through different options.

4. Select the arrow beside **0 (default)** to expand it and list all of the objects on this layer.

5. Scroll down in the object list and locate the objects **Parking Lot Surface**, **Outside Grading**, **Outside Curbing**, **Inside Grading**, **Inside Curbing**, and **Building Pad**.

6. These objects are ground surfaces and part of a group called **Site XREF**. You can verify it by selecting one of these objects such as the **Building Pad** (shown in Figure 2–44) in the

Layer Explorer. Then, click ⬚ (Sort by Hierarchy) to shift to the hierarchy mode. Note that **Site XREF** is expanded and all of the objects in the group are highlighted, as shown in Figure 2–45. Scroll down and note that **Building Pad** is also listed and highlighted**.**

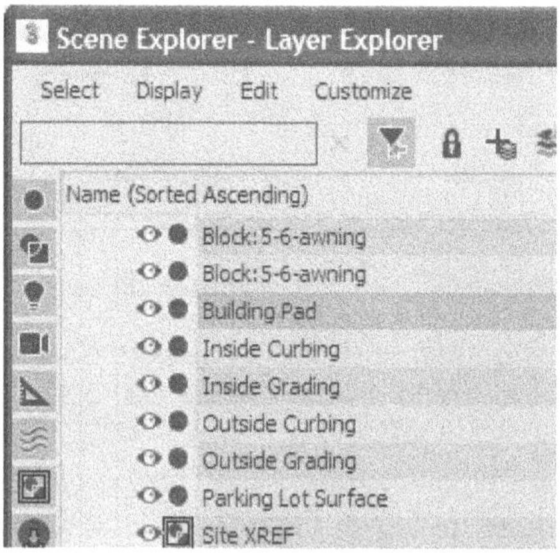

Figure 2–44

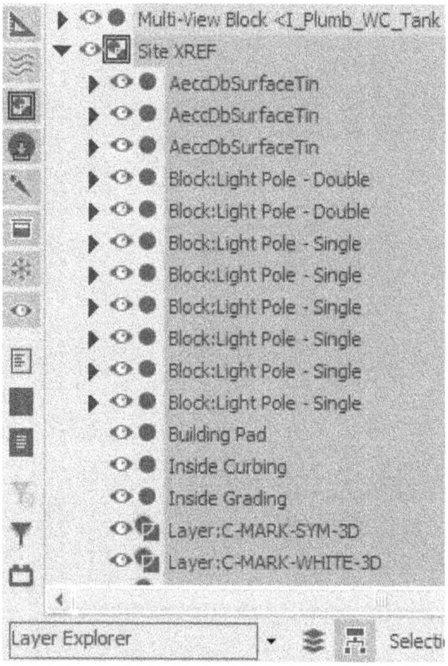

Figure 2–45

7. Zoom out in the viewport so that all the objects are visible.

8. In the Layer Explorer click ⬚ (Sort by Layers).

If you already have objects selected, click in empty space in the viewport to clear selection.

9. In layer **0 (default)**, select **Site XREF**. Note that a number of objects are selected in the viewport and that **1 Group Selected** displays in the Status Bar.

10. With **Site XREF** selected, select **Group>Open** in the menu bar. The Site XREF group is now open. Note that nothing is selected now.

   • To verify this, select **Building Pad** in layer **0 (default)** and

   click ⬚ (Sort by Hierarchy). Note that only the single object is highlighted and the complete group is not highlighted.

11. In the Layer Explorer, click ≋ (Sort by Layers). Select the six ground surfaces by using <Shift> **or <Ctrl>** as shown in Figure 2–46.

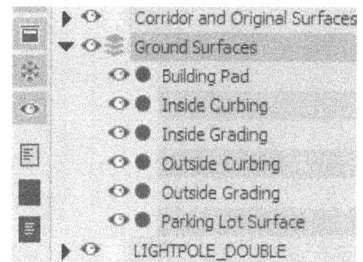

Figure 2–46

12. In the menu bar, select **Group>Detach**.

You can also use

⊕ (Create New Layer) in the Layer toolbar, which opens a dialog box. Verify that ***Move Selection to New Layer*** *is selected and then click* ***OK****.*

13. In the Layer Explorer with the six ground surfaces selected, click ⊕ (Create New Layer). A new layer called **Layer001** is automatically created with the six building surfaces placed in it, as shown in Figure 2–47. Note that the software automatically sets this layer to be the current layer, which is indicated by ≋ (blue icon).

14. Right-click on the layer **Layer001** and select **Rename**. Rename the layer as **Ground Surfaces**, as shown in Figure 2–48.

Figure 2–47   **Figure 2–48**

15. Expand layer **Corridor and Original Surfaces|Surfaces** and note that there are eight ground surfaces in it. Right-click on this layer to open the menu and note that **Delete** is unavailable (grayed out), because the layer contains objects.

You can also select ***Select Child Nodes*** *in the right-click quad menu.*

16. With the **Corridor and Original Surfaces|Surfaces** layer selected, in the Layer Explorer toolbar, click ⊟ (Select Children). This selects all of the objects in this layer.

*You can also select **Add Selection To>New Parent (pick)** and then select the required layer to move.*

17. In the Layer Explorer toolbar, click ![icon] (Add to Active Layer). The eight objects from the **Corridor and Original Surfaces|Surface** layer are moved to the **Ground Surfaces** layer (which is the active layer), as shown in Figure 2–49.

> C-MARK-YELLOW-3D
> Corridor and Original Surfaces|Surfaces
> Ground Surfaces
>   AeccDbSurfaceTin
>   AeccDbSurfaceTin
>   AeccDbSurfaceTin
>   Building Pad
>   Corporate Drive: Asphalt
>   Corporate Drive: Concrete
>   Corporate Drive: Grassed Areas
>   Existing Ground Surface
>   Inside Curbing
>   Inside Grading
>   Outside Curbing
>   Outside Grading
>   Parking Lot Surface
>   Water Surface
> LIGHTPOLE_DOUBLE

Figure 2–49

18. Right-click **Corridor and Original Surfaces|Surfaces** and note that **Delete** is now available. Select **Delete** to remove **Corridor and Original Surfaces|Surfaces**.

19. Select ![icon] (gray layer icon) next to layer **0 (default)** to make the layer active which toggles the icon to ![icon] (blue layer icon).

Task 2 - Set Layer and Object Properties.

Set the ground surfaces so that it does not cast shadows although they will still receive shadows. This simplification can save rendering time without significantly affecting the final output when using relatively flat ground surfaces.

1. In the Layer Explorer, select and right-click on the layer **Ground Surfaces**, and then select **Properties**.

2. In the Layer Properties dialog box, in the *Rendering Control* area, toggle off **Cast Shadows** (as shown in Figure 2–50) and click **OK**

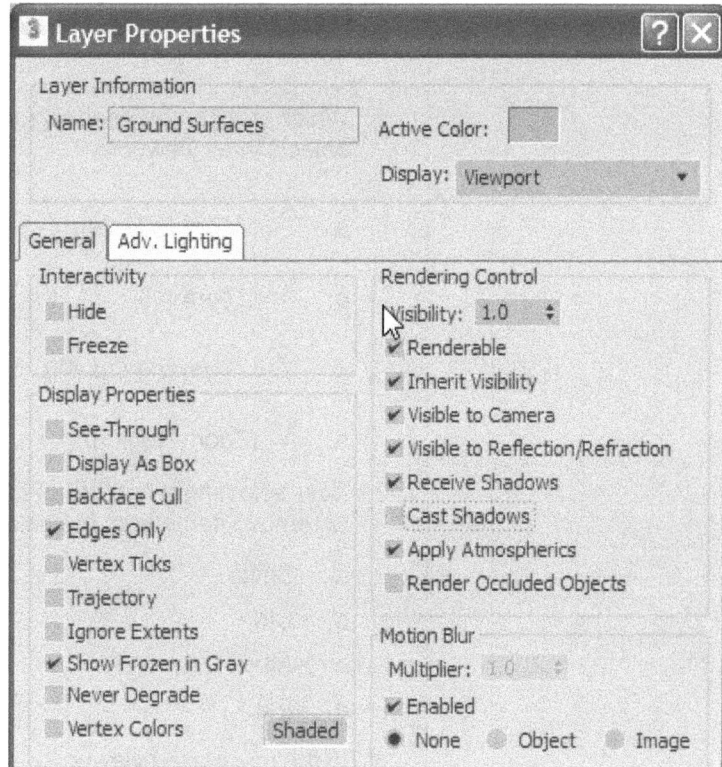

Figure 2–50

3. You can override this setting for one of the ground surfaces. In the Layer Explorer, in the layer **Ground Surfaces**, select and right-click on **Outside Grading**. Select **Properties** to open the Object Properties dialog box.

4. In the Object Properties dialog box, in the *Rendering Control* area, click **By Layer** so that it changes to **By Object**. Verify that **Cast Shadows** for this object is enabled and click **OK**.

5. Close the Layer Explorer.

6. Select **Application menu>Save As**, and save your work as **MyLayers.max**.

Chapter Review Questions

1. Which tool can be used to zoom to the extents of all visible objects in all viewports?

    a. (Zoom Extents)

    b. (Zoom All)

    c. (Zoom Extents All)

    d. (Zoom Region)

2. After selecting a number of objects, which key do you press to remove items from the selection?

    a. <Shift>

    b. <Ctrl>

    c. <Alt>

    d. <Esc>

3. In the maximized viewport display, along with holding <Win>, which key do you need to press to open the viewport overlay where you can switch to a different viewport?

    a. <Shift>

    b. <Ctrl>

    c. <Alt>

    d. <Tab>

4. You should assign the unit scale before adding any geometry to the scene. Changing the **System Unit Scale** later does not rescale objects that are already present.

    a. True

    b. False

5. In the Layer Explorer, which option makes objects unselectable, but leaves them visible in the viewport and renders them normally?

    a. **Hide**
    b. **Freeze**
    c. **Render**
    d. **Radiosity**

6. In the Layer Explorer toolbar, selecting a few objects and then clicking (Create New Layer) creates:

    a. A new inactive layer that is empty.
    b. A new active layer that is empty.
    c. A new inactive layer that contains the selected objects.
    d. A new active layer that contains the selected objects.

Command Summary

Button	Command	Location
Layers		
	Add Selection to Current Layer	• Layers Toolbar
	Add to Active Layer	• Scene Explorer Toolbar
	Create New Layers	• Layers Toolbar • Scene Explorer Toolbar
	Manage Layers	• Main Toolbar • Layers Toolbar
	Select Objects in Current Layer	• Layers Toolbar
	Set Current Layer to Selection's Layer	• Layers Toolbar
Object Selection		
	Crossing	• **Main Toolbar:** Window/Crossing Toggle
	Rectangular Selection Region	• **Main Toolbar**
	Select Object	• **Main Toolbar**
	Select by Name	• **Main Toolbar**
	Window	• **Main Toolbar:** Window/Crossing Toggle
Viewport Navigation		
	Dolly Camera	• **Viewport Navigation Toolbar (Camera Views):** Dolly Camera flyout
	Field-of-View	• **Viewport Navigation Toolbar:** Zoom Region flyout in Perspective and Camera views
	Maximize Viewport Toggle	• **Viewport Navigation Toolbar**
	Orbit Camera	• **Viewport Navigation Toolbar (Camera Views)**
	Orbit	• **Viewport Navigation Toolbar (Non-Camera Views):** Orbit flyout

	Orbit Point of View	• **Viewport Navigation Toolbar (Non-Camera Views):** Orbit flyout
	Pan View	• **Viewport Navigation Toolbar**
	Perspective	• **Viewport Navigation Toolbar (Camera Views)**
	Roll Camera	• **Viewport Navigation Toolbar (Camera Views)**
	Truck Camera	• **Viewport Navigation Toolbar (Camera Views)**
	Walk Through	• **Viewport Navigation Toolbar:** Pan View flyout in Perspective and Camera views
	Zoom	• **Viewport Navigation Toolbar (Non-Camera Views)**
	Zoom All	• **Viewport Navigation Toolbar (Non-Camera Views)**
	Zoom Extents	• **Viewport Navigation Toolbar (Non-Camera Views):** Zoom Extents flyout
	Zoom Extents Selected	• **Viewport Navigation Toolbar (Non-Camera Views):** Zoom Extents flyout
	Zoom Extents All	• **Viewport Navigation Toolbar:** Zoom Extents All flyout
	Zoom Extents All Selected	• **Viewport Navigation Toolbar:** Zoom Extents All flyout
	Zoom Region	• **Viewport Navigation Toolbar (Non-Camera Views)**

Assembling Project Files

The files used in the Autodesk® 3ds Max® software can be modeled directly in the software, referenced by linking, or directly imported from another source. Linking files enables you to incorporate objects or other scene files into the current scene by externally referencing them. Once referenced, the connection between the two files can be maintained. If files are imported, they are merged with the project and no link is established. Understanding the benefits and drawbacks of using external data helps you decide how to best reference it in a project.

Learning Objectives in this Chapter

- Understand the difference between File Linking and File Importing, and edit the linked data files.
- Combine entities from .DWG, .DXF, .FBX, and .RVT files into an active Autodesk 3ds Max scene.
- Understand how to link AutoCAD® DWG, DXF, generic FBX files, and Autodesk® Revit® RVT/FBX files.
- Create and modify presets.
- Incorporate objects or other scene files into the current scene by externally referencing them.
- Manage data using the asset tracking systems.

3.1 Data Linking and Importing

Although the Autodesk 3ds Max software has a robust 2D and 3D modeling system, it might be efficient to link or import some or all of the design data from other Autodesk software, such as AutoCAD®, Autodesk® Revit® Architecture, AutoCAD® Architecture, or Autodesk® Inventor®.

Linking vs. Importing

You can link or import files using the **File Link** and **Import** tools. You can link files such as .DWG, .DXF, .FBX, and .RVT, and import files such as Autodesk® Inventor® (.IPT, .IAM), Autodesk® Alias® .Wire, Autodesk® Showcase® .APF (Autodesk Packet File), LandXML and DEM data files, and Adobe Illustrator (.AI).

- Linked geometry differs from imported geometry in that it remains connected to the source file. If the source file is edited, the Autodesk 3ds Max Scene can be updated to show those changes. Imported geometry maintains no connection to the source file.

- If a source .DWG, .DXF, .FBX, or .RVT file is likely to change (or you would prefer to make changes in the .DWG, .DXF, .FBX, or .RVT directly), then using **File Linking** might be the best way to incorporate this data into the Autodesk 3ds Max software.

- **Importing** can be used as a faster alternative to linking to bring large amounts of data into the software. Complex geometry might be faster to reimport than to update through a file link.

- File links and imports are launched from the Application Menu (as shown in Figure 3–1):

    - Expand (Application Menu), expand **Import**, and select **Link Revit/Link FBX/Link AutoCAD**, or

    - Expand (Application Menu), expand **Import**, and select **Import**.

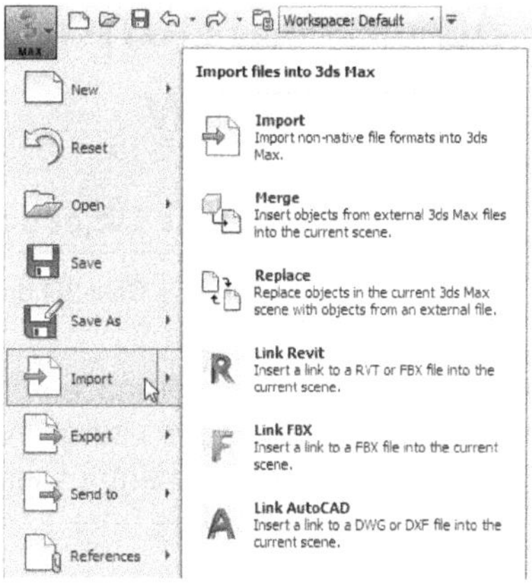

Figure 3–1

Editing Linked Data

- Linked geometry can be edited but not directly deleted from a scene file. Alternatively, the layer on which the objects are placed might be ignored during a reload, or set to **Hide** in the Layer dialog box.

- Edits applied to linked geometry (such as through modifiers) are reapplied after a link is updated. Some complex modifications might not apply as expected, so you should always review your geometry carefully after a link is updated.

- Links to drawing files are not bi-directional, so that changes you make to the data in the Autodesk 3ds Max software do not update the original .DWG, .FBX, .DXF, or .RVT file.

- In linked files that are bound, the geometry stays in the scene file as-is, but the connection to the source file is dropped.

Importing

You can export an .FBX file from the Autodesk Revit software and import it in Autodesk 3ds Max software. The FBX importer is an independent plug-in that is frequently updated. In the FBX Import dialog box, use **Web Update** to check for web updates, download the latest updates, and install them. Close 3ds Max when you do the install.

Merging Autodesk 3ds Max Scene Files

Objects already saved in Autodesk 3ds Max scenes (.MAX files) are imported into the current scene using the **Merge** option (**Application Menu>Import>Merge**). Merging files is a one-directional transfer that does not maintain any connection between the two files. Using the **Merge** option, you can either load a few objects from a scene or you can load a complete scene into the current one.

Practice 3a

Ground Surfaces using Civil View

Practice Objective

- Open a Civil 3D data file in a scene file.

Estimated time for completion: 20 minutes

In this practice you will open a .VSP3D file for importing ground surfaces using Civil View. You will then modify the material assignment for various ground surfaces using the Civil View Explorer.

You must set the paths to locate the External files and Xrefs used in the practice. If you have not done this already, return to **Chapter 1: Introduction to Autodesk 3ds Max** and complete Task 1 to Task 3 in **Practice 1a: Organizing Folders and Working with the Interface**. You only have to set the user paths once.

Task 1 - Initialize Civil View.

It is recommended that you import 3D ground surfaces from Civil/Survey products, such as AutoCAD Civil 3D or Land Desktop using the vsp3d data format.

You have to initialize Civil View once.

1. In the menu bar, select **Civil View>Initialize Civil View**. If you have already initialized Civil View, go to Step 5.

2. In the Initialize Autodesk Civil View dialog box, set the *System Units* to **Feet** because the civil project that you will be opening uses Feet as its unit of measurement. Verify that **Don't warn me about System Units again** is selected.

3. In the *Select a Country Resource Kit* area, select **US IMPERIAL** and verify that *Start Mode for Civil View* is set to **Manual**. Click **OK**. In the Information dialog box, click **OK**.

4. Exit and then restart the Autodesk 3ds Max software.

5. Start Civil View by selecting **Civil View>Start Civil View**.

Hint: Starting Civil View

Although Civil View is initialized next time you launch the Autodesk 3ds Max software, you are still required to start Civil View if the *Start Mode for Civil View* is set as **Manual**. You can change this setting in the Civil View Preferences dialog box, in the *General* tab, by select **Automatically start Civil View?**, as shown in Figure 3–2.

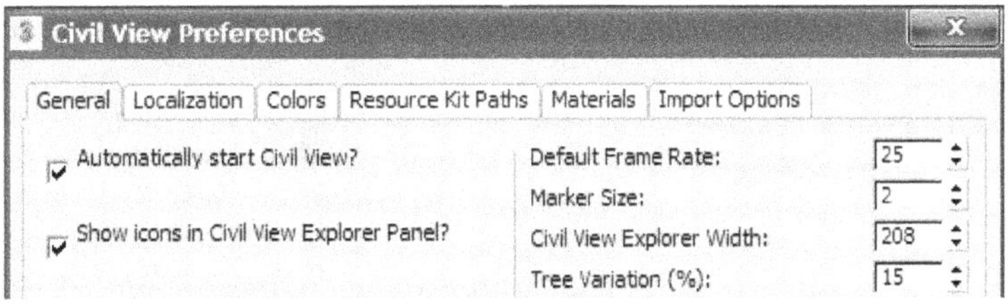

Figure 3–2

Task 2 - Opening a Civil 3D File.

1. Open **Civil Base XRef.max** from the *...\scenes* folder. If a Mismatch dialog box opens, click **OK** to accept the default values. If prompted again, click **OK**. This is an empty scene in which the System Unit Scale has been set to **1 Unit=1.0 Feet**.

2. In the menu bar, select **Civil View>Geometry Import>Civil 3D (VSP 3D) File**, as shown in Figure 3–3.

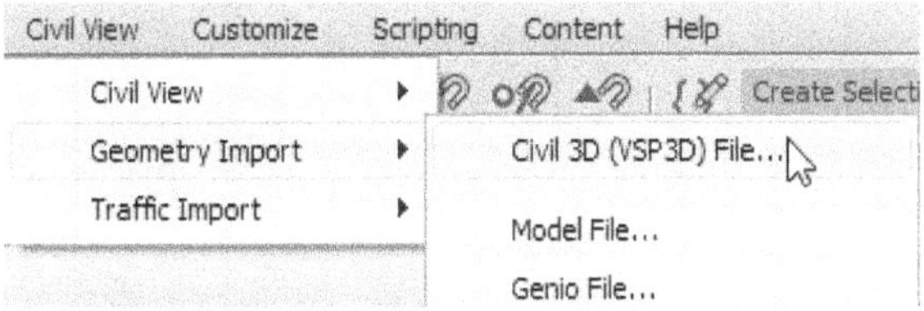

Figure 3–3

3. In the Civil 3D Import Panel dialog box, click **Open**. In the Select a VSP3D File dialog box, browse to the *...\import* folder in the practice files folder and open **Civil surfaces.vsp3d**.

The objects listed include surfaces, site/ grading featurelines, corridor (surfaces, baselines, featurelines etc.),and point groups, etc.

4. In the Civil 3D Import Panel dialog box, a list of objects that are in the AutoCAD Civil 3D file are listed. In the left pane, select **Surfaces [9]** to display all of the surfaces in the right pane. Select **Building Pad**, hold <Shift>, and select **Parking Lot Surface** to highlight the first seven surfaces. Select the checkbox for **Building Pad** to select all seven highlighted surfaces, as shown in Figure 3–4. You can select them individually as well.

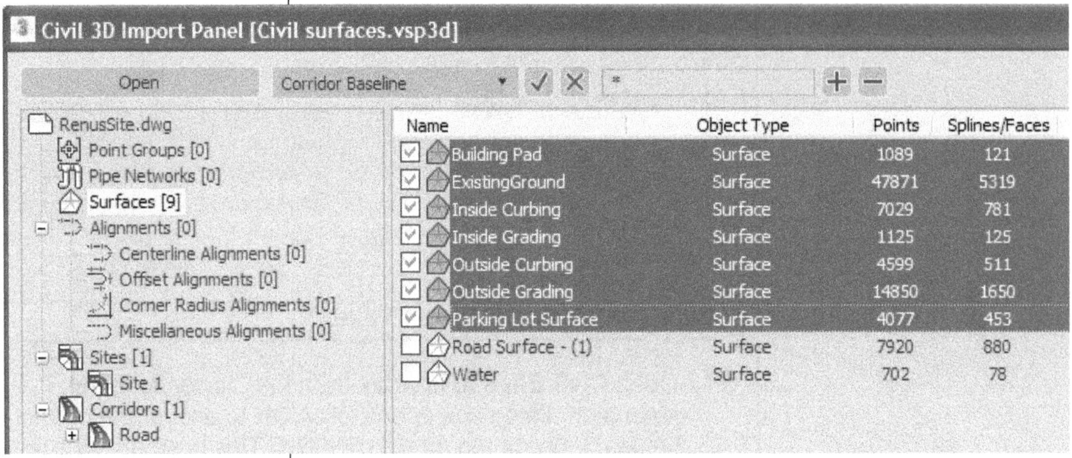

Figure 3–4

5. You will select the corridor surfaces and the baseline. In the left pane, select **Corridors [1]** and in the right pane, click in the checkboxes for **PrimaryAccess**, **Region(1)**, **Region(2)**, and **Region(3)**, as shown in Figure 3–5.

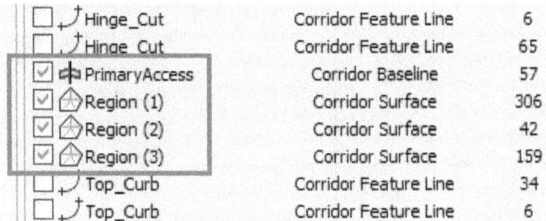

Figure 3–5

6. Click **OK**. In the Civil View Information, click **Yes** to accept the global shift values.

7. Click **Yes** to proceed without a feature interpretation style.

8. In the Warning dialog box, click **OK**. In the Error dialog box, click **OK**.

It takes a few minutes to load the file.

9. The ground surfaces, building pad, corridor, and parking lot are displayed in all of the viewports. If they are not, click

   (Zoom Extents All). In the Perspective viewport, note that only the corridor displays the right surface material but the rest of the surfaces display a checkerboard material.

*Right-click on the title bar and select **Dock>Left**.*

10. In the menu bar, select **Civil View>Civil View>Civil View Explorer** to open the Civil & View Explorer. Dock it along the left side of the screen.

Task 3 - Modify Material Assignment.

---

1. Verify that the *Civil Explorer* tab is selected. Expand **Civil View Objects>Imported Objects**, if not already expanded. Select **Surfaces** and note that the corridor is selected in the viewports. The Object List rollout opens with all of the surfaces listed, as shown in Figure 3–6.

Figure 3–6

A material is not required for the first three corridor regions.

2. In the Object List rollout, select **C3Dsurface-C-TOPO-Building Pad**. In the Surface Parameters rollout, select the *Statistics* tab and note that in the *Face Selection Sets*, in *By Material ID*, **[31] Ground Type 4** has been assigned, as shown in Figure 3–7.

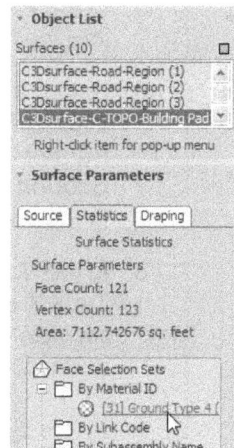

Figure 3–7

The complete list might not be visible in the Explorer. Hover the cursor in empty space in the information area until it displays as a Pan (hand) cursor. Slide up or down, using the hand cursor or the scroll button to display all of the information.

3. Right-click on **[31] Ground Type 4** and select **Modify Material ID Assignment**, as shown in Figure 3–8.

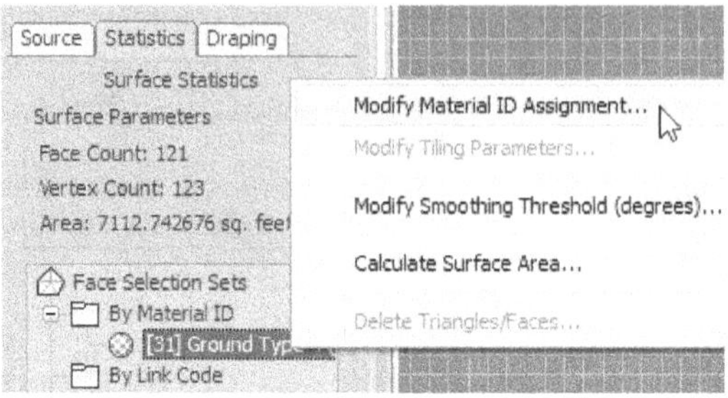

Figure 3–8

4. Click **Yes** in the Warning dialog box.

5. In the Modify material channel dialog box, select **[22] Concrete Type 1** as shown in Figure 3–9. Click **OK**.

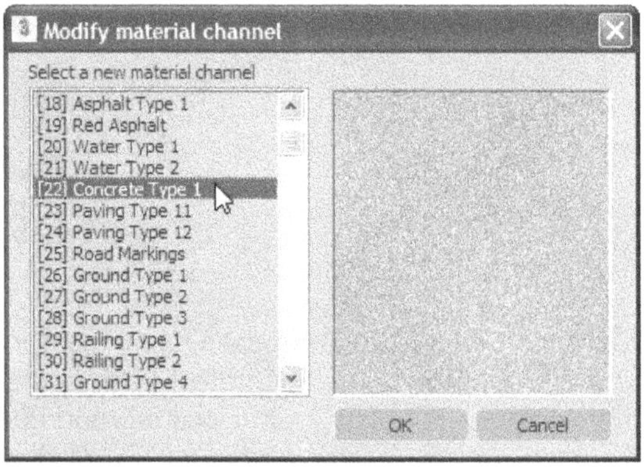

Figure 3–9

6. In the **Perspective** viewport, use **Zoom** and **Pan** to zoom into the building pad. Note how the new material is applied.

7. Select **Surfaces** again and in the Object List rollout, select **C3Dsurface-C-TOPO-Existing Ground**. In the Surface Parameters rollout, in the *Statistics* tab, right-click on **[31] Ground Type 4**, and select **Modify Material ID Assignment**. In the Warning dialog box, click **Yes**.

8. In the Modify material channel dialog box, select **[28] Ground Type 3** and click **OK**. In the **Perspective** viewport, note that the new ground type material is applied to the ground surface.

A material is not required for the first three corridor regions.

9. Similarly, for the other surfaces, apply the material types as follows:
   - C3Dsurface-C-TOPO-Inside Curbing:
     [38] Concrete Type 3
   - C3Dsurface-C-TOPO-Inside Grading:
     [28] Ground Type 3
   - C3Dsurface-C-TOPO-Outside Curbing:
     [38] Concrete Type 3
   - C3Dsurface-C-TOPO-Outside Grading:
     [28] Ground Type 3
   - C3Dsurface-C-TOPO-Parking Lot Surface:
     [39] Asphalt Type 4

You might need to undock the explorer first to close it.

10. Close the Civil View Explorer.

11. Click (Zoom Extents All). In the **Perspective** view, the scene displays as shown in Figure 3–10.

Figure 3–10

12. Save your work as **MyCivil Base XRef.max**.

3.2 Linking Files

File Linking is used to incorporate data from other Autodesk software such as Autodesk Revit and AutoCAD into the Autodesk 3ds Max scene. If the incorporated data is changed in the originating software, the file link enables you to update those changes in the 3ds Max scene. File linking is useful when you are working on a visualization project and know that all design decisions have not yet been made. You can link files using the Manage Links dialog box that can be opened as follows:

- (Application Menu)>Import>Link Revit: Links the .RVT files from the Autodesk Revit Architecture software.

- (Application Menu)>Import>Link FBX: Links the .FBX files that can be created in the Autodesk Revit, Autodesk MotionBuilder, Autodesk Maya, and Autodesk Mudbox software.

- (Application Menu)>Import>Link AutoCAD: Links the .DWG and .DXF files from the AutoCAD software.

- You can also open the Manage Links dialog box outside of the Link commands (**Application Menu>References> Manage Links**) and modify the Link settings.

Linking DWG Files

In CAD data files it is common to have large numbers of objects. When linking or importing AutoCAD .DWG or .DXF files, it is efficient to combine multiple, related objects together into a single Autodesk 3ds Max object to control their display and visibility.

- When multiple entities are combined into compound Autodesk 3ds Max shapes (2D objects) and meshes (3D objects), you can still access and adjust the original geometry using the Sub-object level modifiers, such as **Edit Spline**, **Edit Mesh**, and **Edit Poly**.

- Once multiple entities are combined, you can detach objects or portions of an objects to form new ones for individual editing control.

Linking FBX and RVT Files

The Autodesk Revit and Autodesk 3ds Max software share a mental ray renderer. Both products use the Autodesk Material Library materials.

- The .RVT and .FBX file format supports the import of photometric lights, both interior artificial lights and exterior daylight systems.

- Detailed .RVT and .FBX file formats can become very large in size and importing them as single files cannot be accomplished. In such cases, use a section box in the **3D View** in the Autodesk Revit software to limit the amount of the scene you are exporting.

Manage Links Options

The Manage Links dialog box (shown in Figure 3–11) contains the following tabs:

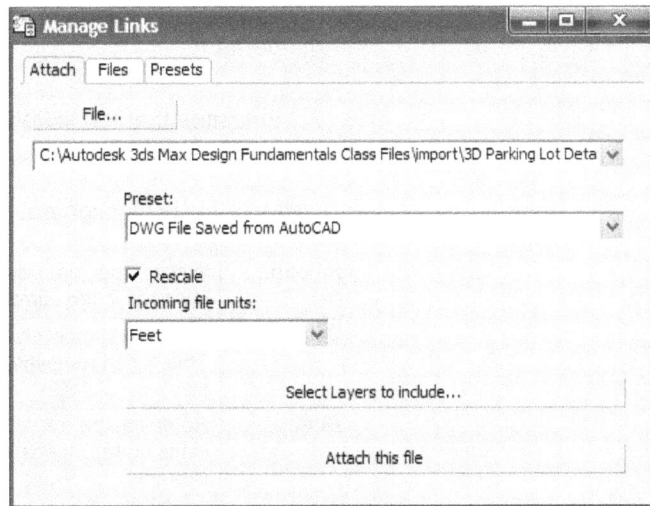

Figure 3–11

Attach Tab

The options available in the *Attach* tab are described as follows:

- **File...** enables you to open a file (.DWG, .DXF, .FBX, or .RVT) for linking. The selected filename and its path display in the File drop-down list. If the file that you selected is a .RVT file with more than one camera view, you are prompted to select a camera view.

- The Preset drop-down list enables you to select the preset settings. The Presets listed here can be created or modified using the *Presets* tab. You can set the units by selecting them in the Incoming file units drop-down list.

- **Select Layers to include** is only available with .DWG and .DXF file formats and enables you to select the layers that you want included with the drawing file.

- **Attach this file** links the selected file with the specified preset settings to the current Autodesk 3ds Max scene.

Files Tab

The *Files* tab displays a list of files that are linked to the current scene with a specific status icon.

- If the linked file has been modified, displays with the linked filename.

- indicates that the linked file is unchanged and does not have any errors.

- When a file is highlighted, the following options are available:

Reload...	When the original file has been changed, it displays the changes in the current scene.
Detach...	Use when you want to remove the link with the original file. This option removes all geometry associated with the linked file.
Bind...	Removes the link with the original file, but the geometry stays in the current scene, although the link between the original file is broken. Changes made to the original linked file cannot be reloaded.

Presets Tab

Many options are available before files are linked to your current scene. These options are configured and saved as **Presets** and can be used when linking files at a later stage. Many of these options require trial and error to find the most appropriate settings. You can link a file and then reload (or detach and relink) with different settings until you achieve the required results.

If you are linking a file for the first time, it is recommended that you create a new preset.

The *Presets* tab lists all existing presets and contains options for creating new presets, modifying existing presets, copying existing ones, renaming and deleting them. You need to select a preset for the **Modify**, **Copy**, **Rename**, and **Delete** options to be available, as shown in Figure 3–12. If no preset is selected, **Copy** is replaced by **New** and is the only available option.

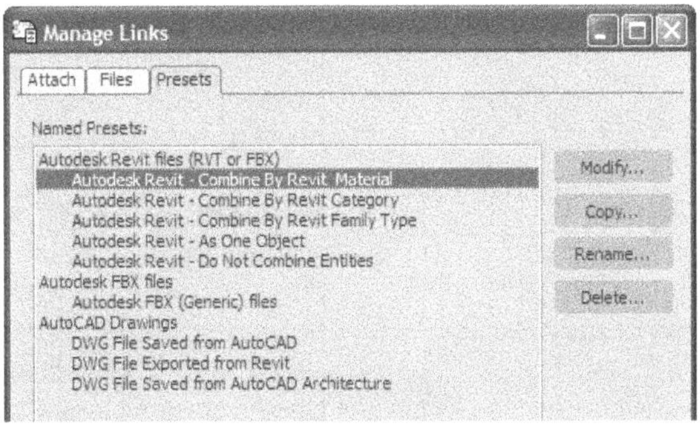

Figure 3–12

Depending on the type of preset selected (.RVT, .FBX, or .DWG), clicking **Modify...** opens a specific File Link Settings dialog box, which enables you to define the way you want the geometry to be linked, what portions of the file are to be modified on **Reload**, and how the geometry is combined.

File Link Settings: DWG Files

In the Manage Links dialog box, in the *Presets* tab, selecting an AutoCAD DWG file preset and clicking **Modify...** opens the File Link Settings: DWG Files dialog box, as shown in Figure 3–13.

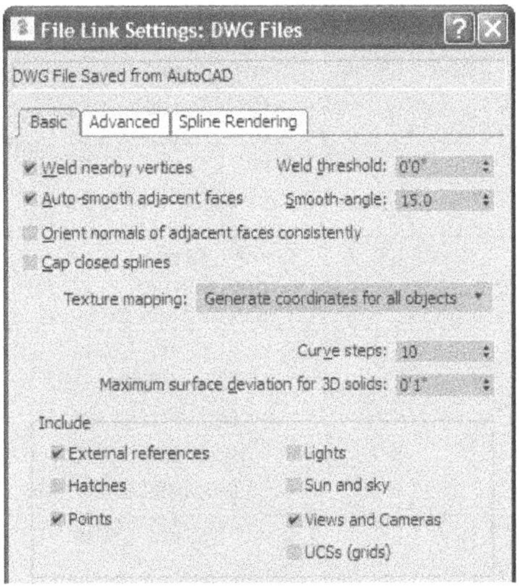

Figure 3–13

Basic Tab

The options available in the *Basic* tab are described as follows:

- **Weld nearby vertices** and **Weld threshold:** Welding joins together vertices of the same object that fall in the weld threshold. If the objects are joined by layer, this option removes duplicate vertices so that the adjacent 2D objects on the same layer are automatically combined into splines. Adjacent 3D objects that are welded become faces in a single mesh that share common vertices.

You can adjust smoothing later if you still encounter smoothing issues after import.

- **Auto-smooth adjacent face** and **Smooth-angle:** Auto-smooth enables adjacent faces in the same 3D mesh to display smooth if the angles of separation between their face normals (a directional vector perpendicular to the face) is equal to or less than the Smooth-angle. Otherwise, the adjacent faces have a faceted edge between them. This is the same smoothing process used in the Edit Mesh and Edit Poly modifiers.

- **Orient normals of adjacent faces consistently:** This option coordinates the face normals of linked objects. This option should be left off by default unless some faces of your 3D objects are missing after the link.

- **Cap closed splines:** It assigns an Extrude modifier to all closed 2D geometry (e.g., circles and closed polylines).

- **Texture mapping:** Texture mapping is used to locate texture maps on objects. Two options are available:

Generate coordinates on-demand	• Links objects without adding any texture mapping. • Adds the mapping when it is first called for by the software. • Enables a faster link but might cause some discrepancies.
Generate coordinates for all objects	• Adds texture mapping to all objects at the time of the link, matching any that might have existed in the original drawing file.

- **Curve steps:** This setting defines the number of segments to subdivide each 2D curve segment into if they are later extruded in the Autodesk 3ds Max software. This setting applies to circles, arcs, polyline curves, spines, and similar curved objects.

- **Maximum surface deviation for 3D solids:** This setting defines the allowed deviation distance from a parametric AutoCAD 3D curve (such as a curved AutoCAD extrusion) and the resulting Autodesk 3ds Max mesh. The lower the value, the more a 3D curve is subdivided. In the Autodesk 3ds Max software, all 3D curves must be segmented.

This value can be set as low, (0.01).

- **Include area options:** These options enable you to select the type of objects to be brought into the scene. Note that the **Lights** option only brings in Lights from AutoCAD drawings pre-2007. If you have Sun and Sky checked, a daylight system is created based on the information in the incoming DWG file from the Autodesk Revit 2009 software.

Advanced Tab

The *Advanced* tab (shown in Figure 3–14) controls the import of AutoCAD primitives and the effect of scene materials while importing.

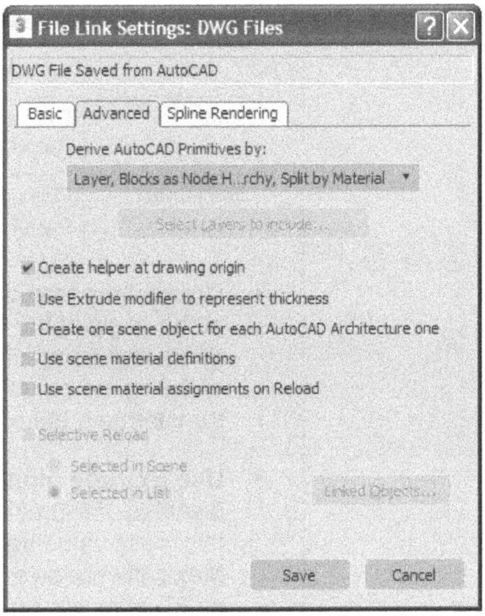

Figure 3–14

The options available in the *Advanced* tab are described as follows:

- **Derive AutoCAD Primitives by:** Controls how AutoCAD objects are combined when linked.

Layer	Creates one object for each AutoCAD layer. Each AutoCAD block links as a single object called a VIZBlock.
Layer, Blocks as Node Hierarchy	This option preserves material assignments in linked AutoCAD blocks. It structures each as a hierarchy of objects rather than single objects.
Layer, Blocks as Node Hierarchy, Split by Material	This option works similarly to the one above but takes into account drawings that have more than one material applied to objects on the same layer. Separate hierarchies are created for each material type on each layer.
Entity, Blocks as Node Hierarchy	This option includes all non-blocks as separate, individual objects. Blocks are preserved as hierarchies, however, organized by layer.
Color	Combines AutoCAD objects by color. All objects of one color are joined in as a single object, regardless of layer.
Entity	Does not combine AutoCAD objects at all. Instead, each AutoCAD object becomes an individual object.
One Object	This option combines all AutoCAD objects into a single object.

- **Create helper at drawing origin:** Adds an origin point helper at the origin of the current coordinate system. All of the linked geometry is part of a hierarchy parented by this helper, so all of the linked objects can be repositioned as one by transforming the helper.

- **Use Extrude modifier to represent thickness:** When disabled, linking 2D AutoCAD objects with a non-zero thickness value translates the objects into the Autodesk 3ds Max software as a 3D mesh. When enabled, objects translate as 2D objects with a parametric extrude modifier. The resulting geometry is the same but when this option is enabled, the extrusion properties (such as height) can be modified after the link or imported using the modifier stack.

- **Create one scene object for each AutoCAD Architecture one:** When unchecked, AutoCAD Architecture and AutoCAD MEP objects are subdivided into separate objects by material.

- **Use scene material definitions:** When unchecked, the Autodesk 3ds Max software includes the current state of any material applied to the linked objects in the AutoCAD software. If selected and the current scene has a material with the same exact name as the AutoCAD material, the scene material is used instead.

- **Use scene material assignments on Reload:** When unchecked, the Autodesk 3ds Max software re-loads the current state of any AutoCAD materials present in the drawing file when the link is updated. When enabled, the Autodesk 3ds Max software maintains the current state of any materials in the scene file after a link is updated. Select this option if you intend to adjust linked materials in the Autodesk 3ds Max software or leave it unchecked if you intend to adjust them the AutoCAD software.

- **Selective Reload:** Enables you to reload a subset of the original file. You can select objects to reload by selecting them in the scene or by selecting them from a list. If you select **Selected in List**, and click **Linked Objects** a list opens.

Hint: Hierarchies and File Linking

Autodesk 3ds Max Hierarchies are collections of objects linked together into parent/child relationships where transform applied to a parent are automatically passed on to its children. Connecting multiple objects in a hierarchical chain can enable sophisticated animations in the Autodesk 3ds Max software, such as the motion of jointed robotic arms.

In the case of the **hierarchy** file link options, incoming AutoCAD blocks are brought into the Autodesk 3ds Max software as multiple objects so that they can maintain multiple material assignments from the AutoCAD software. The parent object itself does not have any geometry and does not render. Most modifiers (such as **Substitute**) must be applied to the objects in the hierarchy rather than the parent.

Spline Rendering Tab

The options available in the *Spline Rendering* tab (shown in Figure 3–15) enable linear objects (2D and 3D lines, polylines, etc.) to display as extruded 3D objects in the viewports or rendering. Normally, splines cannot be rendered because they do not have surface area to interact with scene lighting. These options enable splines to link into the Autodesk 3ds Max software as 3D linear objects with a cross-sectional radius or a rectangular length and width. This provides the surface area for rendering.

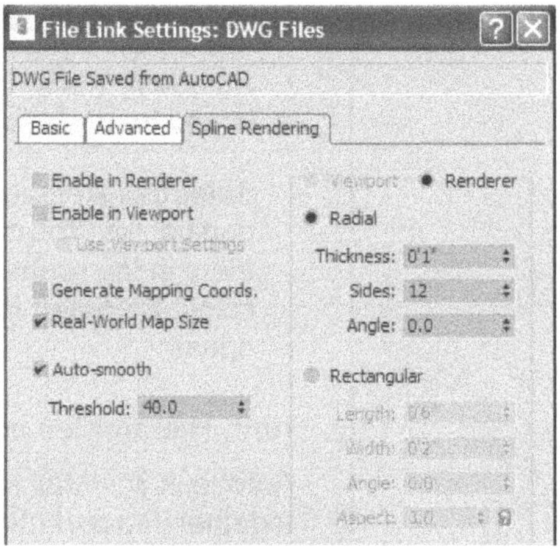

Figure 3–15

- If splines are to be rendered with materials then options such as smoothing, mapping coordinates, and/or real-world map size are often important.

- When enabled, all of the splines linked with this setting are renderable, and all have the same cross-section geometry.

- To make only certain 2D objects renderable (or want some to render differently than others) you could apply a Renderable Spline modifier directly to those objects after linking.

File Link Settings: Revit Files (RVT or FBX)

In the Manage Links dialog box, in the *Presets* tab, selecting an Autodesk Revit file and clicking **Modify...** opens the File Link Settings: Revit Files (RVT or FBX) dialog box, as shown in Figure 3–16. Additionally, you can also select the Autodesk FBX (Generic) file preset and click **Modify...**.This opens the File Link Settings: FBX Files dialog box, as shown in Figure 3–17. This dialog box is similar to the Autodesk Revit Files (.RVT and .FBX) but without a *Geometry* area for controlling the segments and smoothing the linked geometry.

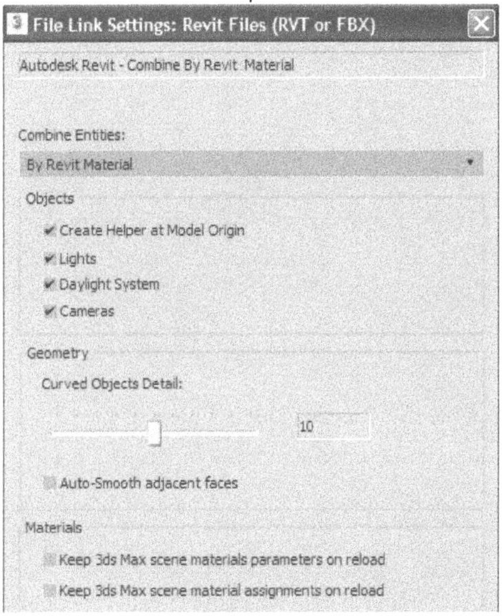

Figure 3–16

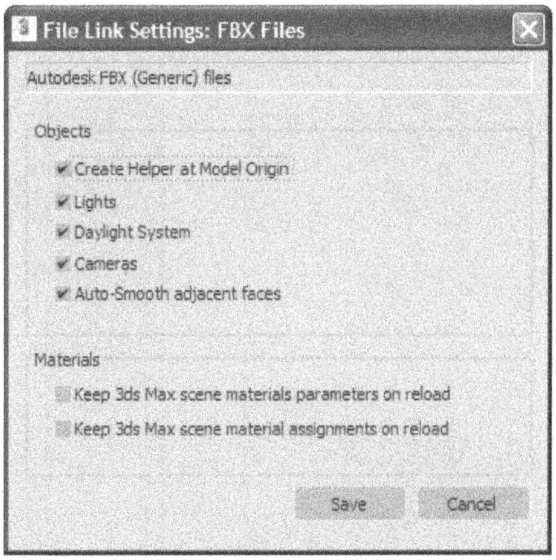

Figure 3–17

The options available in the File Link Settings: Revit Files (RVT or FBX) dialog box are described as follows:

It is recommended that you combine entities to reduce the number of objects.

- **Combine Entities** list: Enables you to select the Autodesk Revit entities that you want to combine, as shown in Figure 3–18. For example, if you select **By Revit Material**, all of the entities that have the same material are linked in the current Autodesk 3ds Max scene as a single object.

Figure 3–18

- ***Objects*** area: The selected options in this area are linked from the .RVT file to your current scene. If the .RVT file or .FBX file contains photometric lights, interior artificial lights, cameras, and exterior daylight systems, you can select the associated options in the File Link Settings dialog box.

- ***Geometry*** **area:** Enables you to set the number of segments for your curved entities and apply auto-smoothing to them.

- ***Materials*** **area:** Enables you to control the material definitions and assignment settings.

Practice 3b

Linking an AutoCAD DWG

Practice Objectives

- Create a preset to link an AutoCAD .DWG file and reposition it.
- Revise the link settings and reload the linked file.

Estimated time for completion: 20 minutes

In this practice you will link AutoCAD geometry to represent the parking lot details, such as pavement markings and other details. You will reposition this file using the Helper object, and will create 3D markings by projecting 2D lines to the elevation of a terrain model.

You must set the paths to locate the External files and Xrefs used in the practice. If you have not done this already, return to **Chapter 1: Introduction to Autodesk 3ds Max** and complete Task 1 to Task 3 in **Practice 1a: Organizing Folders and Working with the Interface**. You only have to set the user paths once.

Task 1 - Link an AutoCAD .DWG File.

If a dialog box opens prompting you about a File Load: Mismatch, click OK to accept the default values.

1. Open **Civil Base.max** from the …\scenes folder.

2. Select **Application Menu>Import>Link AutoCAD**. In the Open dialog box, browse and open the …\import folder in the Practice Files folder. Select **3D Parking Lot Detail.dwg** and click **Open**. The Manage Links dialog box opens with the path and the filename displayed, as shown Figure 3–19.

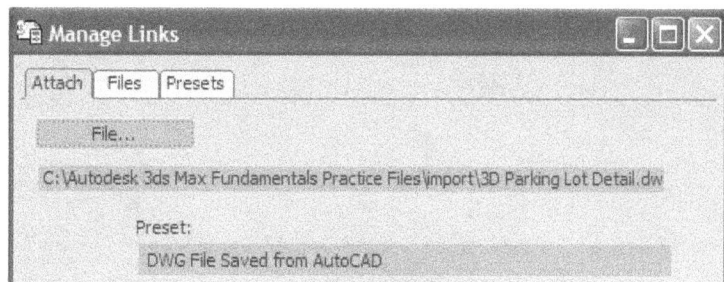

Figure 3–19

If no preset is selected, only New… is available.

3. Select the *Presets* tab and click **New…** to create a new link preset.

4. In the New Settings Preset dialog box, set *New Name* as **AutoCAD – Derive by Layer**. Note that the *Format* is selected as **AutoCAD Drawings**. Click **OK**.

5. In the Manage Links dialog box, select the new **AutoCAD – Derive by Layer** preset, as shown in Figure 3–20. Click **Modify...**.

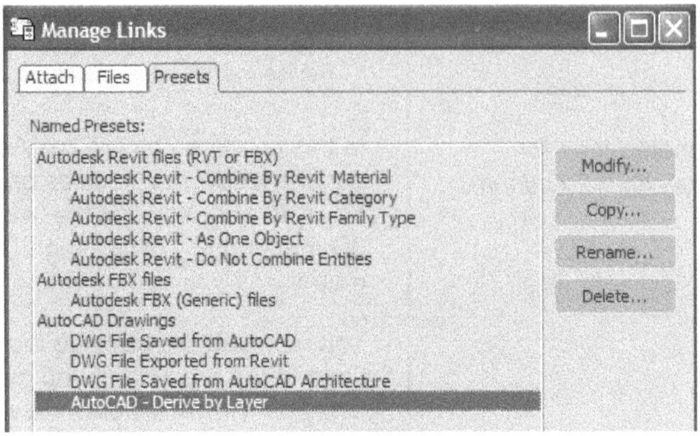

Figure 3–20

*The **Create Helper at drawing origin** option adds a helper object at the origin of the linked file.*

6. In the File Link Settings: DWG Files dialog box, in the *Basic* tab, set the link options, as shown in Figure 3–21. Select the *Advanced* tab and select **Create helper at drawing origin**, as shown in Figure 3–22. Leave all other options as defaults (clear).

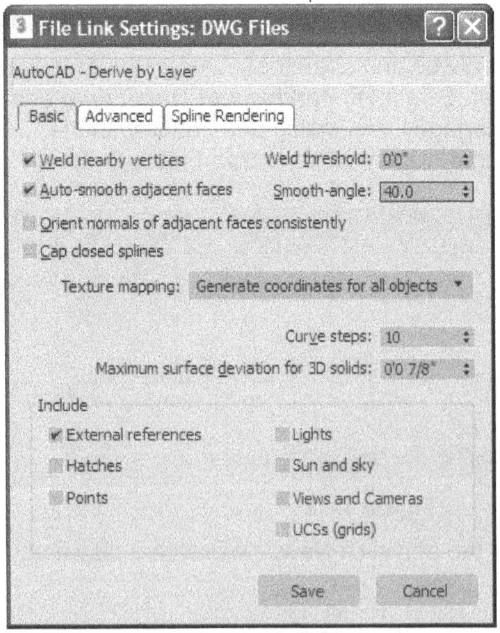

Figure 3–21

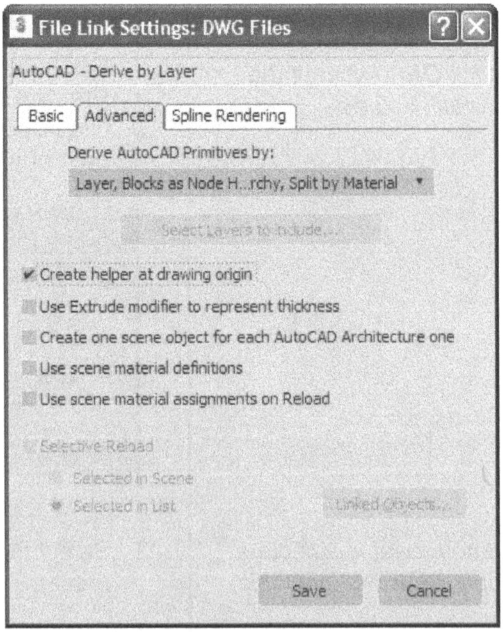

Figure 3–22

7. Select the *Spline Rendering* tab and verify that the link options are set to the defaults, as shown in Figure 3–23.

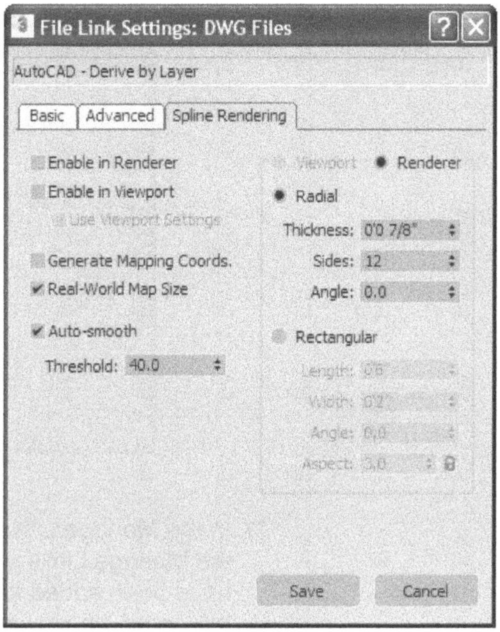

Figure 3–23

8. Click **Save**.

9. In the Manage Links dialog box, select the *Attach* tab. Set *Preset* to **AutoCAD – Derive by Layer**, as shown in Figure 3–24. Click **Select Layers to include...**.

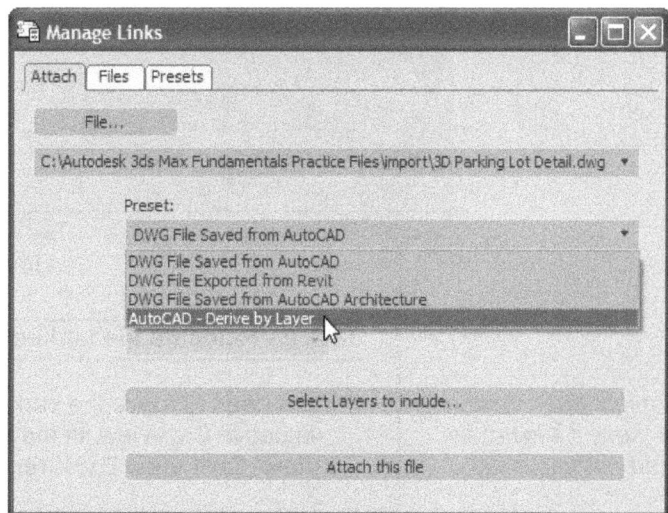

Figure 3–24

10. In the Select Layers dialog box, select **Select from list**. Clear **0** and **DEFPOINTS** and leave all other layers as selected, as shown in Figure 3–25. Click **OK**.

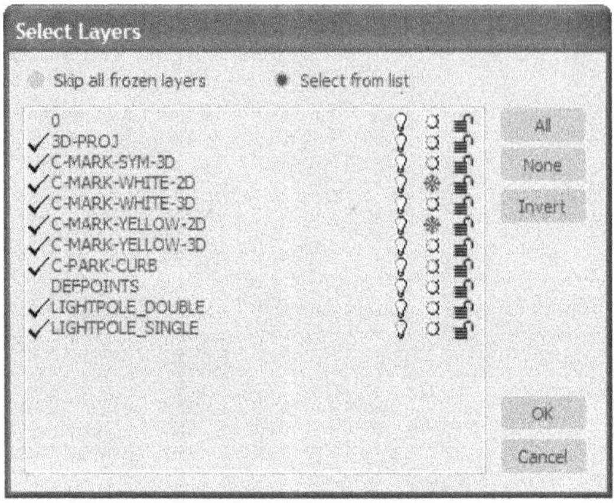

Figure 3–25

11. In the Manage Links dialog box, click **Attach this file**. Close the Manage Links dialog box. Note that the parking lot details have been added to the scene, but are located far away from the origin, as shown in the **Top** viewport in Figure 3–26.

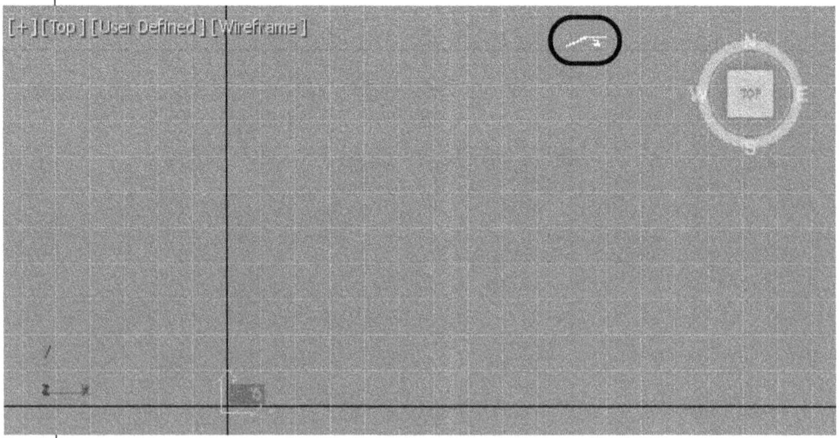

Figure 3–26

Task 2 - Relocate the Linked Geometry.

You might need to start Civil View, if it is not set to start automatically.

1. You need to move the parking lot details by the global shift values in Civil View. In the menu bar, select **Civil View>Civil View>Civil View Explorer**.

2. In the Civil View Explorer, select **Scene Settings**, as shown in Figure 3–27. In the Scene Settings rollout, note the *Global Import Shift* values for *X Shift* and *Y Shift (-9901)*, as shown in Figure 3–28. Close the Civil View Explorer.

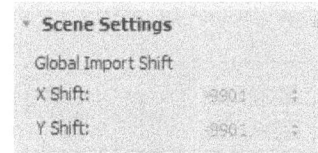

Figure 3–27	Figure 3–28

3. In the Main Toolbar, click 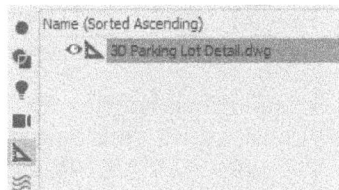 (Select and Move).

If the Scene Explorer is not displayed, select **Tools>Scene Explorer** *and then dock it.*

4. In the Scene Explorer, click (■ (Display None) and

▲ (Display Helpers)), and then select the helper object **3D Parking Lot Detail.dwg**, as shown in Figure 3–29. Note that the **User Coordinate System** icon located at the origin is selected, as shown in Figure 3–30.

Figure 3–29	Figure 3–30

5. In the Status Bar, ensure that ⊞ (Absolute Mode Transform) is displayed. Set the following, as shown in Figure 3–31:
    * *X* edit box: **-9901'0"**
    * *Y* edit box: **-9901'0"**

⊞ X: -9901'0" ♦ Y: -9901'0" ♦ Z: 0'0" ♦

Figure 3–31

6. Press <Enter>.

7. Click ⊡ (Zoom Extents All). Note how the parking lot details are placed exactly on the parking lot surface.

8. In the **Perspective** viewport, use ⌕⁺ (Zoom) and ⌖· (Orbit) to zoom into the Parking lot area and tilt the view to display the area below the surfaces, similar to that shown in Figure 3–32. Note that in addition to the 3D pavement markings, 2D line markings are imported through the link.

Figure 3–32

Task 3 - Revise the Link Settings.

In the Files tab, if the linked file has been modified, 🗎 *displays.*

1. Click **Application Menu>References>Manage Links** to open the Manage Links dialog box.

2. In the Manage Links dialog box, select the *Files* tab and note that the linked file displays 🗎, indicating that the file has not changed. (*Although the linked file has not changed, use* **Reload...** *to revise the link settings.*) Verify that **Show Reload options** is selected, and click **Reload...**.

You can use:
Reload... *to update the file in the scene.*
Detach... *to remove a linked drawing from the scene.*
Bind... *to insert the drawing as is and removes the connection.*

3. The File Link Settings: DWG Files dialog box opens. In the *Advanced* tab, click **Select Layers to include...**. Clear the 2D layers (**C-MARK-WHITE-2Dand C-MARK-YELLOW-2D**), and the two **LIGHTPOLE** layers, as shown in Figure 3–33.

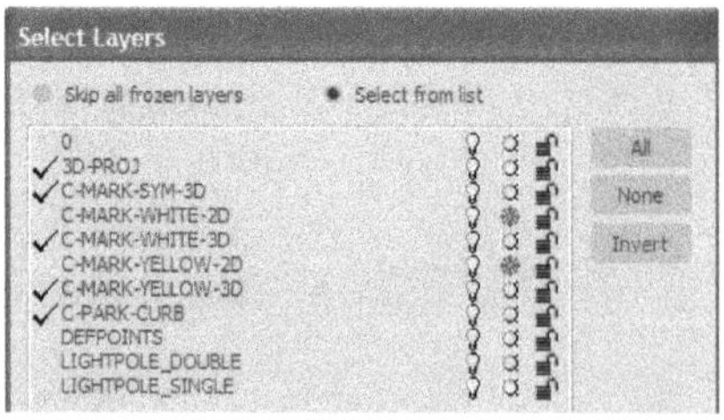

Figure 3–33

The 2D linework should no longer display, keeping the scene smaller.

4. Click **OK** twice to close both dialog boxes. Click ✕ to close the Manage Links dialog box. In the **Perspective** viewport, note that the 2D line markings are not displayed.

5. Save your work as **MyCivil Base.max**.

Practice 3c

Linking and Reloading Autodesk Revit File

Practice Objectives

- Link and reposition an Autodesk Revit file to the current scene.
- Reload a modified .RVT file.

Estimated time for completion: 20 minutes

In this practice you will link a .RVT file into a 3ds Max scene. You will reposition the Revit file using the Helper object. You will then reload a modified version of the .RVT linked file to incorporate the changes made to the original Autodesk Revit file using **Reload**.

You must set the paths to locate the External files and Xrefs used in the practice. If you have not done this already, return to **Chapter 1: Introduction to Autodesk 3ds Max** and complete Task 1 to Task 3 in **Practice 1a: Organizing Folders and Working with the Interface**. You only have to set the user paths once.

Task 1 - Link an Autodesk Revit (.RVT) file.

*If a dialog box opens prompting you about a File Load: Mismatch, click **OK** to accept the default values.*

It might take a few minutes to load the file.

1. Open **Civil Base Link.max** from the *...\scenes* folder.

2. Select **Application Menu>Import>Link Revit**.

3. In the Open dialog box, in the *...\import* folder, select **Revit Building-1.rvt** and click **Open**.

4. The Status Bar is replaced by the Loading file bar, indicating the progress of the file as it loads. Once loaded, the Select Revit View dialog box opens, as shown in Figure 3–34.

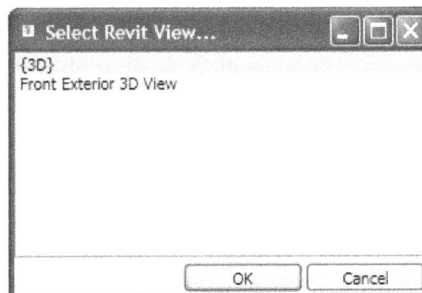

Figure 3–34

5. Select **Front Exterior 3D View** and click **OK**.

*The **Create Helper at Model Origin** option adds a helper object at the origin of the linked file. Selecting and applying transforms (move, rotate, or scale) to the helper object applies the transform to the linked geometry together.*

6. In the Manage Links dialog box, select the *Presets* tab. Click **New...** to create a new preset. In the New Settings Preset dialog box, set the following:
   - *New Name*: **Revit Preset**
   - *Format*: **Autodesk Revit (*.rvt,*.fbx)**.

7. Click **OK**.

8. In the Manage Links dialog box, select **Revit Preset** and click **Modify**.

9. In the File Link Settings dialog box, do the following, as shown in Figure 3–35:
   - In the Combine Entities drop-down list, select **By Revit Category**.
   - In the *Objects* area, clear **Lights** and **Daylight System**.
   - In the *Objects* area, select **Create Helper at Model Origin** and **Cameras**.
   - In the *Geometry* area, set *Curved Objects Detail* to **6**.
   - In the *Materials* area, verify that **Keep 3ds Max scene materials parameters on reload** and **Keep 3ds Max scene material assignments on reload** are cleared.

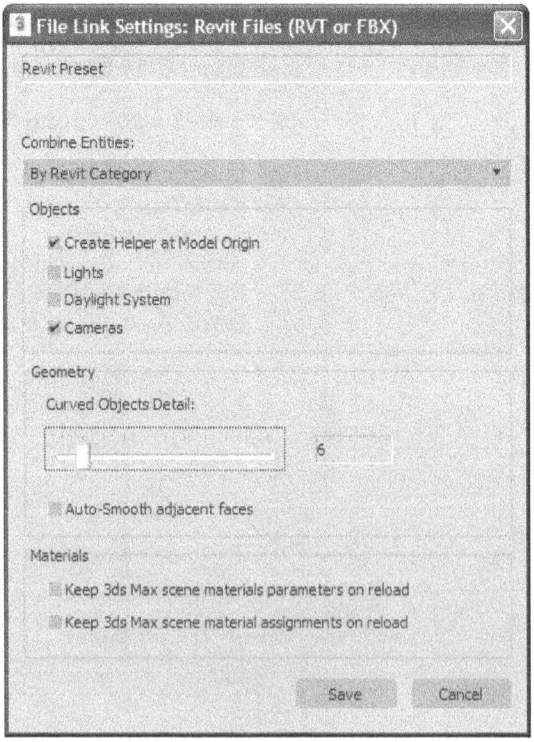

Figure 3–35

10. Click **Save**.

11. Select the *Attach* tab. Expand the Preset drop-down list and select **Revit Preset**.

(It might take a few minutes to load the file).

12. Click **Attach this file**. Note that the Autodesk Revit building and camera are loaded at the 0,0,0 location in the viewports.

13. Click ☒ to close the Manage Links dialog box.

If the Scene Explorer is not displayed, select ***Tools>Scene Explorer*** *and then dock it.*

14. In the Scene Explorer, click ▪ (Display None) and

◢ (Display Helpers) and then select the helper object **Revit Building-1.rvt**, as shown in Figure 3–36.

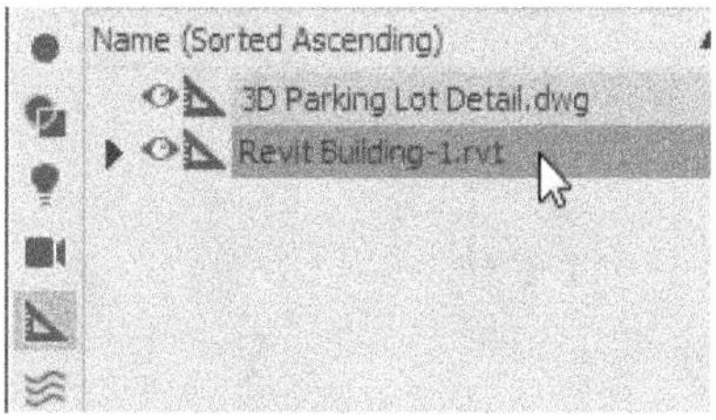

Figure 3–36

15. Right-click on the **Top** viewport to make it active and to

maintain the selection. In the Main Toolbar, click ✛ (Select and Move). The Transform gizmo is displayed at the helper location, which is the origin of the linked Autodesk Revit file.

The position of the building pad from the origin has been calculated.

16. In the Status Bar, verify that ⊞ (Absolute Mode Transform) is displayed. Set the following, as shown in Figure 3–37:
   - *X* edit box: **800'0"**
   - *Y* edit box: **382'0"**
   - *Z* edit box: **154'6"**

Figure 3–37

17. Press <Enter>.

18. Click ⚞ (Zoom Extents All). Note how the building is placed on the building pad.

Grid has been hidden for clarity. Press <G>.

19. In the **Front** viewport, use (Zoom Region) and create a rectangular window around the building to zoom into the building. Select the **User Defined** Visual Style label and select **High Quality.** Select the **Wireframe** Visual Style label and select **Default Shading**. Select the **Default Shading** Visual Style label again and select **Edged Faces** to define the windows and doors. The building should display similar to that shown in Figure 3–38.

Figure 3–38

20. In the **Left** viewport, select the **Wireframe** Visual Style label and select **Default Shading** and then **Edged Faces**.

21. Select the **Left** Point of View label, and select **Cameras>Views: Front Exterior 3D View**, as shown in Figure 3–39.

| Cameras | ▶ | Views: Front Exterior 3D View |
| Lights | ▶ | Views: {3D} |

Figure 3–39

22. Use (Pan Camera) and (Field-of-View) to display the complete building in the **Left** viewport, similar to that as shown in Figure 3–40.

23. In the **Perspective** viewport, use (Zoom) and (Orbit) to zoom into the building and parking lot area so that the display is similar to that shown in Figure 3–40.

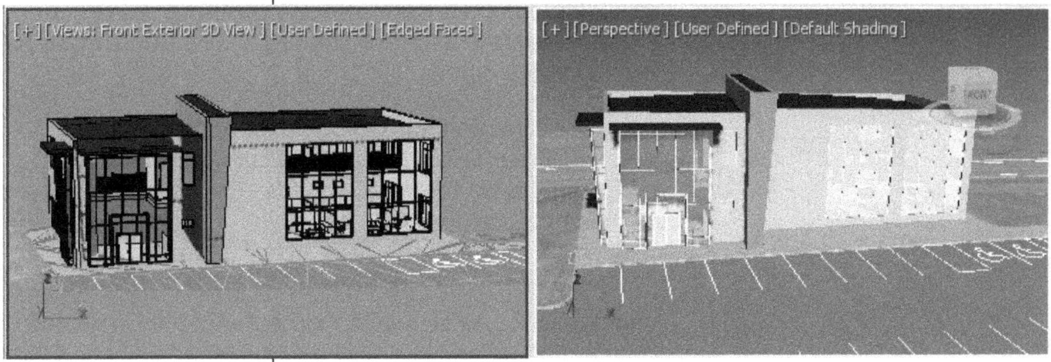

Figure 3–40

Task 2 - Reload the variation of the .RVT file.

A variation to the .RVT linked file (windows have been added) has been included in the ...\import folder.

1. In Windows Explorer, open the ...\import folder.

2. Right-click on **Revit Building-1.rvt** and select **Rename**. Rename the file as **Revit Building-1_ORIGINAL.rvt**.

3. Right-click on **Revit Building-2.rvt**, and select **Copy**. Paste a copy of this file into the same directory. Right-click on the copied file, select **Rename**, and rename the file as **Revit Building-1.rvt**. This must be the same name as the original file that was linked to indicate that the original linked file has changed.

4. Return to the Autodesk 3ds Max software. Select **Application Menu>References>Manage Links** to open the Manage Links dialog box.

5. In the Manage Links dialog box, select the *Files* tab. Note that ⬚ displays in front of the .RVT filename (as shown in Figure 3–41), indicating that changes have been made to the original linked file.

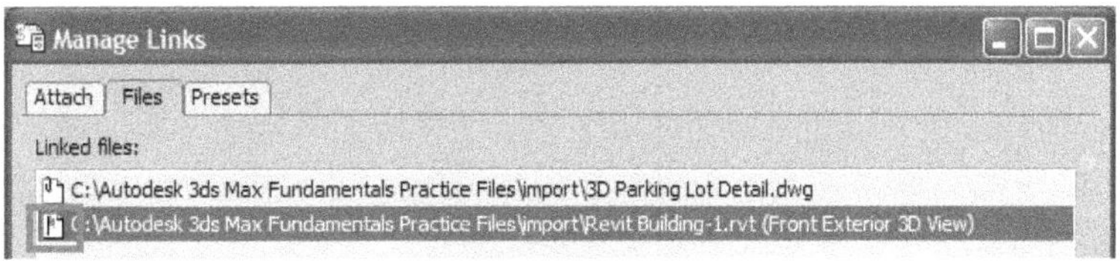

Figure 3–41

6. Select the complete path of **Revit Building -1.rvt** (if not already selected) and click **Reload...**. The Loading file bar displays the progress.

7. In the File Link Settings dialog box that opens, in the *Materials* area, select **Keep 3ds Max scene material assignments on reload**. Click **OK**. The scene is refreshed with the new changes.

8. In the Manage Links dialog box, in the *Files* tab, the icon has changed to 🗋, as shown in Figure 3–42. This indicates that there are no differences between the original file and the linked file.

Figure 3–42

9. Close the Manage Links dialog box.

10. In the viewports, the modified building is displayed. More windows are added to the building, as shown in Figure 3–43.

Figure 3–43

11. Save the file as **MyCivil Base Link.max**.

3.3 References

External References (XRef)

Autodesk 3ds Max Scene files can reference data from other .MAX scene files by expanding **Application Menu> References>XRef Objects or XRef Scene**. The XREF data remains linked to the source (.MAX) scene file so that changes in the source file can be reflected in any scene that contains the XREF.

- External References are useful to break up large projects into more manageable pieces, permit more than one person to work on the same project at the same time in separate files, and to enable the same core scene geometry to be used in multiple files.

- **XRef Scenes** bring in the entire scene. All of the XREF objects are non-selectable and cannot be modified.

- **XRef Objects** enable you to select individual objects (or all) from an XREF scene. These objects remain selectable and modifiable in the XREF scene file.

- You can snap to XREF and use XREF objects with AutoGrid. You can also use XREF objects as alignment targets and you can select an XREF object's coordinate system for object transformation. XREF support parameter wiring and you can XREF the controllers.

- Objects in scenes (.MAX) are imported into other . MAX scenes using the **Merge** option.

Data Management and Asset Tracking

The Autodesk 3ds Max software enables you to manage your data through Data Management (DM) solutions, referred to as Asset Tracking Systems (ATSs).

- DM solutions such as the Autodesk® Vault software enables you to store scene files and any supporting data (such as material maps) in a single database repository.

- These systems can be accessed simultaneously by multiple users with different rights assigned based on their project responsibilities. Data can be checked out for editing by one individual at a time while still being referenced by other users. Users can see who is editing which portion of the project at any time.

- By centralizing the files in a DM system it is much easier to adjust paths for external files such as image maps.

- Data files can be versioned through DM solutions, so that the older versions can be readily accessed, if required.

- For more information see *Asset Tracking* in the Autodesk 3ds Max Help files. Asset Tracking is available through the **Application Menu>References> Asset Tracking**.

Practice 3d

XRef and Merge Objects

Practice Objective

- Link an AutoCAD .DWG file and incorporate objects from another scene file into the current scene.

Estimated time for completion: 15 minutes

In this practice create a new scene file that will contain linked AutoCAD objects and XRef objects from the Civil Base scene. You will then merge objects into the current scene file.

You must set the paths to locate the External files and Xrefs used in the practice. If you have not done this already, return to **Chapter 1: Introduction to Autodesk 3ds Max** and complete Task 1 to Task 3 in **Practice 1a: Organizing Folders and Working with the Interface**. You only have to set the user paths once.

Task 1 - Assemble the Data.

If an unsaved scene is open, you need to save or discard the changes to the scene.

1. Click **Application Menu>Reset** and click **Yes** to reset the scene.

2. For this scene, set the *System Unit Scale* to **Inches**. Select **Customize>Units Setup**. In the dialog box, verify that the following is set:
   - *Display Unit Scale:* **US Standard**, **Feet w/ Fractional Inches**
   - *Default Units*: **Inches**
   - *Lighting Units*: **American**

3. Click **System Unit Setup**. In the System Unit Setup dialog box, set *System Unit Scale* to **Inches**. Click **OK** in both the dialog boxes.

4. Expand **Application Menu>References** and select **Manage Links**.

5. In the Manage Links dialog box, in the *Attach* tab, click **File...**. In the ...*import* folder, select **Exterior AutoCAD Architectural Model.dwg**. Click **Open**.

*The **AutoCAD – Derive by Layer** preset was created in the **Practice: Linking an AutoCAD DWG**. Complete the above mentioned practice to create the preset if not already done so.*

6. In the *Preset* drop-down list, select **AutoCAD – Derive by Layer** and click **Attach this file**. Once the file has been loaded, close the Manage Links dialog box.

   • The AutoCAD Architectural objects were not joined together by layer. Each was subdivided by material type into different objects. Materials previously assigned in AutoCAD Architecture were preserved on these separate objects.

7. Click ▇ (Maximize Viewport Toggle) or use <Alt>+<W> to display the four viewport view.

8. Click ▇ (Zoom Extents All) to display all of the objects in all of the viewports.

9. In the **Front** viewport, select all of the objects by creating a window around the objects. In the Main Toolbar, in the *Named Selection Sets* field, enter **exterior AutoCAD Architectural building**, as shown in Figure 3–44. Press <Enter>.

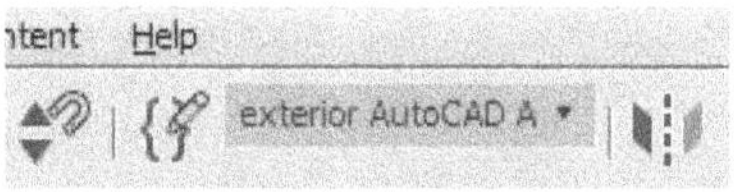

Figure 3–44

You select objects to XREF rather than the entire scene because XREF scene objects cannot be individually selected or modified.

10. Click **Application Menu>References>XRef Objects**. In the XRef Objects dialog box, click ▇ (Create XRef Record from File) as shown in Figure 3–45.

Figure 3–45

11. In the Open File dialog box, select **Parking Lot Detail.max** (from the ...\import folder) and click **Open**.

12. If the Units Mismatch dialog box opens, click **OK**. This rescales the XRef objects to the system units.

13. The Duplicate Material Name dialog box opens prompting you that there is an incoming material with the same name as an existing scene material. Select **Apply to All Duplicates** to keep both materials, as shown in Figure 3–46. Click **Auto-Rename Merged Material**.

Duplicate Material Name

A material name assigned to a merging object is a duplicate of a material in the scene. Do you want to:

Rename Merged Material | Global

Use Merged Material | ✔ Apply to All Duplicates

Use Scene Material

Auto-Rename Merged Material

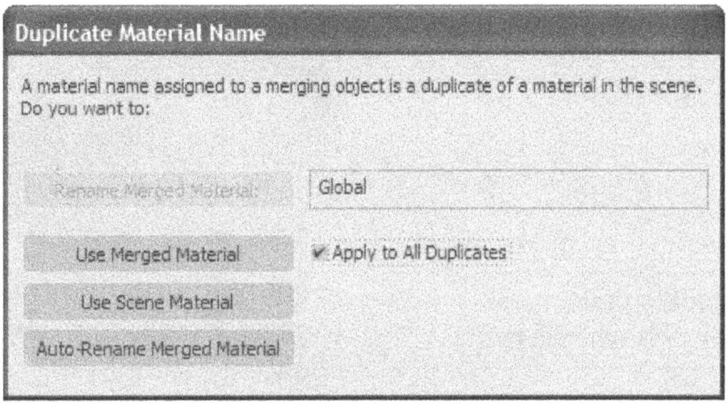

Figure 3–46

14. In the XRef Objects dialog box, note that the .MAX filename is displayed. Click ☒ to close the dialog box.

15. Click ⟐ (Zoom Extents All). Note that the Civil Base objects are located far from the origin. This is a coordinate system discrepancy and not a scale issue. It is common for Architectural drawings to be based in a different coordinate system and scale than the accompanying Civil/Survey drawings.

Task 2 - Coordinate the Data.

In this task you will relocate the Civil Base in the Architectural Data. To line up the data accurately you will need the exact coordinate translation and rotation. You can measure ahead of time in programs, such as AutoCAD by comparing the coordinates of points common to both files.

Alternatively, you can use the Scene Explorer to select all the XRef objects.

1. In the Scene Explorer (■ (Display None) and

   ◉ (Display Object XRefs)), select all of the XRef objects in the list (use <Shift> and then select the first and last).

2. With these XRef objects selected, select **Group>Group** from the menu bar.

3. In the Group dialog box, set the *Group name* to **Site XRef** and click **OK**.

4. In the Main Toolbar, click (Select and Move). In the Reference Coordinate System, select **World**, as shown in Figure 3–47. Click (Use Transform Coordinate Center).

Figure 3–47

The translation coordinates have already been measured in AutoCAD.

5. In the Status Bar, verify that (Absolute Mode) is displayed. In the *Transform Type-in* area, set the following, as shown in Figure 3–48:
   - *X:* **-197'4"**
   - *Y:* **-30'0"**
   - *Z:* **-4'11"**

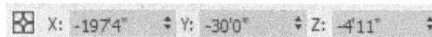

Figure 3–48

6. Press <Enter>.

7. In the Main Toolbar, click (Select Object) to exit the **Move** transform operation.

8. Click (Zoom Extents All).

9. In the **Perspective** viewport, change the Standard visual display to **High Quality** to display the materials.

10. In the **Perspective** viewport, use (Orbit Point of Interest) and click to place a point on the building and then orbit around that point. Using **Pan** and **Zoom**, zoom into the parking lot and building area (as shown in Figure 3–49), and verify that the building is located on the building pad. Although the XREF had a different Unit Scale (feet), it scaled correctly to the active scene (in inches).

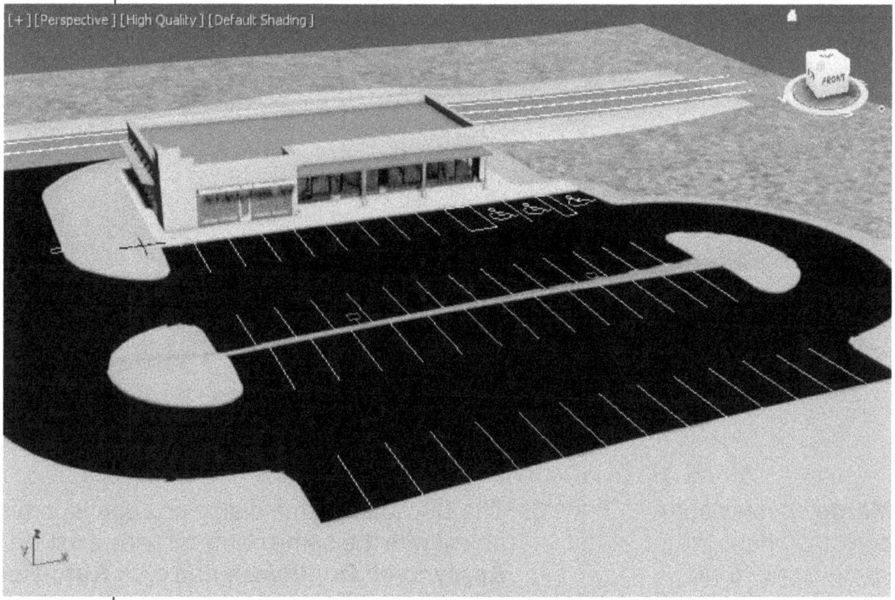

Figure 3–49

11. Save your work as **MyArchitectural Scene.max**.

Task 3 - Merging Objects.

1. Expand **Application Menu>Import>Merge**. In the Merge File dialog box, select **Light Poles for Project1.max** from the ...\scenes folder. Click **Open**.

2. In the Merge dialog box, click **All**, as shown in Figure 3–50. Click **OK**.

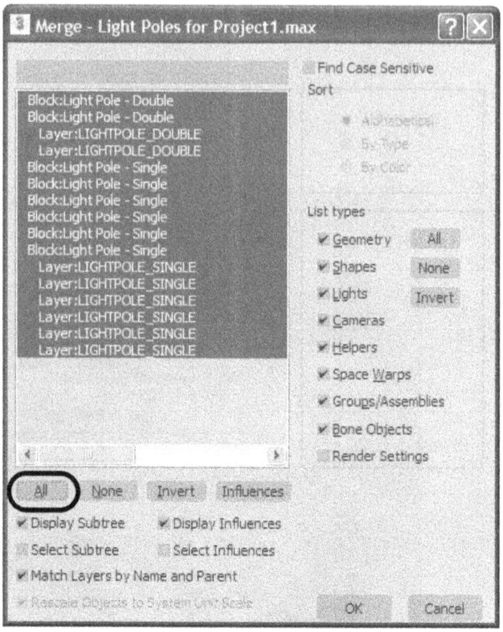

Figure 3–50

Merge enables both objects to have the same name, Skip ignores the incoming object, and Delete Old removes the original object.

3. The Duplicate Name dialog box opens, prompting you that an object with the same name already exists in the scene. Select **Apply to all Duplicates** and click **Auto-Rename**.

4. The light poles are displayed in the scene, as shown in Figure 3–51.

Figure 3–51

5. Save your work.

Chapter Review Questions

1. The following file types can be linked to the current Autodesk 3ds Max scene:

   a. .DWG, .OBJ, .APF, .FBX

   b. .DWG, .DXF, .FBX, .RVT

   c. .DWG, .DXF, .MAX, .RVT

   d. .DWG, .OBJ, .FBX, .RVT

2. In the Manage Links dialog box, in the *Files* tab, which of the following options do you use to remove the link with the original linked file but maintain its geometry in the current scene?

   a. **Reload...**

   b. **Detach...**

   c. **Bind...**

3. Which command do you use to combine objects from a saved Autodesk 3ds Max scene (.MAX file) into your current .MAX scene?

   a. **Import**

   b. **Link**

   c. **Open**

   d. **Merge**

4. While linking Autodesk Revit files in the current Autodesk 3ds Max scene, which of the following options are provided in the Combine Entities List? (Select all that apply.)

   a. By Revit Material

   b. By Revit Layer

   c. As One Object

   d. By Revit Camera

5. When an entire .MAX scene is brought into the current scene using **XREF Scenes**, the XREF objects are selectable but cannot be modified.

   a. True

   b. False

Command Summary

Button	Command	Location
	Absolute Mode	• Status Bar
N/A	Asset Tracking	• Application Menu: References
N/A	Import	• Application Menu: Import
N/A	Link AutoCAD	• Application Menu: Import
N/A	Link FBX	• Application Menu: Import
N/A	Link Revit	• Application Menu: Import
N/A	Manage Links	• Application Menu: References
N/A	Merge	• Application Menu: Import
	Select by Name	• Main Toolbar
	Select Object	• Main Toolbar
	Use Transform Coordinate Center	• Main Toolbar
N/A	XRef Objects	• Application Menu: References
N/A	XRef Scene	• Application Menu: References

Basic Modeling Techniques

Autodesk® 3ds Max® is a rendering and animation software that allows for objects to be directly modeled in the software. Modeling can be accomplished using Primitive Objects or Polygon Modeling tools that are further manipulated using Modifiers and Transforms to move, rotate, and scale them. Additionally, sub-object modes can be used to further modify and control the resulting objects.

Learning Objectives in this Chapter

- Identify the various primitive objects provided with the software.
- Apply changes to the model geometry using modifiers.
- Move, rotate, scale, and place objects, and constrain the movement of the Transform tools.
- Modify objects at a sub-object level.
- Work with various coordinate systems and transform systems.
- Create copies of the same object using various Clone options and create a single unit by grouping multiple objects together.
- Create and modify objects using the Polygon modeling tools.
- Review the status of the overall model and display information about the scene, such as polygon count, number of vertices, etc.

4.1 Model with Primitives

The Autodesk 3ds Max software enables you to create and adjust 3D geometry by creating a complex model from simple 3D objects called primitives, as shown in Figure 4–1.

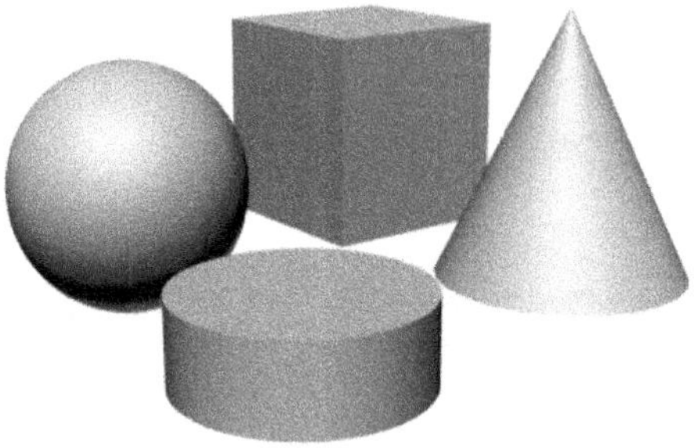

Figure 4–1

- All various types of already built objects (i.e., Standard Primitives, Extended Primitives, Compound Objects, etc.) are listed in the **Create>Geometry** Command Panel, as shown in Figure 4–2. Each of these categories consists of a group of objects that can be modeled and modified to create simple or complex objects.

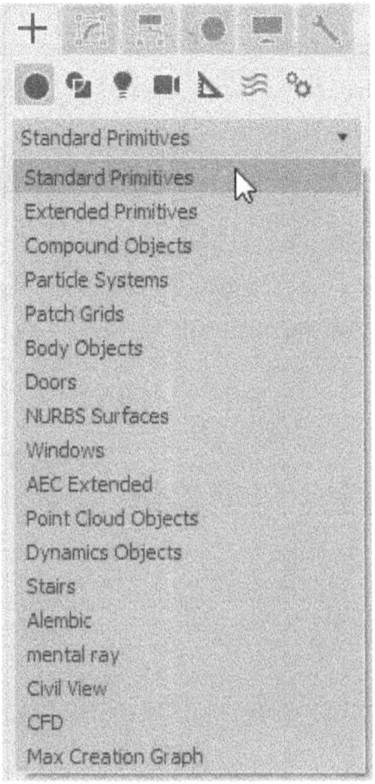

Figure 4–2

- You can model the selected 3D object directly in the viewport by using the mouse to locate and specify the starting point and then dragging the mouse to pick the locations (length, height, etc.).

- You can also enter the precise values in the edit boxes of the Keyboard Entry rollout in the Command Panel (as shown in Figure 4–3), and then click **Create**. You can either enter the values or use the spinner arrows to increase or decrease the values. After entering a value in a field, click in another field or press <Enter> to assign the values to the object.

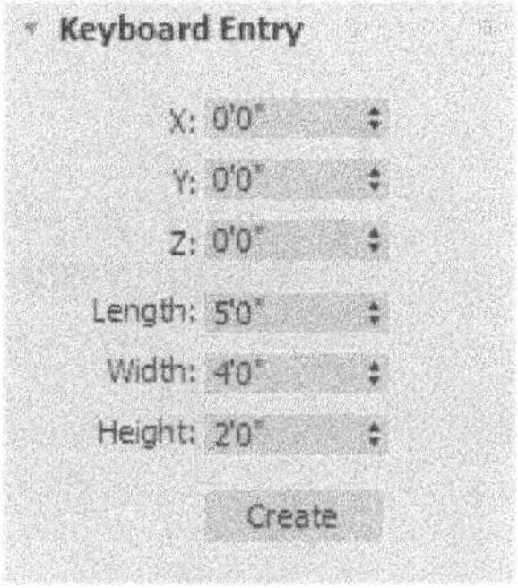

Figure 4–3

- You can also create geometry by modeling with modifiers, creating loft compound objects, or creating a 3D terrain from 2D contour objects.

Practice 4a

Estimated time for completion: 10 minutes

If a dialog box opens prompting you about a File Load: Mismatch, click **OK** to accept the default values.

Modeling with Primitives

Practice Objective

- Create primitive objects by using standard primitives and the modify the object.

In this practice you will model the base for the parking lot light fixtures by modeling the object using a standard primitive and then modifying its parameters using the Modify panel in the Command Panel.

You must set the paths to locate the External files and Xrefs used in the practice. If you have not done this already, return to **Chapter 1: Introduction to Autodesk 3ds Max** and complete Task 1 to Task 3 in **Practice 1a: Organizing Folders and Working with the Interface**. You only have to set the user paths once.

1. Open **Modeling with Primitives.max**. It is an empty base scene file.

2. Click in the **Top** viewport to make it active. The orientation of the object being created depends on the active viewport. For this practice, you will create the cylinder with its height in the Z-axis direction.

3. In the Command Panel, verify that the Create panel (➕) >

    ⬤ (Geometry) is selected with **Standard Primitives** displayed in the drop-down list, as shown in Figure 4–4. In the Object Type rollout, click **Cylinder**.

Figure 4–4

The 0,0,0 location corresponds to the default axes (center of the active grid) of the construction plane. Any value entered for X, Y, and Z, offsets the object by that number in the specified direction.

You can enter the values in their respective fields or use the spinner arrows to increase or decrease the values. After entering a value in a field, click in another edit field or press <Enter> to assign the values to the object.

4. Click on the Keyboard Entry title bar to expand the rollout. Leave the X, Y, Z coordinates at **0'0"**. The software places the base center of the cylinder at 0,0,0, location. Set the following, as shown in Figure 4–5:
   - *Radius*: **1'0"**
   - *Height*: **3'0"**

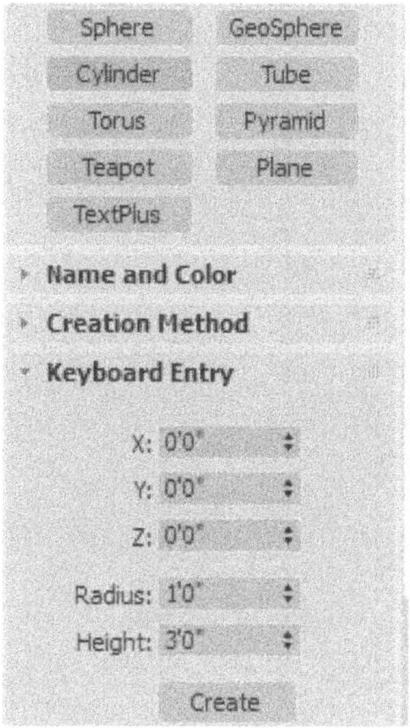

Sphere	GeoSphere
Cylinder	Tube
Torus	Pyramid
Teapot	Plane
TextPlus	

▸ **Name and Color**
▸ **Creation Method**
▾ **Keyboard Entry**

X: 0'0"
Y: 0'0"
Z: 0'0"

Radius: 1'0"
Height: 3'0"

Create

Figure 4–5

5. Click **Create**. Note that a cylinder is created and is displayed in all viewports.

> **Hint: Creating Objects**
>
> After creating an object, you cannot change the parameters in the Keyboard Entry rollout. Changing the parameters in the Keyboard Entry rollout and clicking **Create** adds a second object. If you created another object, in the Quick Access Toolbar, click ↺ ▾ once to undo the creation of the second object. Use the Modify panel () to change the parameters.

6. Click (Zoom Extents All) display the base more clearly. Note that it zooms into the cylinder in all of the viewports.

7. With the cylinder still selected, in the Command Panel, select the Modify panel (). At the top of the modifier list, in the *Name* field, rename the object from *Cylinder001* to **LP Base**.

8. In the Parameters rollout, set the following, as shown Figure 4–6. Note the effect on the geometry:

   - *Radius*: **1'6"**
   - *Height Segments*: **1**
   - *Cap Segments:* **1**
   - *Sides*: **20**

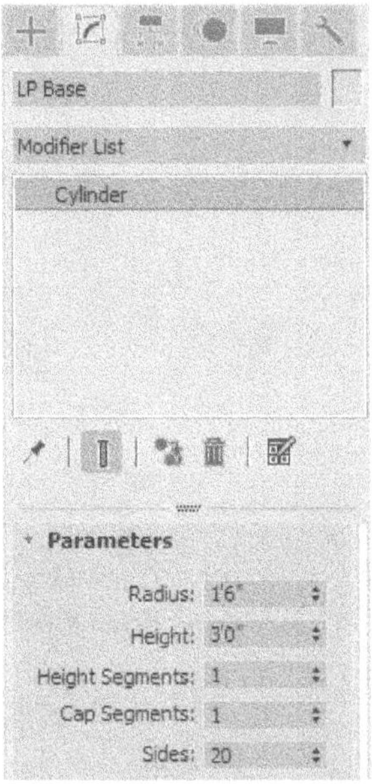

Figure 4–6

9. Select the Create panel (+) and in the Object Type rollout, click **Box** to create the anchor base plate. In the Keyboard Entry rollout set the following, as shown in Figure 4–7:

   - *X* coordinates: **0'0"**
   - *Y* coordinates: **0'0"**
   - *Z* coordinates: **3'0"**

   This will create the center of the base of the box at the 0,0,3 location, which is the top of the cylinder (the height of the cylinder is 3'-0").

   - *Length*: **1'4"**
   - *Width*: **1'4"**
   - *Height*: **0'2"**

10. Click **Create**. A box is created on top of the **LP Base** cylinder, as shown in Figure 4–7.

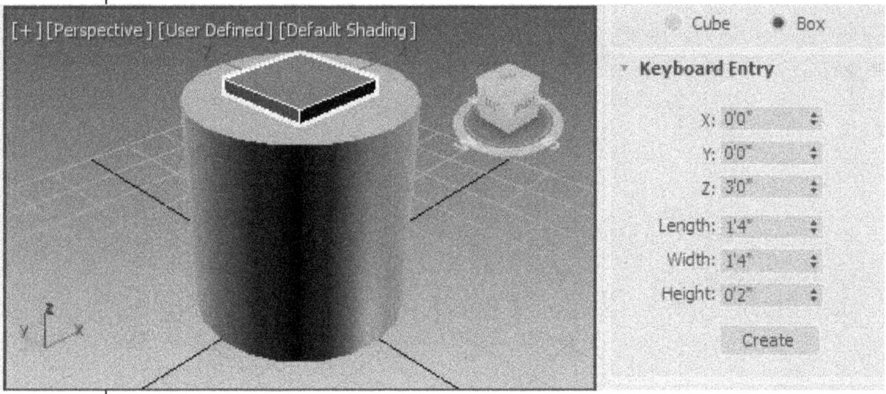

Figure 4–7

11. With the box still selected, select the Modify panel ( ) and rename the *Box001* as **LP Anchor Base**.

12. Save your work as **MyLight Pole.max**.

4.2 Modifiers and Transforms

The Autodesk 3ds Max software includes various modifiers and transforms that enable you to modify your geometry. They are described as follows:

Modifiers	• Adds geometric and property alterations to objects such as Extrude, Taper etc. • Listed in the Modifier Stack and their parameter values are available for adjustment afterwards.
Transforms	• Transforms are used to translate and scale objects in the scene. • Initiated by selecting the required buttons in the Main Toolbar or by using the Transform modes in the right-click quad menu. • Conducted by accessing a transform mode and entering new values, or graphically transforming objects on the screen. • Applied to objects after basic parameters and modifiers have been taken into account (except world-space modifiers). For example, if you scale a box, the **Length** parameter shown in the Modifier Stack does not take into account the effects of the scale transform.

- An object can have any number of modifiers, but only has a single set of transform values at any time.

- Transforms and almost all object and modifier parameters can be animated. For example, a walkthrough animation can be created using Move Transform to move the camera, its target, or both.

Modifiers

Any object that you create can be modified using the modifiers in the Modifier List, as shown in Figure 4–8. This list is located in

the Command Panel's Modify panel ( ) on top of the Modifier Stack. Click the down arrow to display the list and use the scroll bar to navigate through the complete list of modifiers. If you know the name of the modifier, you can enter the first letter to jump to that part of the selection list.

Modifiers are placed in groups and then listed alphabetically.

Figure 4–8

Transform Tools

The Transform tools are available in the Main Toolbar, as shown in Figure 4–9.

Figure 4–9

The available Transform tools are described as follows:

	**Select and Move**
	**Select and Rotate**
	**Select and Scale:** Scaling has three flyout options: (Uniform),  (Non-uniform), and  (Squash). • **Non-uniform:** Enables you to scale one or two axes independently. • **Squash**: Enables you to do the same, but scaling one or two axes applies a simultaneous opposite scaling to the other(s). The Scale Transform gizmo also has the tools for Non-uniform scaling.

Select and Place / Select and Rotate: Enables you to locate and position/locate and rotate an object with respect to the surface of another object.

Right-click on **Select and Place** and use the Placement Settings dialog box (as shown in the image below) to customize how the objects are aligned. Right-clicking on **Select and Rotate** opens the same dialog box with the Rotate option selected.

- **Rotate:** Enables you to click and drag an object to rotate around the local axis that is specified with the object Up Axis.
- **Use Base As Pivot:** Constrains the base of the object as the contact point with the surface of another object. By default, the pivot point of the object is used as the contact point.
- **Pillow Mode:** Enables you to move the objects around each other, but restricts them from intersecting. Useful when moving the object over uneven surfaces.
- **Autoparent:** Automatically links the object that is being placed as a child of the object it is being placed on, creating a hierarchical relationship.
- **Object Up Axis:** The selected up axis is used as the local axis on the object that is being moved.

Hint: XForm Modifier with Scale

To avoid problems in animation, it is recommended that you do not to use the Scale transform directly on objects. Instead, apply an XForm modifier to the objects and then **Scale** the XForm gizmo.

To display a toolbar, right-click anywhere on an empty space in the Main Toolbar and select the required toolbar.

- Transforms can be constrained to one or two axes by selecting one of the buttons in the Axis Constraints toolbar, as shown in Figure 4–10. However, it is more common to use the gizmos or the keyboard shortcuts to constrain the transforms. This toolbar is hidden by default.

- When a transform mode is active, a Transform gizmo displays (as shown in Figure 4–11) on the selected object on the screen.

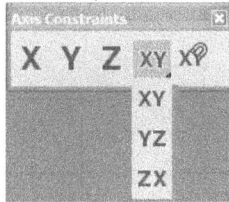

Figure 4–10

Move   Rotate   Scale

Figure 4–11

- Clicking and dragging over the gizmo enables you to perform the transform interactively on the screen. You can also constrain the transform by highlighting an axis handle on the gizmo before clicking and dragging.

- You can change the display size of the transform gizmo interactively in the viewport. Pressing <-> decreases its display size while as pressing <=> increases its display size.

- You can apply a transform accurately by entering (or using spinners) the required transform values in the *Transform Type-In* area, in the Status Bar, as shown in Figure 4–12.

X: 50.0   Y: -32.0   Z: 11.0

Figure 4–12

- In the Main Toolbar, right-click on **Transform** to open its Transform Type-In dialog box, as shown in Figure 4–13 for the Move transform. The Transform Type-In dialog box can be also be accessed by clicking ▢ (Settings) in the right-click quad menu, as shown in Figure 4–14.

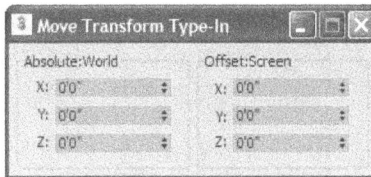

Figure 4–13

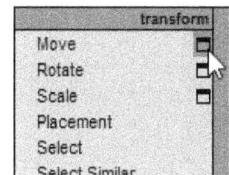

Figure 4–14

- Transform modes remain active until they are canceled by either clicking (Select Object) in the Main Toolbar or by pressing <Q>.

- Click (Select Object) after you have finished a transform to avoid accidentally moving, rotating, or scaling objects while making selections.

Practice 4b

Modeling with Modifiers and Transforms

Practice Objectives

- Create a 2D shape and then extrude it into a 3D object.
- Create primitive solids dynamically and modify objects.
- Transform objects to place them at the right location.

Estimated time for completion: fS30 minutes

In this practice you will refine the parking lot lighting fixture by creating a 2D shape and then extruding it to create a 3D object. You will create primitive objects dynamically in the viewport and then modify the objects using various modifiers in the Command Panel. You will also use Transforms (**Move**, **Rotate**, and **Place**) to place the created objects in the correct scene positions.

You must set the paths to locate the External files and Xrefs used in the practice. If you have not done this already, return to **Chapter 1: Introduction to Autodesk 3ds Max** and complete Task 1 to Task 3 in **Practice 1a: Organizing Folders and Working with the Interface**. You only have to set the user paths once.

Task 1 - Extrude and Adjust the Light Pole.

Modeling 3D geometry from 2D shapes is discussed in detail later in the Student Guide.

To create the rectangular light pole, create a 2D cross-section shape and then extrude it into a 3D object. This approach is another way to create 3D geometry.

1. Open **Modeling with Modifiers and Transforms.max**.

2. Verify that the **Top** viewport is active. In the Create panel

    ($+$), click $\blacksquare$ (Shapes) to create 2D objects. Verify that *Splines* is displayed in the drop-down list and click **Rectangle**, as shown in Figure 4–15.

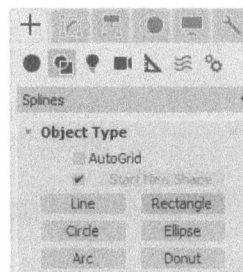

Figure 4–15

The corner radius fillets the corners of the rectangle.

3. In the Command Panel, expand the Keyboard Entry rollout and set the following:
   - *X:* **0'0"**
   - *Y:* **0'0"**
   - *Z:* **3'2"**
   - *Length*: **0'6"**
   - *Width*: **0'6"**
   - *Corner Radius*: **0'1"**

4. Click **Create**. A 2D rectangle is created on top of the base plate.

The modifiers in the Modifier drop-down list are placed in groups and then listed alphabetically. Use the scroll bar to navigate through the list.

5. With the rectangle still selected, select the Modify panel ( ). Expand the Modifier List (click down arrow) and select **Extrude** in the *OBJECT SPACE MODIFIERS* category. Note that Extrude is listed in the Modifier Stack above the Rectangle entry, as shown in Figure 4–16.

Figure 4–16

6. Rename the object *Rectangle001* as **LP Pole**.

7. In the Parameters rollout, set *Amount* to **15'0"** and leave the other parameters as the defaults. Note that the rectangle is extruded and becomes a rectangular-shaped pole.

8. In the **Perspective** viewport, use (Zoom) and **Pan** to get a closer look at the light pole, as shown in Figure 4–17. Note how much detail the light pole's fillet adds to the model.

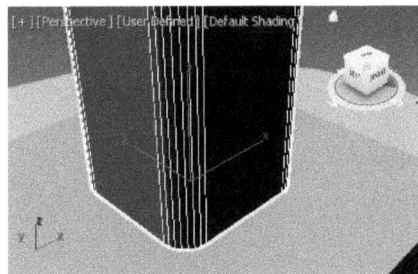

Figure 4–17

Hint: Simple Models

If the object is to be used only as a background item, you should remove any unnecessary detail. Keeping models simple reduces the file size and speeds up software performance and rendering times.

Although the Extrude modifier is listed directly above the Rectangle object in the Modifier Stack, the rectangle's parameters are still accessible and can be changed anytime.

9. In the Modify panel (), in the Modifier Stack, select **Rectangle**. It is highlighted as dark gray. In the Interpolation rollout, change *Steps* to **2** and press <Enter>, as shown in Figure 4–18. The fillet divisions are reduced, as shown in Figure 4–19.

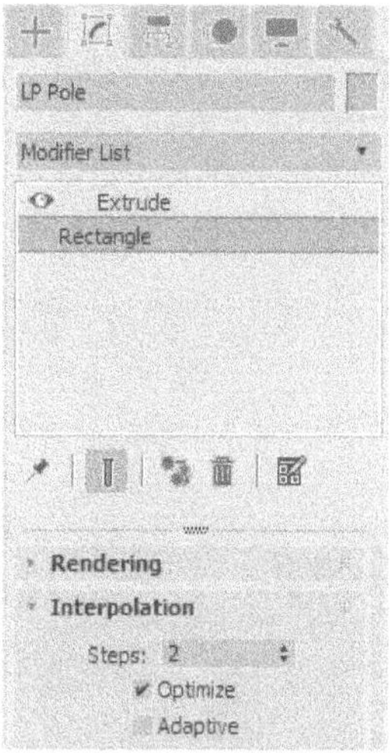

Figure 4–18

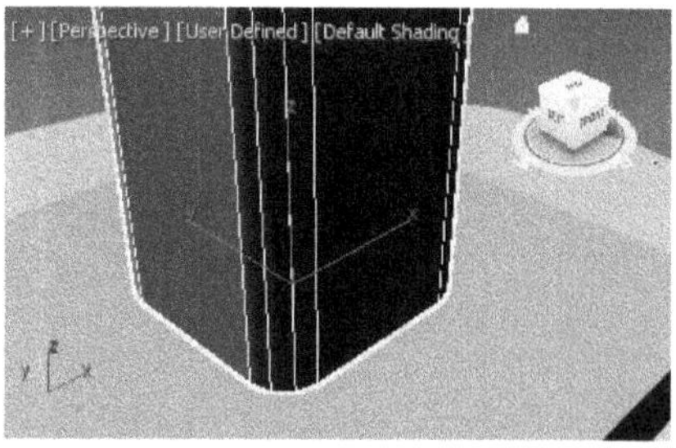

Figure 4–19

10. Save your work as **MyLightPole01.max**.

Task 2 - Taper the Light Pole.

Use the scroll bar to navigate to Taper near the bottom of the list.

1. In the Modifier Stack, select **Extrude** (so that the next modifier *Taper* is applied after it). In the Modifier List, select **Taper**. Note that the *Taper* displays above the *Extrude* in the Modifier Stack, as shown in Figure 4–20. The Modifier Stack lists modifiers in reverse historical order.

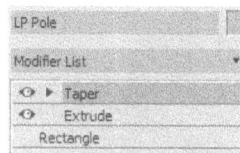

Figure 4–20

2. With Taper selected, in the Parameters rollout, set *Amount* to **-0.5** and press <Enter>. You can still adjust the original **Rectangle** and **Extrude** parameters by selecting them in the Modifier Stack.

3. Click ⬚ (Zoom Extents All) to see all of the objects in the viewports. Note the taper on the pole towards the top.

4. Save your work incrementally as **MyLightPole02.max**.

Task 3 - Create the Fixture Housing and Globe.

---

1. In the **Perspective** viewport, zoom in so that the LP Base object is displayed.

2. In the Create panel (+)> ● (Geometry), in the Standard Primitives drop-down list, select **Extended Primitives** as a sub-category. In the Object Type rollout, click **ChamferCyl**.

You do not have to be accurate because you will modify the dimensions later.

3. In the **Perspective** viewport, next to the base (LP Base), click and drag the left mouse button to size the radius to roughly **2'0"** (Note the Parameters rollout in the Command Panel where the Radius changes interactively as you move the cursor). After releasing the mouse button, move the cursor up the screen slightly to give the cylinder a height of approximately **1'0"**. Click a second time to set the cylinder height. Then move the cursor up and down the screen until you can roughly define a **0'2"** fillet. Complete the object creation process with a third click. The object should display as shown in Figure 4–21.

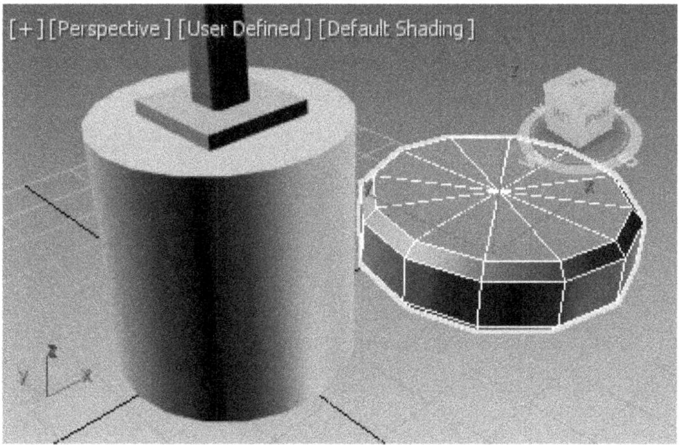

Figure 4–21

4. With the **ChamferCyl** object still selected, in the Command Panel, select the Modify panel ( ). Name the object **LP Fixture Housing** and modify the parameters, as shown in Figure 4–22.

5. In the Create panel ( ), verify that ● (Geometry) is selected. In the drop-down list, select **Standard Primitives.** In the Object Type rollout, click **Sphere** to create the fixture's globe. Click and drag anywhere on the screen to size a sphere of approximately **1'0"** in radius. Select the Modify panel ( ) and assign the parameters, as shown in Figure 4–23.

*A value of **0.5** for the hemisphere creates half a sphere.*

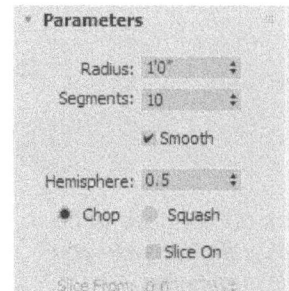

Parameters	
Radius:	2'0"
Height:	1'0"
Fillet:	0'2"
Height Segs:	1
Fillet Segs:	1
Sides:	20
Cap Segs:	1

Figure 4–22

Parameters	
Radius:	1'0"
Segments:	10
	☑ Smooth
Hemisphere:	0.5
● Chop	○ Squash
	☐ Slice On
Slice From:	0.0

Figure 4–23

6. Select **Squash**. This option generates more faces and creates a smoother appearance.

7. Rename the hemisphere **LP Fixture Globe**.

8. Save your work incrementally as **MyLightPole03.max**.

Task 4 - Use Transforms to Position Objects.

---

1. Select the **LP Fixture Housing** (the chamfered cylinder) and in the Main Toolbar, click ✛ (Select and Move).

2. In the Main Toolbar, set the *Reference Coordinate System* to **World** and click  (Use Pivot Point Center), as shown in Figure 4–24.

Figure 4–24

3. The Move gizmo displays over the object, as shown in Figure 4–25. Move the fixture housing by clicking and dragging the gizmo's axis handles and plane handles. By default, the gizmo displays at the object's pivot point, located at the bottom center for this object.

Figure 4–25

The ⊞ *(Absolute Mode) toggles with* ⟳ *(Offset Mode). If the values are entered in* **Offset Mode***, they are added to the current coordinates. This option is useful if you want to move an object a certain distance from the current position.*

4. To position the object correctly, verify that ⊞ (Absolute Mode Transform Type-In) is displayed in the Status Bar. Set the following in the type in edit boxes, as shown in Figure 4–26:
   - *X*: **0'0"**
   - *Y*: **-6'0"**
   - *Z*: **19'0"**

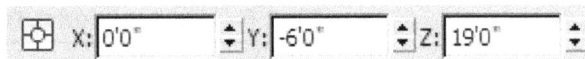

Figure 4–26

5. Click 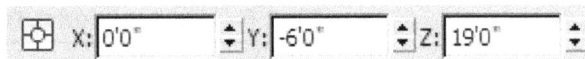 (Zoom Extents All) to display all of the objects in the viewports. In the **Left** viewport, note that the **LP Fixture Housing** (the chamfered cylinder) has now moved to the top right side of the light pole assembly.

6. As the **Move** transform and **Absolute Mode** are already active, select **LP Fixture Globe** (hemisphere) and enter the same X, Y, Z coordinates as you did for LP Fixture Housing (X: **0'0"**, Y: **-6'0"**, Z: **19'0"**). The half globe moves inside the fixture housing.

7. With the half globe still selected, in the Main Toolbar, click

   $\circlearrowright$ (Select and Rotate).

8. In the Status Bar, the X, Y, Z Transform Type-In fields display the current rotations of **0**. Set X to **180** and note the position of the globe is inverted. The object should display as shown in Figure 4–27 in the **Left** viewport.

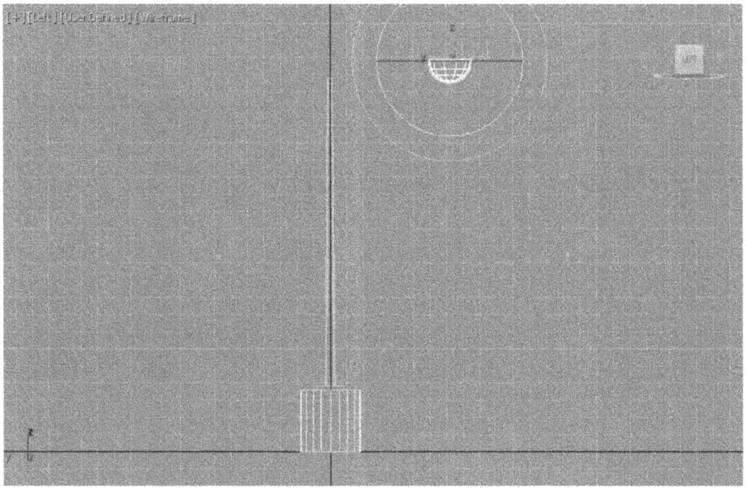

Figure 4–27

9. Click  (Select Object) or press <Q> to end the **Rotate** transform to avoid rotating objects accidentally.

10. Save your work incrementally as **MyLightPole04.max**.

Task 5 - Use Additional Transforms to Place Objects.

You will create a nut and bolt group and place it on the top surface of the anchor plate.

1. In the **Perspective** viewport, zoom into LP Base (base cylinder).

2. In the Create panel (+), ensure that ● (Geometry) and **Standard Primitives** as a sub-category is selected. In the Object Type rollout, click **Cylinder**.

3. In the **Perspective** viewport, using the mouse, create a cylinder that is smaller than the base object.

4. With the new cylinder selected, select the Modify panel (⌐). Rename the new cylinder as **LP Nut** and assign the parameters shown in Figure 4–28.

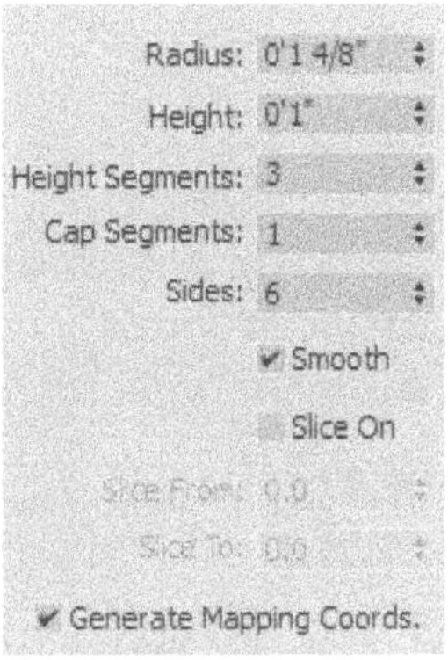

Radius:	0'1 4/8"
Height:	0'1"
Height Segments:	3
Cap Segments:	1
Sides:	6
✔ Smooth	
Slice On	
Slice From:	0.0
Slice To:	0.0
✔ Generate Mapping Coords.	

Figure 4–28

5. With **LP Nut** still selected, click ⊕ (Zoom Extents All Selected) so that it is zoomed in on all the viewports.

6. Click in the **Top** viewport to activate it and clear the selection.

7. In the Command Panel>Create (+)> ● (Geometry), verify that **Standard Primitives** is selected. In the Object Type rollout, click **Cylinder**, and in the **Top** viewport create a small cylinder next to LP Nut (6 sided cylinder).

8. With the new cylinder selected, select the Modify panel ( ). Rename the new cylinder as **LP Bolt** and assign the parameters, as shown in Figure 4–29. The bolt displays as shown in Figure 4–30.

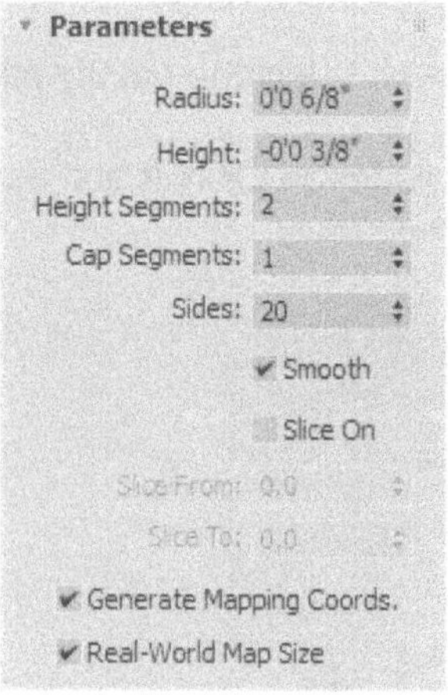

Parameters

Radius:	0'0 6/8"
Height:	-0'0 3/8"
Height Segments:	2
Cap Segments:	1
Sides:	20

☑ Smooth
☐ Slice On
Slice From: 0.0
Slice To: 0.0
☑ Generate Mapping Coords.
☑ Real-World Map Size

Figure 4–29

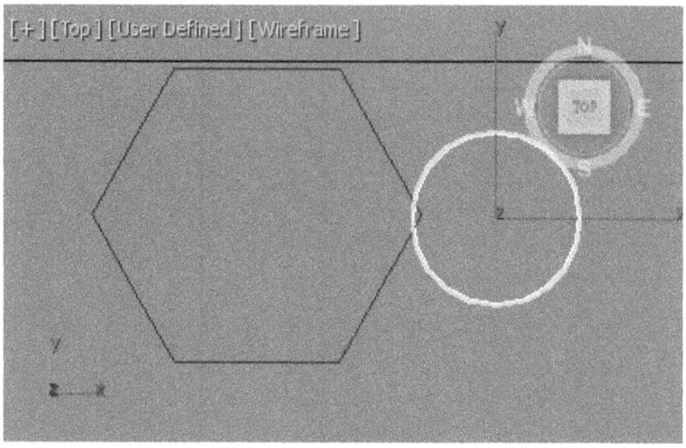

[+][Top][User Defined][Wireframe]

Figure 4–30

9. With **LP Bolt** selected, in the Main Toolbar, click 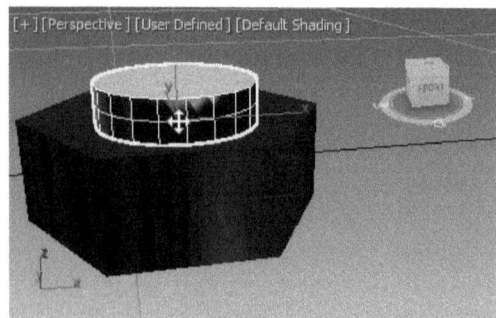 (Select and Place).

10. In the **Perspective** viewport, click and hold ⊕ over the selected **LP Bolt** object. While holding, drag it over the **LP Nut** object. Note that when you move the **LP Bolt** object along the sides of the **LP Nut** object, it automatically flips on its side, as shown in Figure 4–31. Drag the selected **LP Bolt** object along the top surface of the **LP Nut** object and note how it flips so that its base touches the top surface. Place the **LP Bolt** object at the approximate center of the **LP Nut** object, as shown in Figure 4–32.

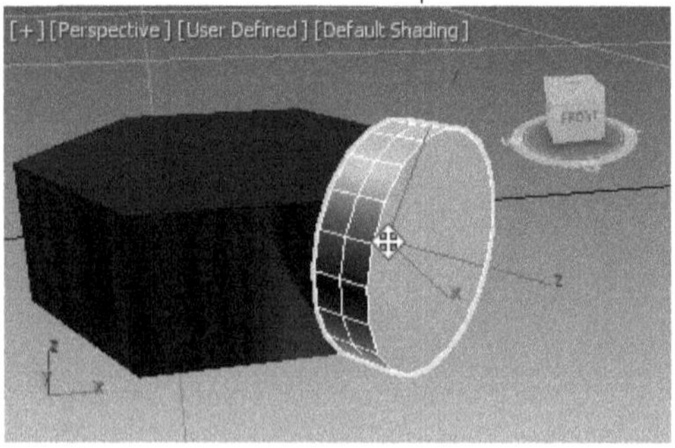

[+][Perspective][User Defined][Default Shading]

Figure 4–31

[+][Perspective][User Defined][Default Shading]

Figure 4–32

11. Click ▧ (Select Object) in the Main Toolbar to exit the Placement command.

12. Select both the **LP Nut** and the **LP Bolt** objects (<Ctrl>) and select **Group>Group**. In the Group dialog box, name the grouped object as **LP Anchor**.

13. Activate the **Perspective** viewport (if not already active) and

    click ▧ (Maximize Viewport Toggle), or use <Alt>+<W> to maximize the viewport.

14. Zoom and pan so that you can clearly see the **LP Anchor** group and the **LP Anchor Base**, as shown in Figure 4–33.

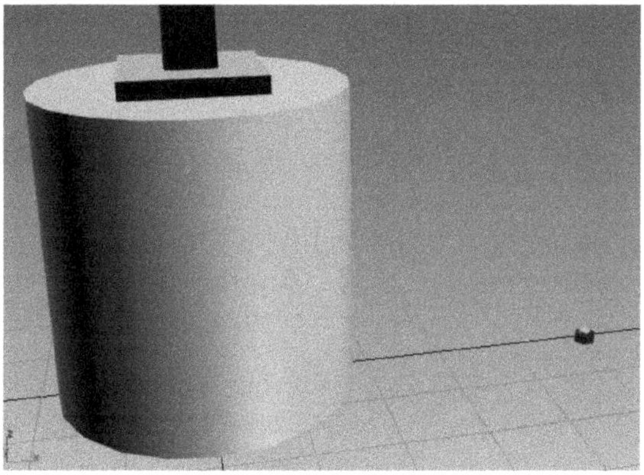

Figure 4–33

15. In the Main Toolbar, click ▧ (Select and Place). Click and hold on the **LP Anchor** group and then drag it on top of the LP Anchor Base plate object. Place the **LP Anchor** group near one of the corners of the plate, as shown in Figure 4–34.

    • Note that the group object is placed halfway inside the LP Anchor Base object.as shown in Figure 4–35.

Figure 4–34

Figure 4–35

16. Right-click on ![icon](Select and Place). In the Placement Settings dialog box, select **Pillow Mode** to activate it.

17. Click on the **LP Anchor** group object and slightly move it. Note how its base now touches the top surface of the anchor plate. Place it in one of the corners, as shown in Figure 4–36.

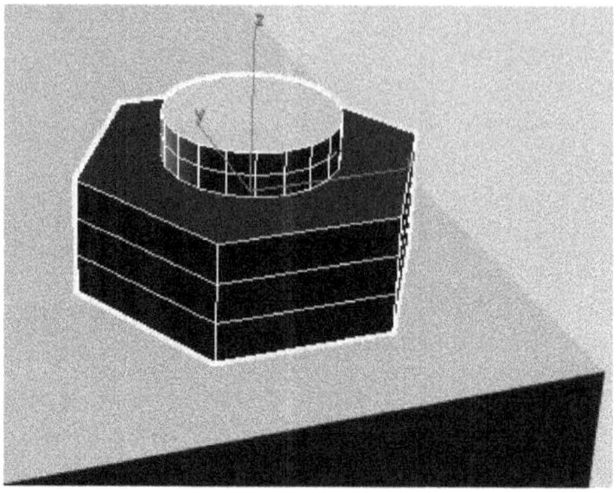

Figure 4–36

It might be easier to copy the object in the ***Top*** *viewport.*

18. Hold <Shift> and then click and drag a copy of the **LP Anchor** group object to place it near the next corner of the plate. Click **OK** in the Clone Options dialog box.

19. While still holding <Shift>, place two more copies of the objects at the other corners of the plate. A total of four **LP Anchor** group objects should now be placed at the four corners of the anchor plate, as shown in Figure 4–37.

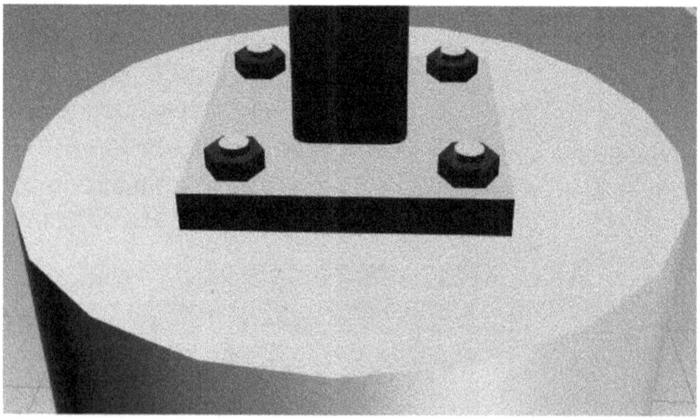

Figure 4–37

20. Save your work incrementally as **MyLightPole05.max**.

4.3 Sub-Object Mode

Many of the objects and modifiers available in the Autodesk 3ds Max software contain sub-objects that can be independently adjusted through transforms and special modifier controls. These sub-objects are adjusted through a special Autodesk 3ds Max state called Sub-object mode. For example, the **Taper** modifier in the column has Gizmo and Center sub-objects (as shown in Figure 4–38) that can be adjusted to position the Taper.

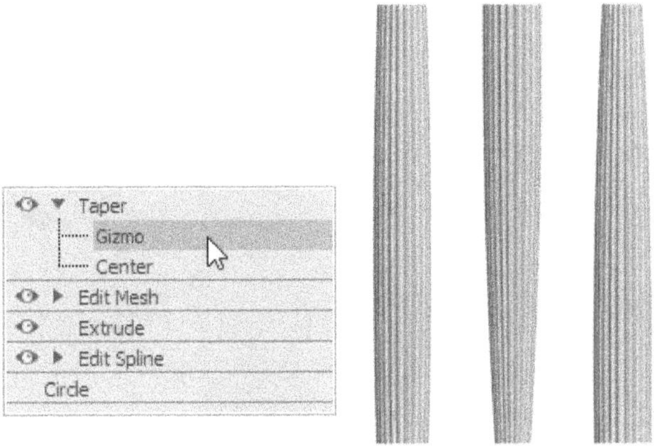

Figure 4–38

Working in Sub-Object Mode

Sub-object mode is activated through the Modifier Stack. You can expand the modifier by clicking ▶ (arrow) next to the object or modifier that has sub-objects, then clicking the sub-object level to be adjusted.

- You can only have one object selected to enter the Sub-object mode. When Sub-object mode is active, the sub-object level (or the modifier name if the sub-object list has not been expanded) is highlighted in blue (with the default user interface settings).

- You cannot clear the currently selected object while in Sub-object mode. Therefore, to edit another object you must first exit Sub-object mode. To do so, click the level of the Modifier Stack presently highlighted in yellow to toggle it off.

Geometric Edits through Sub-objects

A whole range of explicit geometric changes can be made through Sub-object mode.

- Objects imported into the Autodesk 3ds Max software often take the shape of **Editable Splines** or **Editable Meshes**. These have sub-object controls that can be edited directly. For example, a group of vertices in an Editable Mesh can be selected, moved, or deleted separate to the rest of the geometry.

*You can also use the **Polygon Modeling** tools in the ribbon to perform modeling and use modifiers with the **Edit Poly** technique.*

- Many Autodesk 3ds Max objects can also have the controls applied to them through an **Edit Spline** modifier (for 2D objects) or an **Edit Mesh** or **Edit Poly** modifier (for 3D objects). This includes geometry linked to AutoCAD drawings that list only as *Linked Geometry* in the Modify panel.

- Figure 4–39 shows an example of a Box that is being edited geometrically by lowering two of its vertices with the **Move** transform.

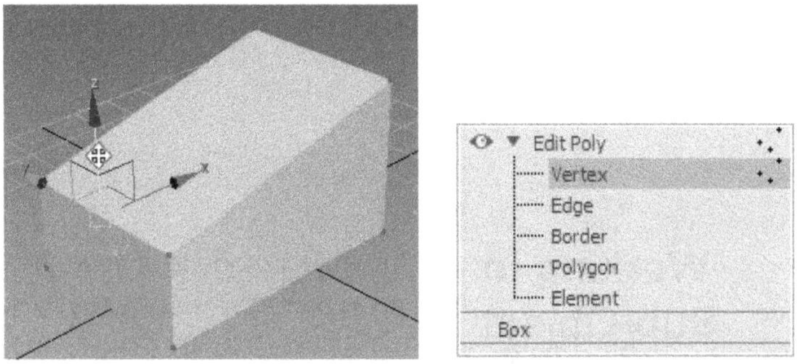

Figure 4–39

- The **Edit Mesh** modifier is best for objects based on a triangular mesh, such as triangulated terrain models.

- The **Edit Poly** modifier is best for objects with faces of more than three vertices, such as rectangular objects.

- To easily review and make changes, it is recommended to adjust objects through their core parameters (such as the length, width, and height of a primitive) and standard modifiers. When required, you can use Spline, Mesh, and Poly for editing.

New in 2017

- A single hotkey can be used to easily and quickly toggle between the various sub-object levels. This speeds up your overall modeling workflow. To use this, to hover your cursor over the required sub-object level and press the hotkey.

Geometric Sub-Objects

The Editable Spline, Editable Mesh, and Editable Poly objects (and any other object with an Edit Spline, Edit Mesh, or Edit Poly Modifier applied to it) share a number of common Sub-object modes. These are described as follows:

	Vertex: The individual 3D points that define an object (Edit Spline, Edit Mesh, or Edit Poly).
	Segment: A single line or curve segment of an Editable Spline.
	Spline: A series of one or more connected Editable Spline segments. Segments are considered connected if they share a common vertex.
	Edge: The linear segments connecting vertices with Edit Mesh or Edit Poly. Three edges are shown in the button.
	Face: The triangular surface area defined by three edges (Edit Mesh only).
	Border: A series of edges that define an opening in an Editable Poly (only).
	Polygon: Enables you to work with coplanar faces (Edit Mesh) or a defined polygon (Edit Poly).
	Element: Enables you to work with all of the faces or polygons that form a contiguous whole (Edit Mesh or Edit Poly).

Smoothing

One of the most important properties controlled at the face or polygon sub-object level is smoothing. Figure 4–40 shows the same geometry without and with smoothing applied.

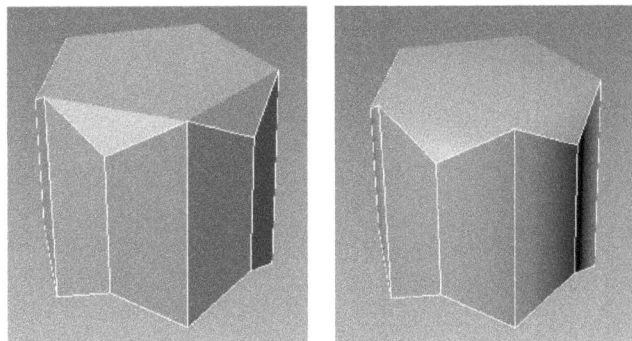

Figure 4–40

- The Autodesk 3ds Max software can have two adjacent faces appear to be smooth or faceted. When smoothed, faces display smooth but the software does not adjust the actual geometry.

- Smoothing is controlled by smoothing groups. Each face or polygon can be a member of up to 32 smoothing groups. If two adjacent faces share a common smoothing group, the software attempts to blend the surfaces together to disguise the edge that separates them.

- Figure 4–41 show an example of the smoothing groups for the selected faces that controls polygon smoothing groups (in Edit Mesh and Edit Poly). When some but not all selected faces fall into a particular smoothing group, that group's box is shown without a number.

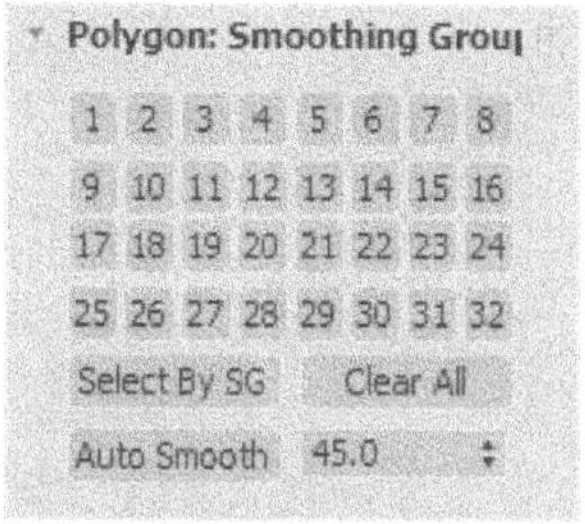

Figure 4–41

- Alternatively, the **Auto Smooth** feature automatically places adjacent selected faces into smoothing groups if their normal vectors have an angle of separation equal to or less than the Auto Smooth angle.

Practice 4c

Modeling with Edit Poly in Sub-Object Mode

Practice Objective

- Modify objects at a sub-object level.

Estimated time for completion: 15 minutes

In this practice you will add some detail to the concrete base of the light pole by chamfering (beveling) the outside top of the cylinder and then add smoothing to it.

You must set the paths to locate the External files and Xrefs used in the practice. If you have not done this already, return to **Chapter 1: Introduction to Autodesk 3ds Max** and complete Task 1 to Task 3 in **Practice 1a: Organizing Folders and Working with the Interface**. You only have to set the user paths once.

1. Open **Edit Poly in Sub-Object Mode.max**.

2. In the **Perspective** viewport, select **LP Base** and click

   (Zoom Extents Selected). Use (Zoom) and

   (Orbit) to display a base similar to that shown in Figure 4–42.

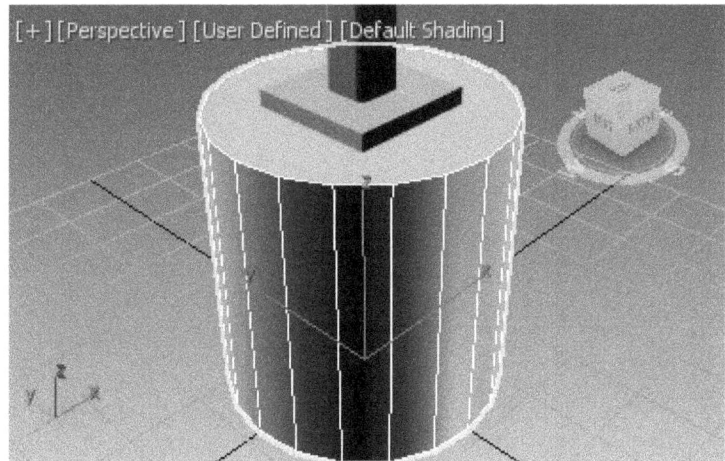

Figure 4–42

3. In the Modify panel (![icon]), select **Edit Poly** from the Modifier List. Click ▶ (arrow sign) for Edit Poly to display its Sub-object modes. Select **Polygon** to activate the Sub-object mode at the Polygon level. The highlighting in the Modifier Stack indicates that you are in the Polygon Sub-object mode, as shown in Figure 4–43.

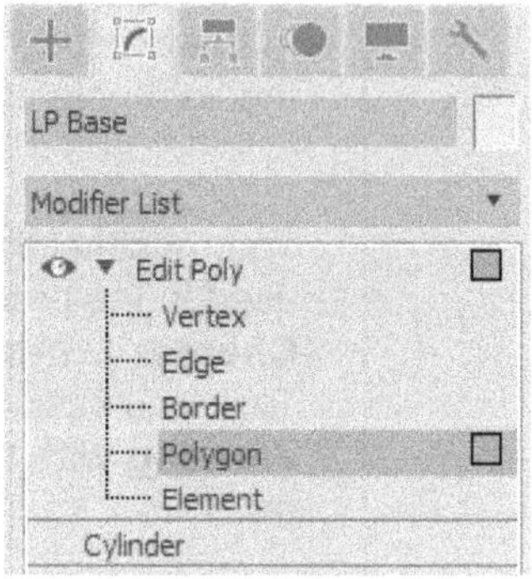

Figure 4–43

Hint: Using Modeling Tools in the Ribbon

You can also perform all of the commands using the **Polygon Modeling** tools in the Modeling ribbon. With the object selected, select the *Polygon Modeling* tab in the *Modeling* tab, in the ribbon. In the drop-down list, select **Apply Edit Poly Mod**, as shown in Figure 4–44. Click ☐ for **Polygon** sub-object level. Note that the selections that you make in the ribbon are reflected in the Command Panel and vice-versa.

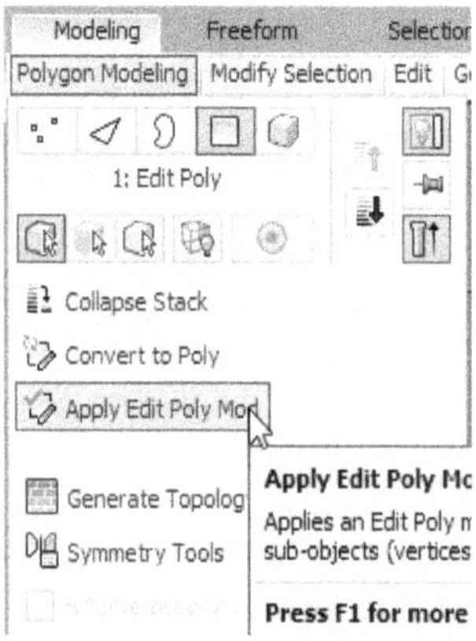

Figure 4–44

---

4. Select the polygon at the top of the cylinder, as shown in Figure 4–45. The selected polygon tuns red.

Figure 4–45

5. Creating a 1" bevel will raise the cylinder top by 1". In preparation, you will first lower the top of the cylinder by that same 1". In the Main Toolbar, click ⊕ (Select and Move). Note that the Move gizmo only displays for the selected polygon.

6. In the Status Bar, click ⊞ (Absolute Mode Transform) to toggle it to 📍 (Offset Mode Transform) and set *Z* to **-0'1"**. Press <Enter>. The cylinder geometry is adjusted by moving the polygon down.

7. Right-click to activate the **Left** viewport (keeping the polygon selected) and zoom into the base area. Note that the base is not touching the base plate anymore.

8. In the Command Panel, scroll down and locate the Edit Polygons rollout. Expand the Edit Polygons rollout, and next to **Bevel** click ▢ (Settings), as shown in Figure 4–46.

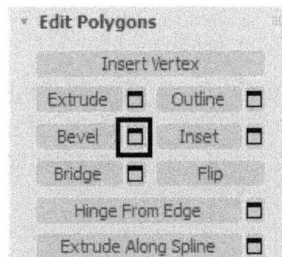

*The rollouts in the Command Panel might extend below the display window. To scroll, hover the cursor over an empty gray area until it displays as a **Hand** icon, then hold and drag the cursor up or down to locate the required rollout.*

Figure 4–46

In the caddy display, when you select the edit box, its icon displays as a spinner and the edit name (Height or Outline) is displayed in addition to the modifier name (Bevel) at the top. You can enter new values in the edit box or use the spinner to change the values.

9. The caddy display opens on the screen, in the **Left** viewport. Hover the cursor over the ⬚ *Height* edit box and set its value to **0'1"** and an ⬚ *Outline* of **-0'1"**, as shown in Figure 4–47. Click ✓. Verify that the caddy display closes and the base is beveled, as shown in Figure 4–48.

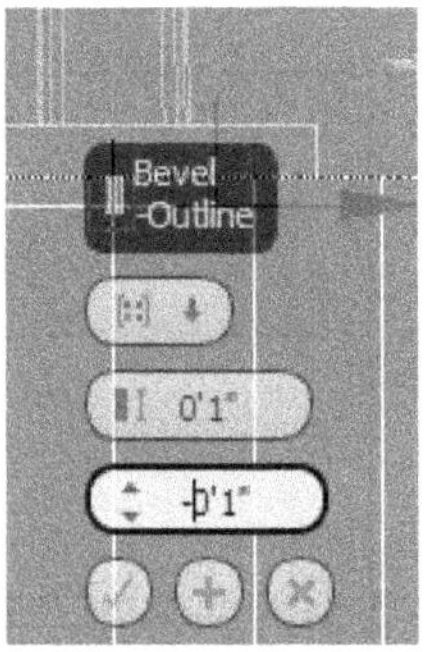

Figure 4–47

Figure 4–48

10. To make the newly created faces smooth you will adjust the smoothing groups. While still in Polygon Sub-object mode, in the menu bar, expand **Edit** and select **Select All** to select all of the polygons in the base object.

11. In the Command Panel, scroll down and locate the Polygon: Smoothing Groups rollout. Click **Clear All** to remove the existing smoothing. Set the *AutoSmooth angle* to **30**, as shown in Figure 4–49. Click **Auto Smooth**.

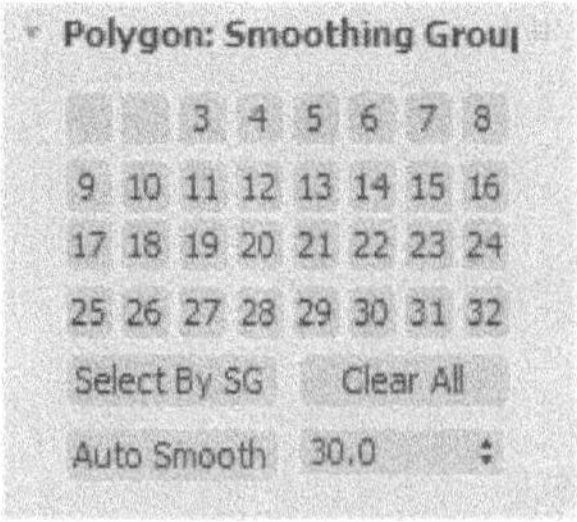

Figure 4–49

12. To end Sub-object mode, in the Command Panel>Modifier Stack, click the **Polygon** that is highlighted in blue to clear the selection.

*To display the smoothing effect, toggle off **Edged Faces** in the Viewport Shading label, if it is enabled.*

13. To display the effect of the smoothing change, in the **Perspective** viewport, clear the object selection by clicking anywhere in empty space. The 30 degrees angle enabled the newly created faces to smooth across each other, but the faces are not smoothed with the top of the cylinder, as shown in Figure 4–50. This is the chamfered appearance that was originally intended. A larger smoothing angle enables the chamfered faces between the top and sides to smooth out.

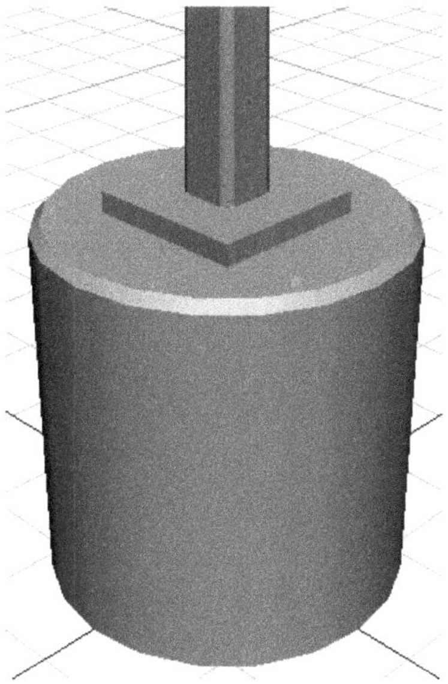

Figure 4–50

14. In the Main Toolbar, click  (Select Object) to end the Move Transform mode as a precaution to avoid moving objects accidentally while making further selections.

15. Save your work as **MyLightPole06.max**.

4.4 Reference Coordinate Systems and Transform Centers

All geometry in the Autodesk 3ds Max software is referenced to a base coordinate system called the Home Grid.

- You can create your own coordinate systems by creating and locating grid objects, available in the Helpers Category in the Create panel.

- You can also create objects in the Auto-grid mode, which creates a temporary 3D Grid aligned to the object directly under the crosshairs. The **AutoGrid** option can be found in the Create panel, in the Object Type rollout, as shown Figure 4–51. If you hold <Alt>, the AutoGrid remains available for future use. If you use AutoGrid without any key pressed, the grid disappears after object creation.

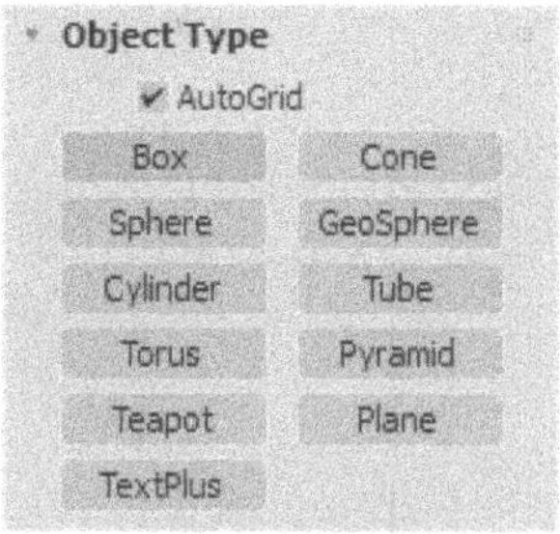

Figure 4–51

Reference Coordinate Systems

Enhanced in 2017

The current Reference Coordinate System might differ depending on which view you are in and which transform is active. It is recommended that new users stay in the **World** system to avoid confusion from changing axis labels. By default, the Reference Coordinate system is set to **View**.

- In the Main Toolbar, the options listed in the Reference Coordinate System drop-down list (shown Figure 4–52) control how transform values are read. Note that A single grid is active at any one time.

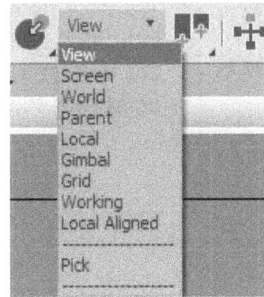

Figure 4–52

- In the **World** coordinate system the X, Y, and Z axes are interpreted based on the Home Grid, even if a user-defined grid is active. To use the coordinates of the active user-defined grid instead, select the **Grid** option.

- In the **Screen** coordinate system the X-axis is always measured along the bottom of the viewport, the Y-axis is always measured along the side, and the Z-axis is measured perpendicularly out of the screen.

- The **View** system is a combination of **World** and **Screen**. In an orthographic view, the **Screen** system is used, while in other views the **World** system is used.

- The **Local** system considers the coordinate system of the selected object. Note that only the Z axis of the object is considered, which can cause unpredictable changes along the X and Y axis.

- The **Grid** system is based on the currently active grid and uses its coordinate system.

- The **Working** option enables you to use the Working Pivot. It is a temporary modeling pivot tool you create from the Hierarchy panel's *Pivot* tab. Generally you need to assign a hotkey to **Use Working Pivot** and **Edit Working Pivot** to make them functional tools.

- The **Local Aligned** option is used with sub-objects in an editable mesh or poly. It calculates all three (X,Y,Z) axes by using the coordinate system of the selected object. It can be used when multiple sub-objects need to be adjusted at the same time.

- The **Pick** option enables you to pick any object in the viewport or from a list and use the reference coordinate system of that object as the reference for transforms. You can use XRef objects with the **Pick** option.

Transform Centers

Transforms are applied through a Transform Center point indicated by the Transform gizmo. The Transform Center options are available in the Main Toolbar, in the Transform Center flyout, as shown Figure 4–53.

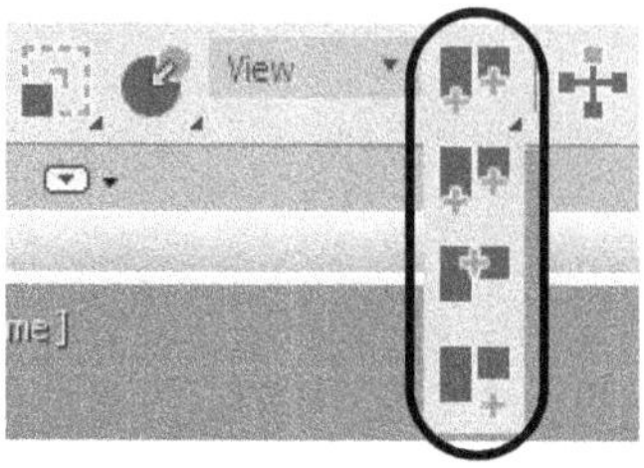

Figure 4–53

Pivot Point Center: Transforms are applied through each selected object's pivot point. Pivots often default to the bottom center or geometric center of objects. Pivot points can be adjusted through controls in the Hierarchy panel. Select this option if you want to rotate many objects, each around its own center.

Selection Center: Transforms are applied through the geometric center of all selected objects.

Transform Coordinate Center: Transforms are applied through the origin point of the current Reference Coordinate System. For example, if you wanted to rotate objects around their individual pivot points about the World Z-axis, you would select the World Coordinate System and Pivot Point Transform Center. Alternatively, to rotate all of the objects around the origin, you would do the same with the Transform Coordinate Center.

- The Transform Center might automatically change depending on whether one or multiple objects are selected, and on the active transform.

- The Reference Coordinate System and Transform Center can be held using **Constant** in the Preference Settings dialog box, in the *General* tab, as shown in Figure 4–54.

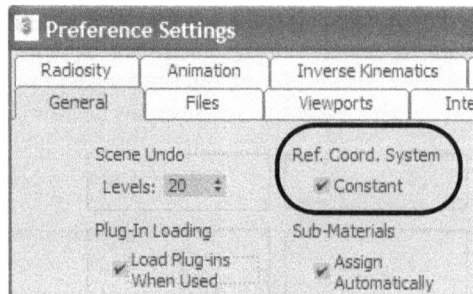

Figure 4–54

4.5 Cloning and Grouping

Cloning

In Autodesk 3ds Max, objects can be duplicated using the **Clone** option (**Edit>Clone**), which opens the Clone Options dialog box, as shown in Figure 4–55. To access the **Clone** command, an object should be selected first, otherwise it remains grayed out.

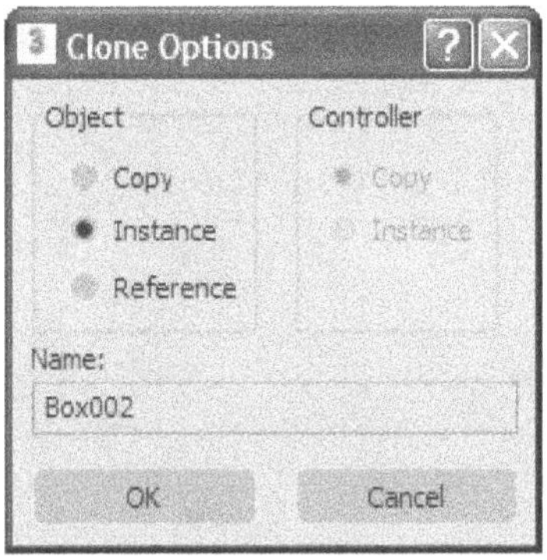

Figure 4–55

Copy	Makes an independent copy without a dynamic link to the source object.
Instance	Makes the duplicate and original Instances of each other. Changes made to any Instance automatically update all Instances, including changes to Modifiers, property changes, and material assignments (except for Transforms).
Reference	A one-directional link where changes made to the original object affect the duplicate. You can apply Modifiers to the Reference without affecting the Source object.

- You can also clone an object by holding <Shift> while transforming through a click and drag on the Transform gizmo. In this procedure, you have an additional option for specifying the number of copies you want to make, which are arrayed at the same Transform value.

- The *Controller* area in the Clone Options dialog box applies to objects in a group or hierarchy.

- Objects that are instanced or referenced display with the Modifier Stack text in bold type. Instancing or referencing can be disabled by right-clicking on the item in the Modifier Stack and selecting **Make Unique**.

Grouping

Enhanced
in **2017**

Grouping enables multiple objects to be treated as a single unit, for selection and transforms. The various grouping options are available in the **Group** menu, as shown in Figure 4–56.

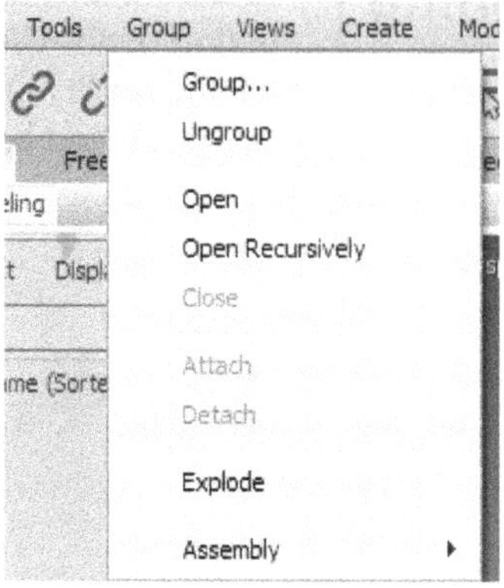

Figure 4–56

Group	Creates a group out of all of the currently selected objects. Groups can have other groups inside them (nested groups).
Ungroup	Dissolves any selected groups back into their constituent objects.
Open/Close	Enables you to select, modify, and transform individual group members as if they were not in a group. The group is still defined; however, it can be Closed to treat the objects as a single unit again.
Open Recursively	Enables you to select, modify, and transform individual members at any level in a group. The group is still defined. Use the **Close** command to restore the original group.
Attach	Enables you to add another object to a group. First select the objects to be attached, then select the **Attach** option in the **Group** menu. When prompted, select a closed group to which to add the objects.
Detach	Enables you to remove selected objects from a group. You must first open the group to select the objects to be detached.
Explode	Dissolves the selected groups and any groups nested inside them.
Assembly	Special case object grouping that are intended for creation of lighting assemblies called luminaires, and for character assemblies.

- Groups are located in the Command Panel's Modify panel, with group name in bold type, and a blank Modifier Stack. The Modifier Stack of individual group members is displayed if it is opened.

- Groups can be copied, instanced, and referenced.

- It is recommended not to use grouping on objects that are linked into a hierarchy and then animated.

Practice 4d

Modeling with Coordinate Systems

Practice Objective

- Create an object and modify the parameters.

Estimated time for completion: 10 minutes

In this practice you will add the Light Pole Mounting Arm to the Light Pole model by creating the model and modifying the parameters.

You must set the paths to locate the External files and Xrefs used in the practice. If you have not done this already, return to **Chapter 1: Introduction to Autodesk 3ds Max** and complete Task 1 to Task 3 in **Practice 1a: Organizing Folders and Working with the Interface**. You only have to set the user paths once.

*If a dialog box opens prompting you about a File Load: Mismatch, click **OK** to accept the default values.*

1. Open **Modeling with Coordinate Systems.max**.

2. Activate the **Front** viewport, if required.

3. Use a combination of **Zoom** and **Pan** to zoom into the top portion, as shown in Figure 4–57. If the Grid is showing in the **Front** view, in the Viewport label, click [+] and select **Show Grids** to clear it. Alternatively, you can press <G> to toggle the grid on or off.

4. In the Create panel (+)> ● (Geometry), click **Box**. Use the cursor to create a small box near the top of the light pole with approximate dimensions for *Length*, *Width*, and *Height*, as shown in Figure 4–58.

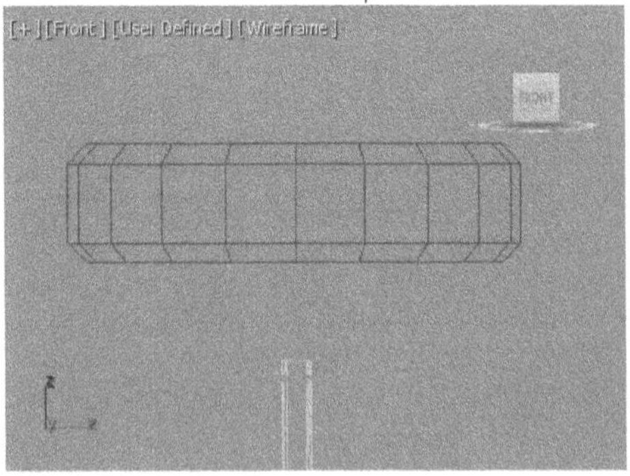

Figure 4–57

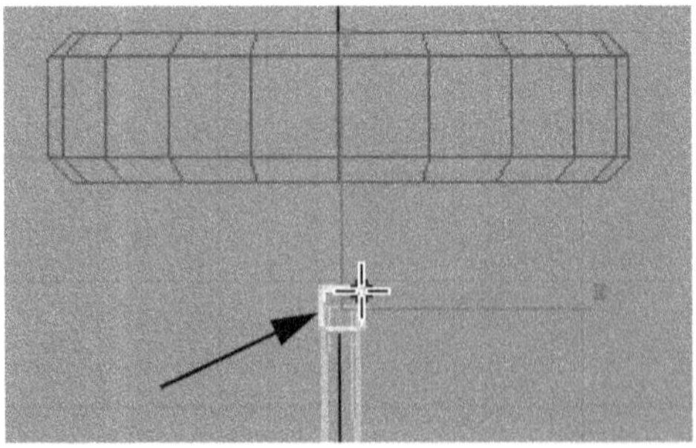

Figure 4–58

The object creation orientation depends on the viewport in which it is being created.

5. With this box still selected, in the Modify panel (), in the Parameters rollout, set the following, as shown in Figure 4–59:

   • *Name:* **LP Mounting Arm**
   • *Length:* **0'3"**
   • *Width:* **0'3"**
   • *Height:* **4'6"**
   • *Height Segs:* **6**

6. In the **Perspective** view, use a combination of **Zoom**, **Pan**, and **Orbit** to zoom into the **LP Mounting Arm**, as shown in Figure 4–59. Since you created the box in the **Front** viewport, the height of the box is measured perpendicular to the view, in this case along the world Y-axis.

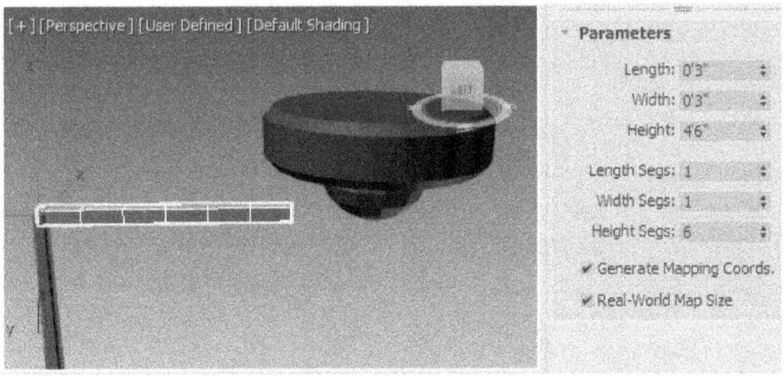

Figure 4–59

7. With the LP Mounting arm selected, click  (Select and Move). In the Status Bar, set the transform mode to

   (Absolute mode) and set the location of the mounting arm with the Z value at **18'0"**, as shown in Figure 4–60.

Figure 4–60

8. In the Modifier List, select **Bend** to curve the arm to the housing. In the Parameters, set the following:

   • *Bend Angle:* **30** degrees
   • *Direction:* **-90** degrees

   Note that the arm is bent and extended.

9. Save your work as **MyLightPole07.max**.

Practice 4e

Cloning and Grouping

Practice Objectives

- Create a single unit of multiple objects.
- Clone an instance of the group and modify it.

Estimated time for completion: 10 minutes

In this practice you will complete the model of the light pole using Cloning and Groups. You will first create a single unit by grouping multiple objects. You will then clone an instance of a group and modify the instance so that the original object is modified as well.

You must set the paths to locate the External files and Xrefs used in the practice. If you have not done this already, return to **Chapter 1: Introduction to Autodesk 3ds Max** and complete Task 1 to Task 3 in **Practice 1a: Organizing Folders and Working with the Interface**. You only have to set the user paths once.

1. Open **Cloning and Grouping.max**.

If the Scene Explorer is not displayed, select ***Tools>Scene Explorer***

or click ▦ *(Toggle Scene Explorer) in the Main Toolbar.*

2. In the Scene Explorer, (■ (Display None) and ● (Display Geometry) to display the scene geometry only. Select **LP Fixture Housing**, **LP Fixture Globe**, and **LP Mounting Arm** (use <Ctrl> to select multiple items), as shown in Figure 4–61. Note that the three items are selected in the viewports.

3. In the menu bar, select **Group>Group** to combine the three objects together into a single, selectable unit. In the Group dialog box, name the group **LP Fixture**, as shown in Figure 4–61. Click **OK**.

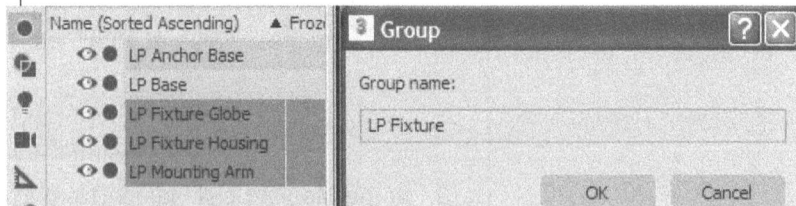

Figure 4–61

4. In the Scene Explorer, note that the group name is identified with the 🖼 symbol and the geometry objects displayed under it, as shown in Figure 4–62. In the Scene Explorer, select the group (**LP Fixture**) and note that all the three objects are selected in the viewport. Similarly, select **LP Fixture Globe** in the Scene Explorer and note that the three objects are still selected in the viewports, as shown in Figure 4–62.

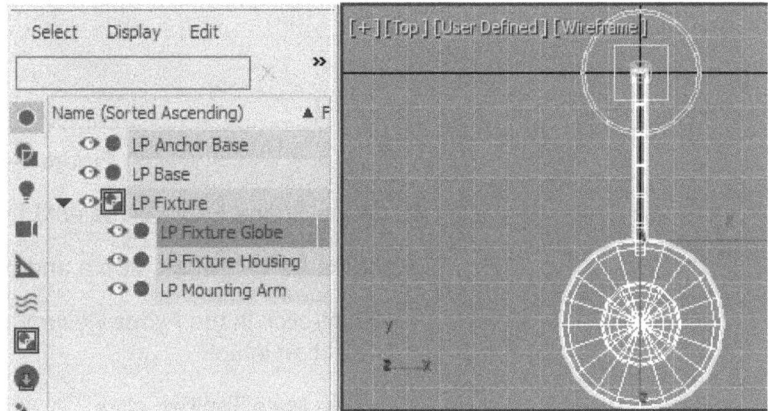

Figure 4–62

5. In the Scene Explorer, select the group (**LP Fixture**) and then in the menu bar, select **Group>Open**. The group remains intact but a pink bounding box encloses the group objects indicating that it is an open group. Here, you can select, manipulate, and transform the three component objects individually.

6. With one or more of the group components selected, in the menu bar, select **Group>Close**. The pink bounding box is cleared with all of the group objects selected, indicating that it is treated as a single object and that the components cannot be modified separately.

7. With the **LP Fixture** group selected, in the menu bar, select **Edit>Clone**.

8. In the Clone Options dialog box, in the *Object* area, select **Instance** (if not already selected) leaving all other options at their default values, as shown in Figure 4–63. Click **OK**.

   • The original and the copy now directly overlay each other. Note that in the Scene Explorer, another group with the name **LP Fixture001** is created.

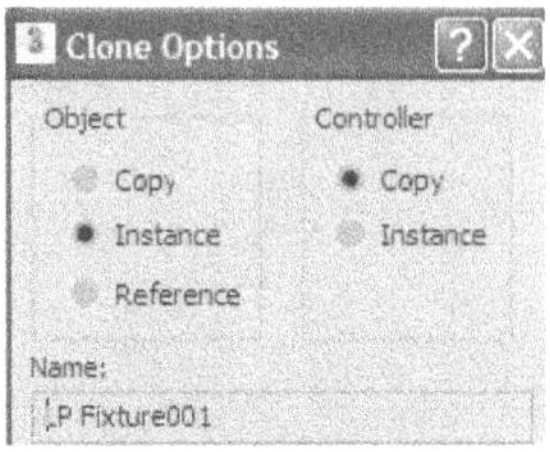

Figure 4–63

9. In the Scene Explorer, select **LP Fixture001**.

10. In the **Left** viewport, zoom and pan to the selected group.

11. Right-click in the **Front** viewport to activate it and keep the selection intact.

12. In the Main Toolbar, click C (Select and Rotate).

13. The position of the Transform gizmo is dependent on the active **Use Transform**. In the Main Toolbar, in the Use

    Transform flyout, click  (Use Pivot Point Center). Note in the **Left** viewport that the Rotate transform gizmo is in the center of the group, as shown in Figure 4–64. This rotation will not place **LP Fixture001** in the correct position.

14. Verify that the **Front** viewport is still active. In the Use

    Transform flyout, click (Use Transform Coordinate Center). In the **Left** viewport, note that the Rotation gizmo moves to the base of the left side, as shown in Figure 4–65.

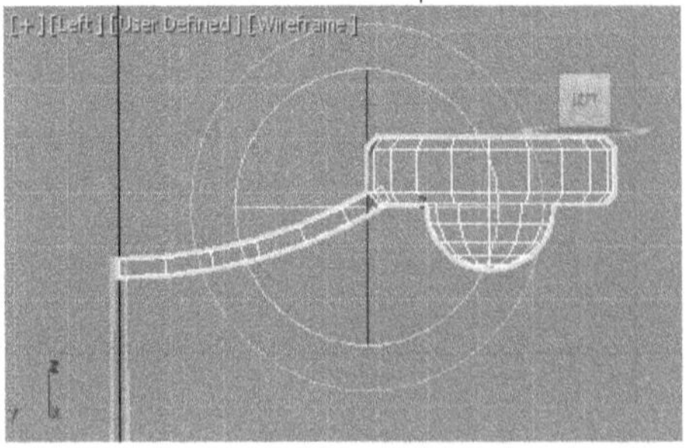

Figure 4–64

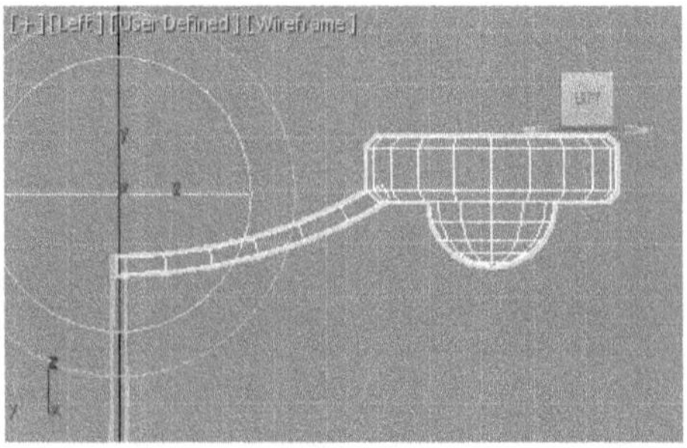

Figure 4–65

15. In the Status Bar, in the *Transform Type-In* area, set *Z* to **180.0** (as shown in Figure 4–66) to rotate **LP Fixture001** by **180°** about the Z axis. Press <Enter>. The round off error might result in a -180° value. This is a common occurrence and is not indicative of a problem.

X: 0.0   Y: -0.0   Z: -180.0

Figure 4–66

- The cloned group is moved opposite to the original group, as shown in Figure 4–67.

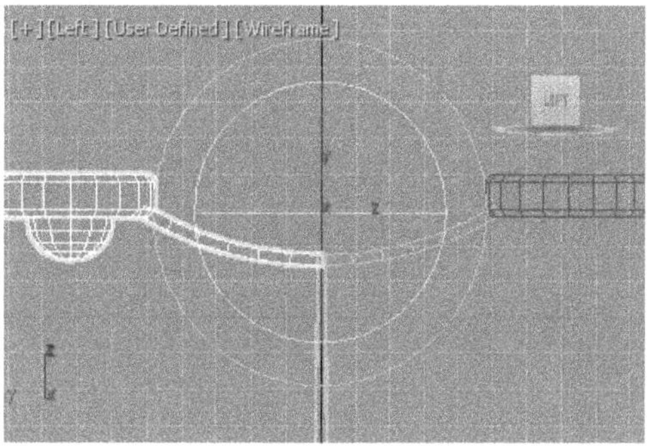

Figure 4–67

16. Click ▨ (Select Object) to end the Rotate transform mode.

17. To verify that the groups are instanced, with **LP Fixture001** selected, select **Group>Open**. A pink bounding box displays around the group.

18. In the Scene Explorer, select **LP Fixture Housing001**.

19. In the Modify panel (⌒), in the Parameters rollout, reduce the *Height* from **1'0"** to **0' 8"**. Both Fixture Housings update and have reduced height as shown in Figure 4–68.

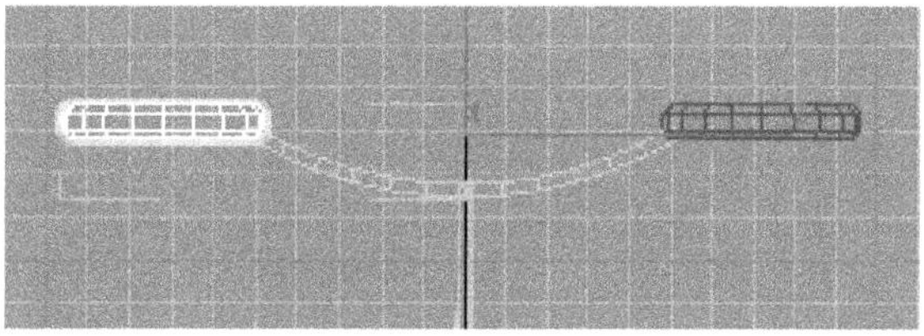

Figure 4–68

20. Select **Group>Close** to close **LP Fixture001**.

21. Save your work as **MyLightPole08.max**

4.6 Polygon Modeling Tools in the Ribbon

The Autodesk 3ds Max software is a powerful environment for creating a variety of 3D models. The box modeling technique, also called polygon modeling or mesh modeling, is an interactive method for creating vertices, edges, faces, and surfaces in a free form way.

- Box modeling can be performed using either the **Edit Mesh** or **Edit Poly** modifiers, or be converted to an **Editable Mesh** or **Editable Poly** object. Any of these methods give you the access to the sub-object levels required to do this type of modeling.

- The **Edit Poly** modifier is a commonly used modeling technique, although you can convert the object to an editable mesh or editable poly object and discard the modifier. You can also use the **Edit Mesh** modifier which is the most stable.

- The Modeling ribbon (*Modeling* tab) provides easy access to polygon modeling tools, including the editing and modification tools used at sub-object level. The ribbon contains many of the commonly used tools that are present in the Command Panel's Modify panel, at the Edit Poly sub-object level. In the *Modeling* tab, the polygon modeling and modifying tools are organized into panels.

- By default, the ribbon can be minimized to the panel tiles by clicking ⌐ and can be docked under the Main Toolbar. By default, **Minimize to Panel Titles** is set in the drop-down list, as shown in Figure 4–69. Click ⌐ to maximize the ribbon. You can also set the ribbon to be minimized to tabs or Panel Buttons by selecting the respective option in the drop-down list.

If the ribbon is not displayed, in the menu Bar, select Customize UI>Show Ribbon or

click ▦ *(Toggle Ribbon) in the Main Toolbar.*

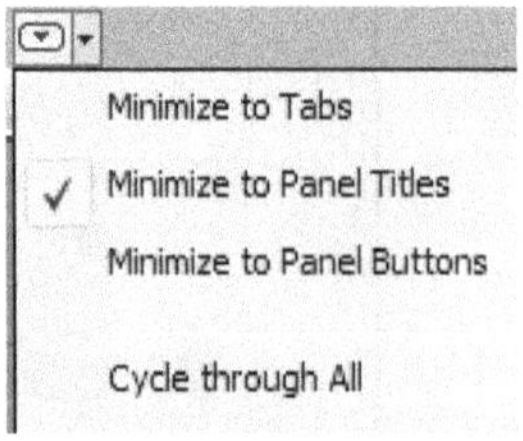

Figure 4–69

Practice 4f

Poly Modeling Using the Ribbon (Optional)

Practice Objective

- Create and modify a model using the box modeling technique.

Estimated time for completion: 40 minutes

In this practice you will learn to create a model using some of the tools and techniques of box modeling. You will also use the **Edit Poly** modifier and the modifier tools available in the ribbon.

Task 1 - Model the Armchair.

*If required, reset the scene by selecting **Application Menu>Reset**.*

1. In the Create panel (+)> ● (Geometry), click **Box** in the Object Type rollout to activate the **Box** tool.

2. In the **Perspective** viewport, create a box of any size by clicking and dragging to define the length and width of the rectangle. Click and continue moving the mouse upwards to define the height.

The model is created in any color.

3. Initially you can use the Parameters rollout in the Create panel to enter the values. After completing a command, you will use the Modify panel (⌐) to edit the values. Set the following:
    - *Length*: **4'2"**
    - *Width*: **2'9"**
    - *Height*: **0'10"**

    Press <Enter>. In the **Perspective** viewport, the box should look similar to that shown in Figure 4–70.

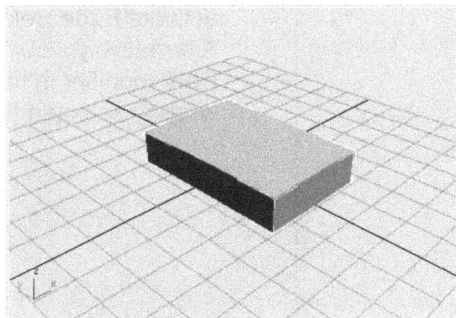

Figure 4–70

4. Name the object **armchair**.

5. To display the edges more clearly, change the display mode to wireframe by selecting the **Visual Style** label and selecting **Wireframe Override**.

6. Press <G> to hide the grid.

7. If the Modeling ribbon is only displaying Panel titles, click ⊡ (Show Full Ribbon).

8. Verify that the *Modeling* tab is active. Ensure that the armchair model is selected. Expand the Polygon Modeling panel and select **Apply Edit Poly Mod**, as shown in Figure 4–71. This adds an Edit Poly modifier to the armchair model. This is also displayed in the Command Panel. Note that the Modify panel ( ) is already open and that the Modifier Stack displays the **Edit Poly** modifier, as shown in Figure 4–72.

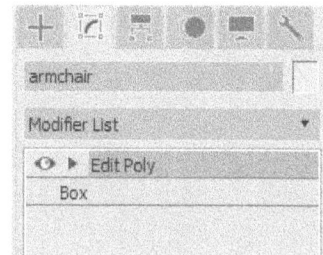

Figure 4–71   Figure 4–72

9. In the Modeling panel of the ribbon, click ◁ (Edge) to activate Edge Selection, as shown in Figure 4–73. Alternatively, you can press <2> to select it. Expand the **Edit Poly** modifier in the Modifier Stack and note that **Edge** is already selected (highlighted in blue).

Figure 4–73

10. In the Navigation toolbar, click (Zoom Extents All Selected) and using **Pan** and **Zoom** fill the viewport with the box.

11. Hold <Ctrl> and select the upper two long edges, as shown in Figure 4–74. The selected edges display in red.

Figure 4–74

In the Caddy display, hover the cursor on the edit box to display the option in its title.

12. Hold <Shift>, and in the ribbon, in the Loops panel, click (Connect) to open the **Connect Edges** caddy display.

13. In the Connect Edges caddy display, set *Segments* to **2** and *Pinch* to **70**. Press <Enter> (leaving *Slide* as **0**). Note that two edges are placed along the two short edges, as shown in Figure 4–75.

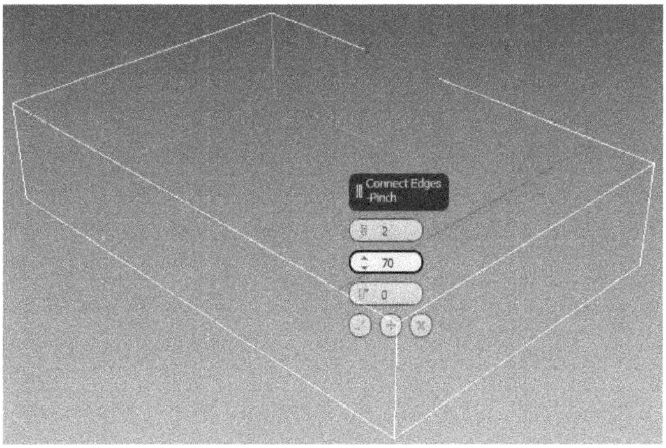

Figure 4–75

Use ⊕ (Apply and continue) when you need to continue in the same tool. If you want to use another tool, use

⊘ (OK) to exit the caddy display.

Pinch moves the lines in opposite directions, while Slide moves both of them in the X-direction

14. If your *Pinch* edit box is still highlighted (white) with the cursor in the edit box, you are required to exit it first. You can also

verify this by hovering the cursor over ⊕.

- If it highlights, then you need to click ⊕ once to apply and continue.

- If it does not highlight, then you need to click ⊕ twice, first to exit the *Pinch* edit box and then to place a new set of segments along the long edge of the box.

15. Leave the *Segments* at **2**. Using the spinner arrows to change the *Pinch* and *Slide* values to create a rectangle towards the back of the armchair, as shown in Figure 4–76. You can drag their slider arrows in either direction viewing the changes dynamically. The values of *Pinch* and *Slide* are approximately **-30** and **-180** respectively. Press <Enter> each time if you enter a new value in the edit box, to see how it

affects the lines. Click ⊘ (OK) to accept the changes and

exit the caddy display. (Hover the cursor over ⊘ and if it

highlights, click ⊘ once. If it does not highlight click ⊘ twice).

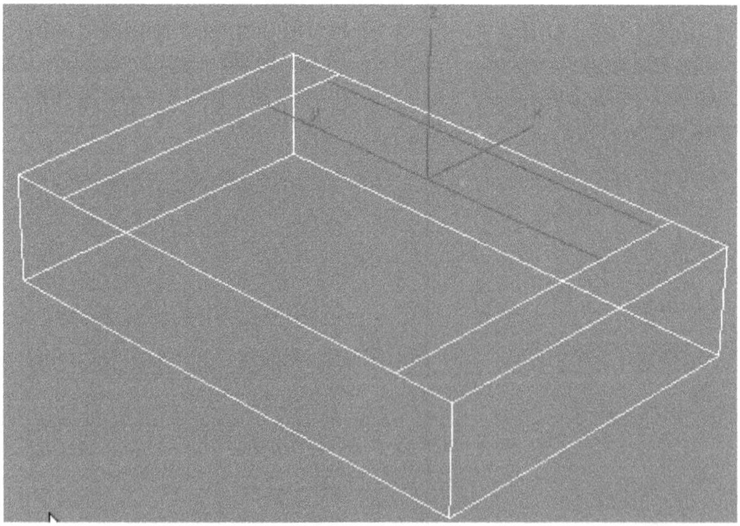

Figure 4–76

16. In the Modeling panel, click ☐ (Polygon), or press <4> to change the sub-object selection level from *Edge* to **Polygon**. Alternatively, select **Polygon** in the **Edit Poly** modifier in the Modifier Stack. In the viewport, right-click and select **Select**. Hold <Ctrl> and select the two polygons along the shorter side of the box, as shown in Figure 4–77.

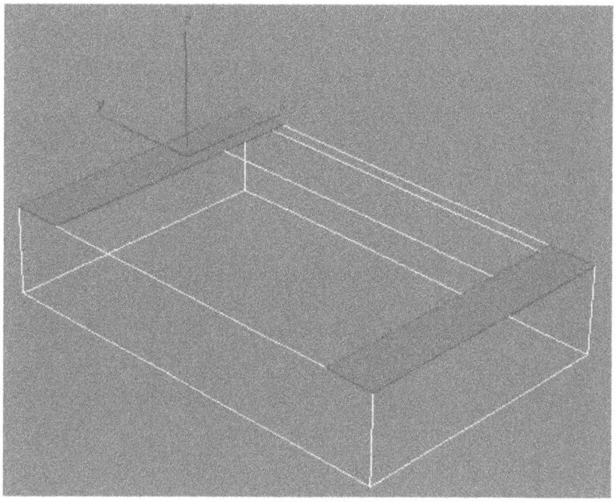

Figure 4–77

Hover the cursor over ✅ *and if it highlights, click* ✅ *once. If it does not highlight click* ✅ *twice). The first time it accepts the values and the second time it exits the caddy display.*

17. In the Modeling ribbon, in the Polygons panel, hold <Shift> and click ⬆ (Extrude) to open the **Extrude Polygons** caddy display. Set *Height* to **0'2"** and click ✅, as shown in Figure 4–78. Click ✅ again to exit the caddy display.

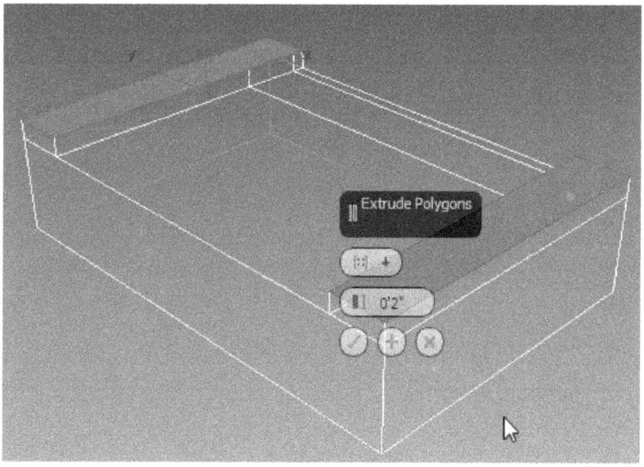

Figure 4–78

18. In the Polygons panel, hold <Shift> and click ⬡ (Bevel) to open the **Bevel** caddy display. Set the following, as shown in Figure 4–79:

- *Height*: **0'1"**
- *Outline*: **-0'1"**

19. Click ✓ to accept the changes and click ✓ again to exit the caddy display.

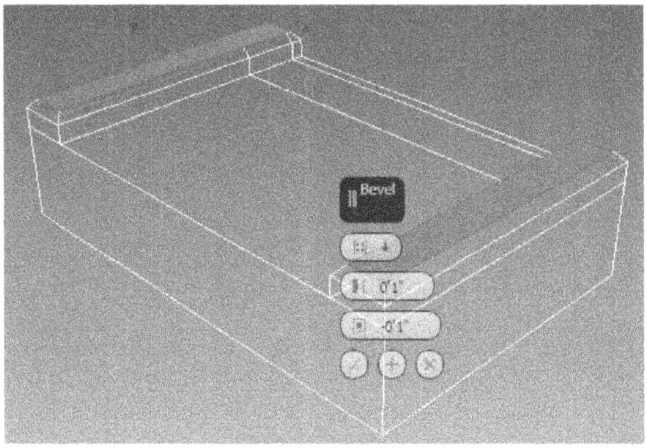

Figure 4–79

The shortcut for Orbit is <Alt> + middle mouse button.

You might need to right-click in empty space to exit the Orbit command first and then select the polygon.

20. In the Navigation toolbar, click 🪐 (Orbit) to orbit in the **Perspective** viewport so that you can see the back of the armchair.

21. Select the long, thin rectangle at the top (along the longer end) for the back of the chair. In the Polygons panel, hold <Shift> and click ⬡↑ (Extrude). In the **Extrude Polygons** caddy display, set extrude to **0'5"** (as shown in Figure 4–80) and press <Enter>. Click ✓ to exit the caddy display.

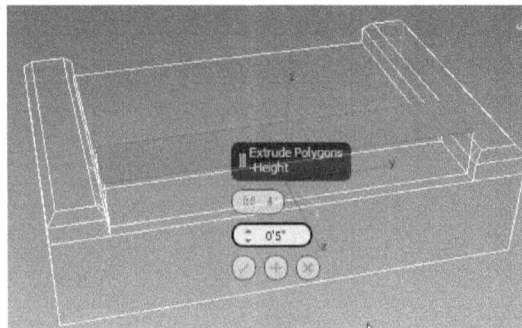

Figure 4–80

22. With the polygon still selected, in the Polygons panel, hold

    <Shift> and click ⬡ (Bevel) to access the Bevel caddy
    display. Bevel up the back of the chair, as shown in
    Figure 4–81. Do not to bevel too much or the edges will
    overlap. The values are approximately **0'7"** for *Height* and

    -0'2" for *Outline*. Press <Enter> and click ⊘ either once or
    twice to exit the caddy display.

Figure 4–81

*Use ⊕ (Orbit) or hold <Alt> and use the middle mouse button to orbit in the **Perspective** viewport for a better view around the object.*

23. In the Main Toolbar, click ✛ (Select and Move) and move
    the selected polygon backwards along the X-axis, as shown
    in Figure 4–82. Orbit the viewport to view the design.

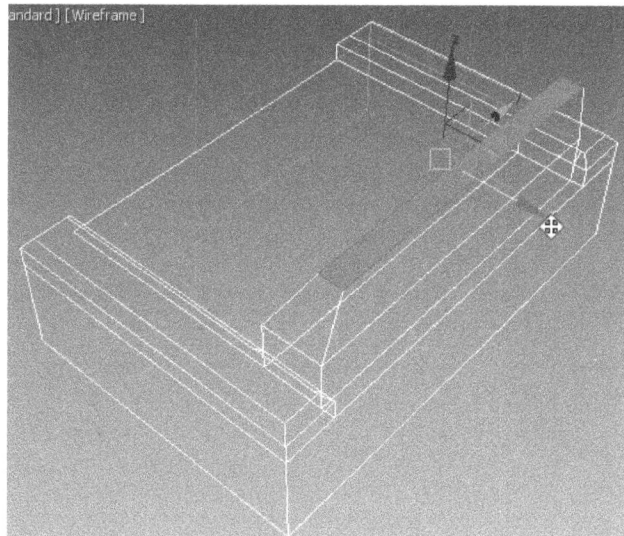

Figure 4–82

Alternatively, click

☐ *(Edge) in the Modeling panel or select* **Edge** *in the Modifier Stack.*

24. Press <2> to change to the **Edge** selection level. If some edge(s) have already been selected, click in an empty area in the viewport to clear the selection.

25. In the Modify Selection panel, click ☐ (Ring Mode) at the bottom of the panel (Ensure that you select **Ring Mode** and not **Ring**). This enables to select a ring of edges when a single edge is selected.

26. Select one of the long edges at the top of the chair back. Because the **Ring Mode** is toggled on, all of the other edges along the first edge are selected and display in red.

27. In the Modify Selection panel, click ☐ (Ring Mode) again to toggle it off.

*Use ☐ (Orbit) or hold <Alt> and use the middle mouse button to orbit in the **Perspective** viewport for easy access for clicking the edges at the back side.*

28. In the Modify Selection panel, click ☐ (Shrink Ring) to clear one edge on either side of the ring. Alternatively, you can hold <Alt> and select one edge in front and one edge in the back to remove them from the selection. Only six edges should be selected, as shown in Figure 4–83.

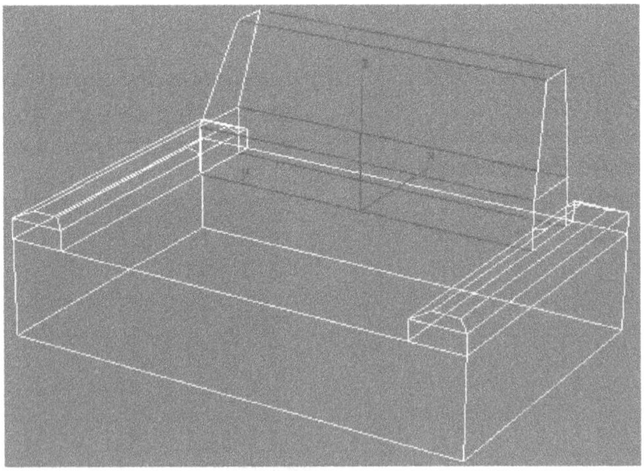

Figure 4–83

29. In the Loops panel, hold <Shift> and click ⊞ (Connect). In the **Connect Edges** caddy display, reset the Pinch and Slide to 0, set the segments to **21** and press <Enter>. This adds 21 vertical segments, as shown in Figure 4–84. Click ⊘ (OK) either once or twice to exit the caddy display.

Sometimes clicking ⊕ *does not work correctly when you need to continue in the same modifier. You can use* ⊘ *and then reopen the modifier.*

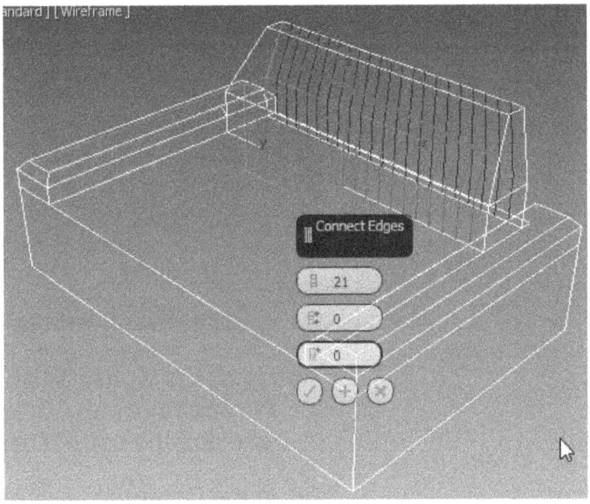

Figure 4–84

30. Hold <Shift> and click ⊞ (Connect) to open the **Connect Edges** caddy display. Change the *Segments* to **3** and press <Enter>. This adds three rows of horizontal segments between two horizontal edges along the armchair back. Click ⊘ either once or twice to exit the caddy display.

31. Clear the selection by clicking in empty space.

32. Maximize the **Left** viewport (Use <Win> + <Shift> to open the overlay). Use the **Zoom** and **Pan** tools to fill the viewport with the model.

33. In the Modeling ribbon, in the Polygon Modeling panel, click ⬚ (Vertex) or press <1>.

Click ↶ (Undo) if you selected the wrong vertices.

34. Click ✛ (Select and Move) and using a selection rectangle, select only the middle vertices in the top row leaving four vertices on each side unselected, as shown in Figure 4–85.

Figure 4–85

- The row of vertices selected display in red.

35. Maximize to display all of the four viewports. In the **Perspective** view, orbit around and verify that you have selected the correct row (only the top most row) of vertices.

36. In the Command Panel, note that you are in the Modify panel with the Modifier Stack indicating that you are at the **Edit Poly>Vertex** level. Expand the Soft Selection rollout and select **Use Soft Selection**. A rainbow color is displayed. The Red/Yellow/Orange/Green vertices will be affected by the selected transform (e.g., **Move**), while the Dark Blue vertices remain unaffected. You can change the Falloff values to add or remove vertices from the affected/unaffected group. Using the spinners in *Falloff,* note that decreasing the falloff changes the cyan colored vertices to a dark blue. Set the *Falloff* similar to that shown in Figure 4–86. Note that the resulting model might differ from that shown.

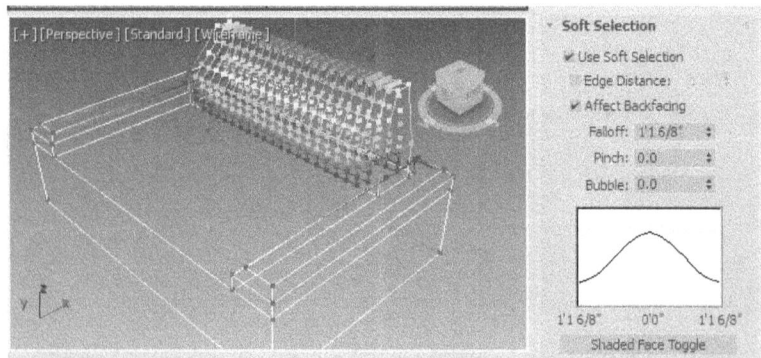

Figure 4–86

You can change the size of the Transform gizmo using the <->(hyphen) and <=> (equal sign).

37. Use ✛ (Select and Move) and move the vertices up by moving the gizmo along the Z-axis, to create the curved chair back, similar to that shown in Figure 4–87. Note that while moving the vertices, the dark blue vertices remain unaffected.

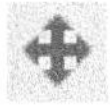

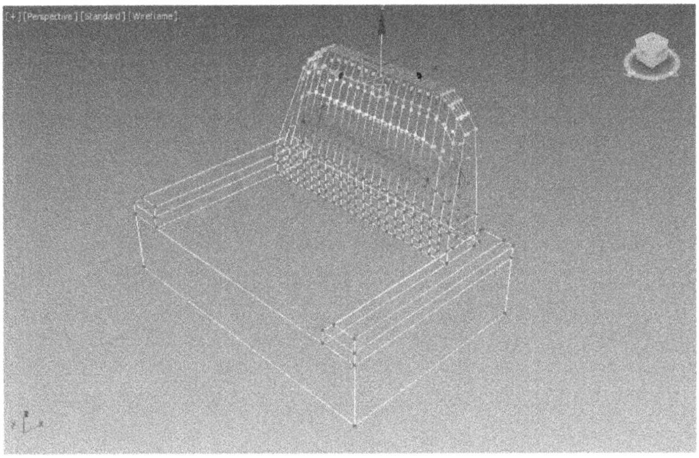

Figure 4–87

Hint: Assign Hotkey

You can assign a hotkey to interactively adjust the Soft selection falloff and pinch in the viewport. To do this, assign a hotkey to **Edit Soft Selection Mode**. Refer to **To edit a soft selection** in the Autodesk 3ds Max Help.

---

38. In the Modifier Stack, select **Edit Poly** to toggle off the sub-object selection

*Alternatively, you can click the **Viewport Shading** menu and select **Realistic** and **Edged Faces**.*

39. Click anywhere in empty space in the **Perspective** viewport to clear the selection. Press <F3> to toggle from *Wireframe* to **Default Shading** mode and press <F4> to toggle on **Edged Faces** mode. The model displays similar to that shown in Figure 4–88.

40. Press <F4> to end the **Edged Faces** mode and display the model using the **Default Shading** mode. In the Display Method label menu, select **High Quality**, as shown in Figure 4–89. Note that there are some problems with smoothing and that the chair looks faceted.

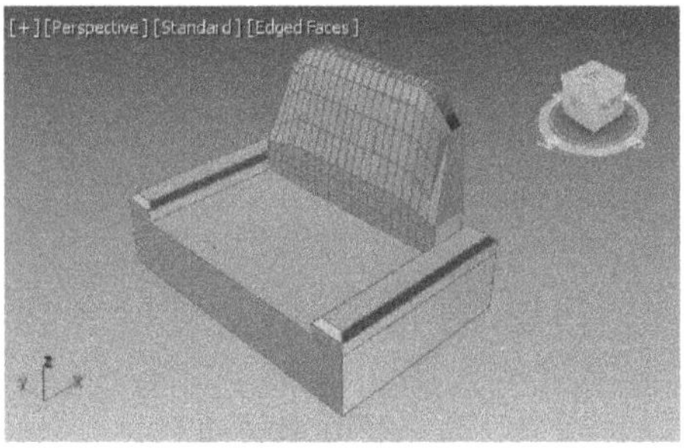

Figure 4–88

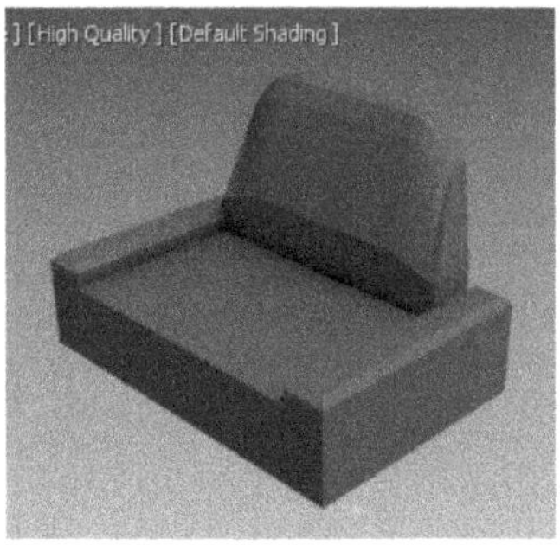

Figure 4–89

41. Select the chair and in the Modifier Stack or ribbon, select **Polygon** or press <4> to access the **Polygon** sub-object level.

42. In the Command Panel, scroll down and expand the Polygon: Smoothing Groups rollout. Press <Ctrl>+<A> to select all of the polygons, and click **Auto Smooth** in the rollout, as shown in Figure 4–90.

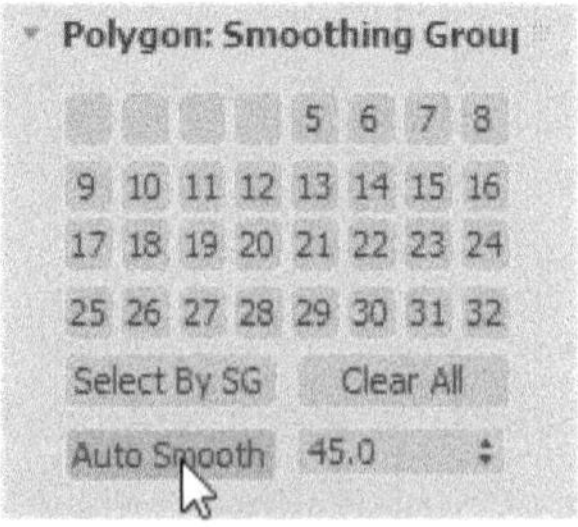

Figure 4–90

43. Click in empty space in the viewport to clear all of the selections. Note that the faceted problem has been fixed, as shown in Figure 4–91.

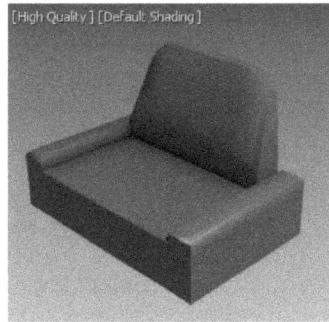

Figure 4–91

Task 2 - Apply Geometric Smoothing.

In this task you will add Geometry Smoothing using the
MSmooth operation.

1. In the **Perspective** view, select the chair, if not already
   selected. In the Modeling ribbon, in the Polygon Modeling
   panel, click [ ] (Polygon), or press <4>.

2. Press <Ctrl>+<A> to select all of the polygons. If they are
   completely displayed in red, press <F2> to only display the
   faces in a red outline (edges).

3. In the Modeling ribbon, in the Subdivision panel, hold <Shift>
   and click [ ] (MSmooth). **Msmooth** changes the geometry
   by adding density to the mesh, as shown in Figure 4–92.

*You can add divisions to
the seat portion of the
chair for the **MSmooth**
modifier to have a
smoother effect. Use
the **Slice** modifier to add
divisions.*

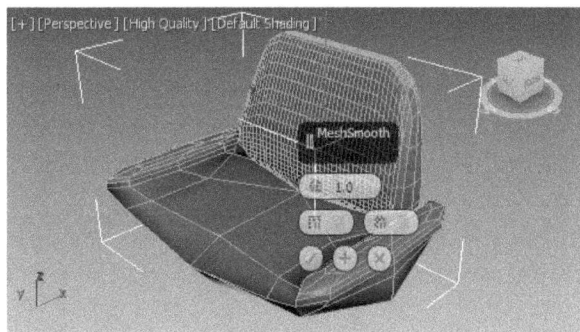

Figure 4–92

4. Click ⊘ to exit the caddy display.

5. Save the file as **My Armchair.max**.

Task 3 - Using Freeform tools. - Optional

If you have time, you can soften the model using the **Freeform** tools.

1. In the *Polygon Modeling* tab, click ☐ (Polygon), if it is not selected. Press <Ctrl>+<A> to select all of the polygons.

2. Select the *Freeform* tab, as shown in Figure 4–93.

Figure 4–93

3. In the Paint Deform panel, click ⊕ (Shift).

4. When you start this command, a Shift Options panel displays on the screen. Also note that the cursor displays as two circles in the active viewport, specifying the brush size. Set the values shown in Figure 4–94.

In the Quick Access Toolbar, click

↶ *(Undo) if you moved the wrong vertices.*

5. Right-click to activate the **Left** viewport (with the selection on) and hover the cursor, which displays as two circles over the top of the back. Stretch the back upward, as shown in Figure 4–95.

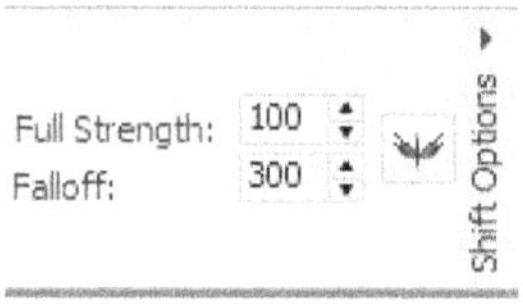

Full Strength: 100
Falloff: 300

Figure 4–94

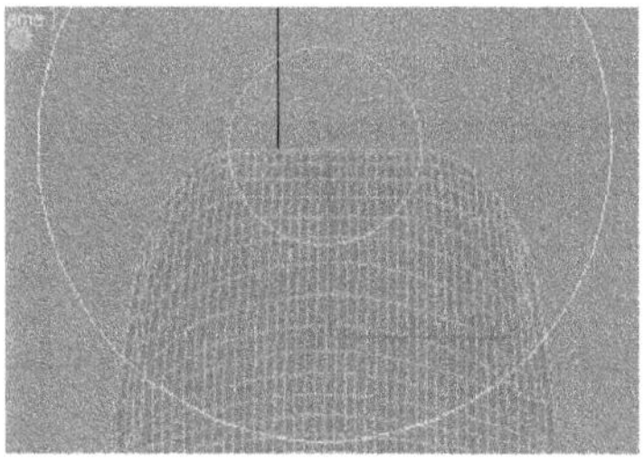

Figure 4–95

Task 4 - Optimize the Mesh.

The shape of the chair has been softened. Now you need to reduce the polycount so the file can be used efficiently. The ProOptimizer modifier will achieve this.

1. Select the **Edit Poly** modifier in the stack to disable Sub-object mode. In the Modifier drop-down list, select **ProOptimizer**, as shown in Figure 4–96.

2. In the Command Panel, in the Optimization Levels rollout, click **Calculate**. Change the *Vertex %* to **22**. Use the spinner to move it up or down as shown in Figure 4–97. Keep watching the viewport and also the statistics are displayed in the rollout.

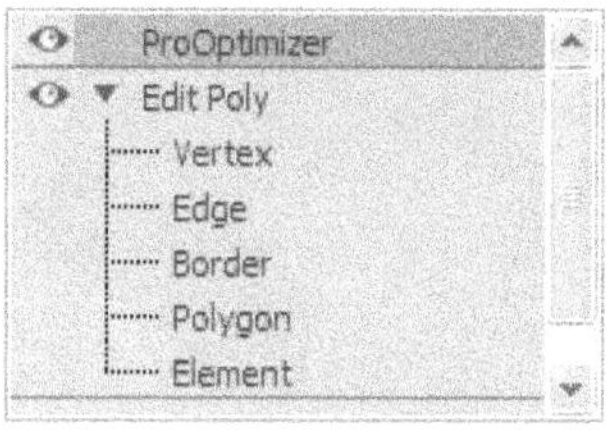

Figure 4–96

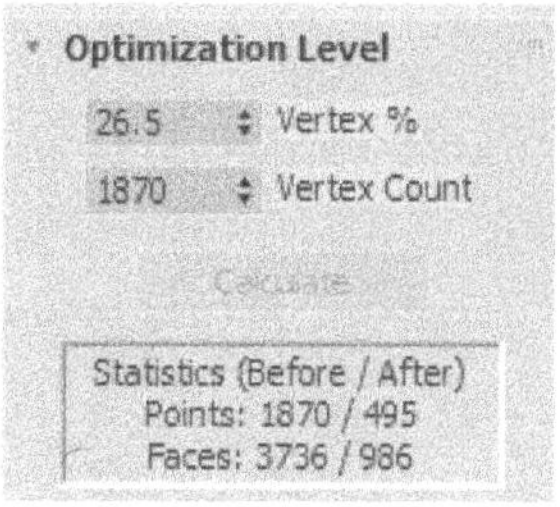

Figure 4–97

3. Save your work as **Myarmchair_softened.max**.

Hint: Using Optimize and MultiRes Modifiers

The **Optimize** and **MultiRes** modifiers are both accessed from the Modifier List. They can be used to reduce the number of vertices and polygons.

- **Optimize:** Reduces the model geometry, but does not critically change the appearance of the model.

- **MultiRes**: Reduces the model geometry and enables you to specify the exact vertex count to be used for reduction. This modifier should be used if you have to export the models to other 3D applications because it maintains the map channels.

4.7 Statistics in Viewport

While Box modeling it is recommended to frequently review the status of your model. You can expand **Application Menu> Properties >Summary Info** to get details about the file. You can also **Show Statistics** directly in the viewport by, clicking **[+]>xView>Show Statistics**. The total number of polygons, vertices, and Frames Per Second are displayed in the viewport (as shown in Figure 4–98), and are dependent on the options selected in the Viewport Configuration dialog box. Alternatively, press <7> to toggle the statistics display in the viewport on and off, in the active viewport.

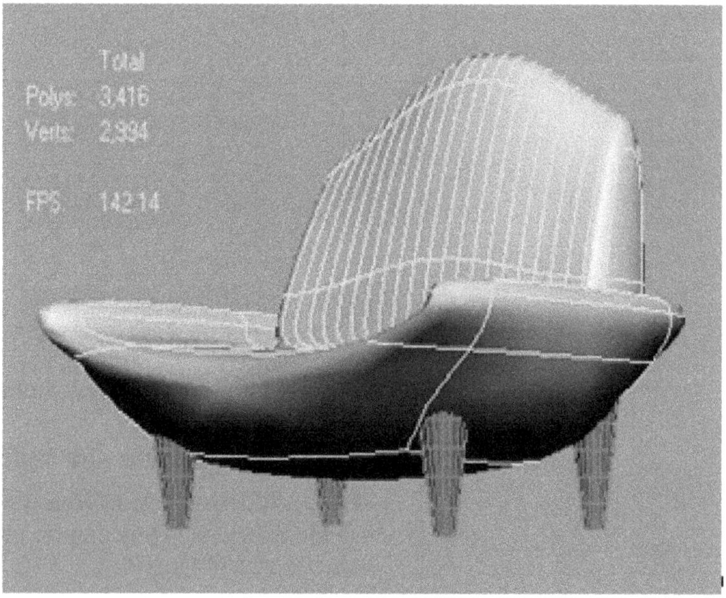

Figure 4–98

The statistics options can be controlled by selecting **Views> Viewport Configuration** and in the *Statistics* tab of the Viewport Configuration dialog box, as shown in Figure 4–99. Here, you can customize the display (e.g., **Polygon Count**, **Triangle Count**, **Edge Count**, **Vertex Count**, etc.).

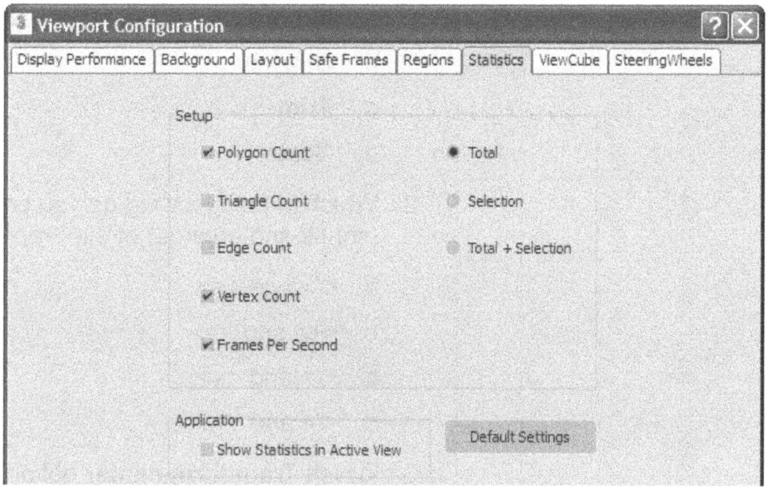

Figure 4–99

Hint: Low Polygon Count

When designing, it is recommended to keep the **Polygon Count** or **Triangle Count** as low as possible to speed up rendering and viewport performance. If you are creating real time models, this impacts the interactive viewport navigation and playback speed.

Performance might be improved if you keep this off when not in use.

- You can toggle the view of the statistics on and off, as required.

Hint: Use Summary Info

Sometimes **Show Statistics** does not give correct results. To check the information, expand **Application Menu> Properties>Summary Info** and then compare the Vertex/Face/Poly count displayed there.

Chapter Review Questions

1. Which of the following are the **Transform** tools in the Autodesk 3ds Max software? (Select all that apply.)

   a. **Move**

   b. **Stretch**

   c. **Trim**

   d. **Scale**

2. Which of the following do you press to change the size (shrink and enlarge) of the Transform gizmo?

   a. <-> and <+>

   b. <+> and <=>

   c. <-> and <=>

   d. </> and <+>

3. Which **Transform center** option do you select if you want to rotate many objects, each around its own center?

   a. (Pivot Point Center)

   b. (Selection Center)

   c. (Transform Coordinate Center)

4. Which clone option creates a one-directional link in which changes made to the original object affect the duplicate, but the modifiers applied to the duplicate do not affect the source object?

   a. **Copy**

   b. **Instance**

   c. **Reference**

5. In addition to the **Polygon Modeling** tools, the *Modeling* tab in the Ribbon contains the commonly used tools from which panel of the Command Panel?

   a. Modify panel ( )

   b. Hierarchy panel ( )

   c. Display panel ( )

   d. Utilities panel ( )

6. Which key on the keyboard can be used as a shortcut to toggle the statistics display in the viewport on and off?

   a. <1>

   b. <3>

   c. <5>

   d. <7>

Command Summary

Button	Command	Location
	Ribbon (Graphite Modeling Tools)	• **Main Toolbar** • **Customize**>Show UI>Show Ribbon
	Select and Move	• **Main Toolbar** • **Edit**>Move
	Select and Place	• **Main Toolbar** • **Edit**>Placement
	Select and Rotate	• **Main Toolbar** • **Edit:**>Rotate
	Select and Uniform Scale	• **Main Toolbar:** Scale flyout • **Edit**>Scale
	Select and Non-uniform Scale	• **Main Toolbar:** Scale flyout
	Select and Squash	• **Main Toolbar:** Scale flyout
	Use Pivot Point Center	• **Main Toolbar:** Transform Center flyout
	Use Selection Center	• **Main Toolbar:** Transform Center flyout
	Use Transform Coordinate Center	• **Main Toolbar:** Transform Center flyout

Chapter 5

Modeling From 2D Objects

In addition to Primitive Objects or Polygon Modeling tools, models in the Autodesk® 3ds Max® software can also be created using 2D shapes that are subsequently used to generate 3D geometry. Tools such as Lathe, Extrude, and Sweep Modifiers enable you to create 3D geometry from a 2D shape.

Learning Objectives in this Chapter

- Create 2D shapes, such as lines and closed shape objects.
- Revolve a profile around an axis using the Lathe modifier.
- Add and subtract shapes using the 2D Boolean operations.
- Add depth to a 2D shape to create 3D geometry using the Extrude modifier.
- Combine two or more 3D objects to generate a third 3D object by performing Boolean operations on their geometry.
- Modify shapes and geometry with precision using various snap modes.
- Create 3D geometry based on a 2D section that follows a series of spline segment paths using the Sweep modifier.

5.1 3D Modeling from 2D Objects

The Autodesk 3ds Max software enables you to create 2D shapes in the form of splines and NURBS, and using various modifiers, to create organic smooth curved surfaces from the shapes. Shapes can be created using ![Shapes icon] (Shapes) in the Command Panel's Create panel (![plus icon]), as shown in Figure 5–1. The splines consist of:

Although the software includes 2D tools, it is not a drafting application.

- Basic shapes: **Line**, **Rectangle**, **Ellipse**, etc.

- Extended shapes: **WRectangle**, **Channel**, **Angle**, etc.

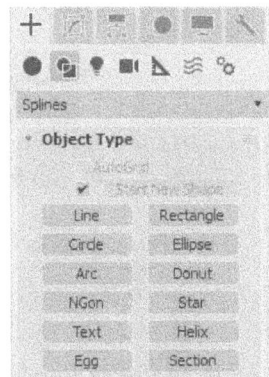

Figure 5–1

The software enables you to draw lines and curves in a freeform interactive manner by clicking points in the viewport. Lines can be drawn to create three kinds of shapes: open, closed, and self-intersecting.

You cannot draw a 2D line that forks or branches.

- Closed shapes can also be created using other shape object types, such as Rectangle, Ellipse, Ngon, or Text.

- Open shapes and self-intersecting shapes can be extruded to create 3D objects, but these objects have mixed face normals. Some faces do not render and might not be visible in the viewport.

- The **Edit Spline** modifier: Enables you to apply edits such as trim, extend, fillet, and chamfer to 2D objects.

- The **Extrude** modifier: Enables you to create 3D objects by extruding closed shapes. The outside of these objects is visible and renderable from all sides. All face normals point away from the center of the object.

- The **Lathe** modifier: Enables you to create 3D objects by using on open shapes where a profile is revolved.

- The Transform Type-In functionality: Enables you to achieve precision using snaps and vertices, which can be shifted after placement.

The **Line** tool has two basic drawing techniques:

Method 1

You can draw straight line segments by clicking and moving the cursor repeatedly. This method does not create any curves at first. All of the vertices created are Corner type. After clicking to set the vertices, you select the line vertices individually or in sets and then change their type from Corner to **Bezier** or **Smooth** to create curves.

> ### Hint: Preventing Self-intersecting Shapes
>
> If you draw too quickly when drawing using Method 1, the program might translate your motions into press and drag, and self-intersecting shapes can be inadvertently drawn. To prevent this, in the Create panel's Creation Method rollout, change the drag type to **Corner**. In doing so, you are not able to drag curves interactively.

Method 2

*You cannot create **Bezier** vertices by clicking, holding, and dragging if both the Initial Type and Drag Type have been set to **Corner** in the Creation Method rollout, in the **Line** tool.*

Draw curves directly by clicking, holding, and dragging to create **Bezier** vertices rather than **Corner** vertices. This is a faster method but harder to control, since you are defining the curve on both sides of the vertex in a single move. Holding <Alt> while dragging enables you to define the curve on the leading side of the vertex, introducing an angle between the vertex handles.

- Using either method, these curved segments are created out of smaller straight line segments. Increasing the segments makes the curve smoother. The *Steps* value in the Interpolation rollout sets the number of segments.

- Drawing while holding <Shift> also draws straight lines and perpendicular lines.

- Press <Backspace> to undo the last drawn vertex in a line.

Practice 5a

Drawing Lines

Practice Objectives

Estimated time for completion: 20 minutes

- Create an open and closed 2D shape.
- Move the location of a vertex and change the shape of a curve.

In this practice you will create, open, and close 2D shapes using the **Line** command. You will then move the location of a vertex and change the shape of a curve using the Bezier handles. Finally, you will create a candlestick model using the 2D shapes drawn.

You must set the paths to locate the External files and Xrefs used in the practice. If you have not done this already, return to **Chapter 1: Introduction to Autodesk 3ds Max** and complete Task 1 to Task 3 in **Practice 1a: Organizing Folders and Working with the Interface**. You only have to set the user paths once.

Task 1 - Drawing 2D lines.

*If a dialog box opens prompting you about a File Load: Mismatch, click **OK** to accept the default values.*

1. Reset the scene.

2. Maximize the **Front** viewport from the layout overlay using

   <Shift> and <Win>. Alternatively use ▨ (Maximize Viewport) or press <Alt>+<W>.

3. Press <G> to hide the grid.

4. In the Command Panel>Create panel (＋), click

   ▦ (Shapes), as shown in Figure 5–2.

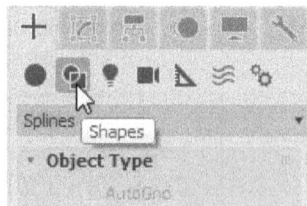

Figure 5–2

5. In the Object Type rollout, click **Line**.

6. In the **Front** viewport, draw a saw-tooth pattern line, as shown in Figure 5–3. Click to set the first point, move the cursor to the next location of the point and click to place the second point. The first line displays. Continue the pattern. Right-click to end, once you have placed the last line. An open shape is created.

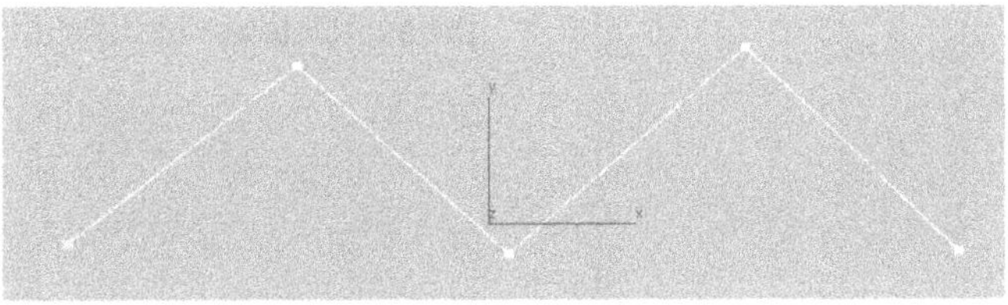

Figure 5–3

7. With the line still selected, delete the lines by pressing <Delete>.

*Closed shapes and open shapes are both used in creating 3D objects. Modifiers, such as **Extrude**, **Lathe**, and **Surface**, can be used to build 3D surfaces based on 2D shapes.*

8. Still in the **Line** command, repeat the drawing process to create a closed shape, as shown in Figure 5–4. Click to set each point and select the starting point (yellow vertex) to complete the shape. In the Spline dialog box, click **Yes** to close the shape. Right-click in the empty space to exit the command. Do not delete this shape.

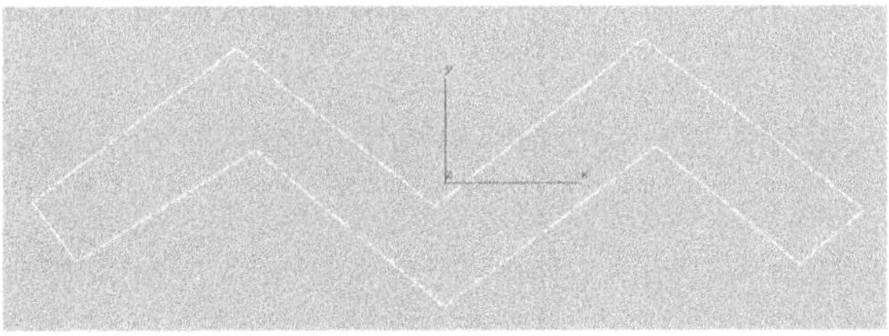

Figure 5–4

9. To draw curved lines, in the Object Type rollout, click **Line**. Then, in the Creation Method rollout, change the *Drag Type* to **Bezier**, as shown in Figure 5–5.

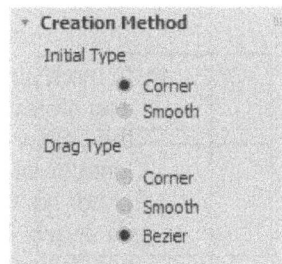

Figure 5–5

10. Click to set the first point, move the cursor, then click and drag to create a Bezier curve running through the second point. Each time you click and drag, the curve extends through the new point. This draws a curve, but it is difficult to control, since dragging affects the curve on both sides of the point at the same time. Draw a curved line similar to the one shown in Figure 5–6. Right-click to exit the command and press <Delete> to delete to this curved line.

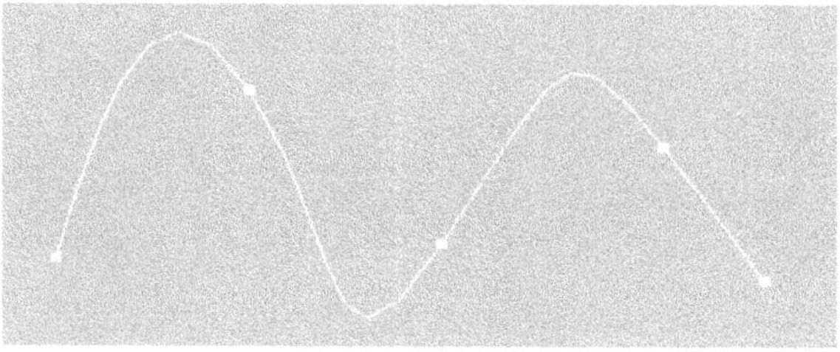

Figure 5–6

11. Right-click in empty space to exit the **Line** command.

12. Select the closed shape that was previously created. In the Command Panel, select the Modify panel ( ). Click ▶ in the Modifier Stack to expand **Line**. Select **Vertex** at the sub-object level, as shown in Figure 5–7.

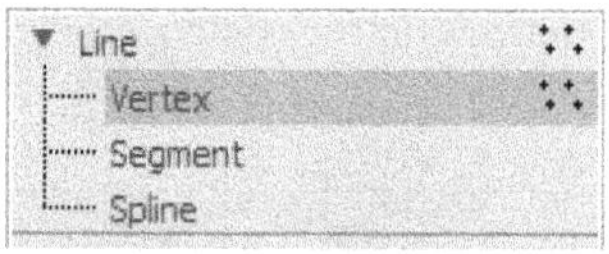

Figure 5–7

13. In the viewport, select one vertex at the top left of the saw tooth pattern. The selected vertex displays in red. Right-click and select **Bezier** in the tools 1 quadrant of the quad menu. Note that the vertex corner is replaced by a Bezier curve and that the Bezier handles are displayed.

14. In the Main Toolbar, click (Select and Move). The Transform gizmo is displayed with the bezier handles. Click the yellow plane at the interior of the gizmo and move the location of the vertex from its initial position. Click and drag either handle end (green square) to modify the curve shape, as shown in Figure 5–8. The handle movement is constrained by the Transform gizmo usage. Note that dragging one handle moves the other handle simultaneously.

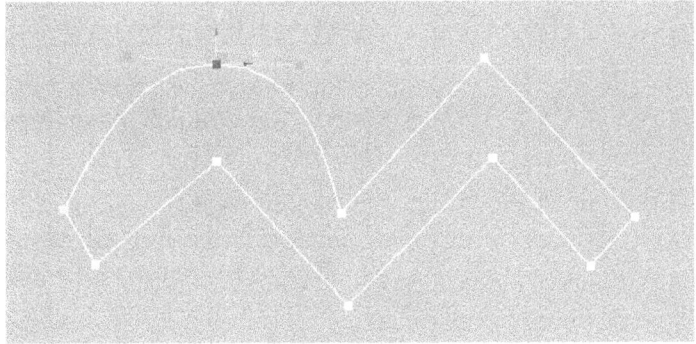

Figure 5–8

Hint: Transform Gizmo Size

<-> (hyphen) and <=> (equal sign) can be used to decrease or increase the size of the Transform gizmo. If the Transform gizmo handles extend beyond the vertex handles, you might have trouble moving the vertex handles.

If you move the Transform gizmo in one axis, the movement of the bezier handles is constrained to that axis. To have the handles move freely, select the yellow square of the gizmo to have movement in the XY-axes. This can also be controlled using the Axis Constraints toolbar.

15. Hold <Shift> and move one of the handles. This changes the command to **Bezier Corner** and enables you to break the continuity of the curve to manipulate the handles on one side of the curve separately from the other, as shown in Figure 5–9. Right-click on the vertex and select **Reset Tangents** to return the original curve shape. To return to **Bezier**, right-click and select it again in the quad menu.

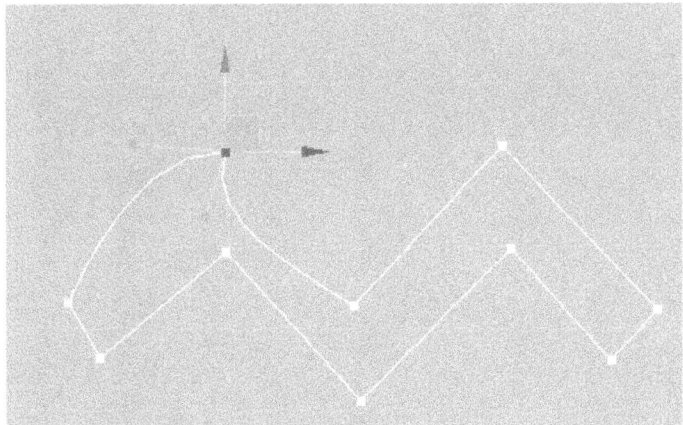

Figure 5–9

Task 2 - Using 2D Shapes to draw a candlestick model.

In this task you will draw a model of a candlestick. A reference photo (**Candlestick_pewter.jpg**) of an actual candlestick as shown in Figure 5–10, is located in the ...\Maps folder.

1. In the Modifier Stack, select **Line** to exit sub-object selection mode. If required, select the shape and any other lines that you might have drawn and delete them using <Delete>.

2. In the Create panel, click (Shapes) and click **Line**. In the Creation Method rollout, in the *Drag Type* area, select **Corner**, if required.

Holding <Shift> creates straight lines at a 90 degree angle (vertical direction) and 180 degree angle (horizontal direction).

3. Start at the bottom right (the yellow vertex indicates the start point) and click to place the first line vertex, as shown in Figure 5–11. Hold <Shift>, move the cursor left, and click to draw the base of the candlestick. Still holding <Shift>, move the cursor up to draw the long straight vertical line segment, and then click to place the vertex. Release <Shift> and continue clicking and drawing in a clockwise direction.

   • Press <Backspace> to undo the points if you make a mistake.

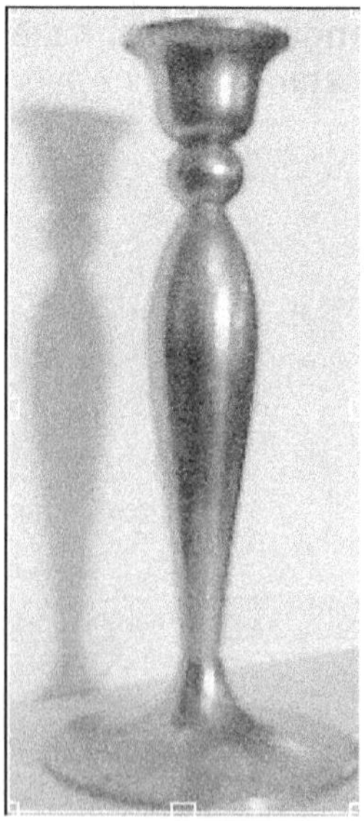

Figure 5–10 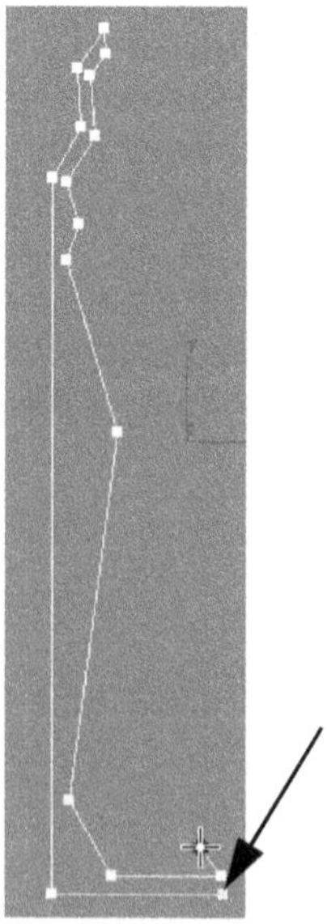   Figure 5–11

4. Continue to place approximately 16 points and close the shape by clicking over the first point. Click **Yes** and then right-click to exit the **Line** command.

5. In the Modify panel ( ), in the Modifier Stack, expand **Line** and select the **Vertex** sub-object level. Hold <Ctrl> and select the four red vertices, as shown in Figure 5–12. Right-click and select **Bezier** in the quad menu. This changes the vertices to **Bezier** vertices with handles

Figure 5–12

6. Adjust the handles of each vertex using (Select and Move) to obtain a shape similar to that shown in Figure 5–13. Move the vertices and handles to get a shape similar to that shown in Figure 5–14.

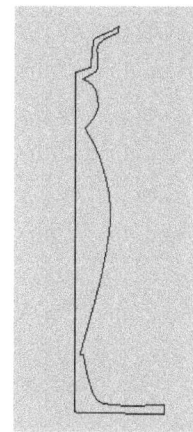

| **Figure 5–13** | **Figure 5–14** |

7. Save your work as **MyCandlestickProfile.max**. For comparison, you can open the file **Candlestick_Profile.max**.

5.2 The Lathe Modifier

The **Lathe** modifier enables you to create a 3D object by revolving a profile (2D shape) around an axis. It can be accessed in the Modifier List, in the Modify panel ( ) in the Command Panel.

How To: Create a 3D Object Using the Lathe Modifier

1. Select a profile (usually a line object).
2. Apply a **Lathe** Modifier.
3. Adjust the axis of revolution.
4. Adjust the alignment of the axis with the profile.

Practice 5b

Estimated time for completion: 5 minutes

*If a dialog box opens prompting you about a File Load: Mismatch, click **OK** to accept the default values.*

*Sometimes, lathed objects display inside-out. If something looks wrong with your candlestick, use the **Flip Normals** option in the Parameters rollout.*

Creating a Candlestick

Practice Objective

- Revolve a 2D shape around its axis.

In this practice you will resolve a 2D shape around its axis, using the **Lathe** modifier to create the solid geometry for the candlestick.

You must set the paths to locate the External files and Xrefs used in the practice. If you have not done this already, return to **Chapter 1: Introduction to Autodesk 3ds Max** and complete Task 1 to Task 3 in **Practice 1a: Organizing Folders and Working with the Interface**. You only have to set the user paths once.

1. Open **Candlestick_Profile.max**.

2. Maximize the **Front** viewport.

3. Select the profile. In the Modify panel ( ), in the Modifier Stack, verify that the **Line** is highlighted and that no sub-object level is highlighted.

4. In the Modifier List, select **Lathe**. The profile revolves around a center point, but the alignment is off, as shown in Figure 5–15.

5. In the Parameters rollout, in the *Align* area, click **Min**. The candlestick should now display as shown in Figure 5–16.

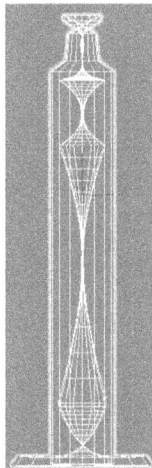

Figure 5–15

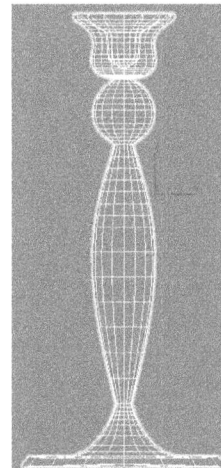

Figure 5–16

6. In the Modifier Stack, expand **Lathe** and select **Axis**. Using

   ✛ (Select and Move), move the X-axis to display the candlestick in various positions.

7. In the Quick Access Toolbar, click ↶ (Undo) or press <Ctrl>+<Z> to undo the axis moves.

8. Select **Lathe** (highlighted) to exit the Sub-object mode. Maximize the viewport to display the four viewports.

9. Assign a color to the geometry by selecting the candlestick first, selecting the color swatch next to the **Line** name, and selecting a color in the Object Color dialog box.

10. In the Viewport Navigation toolbar, click 🪐 (Orbit) and examine the geometry as shown in Figure 5–17.

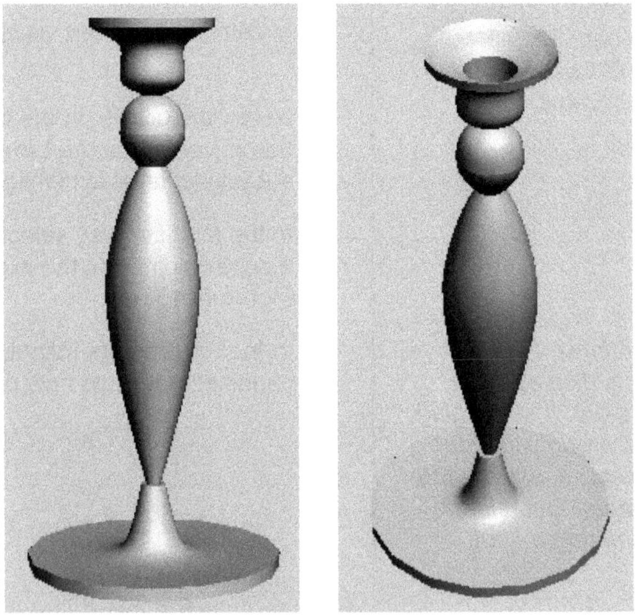

Figure 5–17

11. Save your work as **MyCandlestick.max**.

5.3 2D Booleans

- 2D Boolean operations enable you to create shapes by combining drawn lines and shapes. Using the **Edit Spline** modifier, you can add or subtract shapes at the sub-object level.

- 2D Boolean operations are available in the Spline sub-object level, in the **Geometry** parameters, as shown in Figure 5–18.

- All shapes that are to be combined must be part of a single shape. The **Edit Spline** modifier enables you to convert a shape to an editable spline while the **Attach** command enables you to combine multiple shapes into a single shape.

- When drawing shapes, if you clear the **Start New Shape** option in the Object Type rollout (as shown in Figure 5–19), all of the subsequent shapes that you create are joined into one single shape. If you already have a shape selected, anything you draw becomes part of that shape. By default, the **Start New Shape** option is selected before you start drawing any shapes.

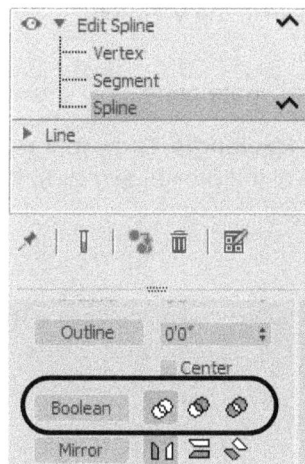

Figure 5–18

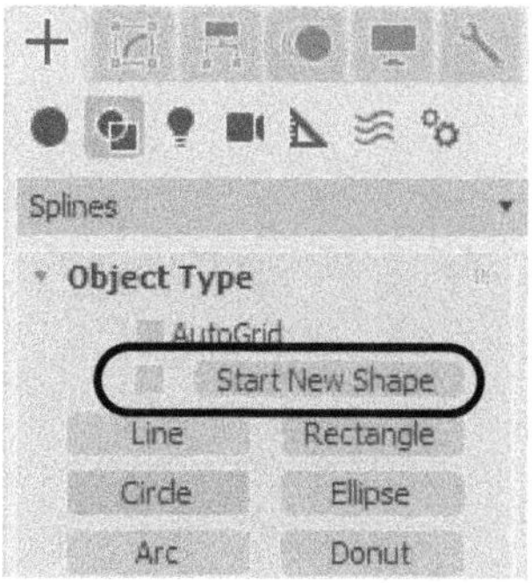

Figure 5–19

- No history is associated with 2D Boolean operations that are saved with the file and you are not able to retrieve the various Boolean components after saving.

Practice 5c

2D Booleans

Practice Objective

- Modify a shape using 2D Booleans.

Estimated time for completion: 5 minutes

In this practice you will add and subtract rectangles using 2D Booleans to change the shape of the profile for the candlestick.

You must set the paths to locate the External files and Xrefs used in the practice. If you have not done this already, return to **Chapter 1: Introduction to Autodesk 3ds Max** and complete Task 1 to Task 3 in **Practice 1a: Organizing Folders and Working with the Interface**. You only have to set the user paths once.

*If a dialog box opens prompting you about a File Load: Mismatch, click **OK** to accept the default values.*

1. Open **Candlestick.max**.

2. Maximize the **Front** viewport and zoom to the extents of all objects.

3. Select the candlestick. In the Modify panel (![icon]( ), in the Modifier Stack, click ![eye]( ) (eye) next to the **Lathe** to toggle the **Lathe** modifier off. The line profile and the **Lathe** axis displays in the viewport.

4. In the Create panel (+), click ![Shapes]( ) (Shapes).

5. Click **Rectangle**. Draw four rectangles intersecting the right edge of the profile, similar to that shown in Figure 5–20.

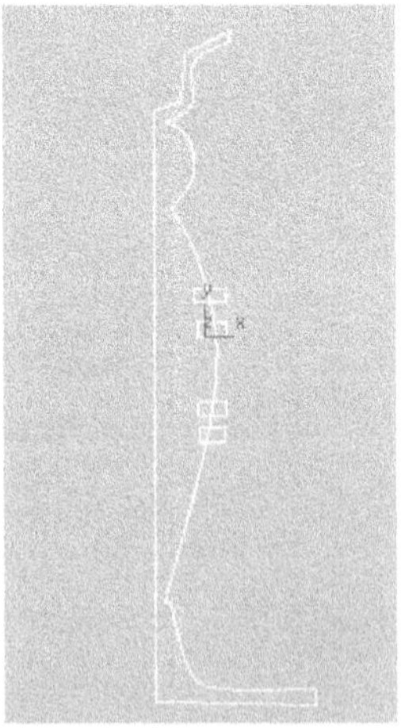

Figure 5–20

6. Right-click to cancel the command.

7. Select the candlestick profile. Open the Modify panel (⬛), and in the Modifier Stack, select **Line**.

8. Scroll down and in the Geometry rollout, click **Attach Mult**.

A blue background in the button means it is active.

9. In the Attach Multiple dialog box, click ⬛ (Display Shapes) to activate it, if not already active. Select all of the four rectangles and click **Attach**. All of the rectangles become part of the candlestick profile spline object.

10. In the Modifier Stack, select the **Spline** sub-object in the **Line** object and select the candlestick profile in the viewport. The selected profile displays in red and the rectangles remain white (unselected).

11. In the Geometry rollout, scroll down and click **Boolean** to activate it. Verify that ⬛ (Union) is already active.

12. In the viewport, hover the cursor over the topmost rectangle, and note that the cursor displays as a Union cursor (⬛). Select the topmost rectangle and then select the second rectangle. Note that in each case, the profile is extended to the right to include part of the rectangle, and the inner part of the rectangle is discarded.

13. In the Command Panel, click ⬛ (Subtraction) to activate it. Hover the cursor over the third rectangle to display the cursor as a Subtraction cursor (⬛).

14. Select the third rectangle and then select the last rectangle. For these shapes, the rectangle is subtracted from the candlestick. The first two rectangles create a rim, and the last two create an inscribed groove, as shown in Figure 5–21.

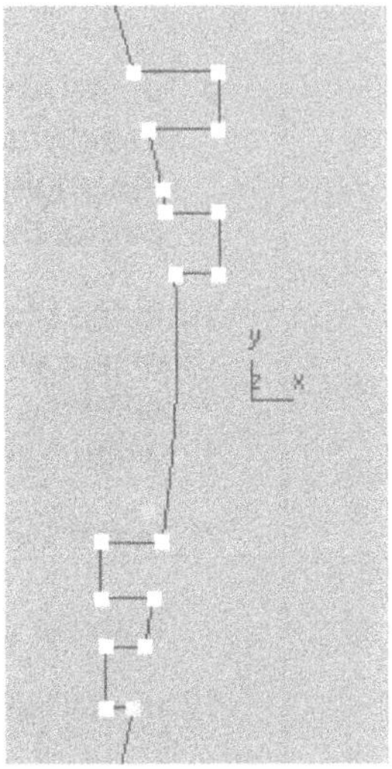

Figure 5–21

15. In the Modifier Stack, select **Lathe**, and then click ⬚ (grayed out eye) next to **Lathe** to toggle it on.

16. Press <Alt>+<W> to return to four viewports. Activate the **Perspective** viewport and review the results in **Default Shading** display mode. The two rims and two grooves are created in the candle stick, as shown in Figure 5–22.

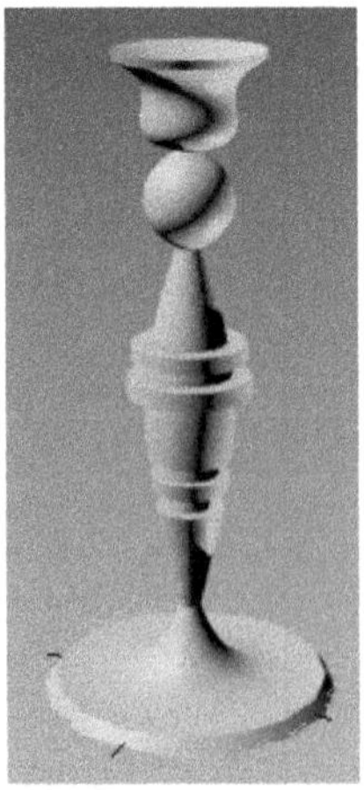

Figure 5–22

17. Save your work as **MyCandlestick01.max**.

18. (Optional) Modify some of the vertices. Select the

    candlestick, if required. In the Modify panel (), select **Line** and **Vertex** sub-objects. Select one of the vertices in the first rim that you created, as shown in Figure 5–23.

19. (Optional) In the Modifier Stack, click  (Show end result on/off toggle), as shown in Figure 5–24. This tool enables you to see the object as an end product.

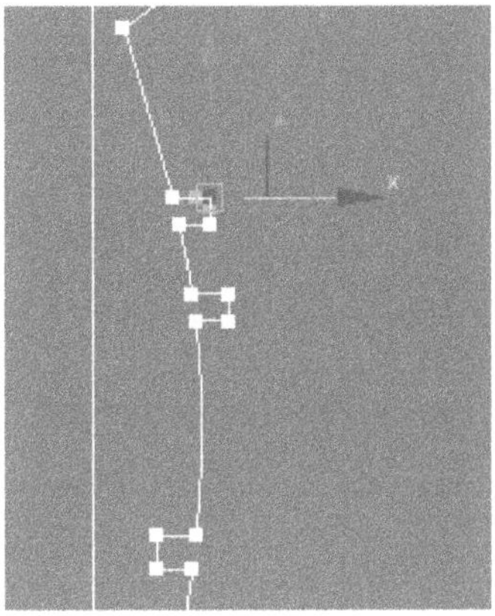

Figure 5–23

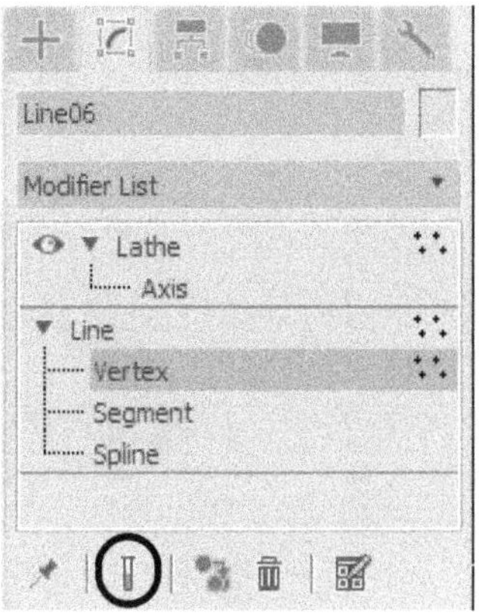

Figure 5–24

20. (Optional) Move the selected vertex in the viewport. You are now sculpting the candlestick in real time, as shown in Figure 5–25.

Figure 5–25

21. Save your work as **MyCandlestick01.max**.

5.4 The Extrude Modifier

The **Extrude** modifier enables you to add depth to a 2D shape to create 3D geometry. As with other modifiers, the Extrude modifier is available in the Modifier List, in the Command Panel's Modify panel (), as shown in Figure 5–26.

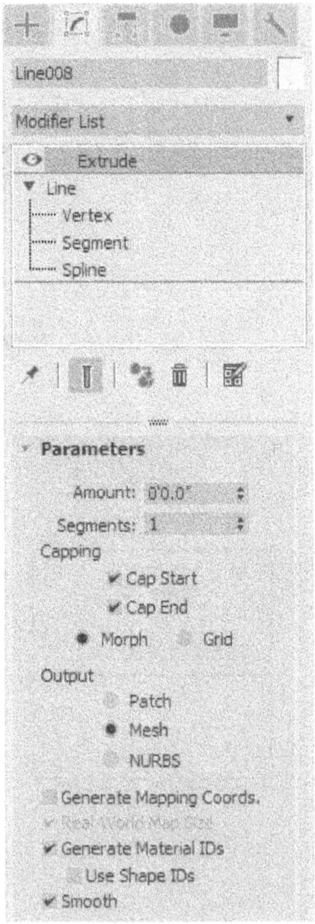

Figure 5–26

Capping area

The capping options are located in the Parameters rollout, in the *Capping* area, as shown in Figure 5–26.

- Capping only applies to closed extruded shapes. Open shapes can be extruded but they cannot be capped.

- Closed shapes often do not cap if they cross themselves or if they have more than one vertex at the same location.

- You can also extrude with a height of **0** to create a flat surface. In this situation, only the start or end cap is required.

- Figure 5–27 shows **various** capping options.

Original Shape   *No Capping*   *Cap Start*   *Cap End*

Figure 5–27

- **Morph** capping type linearly interpolates across the vertices to create the cap, as shown in Figure 5–28. This option creates less geometry and is the default setting.

- **Grid** capping type breaks down the cap into a repeating grid of vertices, in square shapes, as shown in Figure 5–29. The grid method enables more complex modeling on the surface of the cap, but adds a great deal of geometry.

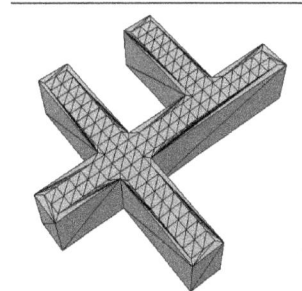

Figure 5–28   **Figure 5–29**

Output area

The *Output* area options controls the kind of object that is derived if you simplify (collapse) the object. It is recommended to select the default **Mesh** option. **Patch** and **NURBS** options are used to create complex curved geometry.

Mapping Coordinates

The options for mapping coordinates and real-world map sizing are described with materials.

- For surfaces that have tiled, repeating textures of a specific size (e.g., carpeting, wall surfaces, metal, etc.) select **Generate Mapping Coords** and **Real-World Map Size**.

- For surfaces meant to show textures that are scaled explicitly (e.g., signs, labels, company logos, paintings, computer screens, etc.) you might use **Generate Mapping Coords option,** but the **Real-World Map Size** option can be cleared.

- Select **Generate Material IDs** to apply a different material to the sides, start, and end cap through a Multi/Sub-object material.

- Selecting **Use Shape IDs** assigns material IDs that have been applied to the segments of the spline that you extruded.

Extruding Nested Splines

When linked or imported geometry is merged together (such as by layer with the weld option) or, when 2D objects become attached to form complex splines, these objects are called **nested splines**. When extruding a nested spline (as shown in Figure 5–30), the enclosed areas form solid masses and can be used for modeling wall systems and similar geometry.

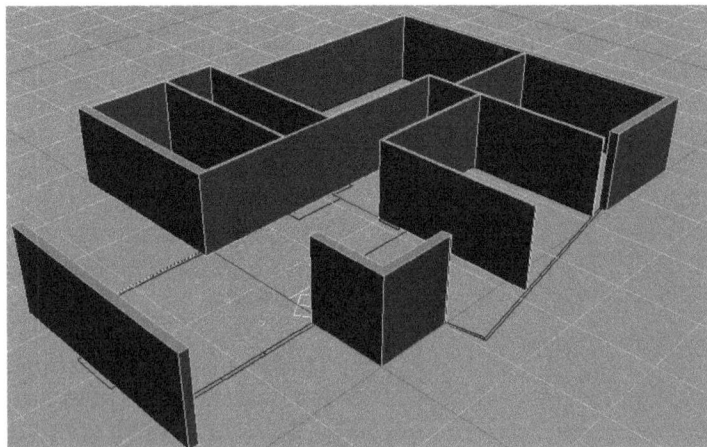

Figure 5–30

5.5 Boolean Operations

Boolean operations enable you to graphically bring together two 3D objects to generate a third 3D object. This is an intuitive way to create complex geometry from simple 3D primitives and extruded 2D shapes.

The Boolean objects are available in the Create panel ($+$), by clicking ● (Geometry) and selecting **Compound Objects** in the drop-down list. You can select the required Boolean object in the Object Type rollout, as shown in Figure 5–31.

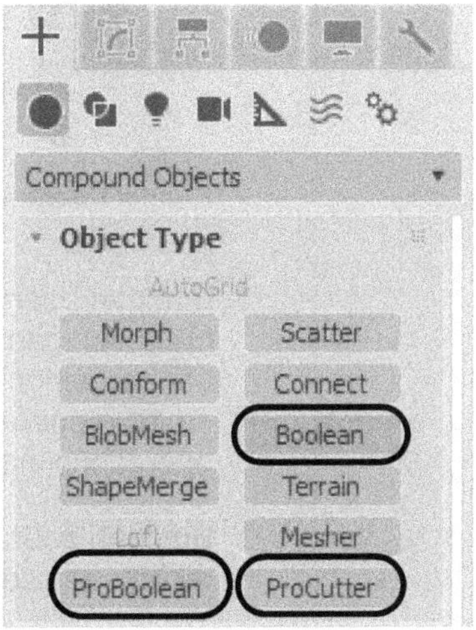

Figure 5–31

The three types of Boolean objects that can be created, are described as follows:

<table>
<tr><td>**Boolean compound object**</td><td>Combines two 3D objects to generate a third 3D object by applying a logical operation. The Boolean compound object offers improved stability.</td></tr>
<tr><td>**ProBoolean compound object**</td><td>Similar to the Boolean compound object, this option has more advanced functionality and alternate workflow.</td></tr>
<tr><td>**ProCutter compound object**</td><td>Enables you to separate objects into pieces so that you can use them in dynamic simulations.</td></tr>
</table>

Enhanced
in **2017**

Boolean Operations

The original objects are referred to as **Operands** and the final result is a **Boolean** object. The operands can be combined in three ways, as shown in Figure 5–32:

- By subtraction of one from the other.

- By finding the intersection where their geometries overlap.

- By the union of the two together.

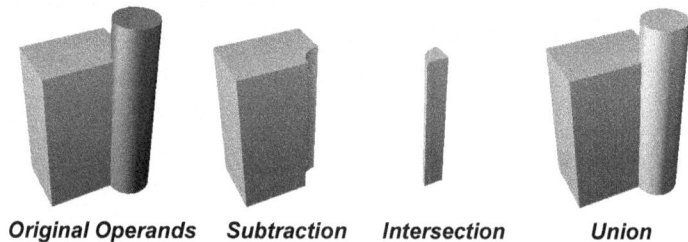

Original Operands   *Subtraction*   *Intersection*   *Union*

Figure 5–32

- Boolean operations can be nested where the results of one operation can be used as input to the next. **ProBooleans** offer superior methodology when creating objects with multiple operands. It enables you to reorder and change the operations interactively.

- Boolean operations can be animated, this is often a technique used to reveal or hide geometry in a presentation.

New in 2017

Boolean Explorer

The Boolean Explorer can help you to keep track of the various operands that are being used, as shown in Figure 5–33. The Boolean Explorer is only available with the Boolean compound object.

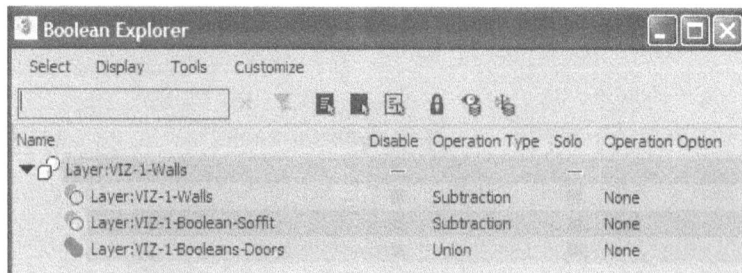

Figure 5–33

- To open the Boolean Explorer, in the Boolean Parameters rollout, click **Open Boolean Explorer**.

- Whenever you add an operand, it is displayed in the Boolean Explorer.

- If you change the order of the operands, the change is reflected in the Boolean Explorer.

Adjusting Boolean Results

The results of a Boolean operation can be adjusted dynamically by making changes to the operands' parameters or modifier stack. This dynamic update requires that operands be identified as a reference or instance on creation (or an extracted operand is selected to be an instance).

- The original operands can be maintained for editing after the fact or they can be reconstituted (extracted) from the Boolean result later on.

- The practical application of adjusting Boolean results is best left for Intermediate course material.

Best Practices

Boolean operations are known to produce unexpected results if the operand geometries had certain issues such as: gaps, irregular face normals, did not overlap each other, etc. It is recommended to avoid the following issues whenever possible:

- Avoid coplanar operands, whenever possible, to minimize Boolean complexity.

- Boolean operations expect water-tight geometry. If the geometry does not cleanly define a volume, the Boolean might not work, as shown in Figure 5–34.

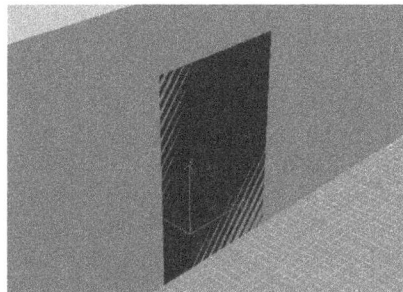

Figure 5–34

Collapsing Booleans

When an object has been sufficiently modeled with Boolean operations you can leave the result as a Boolean object or simplify (collapse) it to a mesh.

- To collapse a Boolean object to an editable mesh, in the Modifier Stack, right-click on the Boolean and select **Convert to: Editable Mesh** or **Convert to: Editable Poly**.

- If you are using a Boolean result as an operand for another Boolean operation and are not getting the expected results, it might help to convert the original Boolean object to an editable mesh before the second operation. It is recommended to use ProBooleans if you have multiple operands.

- Boolean objects that originate from linked AutoCAD geometry might react unpredictably after an updated DWG link.

- Many other kinds of 3D objects besides Booleans can be collapsed to a mesh to simplify them.

- Once an object is converted to a mesh, it loses all of its parametric controls. Therefore, converted Boolean objects cannot be updated by editing instanced operands or a file link update.

If you select a selective reload and avoided the layers used to create your Booleans, any connected Boolean objects would be removed from the scene.

Practice 5d

Estimated time for completion: 20 minutes

Extrude Walls and Create Wall Openings

Practice Objective

- Add depth to a 2D spline to create 3D walls and openings in 3D walls.

In this practice you will extrude walls from a spline to create 3D walls. You will then refine the walls by creating openings for a corridor and doors, using the **Extrude** modifier. Additionally, you will use **ProBoolean** objects to graphically subtract two objects from the walls.

You must set the paths to locate the External files and Xrefs used in the practice. If you have not done this already, return to **Chapter 1: Introduction to Autodesk 3ds Max** and complete Task 1 to Task 3 in **Practice 1a: Organizing Folders and Working with the Interface**. You only have to set the user paths once.

Task 1 - Extrude the Walls.

*If a dialog box opens prompting you about a File Load: Mismatch, click **OK** to accept the default values.*

*If the Scene Explorer is not displayed, select **Tools>Scene Explorer***

or click ▦ *(Toggle Scene Explorer) in the Main Toolbar.*

1. Open **Spline Walls Bound.max**.

2. In the Scene Explorer toolbar, click ■ (Display None) and click ▧ (Display Shapes). Select **Layer:VIZ-1-Walls** and note that the 2D lines for the walls (cyan colored shapes) are selected in the viewport. .

3. In the Command Panel, select the Modify panel (▱). The name **Layer:VIZ-1-Walls** displays in the Command Panel and it is an **Editable Spline**.

4. In the Modifier List, select **Extrude**. In the Parameters rollout, set *Amount* to **11'0"** (the height of the first floor walls), as shown in Figure 5–35. Press <Enter>.

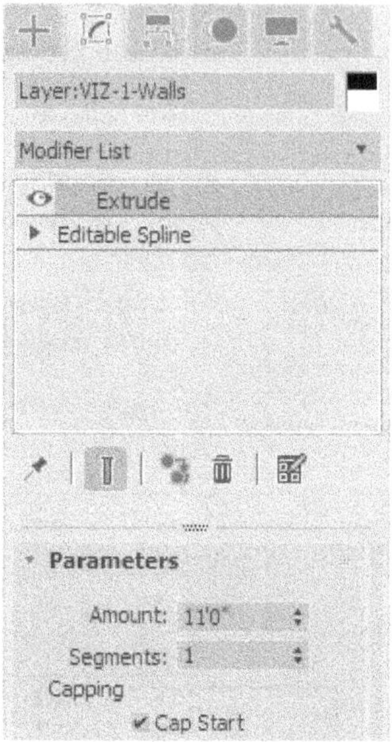

Figure 5–35

The missing wall sections eventually contain curtain walls.

5. Click (Zoom Extents All). Only the areas enclosed by the wall linework are extruded, as shown in Figure 5–36.

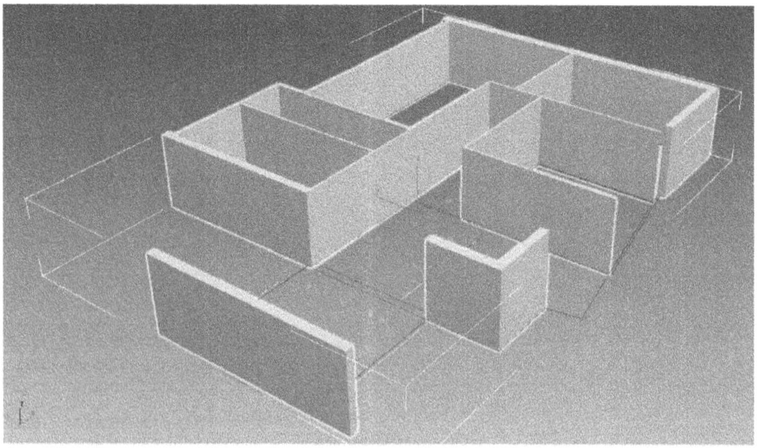

Figure 5–36

Task 2 - Creating the Subtraction Operands.

The Layer Explorer is a modeless dialog box and can remain open while you are working in the viewport.

1. In the Main Toolbar, click ▤ (Layer Explorer). In the Layer Explorer, select the two layers **VIZ-1-Booleans-Doors** and **VIZ-1-Boolean-Soffit**. Right-click on any of the selected layer and click **Select Child Nodes**, as shown in Figure 5–37. These layers contain closed polylines that define the openings to be created. Note that these layers are selected as well.

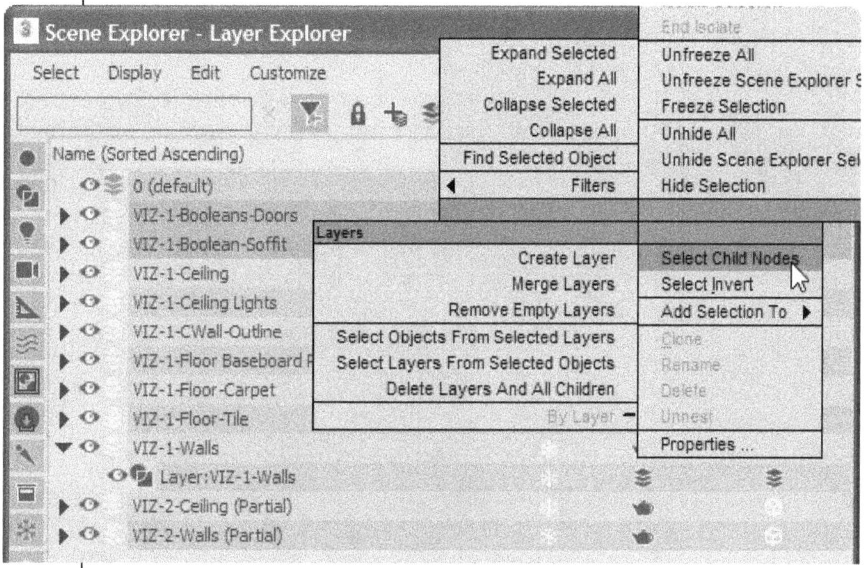

Figure 5–37

2. To avoid a coplanar face along the floor, first move these objects below the floor level. In the Main Toolbar, click

   ✛ (Select and Move). Set coordinate system to **World** and

   click ▤ (Use Transform Coordinate Center), as shown in Figure 5–38.

Figure 5–38

3. In the Status Bar, in the *Transform Type-In* area, activate

   (Offset Mode Transform), enter **-1'0"** in the *Z* field, and press <Enter>.

4. In the Main Toolbar, click  (Select object).

5. Click anywhere in empty space to clear the selection. In the Layer Explorer, highlight only the layer **VIZ-1-Boolean-Soffit**. Right-click on the selected layer and click **Select Child Nodes**. This layer contains a single polyline defining an opening in one of the walls.

6. In the Command Panel>Modify panel (), verify that the name **Layer:VIZ-1-Boolean-Soffit** displays in the panel.

7. In the Modifier List, select **Extrude**. In the Parameters rollout, set *Amount* to **9'0"** and press <Enter> (this is **8'** + the **1'** that was just used to lower the object). The first subtraction operand (8'0") is created, as shown in Figure 5–39.

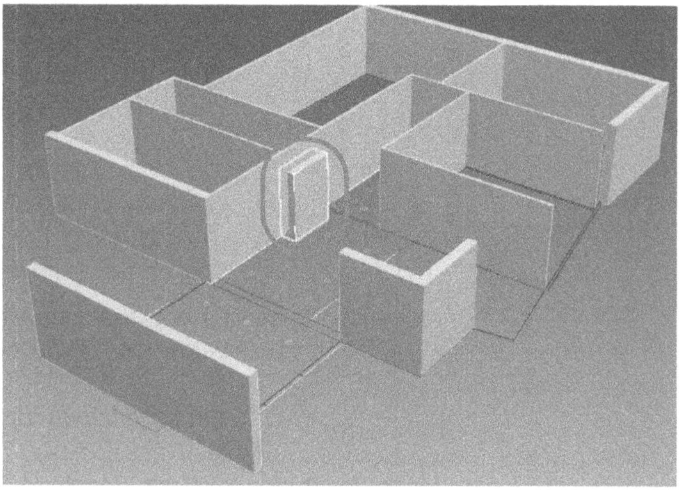

Figure 5–39

8. Repeat Steps 5 to 7 for **VIZ-1-Booleans-Doors**. Select the child layer of **VIZ-1-Booleans-Doors** and extrude it with an *Amount* of **8'0"**. The 7'0" subtraction operands are created, as shown in Figure 5–40.

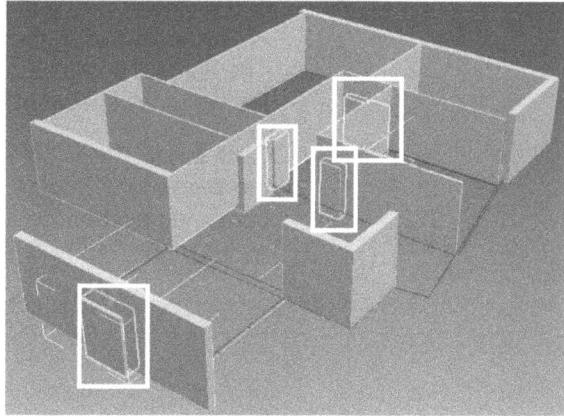

Figure 5–40

Task 3 - Creating the Wall Openings.

1. In the Layer Explorer, select **VIZ-1-Walls.** Right-click on the selected layer and click **Select Child Nodes**.

2. In the Create panel (![+]( ))> ● (Geometry), select **Compound Objects** in the drop-down list, as shown in Figure 5–41. Click **ProBoolean** to convert the wall system into a Boolean object. The selected walls (**VIZ-1-Walls)** are now your Operand A.

3. In the Pick Boolean rollout, verify that **Move** is selected and click **Start Picking**.

4. In the Parameters rollout, in the *Operation* area, verify that **Subtraction** is selected, as shown in Figure 5–42. This subtracts **Operand B** (the soffit opening) from **Operand A** (the walls).

Figure 5–41

Figure 5–42

5. In the viewport, select the Boolean Soffit extrusion (**VIZ -1-Boolean Soffit**, the 9'0" operand that was created first). The volume contained by the Soffit object is removed from the walls, as shown in Figure 5–43.

6. Click any of the **VIZ-1-Boolean-Doors** objects to complete the second ProBoolean subtraction operation. The volume contained by the Doors object is also removed from the walls, as shown in Figure 5–43.

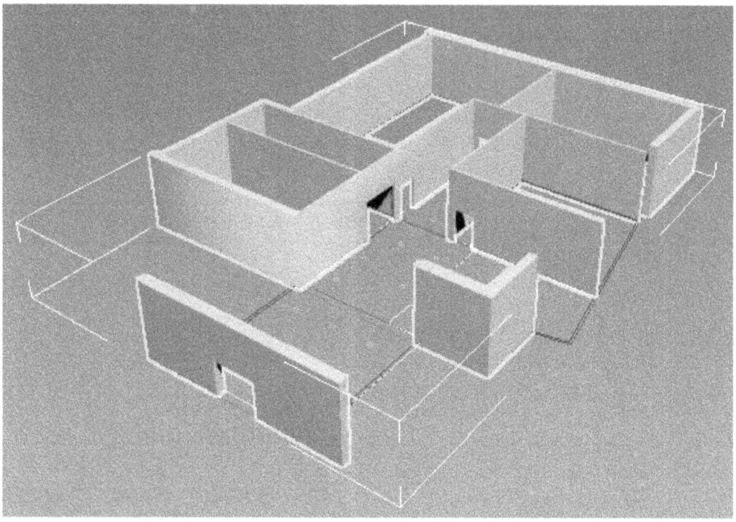

Figure 5–43

7. Click **Start Picking** to end the ProBoolean operation.

8. The ProBoolean operation has the ability to change the way the faces are built in the object using the Quadrilateral Tessellation function. In the Layer Explorer, with the **VIZ-1-Walls** highlighted, right-click on **VIZ-1-Walls** and select **Properties**. In the Object Properties dialog box, verify that the *Name* displays as **Layer:VIZ-1-Walls**. In the *Display Properties* area, click **By Layer** to toggle it to **By Object**. Clear **Edges Only** and click **OK**.

9. Press <F4> to display the edges of the newly created faces, as shown in Figure 5–44. Note the way long triangular faces are created on some of the walls.

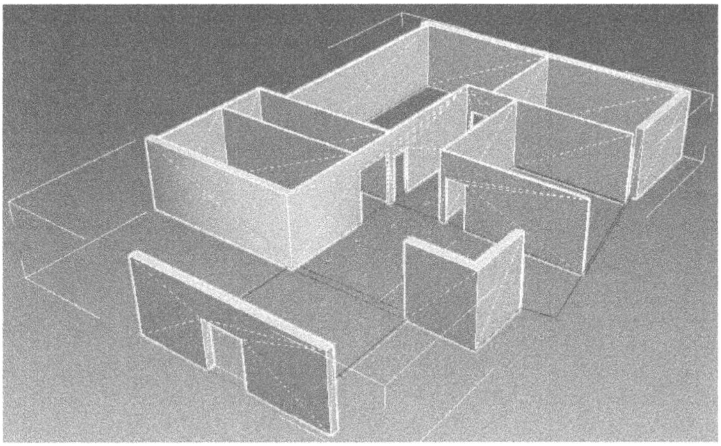

Figure 5–44

10. In the Command Panel>Modify panel (), note that the **ProBoolean** is displayed in the Modifier Stack. Expand the Advanced Options rollout (collapse Pick Boolean and Parameters rollouts). In the *Quadrilateral Tessellation* area, select **Make Quadrilaterals**, as shown in Figure 5–45. Note how the geometry has changed. There are no long triangular faces, as shown on the right in Figure 5–46.

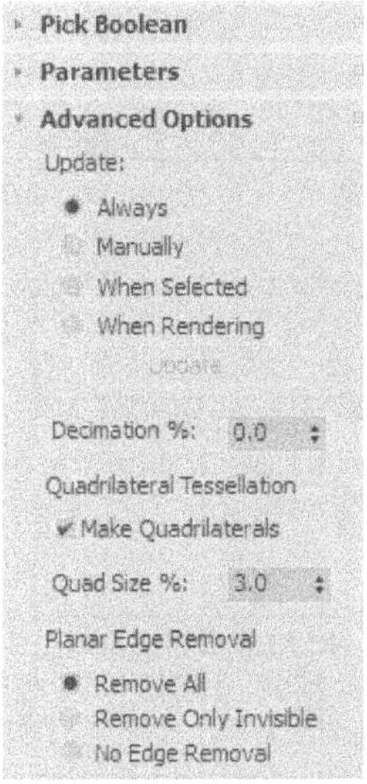

Figure 5–45

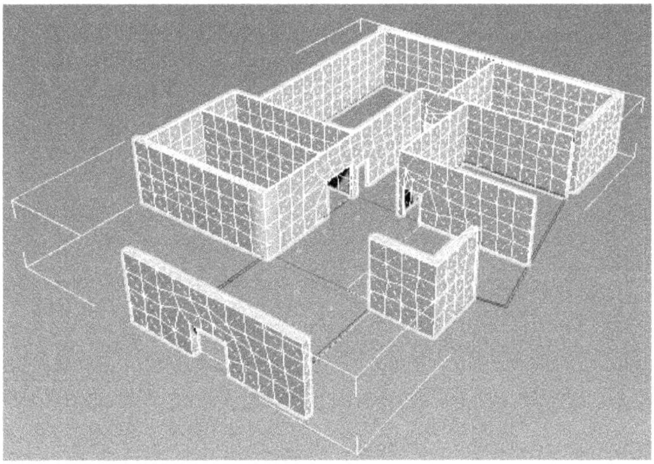

Figure 5–46

11. Increase the *Quad Size %* to **10.0**. This modifies the geometry so that the polygons are bigger, as shown in Figure 5–47.

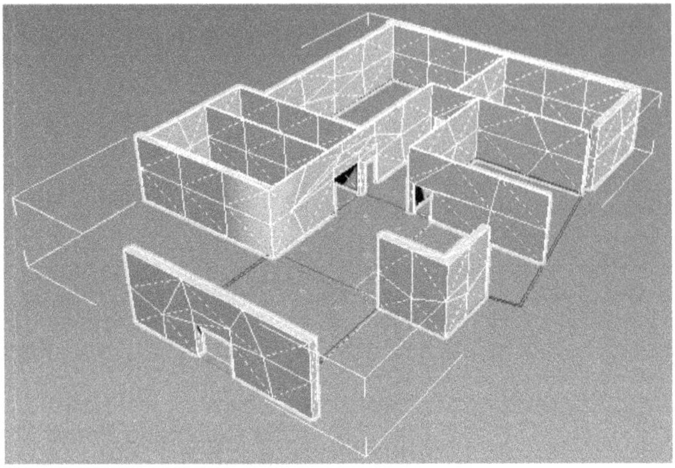

Figure 5–47

12. You can collapse the **ProBoolean** to a simple mesh. In the Modifier Stack, right-click on **ProBoolean** and select **Editable Poly**.

13. Save your work as **MySpline Walls Bound.max**.

Hint: Controlling Edge Line Visibility

After a Boolean or other complex operation, there might be missing or unnecessary edge lines in a wireframe or default shading viewport rendering mode. To easily read the geometry on the screen, only certain edges across your 3D object are visible.

To display the edges, right-click on the object and select **Object Properties**. In the *Display Properties* area, clear **Edges Only**. The **Edges Only** is available in **By Object**. Click **By Layer** to change it to **By Object**.

Alternatively, in the Modify panel, add an **Edit Mesh** modifier to your object and select **Edge** Sub-object mode. In the **Edit** menu, select **Select All**. In the Surface Properties rollout, click **Invisible** to make all edges invisible. Click **Auto Edge** to show only the edges with 24°+ separation. To get required results on curved objects (including curved walls), you might have to enter different separation angles.

5.6 Using Snaps for Precision

Snaps enable you to create, move, rotate, and scale objects with precision and are activated using the buttons in the Main Toolbar, as shown in Figure 5–48. Press <S> to toggle Snaps on and off while drawing lines, creating primitives, or transforming objects.

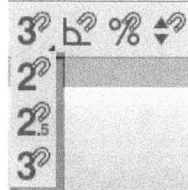

Figure 5–48

The available Toggle options are described as follows:

	3D Snap: This mode snaps to objects in 3D. It is the default option.
	2.5D Snap: This mode snaps to a projection of the selected point at elevation 0 on the current grid.
	2D Snap: This mode enables you to snap to points at elevation 0 on the current grid.
	Angle Snap: This mode enables you to set rotational values (such as a Rotate Transform amount) in angle increments.
	Percent Snap: This mode enables percentile-based values (such as a Scale Transform amount) in percent increments (5%, 10%, etc.).
	Spinner Snap: This mode causes all spinner controls to increment at a set value with a single click. Transform and a host of parameter values can be adjusted by spinners ( ).

- Snap settings, such as the increment values for angle and percent snap, can be set in the *Options* tab of the Grid and Snap Settings dialog box, as shown in Figure 5–49. The dialog box can be accessed by right-clicking on **2D**, **2.5D**, **3D**, **Angle**, or **Percent Snap**, from **Tools>Grids and Snaps>Grid and Snap Settings**, or by holding <Shift> and right-clicking anywhere in the viewport.

- The active snaps are selected in the *Snaps* tab of the Grid and Snap Settings dialog box, as shown in Figure 5–50.

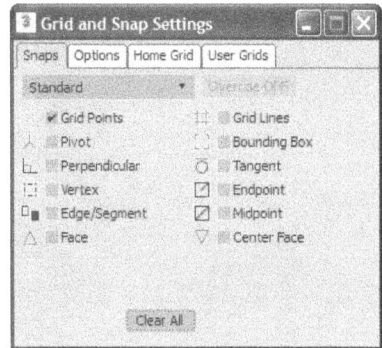

Figure 5–49   **Figure 5–50**

*Right-click on empty space in the Main Toolbar and select **Snaps** in the menu to open the Snaps toolbar.*

- You can activate snaps by selecting buttons in the Snaps toolbar (hidden by default), as shown in Figure 5–51.

Figure 5–51

- You can also activate snaps in the **Snaps** quad menu (hold <Shift>, right-click anywhere in the viewport, and select **Standard**, as shown in Figure 5–52.

Figure 5–52

- The toolbar contains buttons for the most common snap settings. These are described as follows:

	Grid Points: Snaps to grid intersections.
	Pivot: Snaps to the pivot point of an object.
	Vertex: Snaps to vertices on splines, meshes, or similar geometry.
	Endpoint: Snaps to the vertices at the end of a spline segment, mesh edge, or similar geometry. Similar to Vertex except that not all vertices are at the endpoints of spline segments and mesh edges.
	Midpoint: Snaps to the middle of spline segments, mesh edges, or similar geometry.
	Edge/Segment: Snaps to anywhere along spline segments, mesh edges, or similar geometry.
	Face: Snaps anywhere on the surface of a face.
	Snap to Frozen Objects: Enables other snaps to reference frozen objects.
	Snaps Use Axis Constraints: Forces result along the selected axis constraints set in the Axis Constraints toolbar.

- The following additional snaps are available in the Snap and Grid Settings dialog box and the **Snaps** quad menu.

Grid Lines	Snaps to anywhere along a grid line.
Bounding Box	Snaps to the corners of an object's bounding box.
Perpendicular	Snaps perpendicularly to a spline segment.
Tangent:	Snaps tangent to a curved spline segment.
Center Face	Snaps to the center of triangular faces.

By default, these snapping methods are not directly available in the software interface and are required to be added to the toolbar.

- The two additional snap functions available in the Autodesk 3ds Max software are described as follows:

Ortho Snapping: Forces a transform in the horizontal or vertical directions based on the active grid.

Polar Snapping: Forces results to the angle increment set in the Grid and Snap Settings dialog box.

Hint: Adding Snapping modes to toolbar

1. Extend the Snaps toolbar by dragging either edge.
2. Open the Customize User Interface dialog box>*Toolbars* tab (**Customize>Customize User Interface**).
3. Select **Ortho Snapping Mode/ Polar Snapping Mode in** the Action list.
4. Drag the snap mode into the Snaps toolbar.

Hint: Snap to XRef Objects

You can snap to XRef objects just like any other object. In earlier versions, XRef objects were displayed in the scene, but were not recognized by the snap functions.

Practice 5e

Creating a Door with Snaps

Learning Objective

*   Create doors at precise locations using snaps.

Estimated time for completion: 10 minutes

In this practice you will add a door to an opening, using snaps to position it precisely.

You must set the paths to locate the External files and Xrefs used in the practice. If you have not done this already, return to **Chapter 1: Introduction to Autodesk 3ds Max** and complete Task 1 to Task 3 in **Practice 1a: Organizing Folders and Working with the Interface**. You only have to set the user paths once.

*If a dialog box opens prompting you about a Mismatch, click **OK** to accept the default values.*

1. Reset the scene and open **Creating a Door.max**.
    *   The scene contains extruded walls with openings and extruded carpet and tile areas. A camera has also been added.

2. Maximize the **Perspective** viewport.

3. In a **Perspective** viewport, use 🔍 (Zoom) and 🌐 (Orbit) to display the west side of the model (where the space for the outer door is located), as shown in Figure 5–53. Verify that the **Perspective** viewport displays as Default **Shading with Edged Faces**.

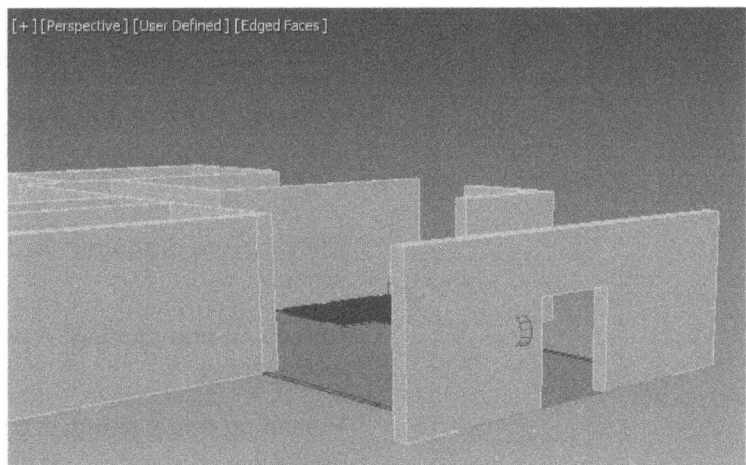

[+] [Perspective] [User Defined] [Edged Faces]

Figure 5–53

4. Using ⊙ (Zoom) and ✋ (Pan), zoom into the doorway opening (as shown in Figure 5–54) to display the points for snapping.

Figure 5–54

5. In the Main Toolbar, click ③ (3D Snaps) to activate it. In the Command Panel, verify that Create panel> ● (Geometry) is open. In the Standard Primitives drop-down list, select **Doors**.

Hint: Create Window and Door Objects

By default, Autodesk 3ds Max Doors and Windows are created by:

- **Clicking and dragging:** To define the width of the door/window.

- **Releasing and picking:** A point to define the depth of the wall opening.

- **Releasing and picking:** A point to define the height of the opening.

---

6. In the Object Type rollout, click **Pivot** to start the door creation process, as shown in Figure 5–55.

*You can also press <Shift> and right-click to open the **Snaps** quad menu and select **Standard>Endpoint**.*

7. Open the Snaps toolbar, and click  (Snap to Endpoint Toggle), as shown in Figure 5–56.

Figure 5–55   **Figure 5–56**

8. Hover the cursor at the bottom left corner of the door opening. Note that when the cursor hovers over the endpoint (corner), it snaps to that point and a small yellow square (endpoint marker) displays, as shown in Figure 5–57.

Figure 5–57

9. Click and hold at this point and then while still holding, drag the cursor over to the lower right corner. Once it snaps to the lower right corner (as shown in Figure 5–58), release the mouse button to define the width of the door.

   - If you have difficulty with this, change the orientation of the **Perspective** viewport, as shown below. You might also want to change to Wireframe display.

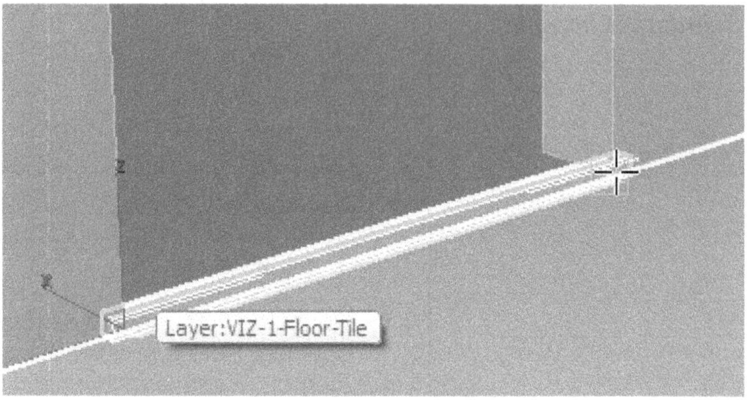

Figure 5–58

10. Move the cursor to the back corner of the door opening and click (not click and drag) to define the depth of the opening, as shown in Figure 5–59.

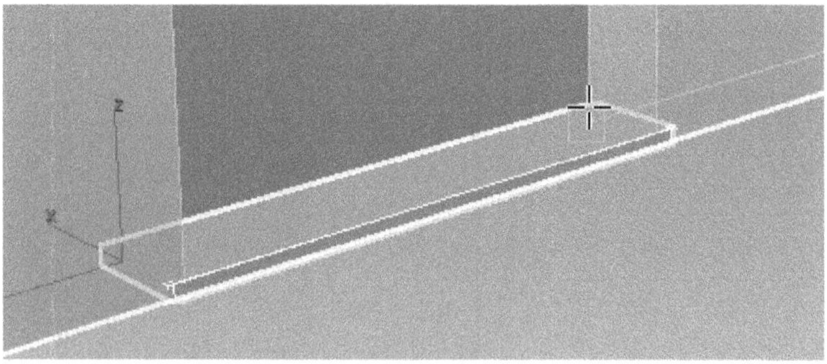

Figure 5–59

11. Move the cursor to the upper right corner of the door opening and click (not click and drag) to define the height, as shown in Figure 5–60. Sometimes this is difficult to do, depending on the angle of your view. You can toggle off the Snap by pressing <S>, then adjust the height using the Parameters rollout.

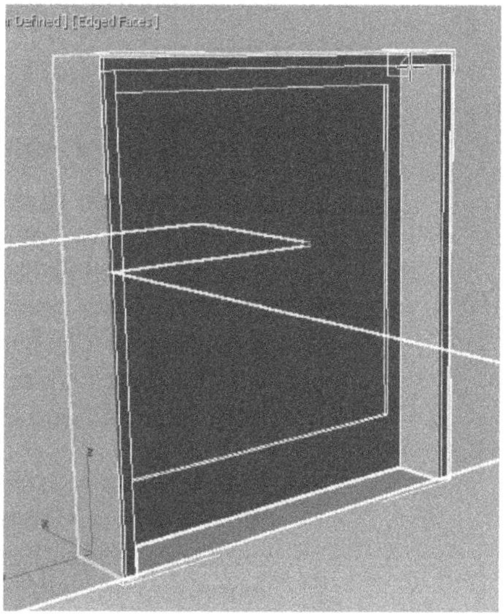

Figure 5–60

12. With the door still selected, in the Command Panel, select the

Modify panel (). In the Parameters rollout, select **Double Doors**. Set the *Open* angle to **45°**. In the Leaf Parameters rollout, in the *Panels* area, select **Beveled**. Note that in the viewport, the door will change to double doors with beveled panels and will be open at a **45°** angle, as shown in Figure 5–61.

Figure 5–61

13. Set the *Open* angle to **0°** to display the panels as closed.

14. Save your work as **MyCreating a Door.max**.

Hint: Holes in Walls using Window and Door Objects

When you use Autodesk 3ds Max Wall objects combined with Window or Door objects, you can automatically create holes for the doors and windows using snaps to align them in place. If you create the door or window away from the wall, you can move it so it intersects with the wall. Use **Select and Link** to link the door or window to the wall to automatically create the hole. You can use Edge snap to align the doors with the walls.

The advantage is that if you move the door or window, the hole moves with it. However, this functionality only works when you create Autodesk 3ds Max wall objects and it is not available when you are extruding linked geometry.

5.7 The Sweep Modifier

The Sweep modifier is a simple and effective option to create 3D geometry based on a 2D section that follows a series of spline segment paths.

- This modifier can create 3D pipe networks, curbing, moldings, and similar types of geometry, very quickly.

- Sweeps are created by adding the Sweep modifier to the path, followed by adjusting cross-section settings and other parameters in the Modify panel.

- You can select a predefined cross-section shape such as, boxes, pipes, tees, and angles, or you can use a custom shape.

- Although this functionality is also available through the Loft compound object, the Sweep modifier is easier to configure.

To use the Sweep modifier, select a spline and then in the Modify panel (), select **Sweep** from the Modifier List. Figure 5–62 shows an example of a wall baseboard created using the Sweep modifier.

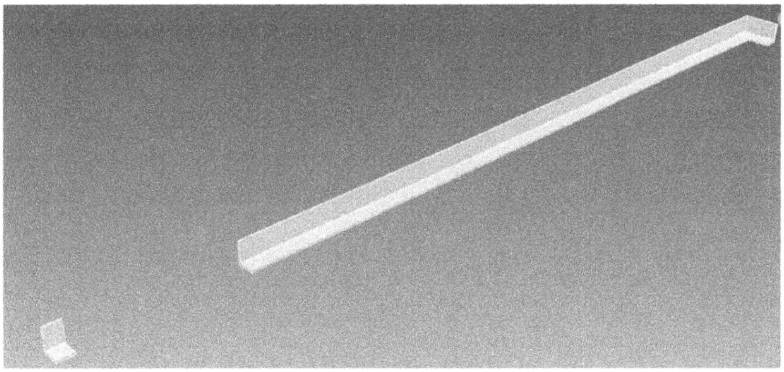

Figure 5–62

Sweep Parameters

Section Type

In the Section Type rollout, you can select the type of profile that you want to sweep along the spline segments.

- If you selected **Use Built-In Section**, a list of precreated cross-sections is available as your profile, as shown in Figure 5–63. The **Angle** is the default cross-section.

Figure 5–63

- You can select **Use Custom Section** to use a custom shapes as your section. You can either create your section in the current scene or obtain it from another .MAX file.

Interpolation

In the Interpolation rollout, you can control the smoothness of the cross-section by adding or removing vertices.

- Steps can be set to **0** for cross-section shapes that have sharp edges (no curves). Otherwise this value should be kept low to reduce complexity. The two options available are described as follows:

Optimize	Groups the supplemented vertices closer to the corners rather than evenly along the shape.
Adaptive	Tessellates (break into segments) curves in the section shape. Select Adaptive results in a wireframe rendering mode to reduce complexity

Parameters

In the Parameters rollout, you can control the size and shape of the predefined cross-sections.

Sweep Parameters

In the Sweep Parameters rollout, you can control the placement and orientation of the cross-section shape along the path object.

- If a sweep result is backwards or upside down, use the two mirroring options to correct it. The options available are described as follows:

Offset	This option enables you to shift the horizontal and vertical position of the sweep geometry away from the spline path
Angle	This options rotates the section relative to the plane. The spline path is drawn as defined by its pivot point.
Smooth Section/ Smooth Path	Selecting these options enables you to make the object smooth, even if the path object or shape are not smooth. In the case of the swept wall baseboard, the section is smoothed to make the cross-section display as filleted, not because the baseboard follows the angled corners of the wall.
Pivot Alignment	This options enables you to anchor the cross-section shape to the path based on the shape's pivot point.
Banking	This options rotates a cross-section shape assigned to a 3D path, similar to an airplane rolling during a turn

Practice 5f

Estimated time for completion:15 minutes

*If a dialog box opens prompting you about a Mismatch, click **OK** to accept the default values.*

*You can also right-click in the viewport and select **Isolate Selection** or press <Alt>+<Q> to activate the Isolate Selection.*

Sweeping the Wall Baseboard

Practice Objective

- Create a wall baseboard by extruding a pre-created cross-section along a selected spline.

In this practice you will create a vinyl baseboard object around the walls using the **Sweep** modifier.

You must set the paths to locate the External files and Xrefs used in the practice. If you have not done this already, return to **Chapter 1: Introduction to Autodesk 3ds Max** and complete Task 1 to Task 3 in **Practice 1a: Organizing Folders and Working with the Interface**. You only have to set the user paths once.

Task 1 - Sweep the path.

1. Open **Sweep Modifier.max**.
   - The scene contains the extruded walls and main door in the closed position. A camera has also been added.

2. Open the Layer Explorer (Main Toolbar> ▤ (Layer Explorer). Select and right-click on **VIZ-1-Floor Baseboard Path**. In the menu, select **Select Child Nodes**. This layer contains a series of lines and polylines that define the base of the wall with gaps at the openings. Close the Layer Explorer.

3. In the Status Bar, click ⊡ (Isolate Selection Toggle) to only display the selected sweep path (2D line). Click anywhere in the **Perspective** viewport to clear the selection. Zoom in so that the path (lines) are displayed as shown in Figure 5–64.

Figure 5–64

4. In the **Perspective** viewport, click on the 2D line to select it.

You can also create a custom profile to be swept along the sweep spline.

5. In the Command Panel, select the Modify panel ([icon]). The name **VIZ-1-Floor Baseboard Path** is displayed. In the Modifier List, select **Sweep**. The **Sweep** modifier displays in the Modifier Stack. In the **Perspective** viewport, zoom in on the left side baseboard. Note that the lines have extruded along an angled cross-section, as shown in Figure 5–65. The shape of the extrusion depends on the selected *Built In Selection* in the Section Type rollout. The **Angle** type is the default selection, as shown in Figure 5–66.

Figure 5–65

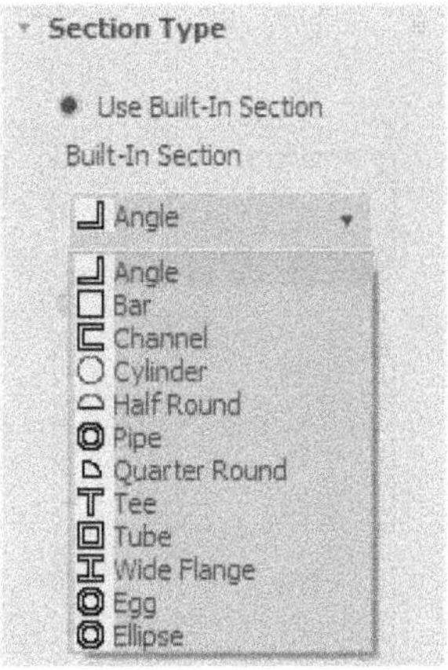

Figure 5–66

6. In the Interpolation rollout, set *Steps* to **0**. (Since all of the wall corners are square, there are no curves required to interpolate along the path.)

7. In the Parameters rollout, set the values shown in Figure 5–67. This shape is meant to create a baseboard with minimal detail. In the viewport, note how the baseboard detail changes.

8. The angle is still facing outward (in the wrong direction). In the Sweep Parameters rollout, select **Mirror on XZ Plane** to reverse the angle face. Clear **Smooth Path** (all of the corners are square and should not display as rounded). Anchor the

   Pivot Alignment option by clicking ⌐ in the lower right corner. This option creates the 3D geometry object by sweeping the lower left corner of the baseboard cross-section along the baseboard path. Select **Gen. Mapping Coords.** and **Real-World Map Size**, as shown in Figure 5–68.

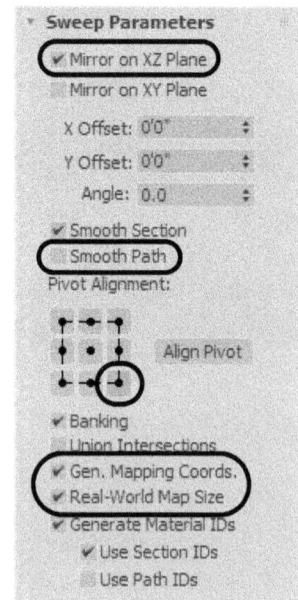

Figure 5–67   Figure 5–68

9. In the Status Bar, click ⌐⌐ (Isolate Selection Toggle) again to clear it. The walls and other geometry are now displayed.

10. In the **Front** viewport, select the **Front** Point of View label and select **Cameras>Camera002-Door**. This displays the door from the inside. Select the **Visual Style** label and select **Default Shading** and **Edged Faces**. Note that the baseboard runs along the entire wall, including the door, as shown in Figure 5–69.

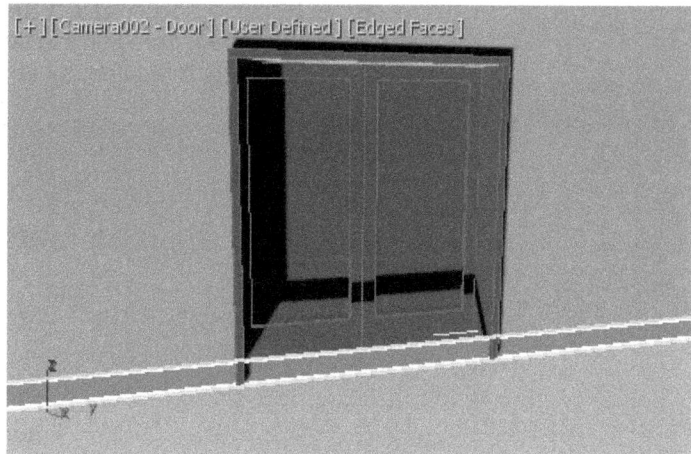

Figure 5–69

Task 2 - Modify the path.

1. Maximize the **Camera002-Door** viewport.

2. Click anywhere on the baseboard to select it. In the Modify
   panel ( ), verify that *Name* displays **Layer:VIZ-1-Floor Baseboard Path**.

3. In the Modifier Stack, in Editable Spline, select **Vertex**. In the viewport, note that the baseboard is not displayed because you have selected an option before the **Sweep** modifier.

4. In the Geometry rollout, click **Refine**.

5. Verify that snap is cleared. In the viewport, click on the spline to place a vertex on either side and outside of the door frame, as shown in Figure 5–70. Once the two vertices have been placed, click **Refine** again to clear it.

Figure 5–70

6. In Editable Spline, select **Segment**. In the viewport, click on the segment between the two vertices, in front of the door. It displays as a red line, as shown in Figure 5–71.

Figure 5–71

7. With the segment selected, press <Delete> to remove the segment.

8. In the Modifier Stack, select **Sweep**. In the viewport, note that the baseboard has been modified and does not pass in front of the door, as shown in Figure 5–72.

Figure 5–72

9. Maximize to open the four viewports display.

10. In the Application Menu, expand **Import**, and select **Merge**. In the Merge File dialog box, select **Interior Furnishings and Detail.max**. Click **Open**. In the Merge dialog box, click **All** at the bottom left to select all of the objects and click **OK**.

11. In the **Perspective** viewport, select the **Perspective** Point of View Viewport label and select **Cameras>Camera001 – Lobby1**. This changes the display to look through the newly merged **Camera – Lobby1**, as shown in Figure 5–73.

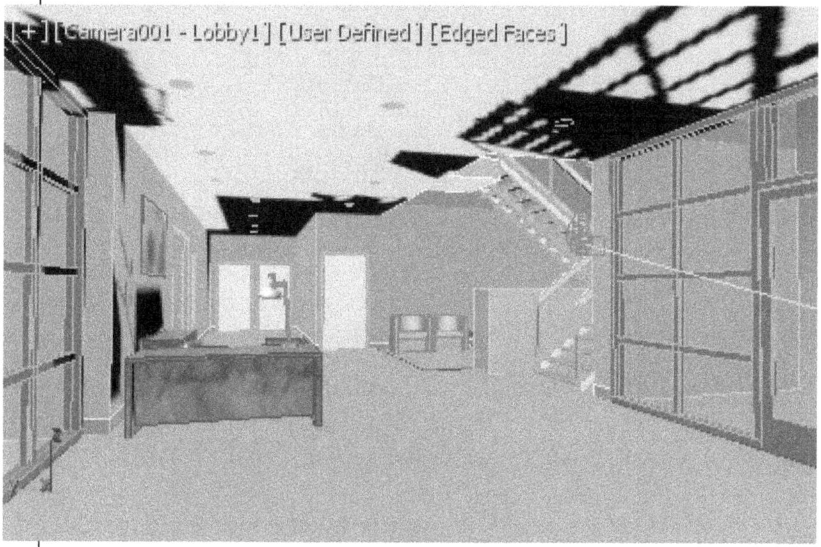

Figure 5–73

12. Select **Edit>Select None** to clear the object selection.

- Note that the desk, chairs, and other furnishings are AutoCAD Architecture 3D blocks. The curtain walls, stairs, and doors are examples of architectural objects that can be created. Save your work as **MySweep Modifier.max**.

Hint: Precreated Objects

Instead of modeling all of your scene content from scratch, look for royalty-free or low-cost objects posted on the Internet. Consider 3D blocks from other software, such as AutoCAD Architecture, Autodesk Revit, AutoCAD Civil 3D, or directly from manufacturer's web sites.

Chapter Review Questions

1. While editing a spline at the vertex sub-object level, which tool enables you to manipulate the handles on one side of the curve separately from the other handle?

   a. **Bezier**

   b. **Bezier Corner**

   c. **Smooth**

   d. **Smooth Corner**

2. To combine shapes using the 2D Boolean operations, which sub-object level in the **Edit Spline** modifier should be selected?

   a. Vertex

   b. Segment

   c. Spline

3. Which **Sweep** modifier option in the Sweep Parameters rollout rotates a cross-section shape assigned to a 3D path?

   a. **Offset**

   b. **Angle**

   c. **Banking**

   d. **Pivot Alignment**

4. Which of the following Snap mode enables you to snap to points at elevation **0** on the current grid?

   a. (Angle Snap)

   b. (3D Snap)

   c. (2.5D Snap)

   d. (2D Snap)

5. You cannot snap to XRef objects as with any other object because the XRef objects are not recognized by the snap functions.

   a. True

   b. False

Command Summary

Button	Command	Location
3	3D Snap	• **Main Toolbar:** Snaps flyout
2.5	2.5D Snap	• **Main Toolbar:** Snaps flyout
2	2D Snap	• **Main Toolbar:** Snaps flyout
	Angle Snap	• **Main Toolbar**
	Isolate Selection	• **Status Bar** • **Keyboard:** <Alt>+<Q>
	Manage Layers	• **Main Toolbar** • **Layers Toolbar**
N/A	Merge	• **Application Menu:** Import
	Offset Mode	• **Status Bar**
	Percent Snap	• **Main Toolbar**
	Shapes	• **Command Panel:** *Create* panel • **Create:** Shapes
	Snap to Edge/ Segment	• **Snaps Toolbar**
	Snap to Endpoint	• **Snaps Toolbar**
	Snap to Frozen Objects	• **Snaps Toolbar**
	Snap to Grid Point	• **Snaps Toolbar**
	Snap to Midpoint	• **Snaps Toolbar**
	Snap to Pivot	• **Snaps Toolbar**
	Snap to Vertex	• **Snaps Toolbar**
	Snaps use Axis Constraints	• **Snaps Toolbar**

Chapter
6

Materials

To create a realistic visualization, materials are used to more accurately represent the model as a realistic real-world design. The Autodesk® 3ds Max® software provides material libraries that can be used to assign materials to objects in a scene or to create and customize materials. Materials control such attributes as color, texture, transparency, and a host of other physical properties that you can adjust to create a realistic representation of the model.

Learning Objectives in this Chapter

- Understand the role of materials and maps in visualization.
- Control the various attributes of a material using various shaders, components, and maps.
- Display and manage all of the materials used in a scene using the Material Explorer.
- Use various types of Standard materials and control the parameters of the material shaders.
- Assign bitmaps or procedural maps to replace the shader parameters in materials.
- Control transparency, embossed or pitted appearance, glass or mirror effect on objects using various mapping techniques.
- Understand the various types of mental ray materials and control their various attributes.

6.1 Understanding Materials and Maps

Introduction to Materials

Materials can be used to create believable visualizations and to dress up geometry so that it resembles objects in the real world. Materials control how light interacts with surfaces in 3D models. If an object is shiny it reflects the light, however, if transparency is applied, the light passes through the object.

- Materials use Maps to paint the surfaces with all types of textures to resemble the actual construction materials for your design.

- Different material types use different material shaders to generate their work. Shaders are algorithms that create the image. Each shader has its own set of parameters.

In the 3D visualization process, to create an image in the viewport or in a image file, a *renderer* is employed. The viewport display uses an interactive viewport renderer however the image is created using an *image* (production) renderer. The renderer determines what the pixel's RGB (red, green, blue) values are in the image based on the material assignments.

Materials and Renderers in the Autodesk 3ds Max software

In the Autodesk 3ds Max software, you can use the scanline, quicksilver, iray renderer, or mental ray renderers as image renderers.

- The viewport renderer can use Nitrous Direct 3D 11 (default), Nitrous Direct3D 9, Nitrous Software, Legacy Direct3D, or Legacy OpenGL graphics drivers to create the real-time interactive display.

- The standard material type is associated with the Autodesk 3ds Max scanline renderer.

- mental ray materials (*Autodesk Material Library/Arch & Design* materials) work with the mental ray renderer.

Materials are deeply interconnected with the renderers. The rendering process is similar for any material type using any renderer. The viewport provides a frame around the image and the output resolution determines the number of pixels to be created in that frame. The renderer then examines the geometry in the scene, first looking at the face normals, removing the faces whose normals face away from the camera (face normals are directional vectors perpendicular to the surface of the face). The remaining faces are z-sorted, the faces in front covering up the ones further away.

- Once the faces are determined, the color, transparency, shininess, texture, reflection, bumpiness, and other values are defined based on the material type, shaders, and map channels.

- The visible faces are calculated using the UVW mapping coordinates and the scene illumination. This determines RGB values, which are applied to the pixels in the image.

Material Components

Materials have several fundamental components. Standard materials have channels that determine the color applied in the calculation based on the lighting interaction. The components available are described as follows:

- The *Diffuse* channel represents those faces that are receiving illumination.

- The *Ambient* channel paints the faces that are in darkness, and it contributes color to all faces in the scene.

- The *Specular* channel determines color based on shininess and lighting information.

- The Shininess is controlled by various parameters, such as **Specularity** and **Glossiness**. Shininess also plays a part in reflection and refraction.

- A Transparency quality is determined by *opacity* values, which can have advanced features such as *falloff* and *additive* or subtractive behavior.

- Materials are defined by maps and other physical properties (diffuse, ambient, shininess, etc.).

Maps

Maps are the key components when working with materials. Maps are based on either 2D image files (bitmaps) or are formula-based, computer-generated images called procedural maps. Some maps can be configured as composites or adjustments to other maps.

- Materials can include multiple maps to serve different purposes.

- Map also serve in other roles, such as an environment background or a lighting projection (a gobo).

When a material containing a map is applied to an object, mapping coordinates are required for the software to render correctly.

- Maps cannot be applied directly to objects in a scene; instead, they are assigned to materials. These materials are then directly applied to objects, as shown in Figure 6–1.

Figure 6–1

- Two of the most commonly used maps types are **diffuse color** and **bump**.

Diffuse Color	Defines the color of objects under normal lighting.
	• Digital or scanned photographs can be used as Diffuse Color maps.
	• The figure below is a brick image map (left) and a rendering of an object with a brick material that uses it (right).

Bump maps	Make objects appear to have texture without modifying object geometry.
	• Bump maps are used to describe indentations, relief, and roughness.
	• In bump maps the lighter-colored areas display projected away from the surface while the darker areas display recessed.
	• The figure below displays a brick bump map (left) and a rendering of an object with a brick material that uses it (right).
	• You can apply both the diffuse and bump map to a single object.

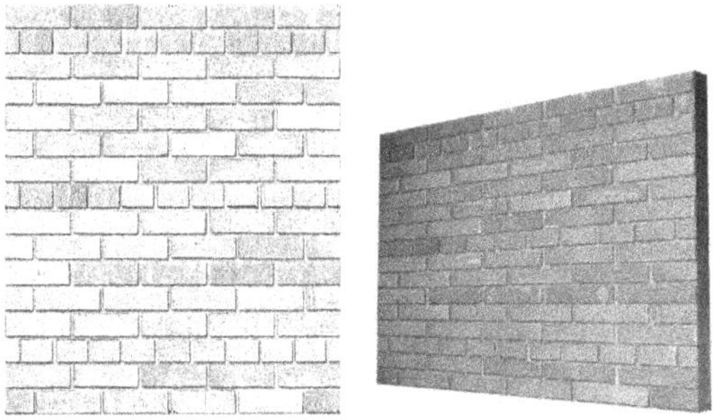

- In addition to these two map types, the Autodesk 3ds Max software can use maps to control many different material parameters that might vary across a surface, including shininess, transparency, and more.

6.2 Managing Materials

Materials are managed through the Material Editor (Slate or Compact). The Slate Material Editor has the Material/Map Browser included with it whereas the Compact Material Editor has an option for accessing the Material/Map Browser.

- Use the Slate Material Editor to design and build materials.

- Use the Compact Material Editor to apply existing materials.

Slate Material Editor Interface

The Slate Material Editor is a graphical interface for listing, creating, modifying, and assigning different kinds of materials. It enables you to graphically create and modify complex materials by wiring the maps and materials to different channels of the parent material. It also enables you to edit and modify the parameters of already created materials. In the Main Toolbar, in the Material flyout, use 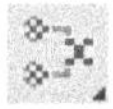 (Slate Material Editor) to open the Slate Material Editor, as shown in Figure 6–2.

You can also select **Rendering>Material Editor>Slate Material Editor**. *Pressing <M> opens the last material editor that was used.*

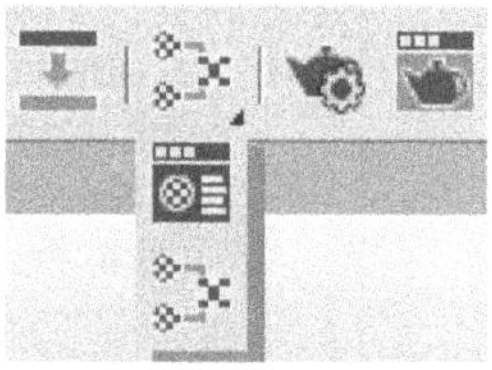

Figure 6–2

The interface of the Slate Material Editor has the following main areas:

Material/Map Browser

The Material/Map Browser area (shown in Figure 6–3) contains an extensive list of predefined materials and maps. You can use the predefined materials directly or as a base for modifying them to get the required material effect.

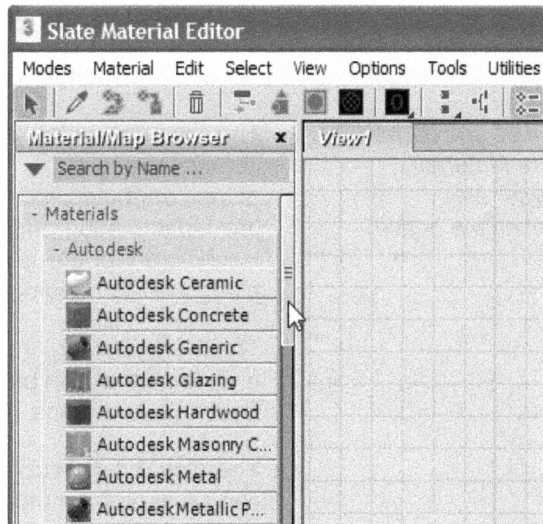

Figure 6–3

You can also open the Material/Map Browser independent of the Material Editor by selecting **Rendering> Material/Map Browser** in the menu bar.

- The Browser displays by default, but you can temporarily close it by clicking ✖ in the title bar. You can open it by selecting **Tools>Material/Map Browser** in the Slate Material Editor's menu bar (as shown in Figure 6–4) or by pressing <O> when the Slate Material Editor is the active window.

- At the top of the Material/Map Browser, click ▼ to open the drop-down list (options menu), as shown in Figure 6–5. It contains options that enable you to control the display of the libraries, materials, maps, and other groups of materials. It also enables you to create and manage new custom libraries and groups.

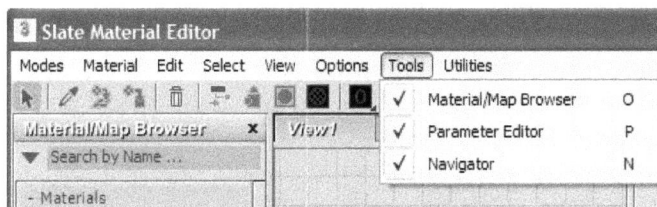

Figure 6–4

Figure 6–5

The materials and maps listed in the Material/Map Browser are dependent on the active renderer.

- The *Search by Name* box enables you to enter the first few characters of the material/map name to display the list of materials/maps that you want to use.

- The materials in the Browser are organized in the form of libraries and groups. The groups are organized on the basis of their attributes such as Maps, Materials, etc and are further divided into subgroups (For example, **Materials>Standard**). Each library or group has a +/- sign, to expand or contract, along with its heading.

- The *Materials* and *Maps* groups contain the type of materials and maps that can be used as templates for creating custom materials and maps.

- The *Controller* group contains the animation controllers that can be used for material animation.

- The Autodesk Material Library contains the mental ray Arch and Design materials and only displays when the active production renderer is set to **NVIDIA iray**, **NVIDIA mental ray**, or **Quicksilver Hardware Renderer**.

- All of the materials used in the scene are listed in the *Scene Materials* group. A solid wedge shaped red band displayed with a scene material name indicates that the **Show Shaded Material In Viewport** option has been selected.

- The materials listed in the Browser are dependent on the type of renderer currently in use. To see all of the materials independent of the renderer, select **Show Incompatible**

  option in the Material/Map Browser drop-down list (click ▼ to open the options menu).

Active View

The Active View is an area in the Slate Material Editor that displays the expanded view of materials with all its elements shown as nodes, as shown in Figure 6–6. You can graphically create and modify complex materials by wiring their nodes together, and further edit their parameters through this view.

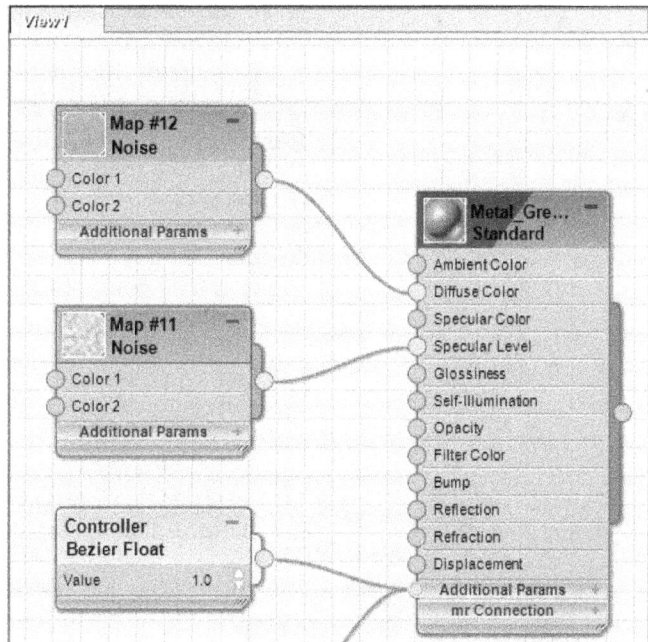

Figure 6–6

You can also double-click on the material in the Map/Material Browser to automatically place it on the View1 sheet.

- To display a material in the active view (*View1*, by default), drag the material from the Map/Material Browser and then drop it on the *View1* sheet. These are called nodes.

- Once the material node is loaded on the active view, the title bar with a preview icon is displayed and the list of various channel slots are listed, as shown in Figure 6–6. You can wire each of these slots to another map or material. On the left side, each node has a number of input sockets (small circles) for each slot. On the right side of each node is a single output socket. These can be wired to the sockets of other material. If a map or material is wired to a channel, the slot displays in green. This material, with its input sockets wired, becomes the parent material and the materials and maps that are wired to the slots become the children. You can further wire the children to other materials to create complex material trees.

- You can also right-click in an empty area of the active view to open a menu containing options for selecting any material/ map/controller listed in the Material/Map Browser.

- The main material node has a blank output socket on the right side that can be used to assign this material to geometry in the viewport. Click and hold the output socket and drag the cursor on to the object. A temporary wire displays indicating that you are assigning the material. Assigning material in this way ignores already selected objects or geometry in the viewport.

- You can use the scroll wheel to zoom in or zoom out on the nodes in the *View1* sheet. Hold the scroll wheel to pan around in the sheet.

- You can also delete wires to cut the connection between the parent material and the child material. To delete a wire, select it and press <Delete>.

- If a white dashed line displays as a border around a node, its Parameter Editor is displayed in the active view.

- The color of the title bar of the node indicates the type of material.

Blue node	Indicates that it is a material.
Green node	Indicates that it is a Map.
Yellow node	Indicates that it is a Controller

- A diagonal line dividing the title bar into two colors (red and blue) indicates that the **Show Shaded Material In Viewport** option is selected for that material.

- Right-clicking on a title bar of a node displays a specific right-click menu containing the options for managing that material or map. The options enable you to control the display and how you want the preview to be displayed on the active sheet. It also enables you to organize the material nodes and their children more efficiently.

- You can select multiple material/map nodes together, then right-click to open the combined menu and use the options for all of the nodes at the same time.

- You can toggle between a large and small material preview icon by double-clicking on the icon in the node title bar.

- The outline of a preview icon indicates whether the material is assigned or not (hot or cold) to objects in the viewport.

	No white boundary around the icon indicates that the material is not used in the scene and is cold.
	Outlined white triangles at the four corners indicate the material is hot and is being used in the scene. Modifying this material interactively displays the modifications in the scene.
	Solid white triangles at the four corners indicate the material is applied to the currently selected object on the scene.

• Additional sheets can be added to the View area by right-clicking on the default *View1* tab and selecting **Create New View**. Using this menu, you can also rename and delete your views. Once multiple sheets exist, you can select the appropriate tab to active it.

Hint: Active View

To organize your working space, it is recommended that you delete any unused materials from the active view. Deleting a material from the active view does not delete the material from the Scene materials list. You can drag and drop (or double-click) the material back to the active view.

• After you have created and applied materials to a scene, the *View* sheets are saved with the .MAX file. When you open the file again, the sheets display the saved material nodes.

Navigator Window

The Navigator window, which displays by default, provides a quick layout of the nodes in the active sheet, as shown in Figure 6–7. It can be used to pan around in the active view by dragging the outlined red box. The colored nodes indicate the same concepts as that of a sheet. A red and blue node indicates that the **Show Map In Viewport** option is selected for that material.

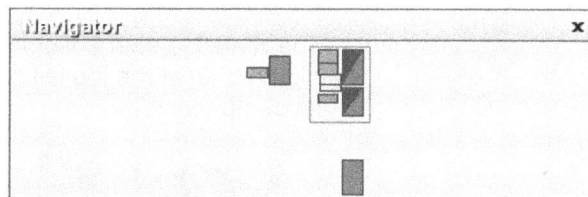

Figure 6–7

Parameter Editor

You can modify a material or a map by adjusting their parameters. Double-click on the material's title bar heading to display the Parameters, as shown in Figure 6–8. A white dashed line border displays around the node indicating that its Parameter Editor is displayed. The parameters are grouped in rollouts and you can click **+** on the rollout name bar to expand the rollout and access its parameters. You can rename the material by entering a new name in the *Name* field of the Parameter Editor.

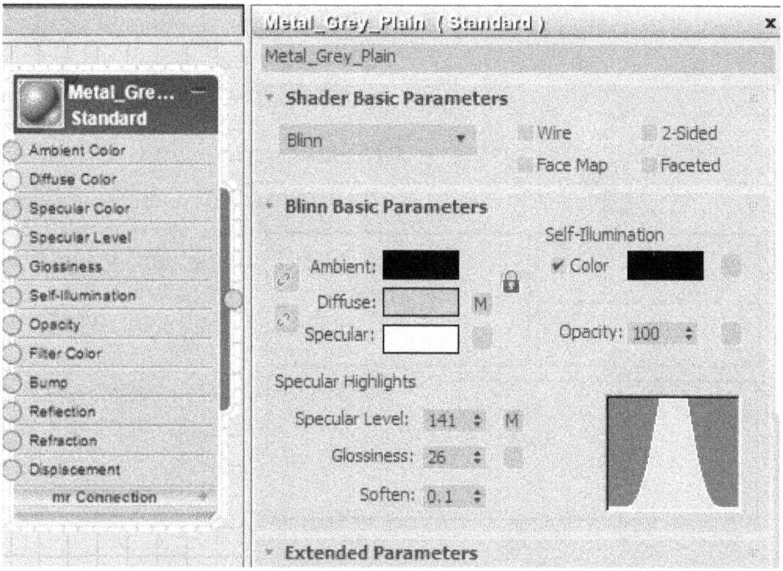

Figure 6–8

Floating the Parameter Editor and hiding the Navigator can help reduce the footprint of the Slate Material Editor on the screen.

- As with any other window, you can move, dock, float, or close the Parameter Editor. To float the Parameter Editor, drag its header outside the Slate Material Editor. To dock it again, double-click on its header.

Toolbar

The Slate Material Editor includes a toolbar (shown in Figure 6–9) at the top left corner of the window and contains the following tools.

Figure 6–9

(Select Tool)	Enables you to select a material node in the Active View. It is the tool that is selected by default.
(Pick Material from Object)	Enables you to pick a material that is assigned to an object in the scene and display it in the active view.
(Put Material to Scene)	Enables you to update objects having an older material whose copy has been edited after it was applied.
(Assign Material to Selection)	Enables you to assign a selected material to selected objects in the viewport.
(Move Children)	Enables you to move the complete material tree when you move the parent material node in the Active View. Clearing this tool, moves the Parent individually and extends the wires as you move the parent
(Show Shaded Material in Viewport)	Enables you to display the maps for the active material. This is helpful when you are modifying the map in the View sheet, you can see the changes interactively in the viewport. You do not have to render to see the map changes.
/ (Lay Out All-Vertical/ Horizontal)	Enables you to organize all of the material nodes and their children in the View sheet either vertically or horizontally.
(Lay Out Children)	Enables you to lay out the children of the currently selected node without changing the position of the parent node.
(Material/Map Browser) (Parameter Editor)	Enable you to control the display of these tools in the Slate Material Editor.
(Select by Material)	Enables you to select objects based on the active material.

Menu Bar

The Slate Material Editor displays a menu bar along the top of the window (shown in Figure 6–10) that contains commands for various actions related to materials.

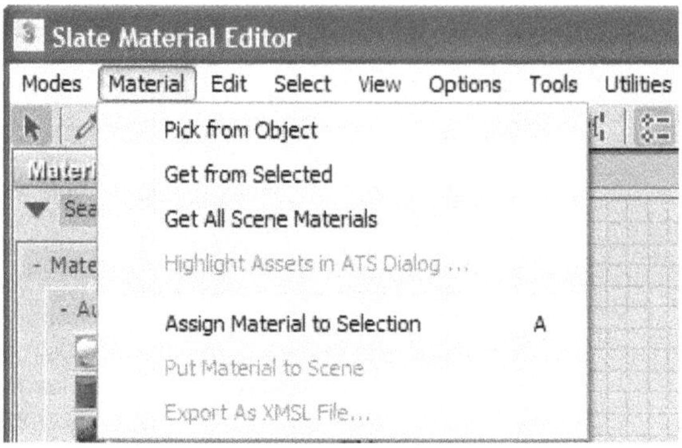

Figure 6–10

Modes	Enables you to toggle between the two editors (Slate and Compact).
Material	Enable you to select a material by picking it from the object in the viewport, by selecting an object in the viewport, or selecting all of the materials used in the scene. You also have the options for assigning materials.
Edit	Enables you to edit the active view and update the preview windows.
Select	Provides different selection options that can be used in the active view.
View	Provides different zoom and pan options and contains options for the layout of the nodes in the active view.
Options	Enables you to further manage the Slate Material Editor.
Tools	Controls the display of the Material/Map Browser, Parameter Editor, and Navigator.
Utilities	Provides the render and object selection options and contains options for managing the materials.

Practice 6a

Introduction to Materials

Practice Objectives

- Load a material library in the Slate Material Editor.
- Create and edit a new material and assign it to objects in the scene.

Estimated time for completion: 20 minutes

In this practice you will assign previously created materials to different objects on the scene. You will then create, edit, and assign new materials to objects in the scene using the Parameter Editor of the Slate Material Editor.

You must set the paths to locate the External files and Xrefs used in the practice. If you have not done this already, return to **Chapter 1: Introduction to Autodesk 3ds Max** and complete Task 1 to Task 3 in **Practice 1a: Organizing Folders and Working with the Interface**. You only have to set the user paths once.

Task 1 - Assigning materials in the Slate Material Editor.

*If a dialog box opens prompting you about a Mismatch, click **OK** to accept the default values.*

1. Open **Intro to Materials and Rendering.max**.
   - The Light pole model is displayed in the viewport.

2. In the Main Toolbar, in the Material flyout, click (Slate Material Editor) to open the Slate Material Editor. Alternatively, you can select **Rendering>Material Editor>Slate Material Editor**.

If you start a new scene file, no materials are listed in the View1 sheet.

3. In the Slate Material Editor, in the *View1* sheet, four materials nodes are displayed, as shown in Figure 6–11. Note that all the materials used in the scene are listed in the *Scene Materials* group (bottom of the list) in the Material/Map Browser.

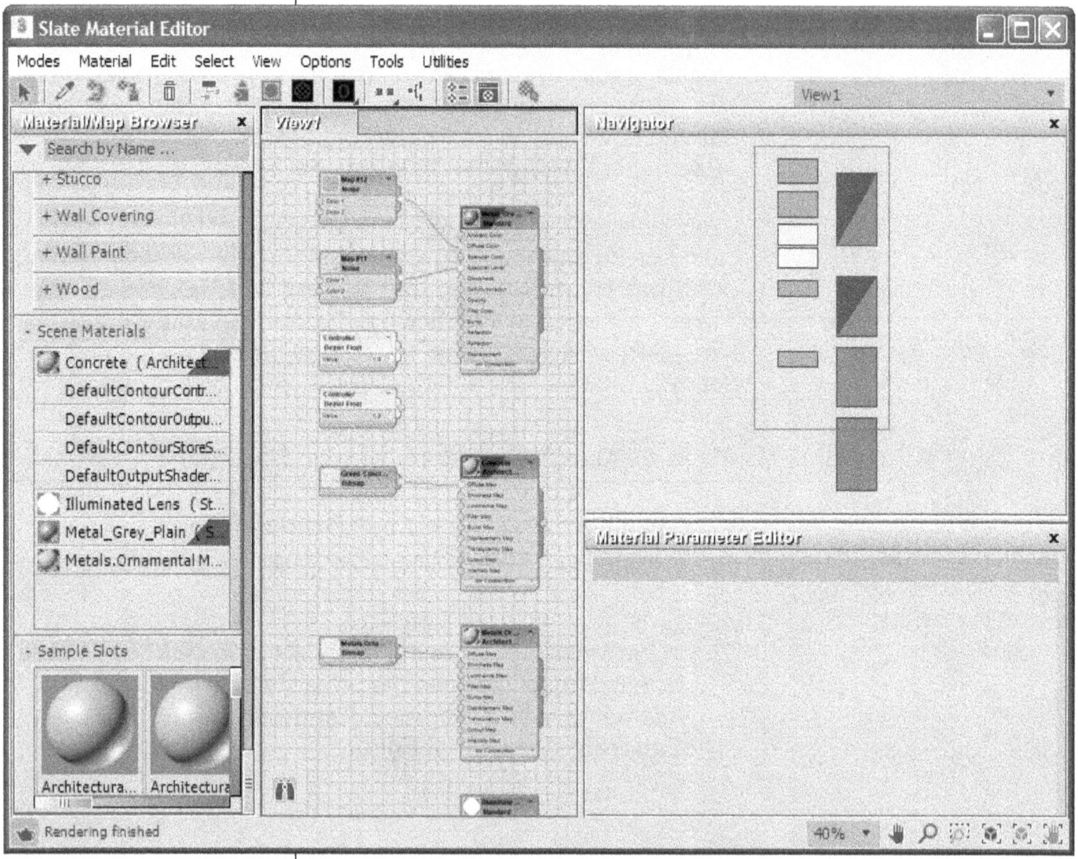

Figure 6–11

A blue node indicates that it is a material, a green node indicates that it is a Map, and a yellow node indicates that it is a Controller.

- A diagonal line dividing the title bar into two colors (red and blue) indicates that the **Show Map In Viewport** option is selected for that material

4. Click in an empty space in the *View1* sheet, and using the scroll wheel on your mouse, zoom into the nodes. Hold the scroll wheel to pan around to see the details of each node. The red bounding box in the *Navigator* area can also be dragged around to quickly access specific areas in the *View1* sheet.

5. Using Zoom and Pan, locate the **Concrete** material (second material node from the top).

You can close the Navigator and Parameter Editor to create more space for displaying the nodes in the active sheet.

6. Move and size the Slate Material Editor in the Drawing window so that you can see both the Material Editor and the model in the viewport window side by side.

7. In the **Concrete** material, click and hold ⬭ (material output socket) on the right side. Drag and drop the **Concrete** material from the *View1* sheet directly to the LP Base object in the viewport window, as shown in Figure 6–12. A temporary wire displays in *View1* indicating that you are assigning the material. (Dragging in this way ignores which objects or geometry are currently selected in the model.) The material is assigned to the object and displays in the viewport.

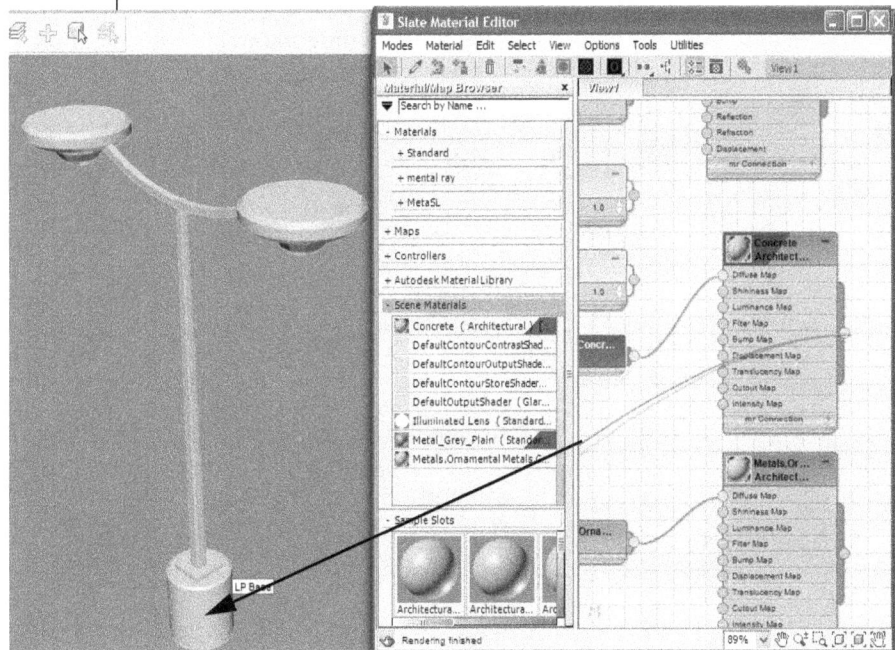

Figure 6–12

Dragging materials in highly complex scenes can be challenging. Instead, you can select objects, select material, and use ⬛ (Assign Material to Selection).

8. Using the Scene Explorer, select the groups **LP Fixture** and **LP Fixture01** (each group contains housing, globe, and mounting arm). You can also select them directly in the viewport.

9. In the Slate Material Editor, in the *View1* sheet, locate **Metal_Grey_Plain** (the first material node). Right-click on the title bar of the material and select **Assign Material to Selection**. The material is applied to all of the objects in the two **LP Fixture** groups.

Hint: Group Objects

To assign a material to individual objects in a group, select the group, select **Group>Open**, and then select the individual object in the group. Then, assign materials to individual parts in the group.

10. Click in the empty space to clear the selection.

11. You can also assign materials directly from the Material/Map Browser. Scroll to the bottom of the Material/Map Browser and expand the *Scene Materials* category, if required, as shown in Figure 6–13. Click and drag **Illuminated Lens** to one of the LP Globe objects in the model. Both globes have **Illuminated Lens** material assigned to them. This method only assigns the material to the object on which you are dropping the material.

Figure 6–13

12. Assign the **Metal_Grey_Plain** material to the LP Base Plate and LP Pole objects using any of the assigning materials method.

13. Orbit and zoom into all objects in the viewport. In the Main Toolbar, click ![Render Production icon] (Render Production) to render the scene. The scene is rendered, as shown in Figure 6–14.

A gradient background was added for visual clarity during rendering.

Figure 6–14

- The globe material was made to look as if it is illuminated, but it does not actually add any light to the scene.

14. Save the file as **MyLightPoleMaterials.max**.

Task 2 - Working with Materials.

When you are starting a new scene or working in an existing scene you will have to create new materials or edit existing materials. In this task, you will be able to use the Slate Material Editor to create and work with materials.

1. The Material/Map Browser of the Slate Material Editor contains an extensive list of predefined materials that you can use directly or use them as a base for creating your custom materials. You can also import your own material library. Scroll through the list of materials that are available in the list.

2. At the top of the Material/Map Browser, click ▼ to open the **Materials/Map Browser Options** menu.

If the material libraries were not installed, there will be no files in the project folder in the \materiallibraries subdirectory.

3. In the **Materials/Map Browser Options** menu, select **Open Material Library**. The Import Material Library dialog box opens in the *materiallibraries* subdirectory. If required, browse to the path under the root installation (usually *C:\Program Files\ Autodesk\3ds Max 2017*) and open the *\materiallibraries* subdirectory.

4. Select and open **AecTemplates.mat**, as shown in Figure 6–15.

   • In the Material/Map Browser, note that a list of materials is added to the top of with **AecTemplates.mat** listed as the title, as shown in Figure 6–16.

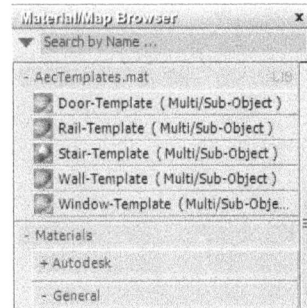

Figure 6–15

Figure 6–16

   • You can remove a library by right-clicking on the category heading and selecting **Close Material Library**. Do not close this library.

Double-clicking on a material in the Material/ Map Browser also displays the material in the View1 sheet, where you can customize the material, as required. Materials do not have to be placed in the View1 sheet unless they are being customized. General materials can be assigned directly from the Material/Map Browser.

5. In the Material/Map Browser, expand the *Materials>General* category. A list of materials is displayed. Right-click on the *General* category and select **Display Group (and Subgroups) As>Medium Icons**. All of the materials in the *General* category now display as thumbnail images. Right-click on the *General* category again and select **Display Group (and Subgroups) As>Icons and Text** to display the materials in the icons and name format.

6. The *View1* sheet already displays the materials used in the scene. To create a new view, right-click on the **View1** label and select **Create New View**, as shown in Figure 6–17.

Figure 6–17

7. Accept the default name, **View2**, and click **OK**. A new empty sheet, *View2,* is added.

*The Autodesk Material Library is not available in the Material/Map Browser when **Scanline Renderer** or **VUE File Renderer** are set as the active renderers.*

8. In the Material/Map Browser, select the *Autodesk Material Library* category.

9. In the list, expand **Metal** and **Steel** to display the materials listed.

10. Double-click on the **Galvanized** material. The material displays as a node on the *View2* sheet, as shown in Figure 6–18.

Figure 6–18

Hint: Add Materials to Sheets

Add materials to sheets if they are going to be modified. If they are simply going to be assigned to an object in the scene, select and drag them directly onto the objects.

---

11. In the *View2* sheet, double-click on the title bar of the **Metal/Steel Galvanized** material.

Note that in the active sheet (View2), the material node is surrounded by a dashed white border, indicating that the Parameter Editor for this material is displayed.

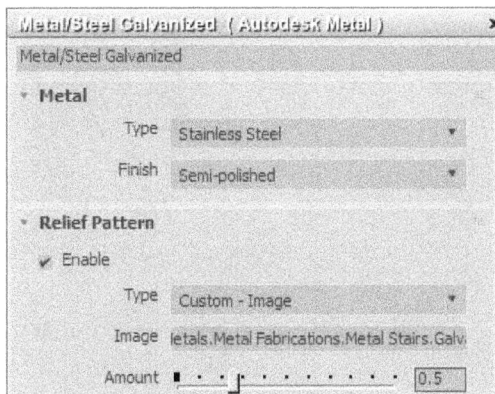

12. The Parameter Editor for this material opens in the Slate Material Editor. In the Relief Pattern rollout, note that *Image* displays the map name as **Metals.Metal Fabrications.Metal Stairs. Galvanized.png**. Use the *Amount* slider or enter the value **0.5** directly in the edit box, as shown in Figure 6–19.

Figure 6–19

Hint: Parameter Editor

You can customize the materials by making changes in the Parameter Editor.

13. In the *View2* sheet, review the preview icon for the material and note that there is no outline around the icon (as shown in Figure 6–20) indicating that it is not assigned to any object and that it is a cold material.

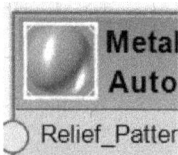

Figure 6–20

14. Using the drag and drop method from the output socket, assign the **Galvanized** material to the **LP Fixture Housings** (the chamfer cylinders) and **LP Mounting Arms** (the arms holding the fixtures to the post).

15. Replace the existing material for the **LP Base Plate** and **LP Pole** with the **Galvanized** material.

16. Review the preview icon for the material. Note that there is now a white outline around the thumbnail, as shown in Figure 6–21. This indicates that the material has been assigned to an object in the scene.

   • Note that this new material is also added to the *Scene Materials* list in the Material Map Browser, as shown in Figure 6–22.

Figure 6–21   **Figure 6–22**

17. Save the file.

6.3 General Materials

General materials are the most basic materials provided with the Autodesk 3ds Max software. They can be accessed by expanding the *Materials>General* categories in the Material/Map Browser, as shown in Figure 6–23.

Depending on the renderer you are using, the list of the materials might differ from the figure shown.

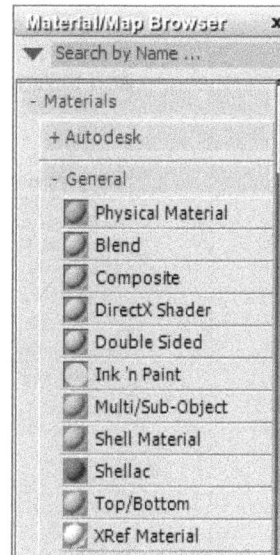

Figure 6–23

- You can use General materials directly as is or customize them by modifying their parameters to create your own materials, as required.

Physical Materials

New in 2017

Physical materials are parameters that create reasonable shading effects and are appropriate for scenes with physically-based lighting. Using Physical materials, you can create materials that are based on the physical properties of a material.

- Physical materials are real world materials that are organized in an easy interface that follows a logical layout.

- Materials are comprised of either a base layer that is assigned a diffuse color with dielectric reflections, or a base color with metallic reflections, as shown in Figure 6–23.

- In addition to the diffuse color, the materials have transparency, sub-surface scattering, self-illumination (emission), and a top clear-coat layer, as shown in Figure 6–24.

- These materials contain both standard and advanced parameters that are designed for physically-based material adjustments.

- These materials work well with ART (Autodesk® Raytracer) and the mental ray renderers.

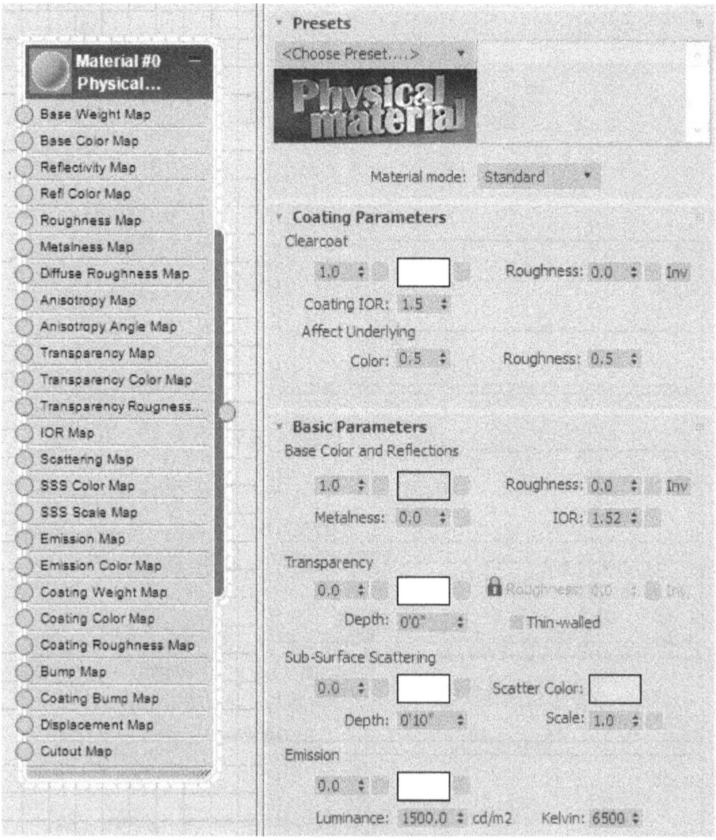

Figure 6–24

Physical Material Parameters

The parameters of the physical materials are easy and follow a simple workflow. The available parameters are:

- The **Coating Parameters** rollout (shown in Figure 6–25) contains options that are used for applying a clear coat onto the finish of the surface.
  - To create a glossy coating on the material, set the *Clearcoat Weight* to **1.0**.
  - *Coating IOR* sets the reflectivity of a clear coat. The higher the value, more reflective the clear coat is.
  - *Roughness* adds a softer sheen and makes a clear coat less glossy.
  - *Affect Underlying* area adds an affect to the base diffuse color.

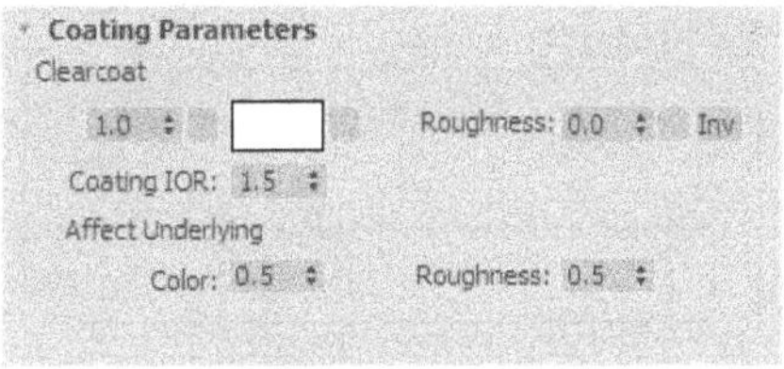

Figure 6–25

- In the **Basic Parameters** rollout (shown in Figure 6–24), the *Base Color and Reflections* area enables you to set the base color of the material surface and add the type and amount of reflectivity.
  - A *Weight* of **0** has no color, and a value of **1** is full color.
  - *Metalness* determines how the surface reflects. A value of **0.0** creates standard reflections (such as for plastics), and a value of **1.0** creates a metal surface (such as for steel or aluminum).
  - *Roughness* and *IOR* work in a similar fashion as the Clearcoat settings, but alter the base surface of the material. A value of **0.0** is a hard surface, and **1.0** is a soft surface.

- In the **Basic Parameters** rollout, the *Transparency* area enables you to create clear materials, like glass.
  - A *Weight* value of **0.0** is completely opaque, and **1.0** is fully transparent.
  - *Thin Walled* creates a glass-like appearance to the surface by making the interior hollow.

- In the **Basic Parameters** rollout, *Sub-Surface Scattering* is a feature that causes light to dissipate through the volume of an object.
  - *Scatter Color* sets the color of the scattered light within the volume of the object.
  - *Depth* sets the distance the light scatters through the object in a real-world distance.

- In the **Basic Parameters** rollout, the *Emission* area enables you to create a material that can emit light and illuminate the scene.
  - An *Emission Weight* of **1** sets the material to full emission and defaults to a *Luminance* of 1500 cd/m² (candelas per meter square).

Multi/Sub-Object Materials

Objects might require different materials on each face. For example, a door or window might need different materials for front and back frames, mullions, and glazing. For this, Multi/Sub-Object materials are used, as shown in Figure 6–26.

- They enable you to stack multiple materials into a single *parent* material, each with a material ID number.

- Faces and polygons of individual objects can have a corresponding ID number assigned through modifiers such as **Edit Mesh** and **Edit Poly**.

- Objects brought into the Autodesk 3ds Max software from vertical applications, such as the AutoCAD Architecture software and the AutoCAD Civil 3D software are divided into multiple objects by material and do not require Multi/Sub-Object materials.

- The Slate Material Editor provides a convenient view that enables you to visually identify all of the materials that make up a Multi/Sub-Object material. Initially, when the material is created, the parent material node opens with 10 default slots. You can wire sub-materials to each slot. Each of the sub-materials can be modified or you can add new materials to the view and rewire into any of the slots. Figure 6–26 shows an example of a Multi/Sub-Object material that is wired to five materials. Slots can be added or deleted using the **Add** or **Delete** options in the Multi/Sub-Object Basic Parameters rollout.

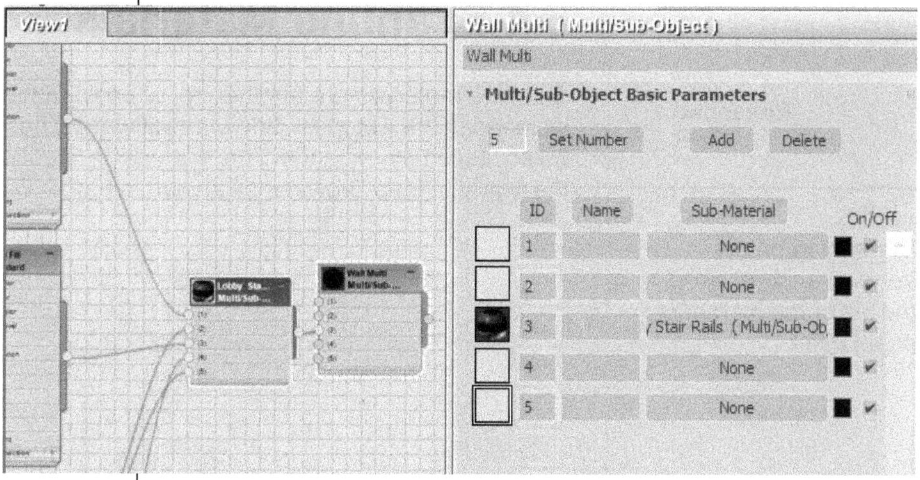

Figure 6–26

Additional Standard Materials

The additional General materials available for use are described as follows:

Blend	Combines two materials to create a third.
Composite	Enables multiple materials to be combined into a single, composite material through additive colors, subtractive colors, or opacity mixing.
DirectX Shader	Enables you to shade objects in the viewport to more accurately display how objects look when exported to real-time viewing.
Double Sided	Enables you to have one material assigned to the outside of objects and another to the inside (the back-facing sides).
Ink 'n' Paint	Creates a flat shaded cartoon rendering with the contours or edges as ink lines.
Shell Material	Used with *texture baking*, which is the process of creating replacement color maps that include the scene illumination (illumination is *baked in*).
Shellac	Superimposes two materials together through additive composition.
Top/Bottom	Assigns different materials to faces with normals pointing *up* and *down*.
XRef Material	Assigns a material applied to an object to another Autodesk 3ds Max scene file. As with Xref scenes and objects, you can only change the material parameters in the original source file.

6.4 Scanline Materials

Enhanced in **2017**

Scanline materials are another set of basic materials that are included in the Autodesk 3ds Max software. These materials can be accessed by expanding the *Materials>Scanline* category in the Material/Map Browser, as shown in Figure 6–27.

Depending on the current renderer used, the list of the materials might differ.

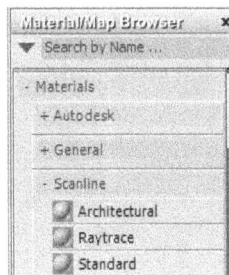

Figure 6–27

Architectural Materials

Architectural materials are a type of Scanline materials (as shown in Figure 6–27) that are appropriate for scenes with physically-based lighting.

Architectural materials are applicable to many different kinds of visualization projects, not only Architectural or Civil/Site projects.

- Architectural materials use a streamlined interface that highlights the parameters and maps that are most likely to change.

- Controls that are not directly available to Standard materials are also available, such as refraction, luminance, and advanced lighting overrides.

Raytrace Material

The Raytrace material is used to create highly configurable, realistic reflections and refractions. These materials support fog, color density, translucency, fluorescence, and other effects. Some Architectural materials (such as ones with the mirror template) automatically generate raytraced results.

Standard Materials

Standard materials are the most basic material and consist of four color components: Ambient color, Diffuse color, Specular color, and Filter color. These materials can be used in most models and can be easily customized.

6.5 Material Shaders

Material Shaders are complex algorithms that describe how light interacts with surfaces. The material color, highlights, self-illumination, and many other features are dependant on the material shaders.

- Standard and mental ray materials enable you to select or use a shader. When using mental ray, a wide range of shaders are available for specific advanced effects. Architectural materials do not provide any shader choice.

- In Standard materials, the shader type is selected through the Shader Basic Parameters rollout, as shown in Figure 6–28.

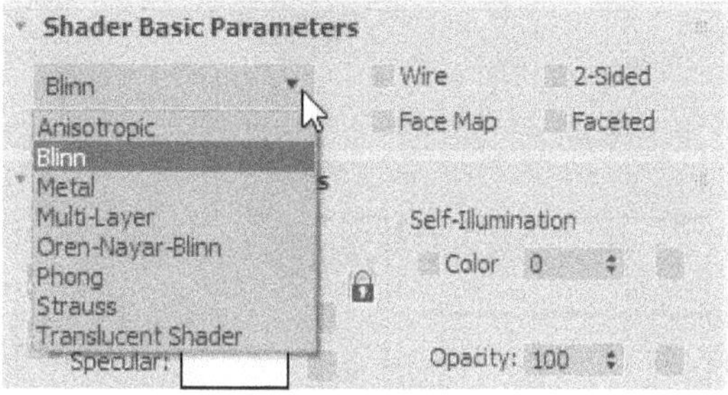

Figure 6–28

- In mental ray materials, shaders can be applied anywhere you might place a map or directly to cameras and lights. They are located using the Material/Map Browser.

- Many shader properties relate to highlights, the bright areas caused by the specular reflection of a light source on the surface of an object.

- The standard shader types are described as follows:

	**Anisotropic**	Shader for materials with elliptical highlights, such as hair, glass, or brushed metal.
	Blinn	General purpose shader for shiny, smooth objects with soft, circular highlights. Blinn is the default shader for Standard materials.

	Metal	For luminous metallic surfaces.
	Multi-Layer	Enables two sets of anisotropic controls for complex or highly polished surfaces.
	Oren-Nayar-Blinn	A variation of the Blinn shader that provides additional controls for matte surfaces such as fabric or terra cotta.
	Phong	Related to the Blinn shader, also used for shiny, smooth surfaces with circular highlights. The Phong shader generates harder, sharper (often less realistic) highlights than Blinn.
	Strauss	For metallic and similar surfaces, Strauss offers a simpler interface than the Metal shader.
	Translucent Shader	Enables you to control translucency, which is the scattering of light as it passes through the material. Appropriate for Semi-transparent materials, such as frosted glass.

- When using the mental ray renderer, you can apply mental ray shaders to materials, which display with a yellow parallelogram, instead of the green symbol used for maps. The mental ray materials display as yellow spheres.

- The mental ray also enables you to attach shaders directly to lights and cameras for a variety of rendering effects such as contour rendering. If the mental ray render is not selected, the various mental ray shaders are not shown as a possible choice. However, in the Material/Map Browser options, when the **Show Incompatible** option is selected, it displays incompatible materials to that renderer in gray.

Shader (Specific) Basic Parameters

Each material shader has a unique combination of parameters (as shown in Figure 6–29) that can be controlled.

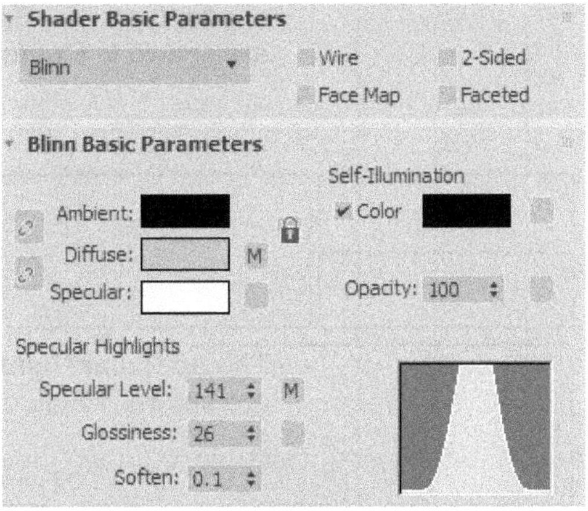

Figure 6–29

- Most of these parameters can be replaced by a map when their values are not constant across the surface. For example, a Diffuse Color Map can be used to replace a single diffuse color for a brick material.

- Colors can be selected by picking on the color swatch next to a color parameter, which opens the interactive Color Selector.

Ambient Color	The color of a material under ambient (background) lighting. It can be assigned globally and through standard lights set to cast ambient light. Ambient and diffuse colors can be locked at the same values, if required.
Diffuse Color	The color of a material under direct lighting. This is the base color of a material (outside of highlights).
Specular Color	The color of material's highlights. It is calculated automatically for the Metal and Multilayer shaders.
Self-Illumination	Values greater than 0 cause materials to appear to be illuminated, but surfaces with this material do not illuminate other objects. This parameter is useful for materials used in light fixtures. Self-illuminated objects do not automatically glow; glows need to be assigned as a special effect (**Rendering>Effects**).
Opacity	This is a percentage measurement of opacity, the opposite of transparency. Materials that have 0% opacity are completely see-through. As an example, a typical clear glass material could have an Opacity between 0-10%.

- Parameters relating to Specular Highlights are listed next to a highlight curve that shows a graphical representation of these settings. Not all of the parameters are available for each shader type. The **Specular Highlights** parameters for Blinn are shown in Figure 6–30.

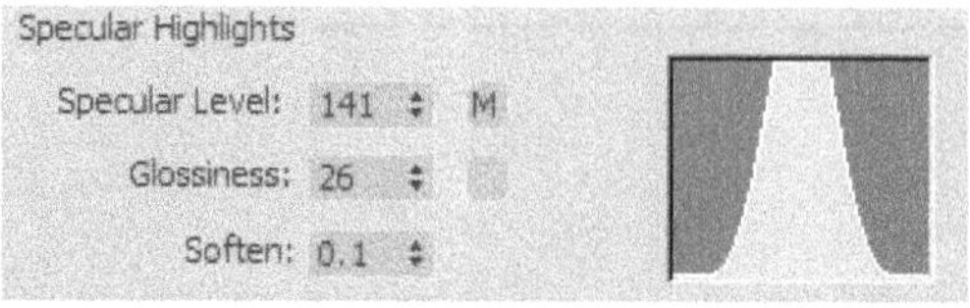

Figure 6–30

- The **Specular Highlights** parameters for Anisotropic shaders are shown in Figure 6–31.

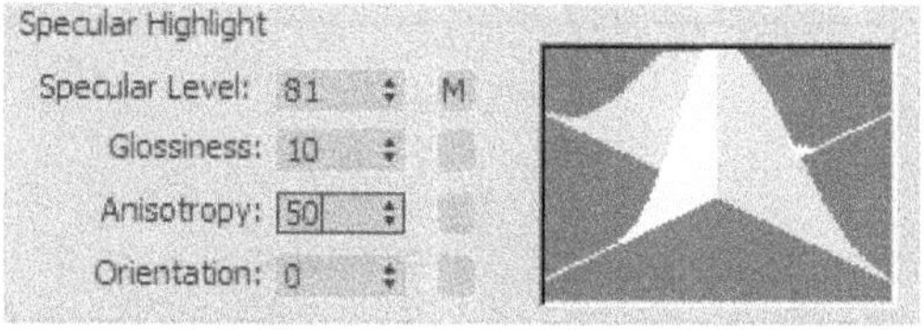

Figure 6–31

Specular Level	A relative measurement of the overall highlight intensity.
Glossiness	A relative measurement of the overall size of highlights. The more glossy an object the smaller and more intense the highlights.
Soften	A relative measurement used to soften the edges of highlights.
Anisotropy	Defines the elliptical shape of Anisotropic highlights, where 0 = round and 100 = a very tight ellipse.
Orientation	Defines the degrees of rotation for an Anisotropic highlight.

6.6 Assigning Maps to Materials

Maps are often assigned to replace the shader parameters, especially Diffuse Color. Maps can be assigned to various materials through the Maps rollout. Figure 6–32 shows the Maps rollout for Standard materials and Figure 6–33 shows the Special Maps and Generic Maps rollout for Physical Materials. Maps include Diffuse Color, Bump maps, Opacity etc.

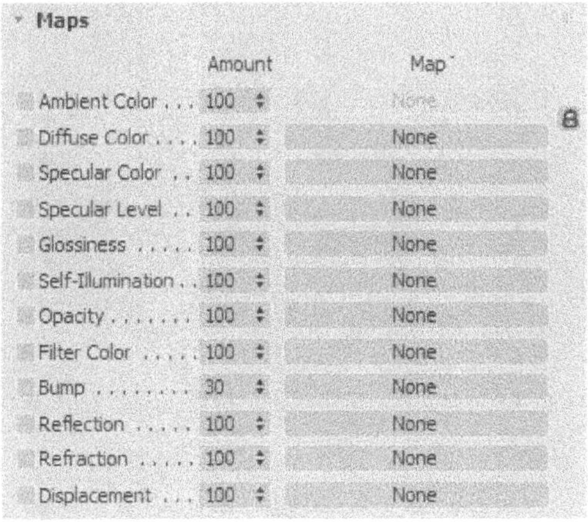

Material #26 (Physical Material)

Material #26

Special Maps

Special Maps

Bump Map	0.3		None
Coating Bump Map:	0.3		None
Displacement	1.0		None
Cutout			None

Generic Maps

Generic Maps

Base Weight	None
Base Color	None
Reflection Weight	None
Reflection Color	None
Roughness	None
Metalness	None
Diffuse Roughness	None
Anisotropy	None
Anisotropy Angle	None
Transparency Weight	None
Transparency Color	None
Transparency Roughness	None
IOR	None
Scattering Weight	None
Scattering Color	None

Maps

	Amount		Map
Ambient Color	100		None
Diffuse Color	100		None
Specular Color	100		None
Specular Level	100		None
Glossiness	100		None
Self-Illumination	100		None
Opacity	100		None
Filter Color	100		None
Bump	30		None
Reflection	100		None
Refraction	100		None
Displacement	100		None

Figure 6–32

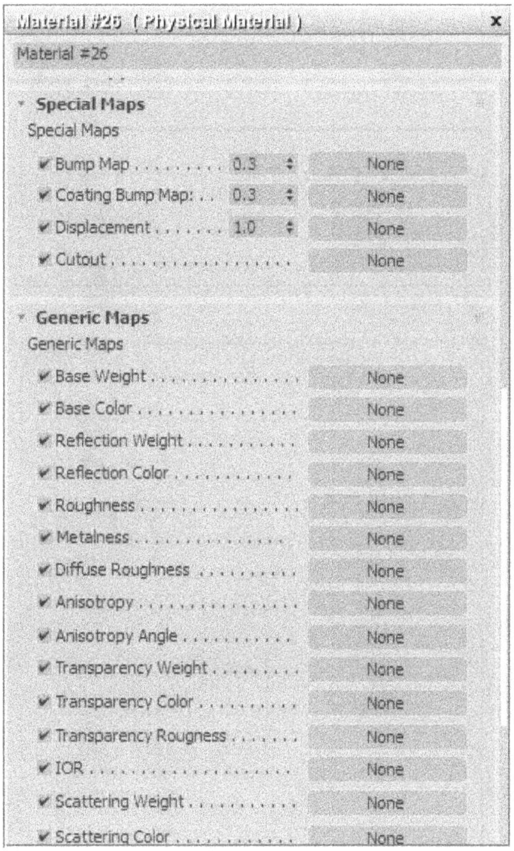

Figure 6–33

Clicking **None** next to a channel opens the Material/Map Browser (shown in Figure 6–34) where you can select a map and assign it or change a map and its settings.

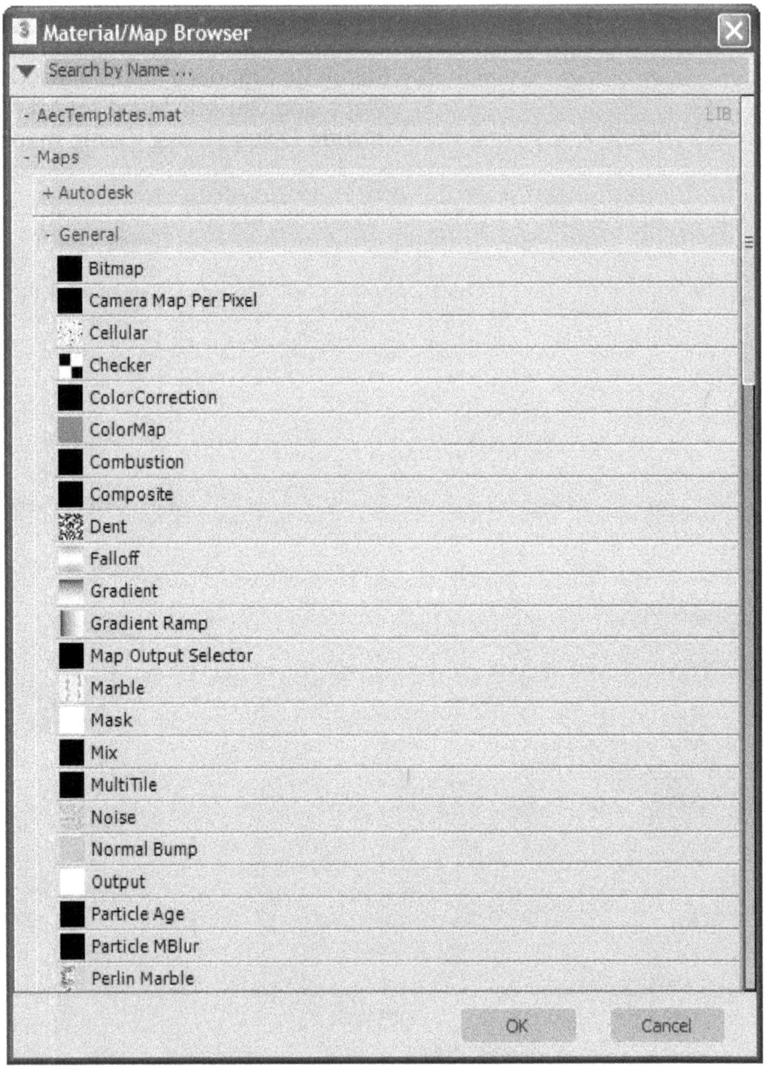

Figure 6–34

- The **Bitmap** map type enables you to assign an external image as a map. Different types of image formats can be used as maps including Windows Bitmaps, JPEGs, PNGs, Targas, TIFFs, and more.

- **Color Map** enables you to make an instance of a solid color swatch. This helps you be consistent in the solid colors that you use in your models. You can also assign a color bitmap instead of creating a color swatch.

- **MutiTile** enables you to assign more than one texture maps into a UV editor. The map is designed so that high resolution textures can be opened and displayed. This map type supports patterns created using Mudbox, Zbrush, and Mari.

- The remainder map types are Autodesk 3ds Max **Procedural** maps, which are automatically generated mathematically rather than from image files.

- When you assign (or edit) a map to a material, individual nodes are created and display the maps assigned to the material components. Wires are created automatically between the map and the material component to which the map has been assigned, as shown in Figure 6–35. Maps can also be added individually and wired into a material to establish a link. To edit any of the parameters in the material or maps, double-click on the title bar heading for the item to access its associated Parameter Editor.

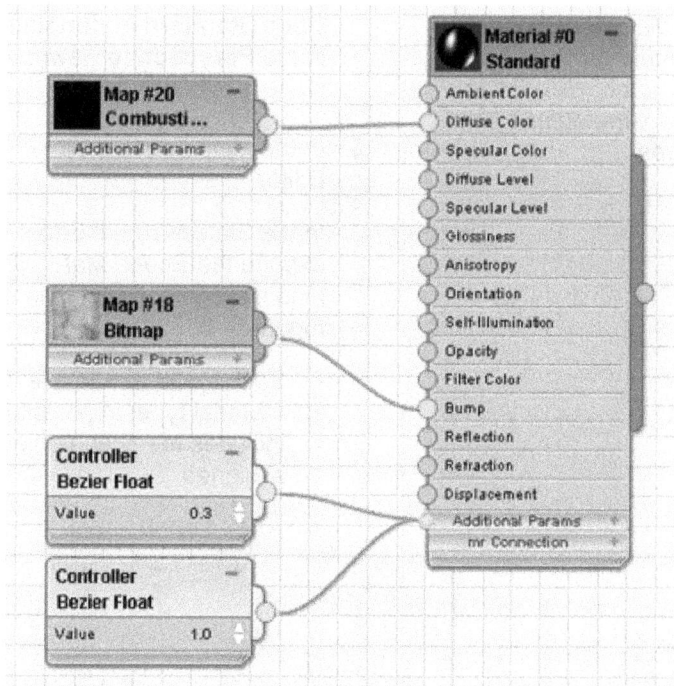

Figure 6–35

Practice 6b

Working with Standard Materials and Maps

Practice Objectives

- Assign a Standard material and modify it.
- Apply an image file and a procedural map to the Diffuse Color of the material.

Estimated time for completion: 20 minutes

In this practice you will assign a Standard material to an object and apply parameter changes to it. You will then apply an image file and a procedural map to an object.

You must set the paths to locate the External files and Xrefs used in the practice. If you have not done this already, return to **Chapter 1: Introduction to Autodesk 3ds Max** and complete Task 1 to Task 3 in **Practice 1a: Organizing Folders and Working with the Interface**. You only have to set the user paths once.

Task 1 - Load Materials into the Material Editor.

*If a dialog box opens prompting you about a Mismatch, click **OK** to accept the default values.*

1. Open **Standard Materials.max**. A model of a guitar displays in the **Perspective** viewport.

2. In the Main Toolbar, click ⬚ to open the Slate Material Editor.

3. In the Slate Material Editor, in the Material/Map Browser, expand the *Scene Materials* category. There are currently nine materials available in this scene, as shown in Figure 6–36.

   - Each material name is listed and is followed by its material type, in parentheses ( ). The square brackets [ ] includes the scene object to which the material has been assigned.

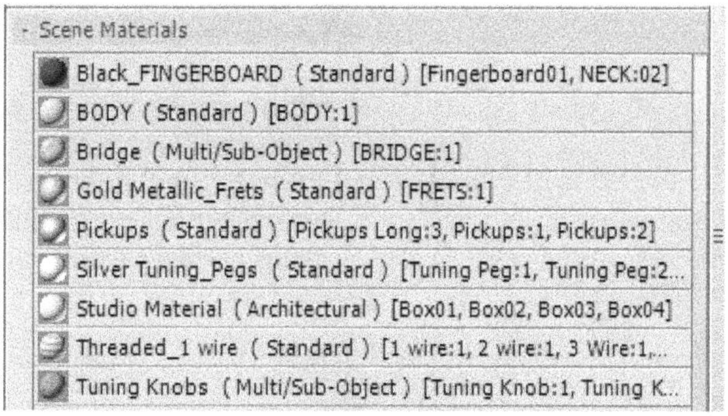

Figure 6–36

4. Note that all of these materials are also displayed in the *View1* sheet and are overlapping each other, as shown in Figure 6–37. In the Slate Material Editor toolbar, click

   (Lay Out All -Vertical) to display the materials vertically in the *View1* sheet.

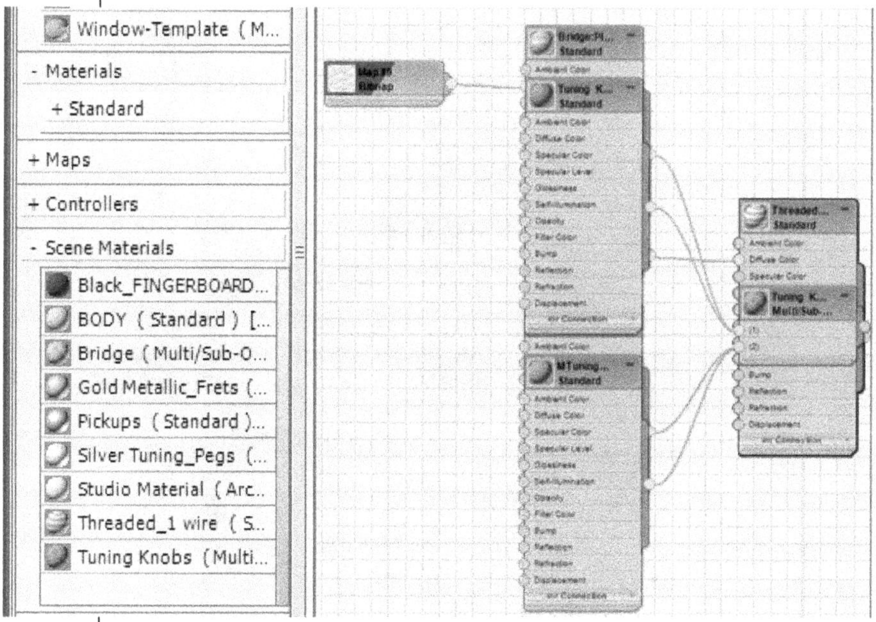

Figure 6–37

Task 2 - Change the material parameters.

1. In the *View1* sheet, using pan and zoom, locate the **BODY Standard** node (name displayed in the title bar), as shown in Figure 6–38. Double-click on the title bar heading to open its Parameter Editor, as shown in Figure 6–39. Note that a white dashed border displays around the node in the *View1* sheet.

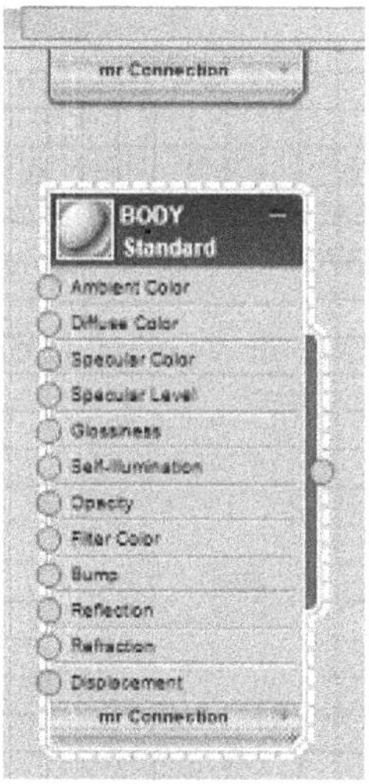

Figure 6–38

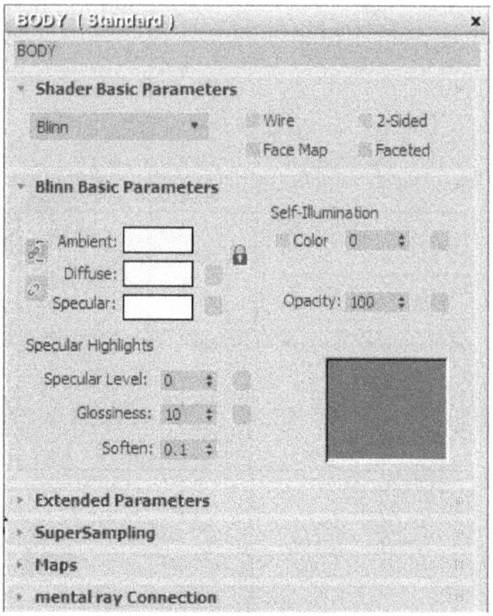

Figure 6–39

2. Note that the **Body** material is a Standard material that uses the Blinn shader. In the Blinn Basic Parameters rollout, select the Diffuse color swatch (currently gray) to open the Color Selector dialog box, as shown in Figure 6–40.

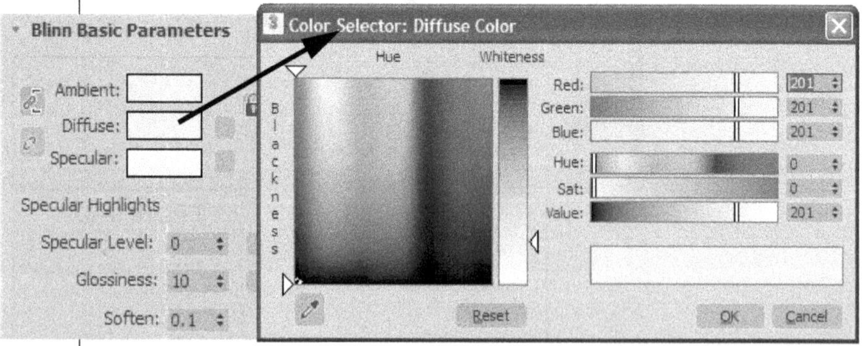

Figure 6–40

The Slate Material Editor is a modeless dialog box that can remain open when you are working in the viewport or performing other operations that do not pertain to the dialog box. You can minimize it to get more space in the viewport and maximize it when you want to work in it.

3. In the Color Selector dialog box you can select a color from the chart or set RGB (red-green-blue) or HSV (hue-saturation-value) levels. Experiment with different colors for the guitar body and click **OK**.

4. Change the *Shading Viewport* (User Defined) to **High Quality**. The guitar is displayed in the viewport with high quality shading and lighting, as shown in Figure 6–41.

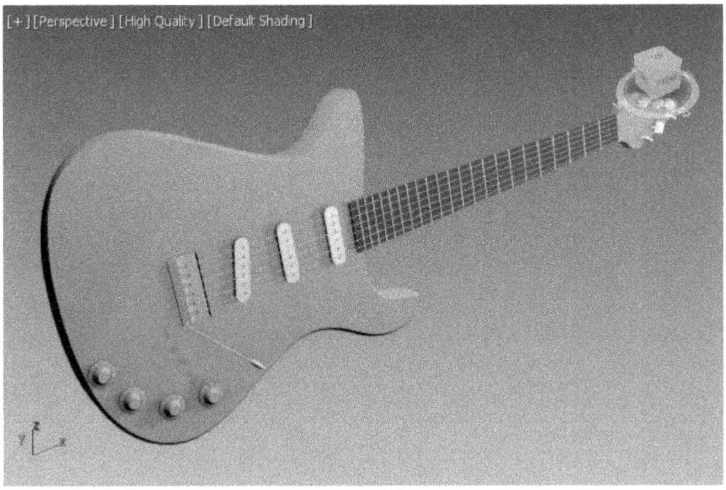

Figure 6–41

5. In the *Specular Highlights* area, the material's *Specular Level* is set to **0**, which is appropriate for a material that is not shiny. To simulate a shiny coating, increase the *Specular Level* to **100**, as shown in Figure 6–42. Note the shiny coating on the guitar body.

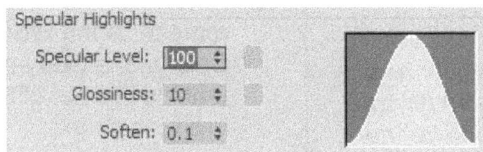

Figure 6–42

6. Change the *Glossiness* to **25**. Increasing the glossy value focuses the highlighting in a smaller area.

7. Click  (Render Production) in the Main Toolbar to display a more realistic rendered image. Close the Render Window.

Task 3 - Applying a procedural map and image file.

A Procedural Map is generated algorithmically. It is not a digital photo or painting. Procedural Maps are useful for terrains or other objects where the texture should not repeat in a tiled pattern.

1. To replace the Diffuse Color with a procedural map that represents a wood grain, verify that the Body material has a white dashed boundary around it indicating that its parameters are displayed. In the Parameter Editor, expand the Maps rollout, as shown in Figure 6–43. Next to the **Diffuse Color** option, click **None**.

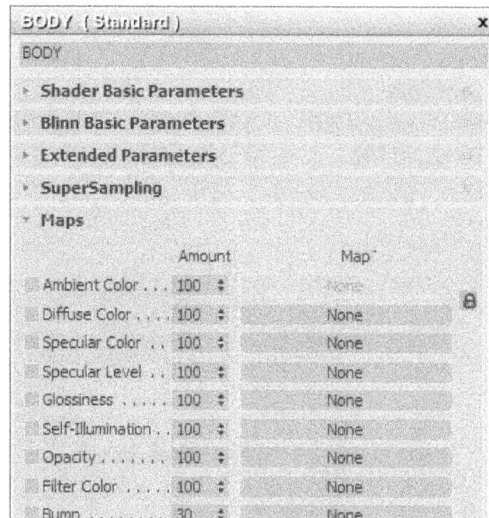

Figure 6–43

2. In the separate Material/Map Browser that opens, expand the *Maps>General* categories and select **Wood**. Click **OK** to assign it as a map to the **BODY** Standard material.

*As with all procedural maps, **Wood** is defined by parameters and formulas, not by an image file.*

*The Map number and name **Map #10 (Wood)** replaces **None** for the Diffuse color in the Parameter Editor.*

3. A new Map node has been added in the *View1* sheet that represents the **Wood** map. The node is wired to the Diffuse Color in the **Body** material, as shown in Figure 6–44. Note that the title bar of this node is green, indicating that the node is a Map node.

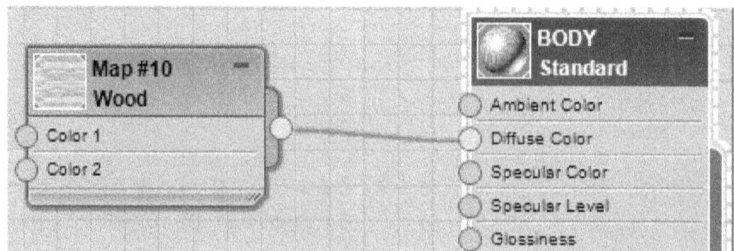

Figure 6–44

4. Double-click on the title bar heading for the **Wood** map. Note that a white dashed border surrounds the Wood Map node, indicating that its parameters are displayed in the Parameter Editor. In the Wood Parameters rollout, set *Grain Thickness* to **8**, as shown in Figure 6–45. This distance is measured in the file's System Unit Scale.

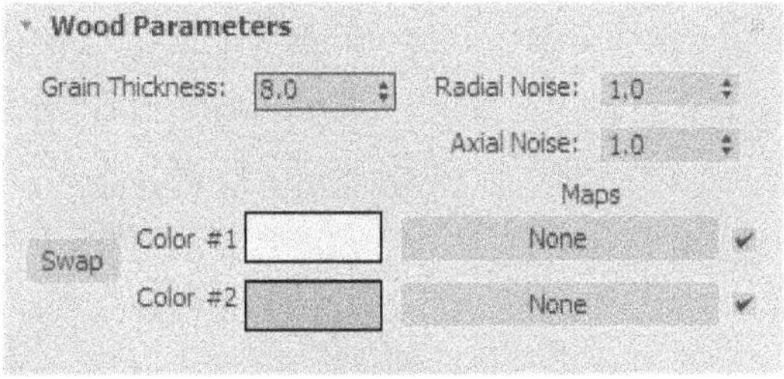

Figure 6–45

*A red and blue node indicates that the **Show Shaded Material in Viewport** option is selected for that material.*

*A red and green node indicates that the **Show Shaded Material in Viewport** option is selected for that map.*

5. The wood grain does not display on the guitar body in the viewport. To display the map in the viewport, in the Slate Material Editor toolbar, click ▣ (Show Shaded Material in Viewport). The wood grain displays on the guitar body in the viewport but it is not accurate. Note that the title header of this node has changed to a half diagonal red area and the rest is green.

6. In the Main Toolbar, click 🫖 (Render Production) to render. The wood map is displayed on the body of the guitar, as shown in Figure 6–46. Leave the modeless Render Window dialog box open.

Figure 6–46

• The display in the viewport might not be identical to the rendered display. This is typical of procedural maps. Procedural maps offer some interesting parameter-driven maps, which maintain the wood grain into the third dimension (across the top of the guitar body).

7. To replace the procedural **Wood** map with an image file, in the *View1* sheet, double-click on the title bar heading for the **BODY** material to open its Parameter Editor. Expand the Maps rollout, right-click on **Map #10 (Wood)**, and select **Clear**. Alternatively, you can drag any **None** onto it. Note that in the *View1* sheet, the wiring between the **BODY** material node and the **Wood** map node has been deleted.

8. Click **None** next to the **Diffuse Color** to open its specific Material/Map Browser.

9. In the Material/Map Browser, double-click on **Bitmap** in the *Maps>General* categories, as shown in Figure 6–47.

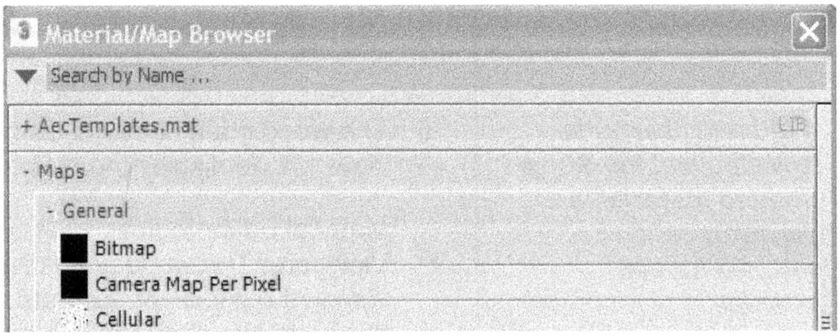

Figure 6–47

You can delete the unused node by clicking its title bar heading and pressing <Delete>. This keeps the active sheet clean. It also removes the material from the active sheet only.

10. The Select Bitmap Image File dialog box opens. Browse to the ...*Maps* folder. Select **GuitarDiffuse.jpg** and click **Open**. A new node for Bitmap is added to the *View1* sheet and its output socket is connected to the Diffuse Color input socket of the **BODY** material node, as shown in Figure 6–48. The new **Bitmap** node and **Wood** Map node might overlap. Select the header of one of the nodes to move them apart.

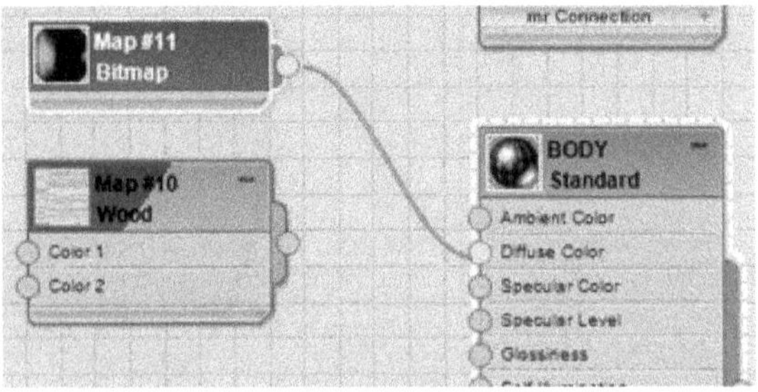

Figure 6–48

11. Double-click on the **Bitmap** node title bar to display its Parameter Editor. In the Coordinates rollout, clear the **Use Real-World Scale** and set the *Tiling* to 1.0 in both **U** and **V**, as shown in Figure 6–49.

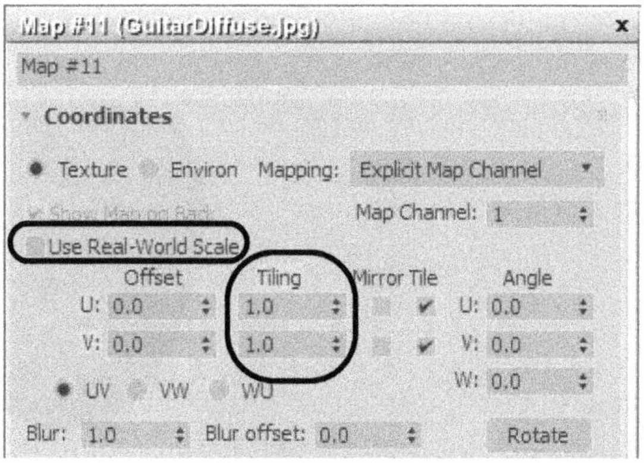

Figure 6–49

12. Click ▣ (Show Shaded Material in Viewport) again to display the **BODY** material with the new map in the viewport.

13. If the Render Window is still open, click **Render**, which is located near the top right corner, to display the effect, as shown in Figure 6–50. If you closed the Render Window,

open it again from the Main Toolbar by clicking 🫖 (Render Production). Leave the dialog box open.

Figure 6–50

Hint: Use Mix Map Type

You could also mix the procedural wood grain with the bitmap by selecting a Mix map type. The mix material on the guitar displays as shown in Figure 6–51.

Figure 6–51

14. To use a Color Correction map along with the Bitmap, In the Material/Map Browser, open the *Maps>General* categories. Double-click on the Color Correction map. A new node for Color Correction is added to *View1*, as shown in Figure 6–52. To relocate a node in the active sheet, hold and drag the title bar heading.

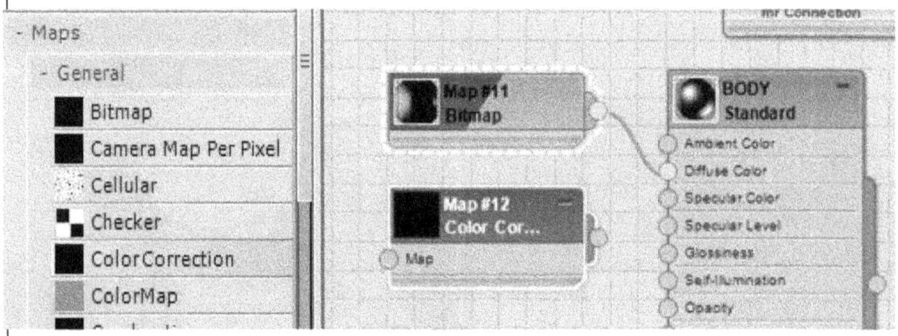

Figure 6–52

15. Select the red wire that connects the Bitmap node to the Diffuse Color of the **BODY** material, press <Delete>.

The input socket of Color correction is used for a Map.

16. For the Bitmap node (**Map # Bitmap**), select the material output socket ⬤ (right socket) and drag/drop the wire to the material input socket (left socket) for the Color Correction node (**Map # Color Correction**), as shown in Figure 6–53. Note that the wired slots display in green.

17. Select ⬭ (material output socket) for the Color Correction node and drag the wire to the material input socket for the Diffuse Color entry in the **BODY** material node, as shown in Figure 6–54.

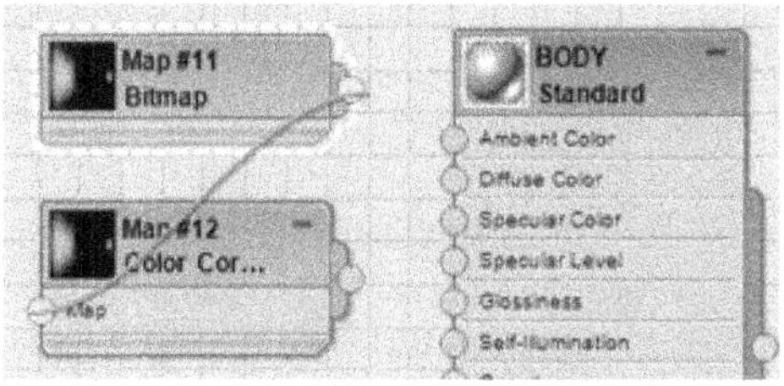

Figure 6–53

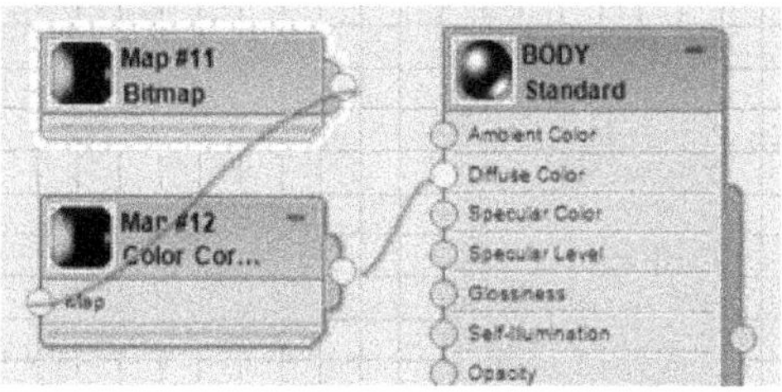

Figure 6–54

18. Select the Color Correction heading and then click

    ▣ (Show Shaded Material in Viewport) to display the map on the guitar in the viewport.

19. Double-click on the Color Correction heading to open its Parameter Editor. In the Color rollout, change the *Hue Shift* slider and note that the guitar changes color interactively in the viewport. Set the slider at any color (such as a green color hue).

20. In the Render dialog box, click **Render** to render the scene, as shown in Figure 6–55.

Figure 6–55

21. Save your work as **MyGuitar.max**.

Practice 6c

Working with Multi/Sub-Object Materials

Practice Objective

- Create a Multi/Sub-Object material and assign different materials to specific faces of a single object.

Estimated time for completion: 20 minutes

In this practice you will create a Multi/Sub-Object material with various materials on different material ID's. You will assign an instanced scene material to all the faces of the wall system, an Autodesk material to some of the outside faces, and an accent paint color to other interior faces using material ID numbers of the Multi/Sub-Object material.

You must set the paths to locate the External files and Xrefs used in the practice. If you have not done this already, return to **Chapter 1: Introduction to Autodesk 3ds Max** and complete Task 1 to Task 3 in **Practice 1a: Organizing Folders and Working with the Interface**. You only have to set the user paths once.

Task 1 - Identify and Apply Multi/Sub-Object Materials.

*If a dialog box opens prompting you about a Mismatch, click **OK** to accept the default values.*

1. Open **Interior Model.max**.

2. In the Main Toolbar, click ⬚ to open the Slate Material Editor.

3. In the Material/Map Browser, expand the *Scene Materials* categories and note that six of the materials in the scene are Multi/Sub-Object materials.

You can leave the modeless Slate Material Editor dialog box open.

4. Click, drag, and drop the **Curtain Wall Doors** material on **PivotDoor07** (door on the left side of the model), as shown in Figure 6–56.

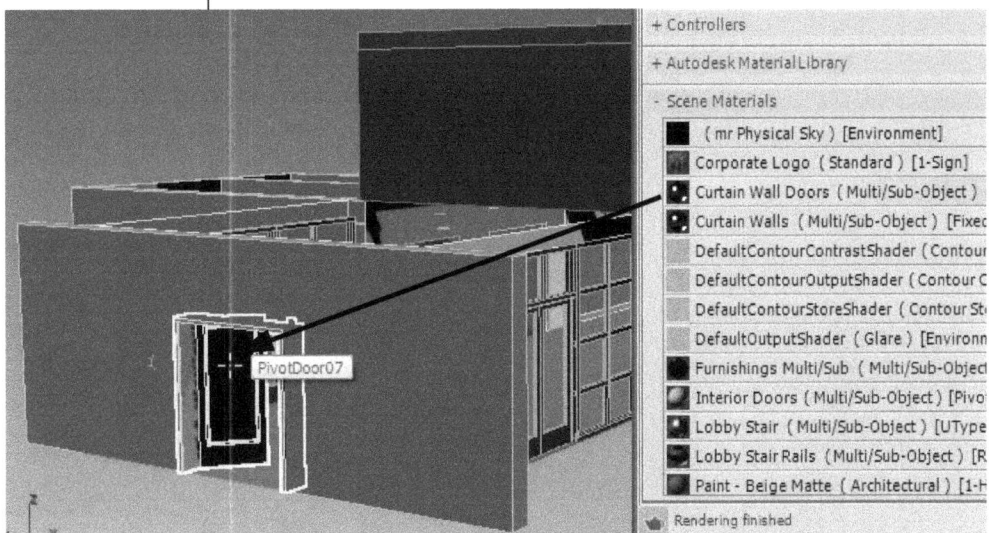

Figure 6–56

5. Select **PivotDoor07** object and click ⬚ (Zoom Extents Selected). The doors have glass panels and solid frames, as shown in Figure 6–57.

Figure 6–57

Task 2 - Create a Multi/Sub-Object Material.

1. In the Material/Map Browser, expand the *Materials>
   General* categories. Double-click on Multi/Sub-Object or drag
   an instance of it to add it to the *View1* sheet, as shown in
   Figure 6–58.

2. Right-click on the title bar heading for the new material, and
   select **Rename**, as shown in Figure 6–59.

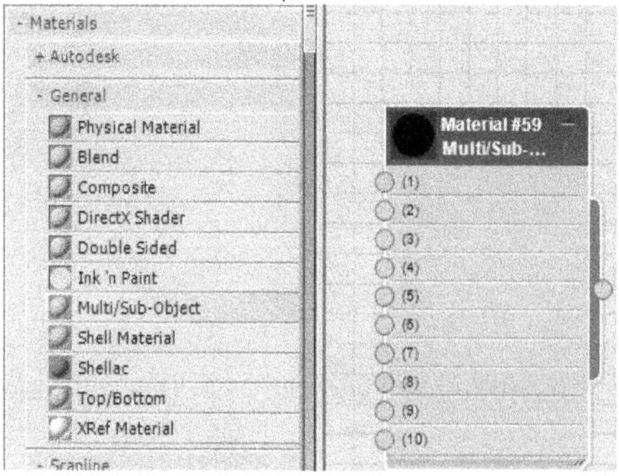

Figure 6–58

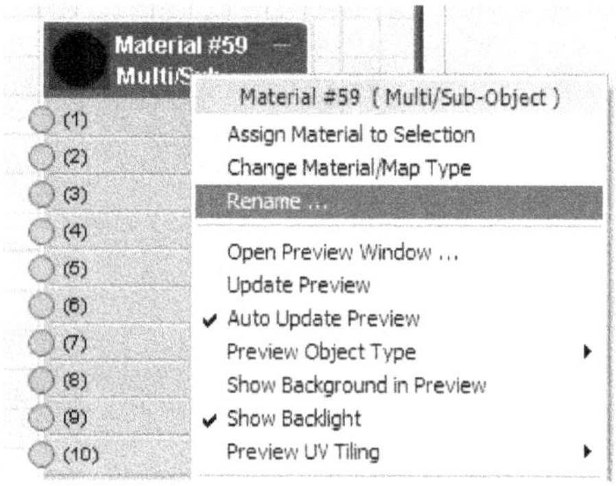

Figure 6–59

3. In the Rename dialog box, enter **Wall Multi** and click **OK**.

4. There are ten default slots in a Multi/Sub-Object material.
   This material only requires five slots. To set the number of
   materials, double-click on the Wall Multi material title bar to
   open its Parameter Editor. Click **Set Number**, enter **5** in the
   Number of Materials edit box and click **OK**. Note that the
   node has only 5 slots now.

*To display all of the
materials in the Scene
Materials, use its scroll
bar.*

5. You will use an instanced copy of the **Paint – Beige Matte**
   material present in the scene for your sub-material 3. (This
   material displays dark brown in this practice but will look
   more like beige when lights are added to the scene.) In
   Material/Map Browser, in *Scene Materials* category, locate
   Paint – Beige Matte, which is an Architectural material.

6. Click and drag the **Paint – Beige Matte** material and place it
   directly on the input socket 3 in the **Wall Multi**
   (Multi/Sub-Object material). When you move the cursor on
   top of the socket, its color changes to green indicating that
   the socket is selected, as shown in Figure 6–60. Drop the
   material on this socket.

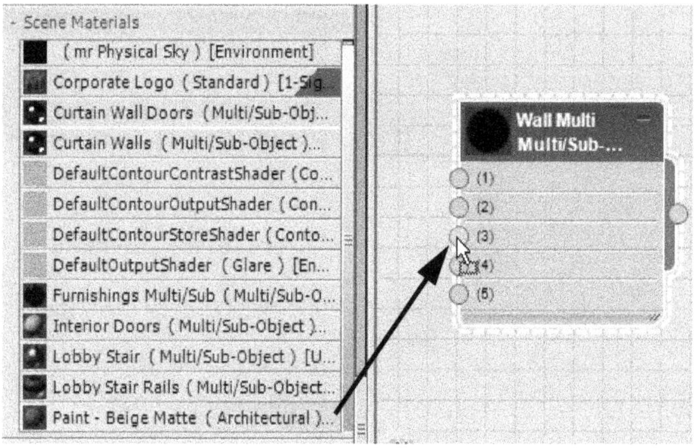

Figure 6–60

7. In the Instance dialog box, verify that **Instance** is selected and click **OK**.

8. The Paint – Beige Matte material node is wired to slot 3 of **Wall Multi** material. Use the pan and zoom (middle mouse button) to display both the material nodes in the *View1* sheet.

9. Verify that the Wall Multi (Multi/Sub-Object material) node has a white dashed boundary indicating that its Parameter Editor is displayed. Note that the **Paint – Beige Matte** material is displayed on the 3 ID slot, as shown in Figure 6–61.

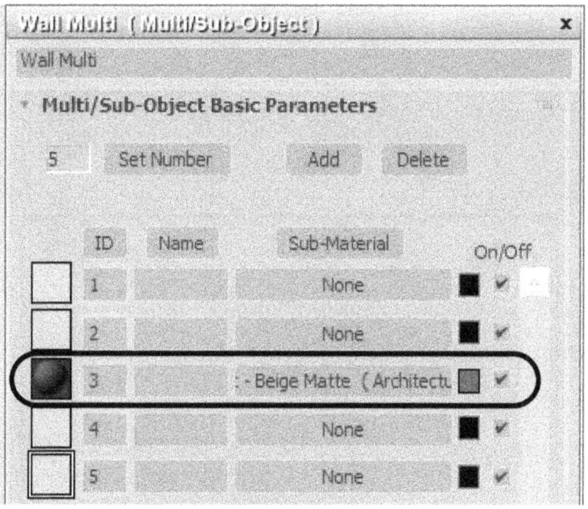

Figure 6–61

10. In the Material/Map Browser, expand the *Autodesk Material Library>Finish* categories and locate **Paint- Varnish** material.

11. Click and drag the **Paint- Varnish** material onto the Wall Multi Parameter Editor and release it over **None** next to *ID* slot 5. Note that the **Paint- Varnish** material is wired to slot 5 of the **Wall Multi** material. Alternatively, you can place the **Paint- Varnish** material on the *View1* sheet and wire it to slot 5.

    - You cannot drag and drop Autodesk materials on the input socket for sub-material 5 directly in the *View1* sheet as you did with the **Paint-Beige Matte** scene material. You need to use the Parameter Editor.

12. Not all the nodes are visible and might be overlapping each other in the active sheet (*View1*). In the Slate Material Editor toolbar, click [icon] (Lay Out All - Vertical) to arrange the sub-materials vertically, as shown in Figure 6–62. Note that in the active view, the input socket 5 of Wall Multi material node is wired to the output socket of the Finish (Paint Varnish) material node. Also, note that in the Parameter Editor of the **Wall Multi** material, the ID5 slot now displays **Paint- Varnish (Autodesk Generic)**, as shown in Figure 6–63.

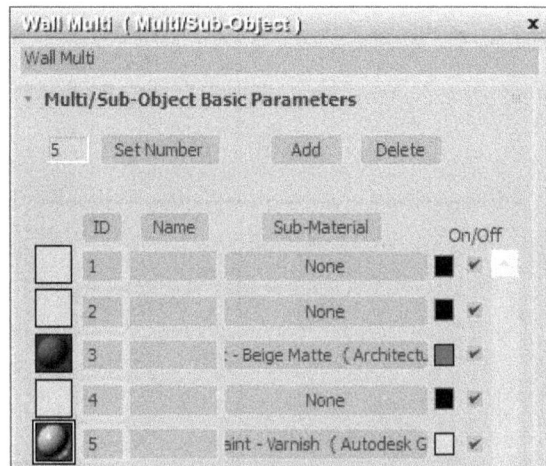

Figure 6–62 **Figure 6–63**

13. You will copy and adjust the **Paint – Beige Matte** material into an accent paint material. In Material/Map Browser, in *Scene Materials* category, click and drag the **Paint – Beige Matte** material and place it on the input socket for sub-material 4 in the **Wall Multi** material.

14. In the Instance dialog box, select **Copy** and click **OK**.

Use 🔳 *(Lay Out All - Vertical), if required.*

15. Double-click on the title bar heading for the new **Paint – Beige Matte** material (slot 4) to open its Parameter Editor.

16. Change the material name to **Paint – Accent**, as shown in Figure 6–64.

17. In the Physical Qualities rollout, select the Diffuse Color swatch. In the Color Selector set *Value* as **255** and press <Enter>. The color changes, as shown in Figure 6–65. Click **OK**.

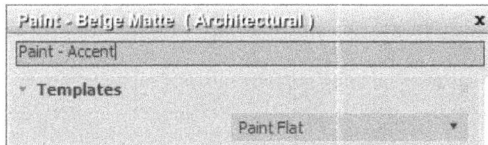

Figure 6–64

Figure 6–65

18. Close the Slate Material Editor.

Task 3 - Assign Material ID Numbers to the Wall System.

---

1. In the **Perspective** viewport, zoom out and pan so that the entire model is displayed in the viewport.

2. In the Scene Explorer (🔲 (Display None) > ⬤ (Display Geometry)), select **Layer:VIZ-1-Walls**, which selects all of the walls in the lower floor in the viewport.

3. In the Command Panel, in the Modify panel (📐), note that it is an Editable Mesh in the Modifier Stack. Select the **Polygon** Sub-object mode, as shown in Figure 6–66.

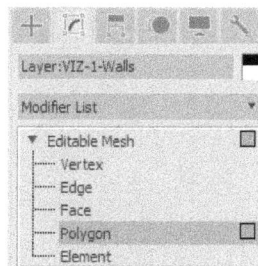

Figure 6–66

---

4. In the viewport, select the **Edged Face** Per-View Preference label and select **Wireframe Override** in the menu. Use

   (Orbit) until your model displays as shown in Figure 6–67. Right-click in empty space to exit the command and maintain the selection.

5. Using <Ctrl>, select the two polygons as shown in Figure 6–67.

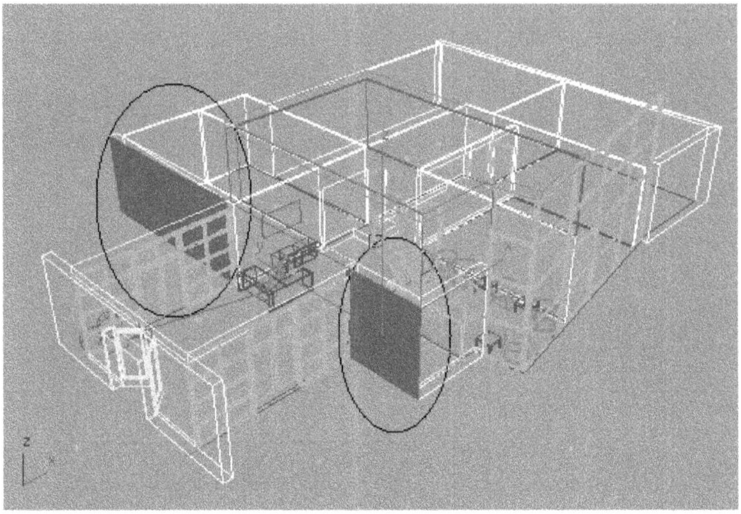

Figure 6–67

6. In the Command Panel, in the Surface Properties rollout, in the *Material* area, set *Set ID* to **5**, and press <Enter>. *Select ID* also changes to **5**, as shown in Figure 6–68. This sets the selected polygons to ID 5 and will associate the Finish (Autodesk Material) with those two walls.

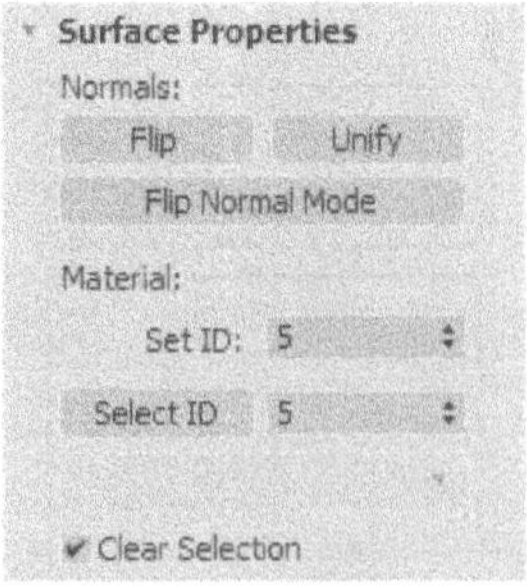

Figure 6–68

7. Clear the selection of the two walls and select the polygon as shown in Figure 6–69. Set *Set ID* to **4** and press <Enter>. This will associate the **Beige - Accent** material with this wall.

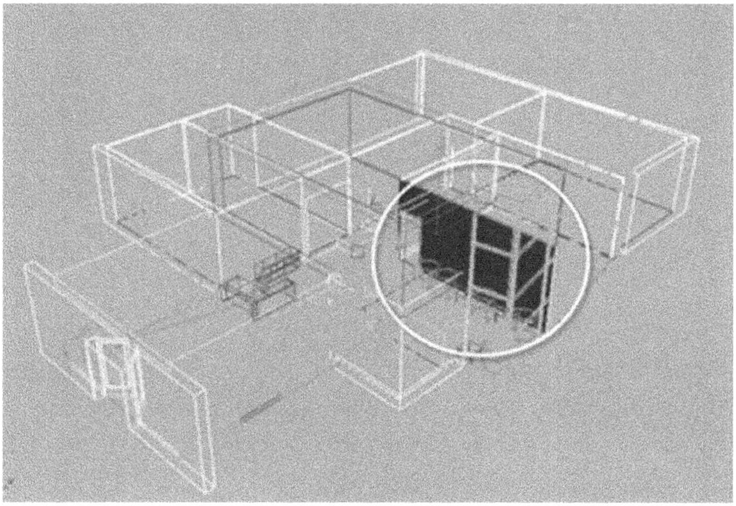

Figure 6–69

8. In the Command Panel, select **Editable Mesh** to exit Sub-object mode.

9. Change the visual display to **Default Shading** and **Edged Faces** by selecting the **Wireframe** (Per-View Preference) label and selecting **Default Shading**. There is no change in the model because the material has not yet been assigned.

10. With the wall object (**Layer:VIZ-1-Walls**) still selected, open the Slate Material Editor, select the Wall Multi material title bar heading in the *View1* sheet. In the Slate Material Editor toolbar, click ![icon] (Assign material to Selection).

11. Note that the interior wall displays in light beige (**Paint – Accent**) and the two exterior brick walls display in grayish brown (**Paint- Varnish**), as shown in Figure 6–70.

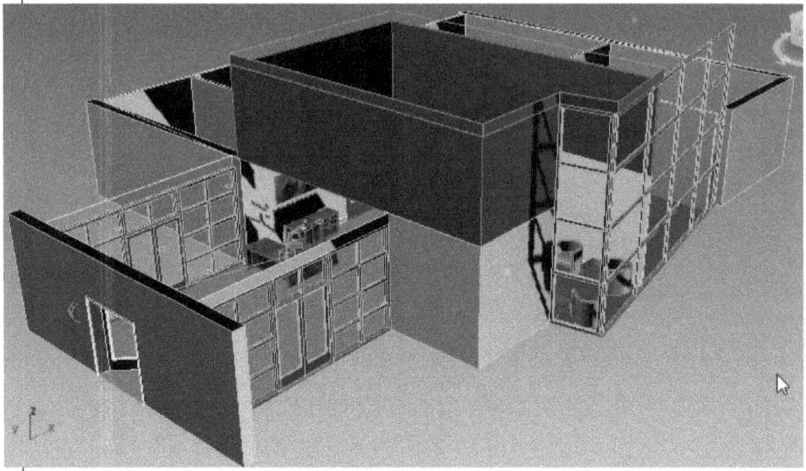

Figure 6–70

12. In the Slate Material Editor, double-click on the **Finish Paint - Varnish** title node to open its Parameter Editor.

13. In the Generic rollout, select the Color bar to open the Color Selector. Change the color to a different one, such as red. In the viewport, note that only the color of the two walls that have ID 5 changes, as shown in Figure 6–71. This indicates that your **Multi-Sub -Object** materials have been applied.

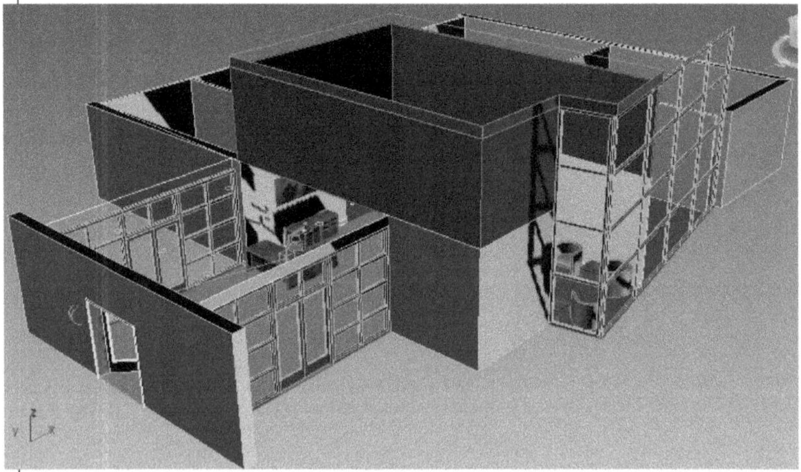

Figure 6–71

14. Save the file as **MyInterior Model MultiMaterials.max**.

6.7 Opacity, Bump, and Reflection Mapping

You can use simple objects with materials and textures applied to them to add detailed effects without adding complex geometry to a scene. For example, leaves on trees or a chain link fence can be generated using a simple model with mapped textures and materials rather that creating it with complex geometry.

Opacity Mapping

Opacity mapping controls the transparency of objects, as shown with the lace curtains in Figure 6–72.

Figure 6–72

To create an Opacity map, add a map to the *Opacity map* channel, under the Maps rollout of the material.

* The black to white values are mapped to the transparent state, where black creates a hole (completely invisible), white makes a surface (100% opaque), and grays create a semi-transparent effect, good for clouds and fabrics.

* If a color image is used as an Opacity map, the RGB color is ignored and only the Luminance value is used. Opacity maps are usually created by taking digital photos and manipulating them in other programs.

Hint: Two-sided Opacity Mapped Material

When you create an opacity mapped material, it is recommended to make the material two-sided to see the backsides of faces if looking inside/through an object.

Bump Mapping

Bump mapping gives the illusion of an embossed or pitted surface without geometry being present on the model, as shown for a braided carpet in Figure 6–73. As with Opacity mapping, it uses black to white values to generate the appearance of a raised surface.

The white value raises the surface fully while the black value does not raise it at all.

- When combined with texture mapping, it helps the scene lighting integrate with the textures to place shadows in cracks, and generally add a veneer of three-dimensionality to the surfaces.

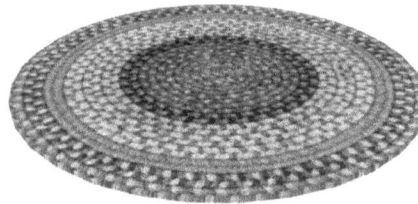

Figure 6–73

Reflection Mapping

Reflection mapping gives a surface the ability to mirror the world surrounding the object, as shown on the glass in Figure 6–74.

- Using Standard materials, you can place a bitmap or a reflection map type in the *Reflection map* channel.

- If you add a bitmap to the *Reflection map* channel, the faces reflect the bitmap based on shininess and scene lighting.

- If you add a Reflect/Refract or Raytrace map, the objects in the scene reflect along with the environment.

Figure 6–74

Practice 6d

Opacity and Bump Mapping

Practice Objective

- Assign a Diffuse Color texture map, Opacity map, and Bump map to an object.

Estimated time for completion: 15 minutes

In this practice you will create a chain link fence using opacity and bump mapping to display the cutouts in a solid piece of geometry. You will then add a map to the *Specular Level* channel to add shininess to the object texture.

You must set the paths to locate the External files and Xrefs used in the practice. If you have not done this already, return to **Chapter 1: Introduction to Autodesk 3ds Max** and complete Task 1 to Task 3 in **Practice 1a: Organizing Folders and Working with the Interface**. You only have to set the user paths once.

Task 1 - Assign the texture map.

If a dialog box opens prompting you about a Mismatch, click OK to accept the default values.

1. Open **start_chainlink.max**.

2. In the *Shading Viewport* (User Defined) label, select **High Quality**.

3. In the viewport, select the object **Line01** (yellow fence object).

4. In the Main Toolbar, click ⬚ to open the Slate Material Editor.

5. In the Material/Map Browser, expand the *Materials>General* categories. In the list, double-click on the **Physical Material** material to add it to the *View1* sheet.

6. Assign the **Physical Material** material to the selected fence object by clicking ⬚ (Assign Material to Selection) in the Material Editor toolbar. Verify that the fence object now displays in gray in the viewport.

7. In the *View1* sheet, double-click on the **Physical Material** material title bar heading to open its Parameter Editor. To open a separate Material/Map Browser, in the Basic Parameters rollout, next to *Base Color and Reflections* color swatch, click ▢ (None), as shown in Figure 6–75.

*Ensure that you select **None** for the Color Map and not the Weight Map*

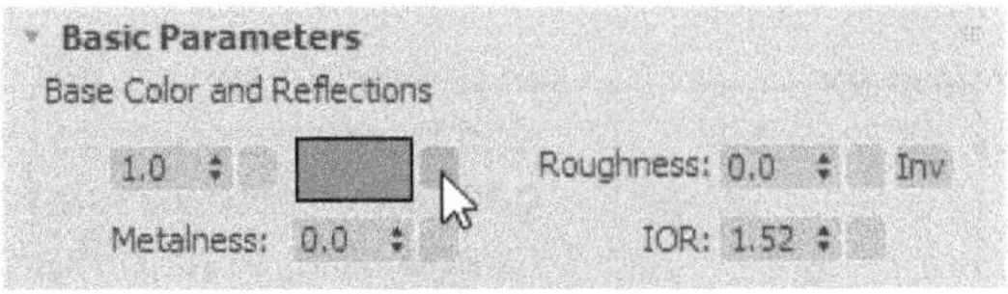

Figure 6–75

8. Expand the *Maps>General* categories and double-click on Bitmap, as shown in Figure 6–76.

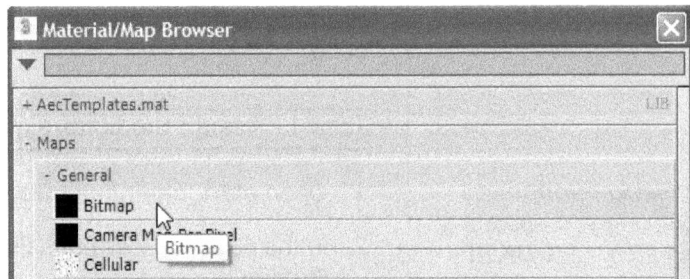

Figure 6–76

The Autodesk Maps are available in your local drive, generally, C:\Program Files\ Autodesk\3ds Max 2017\maps.

9. In the Select Bitmap Image File dialog box, in the Practice Files ...\Maps folder, open **Chain-link.bump.jpg**.

- Note that in the Parameter Editor the icon changes to ▢ᴹ, as shown in Figure 6–77. Also note that in *View1* sheet, the output socket of the Bitmap node is wired to the Base Color Map input socket of the **Physical Material** material, as shown in Figure 6–77.

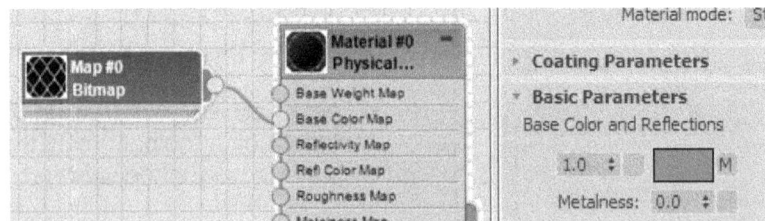

Figure 6–77

10. In the *View 1* sheet, select the **Map # Bitmap** and then click

    ⬛ (Show Shaded Material in Viewport). The **Chainlink** texture should display on the **Line01** object in the viewport, but does not display correctly because the settings need to be changed.

11. In the *View1* sheet, double-click on the **Map # Bitmap** title bar heading to open its Parameter Editor.

12. In the Coordinates rollout, clear **Use Real-World Scale** and set *Tiling* as **U: 6.0** and **V: 3.0**, as shown in Figure 6–78. Press <Enter> for the values to take effect. The **Chainlink** texture should display in the viewport.

    • If it does not display, render the scene once (Main

      Toolbar> 🫖 *(Render Production)). Close the Render*

      Window and then click ⬛ (Show Shaded Material in Viewport) twice to toggle it off and on again..

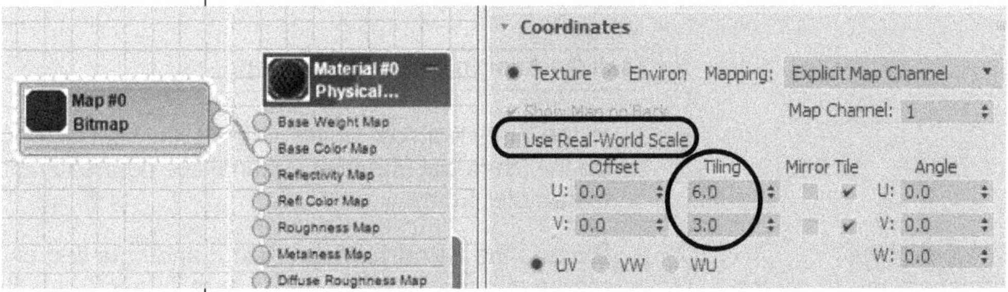

Figure 6–78

13. In the Main Toolbar, click 🫖 (Render Production). The map displays in the Render window. Leave the window open.

14. In the menu bar, select **Rendering>Environment**. In the *Background* area, select the color swatch as shown in Figure 6–79. In the Color Selector, select a new color (cyan) and click **OK**. Close the Environment and Effects dialog box.

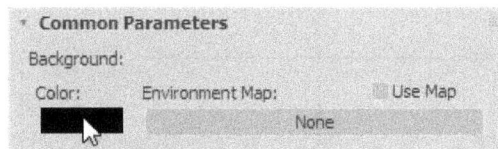

Figure 6–79

15. In the Render window, click **Render**. The Render window should display as shown in Figure 6–80. Leave the window open.

Figure 6–80

Task 2 - Assign the Opacity map.

1. In the Slate Material Editor, in the *View1* sheet, double-click on the **Physical Material** material title bar heading to open its Parameter Editor.

2. Expand the **Generic Maps** rollout and note that chainlink map has already been applied to the *Base* Color channel.

To control the transparency, apply the map to the Opacity channel

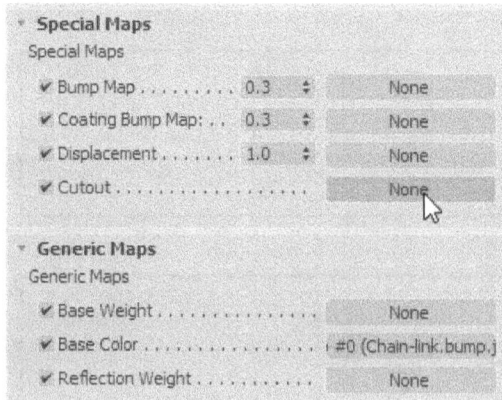

3. Expand the **Special Maps** rollout and click **None** for *Cutout*, as shown in Figure 6–81.

Figure 6–81

The Tiling settings for the Diffuse map and the Opacity map should be the same so that they overlap each other for the cutout to display correctly.

4. In the Material/Map Browser, expand the *Maps>General* categories. Double-click on **Bitmap** to open the Select Bitmap Image File dialog box. Open **Chain-link.cutout.jpg** (from the ...\Maps folder). Note that this bitmap is wired to **Opacity** in Standard material. It also replaces **None** in the Maps rollout of the Parameter Editor.

5. In the *View1* sheet, double-click on **Map #1 Bitmap** (cutout) title bar heading to open its Parameter Editor. In the Coordinates rollout, clear **Use Real-World Scale** and set the *Tiling* to **U: 6.0** and **V: 3.0**. Press <Enter>.

6. Orbit around in the Perspective view so that the fence is facing you. In the Render window, click **Render** to render the scene. Note that the background is displayed through the fence, as shown in Figure 6–82. This is caused by the map on the *Cutout* channel. The chainlink in your rendering might display a little lighter in color than that shown in Figure 6–82.

Figure 6–82

7. Close the Render window.

Task 3 - Assign the Bump map.

1. In the Slate Material Editor, in the *View1* sheet, double-click on the **Physical Material** material title bar heading to open its Parameter Editor. In the **Special Maps** rollout, for *Bump Map,* click **None** .

*You can also drag and drop the map from the Diffuse channel onto the Opacity channel and select **Copy** in the dialog box.*

2. In the Material/Map Browser, in the *Maps>General* categories, double-click on Bitmap to open the Select Bitmap Image File dialog box. Open **Chain-link.bump.jpg** (from the ...*Maps* folder). Note that this bitmap is displayed on **Bump Map**, as shown in Figure 6–83 (the same map was used on the *Base Color* channel). Note that in the *View1* sheet, it is wired to **Bump Map** in **Physical Material** material, as shown in Figure 6–83.

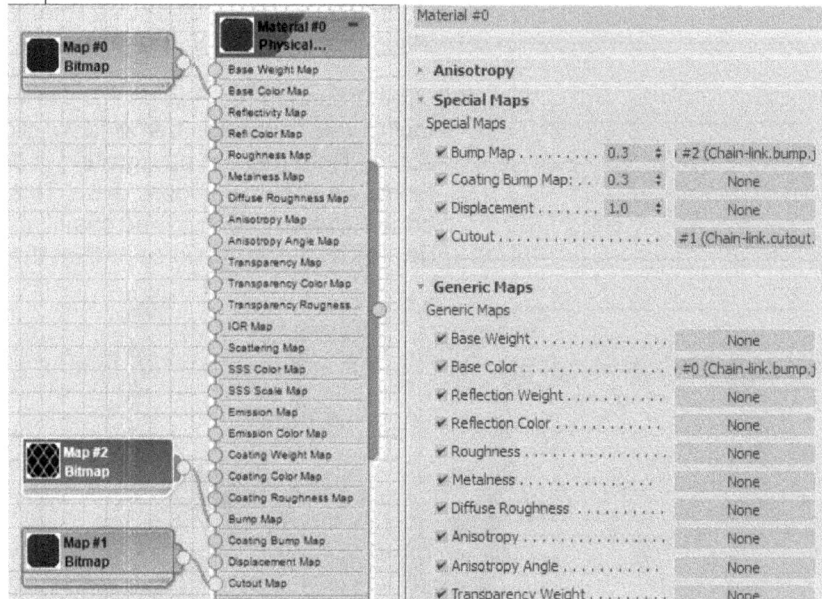

Figure 6–83

If you copied the map, the settings are also copied and you are not required to enter the Tiling values.

3. In the *View1* sheet, double-click on the **Map #2 Bitmap** (*Bump* channel) title bar heading to open its Parameter Editor. In the Coordinates rollout, clear **Use Real-World Scale** and set the *Tiling* to **U: 6.0** and **V: 3.0**.

4. Click (Render Production) to render the scene.

*To display the various maps correctly in the viewport, in the View1 sheet, select the **Material # Physical Material** heading (parent material node) and then click*

 (Show Shaded Material) to switch it on.

5. To make the chain link more realistic (smaller cutouts), set the *Tiling* values for all the three map channels to **U: 18** and **V: 11**. Double-click on each map title bar heading to open its Parameter Editor and change the values.

6. Render the scene again. The rendered scene is similar to one shown in Figure 6–84.

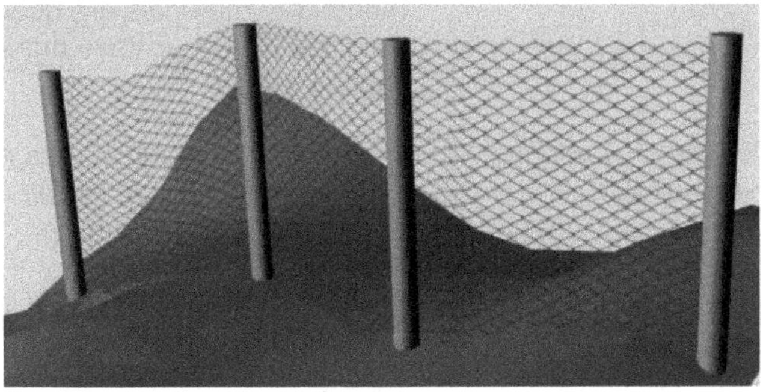

Figure 6–84

There is no light on this side, so the rendering display might be dark.

7. Click ![orbit icon] (Orbit) and navigate in the viewport to the other side of the chain link fence. Render the scene again. Note that the chain link displays. Leave the Render window open.

8. In the viewport, navigate back to the front side of the fence.

9. Save your work as **MyChainLinkFence.max**.

6.8 mental ray Materials

mental ray materials are used with the NVIDIA mental ray renderer to can achieve high-quality images with accurate lighting effects.

*The mental ray material complete list is displayed if the NVIDIA mental ray is assigned to be the current renderer. With ART Renderer, NVIDIA iray, or Quicksilver Hardware Renderer, a limited list of mental ray material is available. The renderer can be made current in the Render Setup dialog box. (**Rendering> Render Setup**).*

- mental ray materials are available in the Material/Map Browser, in the *Materials>mental ray* category, as shown in Figure 6–85.

- **Autodesk** materials are also mental ray materials and are available in a separate *Materials>Autodesk* category, as shown in Figure 6–86.

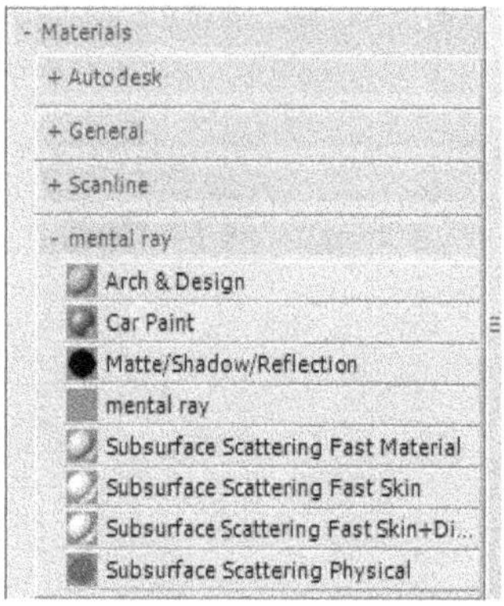

Figure 6–85

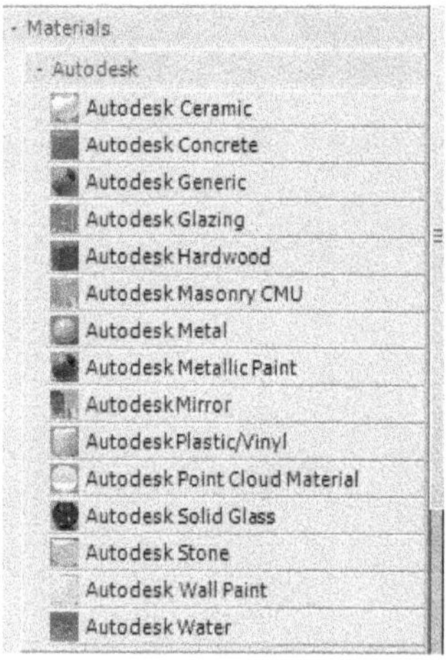

Figure 6–86

Arch & Design Materials

The Arch & Design material type is the most commonly used mental ray material. It provides over 20 different templates for Appearance and Attributes, Finishes, Transparent Materials, and Metals. There are also Advanced Tools for detail enhancement. The Arch & Design templates have default texture bitmaps already assigned when you select them. You can create your own Arch & Design material by modifying its parameters. The templates include the following:

• Matte, Pearl, or Glossy Finish	• Physical Frosted Glass
• Satin or Glossy Varnished Wood	• Translucent Plastic Film with Light Frost
• Rough or Polished Concrete	• Translucent Plastic Film with Opalescent Effect

• Glazed Ceramic/Glazed Ceramic Tiles	• Water, Reflective Surface
• Glossy or Matte Plastic	• Chrome
• Masonry	• Brushed Metal
• Rubber	• Satined Metal
• Leather	• Copper
• Thin or Solid or Physical Glass	• Patterned Copper

Arch & Design materials enable you to do the following:

• Adjust the reflection, refraction, and transparency of the material.

• Control the blurriness of the reflections by using Fast Reflection.

• Control the distance that reflects in a surface.

• Adjust the strength of the reflection based on the angle of viewing (BDRF).

• Add light into the scene using self-Illumination. Unlike standard lights, the self-illumination used with mental ray materials emits illumination in the scene instead of faking the effect.

• Round corners through a post-production pixel shader and an Ambient Occlusion setting that adds subtle detail enhancement to surface corners, cracks, and crevices.

Autodesk Materials

Fifteen **Autodesk** mental ray materials are also available, as shown in Figure 6–86. The materials are:

• Autodesk Ceramic	• Autodesk Mirror
• Autodesk Concrete	• Autodesk Plastic/Vinyl
• Autodesk Generic	• Autodesk Point Cloud Material
• Autodesk Glazing	• Autodesk Solid Glass
• Autodesk Hardwood	• Autodesk Stone
• Autodesk Masonry CMU	• Autodesk Wall Paint
• Autodesk Metal	• Autodesk Water
• Autodesk Metallic Paint	

- In addition to the Autodesk materials in the *Autodesk* category, there are additional categories of Autodesk materials present in the *Autodesk Material Library* category that can be used directly or modified for use in your scenes.

- The Autodesk Material Library materials are simplified versions of the Arch & Design materials. Similar to the Arch & Design materials, Autodesk mental ray materials should also be used with physically accurate (photometric) lights but have a much simpler interface. They contain presets that permit faster selection of specific material parameters and preassigned bitmaps.

- The Autodesk Material Library was designed specifically for architectural visualization and includes material categories for *Ceramic*, *Concrete*, *Fabric*, *Finish*, *Flooring*, *Glass*, *Liquid*, *Masonry*, *Metal*, etc.

- These materials are aligned with the latest release of the Autodesk Revit software, so the materials applied in the Autodesk® Revit® Architecture software display as Autodesk Material Library materials inside the Autodesk 3ds Max software.

Car Paint Material

This is a layered material that provides four layers combining to create one surface treatment. Elements such as a base paint layer, an embedded metal flake layer, a clear-coat layer, and a Lambertian dirt layer, each have their own parameters and rollouts. These enables you to create complex highly reflective surfaces. By using your own texture maps with these base materials, and tweaking the various parameters within each, you can achieve an unlimited variety of materials.

Matte/Shadow/ Reflection Material

This is a mental ray version of the Standard Matte/Shadow material. You can create matte objects by using the Matte/Shadow/Reflection (mi) material included in the Production Shaders library. A photographic plate containing real-world objects can be used as the scene background. The material provides various options for combining the photographic background plate with the 3D scene. The options include ambient occlusion, bump mapping, and indirect illumination.

mental ray Material	This is your basic mental ray material. It provides rollouts that enable you to assign component shaders for materials used with the mental ray renderer.
Subsurface Scattering (SSS) Materials	Enables you to create organic materials like skin that do not reflect light at the surface, but scatter or absorb light below in the surface. There are four different types of Subsurface Scattering materials available for use with the mental ray renderer.

Hint: Output Rollout

The Output rollout of the texture bitmap can be used to great advantage when using mental ray materials. Lighten and brighten the output of the texture by enabling the color map or increasing the Output Amount.

Practice 6e

Working with mental ray Materials

Practice Objectives

- Assign a mental ray material template to an object.
- Assign and modify a mental ray material.

Estimated time for completion: 20 minutes

In this practice you will explore the mental ray materials, shaders, and templates. You will assign an Arch & Design material to an object and modify the material using a map and a color mapping.

You must set the paths to locate the External files and Xrefs used in the practice. If you have not done this already, return to **Chapter 1: Introduction to Autodesk 3ds Max** and complete Task 1 to Task 3 in **Practice 1a: Organizing Folders and Working with the Interface**. You only have to set the user paths once.

Task 1 - Assign the NVIDIA mental ray renderer.

*If a dialog box opens prompting you about a Mismatch, click **OK** to accept the default values.*

1. Open **candleholder.max**. The candle holder is displayed in the four viewports layout. A camera view has already been set up.

2. In the Main Toolbar, click ![icon] to open the Slate Material Editor. In the Material/Map Browser, expand the *Materials* category and note that no mental ray materials or Autodesk materials are available. To work with mental ray materials, you need to set the renderer to mental ray.

3. In the Main Toolbar, click ![icon] (Render Setup) or select **Rendering>Render Setup**.

4. In the Render Setup dialog box, expand the Renderer drop-down menu and select **NVIDIA mental ray**, as shown in Figure 6–87. Close the Render Setup dialog box.

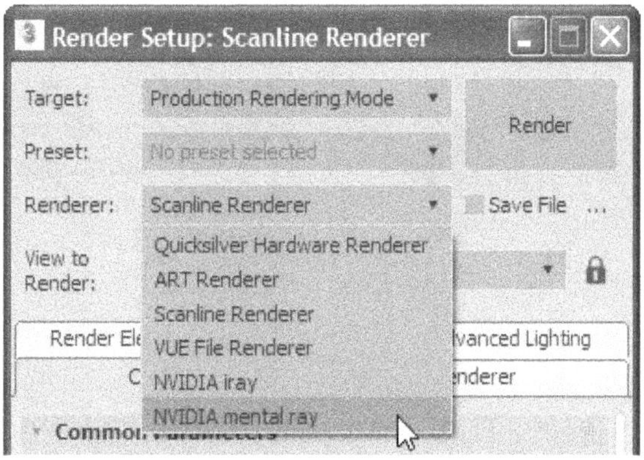

Figure 6–87

Task 2 - Assign the Arch & Design materials.

1. Open the Slate Material Editor, if not already open. In the Material/Map Browser, in the *Materials* category, note that the **mental ray** and **Autodesk** categories are now listed.

2. Expand the *Scene Materials* category at the bottom of the Material/Map Browser. Note that the gray **Standard** materials are being used in the scene.

3. Double-click on each of the gray materials (**CandleHolder**, **Countertop**, **Left Wall**, and **Right Wall**) to place them on the *View1* sheet. They are placed on top of each other. In the

   Material Editor toolbar, click [icon] (Lay Out All - Horizontal) to display the four materials horizontally in the *View1* sheet.

4. To change the color on each of these scene materials, double-click on each material node to open the Parameter Editor. In the Blinn Basic Parameters rollout, select the Diffuse swatch, and select a color in the Color Selector. You can use any color (**Countertop** - dark pink, **Right Wall** - blue, **CandleHolder** - dark blue, and **Left Wall** - green).

5. Verify that the **Camera01** viewport is active (yellow border) and in the Main Toolbar, click ![teapot icon] (Render Production) or press <F9> to render the scene, as shown in Figure 6–88. Note the shadow cast by the candleholder. There is a shadow casting mental ray spotlight already set up in the scene. Leave the Render window open.

Figure 6–88

6. In the Material/Map Browser in the Slate Material Editor, expand the *Materials>mental ray* categories. Double-click on Arch & Design (as shown in Figure 6–89) to add a new material node to the *View1* sheet.

Figure 6–89

7. Double-click on the **Material # Arch & Design** title bar heading to open its Parameter Editor.

8. In the Templates rollout, expand the (Select a template) drop-down list and in the *Metals* sub-category, select **Copper**, as shown in Figure 6–90. The **Copper** material displays as the sample sphere in the material's title bar.

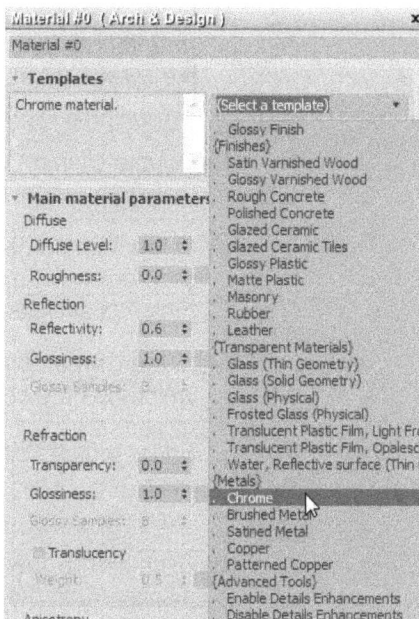

Figure 6–90

*You can select the object in any other viewport but you must activate the **Camera01** viewport before rendering the view.*

9. In the **Camera01** viewport, select the **candleholder** object and in the Slate Material Editor toolbar, click [icon] (Assign Material to Selection).

10. Click **Render** (bottom right of the Render Window), or click

[icon] (Render Production) if the Render window was closed, to render the **Camera01** viewport, as shown in Figure 6–91. The **Copper** material reflects the colors of the walls around it and the lighting in the scene.

*In the Render window, **Render** is located at the bottom right corner of the Settings panel. The rendering time is a little slower due to the calculations for reflections.*

Figure 6–91

11. In the Material/Map Browser, double-click on Arch & Design (*mental ray* category) again to add another material node to the *View1* sheet. Place this new material node to the left of the existing Arch & Design (Copper) node.

12. Double-click on the title bar heading for the new Arch & Design material to access its Parameter Editor.

13. In the Templates rollout, expand the (Select a template) drop-down list and select **Glazed Ceramic Tiles** in the *Finishes* sub-category.

14. In the Camera01 viewport, select the floor object (Box01 which has the countertop material) and in the Slate Material Editor toolbar, click   to assign the new ceramic tile to the floor.

15. Click   (Show Shaded Material in Viewport) to see the tiles displayed on the floor in the viewport.

16. Render the **Camera01** viewport, as shown in Figure 6–92. The **Copper** and **Glazed Tile** materials both display in the scene. The rendering is slower (possibly due to the shadow of the candlestick reflecting on the tiles).

17. Double-click on the title bar heading for the Arch & Design material (Copper template). In the Templates rollout, expand the (Select a template) drop-down list and select **Frosted Glass (Physical)** in the *Transparent Materials* category. This material is automatically assigned to the Candlestick. Render the **Camera01** view again, as shown in Figure 6–93. The render time is significantly slower. The **Translucent** material enables the light to pass through it.

The light is casting a ray-traced shadow, rather than a map shadow.

| Figure 6–92 | Figure 6–93 |

18. Save your work as **Mycandleholder.max**.

Task 3 - Assign a Car Paint material.

To explore the **Car Paint** material, you will load a different file.

1. Open **MR_guitar.max**. This is the guitar with a plain gray material applied to the body.

2. Open the Slate Material Editor, if required. In the Material/Map Browser, expand the *Materials>mental ray* categories. Double-click on the **Car Paint** mental ray material to add it to the *View1* sheet.

3. Select the **BODY:1** object in the viewport (you can select it in the Scene Explorer as well). In the Slate Material Editor toolbar, click ![icon] (Assign Material to Selection) to assign the **Car Paint** material. In the Main Toolbar, click ![icon] (Render Production). The **Car Paint** material is applied to the body, as shown in Figure 6–94.

Your rendering might be slightly different than Figure 6–94. It depends on your monitor display and the Gamma and LUT settings.

Figure 6–94

4. Note that the pickups and strings reflect in the guitar body, but the body looks a little dull. In the *View1* sheet, double-click on the **Material# Car Paint** title bar heading to open its Parameter Editor. In the Diffuse Coloring rollout, select the *Ambient/Extra Light* color swatch to open the Color Selector. Set the *Value* slider to **100**. Click **OK**.

5. Render the scene and note the change in brightness.

6. To add a texture map to a mental ray material, in the Diffuse Coloring rollout, click ☐ for **Base Color** as shown in Figure 6–95.

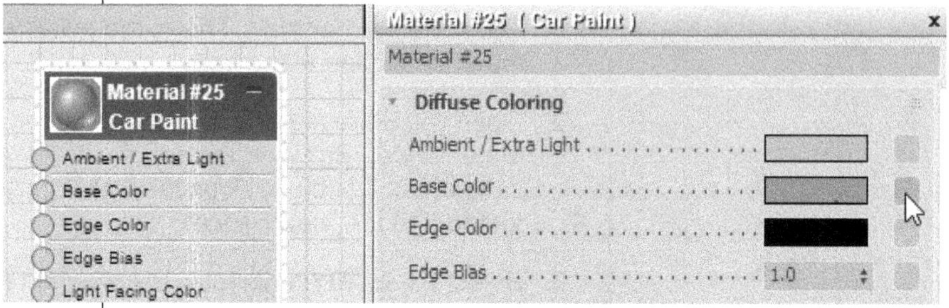

Figure 6–95

7. In the Material/Map Browser, expand the *Maps>Standard* categories and double-click on **Bitmap**. In the Select Bitmap Image File dialog box, browse to the ...*Maps* directory in your Practice Files, open **BURLOAK.JPG**.

8. Render the viewport again. The wood texture is displayed on the guitar body, as shown in Figure 6–96.

Figure 6–96

9. To brighten up the wood texture, in the *View1* sheet, double-click on the **Map # Bitmap** title bar (wired to the Base color of **Car Paint** materials) to open its Parameter Editor.

10. Expand the Output rollout and select **Enable Color Map**. In

the Color Map toolbar, click ⬚ (Add Point) and add a point to the diagonal line at its approximate midpoint, as shown in Figure 6–97.

11. In the Color Map toolbar, click 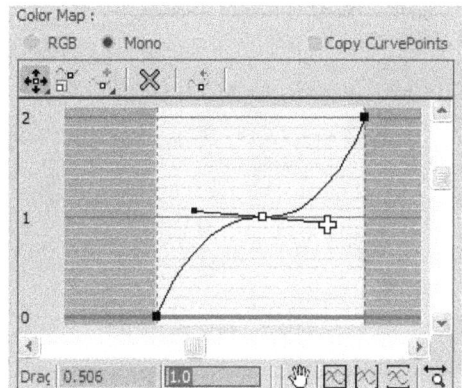 (Move) and drag the right-most point to a *value* of about **2**. You can enter **2** in the right text box at the bottom of graph. Use the **Zoom** tool (located in the lower right corner of the graph window) of the graph to display the point.

12. Move the middle point to **1**, right-click on it and select **Bezier-Smooth**. Move the point and/or handles, as shown in Figure 6–98. The sample sphere for the bitmap updates. Close the Slate Material Editor.

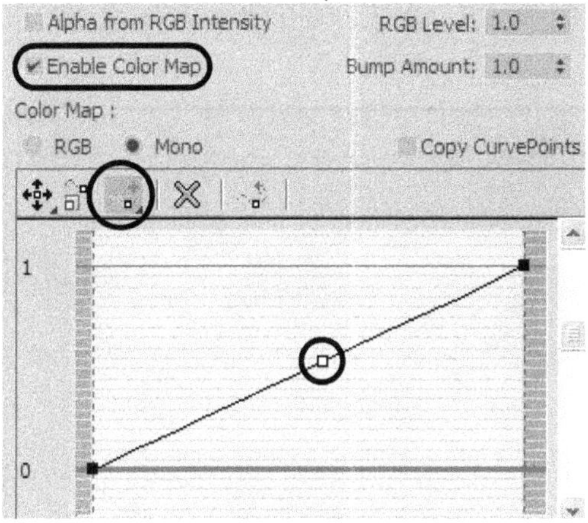

Figure 6–97

Figure 6–98

13. In the viewport, use (Field-of-View) to zoom in on the pickups. Render the scene and note the reflections, as shown in Figure 6–99.

Figure 6–99

14. Save your work as **My_MR_guitar.max**.

6.9 The Material Explorer

The Material Explorer enables you to manage all of the materials used in a scene using. It displays the material's *Name*, *Type*, *Show in Viewport* setting, and *Material ID*, as shown in Figure 6–100.

- You can open the Material Explorer dialog box by selecting **Rendering>Material Explorer**, as shown in Figure 6–100.

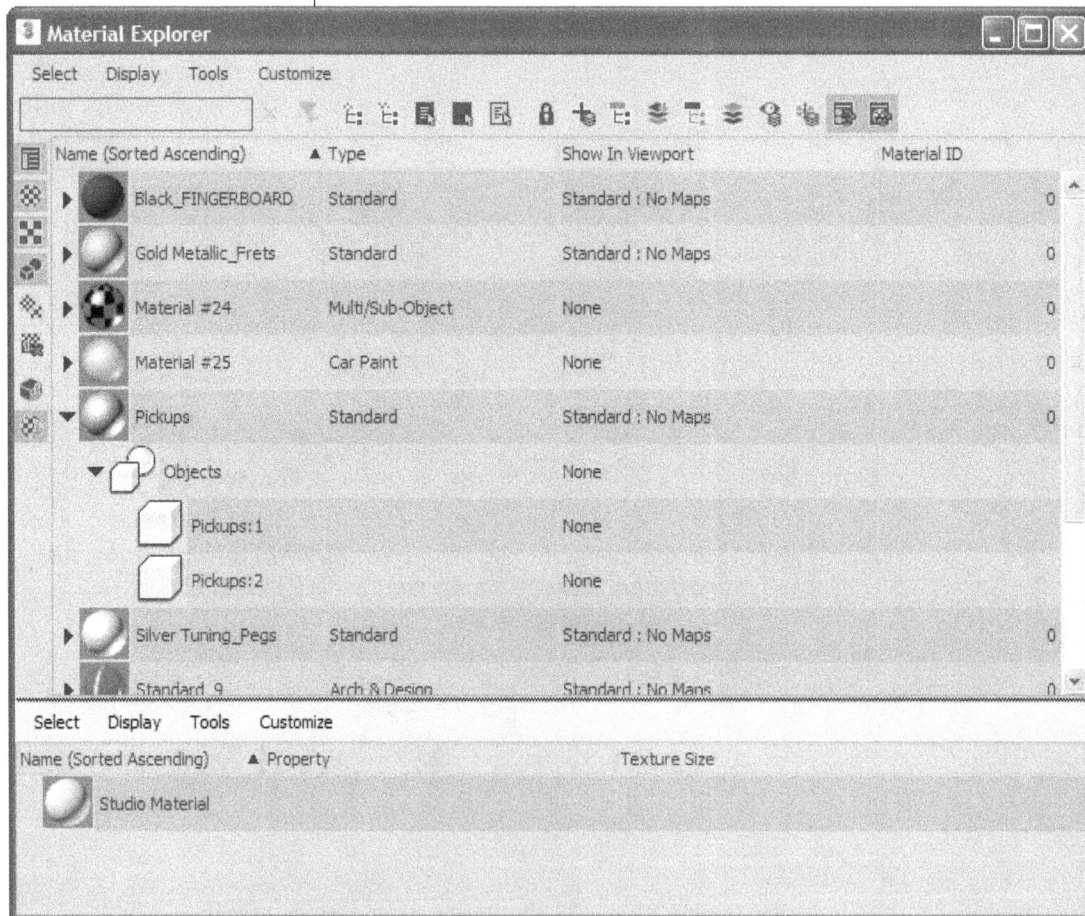

Figure 6–100

- Selecting the various headings sorts the materials in various ways. For example, if you select the *Type* heading, materials of the same type are listed alphabetically according to the material type (such as Architectural, Standard, Arch & Design, etc.).

- The bottom panel of the interface displays information on the maps or other properties of the material. This panel has its own menu that enables you to manipulate each material's properties.

- From the Material Explorer, you can save directly to a new material library (as shown in Figure 6–101) or perform a variety of tasks depending on the type of the material.

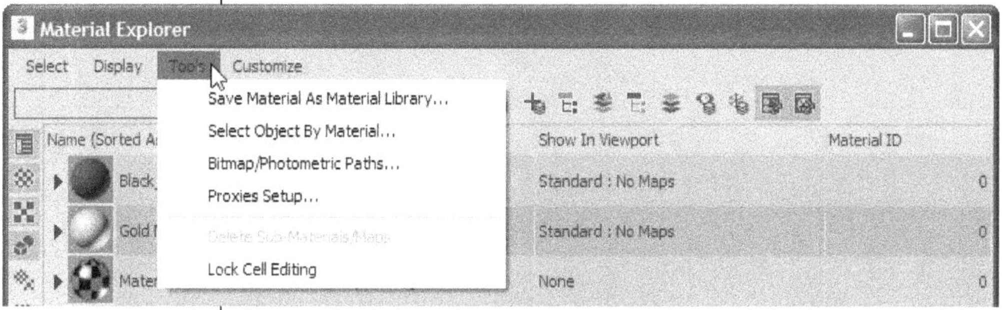

Figure 6–101

Chapter Review Questions

1. What are the three color channels in Standard materials that determine the color applied to an object?

   a. *Ambient, Bump, Specular*

   b. *Bump, Diffuse, Opacity*

   c. *Specular, Opacity, Diffuse*

   d. *Ambient, Diffuse, Specular*

2. The materials and maps listed in the Material/Map Browser are dependent on...

   a. the active scene.

   b. the active renderer.

   c. the active viewport.

   d. the active material editor.

3. In the active view sheet of the Slate Material Editor, the green color (title bar) of a node indicates that it is a...

   a. Material

   b. Map

   c. Controller

   d. Material with the **Show Map In Viewport** option applied.

4. In the active view sheet of the Slate Material Editor, a dashed white border around a material node indicates that the...

   a. Material is being used in the scene.

   b. Map is assigned to one of the channels (socket) of the material.

   c. Parameters of the material are displayed in the Parameter Editor.

   d. Material is a customized material.

5. The Phong shader generates softer, smoother (often more realistic) highlights than the Blinn shader.

   a. True

   b. False

6. Which type of general material enables you to stack multiple materials into a single parent material, each with a material ID number.

    a. Multi/Sub-Object material

    b. Architectural material

    c. Raytrace material

    d. Shell material

7. Which type of mapping gives the illusion of an embossed or pitted surface without actual geometry having to be present on the model?

    a. Opacity mapping

    b. Bump mapping

    c. Reflection mapping

8. Which type of mental ray material is a layered material that provides for four layers (base paint layer, embedded metal flake layer, clear-coat layer, and Lambertian dirt layer) combining to create one surface treatment?

    a. Arch and Design material

    b. Matte/Shadow/Reflection material

    c. Subsurface Scattering (SSS) material

    d. Car Paint material

Command Summary

Button	Command	Location
	Compact Material Editor	• **Main Toolbar** • **Rendering:** Material Editor>Compact Material Editor
N/A	Material Explorer	• **Rendering:** Material Explorer
	Render Production	• **Main Toolbar**: Render flyout • **Rendering:** Render
	Render Setup	• **Main Toolbar** • **Rendering:** Render Setup
	Slate Material Editor	• **Main Toolbar** • **Rendering:** Material Editor>Slate Material Editor

Mapping Coordinates and Scale

When creating a realistic representations of a model, both materials and image texture maps can be used. They can be incorporated in a Material or you can use specific Map Modifiers and Scaling controls to further control how these elements look in a model.

Learning Objectives in this Chapter

- Work with mapping coordinates required for objects with texture maps.
- Assign mapping coordinates using various tools.
- Adjust the size of the image maps using the various map scaling options.
- Assign spline mapping to a curved object.

7.1 Mapping Coordinates

Most of the sample materials provided with the Autodesk® 3ds Max® software are assigned image texture maps, especially the Diffuse Color and Bump maps. Objects that are assigned materials with maps require mapping coordinates to control how the map is projected onto the object. For example, a rectangular sign can use planar or box mapping and a cylindrical can uses cylindrical mapping.

UVW is used instead of XYZ to indicate that the mapping does not need to be aligned with the world XYZ coordinates.

- Mapping is referenced by its own local coordinate system, described by UVW coordinates.

- Many objects (including primitives) are automatically assigned mapping coordinates. This is controlled by **Generate Mapping Coords** in the Command Panel, in the object's Parameters rollout, as shown in Figure 7–1.

- Linked or imported objects with materials assigned in AutoCAD® automatically have mapping coordinates if the **Generate coordinates for all objects** is selected in the import or link preset options, as shown in Figure 7–2.

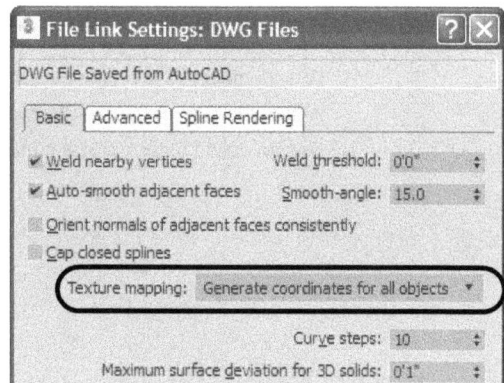

Figure 7–1   Figure 7–2

- The Autodesk 3ds Max software provides a number of different modifiers (such as **UVW Map**, **Unwrap UVW**, and **MapScaler**) that can be used to reassign mapping manually.

- Mapping is often disturbed by editing (as through an Edit Mesh modifier) and by Boolean operations. The Edit Poly modifier has a Preserve UVW's feature that can be toggled on to prevent the need for remapping.

- If you select to render an object without mapping coordinates, you receive a warning message that the maps might not render correctly.

Mapping Controls in Slate Material Editor

At the map level of the Slate Material Editor, in the Parameter Editor of the map (shown in Figure 7–3), there are controls to manipulate the positioning of a map with mapping coordinates. (Some of these controls are duplicated in the UVW Map modifier, which controls only the object it is applied to.)

Use Real-World Scale On

The **Use Real-World Scale** attempts to simplify the correct scaling of textures by specifying the actual height and width (as shown in Figure 7–3) as represented by the 2D texture map. This option requires that the object use UV texture mapping set to **Real World Map Size** and that the Material also have **Use Real-World Scale** selected. It replaces the *Tiling* fields with a Size value for **Width** and **Height**.

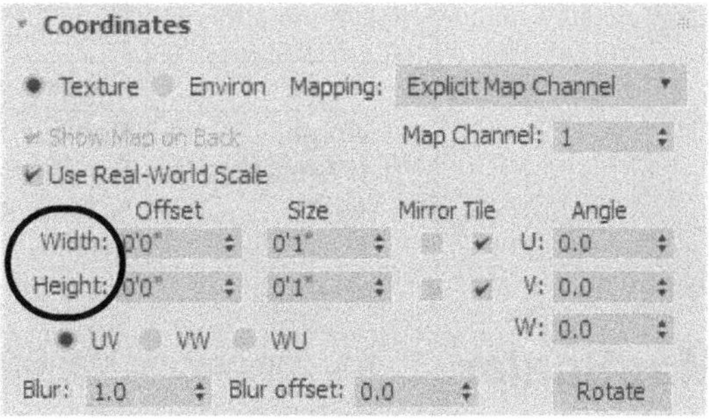

Figure 7–3

Hint: Importing with Use Real-World Scale

Using the **Use Real-World Scale** option when importing from earlier versions of the Autodesk 3ds Max software might cause textures to display incorrectly. It can be due to **Real World Map Size** and **Use Real-World Scale** trying to create an extreme texture. If you leave these on, you need to reset *Tiling* to a different value. You can use **0.01** or a similar small value before you can see the bitmap texture, or go larger and use **10** or **20**. If the texture does not display correctly, it might be easier to toggle off **Use Real-World Scale** and set *Tiling* to **1.0** x **1.0**.

Use Real-World Scale Off

When the **Use Real-World Scale** is toggled off, the map texture is placed with respect to the UV values, as shown in Figure 7–4.

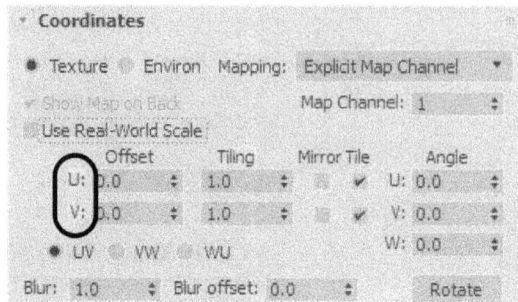

Figure 7–4

Offset	Enable you to move the map on an object relative to the mapping coordinates.
Tiling	Enables you to specify whether the map is repeated or tiled across the surface, in either the U (often width) or V (often height) direction.
Mirror	Causes tiled maps to be mirrored end-to-end as they tile.
Angle (*W-rotation field*)	Controls rotation of the map about the W (local Z) axis. For 2D maps (such as with an image file) this value typically is used to rotate the map on the surface of an object.

MapScaler Modifier

You can use the MapScaler Modifier (Modifier List in the Modify panel (⬚)) to project a map perpendicular to each face of an object. There are two MapScalers:

- **MapScaler World Space Modifier (WSM)** (shown in Figure 7–5) keeps the map scale constant if the object size changes with the Scale transform.

- **MapScaler Object Space Modifier (OSM)** (shown in Figure 7–6) scales the map proportionally.

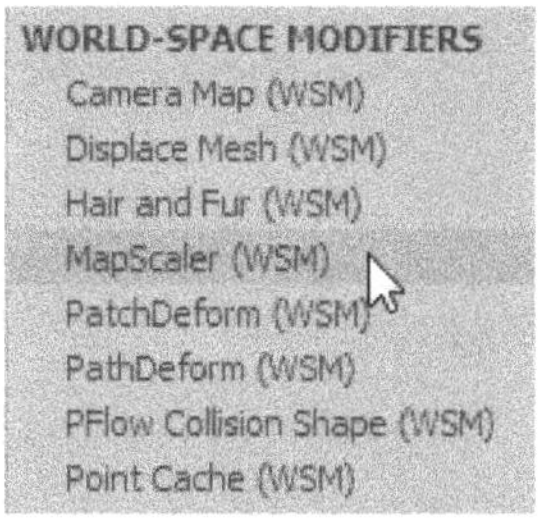

WORLD-SPACE MODIFIERS
Camera Map (WSM)
Displace Mesh (WSM)
Hair and Fur (WSM)
MapScaler (WSM)
PatchDeform (WSM)
PathDeform (WSM)
PFlow Collision Shape (WSM)
Point Cache (WSM)

Lattice
Linked XForm
MapScaler
MassFX RBody
Material
MaterialByElement
mCloth

Figure 7–5 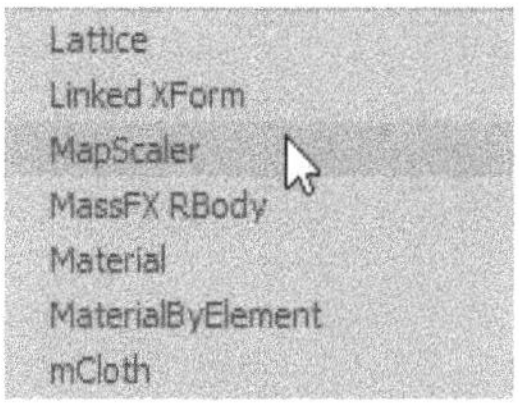   **Figure 7–6**

MapScalers do not always project well on curved surfaces.

- MapScalers enable automatically generated, continuous tiling across complex geometry that might be difficult with UVW Maps. They tend to work well with geometry imported from the AutoCAD Architecture and the Autodesk Revit software.

- One method of repositioning a map on an object assigned a MapScaler is to adjust the U- and V-offset settings in the Bitmap Parameters rollout in the Material Editor. Otherwise, apply a UVW XForm modifier to the object and apply the offsets there instead.

- MapScaler modifiers are generally used on objects that have tiling material maps but do not have a defined beginning or end point, such as concrete pads, metals, asphalt, grass, and sometimes brick.

UVW Map Modifier

The UVW Map modifier (Modify panel ()>Modifier List) enables you to apply a map to an object, where you select a specific shape and location to project the map onto.

- The UVW Map modifier has a gizmo for transforming in Sub-object mode.

- UVW Maps might not project as well as MapScalers on geometry that does not lend itself to the standard projection shapes (planar, box, cylinder, etc.).

Hint: Unwrap UVW

The **Unwrap UVW** modifier is another commonly used mapping method. For more information on *Unwrap UVW*, see the Autodesk 3ds Max Help files.

Practice 7a | Applying Mapping Coordinates

Practice Objective

- Adjust the placement of a map on an object.

Estimated time for completion: 10 minutes

In this practice you will adjust the material mapping using the UVW Map and MapScaler (WSM) modifiers.

You must set the paths to locate the External files and Xrefs used in the practice. If you have not done this already, return to **Chapter 1: Introduction to Autodesk 3ds Max** and complete Task 1 to Task 3 in **Practice 1a: Organizing Folders and Working with the Interface**. You only have to set the user paths once.

*If a dialog box opens prompting you about a File Load: Mismatch, click **OK** to accept the default values.*

1. Open **Light Pole Mapping.max**.

2. In the viewport, select the concrete **LP Base** object and then

   click (Zoom Extents Selected) to zoom into the base object as shown in Figure 7–7. When this cylinder was created, the mapping coordinates were generated automatically.

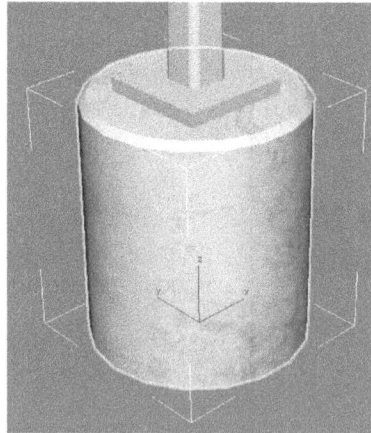

Figure 7–7

*You need to scroll down the list to select the **UVW Map** modifier.*

3. With the **LP Base** object selected, in the Command Panel>

   Modify panel ( ), expand the Modifier list. In the *OBJECT-SPACE MODIFIERS* group, select **UVW Map**, as shown in Figure 7–8.

Turn to Poly
Twist
Unwrap UVW
UVW Map
UVW Mapping Add
UVW Mapping Clear

Figure 7–8

4. In the Parameters rollout, in the *Mapping* area, select **Box,** as shown in Figure 7–9. This projects the concrete map onto the object from all six sides of an imaginary box, causing a seam to form in places, as shown in Figure 7–10.

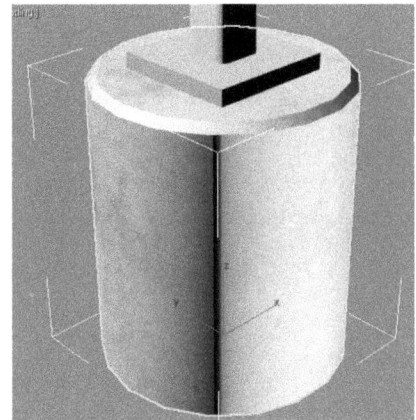

Figure 7–9   **Figure 7–10**

5. Change the projection to *Cylindrical* and then *Planar*, noting the differences.

   • The Cylindrical projection is not handling the beveled top very well, as shown in Figure 7–11.

   • The Planar projection is not displaying the cylindrical base correctly, as shown in Figure 7–12.

Figure 7–11   **Figure 7–12**

6. Remove the UVW Map modifier from the Modifier Stack by selecting it and clicking 🗑 (Remove modifier from the stack), as shown in Figure 7–13.

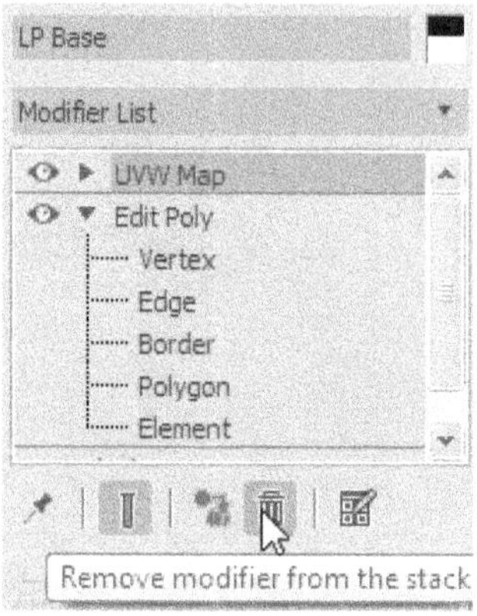

Figure 7–13

7. In the Modifier drop-down list, in the WORLD-SPACE MODIFIERS, select **MapScaler (WSM)**. The MapScalers are automatically projected perpendicular to each face of an object.

8. Change the Shading Viewport (User Defined) label to **High Quality**.

9. In the Parameters rollout, adjust the *Scale* spinner up or down to visually improve the look of the map, as shown in Figure 7–14.

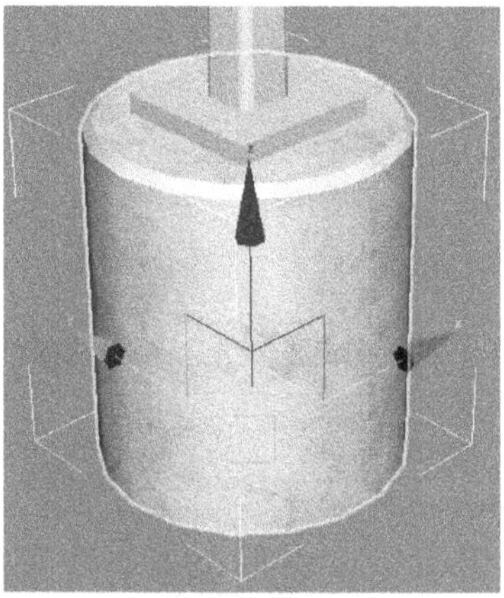

Figure 7–14

10. Save your work as **MyLight Pole Mapping.max**.

Practice 7b

Estimated time for completion: 10 minutes

*If a dialog box opens prompting you about a File Load: Mismatch, click **OK** to accept the default values.*

Mapping a Large Scale Image

Practice Objective

- Assign a map to a model and apply mapping coordinates.

In this practice you will apply a scanned image to a terrain model and map it accurately. You will use the Slate Material Editor and the **UVW Map** modifiers to assign a map to a model, apply mapping coordinates, and adjust the map.

You must set the paths to locate the External files and Xrefs used in the practice. If you have not done this already, return to **Chapter 1: Introduction to Autodesk 3ds Max** and complete Task 1 to Task 3 in **Practice 1a: Organizing Folders and Working with the Interface**. You only have to set the user paths once.

1. Open the file **Mapping a large scale image.max**.

2. If your Units setup is maintained for Imperial, a Units Scale Mismatch dialog box opens. Click **OK** to accept the defaults. The units for this file are set to **Meters** and the *System Unit Scale* is **1 Unit=1 Meter**. This is required because the map that will be used is set for Metric units.

3. In the Main Toolbar, click ⊠ (Material Editor) to open the Slate Material Editor. In the Material/Map Browser, expand the *Materials>Scanline* categories. Double-click on the **Standard** material to add it to the *View1* sheet. Double-click on the title bar heading for this new material to open the Parameter Editor. Change the material name to **Quad Map**.

4. Expand the Maps rollout and for *Diffuse Color*, click **None**, as shown in Figure 7–15. The Material/Map Browser opens.

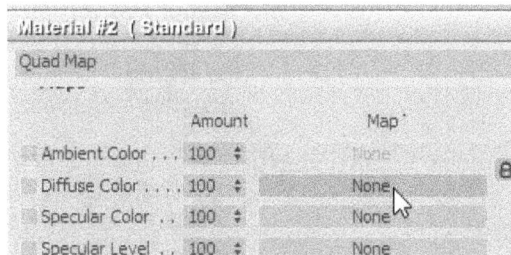

	Amount		Map
Ambient Color . . .	100	÷	None
Diffuse Color	100	÷	None
Specular Color . .	100	÷	None
Specular Level . .	100	÷	None

Figure 7–15

5. In the Material/Map Browser, expand the *Maps>General* categories. Double-click on **Bitmap** to open the Select Bitmap Image File dialog box. Open the image **q257938.tif** from the ...*Maps* folder in the Practice Files folder.

6. In the *View1* sheet, note that the **Map # Bitmap** is wired to the Input socket of *Diffuse Color* of the Quad Map material. Double-click on the Bitmap title bar heading to open its Parameter Editor. In the Bitmap Parameters rollout, in the *Cropping/Placement* area, click **View Image** to open the bitmap. Close the Specify Cropping/Placement window.

7. In the Coordinates rollout, clear **Use Real-World Scale**. Clear *Tile* for both **U** and **V** (as shown in Figure 7–16) because you want this map to display only once and in a specific location.

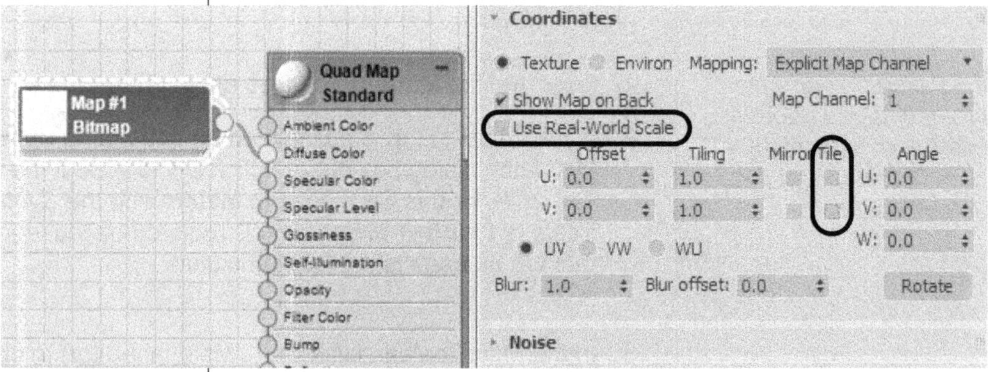

Figure 7–16

8. In the viewport, select the **Terrain01** object. In the *View1* sheet, select the **Quad Map** material and in the Material Editor toolbar, click ![icon] (Assign Material to Selection). The material does not preview in the viewport.

9. In the viewport, right-click on the **Terrain01** object and select **Object Properties**. In the *Display Properties* area, clear **Vertex Channel Display** and click **OK**. Now the gray color of the material is visible on the terrain, and no texture map indicates a mapping issue.

In the Main Toolbar,

click ![teapot icon] *(Render Production).*

10. Render the scene and note the warning message of missing map coordinates. Click **Cancel** in the Missing Map Coordinates dialog box and close the Render window.

11. In the viewport, select the **Terrain01** object, if required. In the Command Panel, select the Modify panel (), and in the Modifier List, select **UVW Map**. Since the diffuse map is not meant to tile, in the Parameters rollout, verify that **Planar** is selected and clear **Real-World Map Size**, as shown in Figure 7–17.

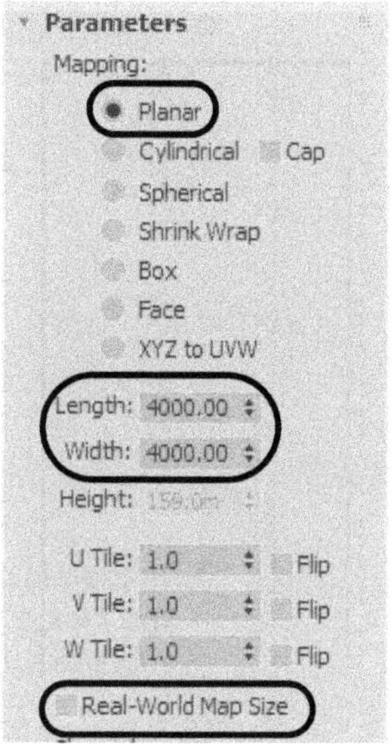

Figure 7–17

12. Render the scene. The terrain model should now resemble a 3D map, as shown in Figure 7–18.

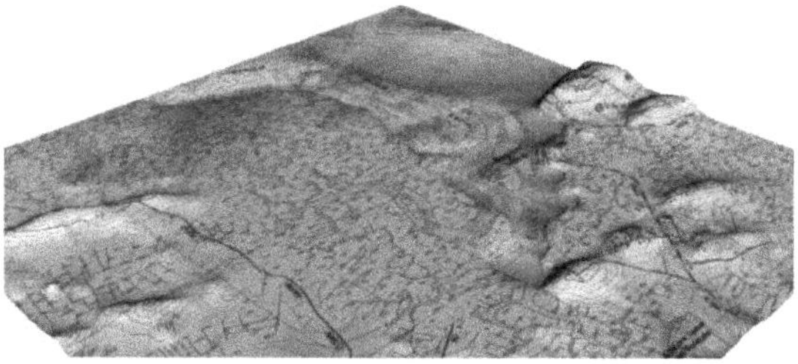

Figure 7–18

- Without any direct manipulation, it appears that this texture map is being applied correctly. This is because the contours used to create the surface were trimmed very close to the geographic boundary of the image file.

13. Close the Render window. If the map does not display in the viewport, in the Slate Material Editor toolbar, click ▣ (Show Shaded Material in Viewport).

14. In the Command Panel, in the Parameters rollout, note that the map was automatically scaled to the correct coordinates displayed in the *Length* and *Width* values.

15. In the Modifier Stack, expand UVW Map and select **Gizmo** to enter Sub-object mode, as shown in Figure 7–19.

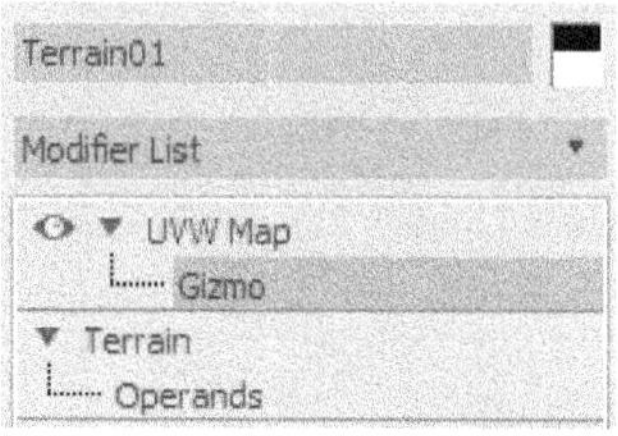

Figure 7–19

16. In the Main Toolbar, click ✛ (Select and Move) and move the image map on the terrain object. You can adjust the map more precisely using the UVW Map gizmo.

17. Save your work as **MyLargeScaleProjectMapped**.

7.2 Mapping Scale

Mapping Scale is directly related to mapping coordinates and both are often addressed at the same time. Objects that use materials with image maps need to have them sized appropriately.

- Procedural maps also need to be scaled, but they are normally controlled by scale parameters at the Map level of the Material Editor.

Explicit Map Scaling

The size parameters of the UVW Map modifier enables you to control the number of times a map is displayed. Examples of this include maps used in materials for 3D models of signs, billboards, computer screens, paintings, etc.

- These kinds of maps are not assigned a real-world scale since they often require to be sized manually for each object. In these situations, clear the **Use Real-World Map Scale** option in the Map Coordinates rollout and clear the **Real-World Map Size** in the **UVW Map** parameters, as shown in Figure 7–20.

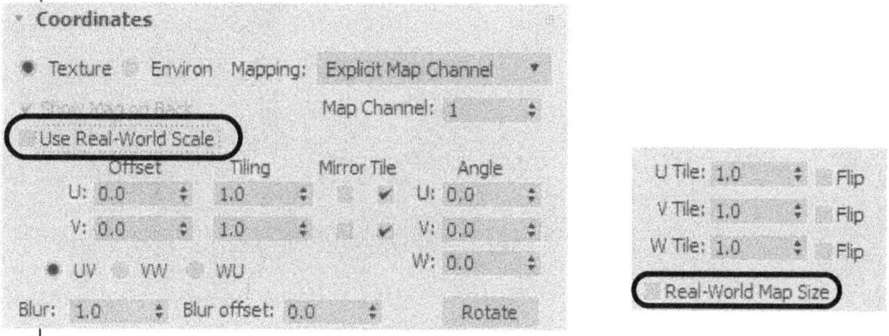

Figure 7–20

- To display the map once, the U and V tile values should be set to **1.0** in both the Map Coordinates rollout of the Material Editor and the **UVW Map** modifier parameters.

- To display the map in the V-direction twice, for example (the map's local Y-direction), set the V tile value to **2** in one of these locations, but not both.

Continuous Map Scaling

When material maps are meant to tile continuously across an object, a continuous approach can be used. The size of these maps can be controlled by a Real World scale that affects all objects using the map, or they can be sized directly using **UVW Map** or **MapScaler** size parameters for each object. Setting a Real World scale makes it easier to affect a global map scale change to multiple objects. You might need to determine the physical size you want to display an image file map in your scene.

Calculating Real World scales

U is the map's local X-axis and V is the local Y.

The **Brick** material uses an image file for a diffuse color map, as shown in Figure 7–21. This image map represents a section of wall that is five bricks wide (measured along the long edges) and 16 courses tall. If you want to use this material to represent bricks that are 11" on center laid in 4" courses, this brick map should be scaled to exactly **4'7" (11" x 5)** in the U direction and **5'4" (4" x 16)** in the V direction.

Figure 7–21

You can set this scale in various ways:

- At a global scale, enable **Use Real-World Scale** and assign appropriate size values in the map's Coordinates rollout, as shown in Figure 7–22.

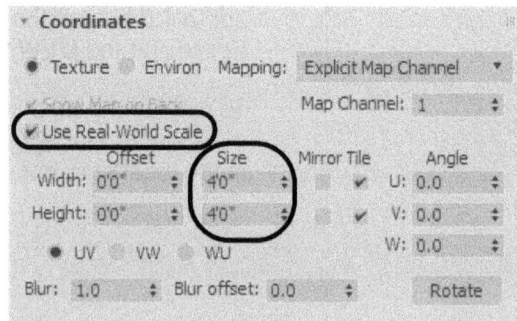

Figure 7–22

- If mapping coordinates are required, apply UVW Maps or Map Scalers to objects displaying this map. UVW Maps should have the **Real World Map Size** option enabled as shown in Figure 7–23. The Map Scalers should be set to a size of one scene unit (such as 1"), as shown in Figure 7–24, in the Parameters rollout of WSM modifier.

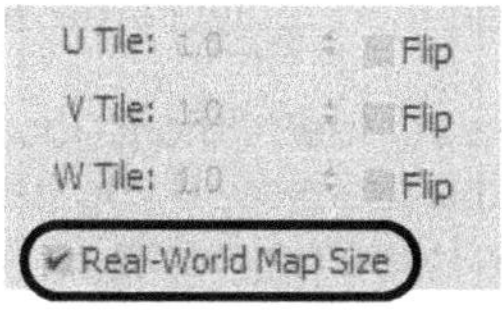

Figure 7–23

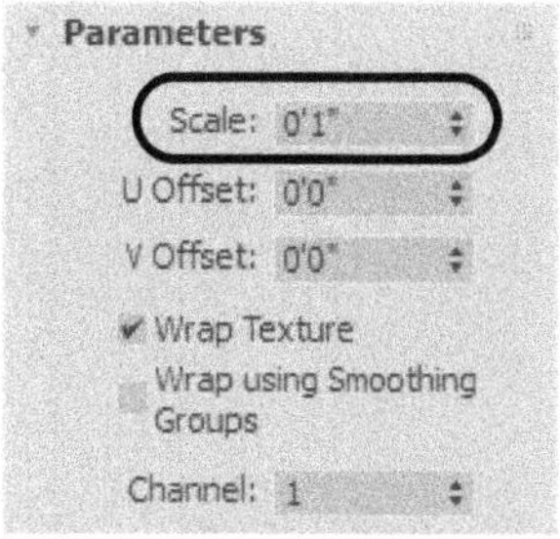

Figure 7–24

- If you want to control map scaling of individual objects through a UVW Map, clear the **Use Real-World Scale** option in the Coordinates rollout and set the *Tiling* values to **1.0**, as shown in Figure 7–25.

- Objects showing map can be assigned sizes directly through the UVW Map modifier's **Length**, **Width** and **Height** parameter values. Clear **Real-World Map Size** in the **UVW Map** parameters.

- If you want to control map scaling on individual objects with a Map Scaler, clear the **Use Real-World Scale** option, set the *U-Tiling* value to **1.0** and the *V-Tiling* value equal to the ratio of the U-scale divided by the V scale, as shown in Figure 7–26.

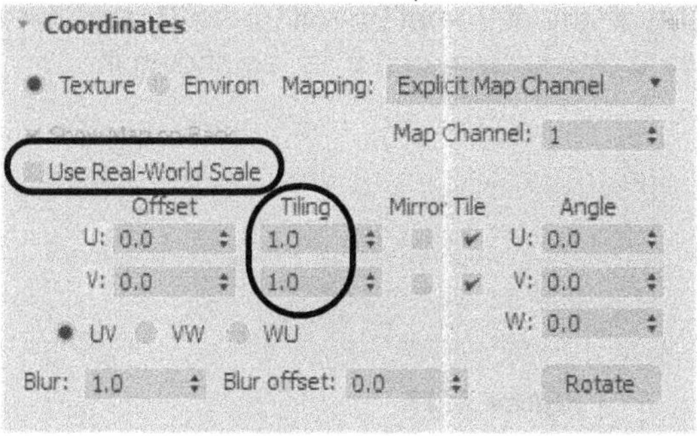

Figure 7–25

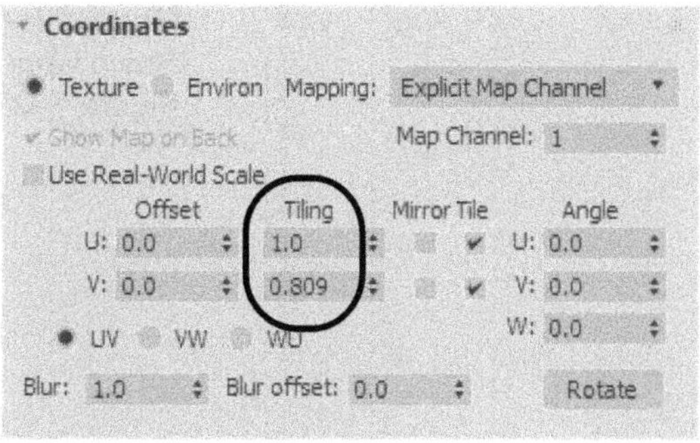

Figure 7–26

- Objects showing this map can be assigned MapScaler modifiers with the **Scale** parameter value set to the U scale.

Practice 7c | Assigning Map Scales

Practice Objectives

- Assign a material that contains an image map.
- Adjust the size of the image maps.

Estimated time for completion: 15 minutes

In this practice you will assign a material containing an image map to an object in a scene. You will then use the **MapScaler (WSM)** modifier to adjust the image map and the scaling options to position it correctly in the scene.

You must set the paths to locate the External files and Xrefs used in the practice. If you have not done this already, return to **Chapter 1: Introduction to Autodesk 3ds Max** and complete Task 1 to Task 3 in **Practice 1a: Organizing Folders and Working with the Interface**. You only have to set the user paths once.

Task 1 - Position and Scale the Brick Maps.

*If a dialog box opens prompting you about a File Load: Mismatch, click **OK** to accept the default values.*

1. Open the file **Interior Mapping.max**. If you completed the Terrain Mapping practice, the *Units* were changed to **Metric**, and a Units Scale Mismatch dialog box now opens. Click **OK** to accept the defaults and adopt the file's units (Imperial).

2. In the Scene Explorer, ■ (Display None) and ● (Display Geometry). Select **Layer:VIZ-1-Walls**, to select all of the walls in the lower floor in the viewport. .

3. In the Modify panel ( ), in the Modifier List, select **MapScaler (WSM)**. In the Parameters rollout, verify that the *Scale* value is set to one system unit **0'1"**, as shown in Figure 7–27.

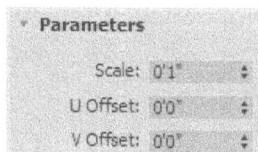

Figure 7–27

4. In the Main Toolbar, click (Material Editor) to open the Slate Material Editor.

5. In the *Scene Materials*, double-click on the **Wall Multi (Multi/Sub-Object)** material to open it on the *View1* sheet. Locate the **Masonry** material, wired to input socket 5 of the **Wall Multi** material, as shown in Figure 7–28. Note that this material has bitmaps wired to the *Diffuse* and *Bump* channels.

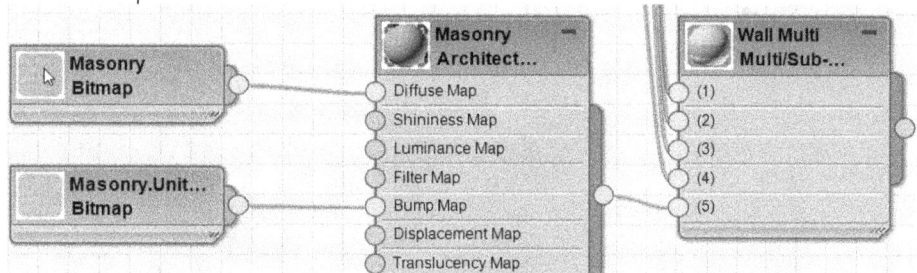

Figure 7–28

6. Double-click on the **Masonry Bitmap** wired to the **Masonry** material's *Diffuse Map* to open its Parameter Editor.

7. In the Coordinates rollout, verify that **Use Real-World Scale** is selected and set the following, as shown in Figure 7–29:
    *   *Width, Size:* **4'7"**
    *   *Height, Size:* **5'4"**

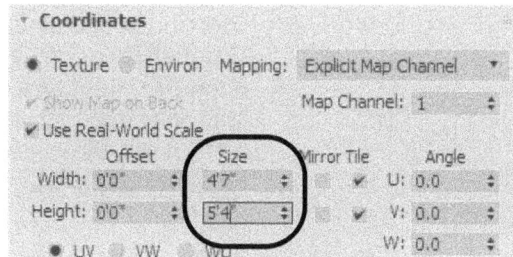

Figure 7–29

8. In *View1* sheet, select the **Masonry Architect** material, click ⬚ (Assign Material to Selection), and click ⬚ (Show Shaded Material in Viewport). Note that the **brick** material has been assigned to the walls because **Layer:VIZ-1-Walls** was selected.

The Slate Material Editor is a modeless dialog box and can remain open while you are working in the viewport or other commands. You can minimize or maximize it, as required.

*The brick texture terminates in acceptable positions along the wall edges. If it does not, move the texture along the wall with the **U-** and **V-** offset parameters in the map's Coordinates rollout, or with a UVW XForm modifier.*

9. In the **Perspective** viewport, use the various navigation tools, such as ⌕ (Zoom), ✋ (Pan), and 🪐 (Orbit), to zoom into and obtain the required orientation of one of the brick walls. The brick texture displays at the correct scale on the wall objects displaying the brick sub-material, as shown in Figure 7–30.

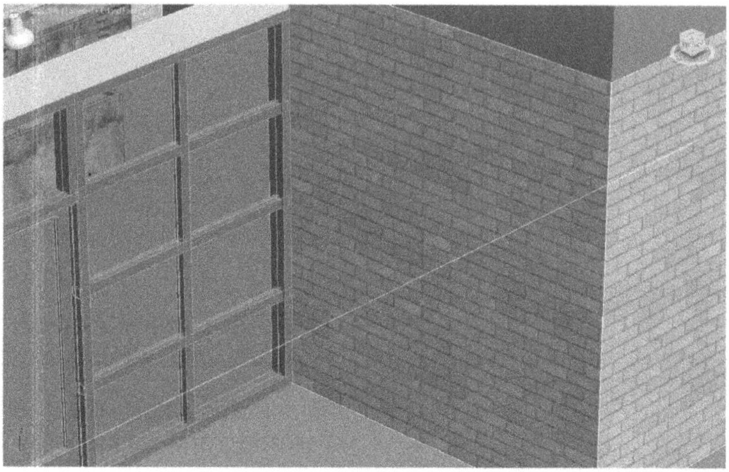

Figure 7–30

10. For images in a material to be aligned, all of their mapping coordinates' parameters should also match. In the Slate Material Editor, double-click on the title bar heading for the **Masonry.Unit** bitmap, wired to the Bump Map of the **Masonry** material. In the Coordinates rollout, set the *Width* and *Height Size* values that were used for the Diffuse Map. This makes the bitmap texture display more realistic.

Hint: Multiple Sets of Mapping Coordinates

In the example, you scaled a Multi/Sub-Object material map with a single MapScaler Modifier. What if another material's map in Wall Multi required a **UVW Map** or different **MapScaler Scale** parameter?

Material maps can be assigned to separate channels in the Material Editor, so that each can be controlled by separate UVW Maps or MapScaler Modifiers. In such a case, you can apply multiple UVW Maps or MapScaler Modifiers to the same object and assign each the applicable channel identified in the **Map** parameters, as shown in Figure 7–31.

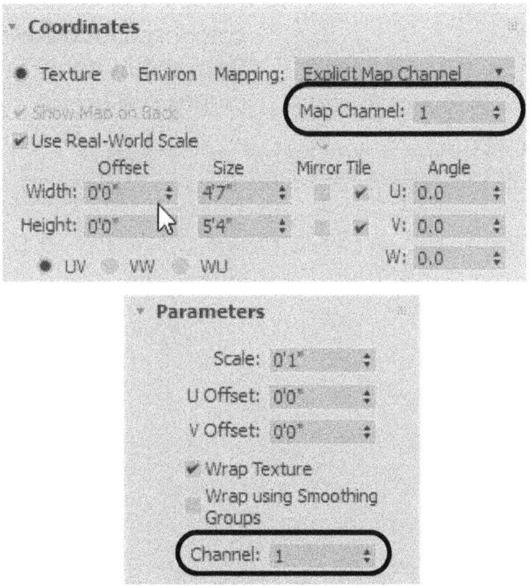

Figure 7–31

Task 2 - Assign the Ceiling Material.

1. Change your current view to the **Camera - Lobby1** camera view, by selecting the **Perspective** POV label and selecting **Cameras>Camera - Lobby1**.

2. Change the Shading Viewport (User Defined) to **High Quality**.

The production renderer should be NVIDIA mental ray, NVIDIA iray, ART Renderer, or Quicksilver Hardware Renderer, to display the Autodesk Material Library.

3. In the Material/Map Browser in the Slate Material Editor, locate the Autodesk Material Library.

   - If the Autodesk Material Library is not listed, in the Main Toolbar, click ![icon] (Render Setup) to open the Render Setup dialog box. In the Renderer drop-down list, select **NVIDIA mental ray** and close the Render Setup dialog box.

4. Right-click on the *View1* label and select **Create New View**. Accept the default view name (*View2*) and click **OK**. The *View2* sheet, which is empty, is the now active sheet.

5. Expand the Autodesk Material Library and the *Miscellaneous* category. Double-click on the **Acoustic Tile - 2x2 White Pebbled** material to display it in *View2* sheet, as shown in Figure 7–32.

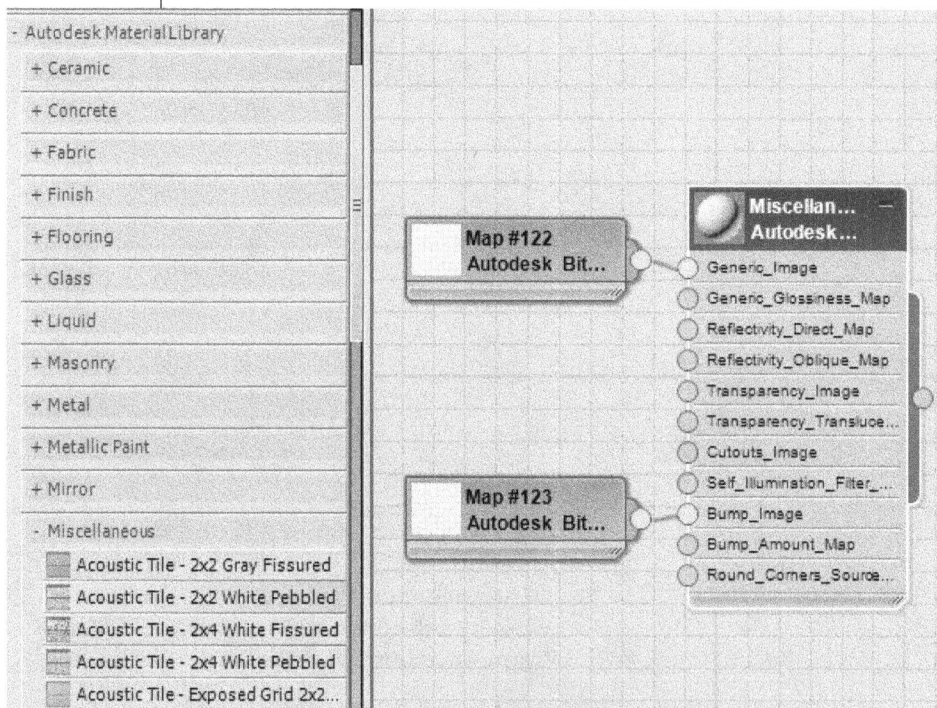

Figure 7–32

6. In the viewport, select the ceiling object and note that **Layer:VIZ-1-Ceiling** is displayed in the Command Panel. In the Command Panel, apply a **MapScaler (WSM)** modifier by selecting it from the Modifier List. In the Parameters rollout, verify that *Scale* is set to **0'1"**.

7. In the Slate Material Editor, in the *View2* sheet, select **Miscellaneous** material by clicking on its title bar and click

   ![icon] (Assign Material to Selection).

8. Note that the ceiling displays in white/gray in the viewport. In the Slate Material Editor toolbar, click ![icon] (Show Shaded Material in Viewport) to preview the diffuse map in the viewport, as shown in Figure 7–33. The ceiling tiles have been sized using the Real-World Map Size that was defined for this material in the Autodesk Material Library (to a 2'x2' grid).

Figure 7–33

9. You can reposition the ceiling texture through the *Offset* fields in the MapScaler modifier. In the Command Panel, in the Parameters rollout, change the *U Offset* and *V Offset* spinner arrows and observe the change in the viewport. Move it so that the left ceiling tile edge coincides with the corner of the ceiling and the left curtain wall window, as shown in Figure 7–34.

Figure 7–34

10. Save your work as **MyInterior Mapping.max**.

7.3 Spline Mapping

Generating mapping coordinates that follow the path of extrusion is useful when a texture needs to follow the curvature of the lofted object. The **Unwrap UVW** modifier enables you to apply spline mapping and to select a spline for the basis of the mapping coordinates. You can use the Mapping gizmo to modify the mapping along the cross-section.

- It is applied at a sub-object level (Polygon or Face), as shown in Figure 7–35.

- It is present in the Wrap rollout of the **Unwrap UVW** parameters, as shown in Figure 7–36.

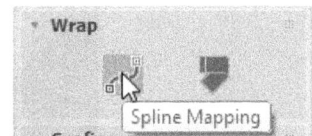

Figure 7–35   Figure 7–36

Practice 7d

Spline Mapping

Practice Objective

- Apply spline mapping to a curved object.

Estimated time for completion: 15 minutes

In this practice you will apply spline mapping to a curved object using the **Unwrap UVW** modifier and adjust the scale and position to place it appropriately.

You must set the paths to locate the External files and Xrefs used in the practice. If you have not done this already, return to **Chapter 1: Introduction to Autodesk 3ds Max** and complete Task 1 to Task 3 in **Practice 1a: Organizing Folders and Working with the Interface**. You only have to set the user paths once.

Task 1 - Position and Scale the Checker Map.

*If a dialog box opens prompting you about a File Load: Mismatch, click **OK** to accept the default values.*

1. Open **Spline Mapping.max**. There are two curved objects. The one on the right has been mapped with spline mapping while the one on the left does not have mapping.

2. Select **Roadshape01** (left object). A spline has already been prepared in this file and it runs (yellow line) through the center of the curved object. You can change the Per-View Preference to **Wireframe Override** to display the spline more clearly and then change it back to **Default Shading**.

3. Expand the Modify panel ( ) and in the Modifier Stack verify that a Line object and an Extrude modifier are listed.

4. In the Main Toolbar, click (Material Editor) to open the Slate Material Editor.

5. In the Material/Map Browser, in the *Scene Materials* category, double-click on **02 - Default** Standard material to place it in the *View1* sheet. This material has already been assigned to the **Roadshape01** object.

6. Double-click on the **02 - Default** title bar to open its Parameter Editor. In the Blinn Basic Parameters rollout, click ▢ (None) for the *Diffuse color* channel, as shown in Figure 7–37.

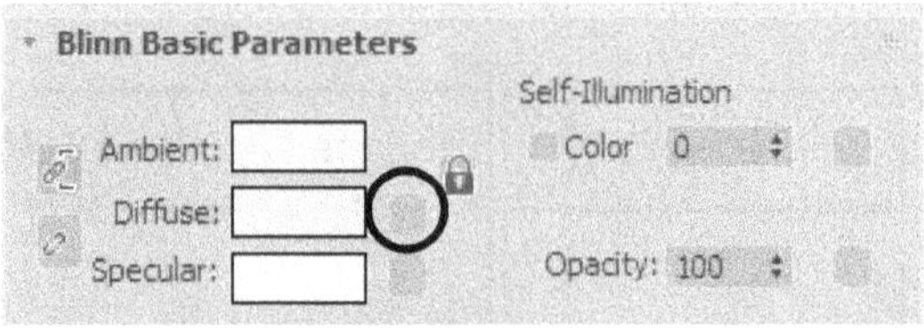

Figure 7–37

7. In the Material/Map Browser that opens, in the *Maps> General* categories, double-click on **Checker**. In the *View1* sheet, note that the Checker node is wired to the input socket of Diffuse Color of the **02- Default** material.

A checker board mapping material is useful for identifying map scaling and orientation issues, which can then be corrected before applying the actual texture map so that it displays correctly.

8. In the Slate Material Editor toolbar, click ▣ (Show Shaded Material in Viewport) to display the checker texture on the road shape in the viewport, as shown in Figure 7–38.

Figure 7–38

- Note that the checker map is projected as a single sheet on top of the rectangular object and not generated to follow the curvature of the spline.

You can minimize the Slate Material Editor so that it is not in the way while you are working in the Command Panel and the viewport and maximize it when you need it again.

9. In the Command Panel>Modify panel (▨), in the Modifier List, select **Unwrap UVW**. Note that the Unwrap UVW is listed above Extrude in the Modifier Stack.

10. In the Modifier Stack, expand Unwrap UVW and select **Polygon**, as shown in Figure 7–39.

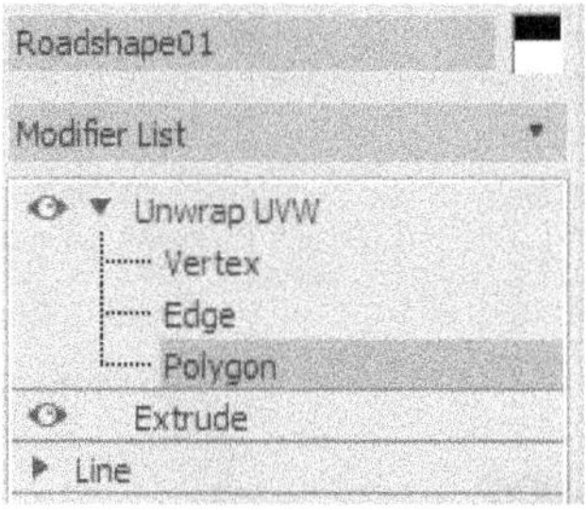

Figure 7–39

11. In the viewport, select the top face along the curve of the **Roadshape01** object. Note that the top checker face is displayed in a red hue indicating that the face is selected.

12. In the Command Panel, pan down to the Wrap rollout. Click

(Spline Mapping), as shown in Figure 7–40.

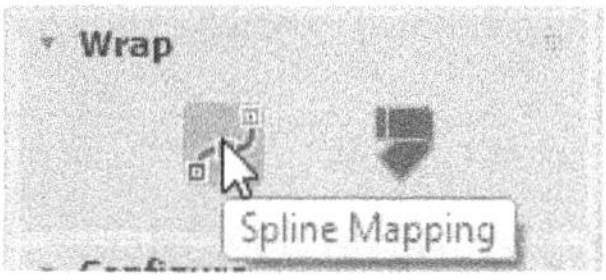

Figure 7–40

*Apply **Planar** for roads and planar surfaces with a line cross-section. Use **Circular** Mapping for objects with a circular cross-section.*

13. In the Spline Map Parameters dialog box, set *Mapping* to **Planar** and click **Pick Spline**, as shown in Figure 7–41.

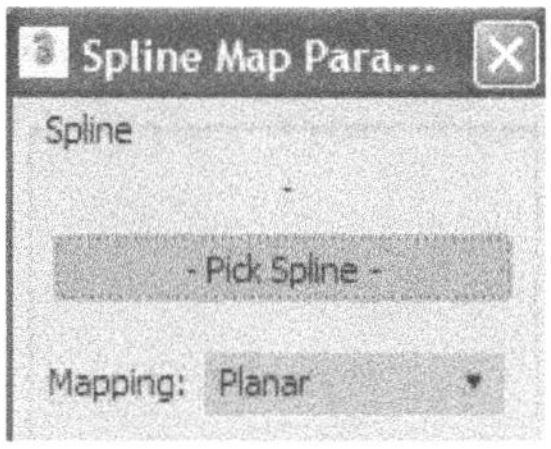

Figure 7–41

14. In the viewport, select the end of the spline (yellow line), which is displayed at either end of the **Roadshape01** object.

15. In the Spline Map Parameters dialog box, click **Commit**.

16. In the Modifier Stack, select **Unwrap UVW** to clear the selection and exit Sub-object mode. The texture is displayed on the shape as a single color indicating that the position and scale need to be corrected.

If the checker map does not display as required, use the spinner for the Size Width to increase or decrease the value and note the interactive changes in the viewport. The checker line should pass through the center, following the curve line.

17. In the Slate Material Editor, in the *View1* sheet, double-click on the **Map # Checker** title bar to display its Parameter Editor. In the Coordinates rollout, set the following, as shown in Figure 7–42:

- *Size Width*: **0'0.8"**
- *Size Height*: **0'0.1"**

Press <Enter> and verify that the *Offset* values are **0'0.0"** for both *Width* and *Height*. It is recommended that you use the spinners to increase and decrease the *Size Width* while checking the interactive display of checker in the viewport.

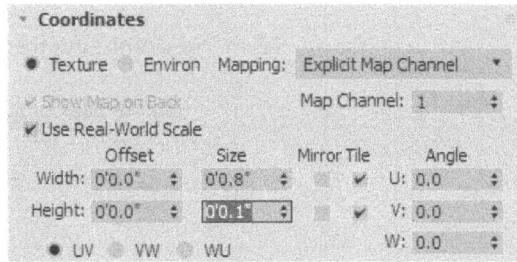

Figure 7–42

The checker map displays as shown in the Figure 7–43. This is the correct position and scale of the **checker** material.

Figure 7–43

Task 2 - Assign the Road Material.

1. In the Material/Map Browser, expand the *Maps>General* categories. Double-click on **Bitmap** to open the Select Bitmap Image File dialog box. Open **TextureForRoad.jpg** (from the ...*Maps* folder).

   - Note that a new node for this bitmap is added in the *View1* sheet.

2. Delete the wire that currently exists between the **Checker** Map and the Diffuse Color of **02 Default** material by selecting the wire and pressing <Delete>.

3. Draw a new wire linking the input socket of the Diffuse Color for **02 Default** material to the output socket of the new Bitmap (**Map #4 Bitmap**), as shown in the Figure 7–44.

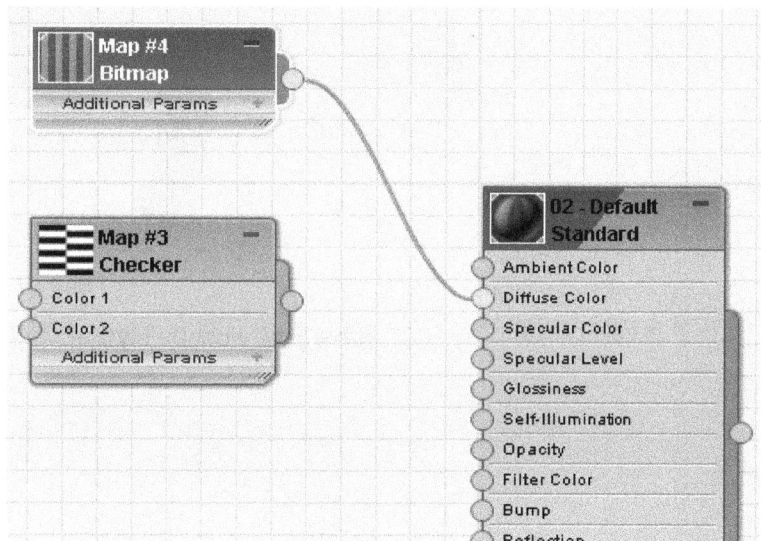

Figure 7–44

4. Select the **02 Default** material title bar and select ▣ (Show Shaded Material in Viewport) to display the road texture on the face on **Roadshape01** object.

5. Double-click on the new **Map # Bitmap (TextureForRoad)** material to open its Parameter Editor. In the Coordinates rollout, clear **Use Real-World Scale**.

6. Set *Tiling* for **U: 2** and **V: 8**. Use the **Offset U** and **V** sliders to center the road. Increasing the **Tiling V** brings the dashes closer to the middle of the road while decreasing it makes the dashes longer and farther apart along the center curve. Use the **Offset U** spinner to increase or decrease the value so that the dashed line is placed along the center of the road. The road shape on the left should now look similar to the road shape on the right as shown in Figure 7–45.

Figure 7–45

7. Save your work as **MyStartSplineMapping.max**.

Chapter Review Questions

1. Which option manipulates the positioning of a map with mapping coordinates at the map level of the Slate Material Editor?

   a. Generate coordinates for all objects.

   b. Generate Mapping Coords

   c. Unwrap UVW

   d. Use Real-World Scale

2. The MapScaler in the World Space Modifier keeps the map scale constant if the object size changes with the Scale transform.

   a. True

   b. False

3. The **UVW Map** modifier enables you to.... (Select all that apply.)

   a. Explicitly apply a map to an object by selecting a shape and location.

   b. Use a gizmo for transforming in Sub-object mode.

   c. Perfectly project on geometry with non-standard projection shapes.

   d. All of the above.

4. Which of the following is the correct method for controlling map scaling of individual objects using a UVW Map? These options are accessed in the Parameter Editor of the map in the Slate Material Editor.

   a. Select **Use Real-World Scale** and assign the appropriate size (*Width* and *Height*) values.

   b. Select **Use Real-World Scale** and assign both the *Width* and *Height Size* values to the U-scale value.

   c. Clear **Use Real-World Scale** and set the *Tiling U* and *V* values to **1.0**.

   d. Clear **Use Real-World Scale** and set the *U-Tiling* value to **1.0** and the *V-Tiling* value equal to the ratio of the U-scale divided by the V scale.

5. Which mapping modifier is used to generate a map to follow the curvature of the spline along which the object was extruded (Spline mapping)?

a. UVW Map

b. Unwrap UVW

c. MapScaler (WSM)

d. MapScaler (OSM)

Introduction to Lighting

Once materials have been added to an Autodesk® 3ds Max® project, lighting can be used to further enhance and create a realistic representation of the model. Projects automatically include default illumination that can be further enhanced or modified to create local or global illumination. Illumination can be accomplished using either photometric or standard lights.

Learning Objectives in this Chapter

- Work with various lighting strategies such as default lighting, local illumination, and global illumination.
- Work with standard lights and control the various parameter settings.
- Control the specific settings of various types of standard lights.
- Work with different types of shadow casting methods available in the software.
- Control the common parameters and set the specific parameters for each type of shadow casting method.

8.1 Local vs. Global Illumination

The Autodesk 3ds Max software provides several different kinds of scene lighting and enables you to add lighting objects that simulate real lights.Commonly used lighting methods provide either local or global illumination.

Default Illumination

By default, the Autodesk 3ds Max software automatically adds light to unlit scenes with invisible, unselectable light objects referred to as default lighting.

- A key light is located in the front and left of a scene and a fill light behind and to the right. These lights act as omni lights that illuminate in all directions. When user-defined light objects are added to a scene, the default lighting is automatically disabled for rendering.

Local Illumination

With a traditional local illumination approach, light sources only affect those objects that they can directly illuminate. They do not account for the diffuse light that bounces off of one surface to illuminate another nor do the effects of this reflected light become mixed together.

- Using a local illumination strategy, also referred to as Standard Lighting, requires arbitrary fill or ambient lights to simulate indirect lighting.

- Using Ray traced materials in a scene lit by standard lighting permits for the calculation of specular reflections between surfaces, which create mirrored effects and highlights on shiny surfaces.

- When a scene is illuminated with standard lighting (local illumination), without ambient or indirect light, the ceiling and shadows are dark as there are no lights pointed directly at those areas, as shown in Figure 8–1. When the ambient lights are added with standard lighting, the ceiling and shadows become softer, as shown in Figure 8–2.

Figure 8–1 **Figure 8–2**

Global Illumination

Global Illumination (GI) algorithms describe how light interacts with multiple surfaces. The illumination and rendering methods that take into account GI include mental ray, radiosity, and raytracing.

- Ray tracing is not used as a stand-alone rendering method but rather to compliment the other rendering methods.

- Radiosity and mental ray are two different lighting/rendering strategies that calculate diffuse inter-reflections of light, automatically generating ambient illumination and light mixing, producing realistic results, especially when daylight is involved.

- Radiosity and mental ray are designed to work with physically based (photometric) lights that have parameters derived from real-world lighting properties.

Figure 8–3 was created with global illumination, showing an interior scene with night time lighting. Figure 8–4 was created with global illumination, showing an interior scene with daytime lighting.

Figure 8–3 **Figure 8–4**

Figure 8–5 shows an example of an indoor scene that uses mental ray lit by physical lighting.

Figure 8–5

Hint: Lighting Analysis

Global Illumination calculations can be rendered as a lighting analysis to reveal illumination levels. Lighting Analysis Assistant generates light meter objects and image overlays based on mental ray physical lighting and materials. This information can be used for green building LEED certification credit 8.1.

Hint: Global Illumination vs Standard Lighting

Although longer to generate, Global Illumination (GI) approaches results are often more realistic. Standard lighting is less time consuming than the GI approaches (although there are exceptions), especially when working with simple scenes that contain a small number of objects or surfaces.

GI approaches are very popular in architecture, interior design, and related fields. However, standard lighting still has a place in these industries for conceptual tasks, projects with short timeframes, or projects that do not require extreme photorealism.

Types of Lights

Two types of lights are provided with the software:

* Standard lights

* Photometric lights

Although both create light objects, there are many different parameters available when you create either type of light. The lights can be created using the Command Panel. In the Create panel (+), click 💡 (Lights), and select the type of light in the drop-down list, as shown in Figure 8–6. Alternatively, you can select **Create>Lights** and then select the type you want to create.

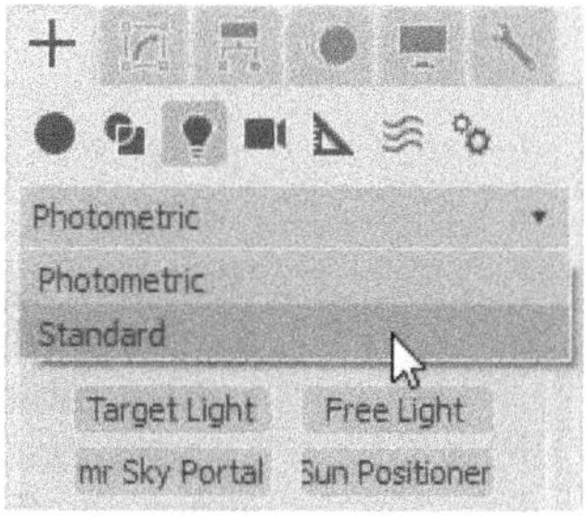

Figure 8–6

8.2 Standard Lighting

Standard lights (as shown in Figure 8–7) are objects based on computer calculations, which imitate lights used in everyday life. The following specifics apply to working with a standard lighting strategy.

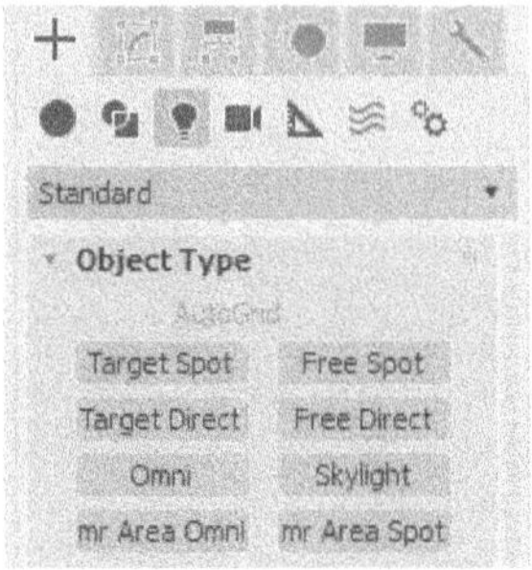

Figure 8–7

- Standard lighting strategies use standard light objects, such as **Spot**, **Directional**, **Omni**, and **Skylights**. They are highly configurable, but are not based on real-world lighting parameters and require arbitrary adjustments to achieve the required effect.

- Objects illuminated with standard lighting can use any material type.

- Scenes lit by standard lighting almost always require additional ambient (fill) lights, either through a global ambient value or ambient light objects.

- Lighting results are calculated at render time and are not stored on the objects. Processing standard lights does not increase file size and mesh subdivision is not required (as with radiosity).

- Standard lighting does not require exposure control. In standard lighting, ensure exposure control is not toggled on as it might result in differences between the viewport display and the rendering result

- Although it also works with mental ray, Standard lighting is designed for use with the Scanline Renderer. The mental ray results are not physically accurate.

- All of the standard lights except for directional lights, are considered Point lights, which cast light from a single point rather than along a line or from an area.

Exposure control is a method of balancing illumination levels in rendered output. It is essential to working with global illumination, using mental ray or radiosity.

Photometric lights are the preferred lighting technique when working with mental ray.

Common Parameters

All standard lights share common General Parameters and Intensity/Color/Attenuation settings. These parameters can be set while creating each type of standard light, as shown in Figure 8–8. Once the lights have been created, you can access these parameters in the Modify panel () in the Command Panel.

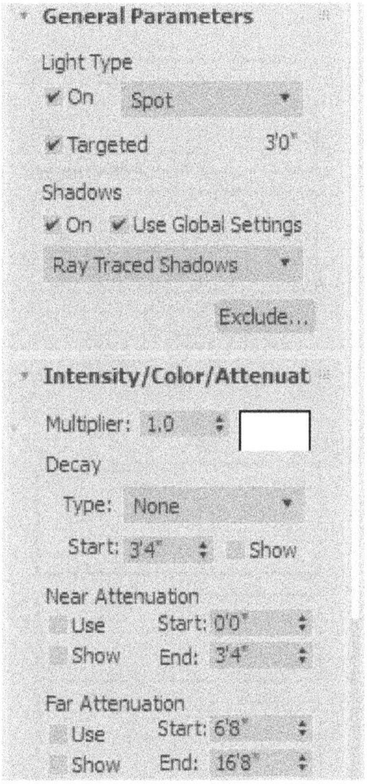

Figure 8–8

General Parameters

Lights cast illumination even if they are on a hidden layer.

The General Parameters rollout enables you to toggle the light on and off in the scene, change the light type (**Spot**, **Directional**, or **Omni**), select to work with a target, and select shadow settings.

Hint: Target Lights

Several types of lights (and some cameras as well) can have a target object. A light always points directly at its target, enabling you to change the direction of the light by moving the target. Target lights are lights with targets and Free lights are lights without targets.

Intensity/Color/Attenuation Parameters

The Intensity/Color/Attenuation rollout provides you with following options:

Multiplier	Controls brightness for standard lights. This is an arbitrary value that needs to be evaluated by trial. Start with a **1.0** value and adjust, as required. Avoid using high Multiplier values, which creates overly bright lighting. The color swatch enables you to select a color to filter the light with.
Decay area	Offers techniques for simulating how light fades over distance.
Far Attenuation area	Provides a similar kind of fading based on explicitly set distances. The *Start* value is where fading begins and the *End* value is the point at which the light fades to zero illumination. Typically you would use either the options in the *Decay* or *Far Attenuation* areas, not both.
Near Attenuation area	Enables you to define a distance from the light where the light starts casting faint illumination and then end with full illumination. Near attenuation does not occur in the real world and is included here as a computer graphics lighting effect
Show (Attenuation option)	Enables a graphical representation of the attenuation distances to remain visible after the object is cleared.

8.3 Types of Standard Lights

The type of standard light objects that can be created are **Spot**, **Directional**, **Omni**, and **Skylights**. They can be selected in the Object Type rollout, as shown in Figure 8–9.

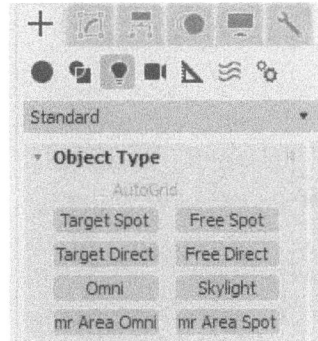

Figure 8–9

Omni Lights

Omni lights (shown in Figure 8–10) are used to represent point lights that cast light equally in all directions, such as an idealized light bulb. Omni lights are also commonly used for ambient fill lights. A single omni light requires six times the computational effort of a single spotlight, so use spotlights in place of omni lights whenever possible.

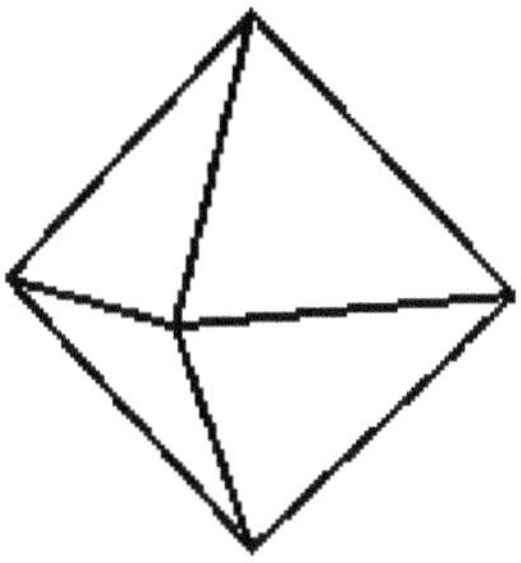

Figure 8–10

Spotlights

Spotlights are used to represent point light sources that cast focused beams of light in a cone with a circular or square base. Figure 8–11 shows an example of a spotlight with a circular base in 2D, and Figure 8–12 shows an example in 3D. Most real world lighting fixtures are more appropriately represented by spotlights rather than omnis or directional lights.

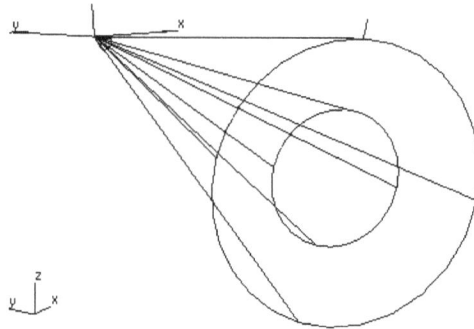

Figure 8–11   **Figure 8–12**

Two types of spotlight objects are available:

* **Target Spot:** Light objects cast focused beams of light pointing directly at a target.

* **Free Spot:** Light object casts focused beams of light pointing anywhere without a target object.

In addition to the Common Standard Parameters, spotlights have specific parameters (as shown in Figure 8–13) to control the distribution of the light they cast.

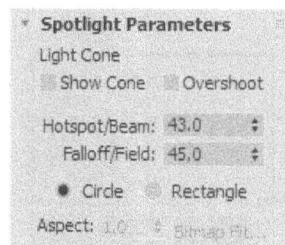

Figure 8–13

* The *Hotspot/Beam* value is the angle over which the full lighting intensity is projected. It is represented as the inner cone, as shown in Figure 8–12.

- The *Falloff/Field* value is the outer angle that illumination projects. It is represented as the outer cone, as shown in Figure 8–12.

- The light fades from full intensity to zero intensity between these two angles. Therefore, when these angles have similar values, the light creates a sharp, defined pool of light. Widely separated angles create a soft, gradual fade.

- The **Overshoot** option enables a spotlight to cast light in all directions (as an omni). However, spotlights only cast shadows within their falloff angle. Overshoot generally looks unnatural and should be used with care.

- The **Aspect** option enables you to define the width and height ratio through a numeric value.

- **Bitmap Fit** enables you to match the rectangular proportions of the lighting area to those of an image bitmap file directly.

Directional Lights

Directional lights are used to represent light sources that cast parallel rays, as shown in Figure 8–14. The best example of parallel light would be the light cast from the sun to an Architectural-scale project or smaller. (The sun could be considered an omni light when dealing with massive visualizations at the continental or global scale.)

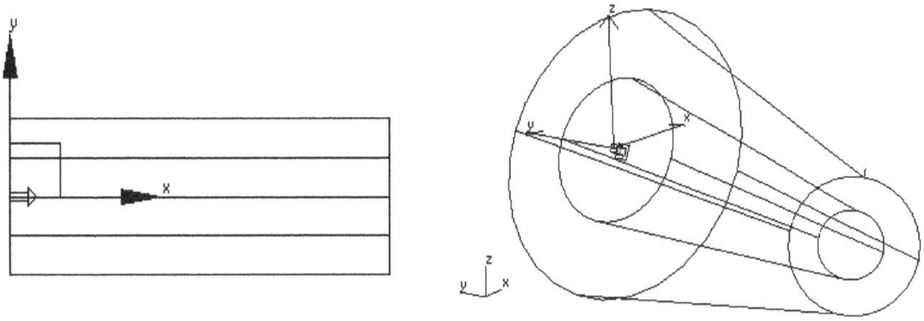

Figure 8–14

Two types of directional light objects are available:

- **Target Direct**

- **Free Direct**

In addition to the Common Standard Parameters, directional lights have specific options available through the Directional Parameters rollout, as shown in Figure 8–15. The Directional Parameters options are nearly identical to those in the Spotlight Parameters rollout options. The only difference is the *Hotspot/Beam* and *Falloff/Field* values. These are measured in terms of a width parameter rather than an angle.

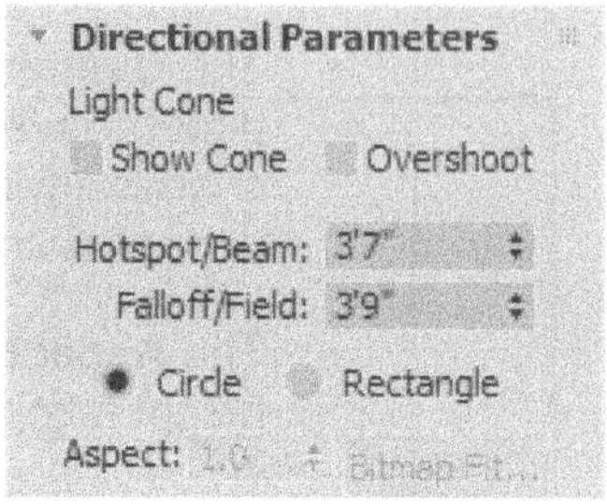

Figure 8–15

Fill Lights

Any light can be used to approximate indirect lighting, which is referred to as a fill light. Fill lights can act as normal lights or they can be specifically set to cast ambient light, by selecting the **Ambient Only** option in the Advanced Effects rollout in the **Standard lights** parameters, as shown in Figure 8–16.

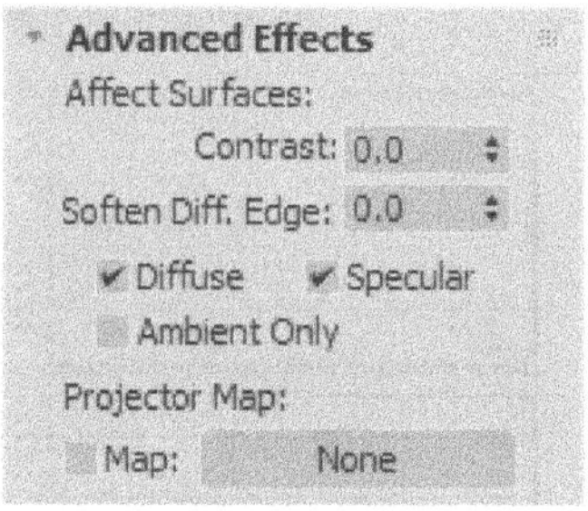

Figure 8–16

- Standard materials have an **Ambient color** parameter that can be used when illuminated using ambient lights. This color can be different from the diffuse color produced by normal (non-ambient) lights. The Ambient color is normally locked to the diffuse or it can be set darker than the diffuse color for emphasis.

- Setting a fill light to cast ambient light automatically disables shadow casting because only real-world light sources (the sun and lighting fixtures) are normally permitted to cast shadows.

- If you want your fill lights to cast normal light (which illuminates a material's diffuse color instead of ambient), do not select the **Ambient Only** option, but rather manually disable shadow casting.

- Architectural materials were designed for radiosity and do not have an **Ambient color** parameter. Otherwise, they function similarly to Standard materials with standard lighting.

- Arch & Design materials were designed for mental ray and also lack an ambient color channel. In mental ray, the concept of ambient lighting is replaced with bounced lighting. It is controlled by the number of diffuse bounces in the Final Gather rollout, as well as reflectivity/transparency, and other material choices.

Skylight and mr Sky

The Standard light category also includes a Skylight object. There is also a mental ray skylight (mr Sky) used with an mental ray sun (mr Sun) to create a sky when rendering with the mental ray renderer. The mr Sky is found in the Photometric category. Both the Skylight and the mr Sky serve as a type of ambient lighting adding global illumination to the scene.

mental ray (mr) Area Omni Light and mental ray (mr) Area Spotlight

Also included in the standard light category are these two area light objects (as opposed to point light objects). They are intended specifically for use with mental ray.

- You can combine the use of mental ray materials and mental ray lighting. This enables for energy-conserving lighting, which is calculated based on the 1st Law of Thermodynamics. mental ray can also use standard lights for rendering.

Practice 8a

Standard Lighting for an Interior Scene

Practice Objectives

Estimated time for completion: 30 minutes

- Create standard lights and adjust their parameters.
- Create ambient fill lighting to brighten the dark areas.

In this practice you will model interior lighting conditions by creating a spot light and array it to position it at various locations around the room. You will adjust the parameters to make the scene realistic and add ambient lighting to brighten areas that are not directly illuminated by your standard light objects.

You must set the paths to locate the External files and Xrefs used in the practice. If you have not done this already, return to **Chapter 1: Introduction to Autodesk 3ds Max** and complete Task 1 to Task 3 in **Practice 1a: Organizing Folders and Working with the Interface**. You only have to set the user paths once.

Task 1 - Create, Array, and Instance Light Objects.

*If a dialog box opens prompting you about a File Load: Mismatch, click **OK** to accept the default values.*

Hold <Win> and press <Shift> repeatedly to cycle through all of the viewports. Release <Win> when the viewport that you want maximized is highlighted.

1. Open **Standard Lighting – Interior.max**.

2. You will add lights in the **Top** viewport such that they point toward the floor. Maximize the **Top** viewport, by selecting it from the overlay (Hold <Win> and press <Shift>).

3. Click ![icon] (Zoom Extents) to refit the model in the **Top** viewport and then zoom into the foyer area (Leftmost area).

4. In the Create panel (![plus icon]), click ![lights icon] (Lights). In the drop-down list, select **Standard** and in the Object Type rollout, click **Free Spot**, as shown in Figure 8–17.

Figure 8–17

The small circles represent the opening for recessed lighting.

5. Click near the approximate center of the upper left circle. A free spotlight is added at that location, as shown in Figure 8–18.

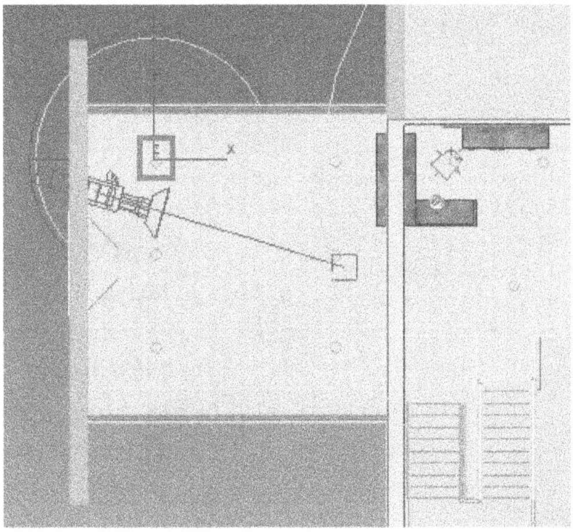

Figure 8–18

6. With the light object still selected, click ✛ (Select and Move).

7. In the Status Bar, verify that ⊞ (Absolute Mode Transform Type-In) is displayed and set the following, as shown in Figure 8–19:
   - *X*: **84'7"**
   - *Y*: **126'10"**
   - *Z*: **9'11"**
   - Press <Enter>

Figure 8–19

In addition to placing the light at the exact center of the recessed fixture, it places the light at a height of 9'11", which is 1" below the ceiling height.

8. In the Command Panel, select the Modify panel (⧉) and name the light **Ceiling Downlight 00**.

- To locate your light objects to the center of the circles representing the recessed fixtures, enter the exact coordinates, which were determined using the **Measure** tool in the Autodesk 3ds Max Utilities. The six lights in the foyer area are 12' apart along the world X-direction and 6' apart along the world Y-direction.

*If the Extras toolbar is hidden, in the Main Toolbar area, right-click in empty space, and select **Extras** in the list of toolbars.*

9. With the light selected, in the Extras toolbar, click

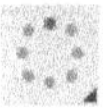

   (Array), as shown in Figure 8–20, or in the menu bar select **Tools>Array**.

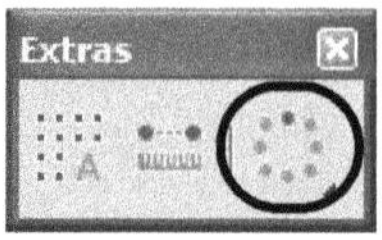

Figure 8–20

10. In the Array dialog box, click **Preview** to enable the previewed display in the scene.

   • For the first dimension of the array, in the *Array Transformation* area, enter *X Incremental* value of **12'0"**.

   • In the *Array Dimensions* area, set *1D Count* to **2** to create two columns of lights.

   • Select **2D**, set *2D Count* to **3**, and *Incremental Row Y* to **-6'0"** to create three rows of lights.

   • In *Type of Object* area, verify that **Instance** is selected so that the parameters of all of the lights can be adjusted at the same time.

   • Note that *Total in Array* is automatically set to **6** (two lights in each of the three rows), as shown in Figure 8–21.

   Note that the six lights are displayed in the viewport because **Preview** is selected.

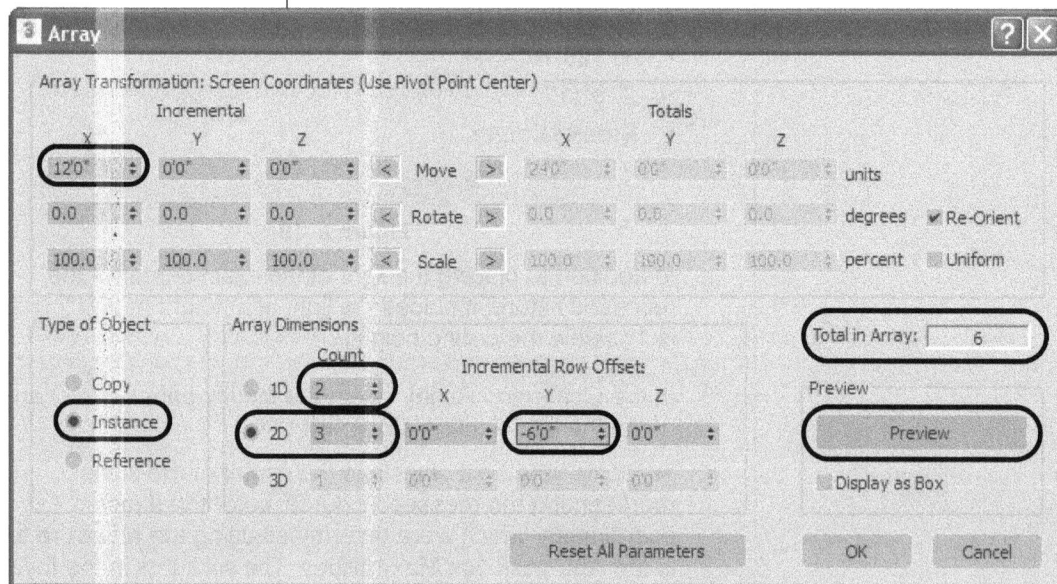

Figure 8–21

11. If the lights preview is in the correct positions (as shown in Figure 8–22) click **OK** in the dialog box.

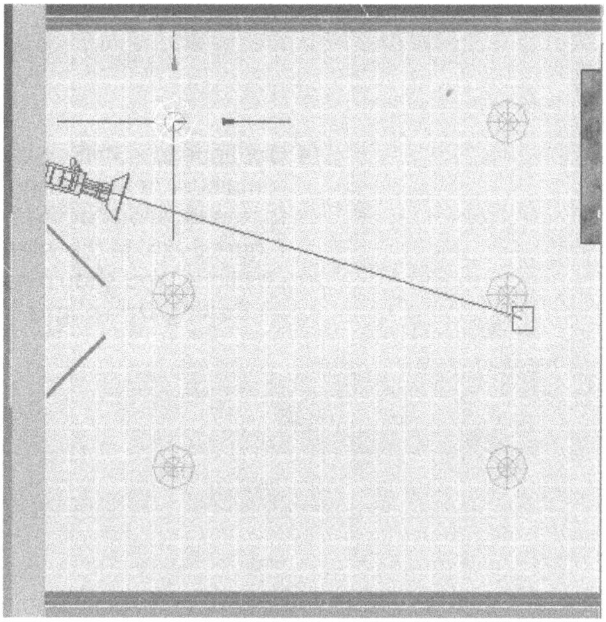

Figure 8–22

When arraying the objects, the software automatically increments the name by 1.

12. Select the light in the upper right corner in foyer (**Ceiling Downlight 001**). Using ⊕ (Select and Move), and holding <Shift>, drag along the Transform gizmo's X-axis to locate the light over the desk area, almost on top of the chair, as shown in Figure 8–23. In the Clone Options dialog box, verify that **Instance** is selected and click **OK**.

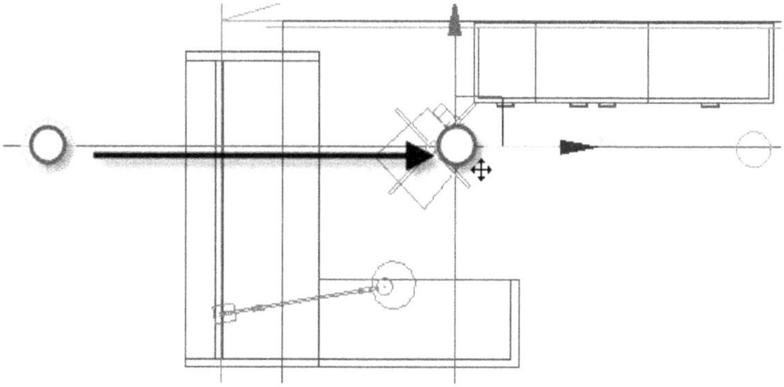

Figure 8–23

13. With the light still selected, in the Status Bar, set the *X* value to **104'7"** and ensure that the *Y* value is set to **126'10"** and and the *Z* value is set to **9'11"**, as shown in Figure 8–24:

X: 104'7"   Y: 126'10"   Z: 9'11"

Figure 8–24

14. Continue to <Shift> + click and drag to instance the remainder of the Ceiling Downlights, to the circles provided for the locations of the recessed lighting, as shown in Figure 8–25. In the interest of time, approximate their positions. You should have 14 lights with the last one named as **Ceiling Downlight 013**.

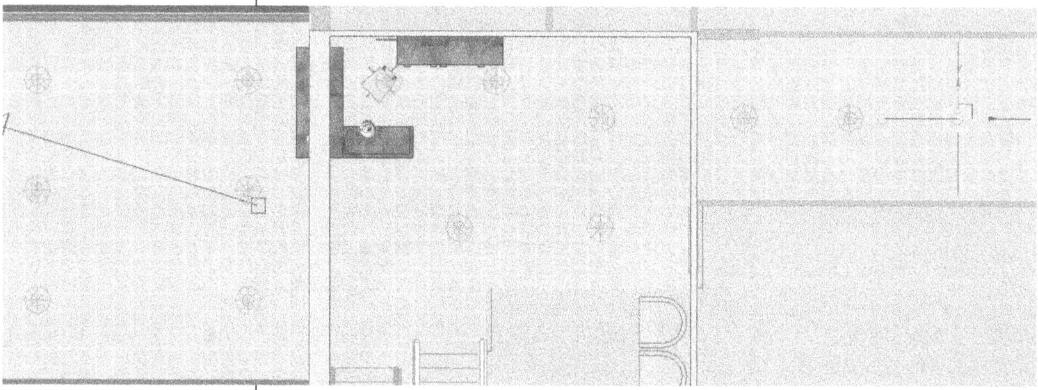

Figure 8–25

Task 2 - Adjust Standard Light Parameters.

In Task 1, you made instances of each of the lights so that their parameters can be adjusted together. You will now adjust lighting levels through light object parameters, avoiding exposure control.

1. Select **Rendering>Exposure Control**. In the Environment and Effects dialog box, in the Exposure Control rollout, clear **Active**, as shown in Figure 8–26. Close the Environments and Effects dialog box.

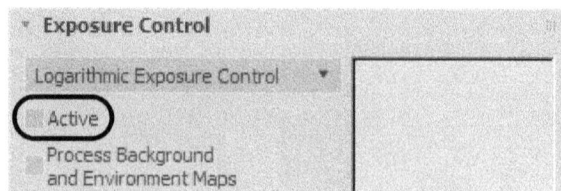

Exposure Control

Logarithmic Exposure Control

Active

Process Background
and Environment Maps

Figure 8–26

2. Select any of the instanced lights. In the Command Panel, verify that the Modify panel (⟲) is open and that **Ceiling Downlight** (any number) name is displayed (i.e., selected). In the Spotlight Parameters rollout, set *Hotspot/Beam* to **45**, press <Enter> and verify that **Circle** is selected. Set the *Falloff/Field* to **47.0**, as shown in Figure 8–27.

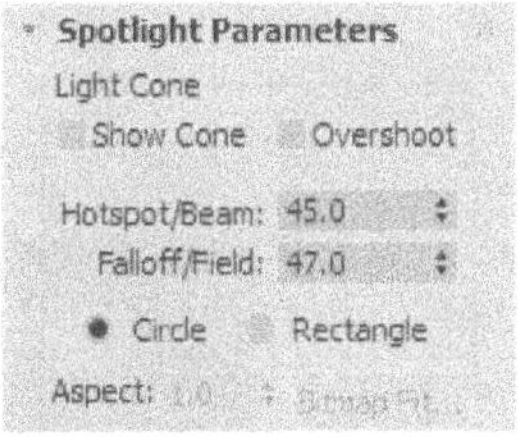

Figure 8–27

3. Change to the **Camera – Lobby1** view by selecting the **Top** POV label and selecting **Cameras>Camera - Lobby1**. In the Main Toolbar, click ![teapot icon] (Render Production). Due to their current hotspot and falloff values, the light objects are only illuminating small pools of light on the floor, as shown in Figure 8–28.

Figure 8–28

The brightness of your rendering might vary as it is dependent on your computer settings.

- The **Layer:VIZ-1-Ceiling Lights** object is formed from extruded circles representing the openings for your recessed lighting. They have been assigned a self-illuminated material to make the openings display brightly lit. The light objects you have just added to the scene do not render.

4. In the viewport, select one of the instanced lights, if not already selected. In the Spotlight Parameters rollout, set the *Falloff/Field* value to **170** degrees and press <Enter>.

*If you need to change some of the parameters and render again, you can leave the Rendered Frame Window open because it is a modeless dialog box. After changing a parameter, click **Render** in the Rendered Frame Window to render the viewport again.*

5. Click ![teapot icon] (Render Production) if you closed the Rendered Frame Window or click **Render** if the Rendered Frame Window is open. The illumination now spreads out, but the floor is being lit too brightly and has lost all of its contrast (sometimes referred to as being washed out), as shown in Figure 8–29. Leave the Rendered Frame Window open.

Figure 8–29

6. In the Intensity/Color/Attenuation rollout, in *Far Attenuation* area, select **Use**. Set the following, as shown in Figure 8–30:
   - *Start*: **0'0"**
   - *End*: **16'0"**

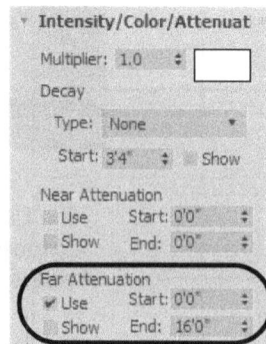

Figure 8–30

7. Click **Render**. The washed out effect is removed but the overall render looks dark, as shown in Figure 8–31.

Figure 8–31

*As with most **Standard Lighting** parameters, attenuation settings are arbitrary and require trial and error to achieve the best result.*

8. Adjust the overall brightness of the lights using the Multiplier. In the Intensity/Color/Attenuation rollout, set *Multiplier* to **2.0**. Click **Render** in the Rendered Frame Window. The surfaces under direct illumination should now become brighter.

Task 3 - Add Ambient Fill Light.

Next use ambient fill lighting to approximate the indirect illumination that would be present in the real world. With a standard lighting approach, fill light is required to brighten areas that are not directly illuminated by your light objects.

1. Add the ambient light globally. Select **Rendering> Environment** to open the Environment and Effects dialog box.

2. In the *Environment* tab, in the Common Parameters rollout, in the *Global Lighting* area, select the **Ambient** color swatch, as shown in Figure 8–32.

Figure 8–32

3. In the Color Selector dialog box, change the *Value* to **25**, and press <Enter>, as shown in Figure 8–33. Leave both the Environment and Effects dialog box and Color Selector dialog box open.

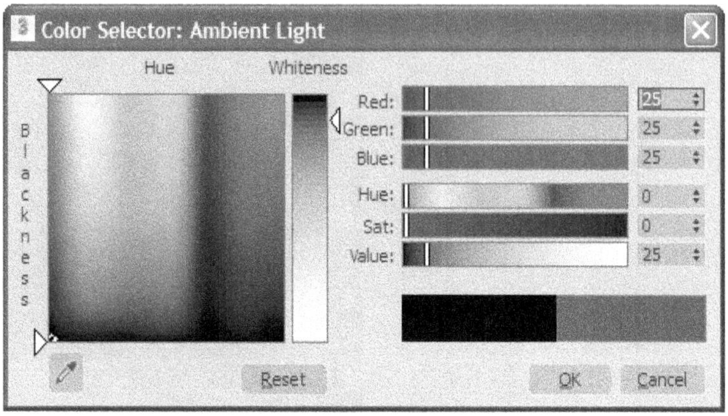

Figure 8–33

4. In the Rendered Frame Window, click **Render** to render the scene. In this rendering many areas have become lighter but the ceiling is still too dark. In the Color Selector dialog box, change the *Value* to **50** and render again. The ceiling is brighter but objects under direct illumination have lost some contrast, as shown in Figure 8–34. The front of the half-wall behind the stairs looks flat because the ambient lighting is so uniform. (This is a pitfall of adding too much global ambient light.)

Figure 8–34

5. This scene might respond better with manually configured ambient light rather than the global settings. In the Color Selector dialog box, set the ambient color *Value* to **0** and press <Enter>. Close all dialog boxes.

6. In the viewport, change to the **Top** viewport by pressing <T> and zoom out to see the floorplan. If 💡 (Lights) is not already active, in the Create panel (✛), click 💡 (Lights). Verify that **Standard** is displayed, and then click **Omni** to create an omni light.

7. Click once in the center of the six lights in the foyer to add an omni light. In the Name and Color rollout, enter **Lobby Fill Light 00** as the name of the light.

8. Click ✛ (Select and Move) and in the Status Bar, change its absolute Z-elevation to **2'0"**.

9. Hold <Shift>, and drag and click to create two instances of the omni light, as shown in Figure 8–35.

Figure 8–35

10. With one of the omni lights selected, in the Modify panel (🔧), in the Advanced Effects rollout, select **Ambient Only**, as shown in Figure 8–36. This setting causes the light to illuminate the ambient color of Standard materials and not to cast shadows.

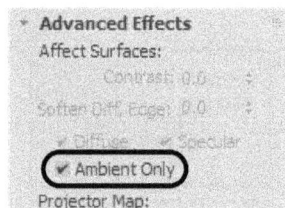

Figure 8–36

11. Change to **Camera – Lobby1** viewport and render the scene. Note that everything is washed out. Ambient lights can wash out a scene with their default settings. Leave the Rendered Frame Window open.

12. With the omni light still selected, in the Intensity/Color/ Attenuation rollout, set *Multiplier* as **0.75** and in the *Far Attenuation* area, select **Use**. Additionally, set the following, as shown in Figure 8–37:

- *Start*: **0'0"**
- *End*: **16'0"**

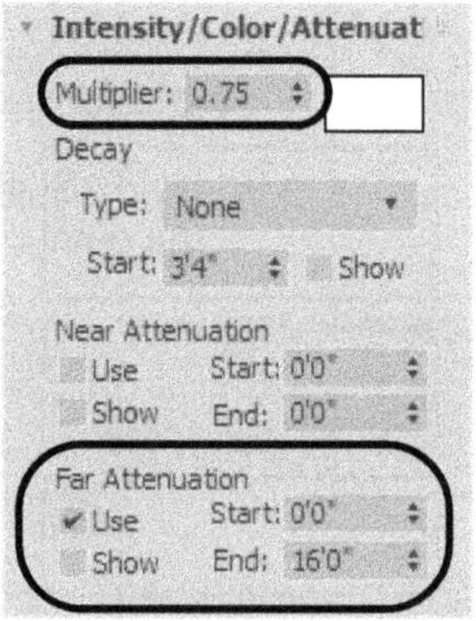

Figure 8–37

Your rendering might not be exactly the same because of your monitor display. You can adjust your Gamma and LUT correction (Preference Settings dialog box> Gamma and LUT tab) to get a similar rendering.

13. Render the scene. The ambient lighting does not look flat, but the floor and desk lamp are illuminated too brightly, as shown in Figure 8–38.

Figure 8–38

14. To resolve the brightness issue, you can exclude these objects from the ambient light. With one of the omni lights (Lobby Fill Light) still selected, in the Modify panel ( ), in the General Parameters rollout, click **Exclude**. The Exclude/Include dialog box opens.

15. Verify that **Exclude** is selected. In the list on the left, select **1-Desk Lamp** and **Layer:VIZ-1-Floor-Tile**. Click **>>** to add them to the Exclude list on the right, as shown in Figure 8–39.

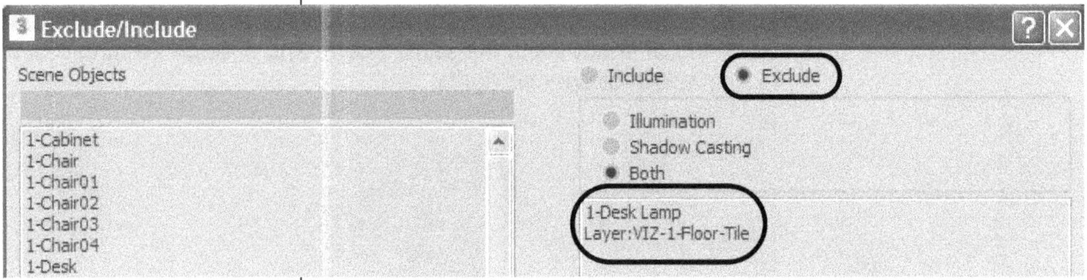

Figure 8–39

16. Click **OK** to close the dialog box.

17. Render the scene. The brightness of the lamp and the floor is removed, as shown in Figure 8–40. Close the Rendered Frame Window.

Figure 8–40

18. Save your work as **MyStandard Lighting – Interior.max**.

8.4 Shadow Types

Autodesk 3ds Max lights are able to cast realistic shadows from opaque objects. There are several shadow-casting methods available, such as Shadow Mapped, Ray Traced, Area, etc. While creating light objects, you can set the type and aspect of shadow by selecting it in the drop-down list (as shown in Figure 8–41), in the *Shadows* area of General Parameters rollout. Alternatively, after creating the light objects, you can control or change them using the Modify panel () parameters of light objects. Individual lights might cast different kinds of shadows in the same scene and shadow casting can be disabled for specific lights.

Figure 8–41

Figure 8–42 shows the shadow-casting methods available.

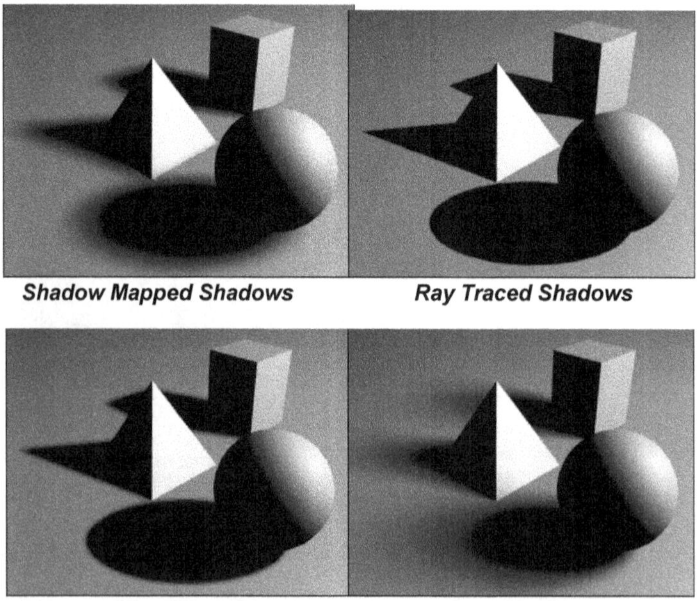

Shadow Mapped Shadows   *Ray Traced Shadows*

Advanced Ray Traced Shadows   *Area Shadows*

Figure 8–42

Shadow Type	Description, Advantages	Disadvantages
Shadow Map	Traditional approach, shadow mapping is relatively fast and creates soft-edged shadows. **Animation:** Shadows only need to be calculated once when scene geometry is not animated. Most efficient shadow type for omni lights.	Not as accurate as other methods; might not be appropriate for shadow studies. Uses a lot of RAM. Does not support materials with transparency or opacity maps.
Ray Traced Shadows	More accurate than shadow maps, supports transparency and opacity mapping. **Animation:** Shadows only need to be calculated once when scene geometry is not animated. In these cases, RT might be best for animations (including animated shadow studies) in terms of rendering time.	Slower than shadow maps, and shadows have sharp edges. Avoid omni lights with Ray Traced shadows whenever possible, as they require 6x the processing time of spot and directional lights.
Advanced Ray Traced	A good, general-purpose shadow type that is an improvement on RT shadows. It is more accurate than Shadow Maps, supports transparency and opacity mapping. Uses less RAM than standard raytraced shadows, therefore is generally faster for producing still renderings. Offers several parameters that can help soften and smooth shadows.	Slower than shadow maps. **Animation:** Shadows must be calculated at every frame, regardless of whether scene geometry is animated or not. Avoid omni lights with Advanced Ray Traced shadows whenever possible, as they require 6x the processing time of spot and directional lights.
Area Shadows	Enables a simulation of shadows cast from an area light (the other methods assume point light sources). Supports transparency and opacity mapping, uses relatively little RAM.	Generally slower than shadow maps, Ray Traced and Advanced Ray Traced. **Animation:** Shadows must be calculated at every frame, regardless of whether scene geometry is animated or not.

mental ray Shadow Maps	A shadow type optimized for the mental ray renderer. This is not covered in this training course.	Not as accurate as Ray Traced or Advanced Ray Traced shadows.

Common Shadow Parameters

The most commonly used shadow parameters in the Autodesk 3ds Max software are:

General Shadow Parameters

All lights have certain general parameters (*Shadows* area in *General Parameters* area) common to all shadow types, as shown in Figure 8–43.

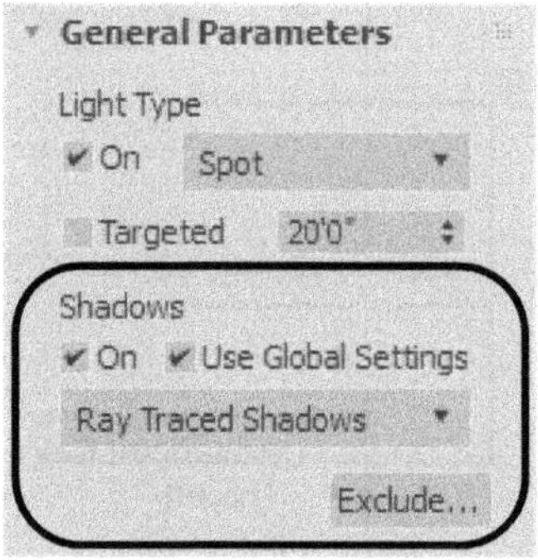

Figure 8–43

On	Enables you to select whether to cast shadows from this light or not and the type of shadows to use.
Use Global Settings	Controls whether the scene's global shadow generator or the light's own individual shadow generator is used.
Drop-down list	Contains all the types of shadows available in the software. Selecting the type provides a shadow specific rollout that can be used to control the advanced settings in the selected shadow type.

Shadow Parameters Rollout

The Shadow Parameters rollout (shown in Figure 8–44) contains settings that are common to all types of shadows.

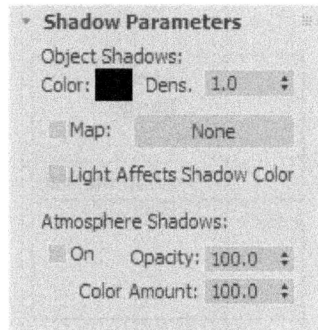

Figure 8–44

Color	Use this swatch to set a shadow to display as a color other than black.
Density	Controls the overall darkness of the created shadows. A density below 1.0 makes shadows lighter, greater than 1.0 makes them darker.
Map	Use this option to have an image map project inside your shadow.
Light Affects Shadow Color	Enables colored light to blend with the assigned shadow color when generating shadows.
Atmosphere Shadows	Enables atmospheric effects to cast shadows.

Shadow Map Parameters

In the General Parameters rollout, in the *Shadows* area, selecting **Shadow Map** in the drop-down list provides a Shadow Map Params rollout, as shown in Figure 8–45. Lights set to cast shadow mapped-shadows have additional controls that are specific to the Shadow Map type of shadow.

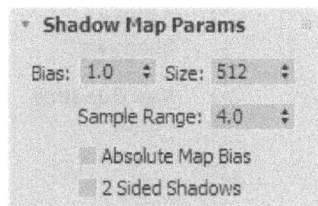

Figure 8–45

Bias	A relative adjustment that can move the shadow closer to or further away from the objects casting them. This value sometimes needs to be adjusted with large scenes.
Size	The height and width (in pixels) of the image map used to create the shadows. Shadow detail and computation time increase as the size increases.
Sample Range	Controls the amount of blending and smoothing. If shadow mapped-shadows appear grainy, increase this value.
Absolute Map Bias	Enables the Bias to be fixed to a value measured absolutely in scene units rather than a relative, normalized value. This option should normally not be used unless shadows flicker and disappear during an animation.
2 Sided Shadows	Enables both sides of a face to cast shadows. Double-sided mode is discussed in the rendering information.

Ray Traced Shadows

In the General Parameters rollout, in the *Shadows* area, selecting **Ray Traced Shadow** in the drop-down list provides a Ray Traced Shadow Params rollout, as shown in Figure 8–46. This rollout contains additional settings for lights set to cast (standard) ray traced shadows.

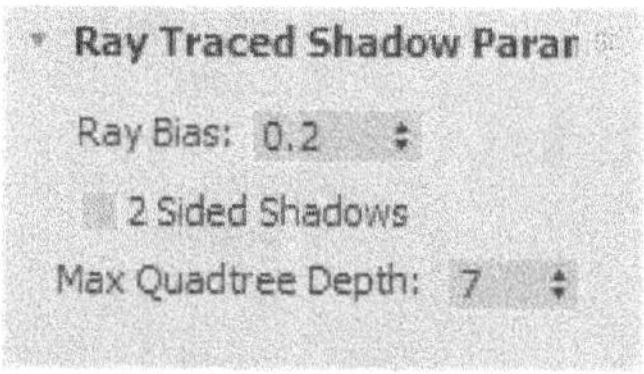

Figure 8–46

Ray Bias	Similar to shadow map bias, ray bias is a relative adjustment to move a shadow closer or further away from an object casting them. This value might need to be adjusted for large scenes.
2 Sided Shadows	Enables both sides of a face to cast shadows.
Max Quadtree Depth	Controls ray-tracing performance. Increasing the quadtree depth can speed up ray-tracing time but requires more RAM. You need to experiment to determine the most efficient quadtree settings for individual scenes (default = 7).

Advanced Ray-Traced Shadows

In the General Parameters rollout, in the *Shadows* area, selecting **Adv. Ray Traced** in the drop-down list provides an Adv. Ray Traced Params rollout, as shown in Figure 8–47 and the Optimizations rollouts, as shown in Figure 8–48. Both rollouts contains additional settings for lights set to cast advanced ray-traced shadows.

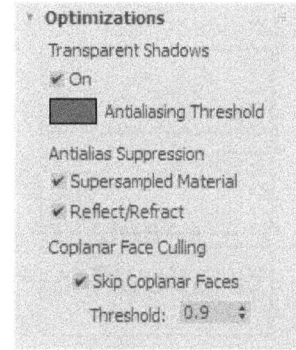

Figure 8–47   Figure 8–48

Adv. Ray Traced Params Options

Basic Options	The menu assigns either a mode without antialiasing (simple), a single or double-pass antialiasing mode. Antialiasing is an additional calculation made to smooth pixilated edges of shadows.
2 Sided Shadows	Enables both sides of a face to cast shadows.
Shadow Integrity and Quality	Controls the number of rays cast in the calculation. Increasing these values can enhance the final result at the expense of longer calculation time.
Shadow Spread	A parameter to blur or soften shadows, measured in pixels.
Shadow Bias	The minimum distance required to cast a shadow. This parameter should be increased as shadow spread is increased.
Jitter Amount	Blurred shadows sometimes cause artifacts to form. Increasing jitter can help break up the patterns of these artifacts and make them less noticeable.

Optimizations Options

Transparent Shadows	When enabled, transparent objects cast colored shadows based on their transparency and diffuse color.
Antialias Suppression	When using supersampling, reflections or refractions, this option disables the second pass in two-pass antialiased mode. This is a good idea to save time since the second pass often adds little in these situations. (Supersampling is discussed in the rendering and animation material.)
Skip Coplanar Faces	Prevents coplanar faces from shading each other (those that lie overlapped in the same plane).

mental ray Shadow Maps

In the General Parameters rollout, in the *Shadows* area, selecting **mental ray Shadow Map** in the drop-down list displays a mental ray Shadow Map rollout, as shown in Figure 8–49. The options should be used with mental ray lights. You only use these for interior shots that render with mental ray and require physical lighting effects, such as caustics or global illumination.

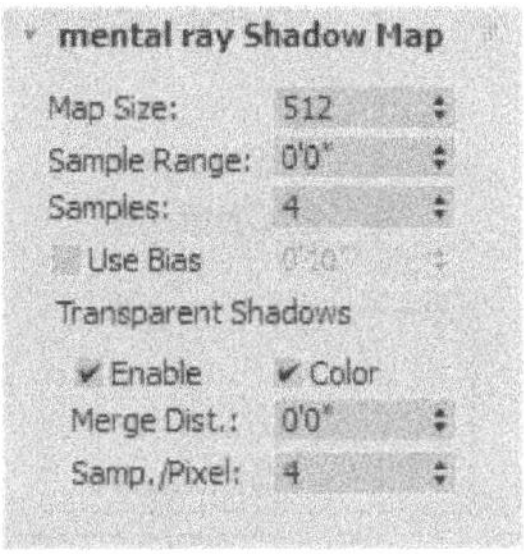

Figure 8–49

Map Size	Determines the resolution of the shadow bitmap. The size of the map is actually the square of this value. It should be in powers of 2 – 256, 512, 1024, 2048 etc.
Sample Range	Used to create soft-edged shadows when using mental ray lights. You must increase this value AND the Samples values greater than zero to get soft shadow effects.
Samples	Determines the number of samples that are removed from the map to make the shadows soft.
Use Bias	Moves the shadow closer or farther from the object.
Transparent Shadows	Provides controls for finer looking shadows. When enabled, you can add transparency and control shadow color. The *Merge Dist* and *Samp./Pixel* fields enable you to increase shadow quality (this result in additional memory consumption and slower renderings).

Practice 8b

Working with Shadow Parameters

Practice Objective

- Understand the different types of shadows casting methods.

Estimated time for completion: 10 minutes

In this practice you will adjust parameters to refine the shadows in a scene.

You must set the paths to locate the External files and Xrefs used in the practice. If you have not done this already, return to **Chapter 1: Introduction to Autodesk 3ds Max** and complete Task 1 to Task 3 in **Practice 1a: Organizing Folders and Working with the Interface**. You only have to set the user paths once.

1. Open **Shadow Parameters.max**.

*If a dialog box opens prompting you about a File Load: Mismatch, click **OK** to accept the default values.*

2. In the Scene Explorer, (■ (Display None) and 💡 (Display Lights)), select one of the Ceiling Downlight objects, such as **Ceiling Downlight 06**.

3. In the Command Panel, select the Modify panel (🖉), and examine its parameters. These lights use the default Advanced Ray Traced shadow type (**Adv. Ray Traced** in General Parameters rollout), as shown in Figure 8–50.

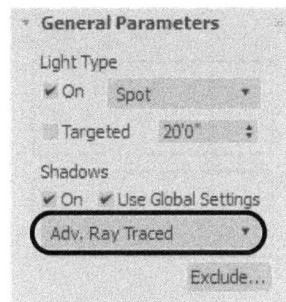

Figure 8–50

4. In the Main Toolbar, click ![icon] (Render Production) to render the scene. In the Rendered Frame Window, zoom and pan to the desk area, as shown in Figure 8–51. The edges of the shadow under the desk display jagged. Leave the Rendered Frame Window open.

Figure 8–51

5. In the Modify panel (![icon]), expand the Adv. Ray Traced Params rollout and in the *Basic Options* area, select **2-Pass Antialias** in the drop-down list. In the *Antialiasing Options* area, set the following, as shown in Figure 8–52:

   • *Shadow Integrity*: **2**
   • *Shadow Quality*: **3**

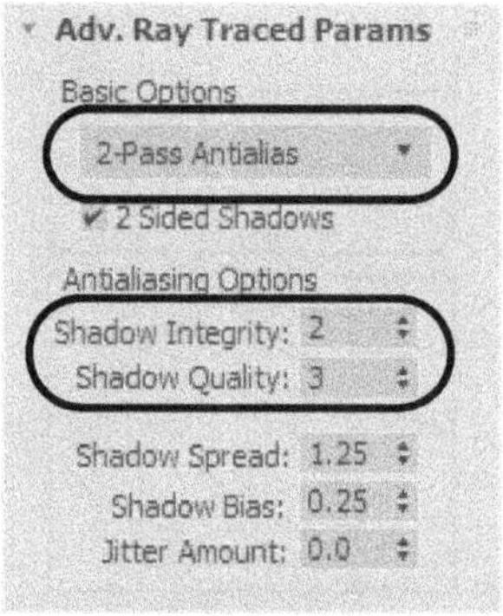

Figure 8–52

6. In the Rendered Frame Window, click **Render**. The shadow edges display more smoothly, but the rendering time has increased.

7. In the General Parameters rollout, in the *Shadows* area, change the type from *Adv. Ray Traced* to **Shadow Map** by selecting **Shadow Map** in the drop-down list.

When soft shadows are required or speed is critical, Shadow maps make a good alternative.

8. Render the scene. These shadows are fuzzier and less accurate (as shown in Figure 8–53) but significantly faster to render.

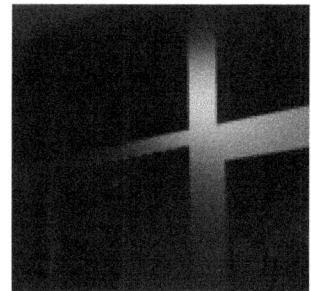

Figure 8–53

9. To make the shadow-mapped shadows better defined, increase the map size. In the Shadow Map Params rollout, double the *Size* from 512 to **1024**, as shown in Figure 8–54.

10. Render the scene. Zoom into the right side and note that the shadow maps are causing rendering artifacts along the curtain wall, as shown in Figure 8–55.

There might not be a huge difference in shadows under the desk.

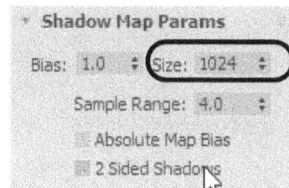

Figure 8–54

Figure 8–55

11. Adjust the Shadow map by setting the following:

   • *Size*: **2048**

   • *Bias*: **0.01**

12. Render the scene again. These settings reduce the problem, but can increase rendering time. Also note that the shadows have become slightly more significant under the desk .

13. Save your work as **MyShadow Parameters.max**.

Chapter Review Questions

1. The default lights (key light and fill light) provided by default in the Autodesk 3ds Max scene, act as:

   a. Omni lights

   b. Spotlights

   c. Directional lights

   d. mental ray area omni light

2. Which type of standard lights are used to represent light sources that cast parallel rays?

   a. Omni lights

   b. Spotlights

   c. Directional lights

   d. mental ray area omni light

3. In the Intensity/Color/Attenuation rollout (shown in Figure 8–56), which has common parameters for all of the standard lights, which option does not occur in the real world and is only included as a computer graphics lighting effect?

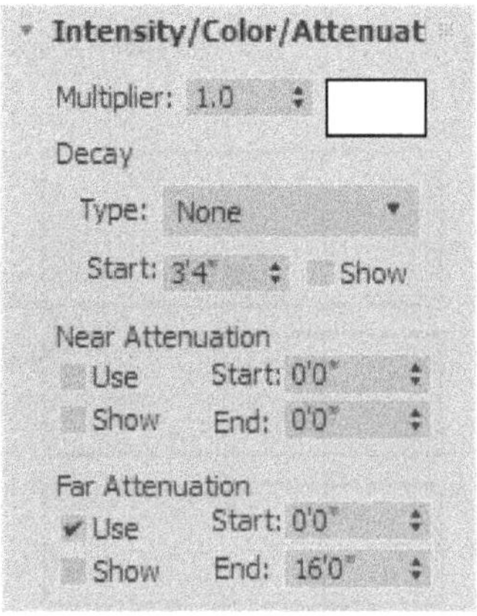

Figure 8–56

   a. Multiplier

   b. Decay options

   c. Near Attenuation options

   d. Far Attenuation options

4. In the Spotlight parameters rollout (shown in Figure 8–57), which option enables a spotlight to cast light in all directions and behave like an omni light? (Hint: Setting this option generally looks unnatural and it should be used with care.)

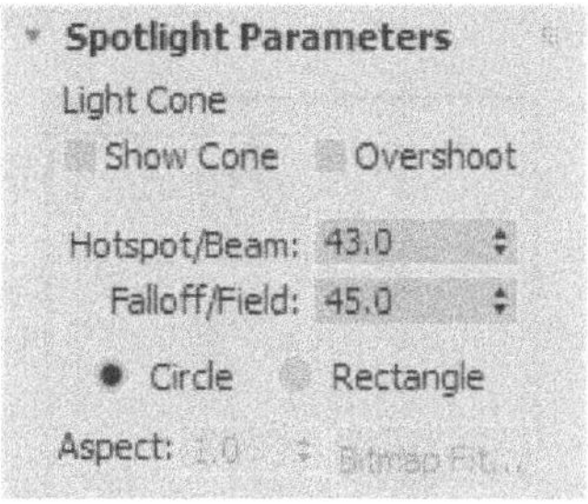

Figure 8–57

   a. Show Cone

   b. Overshoot

   c. Hotspot/Beam

   d. Falloff/Field

5. Which one of the following shadow types does not support materials with transparency and opacity maps?

   a. Shadow Map

   b. Ray Traced Shadows

   c. Advanced Ray Traced

   d. Area Shadows

6. In the Shadow Map type of shadows, a density value below 1.0 makes the shadow darker and a density value of greater than 1.0 makes the shadow lighter.

   a. True

   b. False

Command Summary

Button	Command	Location
	Array	• **Extras toolbar** • **Tools:** Array
	Lights	• **Command Panel:** *Create* panel • **Create:** Lights
	Render Production	• **Main Toolbar** • *Rendering:* Render

Chapter
9

Lighting and Rendering

Photometric lights are generally used to accurately represent real-world lighting. Once added, their parameters can be further modified to create realism in a design. Additionally, the use of sunlight and skylight in a daytime scene and the use of exposure controls can add additional realism.

Learning Objectives in this Chapter

- Create photometric lights and modify them by changing their parameters.
- Work with different methods of Exposure Control and control the method specific parameters.
- Create Sunlight and Skylight and use their parameters to enhance the lighting in a scene.

9.1 Photometric Light Objects

Photometric light objects are based on quantitative measurements of light levels and distribution. They provide a real-world lighting and accurate scene illumination when used with mental ray and other global illumination solutions. In the Autodesk® 3ds Max® software, photometric lights are the default choice for creating lights.

- Photometric lights take advantage of physically-based color, intensity, and distribution properties. They can be defined with real-world lighting parameters in engineering units.

- Since photometric lights are based on real-world calculations of light energy, they are **scale-specific**. Scenes using photometric lights and mental ray/radiosity should have an appropriate system unit scale.

- All photometric lights automatically decay (attenuate) with an inverse-square relationship. Far attenuation can be controlled manually, to save calculation time and energy.

- Photometric lights work for both the scanline renderer and mental ray renderer.

- Exposure control should be used with Photometric lights objects to adjust the brightness of the scene, the Shadow/Midtones, and Highlight areas of the image. If the Exposure control is not on with the Photometric light type, the software prompts you to use the Logarithmic Exposure Control (for Default Scanline renderer) or the mr Photographic Exposure Control (for the mental ray renderer).

Photometric Light Types

*The **mr Sky Portal** is also included in the Object Type rollout but it is not a standard photometric light type.*

In the Command Panel's Create panel ($+$)> 💡 (Lights), **Photometric** is the default light type, as shown in Figure 9–1. The object types for photometric lights are:

- **Target Light**

- **Free Light**

Figure 9–1

While creating a Target Light or a Free Light, you can set different parameters to illuminate the scene accurately and effectively. Once the lights have been created, you can modify the parameters using the Modify panel in the Command Panel.

Templates Rollout

Once you create either a Target or Free light there are Templates to select from, as shown in Figure 9–2. Selecting a template controls the intensity and color temperature of the light.

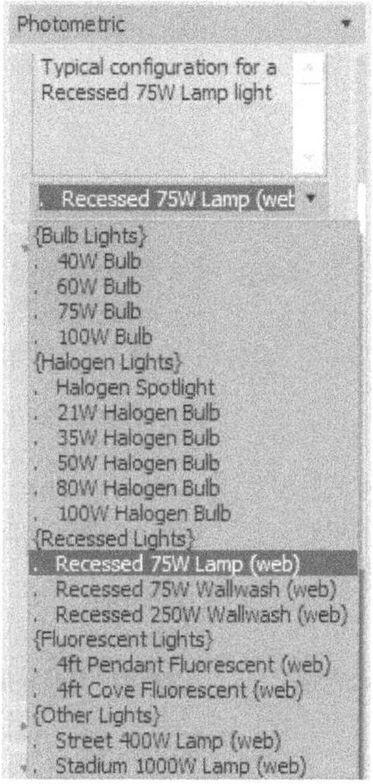

Figure 9–2

General Parameters Rollout

The General Parameters rollout controls some of the basic settings for toggling the light on/off in the scene and the different shadow casting methods (Ray Traced, Adv. Ray Traced, mental ray, Shadow Map, etc.). The options found in the *Light Properties* area and *Shadows* area are similar to the options found in Standard Lights, and can be used in the same manner.

Any Free Light can be changed into a Targeted Light (and vice-versa) by using the **Targeted** option in the *Light Properties* area. When the Targeted option is enabled, a tool tip displays as you move the target indicating the illumination, as shown in Figure 9–3.

Figure 9–3

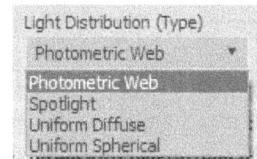

Figure 9–4

*In the General Parameters rollout, many options (Light Properties area options, Shadows area options, and **Spotlight** parameters) are identical or similar to the options used when creating Standard Lights.*

The *Light Distribution* area (shown in Figure 9–4) contains a list of the photometric light distribution types available in the software. These control the way the light illuminates the surrounding space. The options are described as follows:

Uniform Spherical	Casts light in all directions, like a standard Omni light.
Uniform Diffuse	Casts light in one hemisphere only and mimics the way light emits from a surface.
Spotlight	Provides hotspot and falloff parameters identical to standard spotlights.
Photometric Web	Casts light according to a 3D representation of light intensity as determined by a lighting file format, such as IES, LTLI, or CIBSE. These are files provided by lighting manufacturers, usually available via the Internet.

Distribution (Photometric Web) Rollout

If you select Photometric Web in the Light Distribution type list, the Distribution (Photometric Web) rollout displays, as shown in Figure 9–5. Real-world luminaries (lighting fixtures) nearly always cast light in varying amounts in different directions. The Web distribution method enables the Autodesk 3ds Max software to simulate the laboratory-determined light distribution of specific lighting fixtures.

- Photometric lights can make use of web distribution information from IES, LTLI, or CIBSE photometric web data files that can be obtained from lighting manufacturers for specific light fixture models. They are often available directly from manufacturers' web sites.

- Lights with Web distributions are indicated with photometric web icons (as shown in Figure 9–6) that graphically represent the 3D distribution of light cast from the light fixture.

Figure 9–5   Figure 9–6

Web Distribution in Viewports

You can see the web distribution in the viewport. Select the **Shading Viewport** label (such as **High Quality**) and select **Lighting and Shadows>Illuminate with Scene Lights** (as shown in Figure 9–7) to see the lights in the viewport. You can add shadows by selecting **Shadows** and toggle on **Ambient Occlusion** in the viewport to add subtle detail enhancement. These options only take effect in viewport and have no effect on the actual renderings.

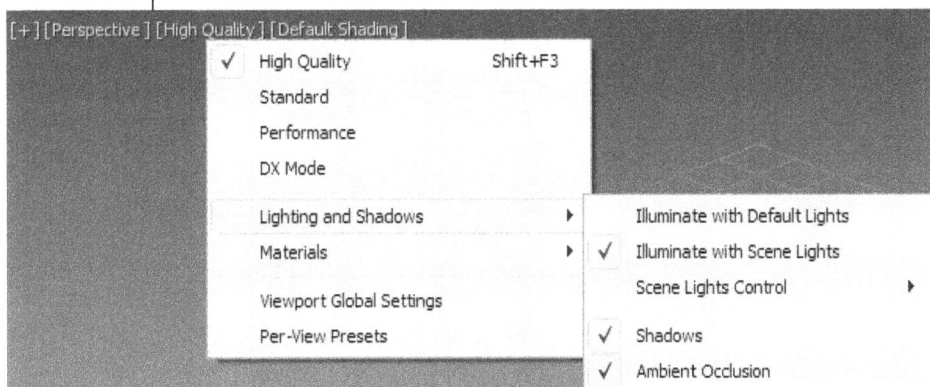

Figure 9–7

Shape/Area Shadows Rollout

The Shape/Area Shadow controls are used to generate a shadow casting shape and to calculate shadows based on a particular shape. The various shapes have different parametric controls and the shapes can be selected in the Shape/Area Shadows rollout, as shown in Figure 9–8.

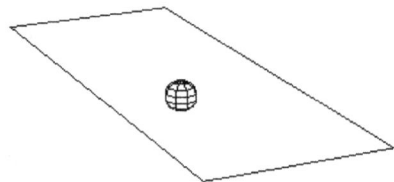

Shape/Area Shadows

Emit light from (Shape)

Line

Point
Line
Rectangle
Disc
Sphere
Cylinder

Figure 9–8

- **Point:** Shadows are created as if the light was one single point, as shown in Figure 9–9.

- **Line:** Shadows are created as if the light was one single line, as shown in Figure 9–10. The size of the line is controlled with the **Length** parameter.

Use this for fluorescent tubes or rectangular ceiling lights.

- **Rectangle:** Shadows are created as if the light was a rectangular area (as shown in Figure 9–11) governed by **Length** and **Width** parameters.

Figure 9–9

Figure 9–10

Figure 9–11

- **Disc:** Shadows are created as if the light was a flattened sphere, as shown in Figure 9–12. A radius control determines the size of the disc.

- **Sphere:** Shadows are created as if the light was a round ball or globe, as shown in Figure 9–13. Again a radius control determines the size of the sphere.

- **Cylinder:** Shadows are created as if the light emitter is cylindrical, as shown in Figure 9–14. **Radius** and **Length** are the two parameters to control the cylinder proportions.

| Figure 9–12 | Figure 9–13 | Figure 9–14 |

In the Shape/Area Shadows rollout, in the *Rendering* area, you can also select the **Light Shape Visible in Rendering** option. This permits the Cylinder, Disc, Sphere, and Rectangle light shapes (as shown on the top in Figure 9–15) to render as objects in the viewport (as shown on the bottom in Figure 9–15). The Point and Line objects do not work with this feature.

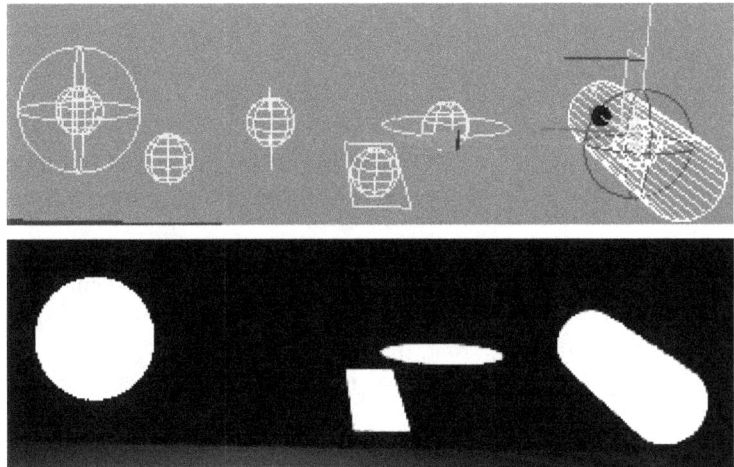

Figure 9–15

Intensity/Color/ Attenuation Rollout

Photometric light color can be assigned through a lamp specification (such as fluorescent, halogen, incandescent, etc.) or through a temperature specified in degrees Kelvin. This color can also be filtered (tinted) through a color swatch. All of these options can be selected in the *Color* area of the Intensity/Color/ Attenuation rollout, as shown in Figure 9–16.

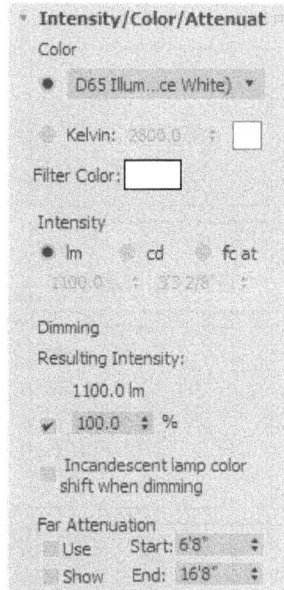

Figure 9–16

The overall brightness of Photometric lights can be specified as one of three intensity values (*Intensity* area):

Luminous flux	The overall output strength of the lamp, measured in lumens (lm).
Luminous intensity	The light energy that is released over time, measured in candelas (cd).
Illuminance	A measurement of how much illumination reaches a surface a set distance away from a lamp with a certain facing. Illuminance is measured in foot-candles (fc, lumens/ft2) or lux (lumens/m2). When using this option, specify both the Luminous flux (lumens) and the distance at which that brightness occurs

Hint: Photometric Lights Data

The Autodesk 3ds Max software ships with a host of sample lighting templates that you can use out-of-the-box.

The Autodesk 3ds Max Help lists a number of sample fixtures in the **Common Lamp Values for Photometric Lights** section.

Lights that combine the geometry of a light fixture with the correct photometric light distribution model are referred to as luminaries. These are assemblies with a hierarchy created so that the photometric light is linked to the geometry. You can obtain luminaries from manufacturer websites (such as ERCO). You can also import lighting fixtures from the Autodesk® Revit® software using FBX import.

The *Far Attenuation* area controls the end location of the Photometric light and the area that is graduated as the end of the range is approached, as shown in Figure 9–17.

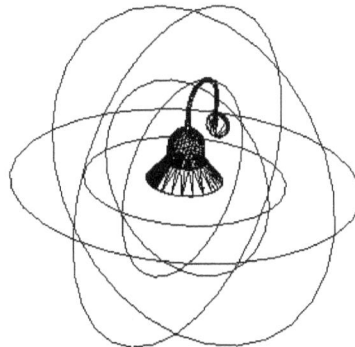

Figure 9–17

Practice 9a

Estimated time for completion: 10 minutes

If a dialog box opens prompting you about a File Load: Mismatch, click OK to accept the default values.

Working with Photometric Lights

Practice Objectives

- Create photometric lights and modify their parameters.
- Use preset lamps and their provided data.

In this practice you will create and adjust photometric lights. You will use different lamp presets to apply realistic lighting to the lobby model.

You must set the paths to locate the External files and Xrefs used in the practice. If you have not done this already, return to **Chapter 1: Introduction to Autodesk 3ds Max** and complete Task 1 to Task 3 in **Practice 1a: Organizing Folders and Working with the Interface**. You only have to set the user paths once.

Task 1 - Create free photometric lights.

1. Open **Photometric Lighting start.max**.

2. Using <Win> and <Shift>, display the **Top** viewport as the maximized viewport. Click (Zoom Extents) to display the floorplan. Change to Wireframe mode by pressing <F3>.

3. In the Create panel ( ), click (Lights) and verify that **Photometric** is displayed in the drop-down list. In the Object Type rollout, select **Free Light**, as shown in Figure 9–18.

Figure 9–18

You can zoom into the area where the yellow circles are placed, which indicate the slots for lights.

4. Click approximately over the upper left light fixture circle to place a light, as shown in Figure 9–19.

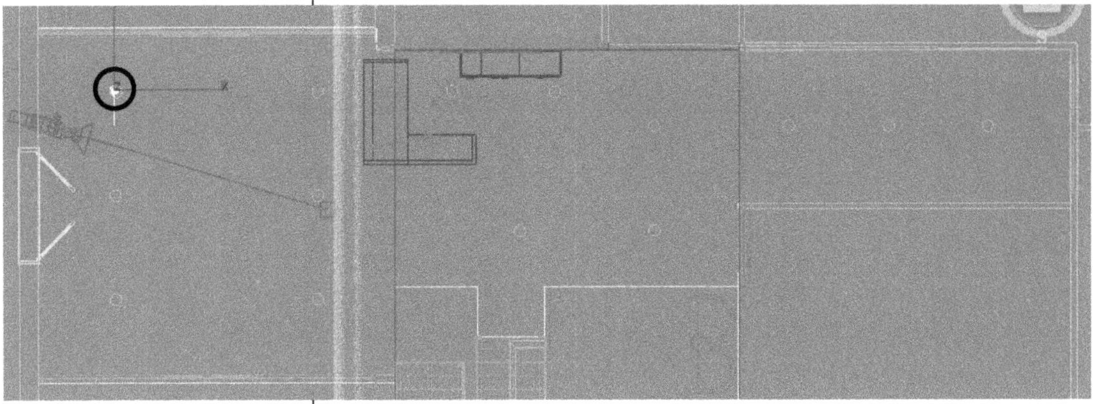

Figure 9–19

Alternatively, right-click

on ✛ *(Select and Move) in the Main Toolbar to open the Transform Type-In dialog box. You can also enter the values in the Status Bar.*

5. In the viewport, right-click on the new light and in the quad menu, next to **Move**, select ▢ (Settings). In the Move Transform Type-In dialog box, in the *Absolute:World* area, set the following, as shown in Figure 9–20:

- *X:* **84'7"**
- *Y:* **126'10"**
- *Z:* **9'11"** (elevation)

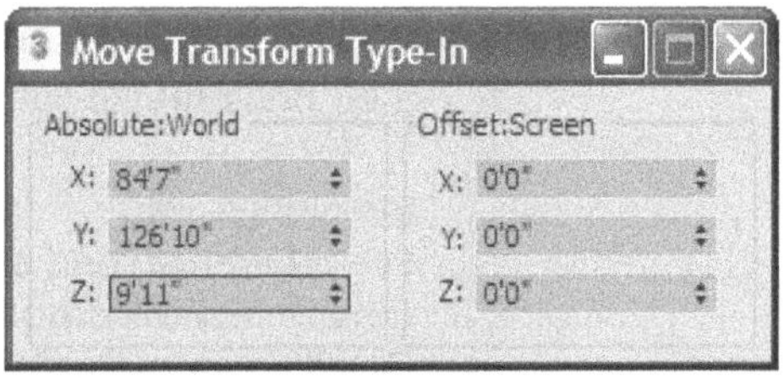

Figure 9–20

6. Close the dialog box. With the light object selected, in the Modify panel (⌐), rename the light object as **Light – Downlight A 00**.

7. In the General Parameters rollout, set *Light Distribution (Type)* to **Spotlight**. Note that the shape of the light object changes in the viewport.

8. In the Intensity/Color/Attenuation rollout, set *Color* to **HID Quartz Metal Halide**, as shown in Figure 9–21.

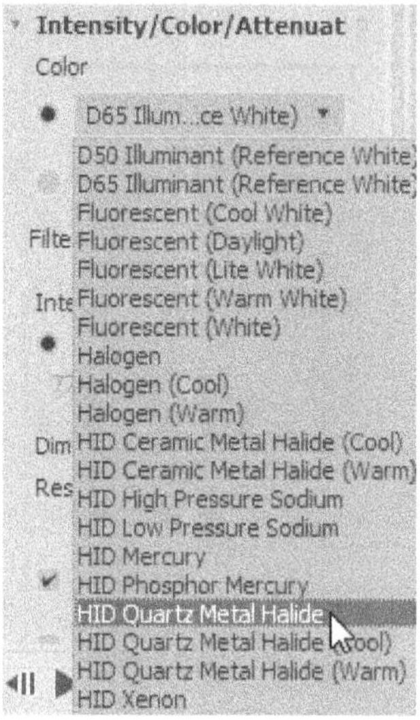

Figure 9–21

Hint: Accessing Photometric Lights Data

When using metal halide lamps, you can find suggestions for their photometric light parameters in the Help system. In the InfoCenter, click in and select **3ds Max Help**. Select the *Search* tab and enter **Common Lamp Values** in the search box. Select **Common Lamp Values for Photometric Lights**. Scroll down to **Par38 Line Voltage Lamps**. The **Medium Beam** has intensities between 1700-4000 candelas, as shown in Figure 9–22. The values for beam and field angles are also displayed.

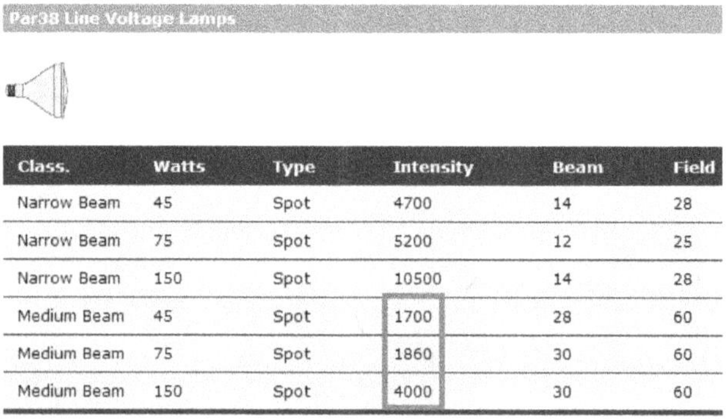

Par38 Line Voltage Lamps

Class.	Watts	Type	Intensity	Beam	Field
Narrow Beam	45	Spot	4700	14	28
Narrow Beam	75	Spot	5200	12	25
Narrow Beam	150	Spot	10500	14	28
Medium Beam	45	Spot	1700	28	60
Medium Beam	75	Spot	1860	30	60
Medium Beam	150	Spot	4000	30	60

Figure 9–22

9. With the new light still selected, click ✛ (Select and Move) and then use <Shift> + click and drag to instance the light (the **Instance** option in the Clone Options dialog box). The lights should correspond to the symbols for Ceiling Lights (circles provided for the locations of the recessed lighting). You can approximate their positions and have 14 lights with the last one named **Light - Downlight A 013**.

10. Select Point of View label (Top) and select Cameras> **Camera - Lobby1** to display the **Camera - Lobby1** viewport. Change the *Shading Viewport* to **Standard** and *Per-view Preference* viewport (Wireframe) to **Default Shading + Edged Faces** to display the 14 spotlights, as shown in Figure 9–23.

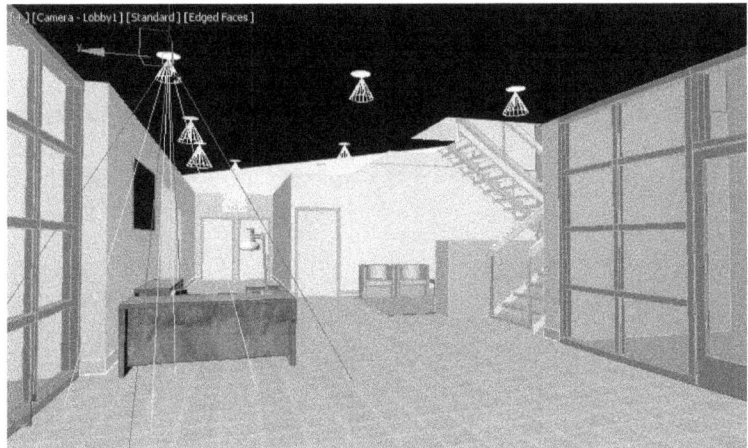

Figure 9–23

11. Select **Rendering>Exposure Control** to open the Environment and Effects dialog box. Note that this being a legacy file, **Logarithmic Exposure Control** is selected in the Exposure Control rollout.

12. In the Exposure Control rollout, select **Active**. Click **Render Preview** and note the render preview.

13. In the Logarithmic Exposure Control Parameters rollout, increase the *Brightness* to **88**, press <Enter>, and watch the render preview update. Close the dialog box.

14. Click 🫖 (Render Production) to render the viewport. Note that the scene is quite dark. Leave the Rendered Window open.

Task 2 - Adjust the light parameters.

1. With one of the lights selected, in the Command Panel, in the Distribution (Spotlight) rollout, note that *Hotspot/Beam* and *Falloff/Field* have default values of **30°** and **60°** as stated in the Autodesk 3ds Max Help.

When changing the Light Distribution Type, the shape of the light object (in the viewport) changes accordingly.

2. If you have access to a photometric data file for a light fixture, you can use it for this light. In the General Parameters rollout set *Light Distribution (Type)* to **Photometric Web**, as shown in Figure 9–24.

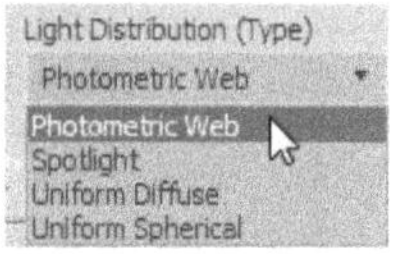

Figure 9–24

3. In the Distribution (Photometric Web) Parameters rollout, click **< Choose Photometric File >** and in the practice files folder, in the ...*sceneassets\photometric* folder, open **sample_downlight.ies**. The thumbnail diagram of the selected web file is displayed, as shown in Figure 9–25.

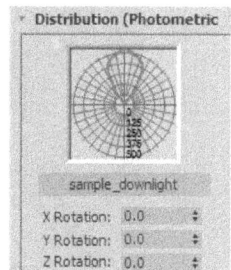

The red shape displays the beam.

Figure 9–25

4. Note that in the Intensity/Color/Attenuation rollout, in the *Intensity* area, the intensity of the light has been updated to **3298.0 cd**.

5. In the General Parameters rollout, in the *Shadows* area, select **Shadow Map** in the drop-down list, as shown in Figure 9–26.

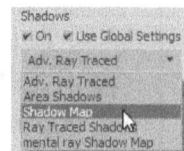

Figure 9–26

*The **Dimming** parameter should be cleared to control the intensity of light.*

6. Click **Render** in the Rendered Window. Note that the dark areas on the floor have been removed and the floor looks washed out.

7. In the Intensity/Color/Attenuation rollout, in the *Intensity* area, set the intensity to **1100** cd and render the scene again, as shown in Figure 9–27. Close the Render Window.

Figure 9–27

*Selecting **Illuminate with Scene Lights** automatically clears **Illuminate with Default Lights** and vice-versa.*

8. The photometric lights representation is displayed in the viewport and you can control their effects individually. Select the *Shading Viewport* label to display the label menu and select **Lighting and Shadows** and **Illuminate with Scene Lights**. In the menu, also expand Scene Lights Control and select **Auto Display Selected Lights**, as shown in Figure 9–28.

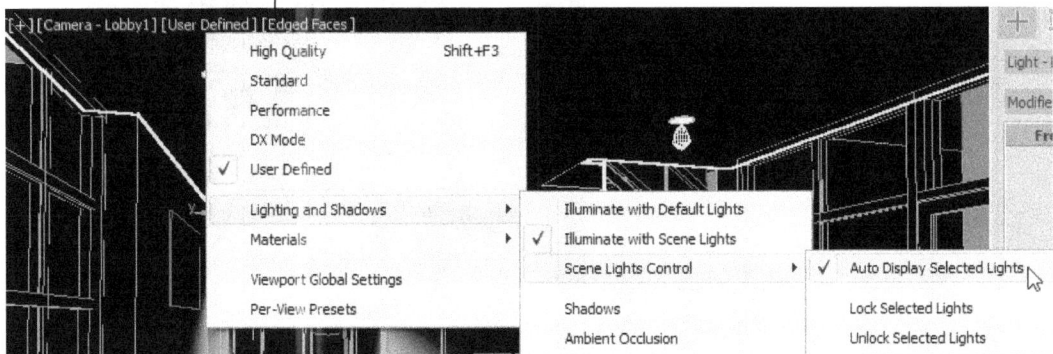

Figure 9–28

If the lights in the viewport are not easily selectable use the Scene Explorer to select the lights.

The display of shadows in the viewport is dependant on the driver you are using. The shadows are previewed in the viewport if you are using Nitrous or the Direct 3D drivers.

9. In the viewport, select one of the lights to enable it. You will see the effect of that light in the viewport. Select another light and see its effect in the viewport. Using <Ctrl>, select a few more lights to activate them together and visually see the effects.

10. In the *Shading Viewport* label menu, verify that **Lighting and Shadows>Shadows** is selected to display the shadows that are cast along with the lighting effect of the light selected.

11. With one of the lights selected, in the Command Panel, in the Templates rollout, select **75 W Bulb**. Note the changes, as shown in Figure 9–29.

Figure 9–29

12. Render the scene. Since the light distribution is spherical, the lighting now illuminates the ceiling and the upper walls, as shown in Figure 9–30.

Figure 9–30

13. In the Templates rollout, select **Recessed 75W Lamp (web)**. This uses a different IES file. Render again. The lighting is dark and moody.

14. Save your work as **MyPhotometricLighting.max**.

Hint: Using Light Lister

The Autodesk 3ds Max software includes a Light Lister utility (as shown in Figure 9–31) (**Tools>Light Lister**) that enables you to view and change light properties without having to select them first. You can change the settings for all lights together or for the selected lights.

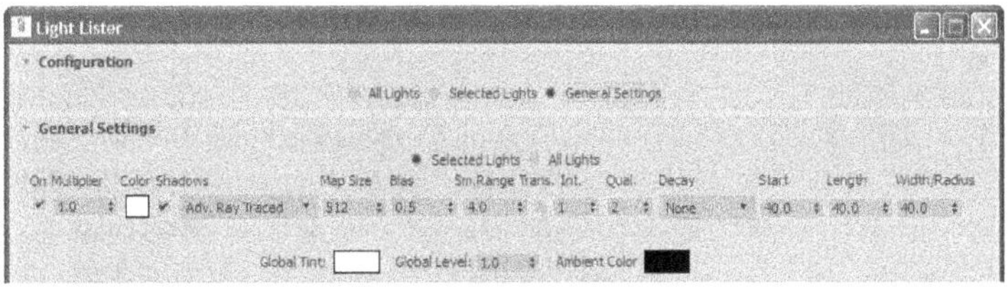

Figure 9–31

Hint: Using mental ray with Standard Lights

The mental ray renderer was designed to be used with photometric light objects. Standard lights can also be used with mental ray, but since they are not physically-based, it cannot achieve accurate results. For better accuracy, it is recommended not to mix standard and photometric lights in the same scene. The following should be considered:

- The luminous intensity of standard lights is equal to the light's multiplier parameter times the Physical Scale value in Logarithmic Exposure Control. (The default Physical Scale value is 1500 candelas in the Logarithmic Exposure Control Parameters rollout in the Environments and Effects dialog box.) You can make drastic changes to the Physical Scale value to compensate for scale problems in lighting a scene. Change this value to 80,000 or 150,000 to brighten a scene.

- To limit the effects of exposure control (i.e., not have the exposure control affect the direct lighting) use the **Affect Indirect Only** option.

- There is an Exposure Control type called **mr Photographic Exposure Control**. In the mr Photographic Exposure Control rollout, in the *Physical scale* area, you can change the scale by selecting **Unitless** and adding a Physical scale value.

Practice 9b

Materials that Create Lighting

Practice Objective

* Create a self illuminating material.

Estimated time for completion: 5 minutes

In this practice you will learn how to toggle on a self-illuminating material and apply it to an object for illuminating the scene.

You must set the paths to locate the External files and Xrefs used in the practice. If you have not done this already, return to **Chapter 1: Introduction to Autodesk 3ds Max** and complete Task 1 to Task 3 in **Practice 1a: Organizing Folders and Working with the Interface**. You only have to set the user paths once.

*If a dialog box opens prompting you about a File Load: Mismatch, click **OK** to accept the default values.*

1. Open **LightPoleSelfIllumination start.max**.

2. Verify that the **Camera01** viewport is active. In the Main

   Toolbar, click [image] (Render Production) and note the rendered image shown in Figure 9–32. Close the Render Frame Window.

Figure 9–32

3. The globes have a standard material with 100% self-illumination. You will replace the standard material with an Arch & Design Material. In the Main Toolbar, click

   [image] (Material Editor) to open the Slate Material Editor.

4. In the Material/Map Browser, expand the *Materials>mental ray* categories, double-click on Arch & Design to create a new material node in *View1* sheet.

5. Double-click on the title bar heading of the node to open its Parameter Editor. Rename the material **mr Illuminated Lens**, as shown in Figure 9–33.

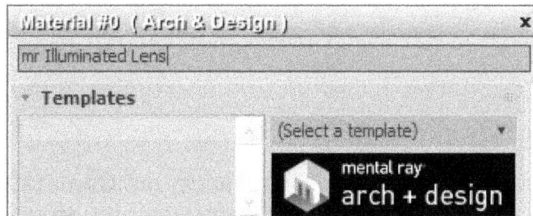

Figure 9–33

Minimize the Slate Material Editor for use again.

6. Scroll down and in the Self Illumination (Glow) rollout, select **Self-Illumination (Glow)**, as shown in Figure 9–34.

7. In the viewport, select one of the globes and in the menu bar, select **Group>Ungroup** to ungroup the objects. Ungroup the second globe group.

8. In the **Camera01** viewport, select the two globes (inverted hemispheres). In the Slate Material Editor, click (Assign Material to Selection) to apply the material to the globes.

9. Render the **Camera01** viewport. Note that the rendering is identical to the rendering before applying the Arch & Design material.

10. In the Slate Material Editor, in the **mr Illuminated Lens** Parameter Editor, in the Self-Illumination (Glow) rollout, in the *Glow options* area, select **Illuminates the Scene (when using FG)**, as shown in Figure 9–35.

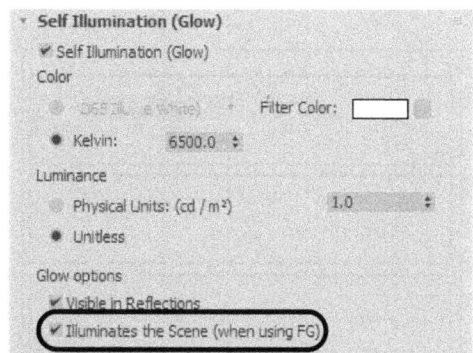

Figure 9–34

Figure 9–35

11. Render the **Camera01** viewport again. The illumination is still not visible.

12. In the Slate Material Editor, in the Self-Illumination (Glow) rollout, in the *Luminance* area, verify that **Unitless** is selected, and increase its multiplier to **10**, as shown in Figure 9–36.

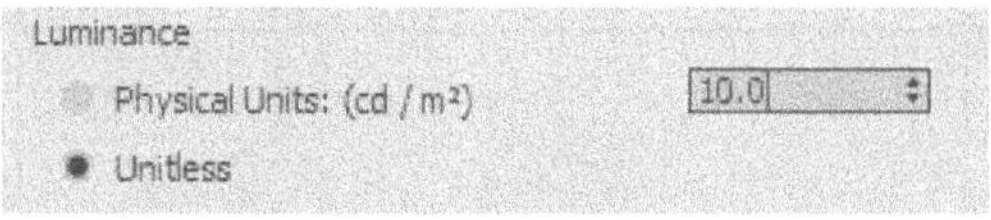

Luminance
  Physical Units: (cd / m²)   10.0
  ● Unitless

Figure 9–36

13. Render the **Camera01** viewport again The illumination is displayed around the globe as shown in Figure 9–37.

Figure 9–37

14. Save your work as **MymrIlluminatedMaterials.max**.

9.2 Exposure Control

Lighting, Materials, and Exposure Control are all used together to produce a real-world rendered image.

- **Exposure Control** parameters are a global adjustment used to modulate the output levels and color range of renderings and viewport display to expected values. Although the exposure control methods are optional when using scanline renderer, they are mandatory when working with mental ray.

- The Autodesk 3ds Max software has the ability to incorporate exposure control in the viewport but is dependant on the driver being used. To display exposure control in the viewport and modify it interactively use the Nitrous or Direct 3D display drivers.

- The Autodesk 3ds Max software calculates real-world illumination values through mental ray. Computer monitors (and printed media) are only able to show a tiny fraction of the total brightness range visible to your eyes.

- Exposure control enables you to adapt the often large dynamic range (the variation of lighting levels) calculated by mental ray into the relatively small dynamic range that can be displayed on a computer screen or printed on paper.

Exposure Control Methods

The various exposure control methods are available in the *Environment* tab in the Environment and Effects dialog box (**Rendering>Environment** or **Rendering>Exposure Control**). In the Exposure Control rollout, select an exposure control method in the drop-down list, as shown in Figure 9–38.

- Exposure Control is used when the **Active** option is enabled.

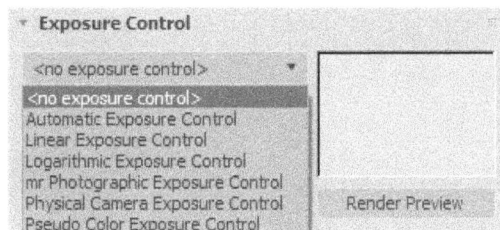

Figure 9–38

Only Logarithmic, mr Photographic, and Pseudo-Color exposure controls are supported by the mental ray renderer.

- **Automatic Exposure Control** attempts to automatically adjust the sample range of lighting levels. It is appropriate for still renderings with very large dynamic ranges. This method can cause flashing when animating, because different frames could be modulated differently.

- **Linear Exposure Control** interprets and adjusts the lighting levels linearly, which might provide better results when working with low dynamic ranges (small variations in lighting levels).

- **Logarithmic Exposure Control** interprets and adjusts the lighting levels with a logarithmic distribution, and provides additional controls that can be used effectively for animations.

- **mr Photographic Exposure Control** gives you the same type of control found in Logarithmic Exposure control, with values such as *Shutter Speed*, *Aperture* (fstops), and *Film speed*. In addition, there is a section that allows for *Shadow*, *Midtone*, and *Highlight* manipulation. Presets automatically adjust the settings, but if a rendering is overly bright or too dark, you can adjust the *Physical scale* setting to **Unitless**, and adjust its value.

- **Physical Camera Exposure Control** interprets and adjusts the exposure value and uses color-response curve to set exposure for physical cameras.

- **Pseudo Color Exposure Control** is used to generate a lighting analysis rendering colorized by luminance (light source brightness) or illuminance (the amount of illumination that arrives at a surface). The different colors in the render (shown in Figure 9–39) give a representation of lighting levels. The red areas depict overlit areas, blue are underlit, and the green areas are at a good lighting level.

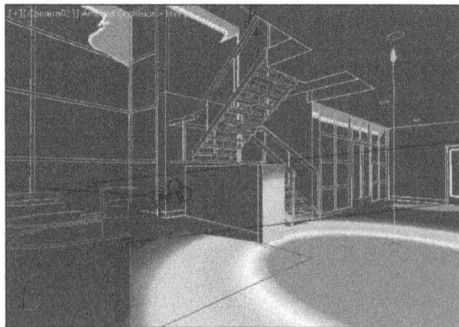

Figure 9–39

Logarithmic Exposure Control Parameters

When **Logarithmic Exposure Control** is selected as the Exposure Control method, a corresponding rollout with parameters that are specific to this method is displayed, as shown in Figure 9–40.

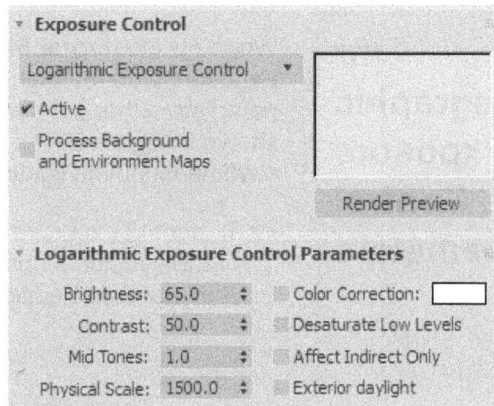

Figure 9–40

Brightness/ Contrast	Adjust the overall brightness and contrast of the rendered image. Brightness controls the perceived illumination of surfaces. Contrast can be used to adjust the difference between light and dark portions of the image. Images that appear washed out (with only a small difference in brightness levels) often benefit from increasing contrast.
Mid Tones	Enables you to shift the brightness levels of the middle portion of the color range. Increasing the midtones value brightens the middle tones of an image and lowering its value darkens them.
Physical Scale	Sets the real-world luminous intensity value of standard lights used with mental ray (multiplied by their multiplier parameter), measured in candelas. This value has no effect on scenes that have only Photometric or IES lights.
Color Correction	Enables you to adjust the color caste of an image so that the color in the swatch displays as white in the final rendering. This adjustment takes place automatically in human vision and is manually adjusted in some real-world cameras using balancing.
Desaturate Low Levels	Converts dark colors to shades of gray, simulating what happens to human vision under dim lighting.
Affect Indirect Only	Enables you to apply exposure control only to indirect lighting, not the direct lighting of your light objects. When working with standard lights this is a helpful option that enables you to manipulate the light object's direct illumination separate from the calculated ambient light.

Exterior daylight	Indicates that you are working with outdoor illumination values, which are much higher than is normally used indoors. When rendering with a camera outside in daylight this option is essential to avoid overexposure.

mr Photographic Exposure Control Parameters

When **mr Photographic Exposure Control** is selected as the Exposure Control method, a corresponding rollout containing parameters that are specific to this method is displayed, as shown in Figure 9–41. This method offers basic presets for daytime/nighttime lighting, and interior and exterior scenes.

- To control exposure, you can enter a single value or use any of the additional options available. These additional options are based on traditional camera and darkroom functionality.

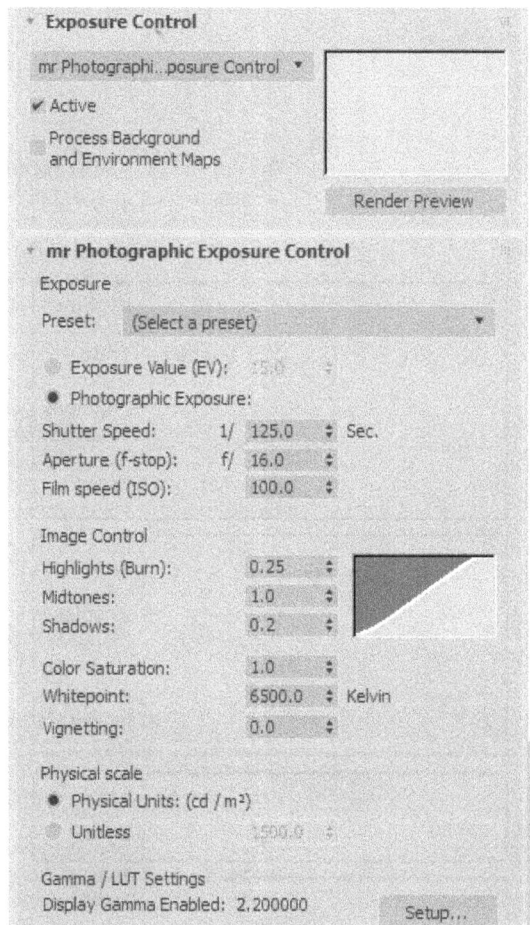

Figure 9–41

Preset	Provides you with predefined sets of values. Lets you select from Physically Based Lighting for Indoor or Outdoor for Daytime or Nighttime, or Non-Physically Based Lighting.
Exposure Value (EV)	Provides you with two options for defining exposure. Exposure Value (EV) is a single value to control the Exposure. Photographic Exposure provides a combination of 3 values to control the Exposure (Photographic Exposure).
Photographic Exposure	Provides three fields (*Shutter Speed*, *Aperture*, and *Film speed*) to control the exposure. The faster the shutter speed, the less light that is admitted into the camera. The lower the aperture (fstop) the wider the opening in the camera lens and thus the more light admitted. With film speed, the higher the number the faster the film, thus more light required.
Image Control	Provides controls similar to a darkroom technique in which you can burn and dodge to control shadows, highlights, and midtones independent of one another. Also provides tools for **Color Saturation** (use 0 for B&W renderings), **Whitepoint** to affect color tinting, and **Vignetting** to create a fuzzy elliptical gradation around the edges of the rendering.
Physical Scale	When this is set to Physical Units, the calculations occur based on the physical lighting and materials in the scene. When Unitless is set, you can enter a numeric adjustment to increase the energy in the scene. Use Unitless whenever the scene seems too dark or bright.
Gamma/ LUT Settings	Accesses the *Gamma and LUT* tab of the Customize> Preferences Viewports dialog box. Gamma is a method to adjust the rendering to suit a particular monitor or output device. Display Gamma, when enabled, controls what the monitor displays. Output gamma controls the brightness and contrast going to the output rendering. Warning: Changing gamma results in images that look one way in the Autodesk 3ds Max software, but look different in other programs such as Photoshop. For this reason be cautious when changing the Gamma.

Practice 9c

Working with Exposure Control

Practice Objective

- Assign NVIDIA mental ray renderer and work with mr Photographic Exposure Control parameters.

Estimated time for completion: 10 minutes

In this practice you will prepare an interior scene for global illumination with mental ray. You will assign NVIDIA mental ray renderer and then apply **mr Photographic Exposure Control** as the exposure control method. You will modify the parameters to adjust the lighting levels in the scene.

You must set the paths to locate the External files and Xrefs used in the practice. If you have not done this already, return to **Chapter 1: Introduction to Autodesk 3ds Max** and complete Task 1 to Task 3 in **Practice 1a: Organizing Folders and Working with the Interface**. You only have to set the user paths once.

Task 1 - Assign NVIDIA mental ray Renderer.

*If a dialog box opens prompting you about a File Load: Mismatch, click **OK** to accept the default values.*

1. Open **mentalray_ExposureControl_start.max**.

2. Verify that the **Camera - Lobby1** viewport is active. In the Main Toolbar, click ![teapot icon] (Render Production). The scene is dark without any calculated ambient light or exposure control, as shown in Figure 9–42.

Figure 9–42

- The object named **Layer:VIZ-1-Ceiling Lights** consists of extruded circles representing the openings for the downlights. The openings display as lit in the renderings because a self-illuminated material has been assigned to them.

3. In the Rendered Frame Window, in the upper left area, click

   ▦ (Save Image) to save this rendering as a JPEG image file. In the Save Image dialog box, save the file in the *renderings* folder of your practice files folder with the name **1_No_Exposure_Control**. In the Save as type drop-down list, select **JPEG File (*.jpg,*.jpe,*.jpeg)**, as shown in Figure 9–43. Click **Save**.

| File name: | 1_No_Exposure_Control | ▼ | + | Save |
| Save as type: | JPEG File (*.jpg,*.jpe,*.jpeg) | ▼ | | Cancel |

Figure 9–43

4. In the JPEG Image Control dialog box, drag the slider to set *Quality* to **Best** (100) and click **OK**. Leave the Rendered Frame Window open for the rest of the practice.

You can also press <F10> to open the Render Setup dialog box.

5. In the Rendered Frame Window, click 🔧 (Render Setup).

   Alternatively, in the Main Toolbar, click 🔧 (Render Setup) or select **Rendering>Render Setup** to open the Render Setup dialog box.

6. In the upper area of the dialog box, in the Renderer drop-down list, select **NVIDIA mental ray** as shown in Figure 9–44. Verify that **NVIDIA mental ray** is displayed in the *Renderer* box.

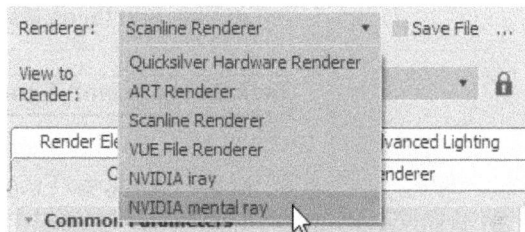

Figure 9–44

The additional panel only displays when NVIDIA mental ray is selected as the production renderer.

7. Note that an additional panel displays at the bottom of the Rendered Frame Window, as shown in Figure 9–45. This panel contains some of the settings for final gather, reflection, etc., which are available in the Render Setup dialog box. This enables you to change the settings easily.

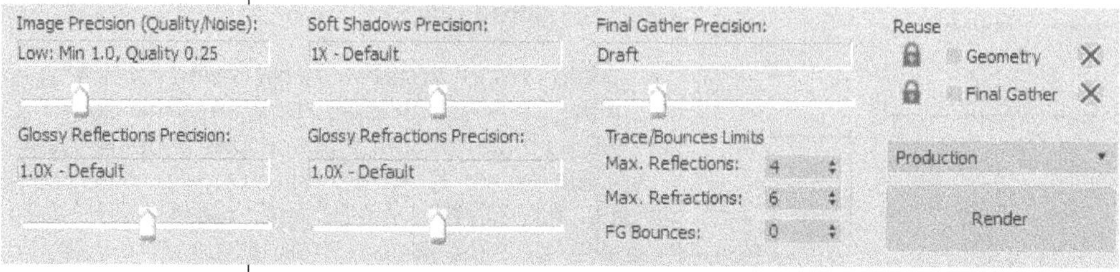

Figure 9–45

8. Click **Render** in the Rendered Frame Window. The rendering takes a little longer but it still looks dark.

9. In the Render Setup dialog box (Main Toolbar> (Render Setup), verify that the *Common* tab is selected. In the Common Parameters rollout, in the *Output Size* area, click **320x240**, as shown in Figure 9–46.

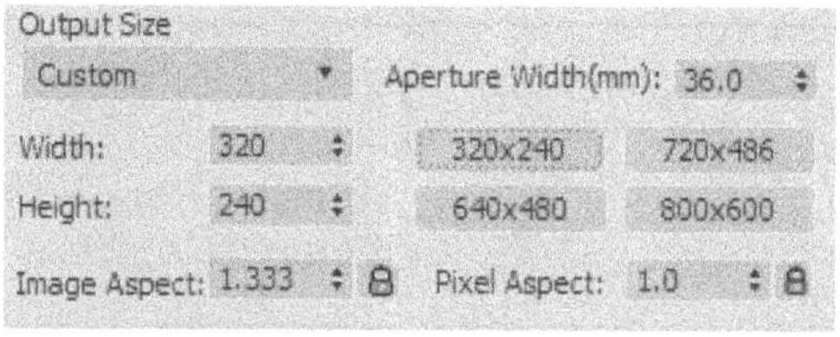

Figure 9–46

10. Close the dialog box.

11. Render the scene and note that the rendered image is smaller and takes lesser time to render.

Task 2 - Work with Exposure Control.

Alternatively, select Rendering> Exposure Control to open the Environment and Effects dialog box.

1. In the Rendered Frame Window, click (Environment and Effects).

2. In the Environment and Effects dialog box, in the Exposure Control rollout, select **mr Photographic Exposure Control** in the drop-down list, as shown in Figure 9–47. Verify that **Active** is selected.

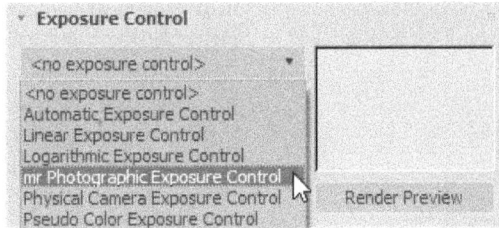

Figure 9–47

3. Click **Render Preview** and note that everything is black.

Use the spinner to reduce the Exposure Value EV and note the Render Preview. It updates interactively as you change this value.

4. In the mr Photographic Exposure Control rollout, in the *Exposure* area, select **Exposure Value (EV)** and using the spinner, reduce the Exposure value and note that the render preview becomes visible. Adjust the EV value until you have a good view of the tile floor in the preview window. You might try a value like EV = **6** or **7,** as shown in Figure 9–48.

Figure 9–48

5. Click **Render** in the Rendered Frame Window. The scene displays brighter than before (as shown in Figure 9–49) under the same lighting conditions. Close the Environment and Effects dialog box.

Figure 9–49

6. In the **Camera - Lobby1** viewport, select any of the **Light–Downlight A-#** (note the name in the Command Panel). In the Command Panel, select the Modify panel ( ). In the Intensity/Color/Attenuation rollout, in the *Color* area, select **HID Ceramic Metal Halide (Cool)**.

7. Render the scene again.

8. In the bottom panel of the Rendered Frame Window, in the *Final Gather Precision* area, verify that the slider is set to **Draft**. Set the *FG Bounces* to **6**, as shown in Figure 9–50.

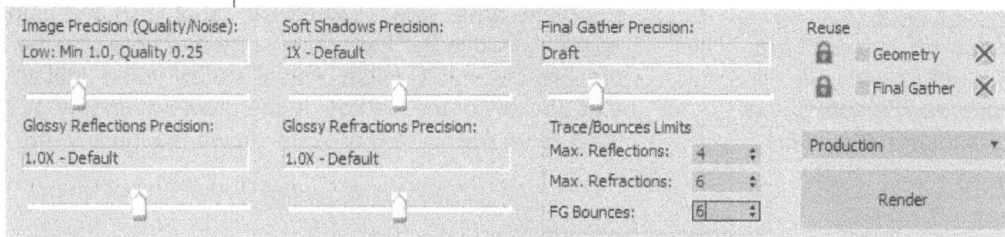

Image Precision (Quality/Noise):	Soft Shadows Precision:	Final Gather Precision:	Reuse
Low: Min 1.0, Quality 0.25	1X - Default	Draft	🔒 Geometry ✕
			🔓 Final Gather ✕
Glossy Reflections Precision:	Glossy Refractions Precision:	Trace/Bounces Limits	
1.0X - Default	1.0X - Default	Max. Reflections: 4	Production ▼
		Max. Refractions: 6	
		FG Bounces: 6	Render

Figure 9–50

9. Click **Render**. Note that there are subtle differences in the lighting in the back of the room, as shown in Figure 9–51.

Figure 9–51

10. In the Rendered Frame Window, click 💾 (Save Image) and save this rendering as **2_Exposure_Control.jpg** in the ...\renderings folder.

11. Save your work as **mymentalray_ExposureControl_start.max**.

9.3 Daytime Lighting

Standard lights can be used to illuminate a nighttime interior scene or a scene that does not have openings to allow in daylight. Nighttime exterior scenes can be lit similarly, with outside light sources such as light fixtures and dim fill lights. Both interior and exterior scenes can be lit with specialized light objects during daytime.

Sunlight represents the direct illumination of the sun, as shown in Figure 9–52 (thick parallel arrows). The light that reflects off of the earth's surface and back down from the atmosphere (and the light that diffuses through the atmosphere on overcast days) is represented as skylight. Skylight illuminates a scene as if it were cast down from a hemispherical dome, as shown in Figure 9–52 (smaller, solid white arrows).

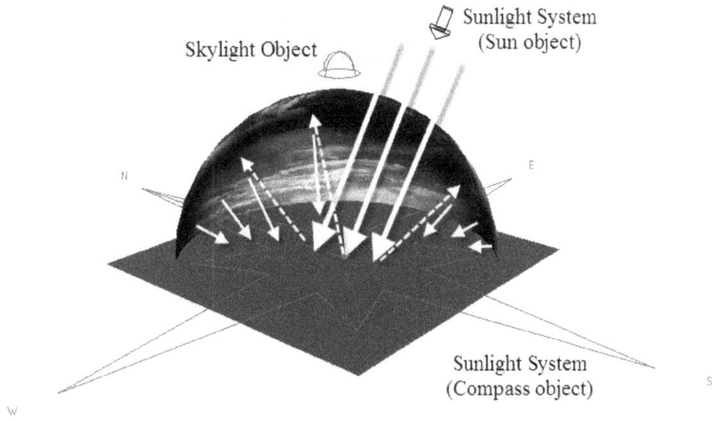

Figure 9–52

In Autodesk 3ds Max, you can create a **Daylight System** using either of the following methods:

- Sunlight and Skylight systems

- Sun Positioner and Physical Sky

Using the **NVIDIA** mental ray renderer, you can create a mental ray daylight system to render a physically based sun and sky lighting.

Sunlight and Skylight System

The Daylight system can be created by combining both Sunlight and Skylight systems.

Sunlight System

Sunlight can be modeled with a Sunlight system that includes a sun object (a direct light) and a compass object that is used to orient the sun in the scene. The angle of the sun's light can be controlled through the date, time, and location parameters. You can also animate the position of the sun over time for shadow studies.

Sunlight and **Daylight** objects are created as System objects, by selecting the Create panel (+) and clicking (Systems), as shown in Figure 9–53.

When creating a Sunlight system, locate the compass over the center of your site at an approximate ground elevation and control the sun's position using the Control Parameters, as shown in Figure 9–54. Once a sun object has been created, these Control Parameters become available in the Command Panel's Motion panel ( ).

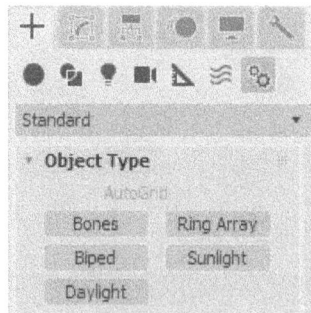

Figure 9–53

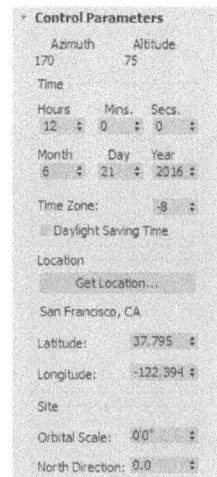

Figure 9–54

- Parameters in the *Time* and *Location* areas enable you to interactively position the sun in the correct location.

- The angle that indicates north in the current coordinate system can be entered in the *North Direction* field. This is used to orient the sunlight to your project geometry.

- The *Orbital Scale* value is the distance from the sun object to the compass (and the ground). The orbital scale should be large enough so that there are no objects behind the sun.

Sun objects are directional lights. Their Modify panel (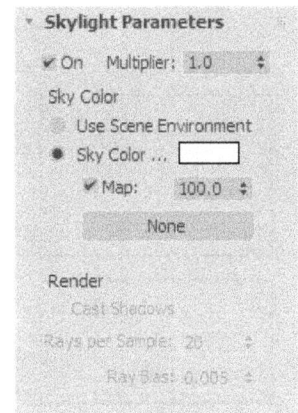) parameters are similar to those for directional lights. To generate shadows correctly, it is sometimes required to clear the **Overshoot** option in Directional Parameters rollout and increase the *Hotspot/Beam* value until it encompasses the entire site.

Skylight System

A Skylight object is not part of the Sunlight system, and is an entirely separate object. With a standard lighting approach, the illumination of a skylight object is not controlled by the date, time, or location settings of the sunlight system. The skylight's brightness (multiplier) parameter can be set manually and animated to change over time.

To create a **Skylight** object as a standard light object, in the Create panel (+), click (Lights), and then click **Standard**, as shown in Figure 9–55. Skylight objects have special controls available in the Skylight Parameters rollout, as shown in Figure 9–56.

Figure 9–55

Figure 9–56

- The light cast from skylights can be colored based on the scene environment map. The **Use Scene Environment** option uses the environment that has been set up in the *Environment* tab in the Environment and Effects dialog box (**Rendering>Environment**).

- The **Sky Color** option enables you to use a single color or a map and it comes with the illumination capabilities in all renderers.

Skylight creates complex shadows that can be realistic and enhance scenes lit with natural lighting. The following settings help control the overall quality (and calculation time) of sky shadows:

Rays per Sample	The number of illuminated rays collected at each sampling point. Lower values result in faster renderings but grainier shadows. Set this value low for test renderings but increase it for the final product (use 15 for still images, but animations might need as much as 20 or 30 to avoid flickering).
Ray Bias	This is the minimum distance between two points for one to cast sky shadows on the other. Increasing this value in scenes with a lot of small detail might speed up rendering time without significantly lowering rendering quality.

Sun and Skylight Options

The following table displays the scene with different sun and skylight options:

	Scene with default lighting (no light objects or shadow casting).
	Scene with Sun (no skylight or ambient light). Note the pitch black shadows.
	Scene with Sun and Skylight; no ambient fill lights or radiosity calculations have been added. Number of Rays = 4.

	Scene with Sun and Skylight; no ambient fill lights or radiosity calculations have been added. Note that the shadows here are less grainy than the ones rendered above. Number of Rays = 10.
	Scene with Sun and Skylight; no ambient fill lights or radiosity calculations have been added. Note that the shadows here are even less grainy than the ones rendered above. Number of Rays = 30. This result took 10x longer to render than the 4 Rays sample.

Sun Positioner Daylight System

New in 2017

A Sun Positioner enables you to create a light system that provides realistic sunlight with a full sky environment. This system uses a simple and intuitive workflow to create a geographically correct positioning and movement of the sun.

To create a **Sun Positioner** object:

1. In the Create panel (+), click (Lights).
2. In the drop down list, ensure that **Photometric** is selected.
3. Click **Sun Positioner**, as shown in Figure 9–57.

- The Sun Positioner creates a Compass rose and a light source that mimics the sun. You can modify the settings of the sunlight system using the sun positioner parameters.

- The Display rollout (shown in Figure 9–58) enables you to control the display of the Compass Rose and set its radius. Using the **North Offset** option, you can set the cardinal direction that is used for placing the sun based on the date and time. In the *Sun* area, you can set the distance of the sun from the compass rose.

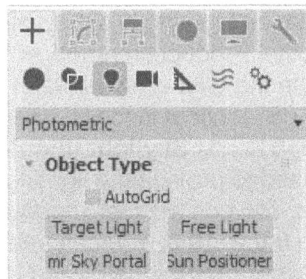

Figure 9–57

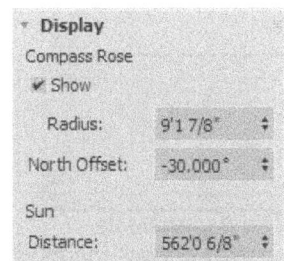

Figure 9–58

- The Sun Position rollout (shown in Figure 9–59) is used to set the position of the sun. The *Date & Time* area enables you to set the time, day, month, and year. You also have the option of using daylight savings time and setting the range of days to be used. In the *Location on Earth* area (shown in Figure 9–60), you can set the location using a database file, or set the Latitude and Longitude coordinates.

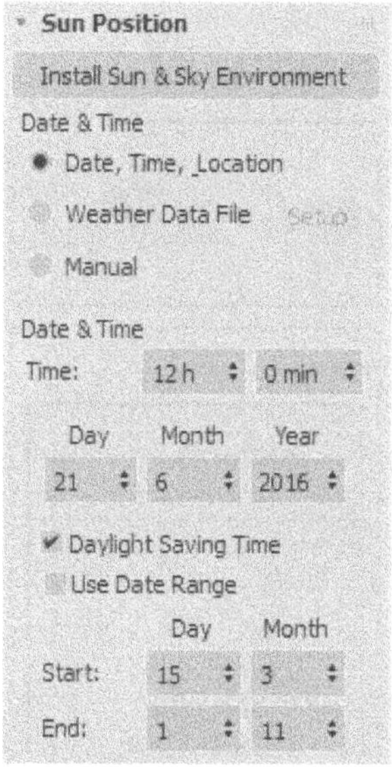

Figure 9–59

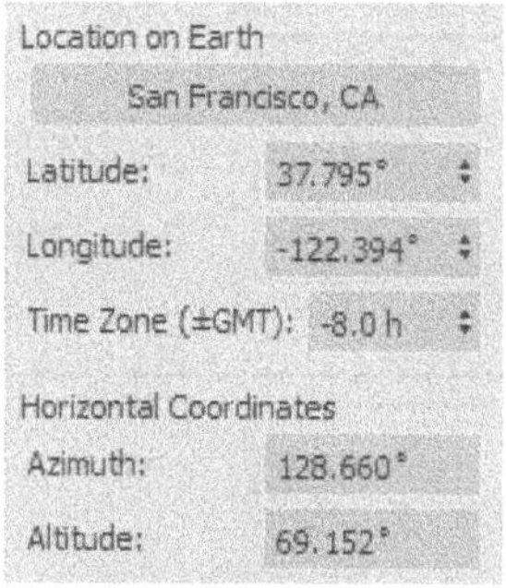

Figure 9–60

Image Based Lighting

Image Based Lighting (IBL) is a rendering technique that involves a scene representation of real-world light information as a photographic image. The image used is typically in a high dynamic range file format, such as, .HDR or .EXR. In the Autodesk 3ds Max software, this image is displayed as an environment map and used to simulate the lighting for the objects in the scene. This enables detailed real-world lighting to be used to light the scene.

Image Based Lighting is only available when **NVIDIA mental ray** is the active Production renderer. You can control the IBL settings in the *Global Illumination* tab>Skylights & Environment Lighting (IBL) rollout in the Render Setup dialog box, as shown in Figure 9–61. The **Skylight Illumination from IBL** is the default option used to provide the lighting information for the mental ray renderer. You can set the *Shadow Quality* by entering a value between **0.0** to **10.0**. You can select a *Shadow Mode* between **Transparent** (better quality and longer render time) and **Opaque**.

The higher value creates crisper shadows and longer render times.

Once the options have been set, you need to add a skylight ((Command Panel, click 💡 (Lights)>**Skylight**) to the scene and select **Use Scene Environment** (Skylights Parameters rollout) to use the lighting from the image.

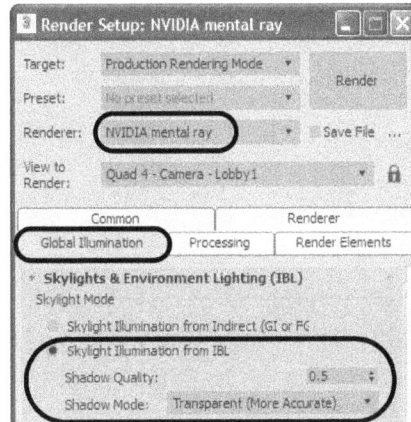

Figure 9–61

Exterior Daylight with mental ray

Using the **NVIDIA** mental ray renderer, you can create a mental ray daylight system to render a physically based sun and sky lighting. The mental ray Daylight System includes a physical sun and sky. This can be seen in the Daylight Parameters in the Modify panel (🔧). mental ray daylight calculates indirect illumination, so that you can illuminate an exterior scene with only a single light source. Early morning and late evening sunlight are tinged with color to create authentic looking renderings. Figure 9–62 shows a mental ray rendering using exterior daylight to illuminate the interior scene.

Figure 9–62

Practice 9d

Image Based Lighting

Practice Objective

- Light a scene using the light in an environment map image.

Estimated time for completion: 15 minutes

In this practice you will learn to light an exterior scene using an HDR image in the Image Based Lighting (IBL) technique for mental ray.

You must set the paths to locate the External files and Xrefs used in the practice. If you have not done this already, return to **Chapter 1: Introduction to Autodesk 3ds Max** and complete Task 1 to Task 3 in **Practice 1a: Organizing Folders and Working with the Interface**. You only have to set the user paths once.

*If a dialog box opens prompting you about a File Load: Mismatch, click **OK** to accept the default values.*

1. Open **Retail Exterior.max**.

2. You need to have NVIDIA mental ray set as your Production Renderer to work with IBL. In the Main Toolbar, click

    (Render Setup) or select **Rendering>Render Setup**. In the upper area of the dialog box, in the Renderer drop-down list, select **NVIDIA mental ray.** Close the Render Setup dialog box.

3. Select **Rendering>Environment** or press <8> to open the Environment and Effects dialog box.

4. In the Common Parameters rollout, in the *Background* area, click **None** for Environment Map.

5. In the Material/Map Browser, expand the *Maps>General* categories and double-click on **Bitmap**.

CountryRoad.hdr has been taken from the Environments folder in the Autodesk Showcase software.

6. In the Select Bitmap Image File dialog box, navigate to the ...\sceneassets\images folder and open **CountryRoad.hdr**. This image will provide the lights for the scene.

7. In the HDRI Load Settings dialog box, in the *Internal Storage* area, verify that **Real Pixels** and **Def. Exposure** are selected, as shown in Figure 9–63. Click **OK**.

Figure 9–63

8. In the Environments and Effects dialog box, note that **None** has been replaced with **Map #9 (CountryRoad.hdr)**. Do not close the dialog box.

9. In the Main Toolbar, click (Material Editor) to open the Slate Material Editor.

10. In the Environments and Effects dialog box, drag and drop **Map #9 (CountryRoad.hdr)** onto the *View1* sheet in the Slate Material Editor.

11. In the Instance (Copy) dialog box, verify that **Instance** is selected and click **OK**. The **Map # Bitmap** node is placed on the *View1* sheet.

12. In the *View1* sheet, double-click on the **Map # Bitmap** title bar to open its Parameter Editor.

13. In the Parameter Editor, in the Coordinates rollout, note that **Spherical Environment** is selected for *Mapping*, as shown in Figure 9–64. The light from the image will illuminate the scene from all directions.

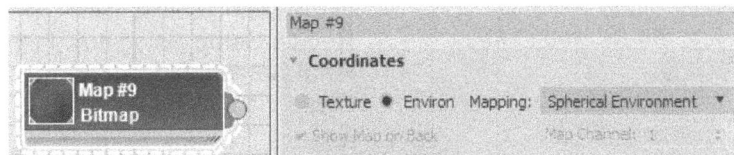

Figure 9–64

14. Close both the Slate Material Editor and Environment and Effects dialog boxes.

15. In the Command Panel>Create panel (✛), click

    💡 (Lights). In the drop-down list, select **Standard** and then select **Skylight**, as shown in Figure 9–65. In the Skylight Parameters rollout, in the *Sky Color* area, select **Use Scene Environment**, as shown in Figure 9–66.

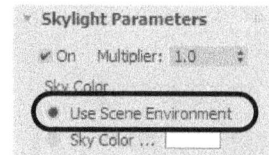

Figure 9–65   **Figure 9–66**

It does not matter where you place the skylight because it is only a helper object.

16. In the **Camera - Southeast View** (the top left viewport), click in one of the parking lines to place the skylight as shown in Figure 9–67.

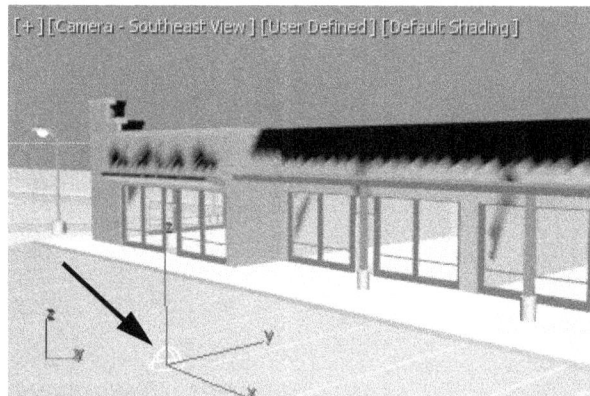

Figure 9–67

You do not require Final Gather if the scene is using the IBL image for lighting.

17. In the Main Toolbar, click 🔧 (Render Setup) to open the Render Setup dialog box. In the *Global Illumination* tab, in the Final Gathering (FG) rollout, clear **Enable Final Gather**. Close the dialog box.

18. Verify that Camera - Southeast View is active. Click

   ✎ (Render Production) to render the scene, as shown in Figure 9–68. Note the environment background that was used and the lighting in the scene with the **Final Gather** disabled.

Figure 9–68

19. Close the Render Frame Window and save the file as **MyIBL.max**.

Practice 9e

Lighting for an Exterior Scene with mental ray Daylight

Practice Objective

- Create a Daylight system with NVIDIA mental ray renderer.

Estimated time for completion: 15 minutes

In general, if you want a daylight system, it is recommended to use the mental ray daylight. In this practice you will create an NVIDIA mental ray daylight system and modify the parameter to get a realistic rendering of the scene.

You must set the paths to locate the External files and Xrefs used in the practice. If you have not done this already, return to **Chapter 1: Introduction to Autodesk 3ds Max** and complete Task 1 to Task 3 in **Practice 1a: Organizing Folders and Working with the Interface**. You only have to set the user paths once.

*If a dialog box opens prompting you about a File Load: Mismatch, click **OK** to accept the default values.*

1. Open **Retail Exterior-Daylight.max**.

2. In the Main Toolbar, click [icon] (Render Setup) or select **Rendering>Render Setup**. In the Render Setup dialog box, in the Renderer drop-down list, select **NVIDIA mental ray** and close the dialog box.

3. Maximize the **Top** viewport and zoom to the extents.

4. In the Create panel (+), click [icon] (Systems). In the Object Type rollout click **Daylight**, as shown in Figure 9–69.

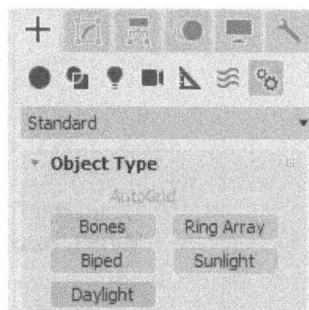

Figure 9–69

The first click is the location of the compass rose. Keep holding the cursor and drag the mouse to resize the compass rose.

5. Near the approximate center of the **Top** viewport, click and drag out to create a compass rose similar to the size shown in Figure 9–70. The north and south points of the compass should approximately touch the top and bottom horizontal lines of the white layout area rectangle. Release the mouse button to complete the creation. You are still in the **Daylight** command.

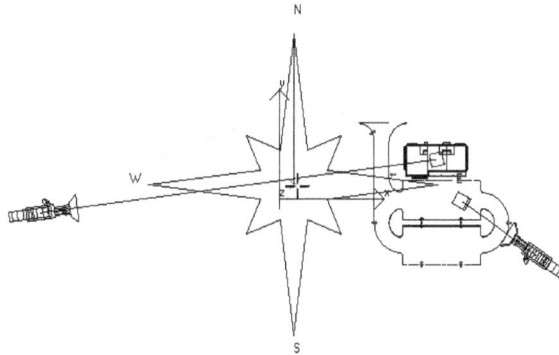

Figure 9–70

6. In the mental ray Sky dialog box, click **Yes**.

7. Note that the sun object is attached to the cursor as you are still in the **Daylight** command (Do not click). Press <L> to change to a **Left** view. Move the cursor up and down to graphically set the initial orbital scale of the sun object. Click when the sun is at a position as shown in Figure 9–71.

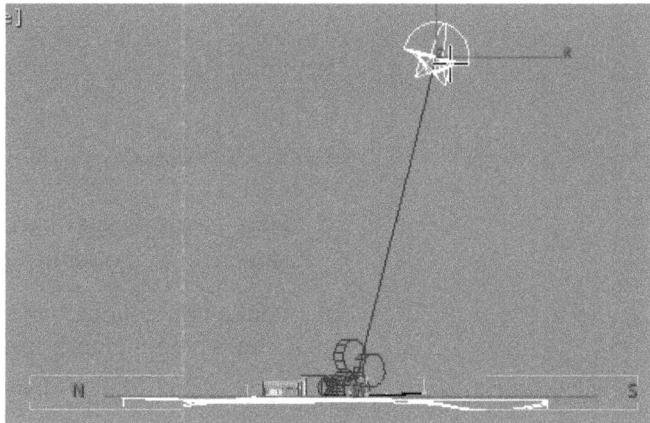

Figure 9–71

Once the Daylight System has been created, these parameters are located in the Motion panel

(*) in the Command Panel.*

8. Sun objects should be placed back from the scene for the shadows to be generated correctly. In the Control Parameters rollout, in the *Site* area, set *Orbital Scale* to **250'0"**, as shown in Figure 9–72.

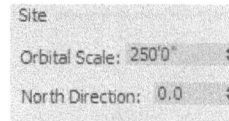

Figure 9–72

9. In the Control Parameters rollout, in the *Location* area, click **Get Location...** and in the Geographic Location dialog box, select **Portland, ME**, and click **OK**.

10. In the Control Parameters rollout, in the *Time* area, set the following, as shown in Figure 9–73:

   - *Hours:* **14**
   - *Month:* **6**
   - *Day:* **21**
   - *Year:* **2016**

   The location of the sun object changes based on the time and date. Press <Esc> to exit the **Daylight** creation command.

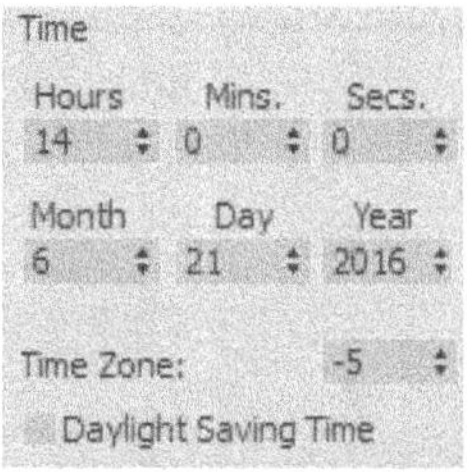

Figure 9–73

11. Maximize **Viewport** to show all four views and activate the

   Camera - Southeast View viewport. Click (Render Production) to render the view.

   - Note that not much is displayed in the rendering and that the rendering is completely washed out.

mr Photographic Exposure Control is the recommended type for the mental ray renderer.

12. In the Rendered Frame Window, click ▧ (Environment and Effects (Exposure Control)). Alternatively, select **Rendering>Exposure Control** to open the Environment and Effects dialog box. In the Environment and Effects dialog box, in the Exposure Control rollout, select **mr Photographic Exposure Control**. In the mr Photographic Exposure Control rollout, select **Exposure Value (EV)** and set it to **13.5** or **14**, (as shown in Figure 9–74) depending on the brightness of your display. Close the dialog box.

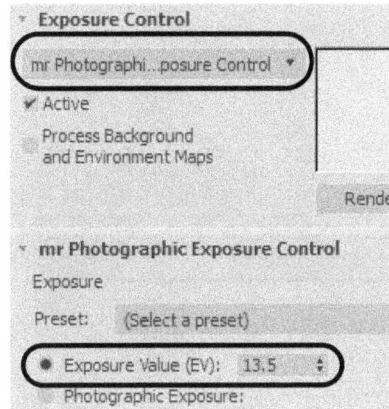

Figure 9–74

13. In the Rendered Frame Window, click **Render**. The rendering looks better.

14. In the bottom panel of the Rendered Window, in the *Trace/Bounces Limits* area, set *FG Bounces* to **2**, as shown in Figure 9–75.

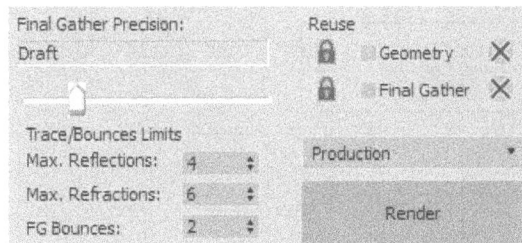

Figure 9–75

15. Click **Render**. Note a slightly brighter rendering, as shown in Figure 9–76.

16. Activate the **Perspective** view and use (Orbit) and pan to orbit to the north direction. Change the time of day to 7 am. In any viewport, select **Daylight001** (sun object) and in the

Command Panel, select the Motion panel ( ). In the Control Parameters rollout, in the *Time* area, set *Hours* to **7**. Activate the **Perspective** viewport and render the scene, as shown in Figure 9–77.

Figure 9–76

Figure 9–77

17. Save your work as **Mymr Daylight.max**.

Practice 9f

Viewport Lighting and Shadows

Practice Objective

- Set the different shading modes to display the shadows in the viewport.

Estimated time for completion: 5 minutes

In the Autodesk 3ds Max software you can view shadows directly in the viewport, without having to render them. In this practice you will learn how to enable Viewport Shading in your models.

You must set the paths to locate the External files and Xrefs used in the practice. If you have not done this already, return to **Chapter 1: Introduction to Autodesk 3ds Max** and complete Task 1 to Task 3 in **Practice 1a: Organizing Folders and Working with the Interface**. You only have to set the user paths once.

*If a dialog box opens prompting you about a File Load: Mismatch, click **OK** to accept the default values.*

1. Open **ViewportShadows_start.max**.
   - This file has a mental ray daylight system already added. The renderer used is also mental ray.

2. In the **Perspective** viewport, select the *Shading Viewport* (User Defined) and select **High Quality.** Note that the **Perspective** viewport display is washed out, although the shadows are displayed.

3. Select the *Shading Viewport* label again and select **Lighting and Shadows** to expand it. Note that **Illuminate with Scene Lights** is selected. This causes the washed out effect because the shadows are based on the scene lights.

For the shadows to be displayed in the viewport, your graphics card should support the Shader Model (2.0 or 3.0) and the display driver should be set to Nitrous Direct3D 11, Nitrous Direct3D 9, or Nitrous Software.

4. Select the *Shading Viewport* label again and select **Lighting and Shadows**. Clear the **Shadows** selection and note how the shadows disappear. Note also that the *Shading Viewport* label automatically changes to **User Defined** because the shadows are always displayed in the High Quality mode. Select **Shadows** to display the shadows in the viewport and change *Shading Viewport* label back to **High Quality**.

5. Select **Rendering>Exposure Control** or press <8> to open the Environment and Effects dialog box. Set the *Exposure Value (EV)* to a number between **13.5** and **15.0**, depending on the brightness of your display. This reduces the washed out effect, as shown in Figure 9–78. Close the dialog box.

Figure 9–78

6. In any viewport, select the **Daylight01** object, or alternatively, use the Scene Explorer to select the **Daylight01** light object.

    In the Command Panel, select the Motion panel ( ). In the Control Parameters rollout, in the *Location* area, change the **North Direction** (using the spinner) and watch the shadows move in the **Perspective** viewport. In viewports, other than the **Perspective**, note that the **Daylight01** object also moves as you change the **North Direction**.

7. In the Control Parameters rollout, note that the month is set to **2** (Feb). Zoom in on the corner of the retail shop to get a closer look at the shadows. Note the long shadows, as shown in Figure 9–79.

Figure 9–79

The shadows get longer in winter months and shorter in summer months.

8. Change the month to **7** (July) and review the shadows, as shown in Figure 9–80. The shadows get shorter.

Figure 9–80

9. Select the **Visual Style** label and select **Lighting and Shadows**. Toggle **Ambient Occlusion** on and off (select and clear). Note the subtle change to the shadows in the viewport.

10. Save your work as **MyViewportShadows_start.max**.

Chapter Review Questions

1. With a Photometric light type, which type of Exposure Control is recommended for the Default Scanline Renderer?

   a. Automatic Exposure Control

   b. Linear Exposure Control

   c. Logarithmic Exposure Control

   d. Pseudo Color Exposure Control

2. Which photometric light distribution type only casts light in one hemisphere and mimics the way light emits from a surface?

   a. Uniform Spherical

   b. Uniform Diffuse

   c. Spotlight

   d. Photometric Web

3. Since photometric lights are based on real-world calculations of light energy, they are not scale-specific.

   a. True

   b. False

4. While using the **Logarithmic Exposure Control** as your exposure control method, which option converts dark colors to shades of gray, simulating what happens to human vision under dim lighting?

   a. Mid Tones

   b. Color Correction

   c. Desaturate Low levels

   d. Affect Indirect Only

5. Which of the following statements is correct?

    a. The angle of the sun's light cannot be controlled using date, time, and location parameters.

    b. The illumination of a skylight object is controlled by date, time, and location settings of the sunlight system.

    c. Skylight objects are directional lights and their modify parameters are similar to those for directional lights.

    d. Sunlight objects are directional lights and their modify parameters are similar to those for directional lights.

6. Which renderer should be the active Production renderer for the Image Based Lighting (IBL) rendering technique to become available?

    a. Scanline Renderer

    b. NVIDIA mental ray

    c. NVIDIA iray

    d. Quicksilver Hardware Renderer

    e. ART Renderer

Command Summary

Button	Command	Location
	Lights	• **Command Panel:** Create panel • **Create:** Lights
	Motion panel	• **Command Panel**
	Render Production	• **Main Toolbar** • **Rendering:** Render
	Render Setup	• **Main Toolbar** • **Rendering**: Render Setup
	Systems	• **Command Panel:** Create panel

mental ray Rendering

The NVIDIA® mental ray® renderer is one of the rendering engines available in the Autodesk® 3ds Max® software. This engine works well for visualization projects due to its global illumination system that enables the use of physically correct lighting and materials. Additionally, customization controls help you to further refine the results that are obtained using this rendering engine.

Learning Objectives in this Chapter

- Create realistic renderings using the NVIDIA mental ray renderer.
- Control the settings for photon mapping and final gather techniques to generate a smooth render.
- Enhance the quality of mental ray renderings using exposure controls and sampling quality.
- Create mental ray proxy objects.

10.1 Fundamentals of mental ray

The NVIDIA mental ray renderer, available with the Autodesk 3ds Max software, is a global illumination system that has been customized specifically for work with design visualization. It calculates physically based lighting using physically correct lights and physically based materials (such as the Autodesk materials or Arch & Design materials).

The mental ray renderer traces the paths of beams of light from their source (the CG light source) to the 3D surface and from the 3D surface onwards to the eye. It computes whether light reflects off the surface, passes through the surface, or is absorbed by the surface based on material definition.

To spread the light through the scene accurately, mental ray scatters points through the scene, which shoot out rays. Averaging occurs over these points with ray calculations to create the color for the pixels in the image. Figure 10–1 shows a mental ray rendering in process.

Figure 10–1

There are two basic methods for distributing light and color through the scene are available in mental ray. These are:

Photons are essential when caustic lighting effects are required.

- **Photon Mapping** is the method that calculates the pixels in a rendering and creates overlapping circular areas based on photon particles distributed by light energy through the scene. These circular areas blend together to create the lighting information in the scene. After calculation, the photon map file can be saved. Once calculated, it can be used in an animation using a moving camera. Photon mapping is useful when rendering interiors are lit by Photometric lights with intricate detail in low light areas.

- **Final Gather** is the method to be generally used for exterior renderings or interiors that are lit by exterior daylight coming through windows. It can be used with Photon Mapping.

mental ray Rendering

A mental ray rendering can approximate the real-world behavior of light. Using photometric lights and physically-based material parameters, mental ray can produce realistic ambient lighting. Some specifications of mental ray rendering are as follows:

- The mental ray renderer is intended to work with Photometric light objects: **Target Lights**, **Free Lights**, **mr Sun**, and **mrSkylight** objects. Standard lights can also be used if they are attenuated.

- The mental ray renderer can work with any material type. However, the Arch & Design materials have built-in mental ray adjustment controls, such as self-illuminance, reflectance, and transmission of light energy.

- mental ray calculates ambient light, thus reducing the time spent configuring ambient lights.

- **mr photographic Exposure Control** is required when lighting with mental ray.

- mental ray results can be stored as an .FGM (Final Gather Map) file and can reuse the calculations. Final Gather results are view-dependent. A mental ray solution can be rendered for multiple viewpoints, but each one must recalculate the Final Gather map for each frame where new geometry is revealed to the eye. When using an animated camera, you need to calculate the final gather map over the course of the animation (usually every 10 or 20 frames).

- The mental ray renderer can a lot of memory. It is recommended to find a balance between the least amount of memory usage and the most acceptable lighting results. Avoid using the **High** quality setting.

- The mental ray Light calculations can be used to create a lighting analysis for energy compliance.

The Autodesk® Revit® and AutoCAD® software use Autodesk materials and can share files with the Autodesk 3ds Max software.

Manually configured ambient light can be added as required, although it is an artistic fix and not a physically accurate solution.

> **Hint: Using .FGM Files**
>
> To speed up the process, calculate the .FGM (Final Gather Map) file using a smaller resolution. Once complete, use the .FGM file for the larger resolution rendering. You can also lower the *Sample per Pixel* **Minimum** and **Maximum** values to save time when calculating the .FGM file. These options are found in the Render Setup dialog box in the Sampling Quality rollout, in the *Renderer* tab.

10.2 mental ray Interior Rendering

Instead of using mental ray lighting when creating interiors without exterior lighting, you can use Photometric lights. When you create daylight and then render an interior scene (as shown in Figure 10–2), there is only direct light from the sun object. To realistically illuminate the interior scene and generate accurate lighting effects, you need to add indirect illumination using the mental ray renderer.

Figure 10–2

Hint: Autodesk Library Materials

It is recommended that you use Autodesk Library materials (which are based on Arch & Design materials) or Arch & Design materials with mental ray to generate the best quality surfaces.

To use mental ray, you should assign the NVIDIA mental ray as

your renderer. In the Main Toolbar, click ![icon] (Render Setup) or select **Rendering>Render Setup**. In the Render Setup dialog box, in the Renderer drop-down list, select **NVIDIA mental ray**, as shown in Figure 10–3. Close the dialog box.

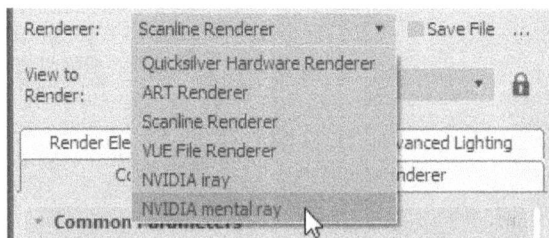

Figure 10–3

Global illumination is included in mental ray as part of generating indirect illumination in interior scenes. It can be obtained by either **photon tracing** or **final gathering**. Both methods use the photon mapping technique.

Photon Mapping

Photons are light particles that reflect, refract, and scatter across the diffuse surfaces based on materials applied to objects. Photons distribute energy quickly in the scene as they bounce from surface to surface.

> **Hint: Practice for Students**
>
> There is no practice using this Photon mapping. However, you can follow along with this lecture by opening **Mental_Interior_ Photons_Start1.max**.

*You should have assigned **NVIDIA mental ray** as your production renderer to display the Global Illumination options.*

Open the Render Setup dialog box, ((Render Setup) or **Rendering>Render Setup**) and select the *Global Illumination* tab. In the Caustics & Photon Mapping rollout, in the *Photon Mapping* area, select **Enable**. By setting *Maximum Num. Photons per Sample* to a small number (1 or 2) and selecting **Maximum Sampling Radius** (as shown in Figure 10–4) you generate (click **Render** in the dialog box) swarms of small white circles that cover the surfaces, as shown in Figure 10–5.

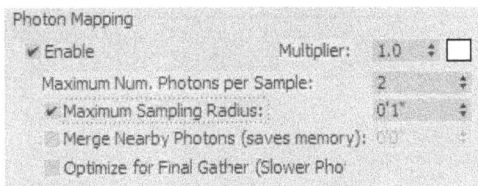

Photon Mapping
✔ Enable   Multiplier: 1.0   ⬦ ☐
   Maximum Num. Photons per Sample: 2   ⬦
   ✔ Maximum Sampling Radius: 0'1"   ⬦
   ☐ Merge Nearby Photons (saves memory): 0'0 ⬦
   ☐ Optimize for Final Gather (Slower Pho

Figure 10–4

Figure 10–5

Slowly increase the **Maximum Sampling Radius** and the circles begin to join and overlap. In Figure 10–6, the *Maximum Num. Photons per Sample* and *Maximum Sampling Radius* are set to **1** and **0'2"** respectively, and in Figure 10–7, the values are set to **5** and **0'5"** respectively.

Figure 10–6

Figure 10–7

Increase the number of photons per sample by an order of magnitude. Continue increasing until you have a smooth photon-based solution. In Figure 10–8, the *Maximum Num. Photons per Sample* and *Maximum Sampling Radius* are set to **50** and **5'0"** respectively, and in Figure 10–9, the values are set to **500** and **5'0"**.

Figure 10–8

Figure 10–9

You might want to reduce the radius and increase the number of photons. The general rule is that when you decrease the radius by 2, you increase the maximum number of photons per sample times by **5.6 (4 x 1.4)**, and in the *Light Properties* area, increase the *Average GI Photons per Light* number by **1.4** photons.

To make the scene smoother, it is recommended that you add final gathering to it. Expand the Final Gathering (FG) rollout (*Global Illumination* tab), in the *Basic* area, toggle on **Enable Final Gather**, and set *Diffuse Bounces* to **2**, as shown in Figure 10–10.

Final Gathering (FG)
Basic
☑ Enable Final Gather   Multiplier: 1.0 ☐
FG Precision Presets:
Draft
Project FG Points From Cam...Position (Best for Stills) ▼
Divide Camera Path by Num. Segments: 9
Initial FG Point Density: 0.1
Rays per FG Point: 50
Interpolate Over Num. FG Points: 30
Diffuse Bounces 2   Weight: 1.0

Figure 10–10

mr Photographic Exposure Control is the recommended exposure control method for the mental ray renderer.

After rendering, note that the brightness in the scene has improved, but is still a little dark because the exposure control options have not been set. In the Environment and Effects dialog box (**Rendering>Exposure Control** or, Rendered Frame Window> 🖼), in the Exposure Control rollout, select **mr Photographic Exposure Control** in the drop-down list, verify that **Active** is selected, and click **Render Preview**. The preview displays dark because no exposure value has been set. In the mr Photographic Exposure Control rollout, activate **Exposure Value (EV)** and using the spinner, set the EV value (**7.0 to 9.5**) until the lighting is improved in the Render Preview, as shown in Figure 10–11. Render the scene as shown in Figure 10–12.

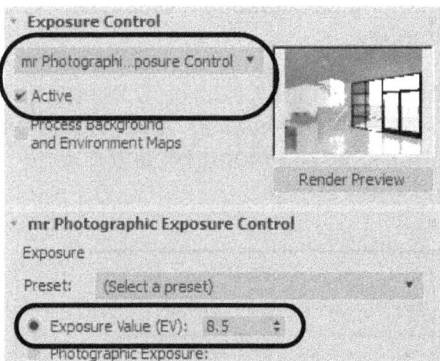

Figure 10–11

Figure 10–12

*If **Read/Write Photons to Photon Map Files** is already selected, click*

[ ] *to specify a folder and filename.*

When you get the required photon solution, you can save a photon map. This calculation is scene-based rather than specific to a viewport. To save a photon map:

1. In the Render Setup dialog box, in the *Global Illumination* tab, expand the Reuse (FG and Photons Disk Caching) rollout.
2. In the *Caustics and Photon Map* area, select **Read/Write Photons to Photon Map Files** in the drop-down list and specify a folder and filename in the Save As dialog box.
3. Click **Generate Photon Map File Now**, as shown in Figure 10–13. The file is saved as a binary .PMAP file (photon-map file).

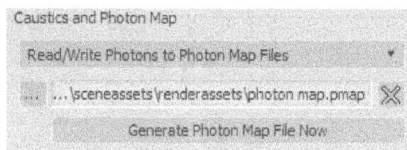

Figure 10–13

In many animations, especially with locked-down (non-moving) camera shots, a photon map saves you considerable rendering time. For interior renderings, photon mapping helps generate light in the scene and can smooth out flashing and shimmering problems in animations.

Photon Merging

Photon merging is similar to adaptive tessellation in radiosity. You can set a merge radius and the photons in that area are merged to conserve memory and calculation time.

For example, if you have two million photons in your scene, you might increase it to 10 million.

• Generally, the workflow for this is to set the merge radius less than 5% of the maximum sampling radius, and increase the number of photons drastically. You can save the photon map once your photon merging calculations are satisfactory and your image looks smooth.

• To enable Photon Merging, in the Caustics & Photon Mapping rollout, in the *Photon Mapping* area, toggle on **Merge Nearby Photons (saves memory)** and enter a radius, as shown in Figure 10–14.

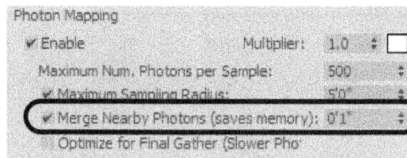

Figure 10–14

- For interior daylight scenes using mr Sky Portals (a photometric light type), you might be able to skip Photon Mapping entirely. However, for interior scenes with artificial illumination, use Photon Mapping to get the required results.

Final Gather

Final Gather is a viewport-based pixel computation that calculates indirect lighting by shooting rays throughout the scene. It creates final gather points that produce rays used to compute the brightness of the lighting.

- Bucket Rendering enables you to see different portions being rendered. If they are not rendered correctly, you can cancel the rendering, make the required modifications, and render again.

- In Render Setup dialog box, *Global Illumination* tab, in Final Gathering (FG) rollout, you can control the **Initial FG Point Density** and **Rays per FG Point** (as shown in Figure 10–15) to develop a smooth rendering. The Final Gather Presets set these numbers for you automatically.

- It is possible to display the final gather points in the renderings. In the Render Setup dialog box, in the *Processing* tab, expand the Diagnostics rollout. In the *Visual* area, select **Enable** and **Final Gather**, as shown in Figure 10–16.

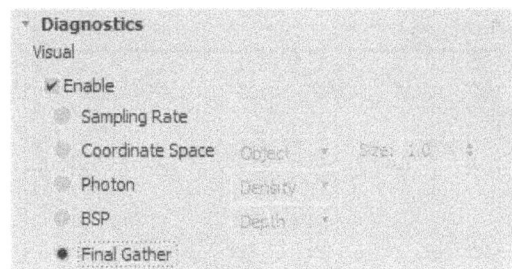

Figure 10–15   Figure 10–16

- When you render the scene, your rendering displays with green dots, as shown in Figure 10–17. Each dot represents a FG point.

Figure 10–17

Final Gather Parameters

The important **Final Gather** parameters are present in the *FG Precision Presets* area, as shown in Figure 10–18 (*Global Illumination* tab>Final Gathering (FG) rollout).

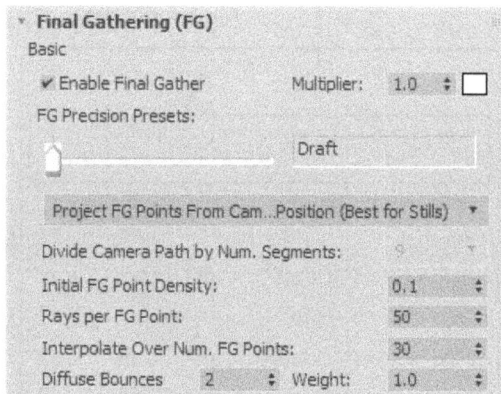

Figure 10–18

- **Initial FG Point Density:** Sets the grid spacing. Using too much density might introduce noise into the image. Remember that each point shoots rays in the scene.

- **Rays per FG Point:** Controls the number of rays shot into the scene from the FG point. If you set the **Interpolate Over Num. FG Points** to **1**, you have a one to one correspondence between Rays and Points. Increase the number of Rays and render to observe the effects. Increase the **Interpolate Over Num. FG Points** gradually to smooth the image. If your scene is evenly illuminated, you can use low values. The number of rays can be set from 50 to 500. If your scene contains a high contrast, you can use much higher values, in the 1000 to 10,000 range.

- **Interpolate Over Num. FG Points:** Determines the radius for smoothing, based on the number of points considered for the light calculation. The larger the number, the more points are considered in a single calculation. Setting this value to something high (between 100 and 250) should result in extremely realistic, artifact-free images. The workflow is to find the minimum radius that achieves realistic results, while maintaining detail in the scene.

- **Diffuse Bounces:** Defines the number of times the light bounces from surface to surface. Typical values range from 5 to 10, depending on the brightness required in the scene. Presets do not affect the *Diffuse Bounces* value.

*You can also use the Final Gather Precision slider directly in the bottom panel of the Rendered Frame Window to control **FG Precision Presets**.*

- **FG Precision Presets:** If you experience splotchiness on the wall, floor, or ceiling of an interior scene, you can increase the Final Gather Presets. Changing the *FG Precision Presets* from **Draft** to **Low** changes the values of **Initial FG Point Density** and **Rays per FG Point**, but all of the other settings remain the same. This eliminates some of the artifacts but increases rendering time. Changing to **Medium** should eliminate almost all artifacts, but can double rendering times. It is not recommended to use **High**, and **Very High** should only be considered when doing large-scale print work.

> **Hint: Additional Options in the Rendered Frame Window**
>
> A panel at the bottom of the Rendered Frame Window is available if the production renderer is set to **NVIDIA mental ray**. In addition to controlling the **Sampling Quality** and **Final Gather Precision**, sliders are available for *Precision of Glossy Reflections*, *Glossy Refractions*, and *Soft Shadows*. This is a global override to speed up rendering in the design stages.

Final Gather Map

Just like the Photon Map, you can write a Final Gather Map using the Render Setup dialog box.

- In the *Global Illumination* tab, expand the Reuse (FG and Photon Disk Caching) rollout. In the *Final Gather Map* area, select **Incrementally Add FG Points to FG Map Files** in the drop-down list and click ▦ to specify a path and filename. Then, click **Generate Final Gather Map File Now** as shown in Figure 10–19. Once the final gather map is generated, you can set the final gather map option to **Read FG Point Only from Existing FG Map Files**. This can be used to save time for long renderings by enabling you to reuse the final gather solution for future renderings without recalculation.

An additional panel displays at the bottom of the Rendered Frame Window when NVIDIA mental ray is selected as the active production renderer.

- You can also access this functionality directly from the Rendered Frame Window. In the bottom panel, select **Final Gather** in the *Reuse* area and click the Lock next to Final Gather, as shown in Figure 10–20.

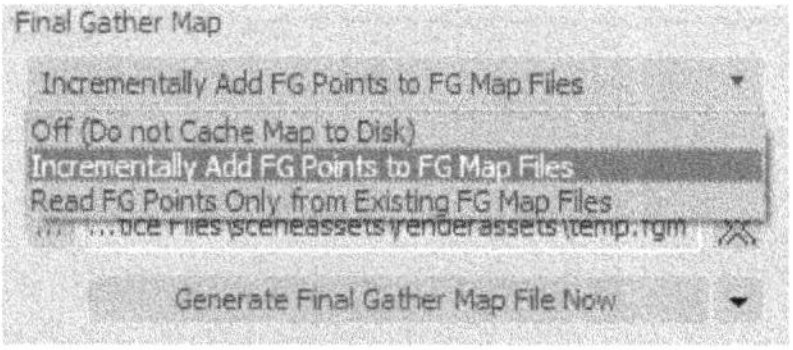

Figure 10–19 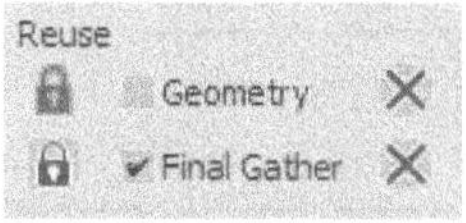   **Figure 10–20**

Exposure Control

Exposure Control (**Rendering>Exposure Control**, Exposure Control rollout) is recommended as part of the mental ray workflow. Select the **mr Photographic Exposure Control** (recommended exposure control method with mental ray), as shown in Figure 10–21. In the mr Photographic Exposure Control rollout, enable **Exposure Value (EV)** and click **Render Preview** to display an image in the thumbnail view. When the image is visible, make adjustments to the **Exposure Value (EV)** spinners and watch the image update interactively in the preview window. Selecting the spinner arrows adjusts the setting in increments of 10. You can also manually enter a numeric value. Controlling one number changes the entire range of values.

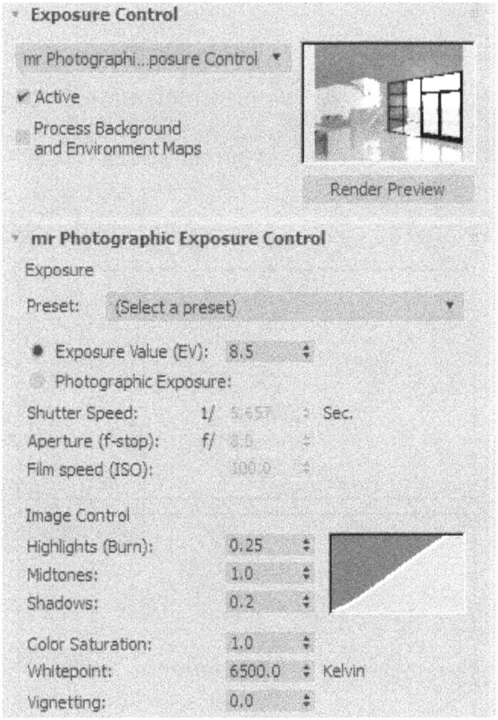

Figure 10–21

The changes can be applied to the whole scene to brighten the whole area, as shown in Figure 10–22. You can also apply Exposure control specifically to the midtone or shadow areas to brighten only those areas, as shown in Figure 10–23.

Figure 10–22

Figure 10–23

Hint: Photographic Exposure

If you are experienced with photography, you can consider using the **Photographic Exposure** option. This is the combination of *Shutter Speed*, *Aperture*, and *Film speed* values consistent with what is used in a traditional 35 mm camera, as shown in Figure 10–24.

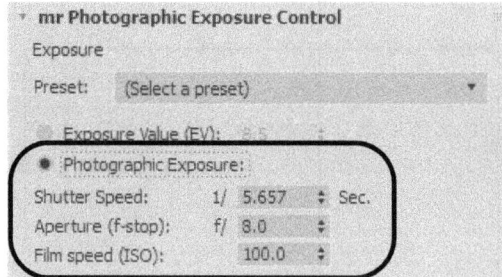

Figure 10–24

Sampling Quality

With mental ray renderer, you can use the Sampling Controls for antialiasing the rendered images. In the Render Setup dialog box, select the *Renderer* tab and expand the Sampling Quality rollout, as shown in Figure 10–25.

You can perform different kinds of sampling, by selecting the *Sampling Mode* in the drop-down list.

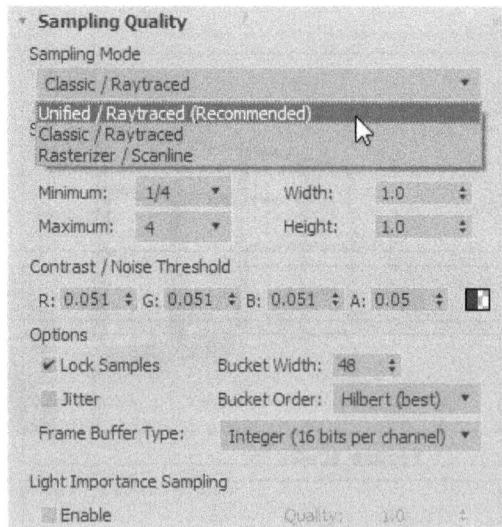

Figure 10–25

The **Unified/ Raytraced (Recommended)** method is used for quick rendering.

• Set the *Quality* of rendering to a range of **0.1 - 20.0** (the higher quality has lesser noise). The *Minimum* and *Maximum* values in the *Samples per Pixel* area (shown in Figure 10–26) provide controls similar to Supersampling in the scanline renderer. Increase the *Maximum* value to smooth out any jagged edges on diagonals. For this method, it is recommended that you adjust the *Quality* values rather than adjusting the *Minimum* and *Maximum* values. You can also access these settings in the bottom additional panel in the Rendered Frame Window and use the *Image Precision (Quality/Noise)* slider, which provides various presets for sample rate combinations, as shown in Figure 10–27.

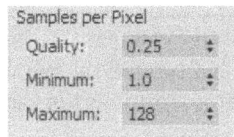

Figure 10–26   Figure 10–27

Do not assign the same value to Minimum and Maximum. The ratio of Minimum to Maximum is typically approximately 1:16.

The **Classic / Raytraced** method controls the antialiasing for the render. This method only uses the *Minimum* and *Maximum* sample rates, as shown in Figure 10–28.

• Consider using low values while determining the initial lighting. Increase these values when you are close to a more finished rendering. Use values, such as *Minimum* **4**, and *Maximum* **64** (or smaller) for a higher quality rendering and values of *Minimum* **1/16**, *Maximum* **1/4** for preview quality.

The **Rasterizer / Scanline** method uses *Shading* to assign a color to the micro-polygons and uses the *Visibility* samples to overset the image, as shown in Figure 10–29. This resolves the motion blur using many samples.

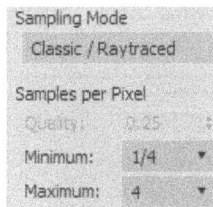 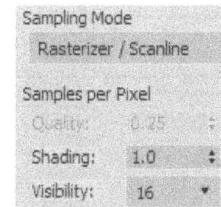

Figure 10–28   Figure 10–29

Ambient Occlusion (A0)

Ambient Occlusion is a type of light calculation that adds a detail enhancement effect by adding gradient shading to bring out subtle differences. It is a material effect that is part of the Arch & Design materials and some of Autodesk Material Library materials. This is enabled in the Special Effects rollout in the Parameter Editor of the material, in the Slate Material Editor, as shown in Figure 10–30.

Special Effects

☑ Ambient Occlusion

Samples:	16
Max Distance:	0'4"

☐ Use Color From Other Materials (Exact AO)

Shadow Color:

● Custom Ambient Light Color

○ Global Ambient Light Color

Figure 10–30

- Ambient Occlusion uses shaders to calculate the extent an area is inhibited by incoming light. It brings out detail in dark corners, along edges, and in bright places exposed to too much light.

- It has a *Max Distance* setting to speed up the rendering by limiting the radius considered. You can combine an extremely low final gather density (e.g., 0.1) with a small AO local radius (e.g., 4") to create quick renderings with good detail and smoothing.

In the film industry, it is common to create a separate Ambient Occlusion pass (called a dirt pass or beauty pass) on top of the rendering to enhance the details. You can create this kind of render pass using **Material Override**. You can enable Material Override in the Render Setup dialog box, in the *Processing* tab, in the Translator Options rollout. Placing an Arch & Design material in that slot temporarily overrides all materials in the scene. In Figure 10–31, the teapot has the Arch & Design material and in Figure 10–32, the teapot has an Override Material with an AO map.

Figure 10–31

Figure 10–32

Hint: Override Material

The **Override Material** can be used to remove the materials temporarily so that you can examine the lighting in your scene in isolation and make changes, as required.

Use **Final Gather** first and see how it looks. If the image has problems, generate a Photon solution to transport light energy into the scene. You can think of this as painting a broad light into the scene. Save a photon map. Use **Final Gather** again. It uses the Photon information and smooths it out into medium size details. Then, use **Ambient Occlusion** in the materials to bring out the small details. This can create quick, smooth, but detailed renderings.

Hint: Ambient Occlusion for Materials

You can apply Ambient Occlusion to the material. In the Slate Material Editor, open the material's Parameter Editor and in the Templates rollout, select **Enable Detail Enhancement**, as shown in Figure 10–33.

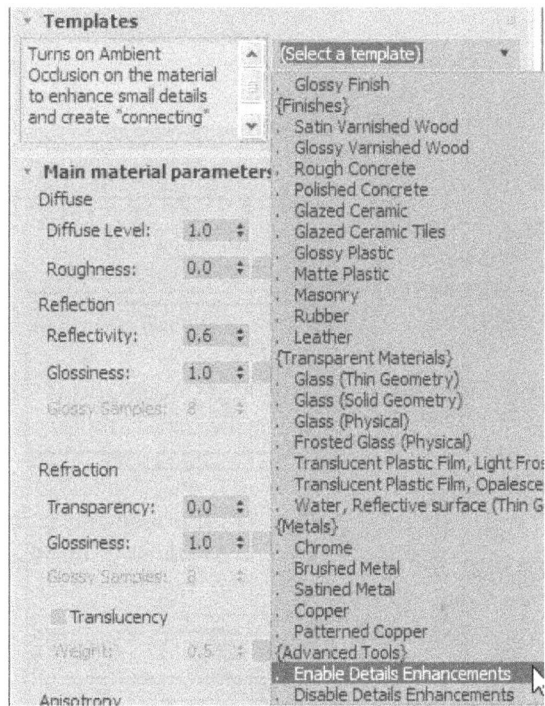

Figure 10–33

Practice 10a

Improving mental ray Speed, Quality, and using Material Overrides

Practice Objectives

- Setup Exposure Control options and Final Gather options.
- Improve the render quality and reuse the existing .FGM file.
- Apply **Material Override** to isolate the materials.

Estimated time for completion: 35 minutes

In this practice you will set Final Gather and exposure controls to get a decent interior render. You will save the Final Gather calculations, and reuse them in future renderings to save time during rendering. You will further enhance the renderings by modifying the Final Gather settings. You will also set the material overrides to temporarily remove materials examining the lighting in the scene.

You must set the paths to locate the External files and Xrefs used in the practice. If you have not done this already, return to **Chapter 1: Introduction to Autodesk 3ds Max** and complete Task 1 to Task 3 in **Practice 1a: Organizing Folders and Working with the Interface**. You only have to set the user paths once.

*If a dialog box opens prompting you about a File Load: Mismatch, click **OK** to accept the default values.*

Task 1 - Working with Render Setup and Exposure Control.

1. Open **Final Gather Map Start.max**.

Leave the Rendered Frame Window open for the rest of the practice (minimize/maximize as required).

2. Verify that the **Camera - Lobby1** viewport is active. In the

While rendering, a Rendering window displays indicating the progress of the rendering. You can cancel the rendering anytime.

Main Toolbar, click (Render Production) to render the viewport. Note that the rendering is washed out and the ceiling is dark. In the Rendered Frame Window bottom panel, note that **Final Gather** is disabled and **Image Precision (Antialiasing)** is displayed indicating that the **Classic/Raytraced** *Sampling* option is used, as shown in Figure 10–34.

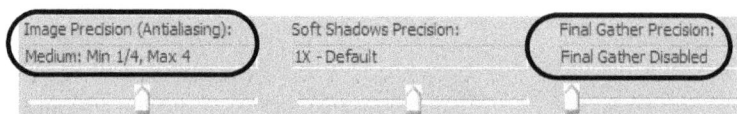

Figure 10–34

You can also press
<F10> to open the
Render Setup dialog
box. Leave the Render
Setup dialog box open
for the rest of the
practice.

3. In the Rendered Frame Window, click ⚙ (Render Setup).

   Alternatively, in the Main Toolbar, click ⚙ (Render Setup) or select **Rendering>Render Setup** to open the Render Setup dialog box.

4. Open the *Global Illumination* tab and expand the Final Gathering (FG) rollout. In the *Basic* area, select **Enable Final Gather**. Then, expand the Skylights & Environment Lighting (IBL) rollout and verify that **Skylight Illumination from (GI or FG)** is selected.

5. Select the *Renderer* tab, expand the Sampling Quality rollout, expand the Sampling Mode drop-down list and select **Unified /Raytraced (Recommended)**, as shown in Figure 10–35.

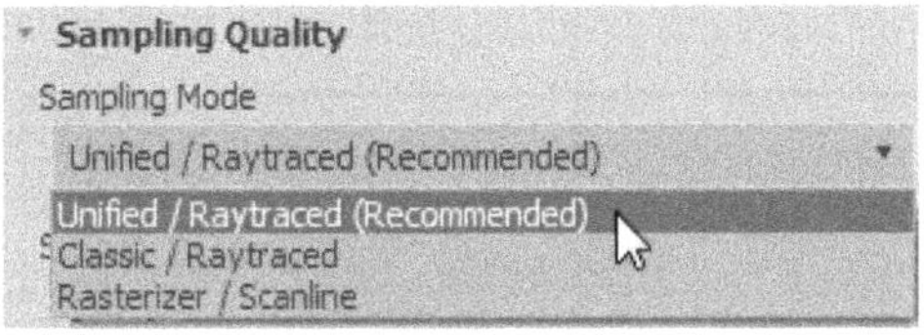

Figure 10–35

6. In the Render Setup dialog box or in the Rendered Frame Window, click **Render**.
   - It will take a few minutes to render because the Final Gather calculates the indirect lighting by shooting rays throughout the scene. Different portions are rendered as Final Gather uses Bucket Rendering.
   - In the bottom panel of the Rendered Frame Window, note that the **Final Gather** is activated and **Image Precision (Quality/Noise)** is displayed, indicating that the **Unified /Raytraced (Recommended)** *Sampling* option is used, as shown in Figure 10–36.

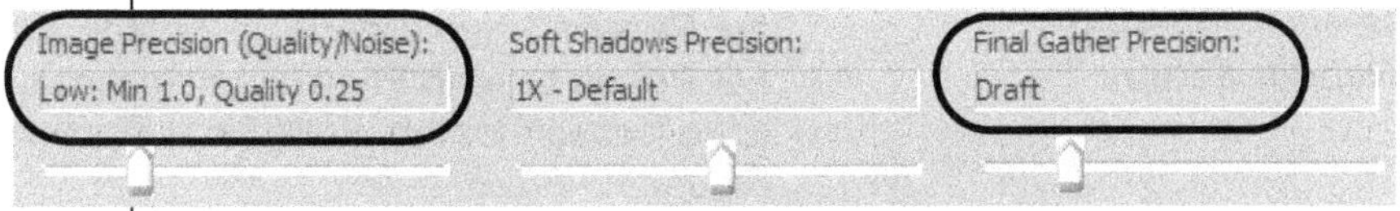

Final Gather (mental
ray) uses Bucket
Rendering, whereas
scanline rendering
renders scanlines
starting from the top of
the image and going
down.

Figure 10–36

7. The rendering is too bright because the Exposure Controls have not been set. In the Rendered Frame Window, click

   ⊡ (Environment and Effects (Exposure Control)). Alternatively, you can select **Rendering>Exposure Control** to open the Environment and Effects dialog box.

8. In the Environment and Effects dialog box, in the Exposure Control rollout, in the drop-down list, select **mr Photographic Exposure Control** and verify that **Active** is selected. Click **Render Preview**, which displays the washed out preview.

9. In the mr Photographic Exposure Control rollout, in the *Exposure* area, select **Exposure Value (EV)** and using the spinner increase the value till you get a better render preview (around **13**), as shown in Figure 10–37. Close the Environment and Effects dialog box.

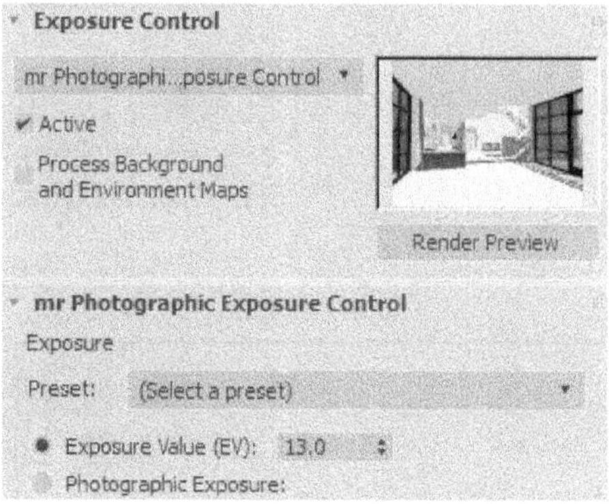

Figure 10–37

Task 2 - Improve rendering speed.

In the Rendered Frame Window, click

(Render Setup). Alternatively, in the Main Toolbar, click

*(Render Setup) or select **Rendering> Render Setup**.*

1. In the Render Setup dialog box, open the *Global Illumination* tab. Expand the Reuse (FG and Photons Disk Caching) rollout.

2. In the *Final Gather Map* area, click as shown in Figure 10–38. In the Save As dialog box, enter **MyFinalGatherMap** as the name of the file. Note that *Save as type* displays **Final Gather Maps (*.fgm)**. Click **Save**. In the Render Setup dialog box, note that **Incrementally Add FG Points to Map Files** is automatically set and that the save location for the .FGM file is displayed, as shown in Figure 10–38.

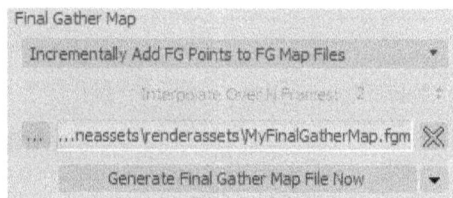

Figure 10–38

---

3. Select the *Common* tab. In the Common Parameters rollout, in the *Output Size* area, change the resolution by clicking **320x240**.

4. Return to the *Global Illumination* tab. In the Reuse (FG and Photons Disk Caching) rollout, in the *Mode* area, select **Calculate FG/Photons and Skip Final Rendering** and click **Generate Final Gather Map File Now**, as shown in Figure 10–39.

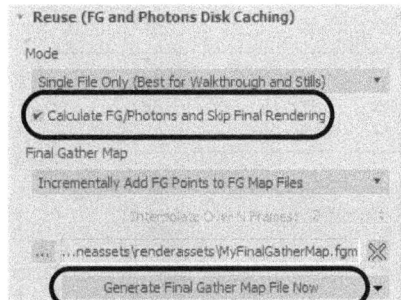

Figure 10–39

- Note that the completed rendering is smaller and does not look like a final rendered image because **Calculate FG/GI and Skip Final Rendering** is selected. It is used to save the Final Gather calculations, which are used in future renderings.

5. When the Final Gather Map calculation is finished, in the Render Setup dialog box, in the Reuse (FG and Photons Disk Caching) rollout, clear the **Calculate FG/GI and Skip Final Rendering** option.

6. In the Rendered Frame Window panel, in the *Reuse* area, verify that **Final Gather** is selected and click 🔒 next to it. This signals the renderer to skip the step of calculating the final gather map, and reuse the saved final gather map. Note that in the Render Setup dialog box, in the *Final Gather Map* area, the option has been automatically changed to **Read FG Points Only from Existing FG Map Files**, as shown in Figure 10–40.

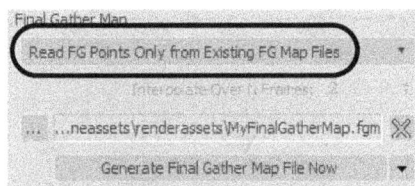

Figure 10–40

7. In the Render Setup dialog box, select the *Common* tab, and in the *Output Size* area, click **640x480** to change the resolution.

8. Click **Render** in the Rendered Frame Window or in the Render Setup dialog box. Note that a bucket rendering is not displayed while rendering because it skips the Final Gather Map calculation. The rendering is displayed as shown in Figure 10–41.

Figure 10–41

If you change to a different view, you should create another .FGM file.

• The rendering is faster but the quality needs improvement. In the same camera view, you can keep reusing the final gather map.

Task 3 - Improve Rendering Quality.

1. In the Render Setup dialog box, open the *Global Illumination* tab. In the Reuse (FG and Photons Disk Caching) rollout, in the *Final Gather Map* area, click [...] and save another FGM file as **MyFinalGatherMap2**.

*You can also change the **Final Gather Precision** in the bottom panel of the Rendered Frame Window.*

2. Expand the Final Gathering (FG) rollout. In the *Basic* area, slide the bar and set the *FG Precision Presets* value to **Medium**, as shown in Figure 10–42.

3. Select the *Common* tab and manually enter a custom output size with the following values, as shown in Figure 10–43:
   • *Width*: **160**
   • *Height*: **120**

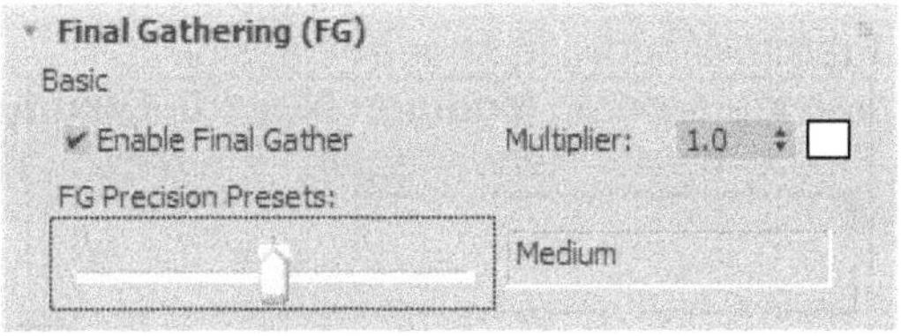

Figure 10–42

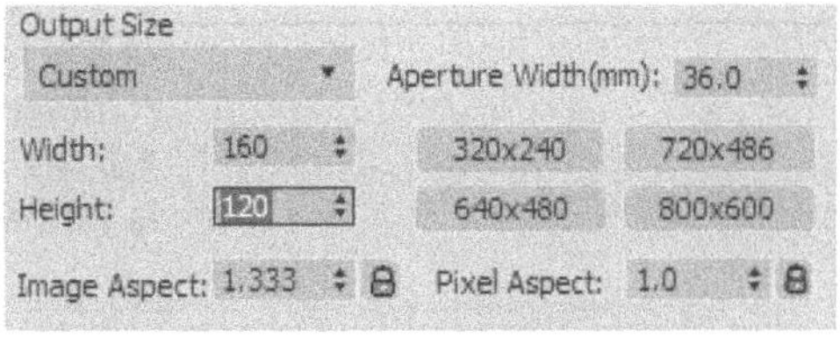

Figure 10–43

4. Return to the *Global Illumination* tab, in the Reuse (FG and Photons Disk Caching) rollout, click **Generate Final Gather Map File Now**. This could take some time to calculate (about 3-5 minutes) because the FG quality has been changed from *Draft* to **Medium**.

5. When the Final Gather Map calculation is finished, verify that in the Render Setup dialog box, in the *Final Gather Map* area, **Read FG Points Only from Existing FG Map Files** is set, as shown in Figure 10–44.

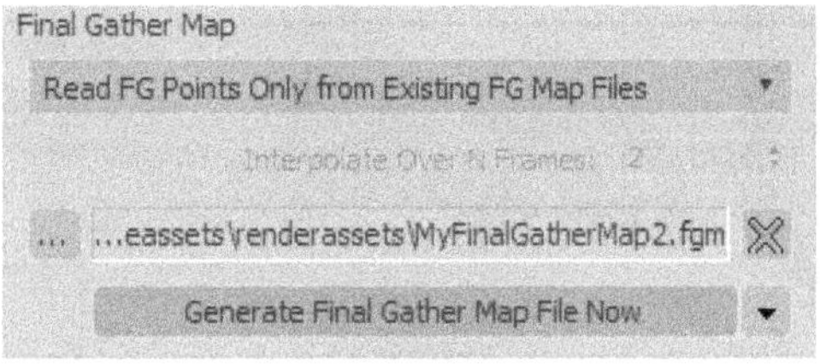

Figure 10–44

6. In the *Common* tab, click **640x480** and render. The rendering only takes little over a minute because it uses the Final Gather points from the saved file. Note that the splotchiness on the ceiling has decreased.

7. The image might still have jagged edges. In the bottom panel of the Rendered Frame Window, in *Image Precision (Quality/Noise)*, drag the slider to **Medium: Min 1.0, Quality 1.0**, as shown in Figure 10–45. Render again. The rendering is further improved.

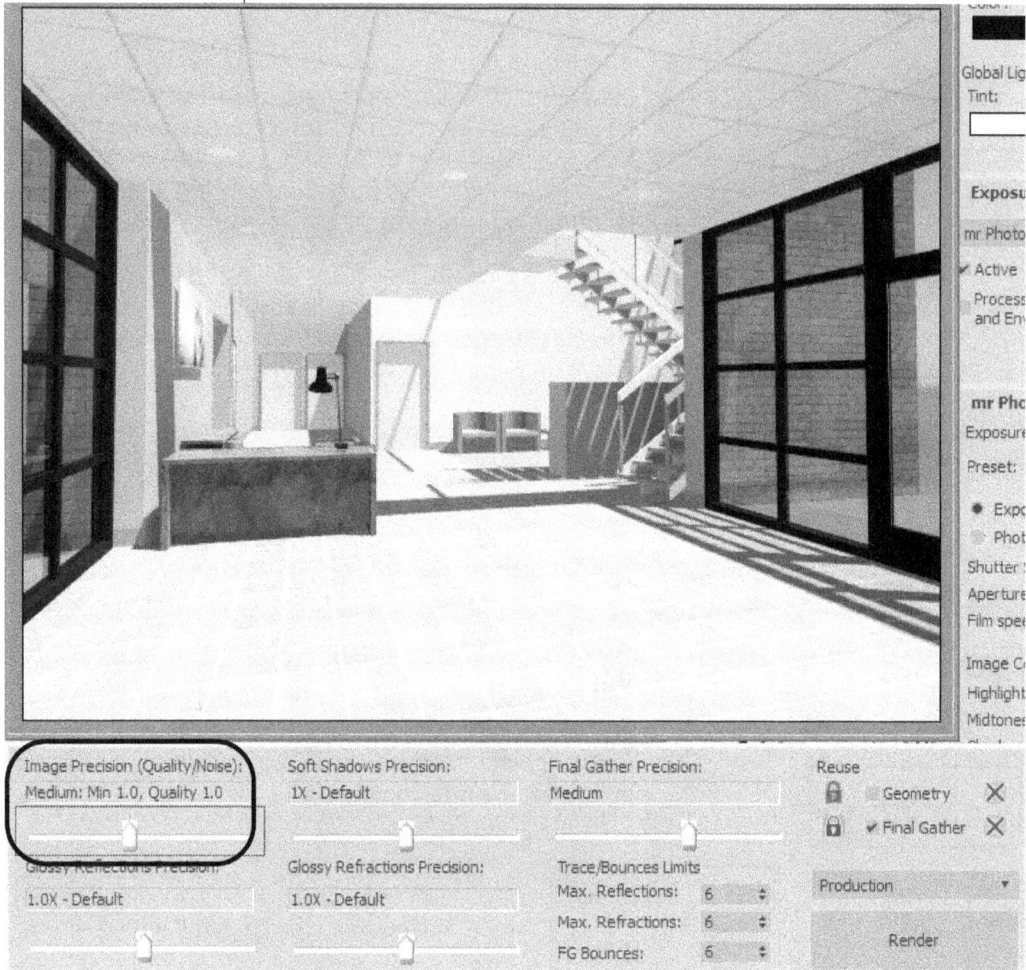

Figure 10–45

Task 4 - Set Material Override.

1. Open the Slate Material Editor.

2. In the Material/Map Browser, in the *Materials>mental ray* category, double-click on Arch & Design to add it as a node to the *View1* sheet and open its Parameter Editor.

3. Set the following, as shown in Figure 10–46:
   - Material name: **Override**
   - *Diffuse* area, *Color*: **white**
   - *Reflection* area, *Reflectivity*: **0**

Figure 10–46

4. Expand the Special Effects rollout and select **Ambient Occlusion**, as shown in Figure 10–47.

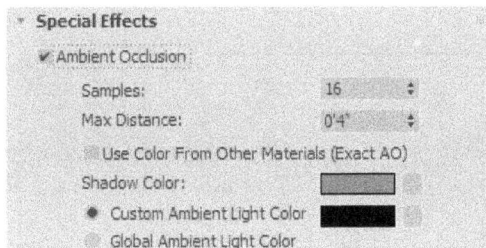

Figure 10–47

5. Move the Render Setup dialog box and place it next to the Slate Material Editor. Verify that the Override material node (*View1* sheet) is visible in the Slate Material Editor, as shown in Figure 10–48.

6. In the Render Setup dialog box, select the *Processing* tab. In the Translator Options rollout, in the *Material Override* area, select the **Enable** option.

The Render Setup dialog box, the Slate Material Editor, and the Rendered Frame Window are modeless dialog boxes and can remain open at the same time.

7. In the Slate Material Editor, in the *View 1* sheet, click and drag the **Override** material's output socket and drop it in the Render Setup dialog box, in the *Material Override* area, on *Material* **None**, as shown in Figure 10–48.

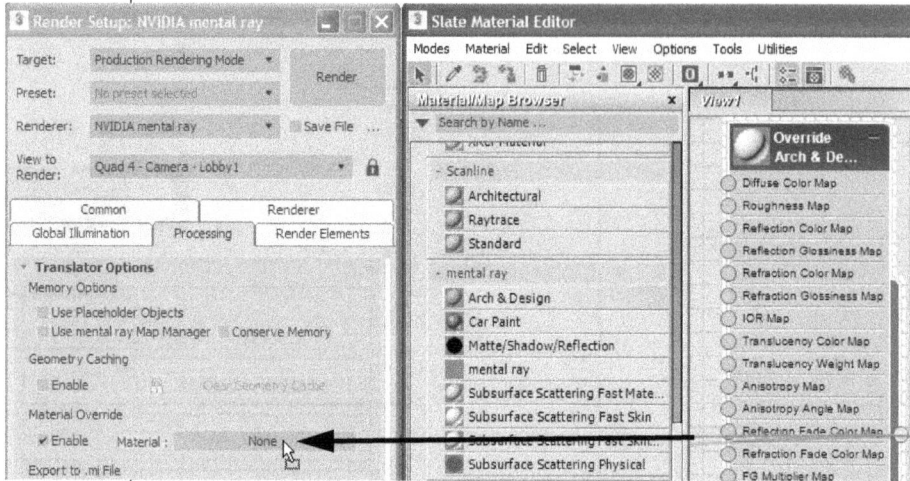

Figure 10–48

8. Verify that **Instance** is selected and click **OK**. Note that in the Render Setup dialog box, **None** is replaced by the material **Override** button, as shown in Figure 10–49.

Figure 10–49

9. Close the Slate Material Editor and the Render Setup dialog box. Minimize the Rendered Frame Window to display the viewports.

10. In the Scene Explorer (■ (Display None)> 💡 (Display Lights)), select **Light Downlight A00**. In the **Camera - Lobby1** viewport, right-click and select **Light On** in the quad menu, as shown in Figure 10–50. Note that in the viewport all of the downlights are displayed in (yellow) because the lights are instanced.

Figure 10–50

11. In the Command Panel, select the Modify panel (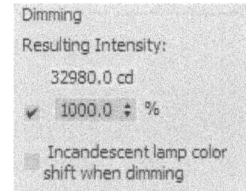). In the General Parameters rollout, in the *Light Distribution (Type)* drop-down list, select **Spotlight** as shown in Figure 10–51.

12. In the Intensity/Color/Attenuation rollout, in the *Dimming* area, enable **Resulting Intensity** by selecting the box before the % edit box and set the % *value* to **1000**, as shown in Figure 10–52.

Figure 10–51   Figure 10–52

13. Restore or maximize the Render Frame Window and click **Render** to render the scene. Note that the materials have been overridden in this scene and a single material is used throughout. This enables you to remove the materials temporarily to examine lighting in your scene. Your rendering might be slightly different than that shown in Figure 10–53.

Figure 10–53

14. Save your work as **MyFinal Gather Map Start.max**.

Practice 10b

Adding a Sky Portal for Interior Lighting from Daylight

Practice Objective

- Add a Sky Portal to incorporate more light to the interior scene from the daylight system.

Estimated time for completion: 20 minutes

In this practice you will apply the Sky Portal object to the surface of the window frame using **AutoGrid**. You will also verify the direction in which the light should be pointing towards the inside of the scene.

The Sky Portal object is a photometric area light that magnifies the outdoor daylight and focuses it into the room. You must have a Skylight object (outdoor mr Sun and Sky Daylight system, Skylight, or IES Sky light) in the scene for Sky Portal to add light to the rendering. Sky Portal is dependent on the exterior lighting energy.

You must set the paths to locate the External files and Xrefs used in the practice. If you have not done this already, return to **Chapter 1: Introduction to Autodesk 3ds Max** and complete Task 1 to Task 3 in **Practice 1a: Organizing Folders and Working with the Interface**. You only have to set the user paths once.

*If a dialog box opens prompting you about a File Load: Mismatch, click **OK** to accept the default values.*

1. Open **SkyPortal_Start.max**.

2. Activate the **Camera01** viewport and in the Main Toolbar,

   click ![render setup icon] (Render Setup) or select **Rendering>Render Setup** to open the Render Setup dialog box. In the *Common* tab, in the Common Parameters rollout, in the *Output Size* area, click **320x240**. Then, click **Render**.

   - Note that Final Gather has been set for the render because the bucket rendering is being performed. The completed render displays light coming through the windows, as shown in Figure 10–54.

3. In the Rendered Frame Window, use the mouse wheel to zoom into the rendering for a closer look at the lamp, as shown in Figure 10–55. You can press, hold, and move the wheel to pan. The desk lamp is completely black (flat) without any lights being reflected. Close the Rendered Frame Window and the Render Setup dialog box.

Figure 10–54   **Figure 10–55**

4. Maximize the **Perspective** viewport and verify that the complete window is displayed in the viewport. Use **Zoom** and **Pan** to position the window, if required.

5. In the Command Panel>Create panel (+), click

   (Lights) and verify that **Photometric** is the default lighting type. In the Object Type rollout, click **mr Sky Portal** and select **AutoGrid**, as shown in Figure 10–56.

Figure 10–56

The rectangular window becomes the Sky Portal object.

6. Position (hover) the cursor over the bottom left corner of **FixedWindow04**. The Transform gizmo displays. Verify that the Y-axis (green) is displaying upward, and the Z axis (blue) is displaying outwards. (You might need to move the cursor slightly to point the gizmo in the right direction). Click at this point and drag the cursor to the upper right corner (as shown in Figure 10–57) to create a window. Release the cursor to display the white portal window. This creates a Sky Portal object that approximately matches the size of the frame.

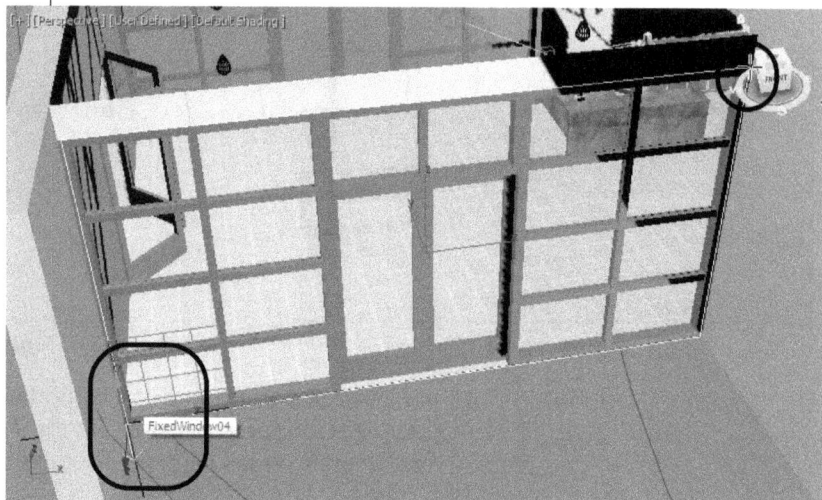

Figure 10–57

7. To verify that the light is pointing toward the correct direction (toward the inside of the room), with the skyportal still selected, click (Select and Move) to display the move Transform gizmo at the center of the skyportal. Zoom into the Transform gizmo and note that a white arrow, overlapping the Y-axis of the gizmo, is pointing toward the building (i.e., through the window), as shown in Figure 10–58. This indicates the light direction is pointing correctly.

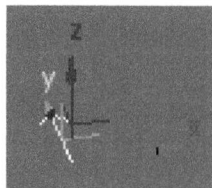

Figure 10–58

• If the light direction arrow is pointing towards the wrong direction, use the **Flip Light Flux Direction** option in the mr Skylight Portal Parameters rollout.

8. Zoom out and use the Y axis to move the sky portal slightly away from the **FixedWindow04** and towards you.

9. Using the viewport overlay, maximize the **Camera01** viewport.

10. Click (Render Production). Zoom in on the lamp, as shown in Figure 10–59. Note the reflectivity and brightness on the lamp.

Figure 10–59

11. Save your work as **MySkyPortal_Start.max**.

- The **SkyPortal_Start.max** file contains the Architectural materials rather than Arch & Design materials. Therefore, the Sky Portal effect might not be drastically different.

- Figure 10–60 shows the materials converted to Arch & Design and the rendering has the *sky portal Multiplier* set to **30** to bring more light into the room.

Figure 10–60

10.3 mental ray Proxies

The mental ray proxy objects enable you to render large quantities of complex objects as instances so that they are only loaded into memory, as required, per bucket during the rendering process. Quick rendering is handy for objects that have a lot of detail and are repeated many times in the scene (such as vegetation and trees). These are proxy objects and can be rendered using **mental ray** in the Create panel

(➕)> ⬤ (Geometry), as shown in Figure 10–61.

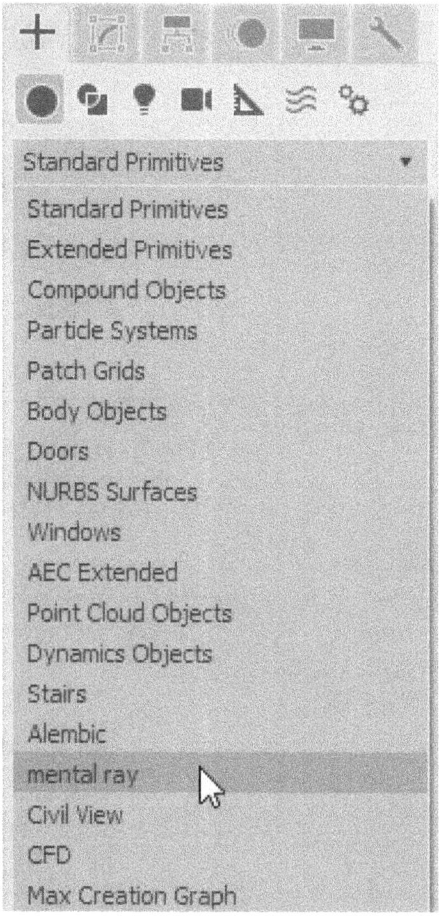

Figure 10–61

Practice 10c

mental ray Proxies

Practice Objective

- Create mental ray proxy objects.

Estimated time for completion: 10 minutes

You must set the paths to locate the External files and Xrefs used in the practice. If you have not done this already, return to **Chapter 1: Introduction to Autodesk 3ds Max** and complete Task 1 to Task 3 in **Practice 1a: Organizing Folders and Working with the Interface**. You only have to set the user paths once.

1. Open **mentalray_proxies_start.max**. This is the far corner of the parking lot of the Retail Exterior file.

2. The scene is displayed in the **Perspective** view. Press <F3> to change to Wireframe mode.

*If a dialog box opens prompting you about a File Load: Mismatch, click **OK** to accept the default values.*

3. In the Command Panel>Create panel (+)>

   (Geometry), select **mental ray** in the drop-down list.

4. In the Object Type rollout, click **mr Proxy**.

5. In the viewport, beside the plant, click and drag to create the mr proxy object (a bounding box will be created), as shown in Figure 10–62.

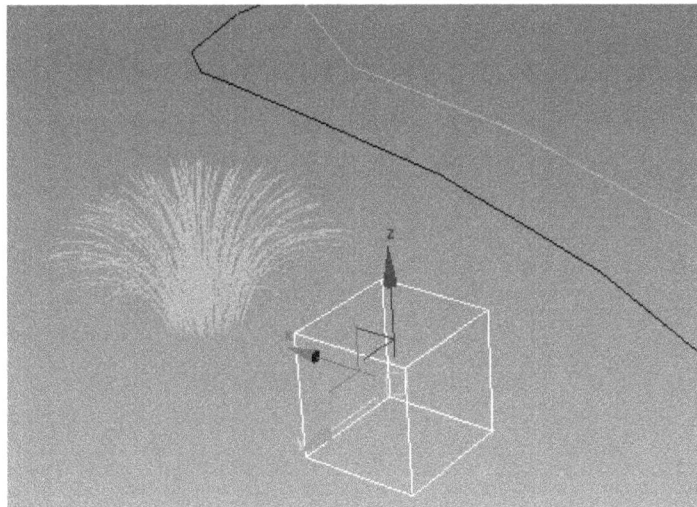

Figure 10–62

6. With this mr proxy object selected, in the Command Panel> Modify panel (![icon]), in the Parameters rollout, in the *Source Object* area, click **None**. In the viewport, select the **Foliage01** object (the plant). The name **Foliage01** displays on **None**, as shown in Figure 10–63.

7. Click **Write Object to File...**. In the Write mr Proxy file dialog box save the file as **RetailExteriorPlanting**. Note that this proxy object will be saved as an **mr Proxy Files (*.mib)** file.

8. In the mr Proxy Creation dialog box, accept the defaults and click **OK**. In the *Display* area of the Parameters rollout, note that a thumbnail and the vertices of the plant is displayed, as shown in Figure 10–64.

Figure 10–63   Figure 10–64

*You can open the Extras toolbar by right-clicking in an empty area in the Main Toolbar and selecting **Extras**.*

9. In the *Display* area, increase the *Viewport Verts* value to **1000** and press <Enter>.

10. Toggle to the four viewports views and in the Top viewport, use ![icon] (Zoom Extents Selected). Zoom out slightly and move the proxy image to follow the curve of the path (green and black lines), as shown in Figure 10–65.

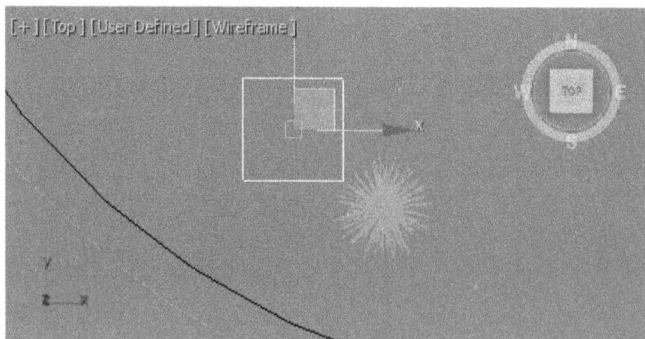

Figure 10–65

11. You can use the **Spacing** tool to plant a row of these proxies. Open the Extras toolbar, in the Array flyout, click

    (Spacing Tool), as shown in Figure 10–66.

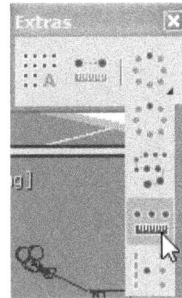

Figure 10–66

12. In the Spacing Tool dialog box, click **Pick Path** and select the green line (Line01) drawn on the grassy area, as shown in Figure 10–67. Note that **Pick Path** is replaced by **Line01** in the dialog box. In the *Parameters* area, verify that **Count** is selected, increase the *Count* to **25** and press <Enter>. Click **Apply** and close the dialog box.

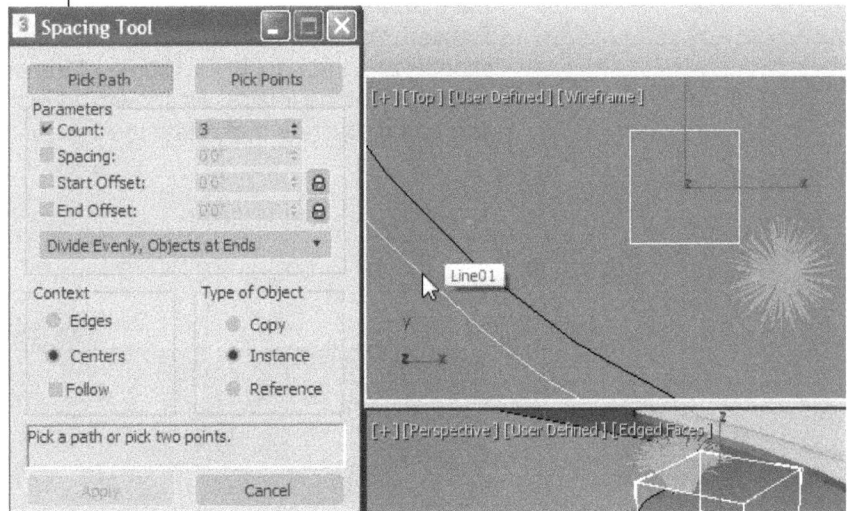

Figure 10–67

13. The plant proxies are placed along the Line01 path.

14. Activate the Perspective viewport and click ![teapot icon] to render the scene, as shown in Figure 10–68.

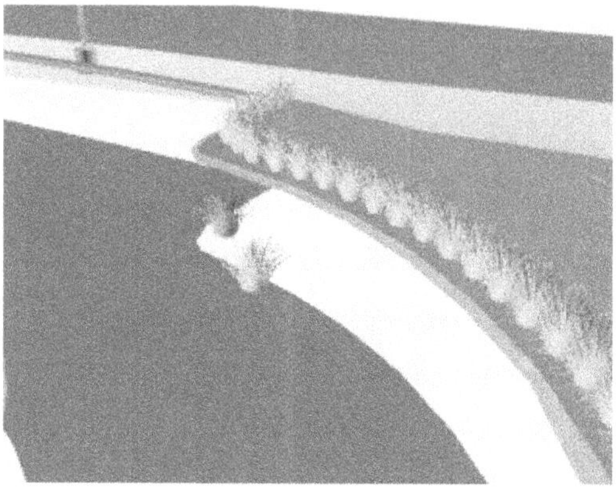

Figure 10–68

15. Save your work as **Mymentalray_Proxies.max**.

Hint: Modify the Proxies to Add Variety

You can use the **Eyedropper** icon in the Material Editor to get the material from the original object and then apply it to the mr Proxies. You can make copies of this material, change it slightly, and then apply it to some of the proxies to break the monotony of the image, as shown in Figure 10–69. For variety, you can also scale and rotate the plants.

Figure 10–69

Chapter Review Questions

1. In mental ray, which option can be used to obtain global illumination?

   a. **Final Gather**

   b. **Exposure Control**

   c. **Sampling Controls**

   d. **Ambient Occlusion**

2. Which Sampling Mode uses *Quality*, *Maximum*, and *Minimum* values for adjusting antialiasing and motion blur?

   a. Unified / Raytraced (Recommended) mode

   b. Classic / Raytraced mode

   c. Rasterizer / Scanline mode

3. What does Ambient Occlusion use to calculate the extent of an area that is inhibited by the incoming light?

   a. Photons

   b. Glossiness

   c. Shaders

   d. Diffuse

4. What type of light object is required for the mr Sky Portal object to add and gather light in the scene?

   a. Omni light

   b. Spotlight

   c. Directional light

   d. Skylight

5. mental ray proxy objects enable you to render large quantities of only simple objects as instances?

   a. True

   b. False

Command Summary

Button	Command	Location
	Environment and Effects dialog box	• **Rendered Frame Window** • **Rendering:** Exposure Control
	Render Setup	• **Main Toolbar** • **Rendering:** Render Setup
	Spacing Tool	• **Extras Toolbar:** Array flyout

Rendering and Cameras

The Autodesk® 3ds Max® software is set so that the default rendering options provide excellent rendering results; however, understanding the different rendering options and presets that you can use to customize and save rendering settings will help you further control the results obtained in your renderings. Additionally, the use of cameras and background images can be included for further customization.

Learning Objectives in this Chapter

- Set the common options available in all of the renderers.
- Control specific options for NVIDIA® iray®, Scanline Renderer, and ART Renderer.
- Understand surface normals and their effects while rendering objects.
- Resolve face normal issues using various settings and rendering modes.
- Create scene states and render pass states using the State Sets feature.
- Create different types of cameras and control their parameters.
- Apply background images to viewports.
- Set the print resolution, paper size, and other options for a rendering.

11.1 Rendering Options

You can set, modify, and change the different options in the Render Setup dialog box, as shown in Figure 11–1. There are four ways to open the Render Setup dialog box:

To quickly re-render the last rendered viewport (regardless of the active viewport) press <F9>. This eliminates the use of the Render Setup dialog box.

- Select **Rendering> Render Setup**.

- Press <F10>.

- In the Main Toolbar, click (Render Setup).

- In the Rendered Frame Window, click (Render Setup).

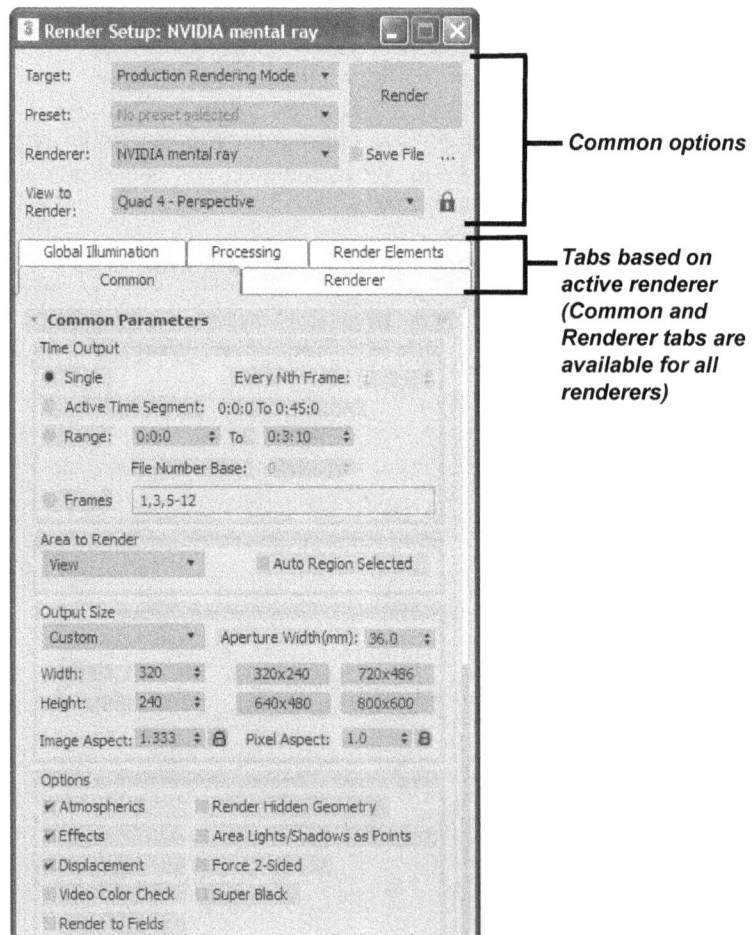

Common options

Tabs based on active renderer (Common and Renderer tabs are available for all renderers)

Figure 11–1

Common Options

Common options are available for all the renderers and are located at the top of the dialog box. These include:

- The **Target** drop-down list enables you to select the rendering options such as, Production, Iterative, A360 Cloud etc, as shown in Figure 11–2.

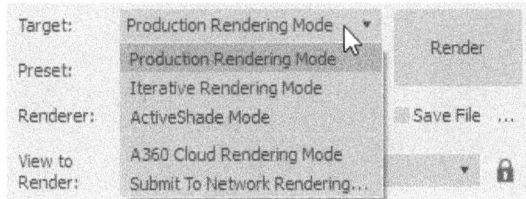

Figure 11–2

- The **Preset** drop-down list (as shown in Figure 11–3) enables you to swap between the available preset files or create, load, and save presets as RPS files using **Load Preset** and **Save Preset**. These presets are also accessed from the Render Shortcuts toolbar, as shown in Figure 11–4. When using the toolbar, you can save the current rendering settings as preset A, B, or C by selecting one of the corresponding buttons in the toolbar while holding <Shift>.

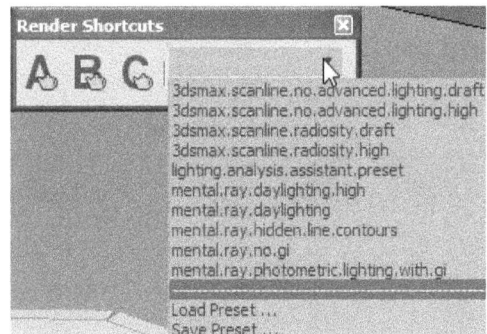

Figure 11–3   Figure 11–4

You can also select the rendering system in the Assign Renderer rollout in the Common tab of the dialog box.

- The **Renderer** drop-down list enables you to select the required rendering system, as shown in Figure 11–5.

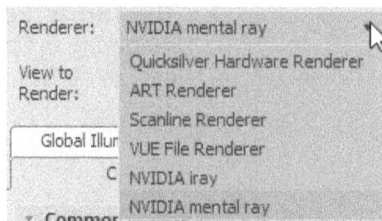

Figure 11–5

New in 2017

Quicksilver Hardware Renderer	Uses the system's graphics hardware (GPU) to quickly produce high-quality images. In order to use this renderer your graphics hardware must support Shader Model 3.0 (SM3.0) or a later version.
ART Renderer	A physically based renderer that uses the CPU only and renders the scene quickly.
Scanline Renderer	Intended to be used with both standard lighting (local illumination) and radiosity-based lighting.
VUE File Renderer	A legacy functionality that is not a graphical renderer. It uses ASCII text files to describe the position and transformation of objects, lighting, etc.
NVIDIA iray	Uses the NVIDIA iray rendering technology to accurately render racing light paths.
NVIDIA mental ray	A separate lighting and rendering system that determines illumination through the distribution of photons.

The tabs in the Render Setup dialog box change according to the active renderer.

Common Tab

The *Common* tab contains settings applicable to all rendering systems. Some of the options are described as follows:

Common Parameters rollout

- The *Time Output* area designates whether you are rendering a still frame (Single) or an animation. When rendering an animation you can specify to render the entire animation (Active Time Segment), a certain range (Range) or specify individual frames (Frames).

- The *Area to Render* area enables you to define what portion of the scene is rendered, such as View, Selected, Region, Crop, or Blowup.

- The *Output Size* area contains the render size options.

- The *Options* area enables you to select the objects and effects to render (**Atmospherics**, **Render Hidden Geometry**, etc.). You can also select the overrides (**Area Lights/Shadows as Points**, **Force 2-Sided**).

- The *Advanced Lighting* and *Bitmap Performance and Memory Options* areas provide additional options to further customize the rendering.

- The *Render Output* area enables you to specify a filename before rendering. Some of the commonly used file formats in which the rendering images are saved are as follows:

JPEG	The JPEG is a lossy format, which sacrifices quality in exchange for a smaller file size.
BMP	Windows Bitmap (24 bit, 16.7 Million Colors).
TGA	Targa (as 24 or 32 bit uncompressed).
PNG	Portable Network Graphics (as 24 or 48 bit color, no interlacing). This has the best file size to quality ratio as it offers the highest color depth with a smaller compression.
TIFF	Tagged Image File Format (24 bit color without compression).

Assign Renderer Rollout

In this rollout you can switch rendering systems and select the ActiveShade renderer that you want to use.

*Alternatively, they can be changed using the **Renderer** drop-down list in the Common area near the top of the Render Setup dialog box.*

Email Notifications Rollout

In this rollout you can set the option of having an email notification sent to you or another user whose email address has been specified. This is useful when the render is run without being monitored, in the case of lengthy renders.

Scripts Rollout

In this rollout you can enable the software to run a selected script before a rendering process has begun or after the process has been completed. The valid scripts that can be run are MAXScript file (.MS), macro script (.MCR), batch file (.BAT), and executable file (.EXE).

Renderer Tab

The *Renderer* tab displays renderer-specific options. It is provided for all of the renderers with render-specific options.

11.2 NVIDIA iray Renderer

The NVIDIA iray supports Sky Portal objects, translucency, and glossy refractions. The physically accurate renderer renders by tracing the light paths. Different from mental ray renderer that renders in buckets, iray renders by progressively refining the image until it has completed the render. Setup is minimal and simple, like a point and shoot camera.

- The iray renderer supports all of the mental ray materials, but only supports a subset of the Standard materials. Materials such as Arch & Design and Autodesk Library materials are available (with the exception of Autodesk Metallic Paint).

- The iray renderer supports Photometric lights (including mental ray daylight), mr Photographic Exposure Control, Batch rendering, Command Line rendering, and Backburner.

- When you select **NVIDIA iray** as the active renderer, the *Common* tab, *Renderer* tab, and *Render Elements* tab are available in the Render Setup dialog box.

Renderer Tab

The approach of the iray renderer is based on any of the three forms of time.

- In the iray rollout (shown in Figure 11–6) you can specify the length of time (in hours, minutes, and seconds), specify the number of iterations to complete, or you can run the rendering for an unlimited amount of time, enabling you to stop the rendering when you want.

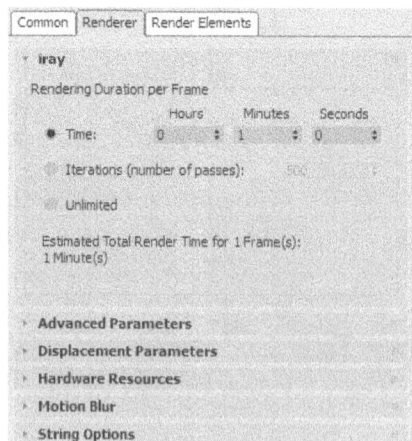

Figure 11–6

The fact that you have a CUDA enabled GPU does not mean that it is used in your render calculations. As of the writing of this student guide, the complete Autodesk 3ds Max scene has to fit in the GPU memory for it to be used. A good measuring stick for the calculation's requirements is 1GB of video memory per 8 million triangles, and 3 bytes per pixel for any referenced bitmaps.

- In the Motion Blur rollout, you can enable the **Motion Blur** option to apply it to objects in a scene. You can specify the Shutter Duration that imitates the shutter speed of a camera. You can also set the number of segments for the blur and the number of iterations before the scene is updated to the next time sample.

- The Hardware Resources rollout displays information about your system's graphics support, as shown in Figure 11–7.

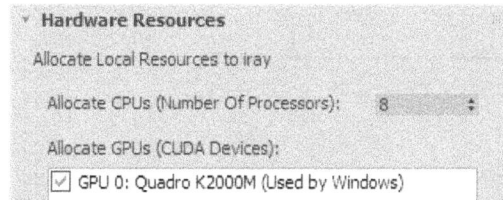

Figure 11–7

- A graphics card with CUDA enabled Graphics Processing Unit (GPU) can be used to speed up rendering.

- The String Options window in the String Options rollout enables you to specify various iray settings, which are saved with your current 3ds Max scene.

Render Elements Tab

In the *Render Elements* tab, you can render various elements. Up to 19 render elements can be rendered at a time including the alpha channel, irradiance data, normals etc.

11.3 Scanline Renderer

The Scanline renderer generates a render by calculating a series of lines starting at the top and moving down. It is intended to be used with both standard lighting and radiosity based lighting.

Renderer Tab

The *Renderer* tab for the Scanline Renderer displays its specific options, as shown in Figure 11–8.

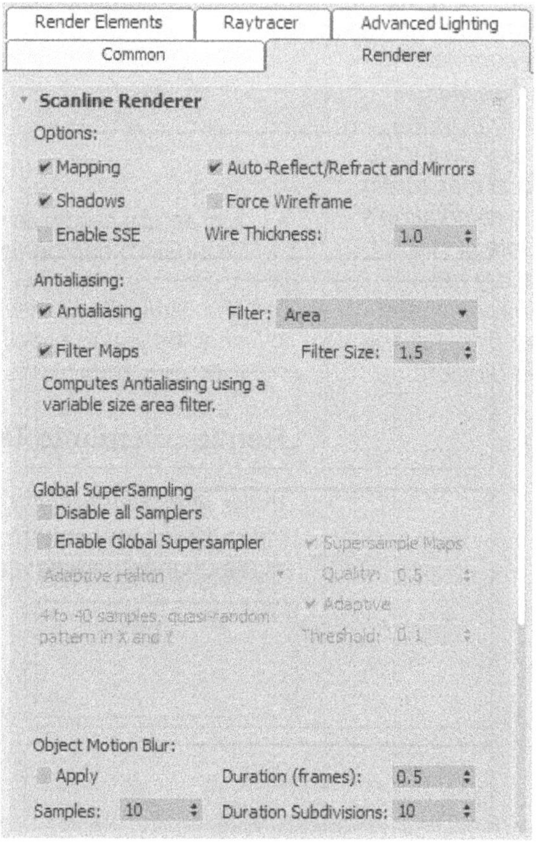

Figure 11–8

- The *Options* area enables you to globally enable or disable the use of all image maps (**Mapping**) or the calculation of all shadows (**Shadows**). The **Force Wireframe** option causes the scene geometry to render as wireframe objects with the **Wire Thickness** parameter listed below.

- The *Antialiasing* area contains options for antialiasing that smooths the jagged diagonal lines and curves in renderings but at a reduced quality, as shown on the left in Figure 11–9.

Antialiasing On   **Antialiasing Off**

Figure 11–9

- SuperSampling (*Global SuperSampling* area) is an additional antialiasing pass applied to material textures. SuperSampling cuts down on noise, flickering, and moire patterns caused by dense material maps, as shown in Figure 11–10.

Supersampling Off   **Supersampling On**

Figure 11–10

Raytracer Tab

mental ray is recommended when a raytrace effect is required, rather than using the Scanline Raytrace features. mental ray has its own set of Raytracing controls.

Raytracing is a rendering method used to calculate accurate reflections, refractions, and shadows. Raytracing is used for raytrace materials and some Architectural materials with shiny, transparent, or mirrored templates (e.g., glass, mirrors, etc.). Raytraced and area shadows cause raytracing to take place and for Scanline Renderer these are managed by the options in *Raytracer* tab, (as shown in Figure 11–11).

Figure 11–11

Several of these options relate to rendering performance. In many ways, these are black box parameters that need to be adjusted through trial and error for individual scenes.

- The **Maximum Depth** option is a measurement of how many reflections of reflections you want to permit. The default value of **9** might be excessive, while **3** might be as effective and requires much less rendering time.

- The **Cutoff Threshold** option is a percent value that causes the software to ignore rays that only contribute that percent or less of a pixel's color in the final rendering. Increasing this value reduces rendering time at a cost of lower accuracy.

Shadow types such as Advanced Raytraced also have antialiasing options.

- If you find that your raytraced reflections or shadows have jagged diagonal lines or curves, you can enable **Global Ray Antialiasing** to add smoothness.

- When cleared, the **Enable Raytracing** option disables all raytracing in the scene.

New in **2017**

11.4 ART Renderer

The Autodesk Ray Trace (ART) renderer is a path tracing renderer which generates fast and accurate renderings using few settings. ART is a physically based renderer and uses the computers CPU only. It supports photometric lights, the Sun Positioner, and physical material. ART is compatible with the Autodesk® Revit® software and is capable of creating highly accurate renderings of architectural scenes due to ART's support of the photometric and day lighting features in the Autodesk Revit software.

When you select **ART Renderer** as the active renderer, the *Common* tab, *ART Renderer* tab, and *Render Elements* tab are available in the Render Setup dialog box, as shown in Figure 11–12.

ART Renderer Tab

The *ART Renderer* tab displays the renderer-specific options, as shown in Figure 11–12.

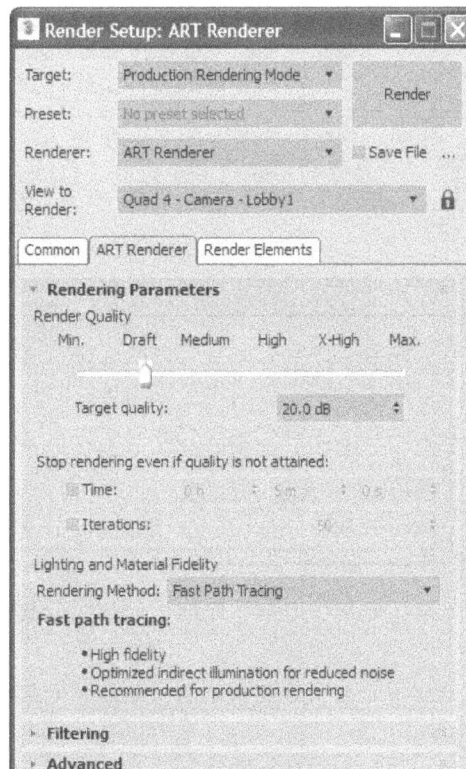

Figure 11–12

- The **Rendering Parameter** rollout enables you to set the *Target Quality,* which is measured in decibels (dB). A lower value is lower quality with more noise in the final image. A higher quality reduces the amount of noise in the final image, but the image takes longer to render.

- You can limit the time or number of iterations for a rendering in the *Stop rendering even if quality is not attained* area. This would prevent an image from taking too long to complete, but the resulting image might not have the desired quality.

- The *Lighting and Material Fidelity* area options are used to create image renderings. You can use the **Fast Path Tracing** method to render high fidelity, indirect illumination, or use the **Advanced Path Method** to generate final renders for true high fidelity images.

- The **Filtering** rollout enables you to activate **Noise Filtering** on final renderings. The **Anti-Aliasing** option sets the *Filter Diameter* in pixels and determines how the ART Renderer anti-aliases the edges in the image.

- The **Advanced** rollout has options to set the size of point lights in scene lighting using the **Point Light Diameter** value. You can also use the **Animate Noise Pattern** option to keep the noise pattern from being static in the final rendering.

Practice 11a

Working with Scanline Rendering Options

Practice Objective

- Set various rendering options to improve the rendering of the scene.

Estimated time for completion: 10 minutes

In this practice you will set some of the Rendering options. This practice uses the Default Scanline Renderer as the active renderer.

You must set the paths to locate the External files and Xrefs used in the practice. If you have not done this already, return to **Chapter 1: Introduction to Autodesk 3ds Max** and complete Task 1 to Task 3 in **Practice 1a: Organizing Folders and Working with the Interface**. You only have to set the user paths once.

*If a dialog box opens prompting you about a File Load: Mismatch, click **OK** to accept the default values.*

1. Open **Rendering Options.max**.

2. In the Main Toolbar, click 　　 (Render Setup) or select **Rendering>Render Setup** to open the Render Setup dialog box.

   - Near the top of the dialog box, in the common options, note that the *Renderer* is set as **Scanline Renderer**, as shown in Figure 11–13.

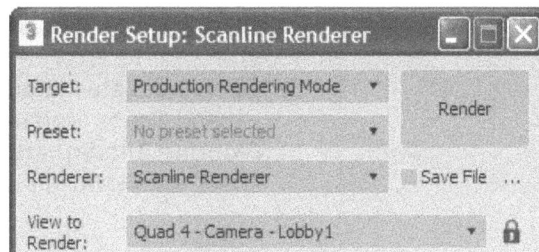

Figure 11–13

If this option is enabled, the software will recalculate radiosity for the material adjustments you make. They are very subtle, so you can ignore the recalculations for this practice.

3. In the *Common* tab, in the Common Parameters rollout, in the *Advanced Lighting* area, verify that **Use Advanced Lighting** is enabled, as shown in Figure 11–14. Clear **Compute Advanced Lighting when Required**, if required.

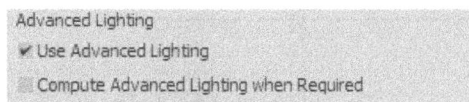

Figure 11–14

You can also click

(Render Production) in the Main Toolbar.

4. Ensure that the **Camera – Lobby1** viewport is active. In the Render Setup dialog box, in the *View to Render* edit box, ensure that **Quad 4 - Camera - Lobby1** is selected. Click **Render** in the Render Setup dialog box.

5. In the Rendered Frame Window, use the mouse wheel to zoom into the floor. Note that a moire pattern has formed on the tile floor, as shown in Figure 11–15.

Figure 11–15

6. In the *Renderer* tab, in the Scanline Renderer rollout, in the *Global SuperSampling* area, ensure that **Enable Global Supersampler** is cleared (as shown in Figure 11–16) to avoid calculating Supersampling for all materials.

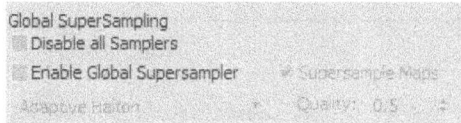

Figure 11–16

7. Open the Slate Material Editor. In the Material/Map Browser, expand Scene Materials and double-click on **Finishes. Flooring.Tile.Square.Terra Cotta** to display it in *View1* sheet, as shown in Figure 11–17.

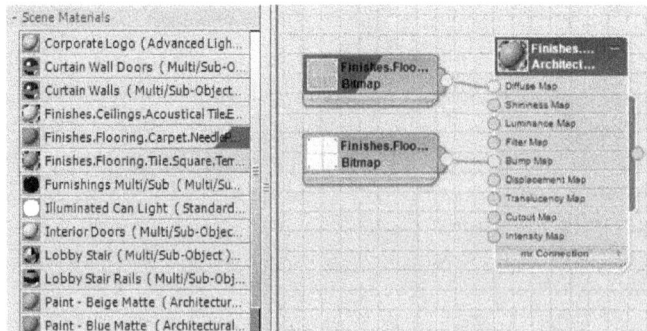

Figure 11–17

8. Double-click on the title bar of the material to open its Parameter Editor.

9. Expand the SuperSampling rollout and clear **Use Global Settings**, as shown in Figure 11–18. Use the default parameters including **Adaptive Halton** as the local supersampler.

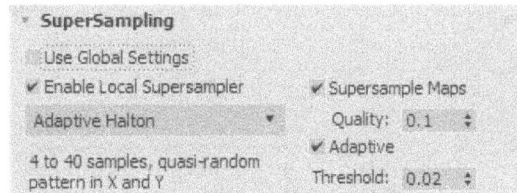

Figure 11–18

10. Render the **Camera – Lobby1** viewport and note that the moire pattern is somewhat reduced, but that the rendering time has increased. The visible edges of the sun's highlight area are also much better defined and antialiased. Some jaggedness displays along the rails in the curtain wall, as shown in Figure 11–19.

Figure 11–19

Clearing Raytraced self-reflections prevents the rails and mullions from reflecting in the glass.

11. Part of this jaggedness is caused by reflections of the shadows being cast near the glass. In the Render Setup dialog box, in the *Raytracer* tab, clear **Enable Self Reflect / Refract**, as shown in Figure 11–20.

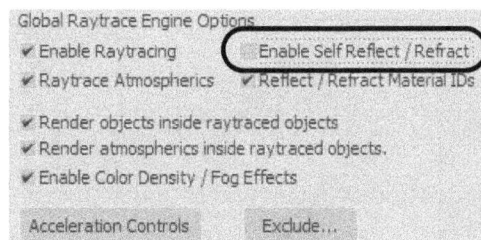

Figure 11–20

12. Render the scene. Note that the outside wall is jagged, and half of it is turned dark (as shown in Figure 11–23) as there is a significant refraction of the outside walls through the glass.

13. In the Slate Material Editor, in the Material/Map Browser, in the Scene Materials, double-click on Curtain Walls and Curtain Wall Doors to display in the *View1* sheet. Click ![icon] (Lay Out All - Vertical) to arrange the materials vertically, as shown in Figure 11–21.

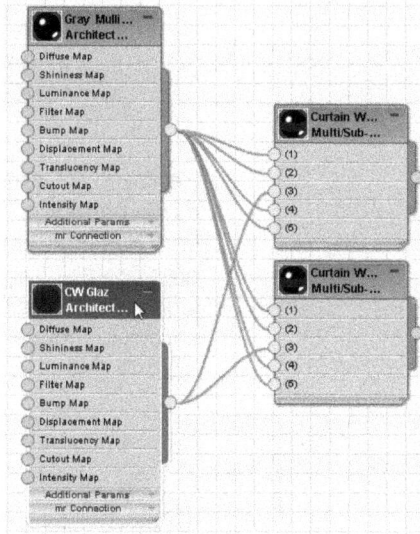

Figure 11–21

With a Raytrace material you could disable refraction, whereas for an Architectural material reduce the Index of Refraction.

14. Double-click on the title **CW Glaz** (Architectural material) to open its Parameter Editor. In the Physical Qualities rollout, set the *Index of Refraction* to **1.0** (as shown in Figure 11–22) which results in no refraction.

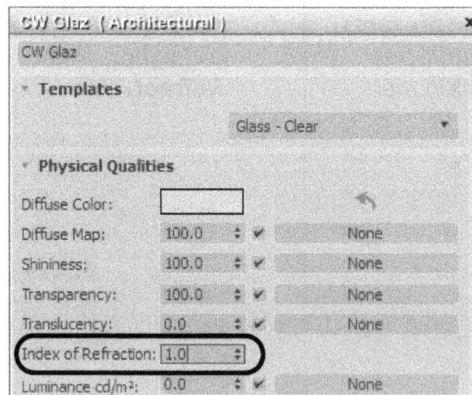

Figure 11–22

15. Render the scene again, as shown in Figure 11–24. The outside wall and rails are less jagged and the glass is less shiny than before.

Index of Refraction: 1.5

Figure 11–23

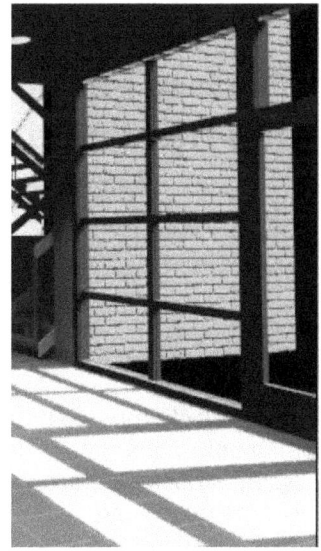

Index of Refraction: 1.0

Figure 11–24

16. Save your scene file as **MyRendering Options.max**.

11.5 Single vs. Double-Sided Rendering

Surface Faces and Rendering Modes

Autodesk 3ds Max 3D objects are treated as surface models rather than solids, to make calculations faster. 3D geometry is resolved into triangular faces when rendered.

Figure 11–25 displays two identical Box objects with the one on the right has all of its edges as triangular faces. To display triangular faces, right-click on the object, and select **Object Properties**. In the *General* tab, in the *Display Properties* area, clear **Edges Only**. If the viewport is set to Edged Face mode (<F4>), the triangular faces are displayed.

*In the Object Properties dialog box, in the Display Properties area, all of the options are grayed out if it is set to **By Layer** Change it to **By Object** for the options to be available.*

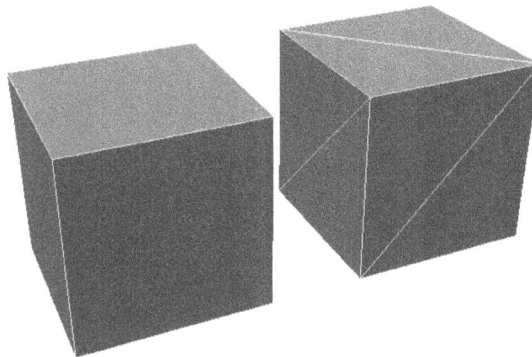

Figure 11–25

- In single-sided rendering mode, the faces are only displayed in the viewport and in renderings from the outside of the object. Therefore, no time is spent on calculating the inner faces of the object.

Working in single-sided mode is a more efficient way to render. It is recommended to use single-sided mode whenever possible.

- When using the scanline renderer, rendering in double-sided mode forces the Autodesk 3ds Max software to determine what the inside and the outside of each face looks like, adding significant rendering time.

Surface Normals

The Autodesk 3ds Max software determines which side of a face is visible in single-sided rendering mode using surface normals.

- Normals are imaginary vectors located perpendicular to one side of each face. The side that the normals project from is considered the front side or outside of the face.

- In single-sided mode, the Autodesk 3ds Max software renders faces whose vectors point towards the camera even if at very oblique angles, as shown in Figure 11–26.

- 3D objects such as primitives like these boxes automatically have their face normals pointing to the outside.

- Single-sided rendering mode can cause problems when object normals are inconsistent (inverted). In Figure 11–27, the box on the right has its top face normals pointing down instead of up. This can cause the box to have missing faces. (The back-facing edge lines are shown here for clarity but normally would not be visible.)

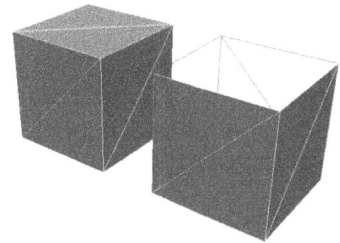

Figure 11–26   **Figure 11–27**

The viewport behavior might vary depending on your video driver.

- The faces with inverted face normals display in black in the viewport, but are invisible in the rendering To see through the faces that point away, right-click on the object, select **Object Properties** and in the *Display Properties* area, select the **Backface Cull** option.

Inconsistent face normals are a common result of importing 3D data from other applications.

- CAD software packages generally do not assign surface normals to 3D geometry. When you import this data into the Autodesk 3ds Max software, surface normals are automatically assigned to faces based on the order in which the vertices were created, which can result in inconsistent facings.

- When linking or importing 3D blocks and drawing from other software, there might still be inconsistent or inverted face normals, which need to be corrected.

Steps to Resolve Face-Normal Issues

If you experience missing faces due to inconsistent normals when working in a single-sided rendering mode, you can resolve them in several ways.

- If the data was imported or linked (.DWG or .DXF file), delete and re-import or reload the linked file and in the Import Options dialog box, select **Orient normals of adjacent faces consistently**, as shown in Figure 11–28. This option should be left off unless face-normal issues are present.

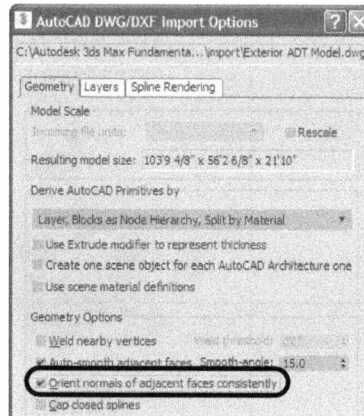

Figure 11–28

- If re-importing or reloading data is not feasible (or the data was not imported/linked) the Normal modifier can be used to unify faces. This object-space Modifier has the ability to flip all of the face normals when an object is completely inside out.

- If you have a small number of faces with normals pointing the wrong way (or a large number and some time to spend) you could manually flip and unify face normals. Using the **Edit Mesh** and **Edit Poly** modifiers, select the inverted polygon and then in the Surface Properties rollout use the **Flip** and **Unify** options, as shown in Figure 11–29.

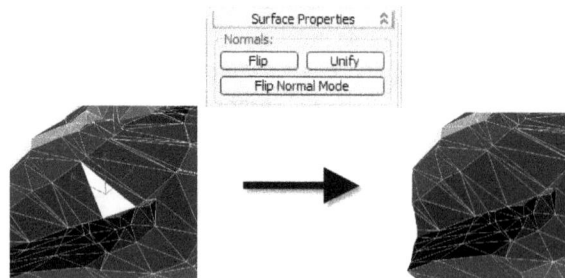

Figure 11–29

Enabling Double-Sided Mode

If you only have certain objects with face-normal issues that cannot be easily fixed, use **2-sided** materials. This renders the objects as double-sided that have double-sided materials, while rendering the rest of the scene geometry as single-sided. Different materials have the 2-sided options in different rollouts of the Parameter Editor.

- **Scanline>Standard** materials have the **2-Sided** option in the Shader Basic Parameters rollout, as shown in Figure 11–30.

- **Scanline>Architectural** materials have the **2-Sided** option in the Physical Qualities rollout, as shown in Figure 11–31.

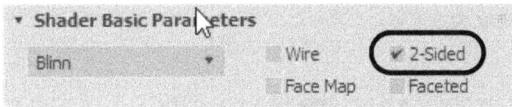

Figure 11–30

Figure 11–31

- **mental ray>Arch & Design** materials are two-sided by default. To have one-sided behavior, select **Back Face Culling** in the material's Advanced Rendering Options rollout, as shown in Figure 11–32. This can be handy in a viewport, but ensure the faces are the right direction if using mental ray.

- To render a scene double-sided, in the Render Setup dialog box, in the *Common* tab, in the *Options* area, enable **Force 2-Sided**, as shown in Figure 11–33. (When not selected, the Autodesk 3ds Max software renders in single-sided mode, regardless of any viewport settings.)

You can enable double-sided mode globally to display the missing faces. Double-sided options are specific to each individual scene file.

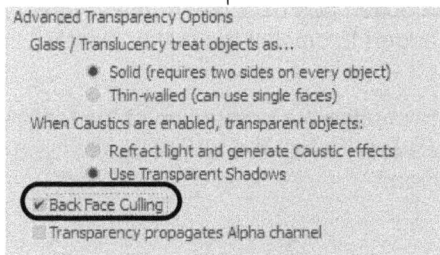

Figure 11–32

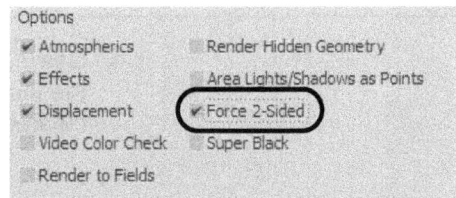

Figure 11–33

Practice 11b

Estimated time for completion: 5 minutes

At the university of Utah in 1975, Professor Martin Newell developed the teapot object. It was used for testing rendering algorithms. Today, the (Newell) teapot still exists in many 3D applications, including the Autodesk 3ds Max software.

Double-Sided Rendering Mode

Practice Objective

- Render an object as double-sided using a double-sided and single-sided material.

In this practice you will render an object as double-sided using a double-sided and single-sided material.

Task 1 - Assigning a double-sided material.

1. Reset the scene.

2. In the Command Panel>Create panel,($+$), click

   ⬤ (Geometry), and in the Object Type rollout, click **Teapot**. In the **Perspective** viewport, click and drag to create the teapot object of any size.

3. With the teapot selected, select the Modify panel ( ) and in the *Teapot Parts* area of the Parameters rollout, clear **Lid**, as shown in Figure 11–34 to display the inside of the teapot, as shown in Figure 11–35. The faces on the inside of the teapot are visible because the **Backface Cull** option is not set by default.

| Figure 11–34 | Figure 11–35 |

- The teapot selection has been cleared and its orientation has been changed to display the inside clearly.

4. Use (Orbit) to change the orientation of the teapot so that the inside is displayed. Select the teapot again if you had cleared its selection.

*In the Object Properties dialog box, in the Display Properties area, all of the options are grayed out if it is set to **By Layer**. Change it to **By Object** for the options to become available.*

5. Click ⚙ to open the Render Setup dialog box and ensure that the *Renderer* is set to **Scanline Renderer**.

6. Right-click on the selected teapot and select **Object Properties**. In the *General* tab, in the *Display Properties* area, click **By Layer** to change it to **By Object**, if required. Select **Backface Cull** (as shown in Figure 11–36) and click **OK**. The inside faces of the teapot become invisible.

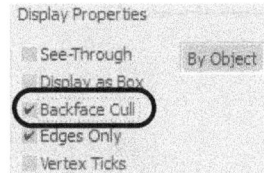

Figure 11–36

7. Click 🫖 to render the scene. Note that the inside of the teapot is black, due to the black background, as shown in Figure 11–37. Leave the Rendered Frame Window open.

Figure 11–37

8. In the Rendered Frame Window, click ⊞ to open the Environment and Effects dialog box. In the Common Parameters rollout, in the *Background* area, click the **Color** swatch. In the Color Selector, change the color to white. Click **OK** and close the Environment and Effects dialog box.

*You can also open the Environment and Effects dialog box by selecting **Rendering> Environment**.*

9. Render the scene again. The faces inside the teapot are missing and display as white because of the background color.

10. Open the Slate Material Editor. In *Materials>General* categories, select the material **Double Sided**. Both the Facing and the Back materials are gray. Double-click on the **Facing** material node and assign a blue color to the **Diffuse** swatch. Similarly, double-click on the **Back** material node and assign a red color to the **Diffuse** channel. Drag and drop, or use 🎨 to assign the material to the teapot.

11. Render the scene. The inside faces are now visible in the rendering, as shown in Figure 11–38. The Object properties are overridden by the double-sided material.

Figure 11–38

Task 2 - Using the double-sided rendering option.

1. In the Slate Material Editor, select **Standard** in the *Materials>Scanline* list. The **Standard** material is not double-sided. Double-click to open the Parameter Editor and assign the color red to its **Diffuse** channel. Assign this material to the teapot. Close the Slate Material Editor.

2. Render the scene. The faces inside the teapot are missing and display as white because of the background color.

To open the Render Setup dialog box, click

*(Render Setup) in the Main Toolbar, or select **Rendering> Render Setup**.*

3. Open the Render Setup dialog box. In the *Common* tab, in the Common Parameters rollout, in the *Options* area, select **Force 2-Sided,** as shown in Figure 11–39.

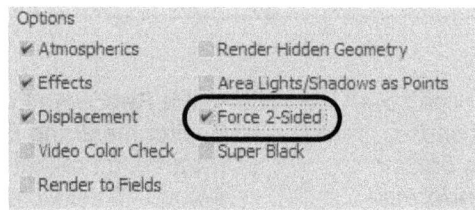

Figure 11–39

4. Render the scene. The teapot renders double-sided, as shown in Figure 11–40.

Figure 11–40

5. Save your work as **MyTeapot.max**.

11.6 State Sets

State Sets is a scene management/render pass manager in the Autodesk 3ds Max software. The State Sets dialog box enables you to record the changes made to the scene at different intervals and saves them in an hierarchical form. Select

Rendering>State Sets or click {⑥} in the State Sets toolbar to open the State Sets dialog box, as shown in Figure 11–41. It opens in the tree view called *States* in which the states are recorded and managed.

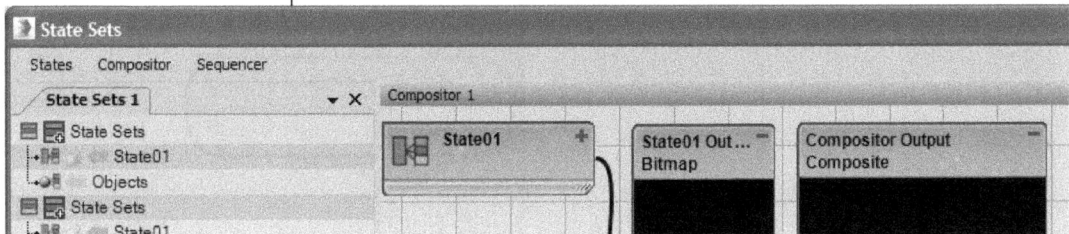

Figure 11–41

Some of the changes, such as using transforms, are not recordable by State Sets. See the Autodesk 3ds Max Help for a list of properties that can be used with the State Sets.

• The tree view opens with the master state at the top, which is displayed as ▣ ⧾ State Sets , and contains the **State01** state.

• You can add a new state by clicking ⧾ next to the master state or by selecting **States>Add State**. A new state with the name **State02** is added in the tree view, as shown in Figure 11–42.

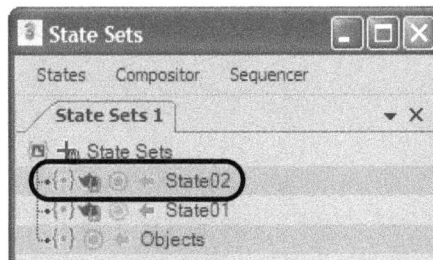

Figure 11–42

• To make a state current, click on the gray arrow. An active state is indicated by a green arrow.

- To record changes to a state, click ◉ (gray circle) next to the state. The ◉ (gray circle) changes to ◉ (black circle), indicating that the state is being recorded, and that you can start making changes to the scene. Once you have made your changes, click ◉ (black circle) to stop recording. The recorded changes are displayed as a children for this state, as shown in Figure 11–43.

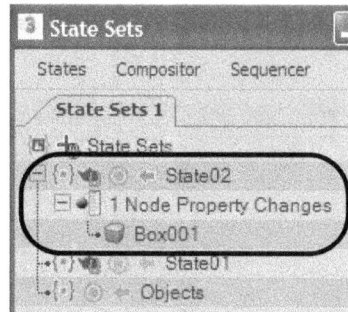

Figure 11–43

- You can add states and record changes in those states.

- To render all of the recorded states, in the State Sets menu bar, select **States>Render All States**, as shown in Figure 11–44. The states are rendered to files and saved in the path and filename specified in the Render Outputs panel.

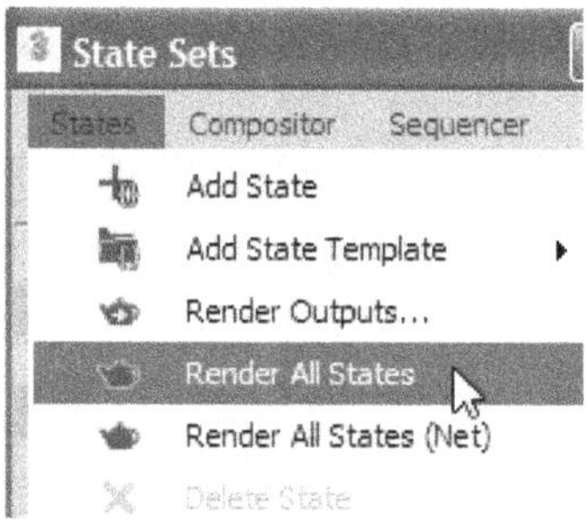

Figure 11–44

- To set a name and path for the output files, select **States>Render Outputs** to display the render outputs panel where you can browse and set the path for the files.

State Sets can bi-directionally interoperate with the Adobe After Effects CS4 (32-bit) and Adobe After Effects CS5/CS5.5 (64-bit). This requires that the files are copied from the Autodesk 3ds Max install folder into the After Effects install folder.

Compositer View

You can display the Compositor View by selecting **Compositor> Compositor View** in the dialog box menu bar with similar functionality to the View sheet in the Slate Material Editor.

Note that in the Compositor View, all of the wired states are displayed. You can modify the composition by modifying the nodes. You can select **Compositor>Compositor Link** to output the composition to the After Effects software or select **Compositor>Create PSD** to output the composition to an Adobe Photoshop .PSD file, as shown in Figure 11–45.

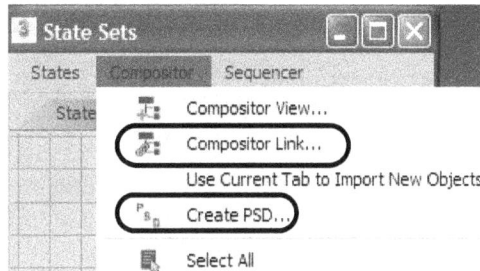

Figure 11–45

Camera Sequencer

You can use the Sequencer mode to set up an animation using multiple camera views. Select **Sequencer>Sequencer Mode** to activate a window along the bottom of the viewports with a track window indicating the cameras that are in use along with the range of frames for active cameras, as shown in Figure 11–46.

To add a camera, use to add a state and then click on **None** and select camera from the menu. Click on the check box to enable the camera track.

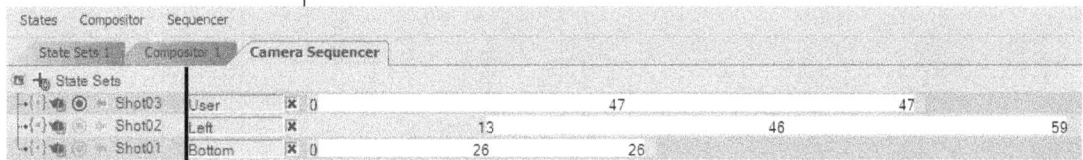

Figure 11–46

State Sets Toolbar

The State Sets toolbar (shown in Figure 11–47) enables you to quickly access the State Sets features.

Figure 11–47

- Click {⊕ to open or close the State Sets dialog box. When you toggle it on and then select **Render All States** from the **States** menu in the State Sets dialog box, the state is rendered with the changed properties.

- Click 🎥 to toggle the state render on or off. When you toggle it on and then select **Render All States** from the **States** menu in the State Sets dialog box, the state is rendered.

- Use the drop-down list to activate a state or access other controls.

- Click 🗃 to open the Select Composite Link File dialog box where you can browse and use the selected .SOF (state output file).

11.7 Cameras

Cameras are created using ![icon] (Cameras), in the Command Panel, in the Create panel (![icon]), as shown in Figure 11–48.

- Target cameras have a target object that can be selected and transformed separately from the camera itself.

- Free cameras do not have a target object.

- Physical cameras includes exposure control and other effects while framing the scene.

*Alternatively, you can create a camera by selecting **Create> Cameras**.*

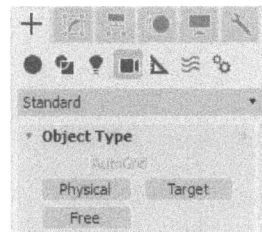

Figure 11–48

- Cameras can also be created on the fly to match a **Perspective** viewport using the **Views>Create Standard Camera From View**.or **Views>Create Physical Camera From View.**

Target and Free Camera Parameters

As with any other object, the **Camera** parameters are available in the Command Panel, in the Modify panel (![icon]), as shown in Figure 11–49.

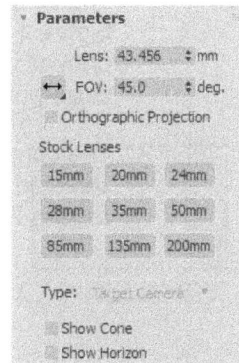

Figure 11–49

The **Camera** parameters found in the Parameters rollout for the Target and Free camera are:

- The focal length of real-world cameras is the distance between the focus point (the film or light-sensitive media) and the optical center of the lens. The **Lens** option available governs how much of the scene is visible to the camera. This corresponds to the focal length of real-world cameras.

- The camera focal lengths are directly related to that camera's field of view (FOV); an angular measurement of how much of the horizon can be seen by the camera. The field of view can be measured horizontally, vertically, or diagonally using the different field of view options, as shown in Figure 11–50.

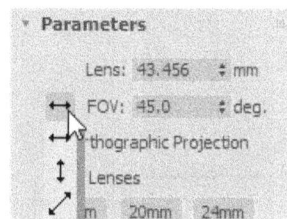

Figure 11–50

- Human vision is often approximated with a 45° field of view; it in fact varies from 60 degrees above to 75 degrees below the horizontal meridian. A focal length of 50mm is very commonly used in real-world cameras, which relates to about a 40° field of view in the Autodesk 3ds Max software.

- Other stock focal lengths are provided in the Autodesk 3ds Max software as button presets. Focal lengths below 50mm are considered short or wide-angle lenses, while those above 50mm are called telephoto lenses.

- The **Orthographic Projection** option (shown in Figure 11–51) causes a camera view to display as an orthographic or user view (axonometric rotated) rather than a three-point perspective.

- The camera's cone of vision is visible when the camera is selected, as shown in Figure 11–52. The **Show Cone** option causes it to remain visible after the camera is not selected.

- The **Show Horizon** option (shown in Figure 11–53) displays a dark gray line in the camera viewport representing the horizon in the camera view. It is helpful when aligning a camera to a background image.

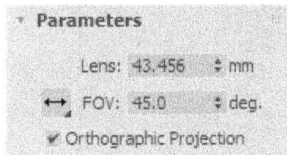

Figure 11–51

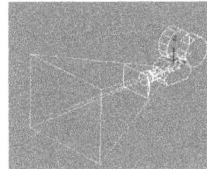

Figure 11–52

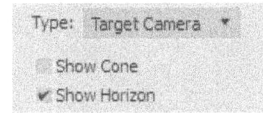

Figure 11–53

Hint: Two-Point Perspectives Through Cameras

By default, camera and perspective viewports show three-point perspective views. You can display a two-point perspective by adding a Camera Correction modifier to the camera object; select **Camera Correction** in **Modifiers>Cameras**, as shown in Figure 11–54. Two-point perspective causes vertical lines to remain vertical rather than converge over distance.

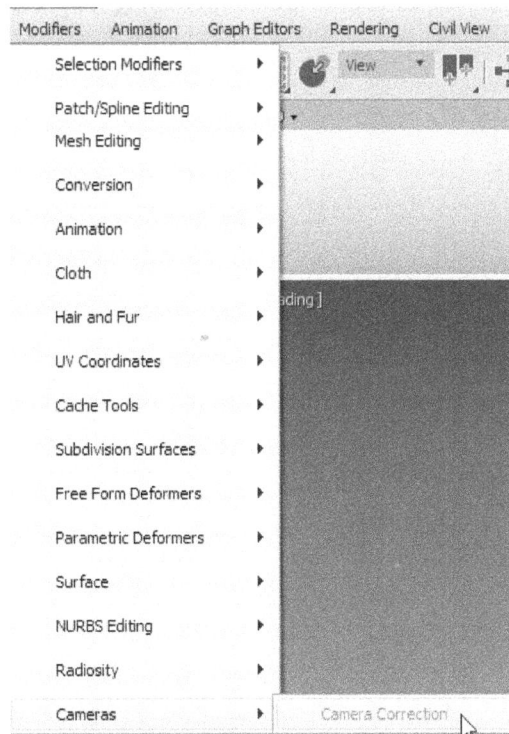

Figure 11–54

There are some additional **Camera** parameters, as shown in Figure 11–55.

Figure 11–55

- The *Environment Ranges* area contains the distances measured from the camera between which you want to show any atmospheric effects assigned in the Atmosphere rollout of the *Environment* tab in the Environment and Effects dialog box (**Rendering>Environment**).

- The *Clipping Planes* area contains the cutoff distances for the geometry that displays in the camera. When enabled, only geometry between the clip distances is visible.

Depending on the selected effect, a Parameters rollout specific to that effect (Depth of Field Parameters or Motion Blur Parameters) opens below the Cameras Parameters rollout.

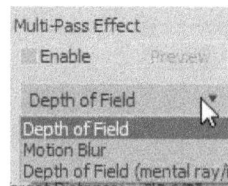

- The *Multi-Pass Effect* area (default is Depth of Field) is a camera-specific rendering effect that causes distance blurring, where only a certain point is in focus. This effect simulates how areas away from the focal point display blurred in human vision and photography. You can either select **Depth of Field (mental ray)**, **Depth of Field**, or **Motion Blur** (as shown in Figure 11–56) as an effect to be used in the rendering. You can also select the native Depth of Field effect of either mental ray, iray, or Quicksilver renderer.

Figure 11–56

Physical Camera

The Physical Camera (as shown in Figure 11–57) is the best option for setting up photorealistic, physically based scenes. Physical Camera integrates framing the scene with per-camera exposure control, perspective control, distortion, depth of field, and motion blur. The options that can be incorporated while using the Physical camera is dependent on the active renderer.

The **Physical Camera** parameters (shown in Figure 11–58) are described as follows:

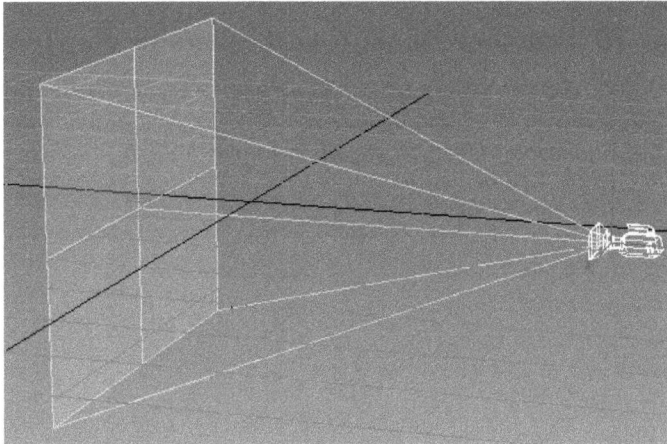

Figure 11–57

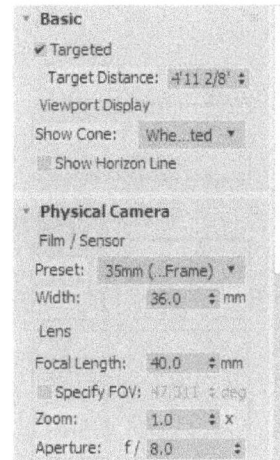

Figure 11–58

Basic rollout	When Targeted is selected, it defines properties for a target camera, and viewport display options.
Physical Camera rollout	Contains properties to define the scene view using real world camera values for accurate reproduction of a camera shot scene. Presets are available for common camera types which define Lens properties, focus, and shutter speed.
Exposure rollout	Defines exposure properties to be used with the physical camera. These properties do not affect the global exposure settings in the Environment settings.
Bokeh (Depth of Field) rollout	Properties to create a blurring effect in areas of the image that are out of focus. This effect is most apparent when the out-of-focus areas of the scene have small points of high contrast, typically from light sources or bright objects.
Perspective Control rollout	Properties to shift the perspective of the camera scene without changing the location or orientation of the camera.
Lens Distortion rollout	Settings to apply a camera distortion effect to the rendered image using cubic, or texture distortion.
Miscellaneous rollout	Enables clipping planes and modifies near and far environment ranges.

11.8 Background Images

The Autodesk 3ds Max software can use image files as viewport and rendering backgrounds. Background images are used to add detail to a scene or show a proposed construction project in its real-world context. You can load an image into the viewport background, independent of the rendering background (the environment map) or load it to both the viewport and rendering backgrounds.

How To: Enable a Background Image to Viewports

1. Select **Views>Viewport Configuration>*Background* tab** (<Alt>+<B>) to open the Viewport Configuration dialog box in the *Background* tab, as shown in Figure 11–59.

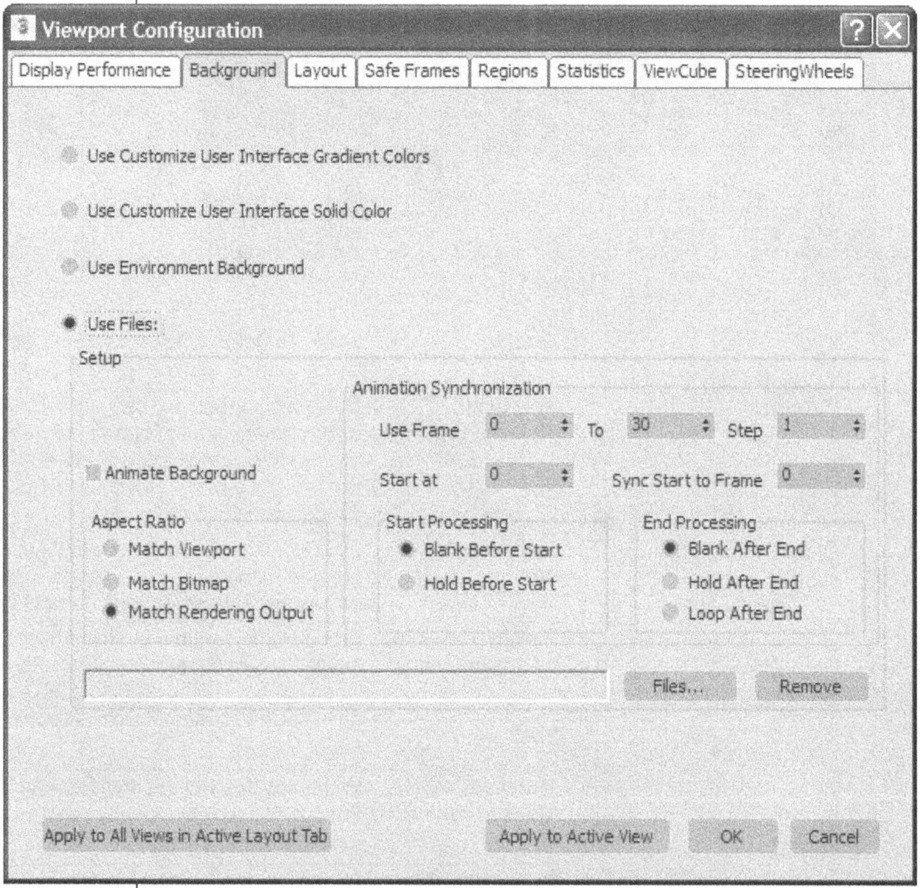

Figure 11–59

*If any option other than
the **Use Files** option is
selected, the Setup area
is grayed out.*

2. Select **Use Files** to make the *Setup* area available for use.
3. In the *Aspect Ratio* area, select **Match Bitmap** to keep the aspect ratio of the image file constant.
4. Click **Files...** to browse for the image file and open it.
5. Click **Apply to Active View** or click **Apply to All Views in Active Layout Tab** to only display the image in the active viewport or to display it in all of the viewports.
6. Click **OK**.

How To: Assign an Environment Map to a Viewport

*Select **Rendering>
Environment** to open
the Environment and
Effects dialog box.*

1. To enable an environment map to display in a viewport, you need to select the **Use Map** option and load a map using the *Environment Map* slot in the Environment and Effects dialog box, as shown in Figure 11–60. You can adjust the map parameters using an Instance of the map in Slate Material Editor, and opening its Parameter Editor.

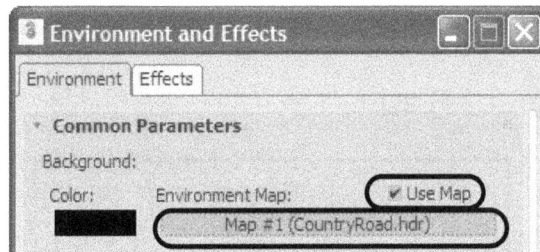

Figure 11–60

*Select **Views>Viewport
Configuration** or press
<Alt>+<B>.*

2. Select the viewport in which you want to display the map.
3. In the Viewport Configuration dialog box (*Background* tab), select **Use Environment Background** and click **OK**.

Hint: Updating a Background Image

Certain changes (e.g., change in resolution or aspect ratio) do not update the background image automatically. You should use <Alt>+<Shift>+<Ctrl>+<B> to update the background image in the active viewport. This command is not available if the active viewport does not display a background image.

Hint: Assign Background Image from Windows Explorer

You can also assign a background image directly from Windows Explorer by dragging and dropping the image file onto a viewport. A Bitmap Viewport Drop dialog box opens prompting you to select it as a viewport background or an environment map or both, as shown in Figure 11–61.

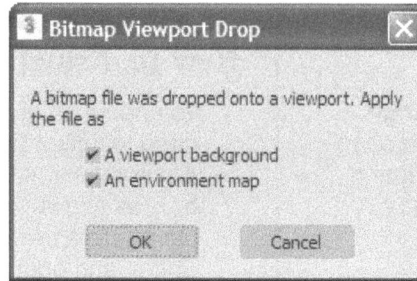

Figure 11–61

Aspect Ratio

The Autodesk 3ds Max software uses an aspect ratio to describe image proportions. It is the relationship between length and width of images, renderings, and viewports. For example, HDTV video can be created at a resolution of 1920 x 1080 pixels (1080p), which has an aspect ratio of 1.78 (1920 / 1080 = 1.78).

It is recommended to match the aspect ratio of a background image to the aspect ratio of a viewport and the rendered output. This enables you to see a more accurate representation of the final output in the viewports. The composition of a massing study displays different in the viewport (as shown in Figure 11–62) than it does in the rendered output (as shown in Figure 11–63) when their aspect ratios do not match.

Figure 11–62

Figure 11–63

You can maintain the aspect ratio of the viewport background using the options in the *Aspect Ratio* area in the Viewport Configuration dialog box, in the *Background* tab, as shown in Figure 11–64.

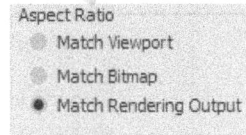

Figure 11–64

Match Viewport	Enables you to match the aspect ratio of the image to the aspect ratio of the viewport,
Match Bitmap	Enables you to lock the original aspect ratio of the image.
Match Rendering Output	Enables you to match the aspect ratio of the image to the active rendering output device.

Safe Frames

Safe Frames is a viewport display option that defines the portions of the viewport for rendered display. To enable this option, select the Viewport **+** label, and select **Configure Viewports** or select **Views>Viewport Configuration**. When the Viewport Configuration dialog box opens, select the *Safe Frames* tab, as shown in Figure 11–65.

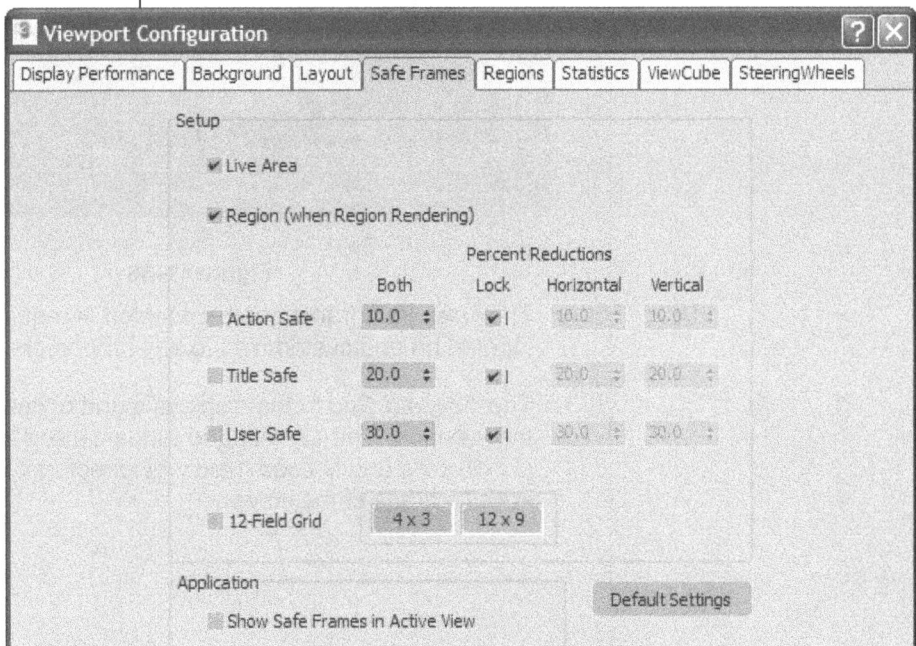

Figure 11–65

The *Safe Frames* tab provides setup options that relate to safe areas for animated action and titles when creating graphics for television. When set, these are displayed as rectangles in the active view, as shown in Figure 11–66:

- The outer rectangle is the *Live area*; the limits of what is rendered.

- The middle rectangle is the *Action safe area*, the recommended area for any animated action when creating graphics for television.

- The inner rectangle is the *Title safe area*, the recommended area for titles when creating graphics for television.

Figure 11–66

- The *User Safe* frame can be enabled, if required. It can be toggled on and customized to any proportion.

- The *12-Field Grid* frame displays a grid of cells (or fields) in the viewport. The 12-field grid yields either 12 (4x3) or 108 (12x9) cells and is used mainly by directors to reference specific areas of the screen.

Assigning Size and Aspect Ratio for Rendered Output

The rendering size (in pixels) and the aspect ratio of rendered output can be assigned in the *Output Size* area of the Render Setup dialog box, as shown in Figure 11–67 (**Rendering> Render Setup>***Common* tab). There are several different presets available for output size.

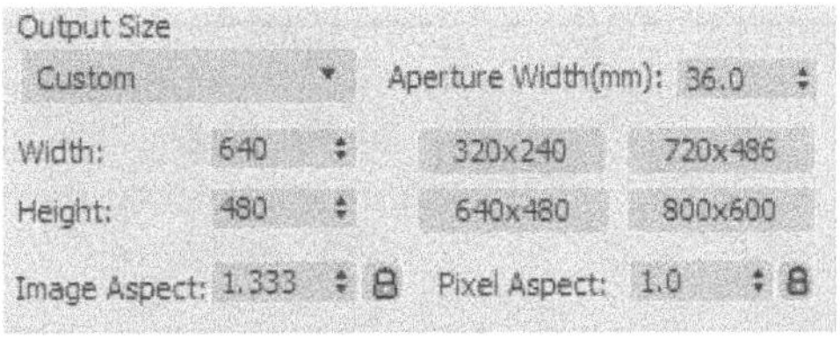

Figure 11–67

The pixel aspect ratio is determined by the image width and height.

Do not confuse the Image Aspect Ratio with the Pixel Aspect ratio. You can define the proportions of the pixel rectangle independent from the image. Consider the pixels to be individual tiles in a mosaic. The tiles can be narrow, long, or short and wide.

Hint: Use Standard Aspect Ratios

Be cautious about selecting random width and height values. Most output has a required width and height value for a particular media type. Problems occur because non-standard choices have been made for the rendering aspect ratio.

Practice 11c

Cameras and Background Images

Practice Objectives

- Apply a bitmap image as a background for the scene.
- Create a Physical Target Camera and modify the parameters.

Estimated time for completion: 20 minutes

In this practice you will apply a bitmap image as an Environment Map in a rendered scene, and as a Background Image in a viewport. You will then create a Physical Camera and modify its parameters to correctly display scene objects on top of the background image.

You must set the paths to locate the External files and Xrefs used in the practice. If you have not done this already, return to **Chapter 1: Introduction to Autodesk 3ds Max** and complete Task 1 to Task 3 in **Practice 1a: Organizing Folders and Working with the Interface**. You only have to set the user paths once.

Task 1 - Apply an Environment Map.

You will first configure an Environment Map to serve as a viewport and rendering background.

*If a dialog box opens prompting you about a File Load: Mismatch, click **OK** to accept the default values.*

1. Open **Rendering and Animation.max**.
   - This is the retail exterior scene with standard exterior lighting.

2. In the menu bar, select **Rendering>Environment**. The Environment and Effects dialog box opens.

3. In the *Environment* tab, in the Common Parameters rollout, in the *Background* area, click **None** for *Environment Map*.

4. In the Material/Map Browser, open the *Maps>General* categories and double-click on **Bitmap**.

5. In the Select Bitmap Image File dialog box, open **Background.jpg** (from the ...\Maps folder).

- Note that **None** is replaced with **Map #9 (Background.jpg)** and **Use Map** is automatically enabled, as shown in Figure 11–68.

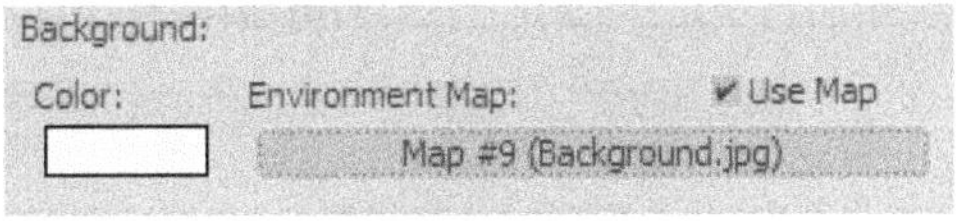

Figure 11–68

6. Close the Environment and Effects dialog box.

7. Activate the **Perspective** viewport and click (Render Production). The tree line displays behind the model, as shown in Figure 11–69.

Figure 11–69

- Note that the image file is only displayed in the rendering as a background and not in the viewport.
- The position of the background image is not correct.

8. Close the Rendered Frame Window.

9. Ensure that the **Perspective** viewport is active, and then select the General viewport label (+)>**Configure Viewports**. In the Viewport Configuration dialog box, select the *Background* tab, if required.

You can also press <Alt>+<B> or select **Views>Viewport Configuration** *to open the Viewport Configuration dialog box.*

10. Select **Use Environment Background**, as shown in Figure 11–70. Click **OK**.

- Note that the image displays behind the scene in the **Perspective** viewport, but is not in the correct position.

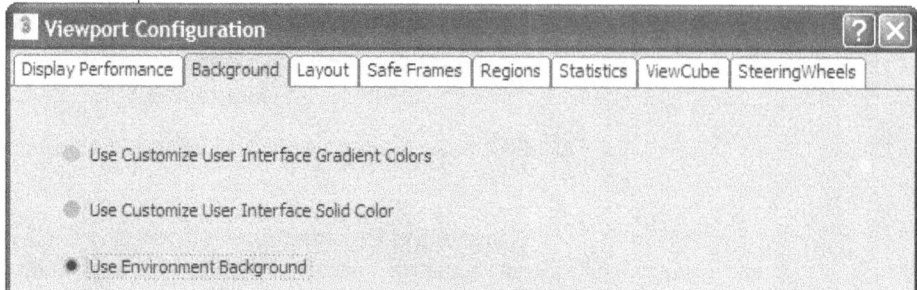

Figure 11–70

11. To modify the image, open the Slate Material Editor.

12. In the Material/Map Browser, in the *Scene Materials* category, double-click on **Map # (Background.jpg) [Environment], to** place its node on the *View1* sheet, as shown in Figure 11–71.

Figure 11–71

13. Double-click on the **Map # Bitmap** title bar to open its Parameter Editor.

14. In the Bitmap Parameters rollout, click **View Image**, as shown in Figure 11–72.

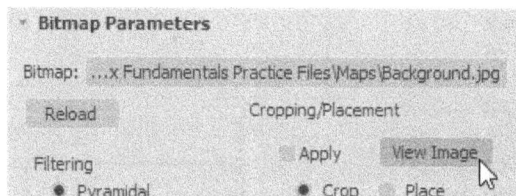

Figure 11–72

Programs such as Adobe Photoshop can be used to remove features that are not required in a background image.

- The Specify Cropping/Placement viewer displays a grassy field with the top of a trailer, as shown in Figure 11–73.

Figure 11–73

- In the Specify Cropping/Placement viewer, you can specify the image cropping (the limit of the area to be displayed) by re-sizing the red rectangle around the image. When required, cropping is enabled in the Bitmap Parameters rollout, in the *Cropping Placement* area, using the **Apply** option.

The Aspect value indicates if the image is being stretched or not.

15. Right-click and hold over the image to access the color and other image data information, as shown in Figure 11–74. The image is currently 1200 pixels wide by 750 pixels high. The Aspect value of 1.00 shows that this image is displaying normally. Close the Specify Cropping/Placement viewer.

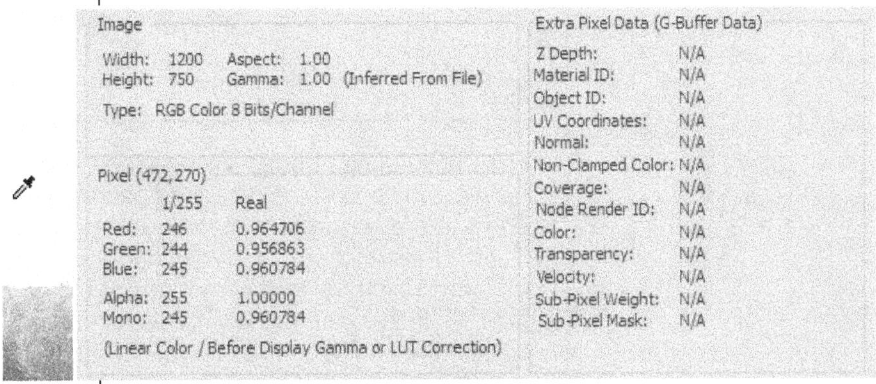

Figure 11–74

16. In the Map Parameter Editor (Slate Material Editor), in the Coordinates rollout, verify that **Environ** is selected. This indicates that the map is used as a 2D backdrop. In the Mapping drop-down list, select **Screen**, as shown in Figure 11–75. Close the Slate Material Editor.

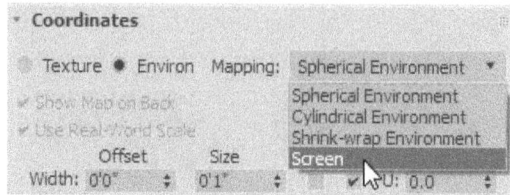

Figure 11–75

- In the **Perspective** viewport, note that the background image has updated and that a small portion of the tree line displays behind the right side of the building.

17. Render the **Perspective** viewport. The tree line in the image should display partially behind the model, as shown in Figure 11–76 (although the image is not yet in the correct position). Close the Rendered Frame Window.

Figure 11–76

Task 2 - Create a Camera.

The background photograph was taken from about the center of the westerly end of the proposed parking lot curb island location. The camera was approximately eleven feet above the proposed first floor elevation (on a ladder) and pointed horizontally towards a proposed interior wall corner and vertically to the level of the horizon. In this task you will create a camera approximately lined up with the background image. This type of approximation is required when exact measurements of camera position and other existing features are not available.

1. Activate the **Top** viewport and maximize it.

2. In the Command Panel>Create panel (✛), click

   ▆◀ (Cameras), and click **Physical**. Start with the approximate camera location (to the left of the middle double parking lot), click and drag to locate the target approximately over the model's back wall, and release to place the target, as shown in Figure 11–77.

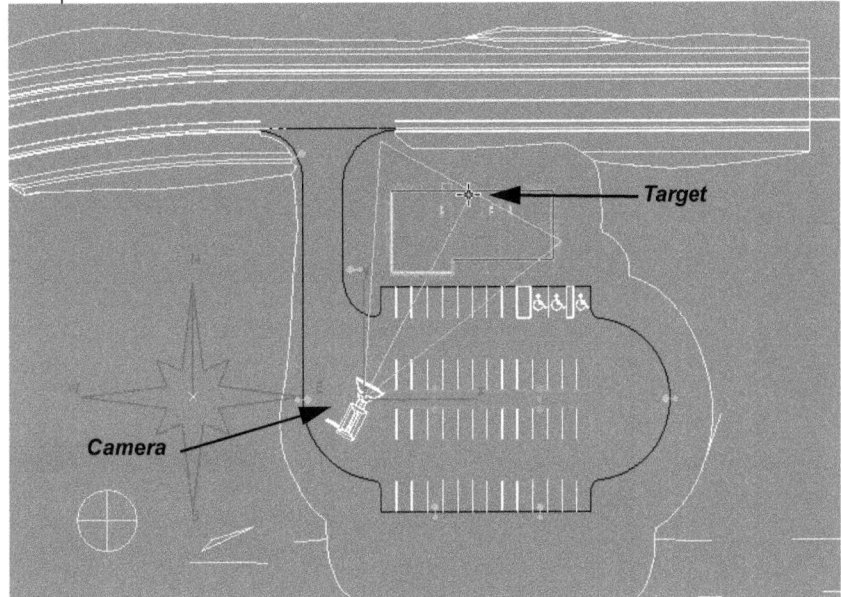

Figure 11–77

3. Maximize to the four viewports. Press <Esc> to exit the **Cameras** command and then activate the **Perspective** viewport.

4. Select the **Perspective** POV label and select **Cameras> PhysCamera001**. Note that the background image is visible in the viewport with the building being viewed at an angle from the bottom up, and that the top of the trailer might be visible in the front.

5. in the Scene Explorer, select the camera object by selecting

   PhysCamera001. In the Main Toolbar, click ✛ (Select and Move). In the Status Bar, note that *Z* elevation is **0.0**. Set Z to **11'0"**. Note that the tree lining is now visible behind the building along the left side and the trailer top is not visible.

6. You can now adjust the camera to display the image with respect to the building. In the **Top** Viewport, move the Camera object and keep looking in the **PhysCamera001** viewport until you get the scene similar to that shown in Figure 11–78.

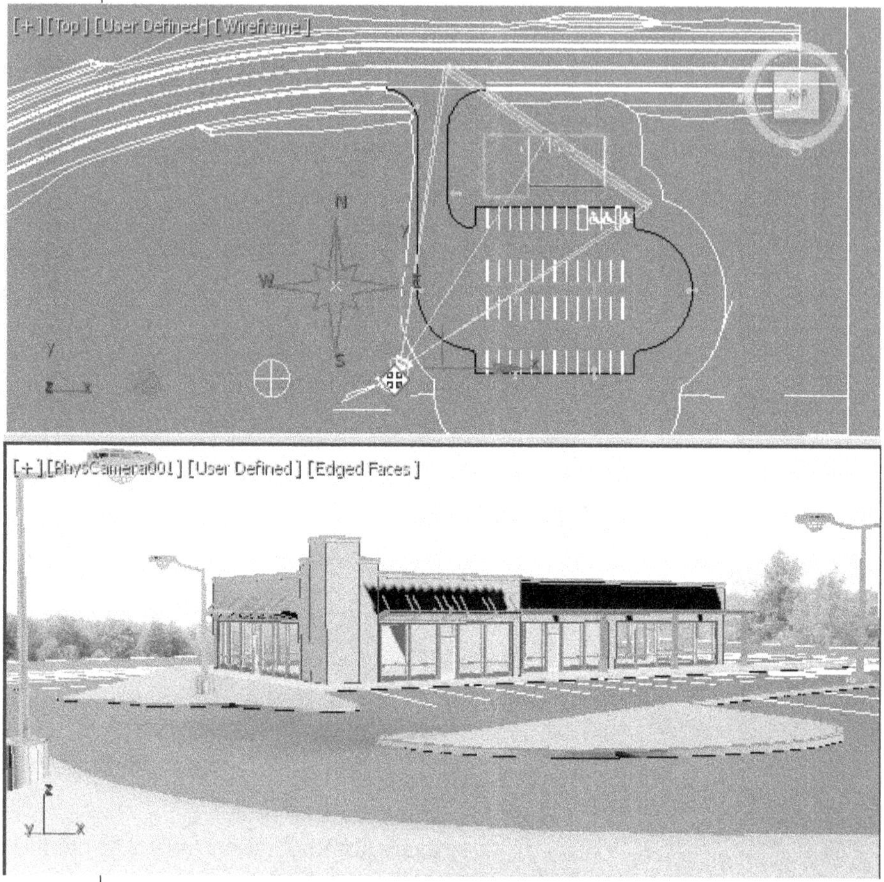

Figure 11–78

Task 3 - Approximately Match the Camera to the Background.

The background image has an aspect ratio of 1.6 (1200 pixels wide/750 pixels high). You will match the viewport and rendering to this aspect ratio.

1. In the Main Toolbar, click ![icon] (Render Setup) or select **Rendering>Render Setup**.

2. In the Render Setup dialog box, in the Common Parameters rollout, in the *Output Size* area, set *Image Aspect* to **1.6.** Click

   ⊟ next to it to activate it. Then, set the *Width* to **600** pixels and press <Enter>, as shown in Figure 11–79. Note that the *Height* is automatically set to **375** because the *Image Aspect* is locked at **1.6**.

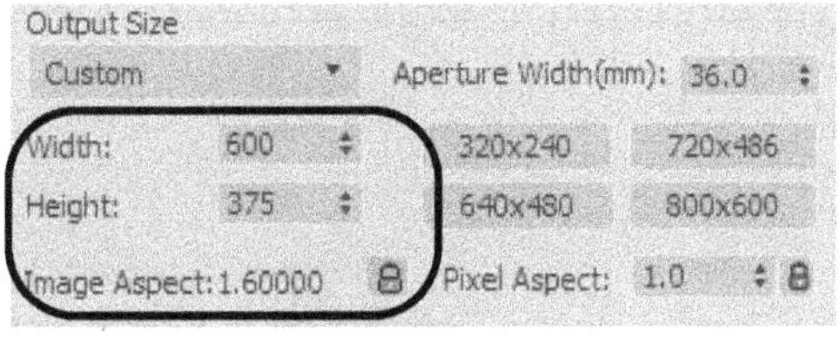

Figure 11–79

3. Close the dialog box. Activate the **PhysCamera001** viewport and render the scene to see the results.

4. Select the **PhysCamera001** POV label and select **Show Safe Frames**. Note the safe frames in the viewport, as shown in Figure 11–80.

Figure 11–80

Real-world 35mm cameras are named because of the diagonal measurement of their film, not their focal length.

5. Select the camera object in any viewport, if required, and in the Command Panel, select the Modify panel ( ). In the Physical Camera rollout, note that in the Film/Sensor area, the Preset is set as **35mm** (Full Frame). This indicates that the photo was taken with a 35mm camera that had an adjustable lens.

6. In the Exposure rollout, click **Install Exposure Control.** In the Warning dialog box, click **OK** to replace the exposure control with the Physical camera exposure control.

7. Render the **PhysCamera001** viewport and note that the rendering is washed out.

8. In the Exposure rollout, change the Target EV value to around 8.5 - 9.5, as shown in Figure 11–81. Render the scene and note that the rendering is not washed out anymore.

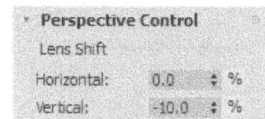

Figure 11–81

9. In the Basic rollout, in the *Viewport Display* area, select **Show Horizon Line**, as shown in Figure 11–82. In the **PhysCamera001** viewport, note that a black line displays across the middle of the viewport. It represents the horizon of the 3D model as seen by the camera.

10. You will adjust the position of the horizon. In the Perspective Control rollout, in the *Lens Shift* area, set the Vertical % value to **-10 %**, as shown in Figure 11–83. Note that the tree line is visible behind the building.

Figure 11–82   **Figure 11–83**

11. Verify that the **PhysCamera001** viewport is active and render the scene. Note that, with the help of some assumptions you have reasonably located the model over an existing photograph, as shown in Figure 11–84.

Figure 11–84

12. Save your work as **MyRenderingandAnimation.max**.

11.9 The Print Size Wizard

When you create renderings for print, the Print Size Wizard (shown in Figure 11–85) can help you select an appropriate rendering based on a required output resolution. To access the wizard, select **Rendering>Print Size Assistant**.

Figure 11–85

- A rendering's print resolution describes how many pixels show per printed inch, often referred to as pixels-per-inch on screen (ppi) or dots-per-inch on paper (DPI). Select the required dpi in the *Choose DPI Value* options.

Trial and error might be required to determine an appropriate resolution.

- Rendering time increases exponentially with size, so select the lowest resolution that provides an acceptable result.

- Many laser printers and plotters output between 300-600 DPI, however, when rendering values such as 72-150 DPI you can also get good results. High-end equipment plotting at 1200 DPI or better creates outstanding prints at 200-300 dpi and on high-quality paper.

- Higher quality paper can get better results than increasing resolution.

Practice 11d | Using the Print Size Wizard

Practice Objective

- Set the print resolution, paper size, and other options for a rendering.

Estimated time for completion: 5 minutes

In this practice you will prepare a rendering for an A-size, 8.5"x11" print at 72 DPI. You want at least a 1/2" border around all sides and the aspect ratio of 1.6. Using the Print Size Wizard, you will set all the options to get the required print.

You must set the paths to locate the External files and Xrefs used in the practice. If you have not done this already, return to **Chapter 1: Introduction to Autodesk 3ds Max** and complete Task 1 to Task 3 in **Practice 1a: Organizing Folders and Working with the Interface**. You only have to set the user paths once.

*If a dialog box opens prompting you about a File Load: Mismatch, click **OK** to accept the default values.*

1. Open **Print Wizard.max**.

2. Open the Print Size Wizard by selecting **Rendering>Print Size Assistant**. Verify that the printing units (*Choose Unit*) are set to **inches** and the orientation is set to **Landscape**.

3. In the Paper Size drop-down list, select **A – 11x8.5in**. Note in the viewport that this setting changes the aspect ratio (11"/8.5" = 1.29). Change the Paper Size back to **Custom**.

4. Set the *Paper Width* to **10** (11" minus a half-inch border on each side). When printing, the 1/2" border displays along both sides as long as you print this image centered on an 8.5" x 11" page at 72 DPI. On a hand-calculator work out the required rendered height 10"/1.6 = 6.25".

5. Set the *Paper Height* to **6.25** and select the *DPI* value of **72**, as shown in Figure 11–86. Press <Enter>. Note that the rendering size changes to 720 x 450 pixels.

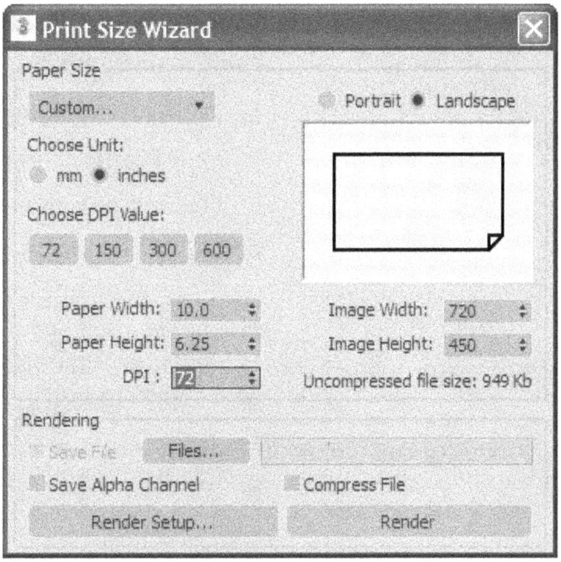

Figure 11–86

6. Click **Render**.

   - Once rendered, you save the image and open it in an image editor or layout program to add your company logo, titles, labels, and other additional details.
   - You can also print directly to the current system printer by clicking 🖨 (Print Image) in the Rendered Frame Window.

7. Save the file as **MyPrint Wizard.max**.

Chapter Review Questions

1. Which renderer in the Autodesk 3ds Max software is not a graphical renderer and uses ASCII text files to describe the position and transformation of objects, lighting, etc.?

    a. Scanline Renderer

    b. VUE File Renderer

    c. Quicksilver Hardware Renderer

    d. NVIDIA mental ray renderer

2. When saving a rendering as an image file, which of the following format offers highest color depth with a smaller compression? In other words, this image file format is the best choice regarding file size to quality ratio.

    a. JPEG

    b. BMP (Bitmap)

    c. TGA (Targa)

    d. PNG (Portable Network Graphics)

    e. TIFF (Tagged Image File Format)

3. In rendering, which of the following is used to calculate accurate reflections, refractions, and shadows?

    a. Antialiasing

    b. SuperSampling

    c. Motion Blur

    d. Raytracing

4. In single-sided mode, the Autodesk 3ds Max software renders faces whose vectors point towards the camera.

    a. True

    b. False

5. What is the most commonly used focal length in real-world cameras?

    a. 30mm

    b. 50mm

    c. 70mm

    d. 90mm

6. For background images, which keys do you press to update the active viewport with the specific changes made to the image (the changes that do not update automatically)?

    a. <Alt>+<B>

    b. <Alt>+<Ctrl>+<B>

    c. <Alt>+<Shift>+<B>

    d. <Alt>+<Ctrl>+<Shift>+<B>

Command Summary

Button	Command	Location
	Cameras	• **Command Panel:** *Create* panel • **Create:** Cameras
	Effects and Environment dialog box	• **Rendered Frame Window** • **Rendering:** Environment
	Render Setup	• **Main Toolbar** • **Rendering:** Render Setup
	State Sets	• **State Sets Toolbar** • **Rendering:** State Sets
N/A	Viewport Configuration dialog box> *Background* tab	• **Views:** Viewport Background> Configure Viewport Background • **Keyboard:** <Alt>+<B>

Chapter

12

Animation

Animations created in the Autodesk® 3ds Max® software involve the use of Animation and Time Controls. These enable you to animate and keyframe a camera to create a walkthrough animation or to create single-frame images and then assemble them to create a movie.

Learning Objectives in this Chapter

- Work with Animation and Time Controls and set various options.
- Create animation output using the various approaches available.

12.1 Animation and Time Controls

Animations in the Autodesk 3ds Max software are created by playing back a number of still frames in rapid succession using desktop animation files such as .AVIs and .MOVs.

The Autodesk 3ds Max animation system offers powerful controls to create animations, ranging from simple camera movements to extremely complex sequences.

- Traditional movies play back a sequence of still images in rapid succession.

- Computer movie formats compile a sequence of still images into a compressed format, keeping track of the changes from frame to frame at the pixel level.

- Animations are based on Key Frames (or keys), which are time indexes at which objects change their position, rotation, scale, and/or a limited number of object parameters.

- The Autodesk 3ds Max software generates animations by interpolating between a small number of user-defined key frames – smoothly or otherwise.

- The animation controls enable you to create and play back a preview animation in one or more viewports.

Time Slider and Track Bar

The time slider and the track bar (shown in Figure 12–1) are found below the viewports and enable you to advance and reverse along an animation forward or backwards in time.

- The numbers below the time slider indicate the current time or frame number. Use the greater than (>) and lesser than (<) keys as shortcuts for moving the time slider a frame at a time.

- The shortcut menu in the Track bar contains the key properties and the controller properties. Selecting a key and then right-clicking displays all of the values for that key. Using the shortcut menu, you can also delete keys and use filter options for the display of the track bar.

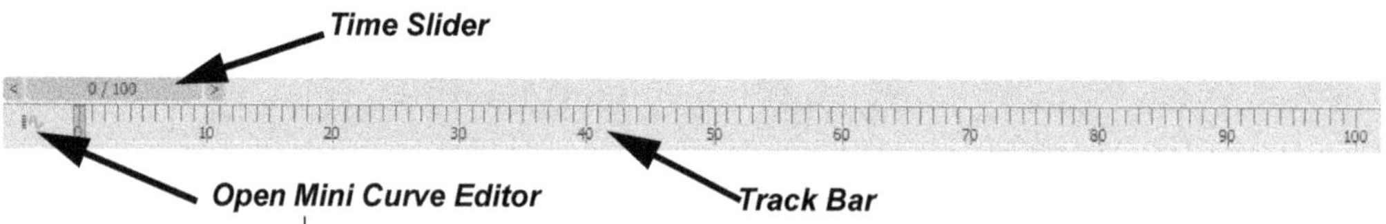

Figure 12–1

Enhanced
in 2017

- On the left side of the track bar, clicking ⚡ (Open Mini Curve Editor) opens the Mini Curve Editor (as shown in Figure 12–2), which replaces the track bar and the time slider. The Curve Editor contains a menu bar, toolbar, controller window, and the key window. You can collapse the Curve Editor by clicking **Close** at the left end of the Curve Editor toolbar.

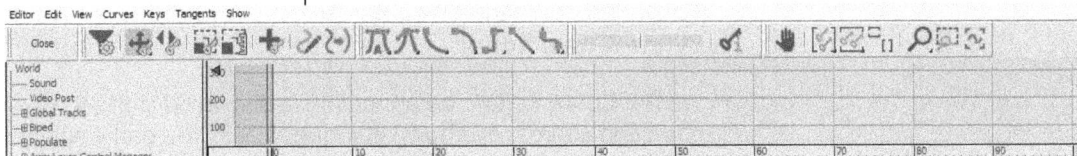

Figure 12–2

Enhanced
in **2017**

Hint: Track View: Using the Curve Editor and Dope Sheet

The Curve Editor and Dope Sheet are two animation data editors which graphically display and enable you to modify the animation controllers that are used to interpolate the objects in a scene.

- To open the Track View - Curve Editor, in the Main toolbar,

  click ![icon], or in the Menu Bar, select **Graph Editors>Track View- Curve Editor**.

- In the Curve Editor, the animation is displayed in the form of function curves, as shown in Figure 12–3. You can visualize and modify the motion by controlling the curves (i.e., tangent handles) at various keys.

Figure 12–3

- To open the Track View - Dope Sheet, in the Menu Bar, select **Graph Editors>Track View- Dope Sheet**.

- In the Dope sheet, the animation is displayed in the form of a spread sheet displaying keys and ranges, as shown in Figure 12–4. You can visualize and modify the motion by controlling the keys directly.

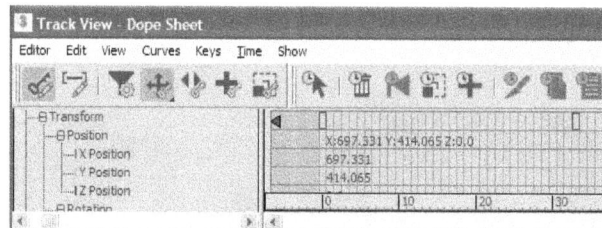

Figure 12–4

Animation and Time Controls

The Animation and Time Controls (shown in Figure 12–5) are found at the bottom right corner next to the Navigation Controls.

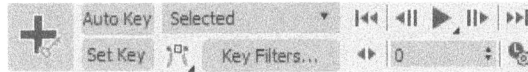

Figure 12–5

The various Animation and Time controls are described as follows:

*When either **Auto Key** mode or **Set Key** mode is active, their corresponding buttons display in red, indicating that you are in the animation mode.*

 +	Enables you to manually add an animation key at the time shown in the time slider.
Auto Key/ Set Key	Activates either **Auto Key** or **Set Key** Animation Modes. • When **Auto Key** mode is active all movement, rotation, and scale changes are automatically stored as keys at the current frame. This method is more widely used by design visualizers. Press <N> as a shortcut to toggle on the mode. • The **Set Key** mode enables you to create keys, set key information, and offers more control over the kinds of keys you create through filters by using  + . Its functionality was added primarily for character animators who used this methodology in other packages. Press <'> (single apostrophe) as a shortcut to toggle on the mode.
Previous/ Play/ Next	Enable you to play an animation in your viewport(s) and advance to the next or previous frame/key. • When you click ▶ (Play Animation), the software plays the animation in the active viewport and replaces this icon with II (Stop Animation). • ▶ (Play Animation) is a flyout and contains ▶ (Play Selected), which only plays the selected objects in the active viewport.

◄► (Key Mode Toggle)	Enables you to move between frames or keys. • When you are in Key mode (active), the Previous and Next icons display as ◄ ▶ ▶I and enable you to jump to the previous or next keyframe. • Keyframes are set in the Time Configuration dialog box (Key Steps area). When Key mode is off, the Previous and Next icons are displayed as ◄II ▶ II▶ and you can jump to the previous and next frame.
I◄◄ (Go to Start)/ ▶►I (Go to End)	Enable you to move directly to the beginning or end of an animation. The time slider jumps to the selected location.
86 ▲▼ (Current Frame)	Enables you to advance to a specific frame or time in the animation.
Key Filters...	Opens the Set Key Filters dialog box, which enables you to select the tracks on which the keys can be created. The track sets are created with the **Set Key** mode. The Selected drop-down list contains the created track sets and selection sets and enables you to select the required one quickly.
(Default In/Out Tangents for New Keys)	Contains a list of tangent types.
(Time Configuration)	Opens the Time Configuration dialog box.

Time Configuration

Clicking (Time Configuration) opens the Time Configuration dialog box (as shown in Figure 12–6) where you assign an animation, its length, playback rate, and other critical parameters. It is recommended to adjust these parameters before you start configuring an animation.

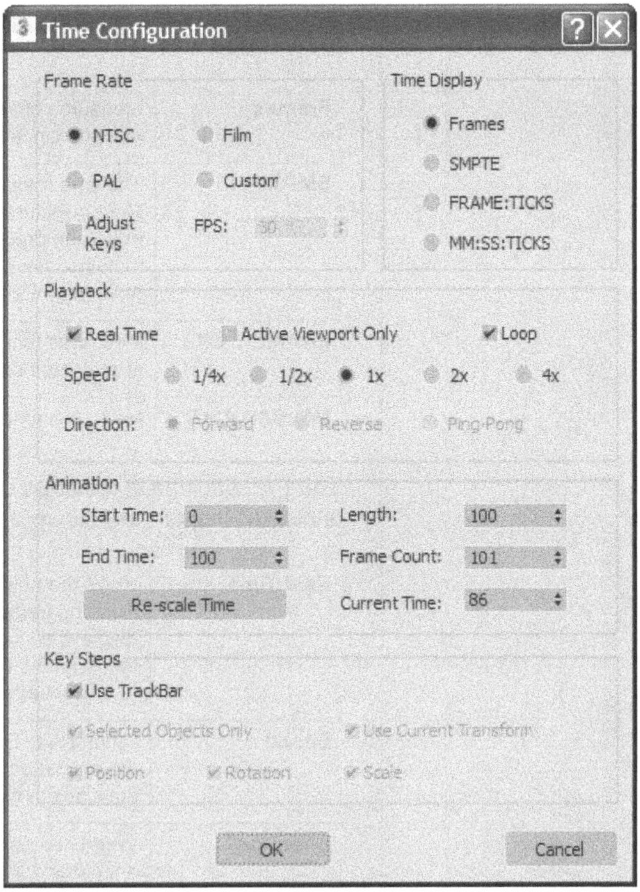

Figure 12–6

The *Frame Rate* area provides options to define how many still frames to show per second (FPS). When setting a frame rate, the goal is to create an animation that flows smoothly without rendering additional frames. The best choice for frame rate depends on the medium where you intend to play your animation.

NTSC	**National Television Standards Committee:** the standard television frame rate used across most of the Americas and Japan: 30 FPS.
PAL	**Phase Alternate Line:** the standard used across Europe: 25 FPS.
Film	Assigns the frame rate used in film production: 24 FPS.
Custom	Enables you to select a specific frame rate. Animations created for desktop and web-based presentations are often set 12-25 FPS.

The *Time Display* area provides options to select how you want to measure time during your animation.

Frames	Measures time in the number of frames that have elapsed since the beginning of the animation.
SMPTE	The time measurement standard used by the Society of Motion Picture Technical Engineers for video and television productions. This standard measures time in minutes, seconds, and frames separated by colons (such as 1:22:43).
FRAME:TICKS	Measures time in frames and ticks only. A tick is a unit of animated time that equals 1/4800 of a second.
MM:SS:TICKS	Measures time in minutes, seconds and ticks.

The *Playback* area provides options to control how the animation is played back in the viewports.

Real Time	Plays the animation at the real world playback rate, skipping frames, if required. Clearing this option displays all frames in sequence, even if it slows down the animation preview. This is used by most animators to inspect every frame for problems.
Speed	When **Real Time** is enabled, speed up or slow down the animation using this option or continually play using the **Loop** option.
Direction	When not using **Real Time** you can select to play the animation forwards, backwards, or ping-pong (forwards and backwards again) using the **Direction** option.
Active Viewport Only	Limits the animation preview to the active viewport, which might be required if system resources are taxed by the animation playback.

The options in the *Animation* area define the active time segment (the current animation length) between the starting and ending time.

Start Time	Can be equal to 0, a positive, or negative time value as required.
End Time	Can be equal to 0, a positive, or negative time value as required.
Length	The calculated time between the starting and ending points.
Frame Count	A value equal to the animation length + 1 frame, to account for the rendering of frame 0.

Current Time	Provides the frame you are on in the animation. Use this field to change to a different frame without exiting the dialog box.

When animation times are changed in this dialog box, the existing keys do not automatically scale to the new time. For example, if you lengthen an existing animation by increasing the end time, the current animation still stops at the old end time (unless you then manually adjust the keys).

To expand or contract an animation's overall length, click **Re-scale Time**, to open the Rescale Time dialog box, as shown in Figure 12–7. Changing the animation times spaces the existing keys along the new animation length.

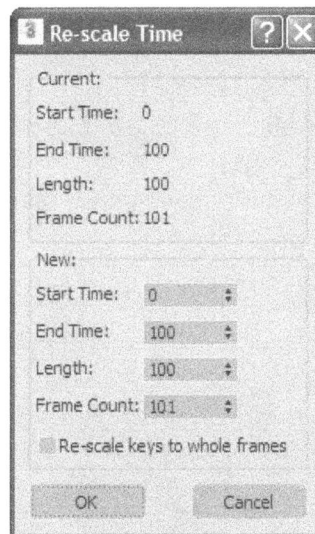

Figure 12–7

The *Key Steps* area provides options to limit how and which animation keys are created in Key mode. Leave the **Use TrackBar** option enabled to not limit key creation.

Progressive Display and Adaptive Degradation

The Progressive Display (only for Nitrous drivers) and Adaptive Degradation is a display option that can be very useful when playing animations in the viewport or when navigating large files in the viewport. When enabled (in the Status Bar, click ⬡ , or use <O> to toggle it on/off) it degrades an animation preview to a simpler display method to display the correct playback rate. It enables you to play a complex animation in a viewport at the correct speed, even if it means simplifying the display to a less detailed display mode, such as wireframe.

If you are using one of the legacy display drivers (Direct3D or Open GL), the Adaptive Degradation tab replaces the Display Performance tab in the Viewport Configuration dialog box.

In the Status Bar, right-click on ⬡ (Adaptive Degradation) to open the Viewport Configuration dialog box in the *Display Performance* tab, as shown in Figure 12–8. You can also open this dialog box by selecting **Views>Viewport Configuration** and then selecting the *Display Performance* tab. Alternatively, in the Viewport label, click [+] to display the label menu and select **Configure Viewports**. Using the menu bar or the Viewport label menu opens the dialog box in the *Visual Style & Appearance* tab. Select the *Display Performance* tab.

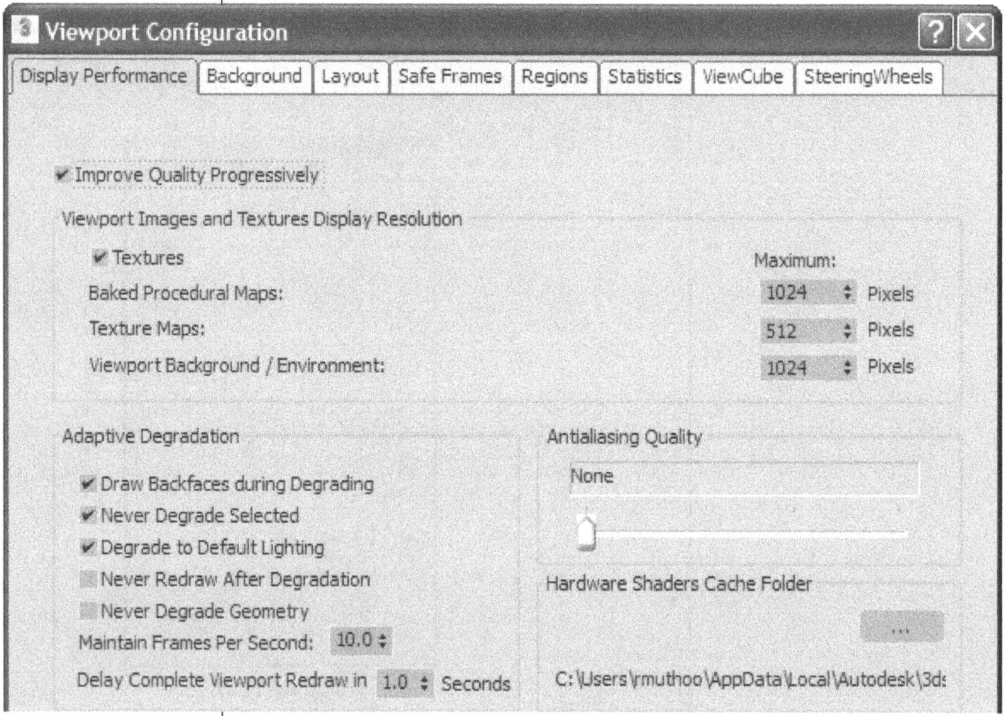

Figure 12–8

Improve Quality Progressively

This option (only available for Nitrous display drivers) enables you to improve the viewport quality through successive iterations. Once the iterations have been completed, a high quality rendered image is displayed in the viewport. You can also activate or clear this option in the menu bar (**Views> Progressive Display**).

Viewport Images and Textures Display Resolution

This area contains the following options:

Baked Procedural Maps	Enables you to set the resolution, in pixels, that is used to display the procedural maps in the viewports.
Texture Maps	Enables you to set the resolution in pixels, that is used to display the texture maps in the viewports.
Viewport Background / Environment	Enables you to set the resolution in pixels, that is used to display the environment and background maps.

Adaptive Degradation

The *Adaptive Degradation* area has the following options:

- When **Draw Backfaces during Degrade** is toggled on, the software draws the backface polygons while degrading the objects.

- When **Never Degrade Selected** is toggled on, the software does not degrade the selected objects.

- When **Degrade to Default Lighting** is toggled on, the software turns off all of the lights in the viewport with only the default lighting toggled on.

- When **Never Redraw after Degrade** is toggled on, the degraded objects display as is and do not redraw.

- When **Never Degrade Geometry** is toggled on, the geometry in the viewport is not degraded.

- The **Maintain Frames Per Second** option enables you to set the frame rate. The software maintains this frame rate through degradation.

- The **Delay Complete Viewport Redraw** option enables you to set a time in seconds, during which the viewports are not redrawn when degradation is complete.

> **Hint: Bitmap Proxy Images**
>
> Using Proxy images enables you to reduce the memory required for the 2D texture and increase the rendering speed. Expand Application Menu, select **References**, and select **Asset Tracking** to open the Asset Tracking dialog box. Use **Bitmap Performance and Memory>Global Settings** to set the proxy resolution.

Antialiasing Quality

Enables antialiasing in the viewport, which attempts to soften the rough edges in 3D Geometry. Note that higher quality settings can reduce system performance.

Hardware Shaders Cache Folder

The folder along with the complete path where the hardware shaders are saved is displayed. Click **...** to open the Configure System Paths dialog box and select a different location for saving your hardware shaders.

12.2 Walkthrough Animation

When animating cameras, it is often easier to have a camera follow a linear path than to configure the camera's position manually. For example, in Figure 12–9, you can animate a camera following a path going up a street to the house.

Figure 12–9

- To animate a target camera following a path, you create a helper object called a Dummy object, as shown in Figure 12–10. While a Dummy object is not required, it provides more control.

- The path can be a spline (shown in Figure 12–10) created in the Autodesk 3ds Max software or a linked/imported object. You then create a target camera and Dummy object and align them so they share a similar orientation. Multiple paths can be assigned and weighted during an animation.

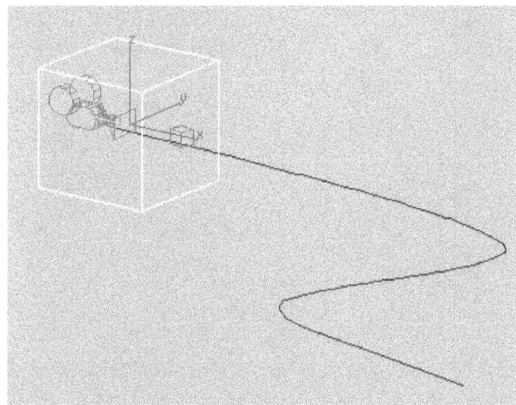

Figure 12–10

- To create a Dummy object, in the Command Panel>Create panel (+), click ▲ (Helpers). In the Object Type rollout, click **Dummy**. A Dummy object is usually drawn in the **Top** viewport to ensure orientation with world space. Dummies have no parameters in the Modify panel and do not render in your final animation.

- In the Main Toolbar, use 🔗 (Select and Link) to link the Camera and Dummy.

- To animate the Dummy object and Camera, define a Path Constraint (**Animation>Constraints>Path Constraint**). A dotted line displays in the viewport, as shown in Figure 12–11. Select the spline to be used as the path. If you cannot see the path, you can press <H> to select the path by name from the Select From Scene dialog box.

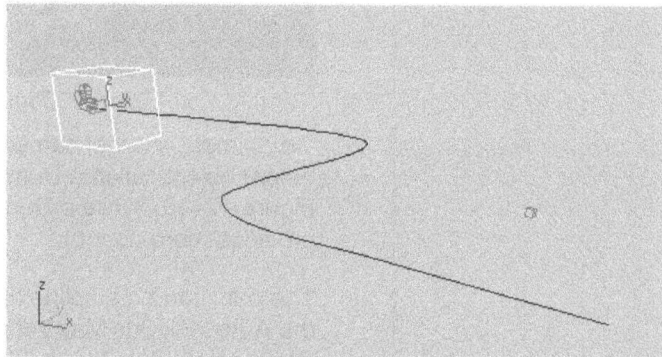

Figure 12–11

- Alternatively, the target object can be positioned over the subject and left unanimated. In this case, the target stays fixed over the building and the Dummy and Camera back animate along the path.

- The Dummy can follow the path using the **Follow** checkbox in the Motion panel.

Practice 12a

Creating a Turntable Animation

Practice Objective

- Animate a building by rotating a camera around it at keyframe intervals.

Estimated time for completion: 20 minutes

In this practice you will animate a camera rotating around the retail exterior building. You will add a dummy object on the building and set the key frames. Then apply rotation at the keyframes. You will then add interpolation to the keys using the dialog box and the Mini Curve Editor. This creates the illusion that the viewer is standing still and the building is revolving as if on a turntable.

You must set the paths to locate the External files and Xrefs used in the practice. If you have not done this already, return to **Chapter 1: Introduction to Autodesk 3ds Max** and complete Task 1 to Task 3 in **Practice 1a: Organizing Folders and Working with the Interface**. You only have to set the user paths once.

*If a dialog box opens prompting you about a File Load: Mismatch, click **OK** to accept the default values.*

1. Open **Turntable_Animation_Start.max**.

2. Verify that the **Top** viewport is active and maximize it.

3. Select the camera (**Turntable camera** is the only camera object) in the viewport. Click ⬚ (Zoom Extents All Selected) to display the camera, its target, and the entire building, as shown in Figure 12–12.

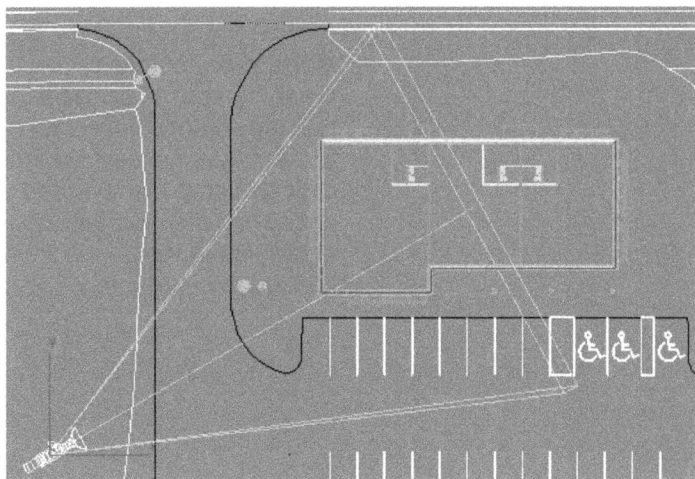

Figure 12–12

4. In the Command Panel>Create panel (+), click

   ▲ (Helpers).

5. In the Object Type rollout, click **Dummy**. Starting from the camera target by clicking on the target (the small blue square in the center of the building), drag to create a dummy object (a square box) large enough to approximately extend beyond the two horizontal walls of the building, as shown in Figure 12–13.

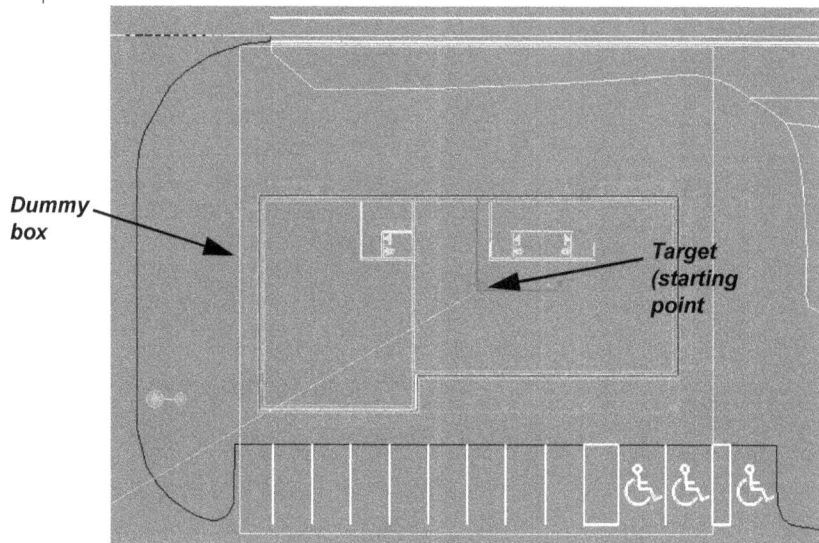

Figure 12–13

6. In the Main Toolbar, click 🔗 (Select and Link). In the viewport, select **Turntable camera** (camera object). Note that the cursor displays as two linked squares when you hover it over the selected camera. Starting from the camera, click and drag the cursor to the Dummy object (box). A white dotted line displays between the camera and the dummy, as shown in Figure 12–14. Release the mouse to link the camera to the dummy.

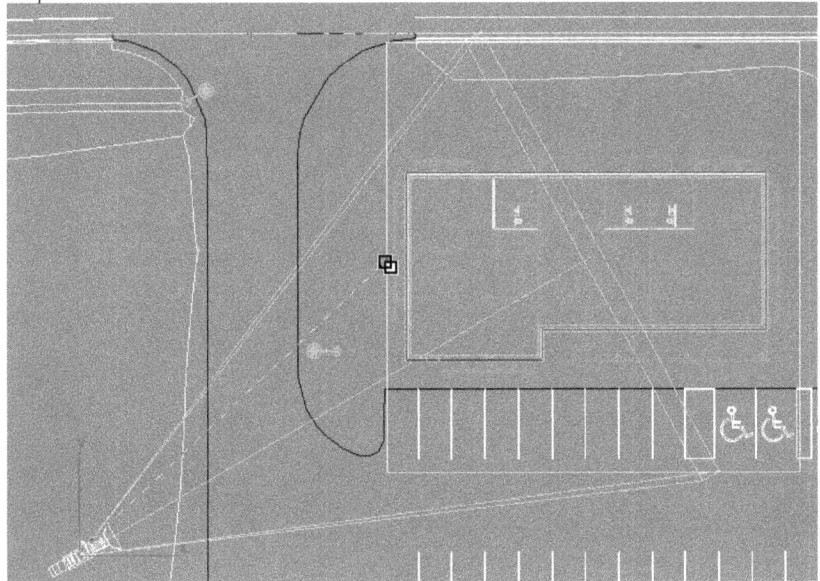

Figure 12–14

7. To test it, click (Select and Move) and move the Dummy object. The camera should move with it. Undo the move after the test and click (Select Object) to exit the **Move** command.

8. In the Animation playback controls, click (Time Configuration) to open the dialog box. Set the following:

   • *Time Display*: **Frames**
   • *Animation* area - *End Time*: **99**

9. Click **OK**. Near the bottom of the viewport, note that the Time Slider displays as **0/99**.

10. Using the layout overlay, maximize the **Turntable camera** viewport.

*Click **Auto Key**. It displays in red, indicating that you are in the **Auto Key** animation mode. The slider bar area displays in red and a red border surrounds the current viewport.*

11. In the Animation controls, click **Auto Key** (it displays in red) and drag the Time Slider to **frame 33**. The Track Bar displays a blue rectangle at frame 33, as shown in Figure 12–15.

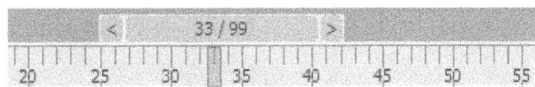

Figure 12–15

You can also use the Rotate gizmo to rotate the dummy object horizontally until the values on the screen display as [0.00, -0.00, -120.00].

12. In the Scene Explorer, using ■ (Display None) and ◢ (Display Helpers), select **Dummy001**. Verify that Dummy001 is displayed in the Name and Color rollout.

13. Click ↻ (Select and Rotate). In the Status Bar, in the Z field, enter **-120**, and press <Enter>, so that the building is rotated as shown in Figure 12–16.

Figure 12–16

14. Drag the Time Slider to frame **66** and rotate the dummy object another 120 degrees, by entering **-240** in the Z field of the Status Bar and press <Enter>, as shown in Figure 12–17.

Figure 12–17

15. Drag the Time Slider to frame **99** and rotate the dummy object another 120 degrees, by entering **-360** in the *Z* field.Press <Enter>.

16. Play the animation by clicking ▶. Note that there is a pause with each revolution of the camera. Stop the animation by clicking ▮▮.

17. If your animation has a lag, in the Status Bar, click ⬡ (Adaptive Degradation).

The working of the Adaptive degradation depends on your system configuration. You might not see the wireframe model while using Adaptive Degradation.

18. In the Animation controls, click ▶. Note that over time, the objects change into a wireframe model and animate smoothly. Stop the animation by clicking ▮▮. Note that the model is redrawn as shaded almost immediately.

19. Right-click on ⬡ (Adaptive Degradation) to open the Viewport Configuration dialog box in the *Display Performance* tab. In the *Adaptive Degradation* area, set *Delay Complete Viewport Redraw in* to **5.0** seconds. Click **OK** to close the dialog box

If the animated object is not selected, the modified keys (green) is not displayed in the timeline.

20. Click ▶. Let the animation play in the viewport until the complete model has been degraded to a wireframe model and then click ‖. Note that the model remains a wireframe for 5 seconds before it is redrawn as a shaded model.

21. Verify that the Dummy object is selected. To fix the pause at each revolution, right-click on the green key in the timeline at frame 99 and select **Dummy001: Z Rotation**, as shown in Figure 12–18. You can Pause the animation, if it is still running.

22. In the dialog box that opens, expand the *In* interpolation to display the interpolation tools flyout, as shown in Figure 12–19. Click ◢ (Linear interpolation).

Figure 12–18

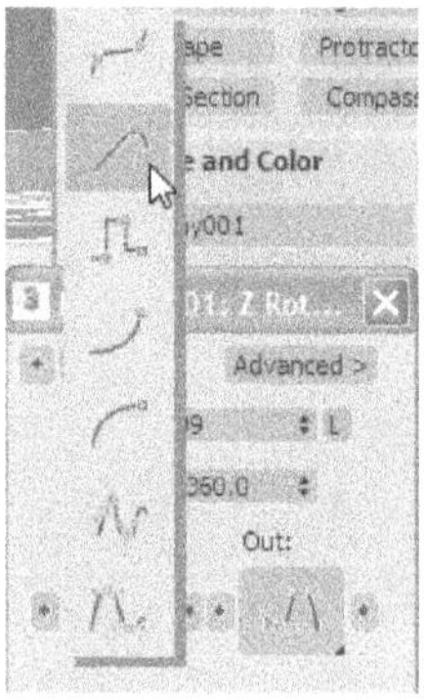

Figure 12–19

23. Similarly, change the *Out* interpolation to ◢ (Linear interpolation), as shown in Figure 12–20.
   • This sets the interpolation to Linear at frame 4 (99).

24. You will set the interpolation to Linear for the other three frames (0, 33, 66). In the upper left corner of the dialog box, click ◂ (left arrow) (as shown in Figure 12–20), to advance to key **1**, which is the key number. The *Time* displays as **1** and the *Value* displays as **0.0**, as shown in Figure 12–21. Set the *In* and *Out* Interpolation to **Linear** for key 1.

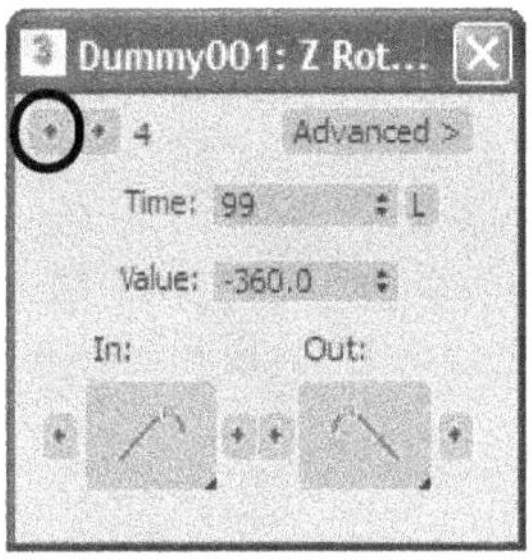

Figure 12–20

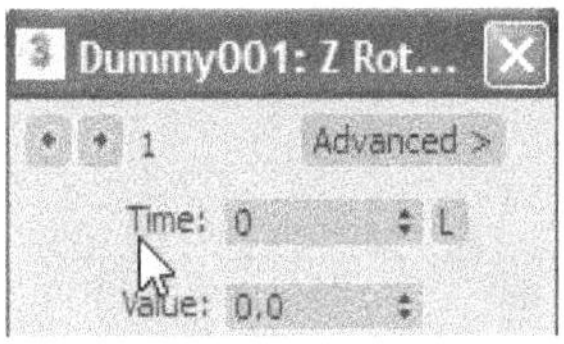

Figure 12–21

25. Repeat for the remaining keys **2** and **3** (frames 33 and 66), using (right arrow) to move to the required key. Close the dialog box.

26. Click to play the animation. It should loop without any pause.

27. Click to stop the animation.

28. In the Main toolbar, click (Track View) to open the Curve Editor. It displays the key window (right side) containing keys (small gray squares) and the linear slanting line (blue line) that displays the animation, as shown in Figure 12–22. You might have to zoom and pan inside the key window for the keys to display.

29. Hover the cursor over the Controller window (left side). It displays as a **Hand** icon. Hold and drag it up until the dummy object is listed with its applied Transforms, as shown in Figure 12–22.

30. In the Rotation node of the dummy object, select **X Rotation**, **Y Rotation**, and **Z Rotation**, if not already selected, as shown in Figure 12–22.

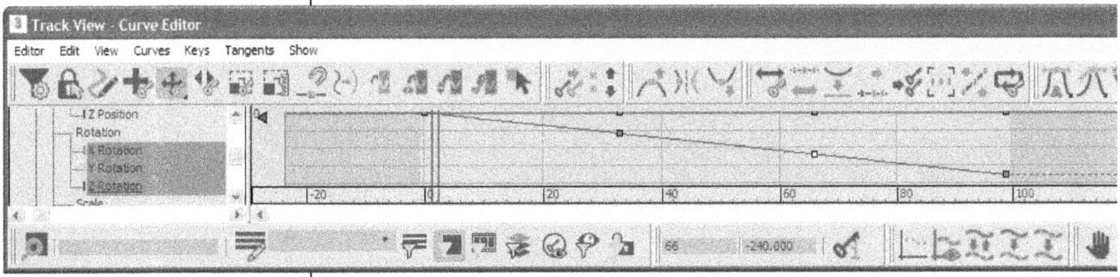

Figure 12–22

The selected key in the Curve Editor is represented as white in color.

31. In the Key window, on the blue line, select the key (small gray square) at frame 33. It displays in white indicating that it has been selected, as shown in Figure 12–23. In the Curve Editor toolbar, click ⬎ (Set Tangents to Slow).

- Note that a slight curve is added at this frame 33.

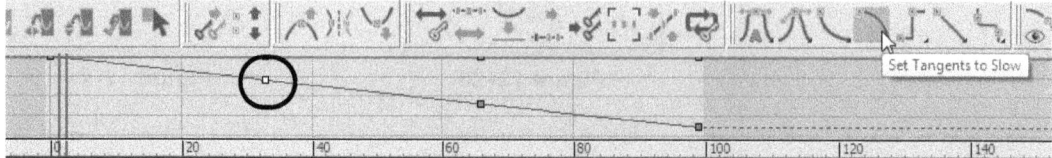

Figure 12–23

32. Click ▶ to play the animation and note that the animation slows down slightly when it reaches frame 33. Click ⏸ to stop the animation.

33. Add **Set Tangents to Slow** to the keys at frame 0, 66, and 99. Slight curves are added to these frames, as shown in Figure 12–24.

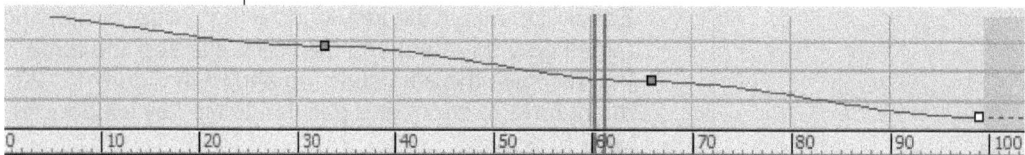

Figure 12–24

34. Click ▶ to play the animation and click ⏸ to stop.

35. Click **Close** at the left end of the Curve Editor toolbar to close the Curve Editor.

36. Save your work as **MyTurntable_Animation.max**.

Practice 12b

Keyframing a Camera Animation

Practice Objective

- Animate a camera to fly over the site.

In this practice you will add a camera to the scene and set the animation for the camera. You will then modify the animation by creating a new key and modifying the camera position at this key. This approach is similar to manually configuring a walkthrough or driveby animation.

You must set the paths to locate the External files and Xrefs used in the practice. If you have not done this already, return to **Chapter 1: Introduction to Autodesk 3ds Max** and complete Task 1 to Task 3 in **Practice 1a: Organizing Folders and Working with the Interface**. You only have to set the user paths once.

Estimated time for completion: 20 minutes

*If a dialog box opens prompting you about a File Load: Mismatch, click **OK** to accept the default values.*

*To display the toolbar, right-click anywhere in the blank area of the Main Toolbar and select **Render Shortcuts**.*

Task 1 - Save the Previous Render Options as a Preset.

1. Open **Presets.max**.

2. Before you configure the animation you should save all of the rendering settings for the still rendering. In the Render Shortcuts toolbar, in the Presets drop-down list, select **Save Preset**, as shown in Figure 12–25.

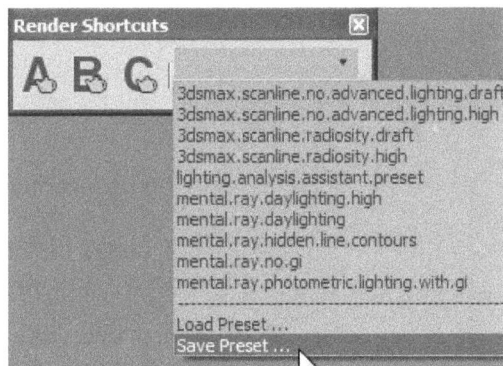

Figure 12–25

3. In the Render Presets Save dialog box, in the *File name* edit box, enter **Retail_Exterior_with_Background** to save your current render settings and click **Save**.

4. In the Select Preset Categories dialog box that opens, leave all of the preset categories as highlighted and click **Save**.

Task 2 - Configure the Camera Animation.

1. Maximize the **Top** viewport and zoom out till the building, parking lot, and the end of the road on the left side is displayed.

2. In the Command Panel>Create panel (➕), click

   📷 (Cameras). In the Object Type rollout, click **Target**. Create a camera and the target in the approximate positions, as shown in Figure 12–26.

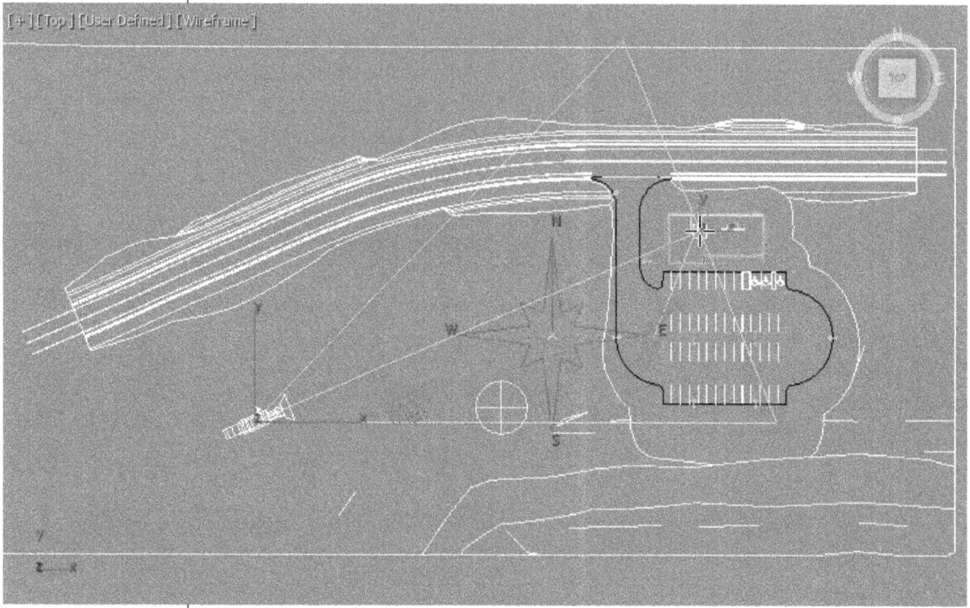

Figure 12–26

3. With the new camera selected, select the Modify panel

   (🖊). Leave the camera with the default parameters but change its name to **Camera - Flyover**.

4. Maximize to display all four viewports. Right-click in the **Front** viewport to activate it. Change that view to show the **Camera - Flyover** view (as shown in Figure 12–27) by selecting the **Front** Point of View label and selecting **Cameras>Camera – Flyover**.

Figure 12–27

5. In the Animation controls, click ![icon] (Time Configuration). In the *Frame Rate* area, select **Custom**, set *FPS* to **20**, and in the *Animation* area, set *End Time* to **0:30:0**, as shown in Figure 12–28. Verify that all of the other values match the values in Figure 12–28. Your animation is 30 seconds long and intended for desktop playback at 20 FPS. Click **OK**.

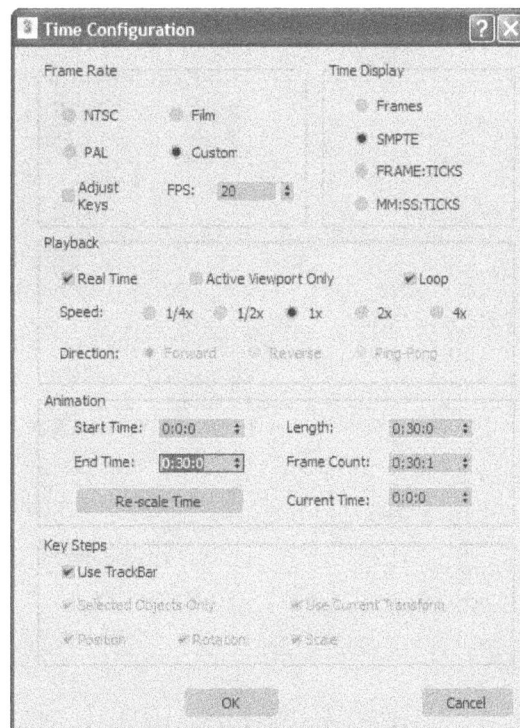

Figure 12–28

6. Verify that the Time Slider is currently located at time **0:0:0**, as shown in Figure 12–29.

Figure 12–29

7. Click **Auto Key**. It displays in red. Note that the Time Slider and outline of **Camera - Flyover** viewport also display in red.

8. Drag the Time Slider all of the way to the *end time* of **0:30:0**, as shown in Figure 12–30. Note the blue marker on the scale.

Figure 12–30

9. Verify that the **Camera - Flyover** object is selected (note the name in the Modifier Stack. Click (Select and Move) and in the Status Bar, in the *Transform Type-In* area enter **X = 300'0"**, **Y = 0'0"**, and **Z = 0'0"**, as shown in Figure 12–31. The roundoff error might change your X-coordinate to a value just below 300' (this often happens, but does not significantly affect this animation).

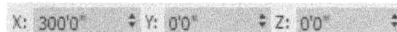

Figure 12–31

10. Click **Auto Key** again to toggle off Auto Key mode.

11. Slide (scrub) the Time Slider left and right and watch the camera move. With the **Camera - Flyover** viewport active, click to see a preview of the animation.

12. is changed while the animation is playing. Stop the animation by clicking . Move to the beginning by clicking .

*If you do not click **Auto Key** again to toggle the mode off, you create an unintended animation. The camera's animation keys are visible along the time slider as colored boxes (as long as the camera is selected). Right-click to modify or delete a key.*

Task 3 - Modify the Animation by Adding a New Key.

You are currently skimming at elevation 0 which makes you fly directly through some slopes of the terrain. To make the animation look more like a flyover you will add another key in the middle of the animation and raise the camera up in the Z-direction at that point.

1. Verify that the **Camera – Flyover** camera is selected.

2. Move the Time Slider to exactly **0:15:0** (the midpoint of the animation) and click ⊕ (Set Keys). A new key is created at this point.

3. In the Time Slider, right-click on this new key and select **Camera – Flyover: Z Position**. Set the *Value* to **30'0"**, press <Enter> and close the dialog box.

4. Click |◄◄ to return to the beginning and click ▶ to preview the animation. Note the vertical change has been adjusted but now at around the midpoint the camera is too close to the building. You will pull the camera back from the building at the midpoint. Stop the animation by clicking ❚❚

5. Drag the Time Slider to exactly **0:15:0** and click **Auto Key**.

6. Right-click in the **Top** viewport and verify that the **Camera – Flyover** camera is still selected (if not, then select it). Click ⊕ (Select and Move) and in the Status Bar, in the *Transform Type-In* area, set the following, as shown in Figure 12–32:
   * *X:* **15'0"**
   * *Y:* **-120'0"**
   * *Z:* **30'0"**

This moves the **Camera – Flyover** camera away from the building. Since this is done in **AutoKey** mode the camera's existing key at 0:15:0 is updated with this new position.

If done without being in Auto Key mode you would move the camera at frame 0 and at all other keys.

X: 15'0" ⬍ Y: -120'0" ⬍ Z: 30'0" ⬍

Figure 12–32

7. Click **Auto Key** to toggle it off. Click ⏮ to return to the beginning and click ▶ to preview the animation. Stop the animation by clicking ⏸.

8. Click ⚙ (Render Setup) to open the Render Setup dialog box. In the *Common* tab, in the Common Parameters rollout, *Output Size* area, set *Width* to **300** and press <Enter>, as shown in Figure 12–33. With the aspect ratio locked at 1.6 a rendering *Height* of **188** is automatically calculated.

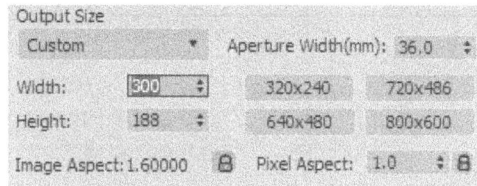

Output Size

Custom ▼	Aperture Width(mm):	36.0 ⬍
Width: 300 ⬍	320x240	720x486
Height: 188 ⬍	640x480	800x600
Image Aspect: 1.60000 🔒	Pixel Aspect: 1.0 ⬍ 🔒	

Figure 12–33

9. In the *Time Output* area select **Active Time Segment** (entire animation). Normally you select a filename and location to render to.

10. Near the top of the dialog box, in the Preset drop-down menu, select **Save Preset** and save the rendering settings as **RetailExteriorAnimation.rps**. Save all preset categories.

11. Save the file as **MyCameraAnimationFlyover.max**.

Practice 12c

Creating a Walkthrough Animation

Practice Objective

- Animate a camera object along a path in a scene.

Estimated time for completion: 10 minutes

In this practice you will merge a .MAX file, which has a hemispherical dome with a simple sky texture and ground color applied to be used as a background for the current scene. You will also merge a file in which the path has been created.

You must set the paths to locate the External files and Xrefs used in the practice. If you have not done this already, return to **Chapter 1: Introduction to Autodesk 3ds Max** and complete Task 1 to Task 3 in **Practice 1a: Organizing Folders and Working with the Interface**. You only have to set the user paths once.

*If a dialog box opens prompting you about a File Load: Mismatch, click **OK** to accept the default values.*

1. Open **Camera Animations.max**.

2. In the **Application Menu>Import**, select **Merge**. In the dialog box, select **Sky and Ground Dome.max** from your practice files folder. Click **Open**.

3. In the Merge dialog box, select **Sky and Ground Dome** and click **OK**.
   - The Dome object has been turned inside-out by the normal modifier so that in single-sided rendering mode its surfaces can only be seen from the inside. This enables the dome to be seen in the renderings when a camera is inside the dome.

4. In the **Application Menu>Import>Merge,** select **Animation Path.max**. Click **Open**.

5. In the Merge dialog box, select **Animation Path 3D** and click **OK**. This 3D path is located along the proposed ground surface of the access road, as shown in Figure 12–34.

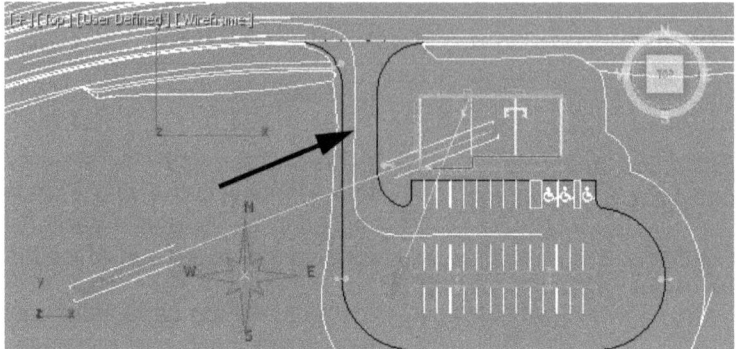

Figure 12–34

6. Maximize the **Top** viewport.

7. Using the Scene Explorer, select the object group **_Site Model** (▪ (Display None) and ▣ (Display Groups)).

8. Right-click in the viewport and select **Freeze Selection** in the quad menu. The Site model geometry displays in a dull gray color and you can easily see the blue path that travels along the street. If required, use **Pan** to display the complete path in the viewport.

9. In the Command Panel>Create panel (+), click ▣ (Cameras). In the Object Type rollout, click **Target**. Click near the left end of the path to place the camera, drag to the center of the building and release to set the target, as shown in Figure 12–35. In the Name and Color edit box, enter the name of the camera as **Walkthrough_Cam01**.

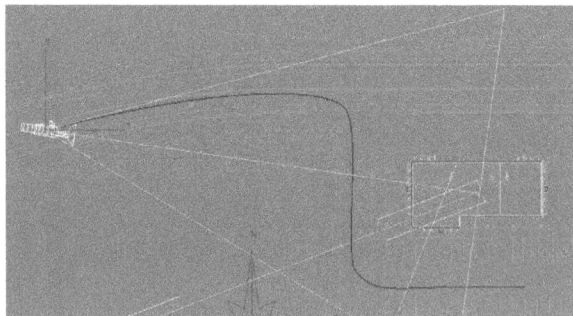

Figure 12–35

10. In the viewport, zoom into the Camera object. Click in the viewport to clear any selection.

11. In the Command Panel>Create panel (✛), click

 ◢ (Helpers). Click **Dummy**.

If you were flying a camera through the interior of a design you would align the camera to the dummy at this point. In this animation it is not required for this type of exterior flyby.

12. Click and drag to create the Dummy object around the Camera by starting at the beginning of the animation path spline, as shown in Figure 12–36.

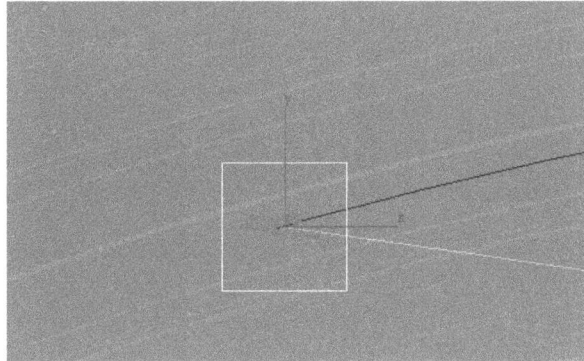

Figure 12–36

13. In the Main Toolbar, click 🔗 (Select and Link).

14. In the viewport, select and hold the newly created **Walkthrough_Cam01** object to define it as the child object. Drag the cursor to the outline of the **Dummy**. A dotted line displays between the cursor and the object, and the dummy object turns yellow, as shown in Figure 12–37. Release to link the camera to the **Dummy**.

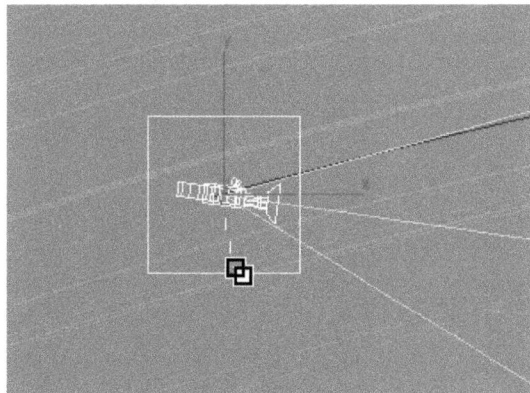

Figure 12–37

15. To check it, in the Main Toolbar, click ⊕ and move the Dummy. You should see the Camera move with it. This confirms that the linkage is correct. Undo the move.

When you hover the cursor over the path, it should turn yellow to show that it is going to be selected. Once it turns yellow, click to select it.

16. Now you will constrain the dummy to the path. Select the Dummy object in the viewport and select **Animation> Constraints>Path Constraint**. The cursor is connected with a dotted line to the pivot point of the Dummy object. Click anywhere over the blue spline (Animation Path 3D) to select it as the animation path, as shown in Figure 12–38. The pivot point of the dummy automatically shifts to coincide with the start point of the path.

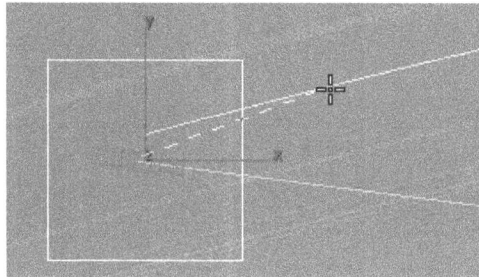

Figure 12–38

17. Zoom out till the entire blue path is displayed. Click ▶ to play the animation. The Dummy and the camera animates along the path, as shown in Figure 12–39. Click ⏸ to stop the animation.

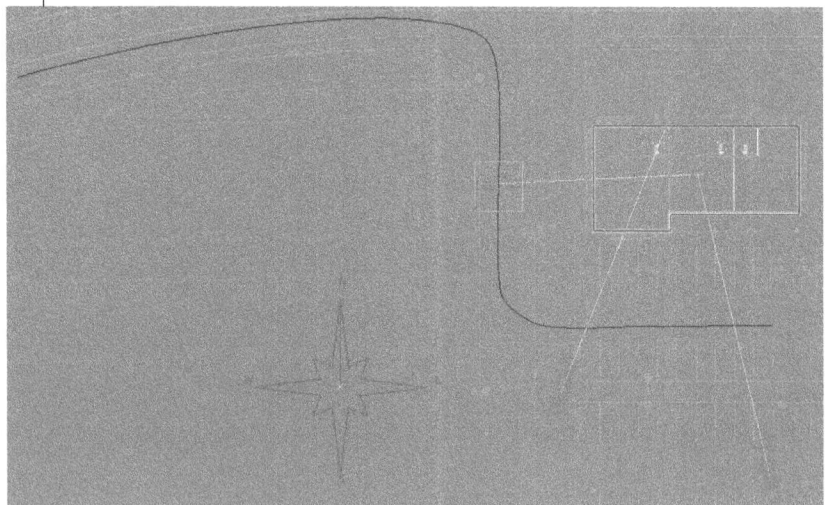

Figure 12–39

18. Maximize to display all four viewports. Activate the **Camera01** viewport and change it to the **Walkthrough_Cam01** viewport (select the **POV** label and select **Cameras>Walkthrough_Cam01**).

19. Click ▶ to play the animation. The animation might be improved if the camera was higher off the ground.

20. Click |◀◀ to go to the start of the animation, at frame zero.

Use the Scene Explorer, use ◼ (Display Cameras) and select Walkthrough_Cam01, child of Dummy001.

21. Since the Camera is a child of the Dummy you can add transforms to the Camera without affecting the Dummy's animation. Select **Walkthrough_Cam01.Target** object and in the Modify panel rename it as **Camera_Flyby**.

22. With the **Camera_Flyby** object selected, in the Main Toolbar, right-click on ✛ (Select and Move) to open the Move Transform Type-In dialog box.

23. In the Absolute:World, change the Z-value to **6'0"**. Close the dialog box. Since **Auto Key** is off this lifts the Camera for the entire animation.

24. Play the animation in the **Camera_Flyby** viewport. Stop the animation.

25. Right-click on the viewport and select **Unfreeze All**. The Site model is displayed with full color. Play the animation again.

26. Save your work as **MyCameraAnimationFlyby.max**.

12.3 Animation Output

There are two strategies for creating animation output:

* Render directly to a single, composite animation file such as a .MOV or .AVI. This is generally recommended for previews.

* Render each still image (such as .PNG, .JPEG, .BMP, .TIFF, etc.) and later combine the stills into a composite animation using the Autodesk 3ds Max RAM Player, Video Post, or 3rd party post-production software.

You can select an animation output option in the Render Output File dialog box. To open this dialog box, open the Render Setup dialog box and expand the Common Parameters rollout in the *Common* tab. In the *Render Output* area, click **Files...**, as shown in Figure 12–40.

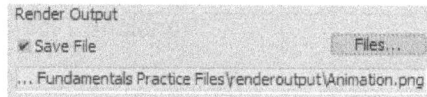

Figure 12–40

The Render Output File dialog box opens. In the Save as type drop-down list (shown in Figure 12–41), you can select to render to a single, compressed animation file (.MOV or .AVI) or to individual frames (such as .PNG, .JPEG, .BMP, .TIFF, etc.). If you select to render as individual frames, you need to provide the name once and the software automatically creates individual files for each frame, which are numbered sequentially.

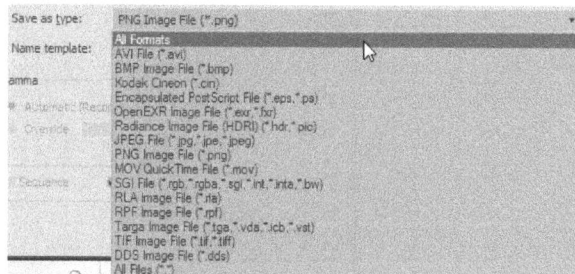

Figure 12–41

Assembling Animations

It is recommended to render files individually and then combine them into an animation. The Autodesk 3ds Max RAM player is a utility used for comparing two images side-by-side, or for previewing and compiling animations.

The RAM player (shown in Figure 12–42) can be opened in the menu bar by selecting **Rendering>Compare Media in RAM Player**.

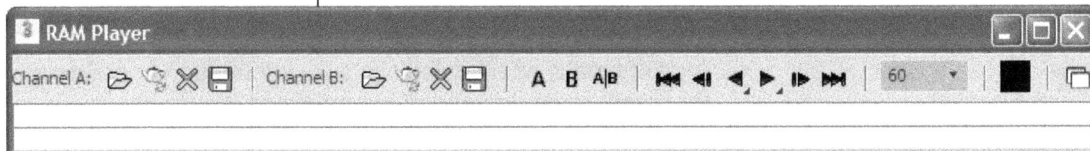

Figure 12–42

Click (Open Channel A) to open the Open File dialog box, shown in Figure 12–43. Enter the path and the first filename of the sequentially numbered image files. Selecting the **Sequence** option opens all of the files, which are named as specified in the *File name* field.

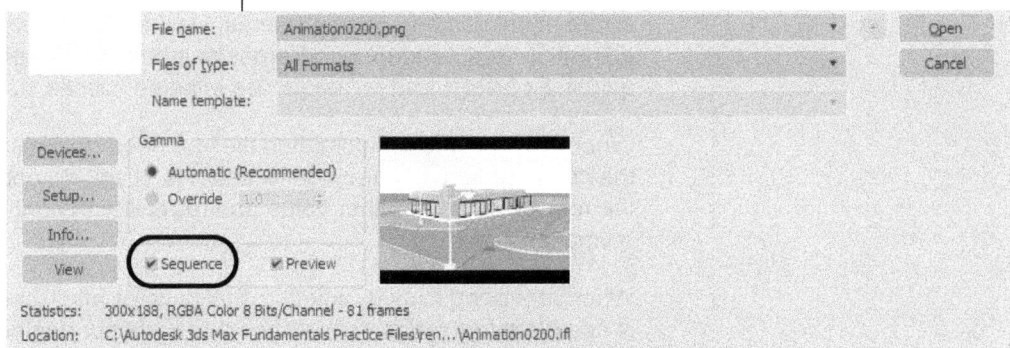

Figure 12–43

An image file list (.IFL) is an ASCII list of which files were used and in which order.

Once you open the specified image file, the Image File List Control dialog box opens (as shown in Figure 12–44), which displays the folder where the image file list (.IFL) is being created. The dialog box also provides you with options to limit the animation to certain frames.

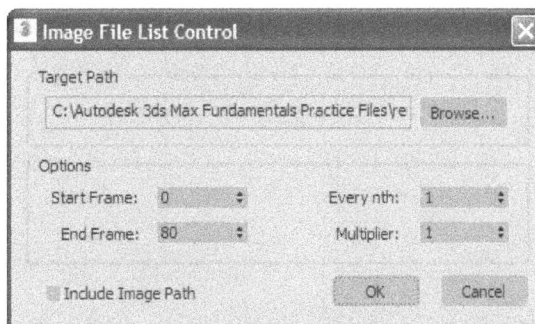

Figure 12–44

Use the various playback options in the RAM Player to play the created animation.

Rendering files individually and then combining them into an animation later has various advantages, such as:

- A lot of time is spent calculating the information to create a rendered frame. Instead of compressing the frames, save them as a sequence of still images for access to all of the information later.

- When rendering individual frames, all of the previously saved frames remain available after a catastrophic error such as a system crash, disc error, power outage, etc. Therefore, you only need to re-render the missing frames required to complete your animation.

- When rendering animations, material, lighting or geometry, errors might occur in certain frames. Unlike compressed animation files, rendering to frames enables you to easily adjust, fix errors, and re-render the affected frames.

- When rendering to an animation file you need to first select the compression or video quality settings. If you do not like the results, select another value and re-render the entire animation.

- When rendering to stills, select a quality value after rendering is complete to try different settings and save out another composite file from the same still renderings.

- Rendering to a still image file format that supports an alpha channel (transparency) enables you to use a compositing package such as Combustion or Adobe After Effects for post-production processing and assembly.

Practice 12d	# Creating Animation Output

Practice Objective

- Create an animation preview and create single-frame file images.

In this practice you create single-frame file images at 5 frame intervals and save them as .PNG file format. You will then assemble the individual frame images to create a movie using the RAM Player.

Estimated time for completion: 15 minutes

You must set the paths to locate the External files and Xrefs used in the practice. If you have not done this already, return to **Chapter 1: Introduction to Autodesk 3ds Max** and complete Task 1 to Task 3 in **Practice 1a: Organizing Folders and Working with the Interface**. You only have to set the user paths once.

Task 1 - Create Still Frames.

If a dialog box opens prompting you about a File Load: Mismatch, click OK to accept the default values.

1. Open **Camera_Animation_Start_Render.max**.

2. Make the **Camera - Flyover** viewport active.

3. Click (Time Configuration) to open the Time Configuration dialog box. Change the *Time Display* to **Frames**.

4. In the *Animation* area, note that the *End Time* is set to **600** indicating that you have a 600 frame animation. Click **OK**.

5. Note that the *Time slider* should display as **0/600**, but it does not. Open the Time Configuration dialog box again ( ) and click **Re-scale Time** in the *Animation* area. The Re-scale Time dialog box opens. Click **OK** in both of the dialog boxes, and note that the *Time slider* is updated to display **0/600.**

*Rendering 600 frames might take a long time. You can select a shorter range and set the **Every Nth Frame** option to make it manageable.*

6. Click (Render Setup) to open the Render Setup dialog box. In the *Common* tab, verify that the Common Parameters rollout is expanded and do the following, as shown in Figure 12–45:

   - In the *Time Output* area, select **Range**.
   - Set a *Range* of **200** to **600**.
   - Set *Every Nth Frame* to **5**.

   This renders every 5th frame between 200 and 600, which is a total of 81 frames of animation.

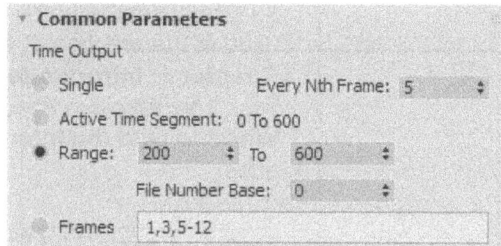

Figure 12–45

In the Render Output File dialog box, in the Save as type drop-down list, you can select to render to a single, compressed animation file (.MOV, .AVI), or to individual frames. If you select a single-frame file format (such as .PNG, .JPEG, .BMP, .TIFF, etc.), you will then automatically create individual files for each frame, numbered sequentially.

7. In the *Render Output* area, click **Files...**.

8. The Render Output File dialog box opens. Locate the ...\renderings folder. Set the *Save as type* to **PNG Image File (*.png)**, and in the *File name* enter the name **Animation**. Click **Save**.

9. In the PNG Configuration dialog box, select **RGB 24 bit** and leave **Alpha channel** enabled. Click **OK**.

10. In the Render Setup dialog box, click **Render** to begin creating individual renderings for each frame.

11. The Rendered Frame Window opens with each frame being rendered and the Rendering dialog box opens (as shown in Figure 12–46), displaying information about the renderings, number of files to be rendered, estimate of the remaining rendering time, render settings, etc.

    - It might take some time to complete the 81 frames of the animation, so you can stop the process with some frames completed or let it continue until all of the frames have completed.

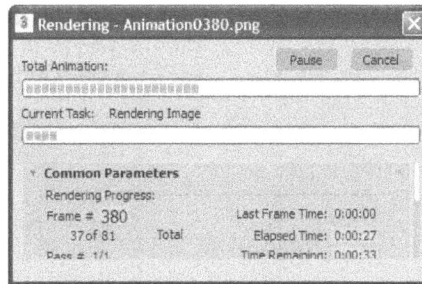

Figure 12–46

12. Close the Rendered Frame Window and Render Setup dialog box.

Task 2 - Assemble the Final Animation.

It is called a RAM player because it loads these images into RAM.

1. In the menu bar, select **Rendering>Compare Media in RAM Player** to open the RAM player. The RAM player is a utility used for comparing two images side-by-side or previewing and compiling animations.

2. In the *Channel A* area, click ☞ (Open Channel A), as shown in Figure 12–47.

Figure 12–47

3. In the Open File, Channel A dialog box, browse to the *...\renderings* folder. Select **Animation0200.png** and verify that **Sequence** is enabled, as shown in Figure 12–48. Click **Open**.

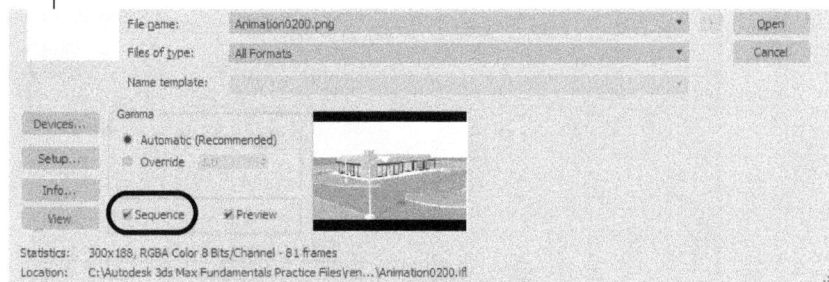

Figure 12–48

- The **Sequence** option enables the system to open all of the PNGs named **Animation*.png**.

4. The Image File List Control dialog box opens, as shown in Figure 12–49. It displays the folder where the image file list (.IFL) is being created. Click **OK**.

Figure 12–49

5. The RAM Player Configuration dialog box opens. It enables you to change the image size or aspect ratio on import, and to limit the number of frames to use and the maximum amount of RAM you want to dedicate to this process. Click **OK**.

6. After the animation has loaded into the RAM player you can play back the animation at different frame rates by selecting a number in the drop-down list, as shown in Figure 12–50.

    Click ▶ (Playback Forward) to play the animation. Select different frame rates and play the animation to see the effect.

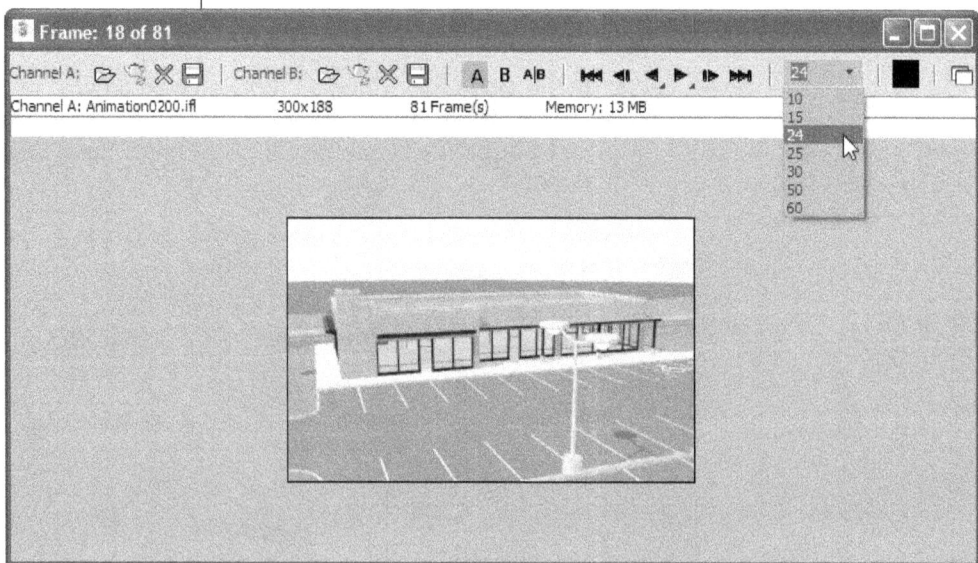

Figure 12–50

7. To save a desktop animation file, click ⊟ (Save Channel A).

8. In the Save File, Channel A dialog box, browse to the ...\renderings folder. Set *Save as type* to **AVI File (*.avi)**. Save the animation as **FlybyAnimation**.

9. In the AVI File Compression Setup dialog box, for the *Compressor*, select **MJPEG Compressor**, set the *Quality* to **60**, and click **OK**.

10. Save your work as **MyCameraAnimation.max**.

11. Navigate to your renderings folder and play **Flyby Animation.avi** file to watch the animation.

If the quality of the animation is not as required, you could try other methods or qualities until you have an acceptable result.

Chapter Review Questions

1. Activating (toggling on) which option in the Animation Controls changes **Previous**, **Play**, **Next Frame** ( ) to **Previous**, **Play**, and **Next Keyframe** ( )?

   a. **Auto Key** animation mode

   b. **Set Key** animation mode

   c. (Key Mode)

   d. (Set Keys)

2. A frame rate of 30 frames per second (FPS) is best suited for which medium?

   a. NTSC

   b. PAL

   c. Film

   d. Custom

3. When animation times are changed in the *Animation* area in the Time Configuration dialog box, the existing keys automatically scale to the new time.

   a. True

   b. False

4. Which category in the Create panel (+) contains **Dummy** as its Object Type?

   a. (Geometry)

   b. (Shapes)

   c. (Cameras)

   d. (Helpers)

5. If you render each still image (such as .PNG, .JPEG, etc.), which utility can you use to combine the stills into a composite animation?

   a. Media Player

   b. RAM Player

   c. Batch Render

   d. Panorama Exporter

Command Summary

Button	Command	Location
Auto Key	Auto Key animation mode	• Animation Controls Toolbar
	Cameras	• Command Panel: *Create* panel • Create: Cameras
	Curve Editor	• Main Toolbar • Graph Editors: Track View - Curve Editor
	Default In/Out Tangents for New Keys	• Animation Controls Toolbar
N/A	Dope Sheet	• Graph Editors: Track View - Dope Sheet
	Go to End	• Animation Controls Toolbar
	Go to Start	• Animation Controls Toolbar
	Helpers	• Command Panel: *Create* panel
	Key Mode	• Animation Controls Toolbar
	Mini Curve Editor	• Track bar
	Previous, Play, Next Frame	• Animation Controls Toolbar
	Progressive Display	• Status Bar
	Render Setup	• Main Toolbar • Rendering: Render Setup
	Select and Link	• Main Toolbar
Set Key	Set Key animation mode	• Animation Controls Toolbar
	Set Keys	• Animation Controls Toolbar
	Time Configuration	• Animation Controls Toolbar

Optional Topics

There are some additional tools available in the Autodesk® 3ds Max® software that you can use when creating and rendering models. This appendix provides details about several additional tools and commands.

Learning Objectives in this Appendix

- Access Autodesk 3ds Max Help and use the various Help tools.
- Work with Architectural materials and the Compact Material Editor.
- Replace objects in a scene with AutoCAD® blocks or other Autodesk 3ds Max objects.
- Create a Lighting Analysis using the Lighting Analysis Assistant.
- Create hierarchies by collecting objects together with parent/child relationship.
- Customize the user interface elements.

A.1 Getting Help with Autodesk 3ds Max

The Help menu contains an extensive list of help options, which are organized as submenus so that finding information is easy. Some of the available help options are as follows:

You can also press <F1> or select Help>Autodesk 3ds Max Help.

1. The **Autodesk 3ds Max Help** is robust, well illustrated, and often the fastest way to find what an option or parameter controls and how to use it. This help is in the form of HTML files at autodesk.com website. There are a variety of ways to access this help. In the InfoCenter, click (?) or expand

   ▼ and select **3ds Max Help**.

2. The **Autodesk 3ds Max Tutorials** (select **Help>Tutorials**) offer thorough and comprehensive learning materials to get you started with almost all of the features in the Autodesk 3ds Max software. The tutorials are in the HTML format at autodesk.com website. You can download the Tutorials and the files required for the tutorials from http://www.autodesk.com/3dsmax-tutorials-scene-files-2016. Install the files on your local hard drive for use as you are completing the tutorials.

3. **3ds Max Communities:** Select **Help>3ds Max Communities>AREA Product Community** and **AREA Discussion Forums** provides a single location for users to closely interact. In addition to the Autodesk 3ds Max forum, the AREA contains forums for other entertainment products, such as Mudbox, Motionbuilder, FBX, Maya.

4. **3ds Max Services and Support**: Select **Help>3ds Max Services and Support>SupportCenter** to connect to the support site. It has many frequently updated technical support articles available. There might also be documents describing how to fix commonly occurring problem. Autodesk Subscription customers also have access to email support directly from Autodesk. You can also connect with other Autodesk 3ds Max users and share information using the Autodesk 3ds Max Facebook page.

5. **3ds Max Resources and Tools:** Select **Help>3ds Max Resources and Tools**, as shown in Figure A–1 to access White Papers, the downloadable Vegetation Library, a Keyboard Shortcut Map, etc.

6. **Feedback:** The Autodesk 3ds Max software provides various **Speak Back** options, as shown in Figure A–2. Selecting an option connects you to web pages for reporting a bug in the software or making a request for small enhancements and new features. It also enables you to activate the Desktop Analytics Program.

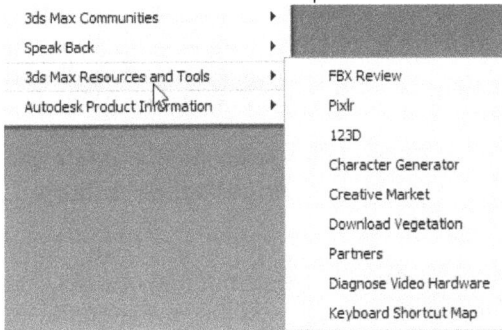

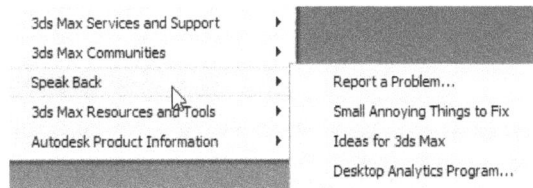

| Figure A–1 | Figure A–2 |

7. **Other web communities:** There is a lot of information available on the Internet for the Autodesk 3ds Max software. Simple keyword searches can quickly find other sites that provide tutorials and helpful tips.

A.2 Compact Material Editor

- The Autodesk 3ds Max software contains two editors for working with materials:

    - Slate Material Editor: Used to design and build materials where the material components are displayed graphically.

    - Compact Material Editor: Used when the materials have already been created and you just need to apply them.

- The Compact Material Editor can be opened by clicking

    ▣ (Compact Material Editor) in the Main Toolbar (Material Editor flyout), or by selecting **Rendering>Material Editor> Compact Material Editor**.

You can also use

✐ (Pick Material from Object) in the Material Editor and select the object in the viewport.

- It is possible to have a material in the scene that has not been loaded into the editor. You can add a scene material to

    the editor by using ▦ (Get Material).

- **Options>Options…** in the Material Editor offers controls that can help speed up performance when several large or complex materials are present in the editor.

- A material shown in a sample slot is previewed as applied to a 3D object. A map previewed in a sample slot is shown as a flat 2D rectangle.

*It is recommended that the sample material contain a scene material for the **Select by Material** option to be available. The Highlight Assets in ATS dialog is available if the material contains a map.*

- Figure A–3 shows the various options available in the shortcut menu. The options enable you to copy the materials from one slot to another, rotating and resetting the rotation of the material sample, and set the number of slots.

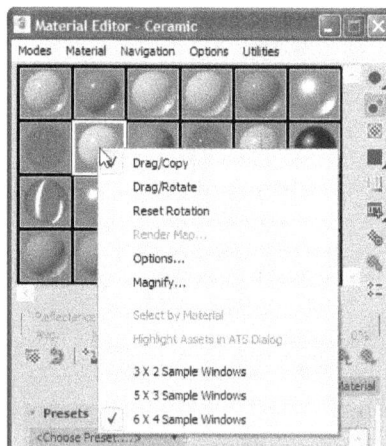

Figure A–3

- The Material Editor toolbars (shown in Figure A–4) work in the same way as the tools present in the Slate Material Editor.

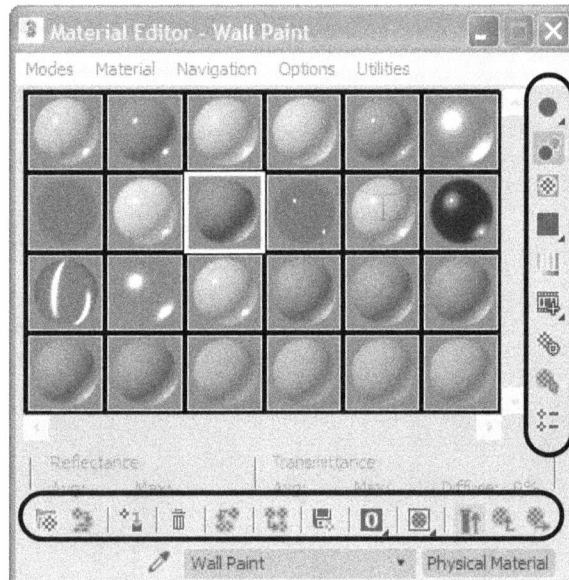

Figure A–4

The Material/Map Browser is embedded in the Slate Material Editor.

*You can also open the Material/Map Browser independently by selecting **Rendering> Material/Map Browser** in the menu bar.*

- The Material/Map Browser can be accessed by clicking

  ![icon] (Get Material). Once you have located a required material in the browser, drag it from the browser to a scene object or to a sample slot in the Material Editor.

- Previews of the materials can be shown in a list, or as buttons. The display can be changed in the right-click menu, as shown in Figure A–5.

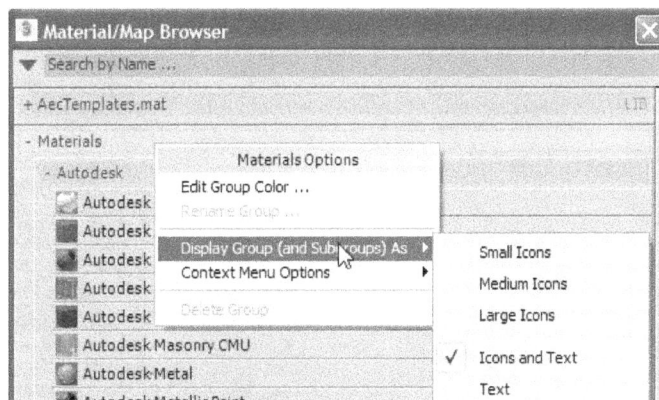

Figure A–5

A.3 Architectural Materials

Materials assigned in other software legacy translate into the Autodesk 3ds Max software as Architectural materials. All materials now import as Autodesk Materials.

Architectural materials offer a simplified interface over Standard materials because they have limited control (directly selecting a shader, some specular parameters, etc.). Architectural materials offer additional, built-in controls for translucency, refraction, and global illumination renderers.

Architectural Material Parameters

Architectural materials use Templates to assign shaders, which are predefined with many common material types (such as metals, paint, plastic, masonry, etc.). Selecting a template automatically populates other values in the Physical Qualities rollout, as shown in Figure A–6.

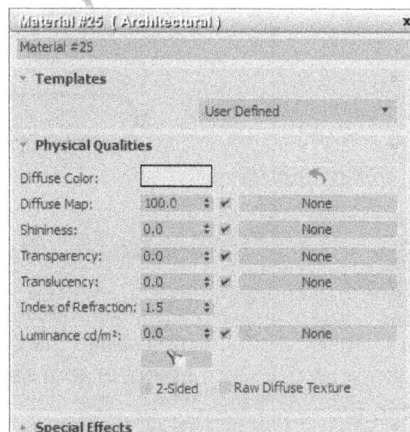

Figure A–6

Diffuse Color/ Diffuse Map	Located at the top of the Physical Qualities rollout, which are identical to those for Standard materials.
Shininess	Similar controls to the Specular Level of Standard materials. Architectural material highlights are generated through the **Shininess** and **Index of Refraction** parameters.
Transparency	The overall percentage that a material is transparent. For example, clear glass materials could be assigned transparencies between 90 and 100%.
Translucency	A measure of how much light is scattered as it passes through the object.
Index of Refraction (IOR)	Controls refraction and reflection. Typical values include 1.0 for air (effectively no refractive distortion), 1.33 for water, 1.5-1.7 for thick glass, and 2.5 for diamond.

Luminance	The amount of physically-based light the material emits. Unlike the Self-Illumination parameter of Standard materials, objects assigned Architectural materials can actually add light to scenes through this parameter as if they were light objects. (For example, illuminated materials are often used to represent neon tubes.)
Bump Maps	Can be assigned in the Special Effects rollout.

Architectural materials do not have Ambient Color controls because these materials are designed to work with radiosity, which directly calculates ambient illumination.

Architectural materials indicate when a reflectance value is out-of-range by colorizing the value in the Material Editor (based on the selected material template). Values that are too low are shown in blue and those that are too high are shown in red. Reflectance values that are out-of-range can be adjusted in a number of ways:

- When using a simple diffuse color (no diffuse image map), lower the overall value (V) of the color.

- The reflectance of Architectural materials can be reduced by entering a lower value for the *Reflectance Scale* in the Advanced Lighting Override rollout, as shown in Figure A–7.

- To lower reflectance when using a diffuse color map with Standard materials, assign the diffuse color to black and enter a value less than 100% for the diffuse color map. A value such as 95%, would reduce the brightness of the map by approximately 5%, as shown in Figure A–8.

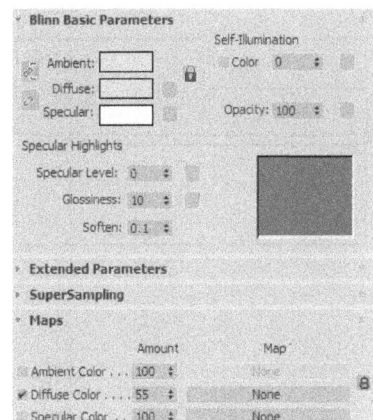

Figure A–7   Figure A–8

Hint: Converting Materials

You can manually convert the Architectural materials to Arch & Design materials by rebuilding them individually.

A.4 Object Substitution

Linked or imported AutoCAD Blocks can be automatically replaced with 3D objects using the **Substitute** modifier.

- The Objects to be replaced (such as linked AutoCAD blocks) should be located with the correct 3D coordinates (including elevation) and rotation for the replacing object.

- The substituting object needs to be one object. For example, the light pole could be used if it was collapsed to a single mesh object. (To do so, right-click on the base object in the Modifier Stack and select **Convert to Editable Poly or Mesh**. Then use the object's **Attach** in the Command Panel to join the other parts to the mesh. Materials and mapping can be preserved during this operation).

- The substitute object can be present in the same scene as the object to be replaced or it can be XRefed in from another scene.

- Although this is commonly used for AutoCAD blocks, other Autodesk 3ds Max objects can be substituted as well with this modifier.

Practice A1

Substituting the Parking Lot Light Poles

Practice Objective

* Replace 2D symbol based objects with 3D photorealistic object blocks.

Estimated time for completion: 10 minutes

In this practice you will substitute completed 3D light pole objects for 2D blocks in a scene using the **Substitute** modifier.

You must set the paths to locate the External files and Xrefs used in the practice. If you have not done this already, return to **Chapter 1: Introduction to Autodesk 3ds Max** and complete Task 1 to Task 3 in **Practice 1a: Organizing Folders and Working with the Interface**. You only have to set the user paths once.

*If a dialog box opens prompting you about a File Load: Mismatch, click **OK** to accept the default values.*

1. Open **Substitution_Start.max**.

2. Switch the viewport to **Wireframe shading** by pressing <F3>.

3. Zoom out on the area of the parking lot to display the flat, circular, and square symbols joined by a line (green), as shown in Figure A–9. These objects in the parking area are 2D light pole blocks. The parking lot surface has been hidden so that you can see the lamp symbols.

Figure A–9

4. In the Scene Explorer, use ■ (Display None)> ▣ (Display Shapes) and expand any one of **Block:Light Pole - Single**. Select the **Layer:LIGHTPOLE_SINGLE**, as shown in Figure A–10.

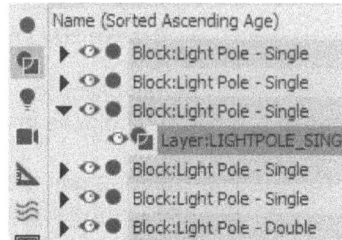

Figure A–10

5. In the Command Panel, select the Modify panel ( ) and then select **Substitute** in the Modifier List. Only one 2D object is required to be selected because AutoCAD blocks link in as instances of each other, as indicated by the bold type in the Modifier Stack, as shown in Figure A–11.

6. Verify that the **Substitute** parameters match the parameters, as shown in Figure A–12 (default). Click **Select XRef Object...**.

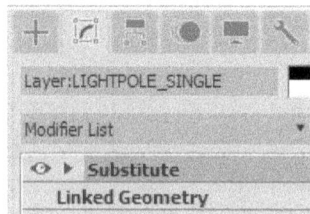

Figure A–11

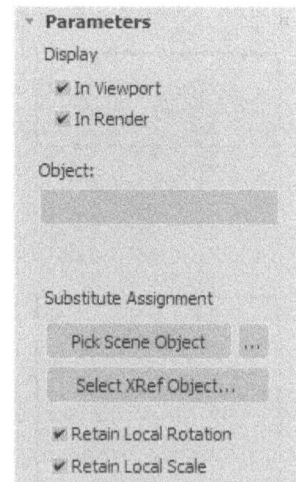

Figure A–12

7. In the Open File dialog box, open the source file, **Light Poles for Substitution.max** from your practice files folder.

8. In the XRef Merge dialog box, select the object named **LP_Single** and click **OK**.

9. In the Warning message dialog box, select **Apply to All Duplicates** to keep both materials, and click **Auto-Rename Merged Material**.

10. In the Substitution Question dialog box, click **Yes** to enable the substitute object's material to be used in this scene. Note that the 2D light pole blocks are replaced by the 3D single lightpole objects.

11. Repeat this process for one of the **Layer:LIGHTPOLE_ DOUBLE** objects (expand **Block:Light Pole - Double**), substituting **LP_Double** from **Light Poles for Substitution.max**.

12. In the viewport, change to **High Quality** in the *Shading Viewport* and **Default Shading** in the *Per-View Preference* label menu. Both the single light poles and double light poles are displayed, as shown in Figure A–13.

    • The **Substitute** modifier enables you to take a 2D symbol on an instanced object and replace it with a 3D photorealistic one several times in a scene, thus saving memory.

Figure A–13

13. Save your work as **MyCivilBaseSubstitution.max**.

A.5 Lighting Analysis

*The **NVIDIA mental ray** is required to be the active renderer for Lighting Analysis. It also requires mental ray materials with physically correct settings.*

In the Quick Access Toolbar, select Default with Enhanced Menus in the Workspaces drop-down list.

The Autodesk 3ds Max software can create a lighting analysis rendering colorized by illumination or luminance values. The lighting analysis can be done using mental ray to physically correct lights and materials. Light meter objects can be placed in the scene to measure lighting. All of this is controlled using the Lighting Analysis Assistant dialog box, as shown in Figure A–14, (**Enhanced Menu Bar>Lighting Analysis>Lighting Analysis Assistant**).

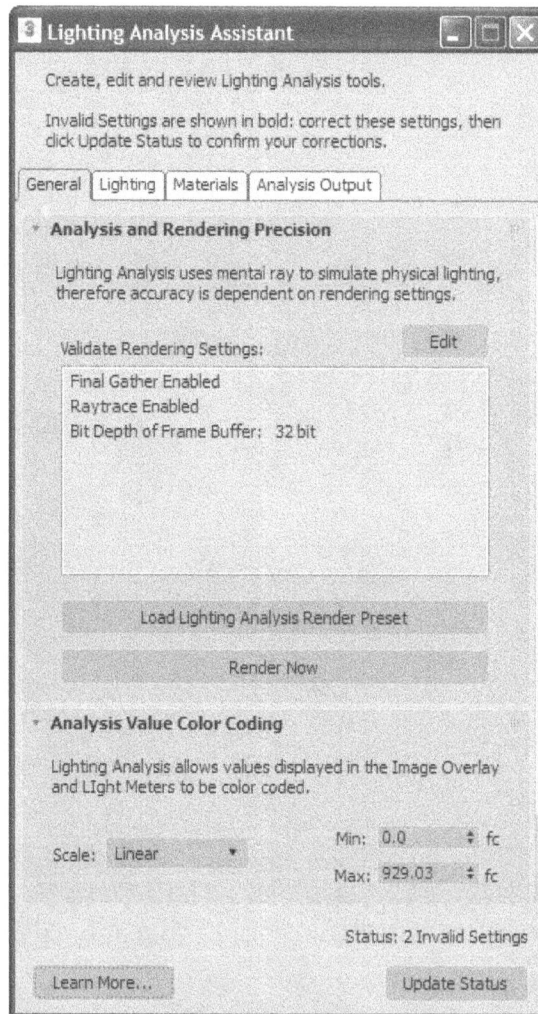

Figure A–14

There are four tabs in the Lighting Analysis Assistant dialog box: *General*, *Lighting*, *Materials*, and *Analysis Output*.

General Tab

The *General* tab validates that the rendering settings are correct. You must have Final Gather and Raytrace enabled and Bit Depth must be set to 32 bit. If any of these settings are incorrect, they are flagged in the Analysis and Rendering Precision rollout and must be corrected by recalculating the validation/ approval.

The Analysis Value Color Coding rollout enables you to adjust the color values displayed in the viewport, as shown in Figure A–15. By lowering the maximum value you can quickly find a pleasing range of colors for your output.

Figure A–15

Lighting Tab

In the *Lighting* tab (shown in Figure A–16), you can create mr Daylight System if one does not exist. You also have quick access to the settings for the sun/sky and daylight positions. If you are doing artificial light calculations (interiors) you can also create photometric lights from here. This dialog box checks for lights that have invalid settings and enables you to select and correct them.

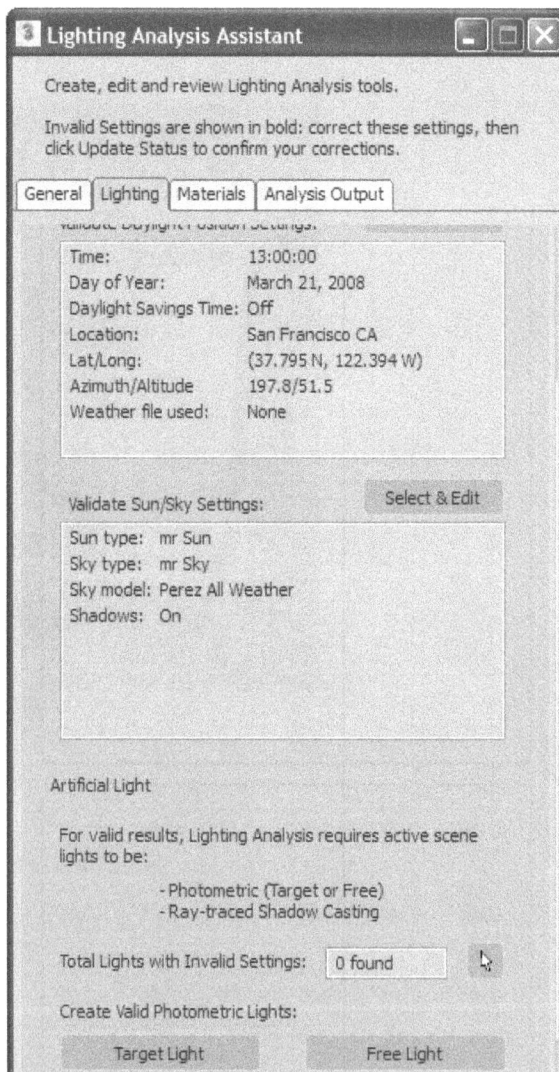

Figure A–16

Materials Tab

The *Materials* tab (shown in Figure A–17), validates the Materials in the scene.

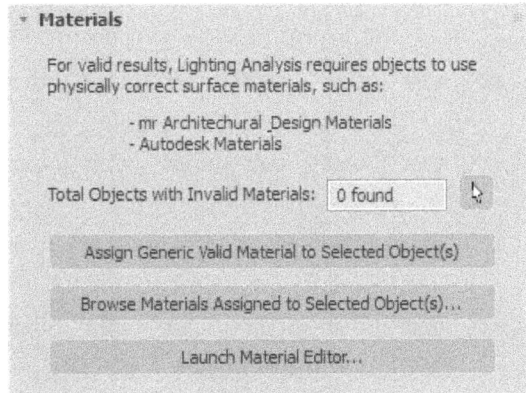

Figure A–17

The Lighting calculations require mr Arch & Design materials or Autodesk materials. If you have a scene that does not have the correct materials, they are flagged in the *Total Objects with Invalid Materials* field. Click the select arrow to select these objects in the viewport. You can then assign new materials to them yourself using the Material Editor or Material/Map Browser. If you do not care about the specific qualities of the material, you can use **Assign Generic Valid Material to Selected Object(s)**.

Hint: Adding Materials

Do not use **Assign Generic Valid Material to Selected Object(s)** on all of the selected objects in an interior. Doing so removes the glass from the windows and skylights. It is a better practice to add your own materials.

Analysis Output Tab

The *Analysis Output* tab (shown in Figure A–18) enables you create light meter objects.

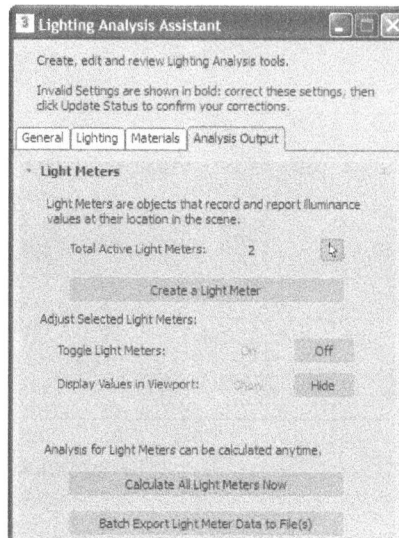

Figure A–18

To create a Light Meter object, click **Create a Light Meter** and drag a window around the objects in the viewport, as shown in

Figure A–19. You can create light meters using (Helpers) in the Command Panel's Create panel, which is a shortcut to the function. Alternatively, you can select **Lighting Analysis>Create>Light Meter**. You can use **AutoGrid** to create light meters over windows or other surfaces. Once the light meter is created, ensure that it is selected and go to the Modify panel and adjust the parameters to create the density of the value output.

Figure A–19

You can calculate all of the Light Meters at once or batch export the light meter data to files. These files can be used for LEED 8.1 Certification for energy compliance of government standards.

You can see the values of the light meters in the viewport or you can add them to your rendering as an Image Overlay. In the Image Overlay rollout, click **Create Image Overlay Render Effect**, to create an Image Overlay. All of the Image Overlay settings and the output settings are listed.

The render effect that adds the printed values on top of the picture that you render displays as shown in Figure A–20.

Figure A–20

Practice A2

Conduct a Lighting Analysis

Practice Objective

- Create a Lighting Analysis for a scene by creating light meter objects.

In this practice you will create lighting Analysis for a scene by creating light meter objects. You will then overlay the values over the render.

You must set the paths to locate the External files and Xrefs used in the practice. If you have not done this already, return to **Chapter 1: Introduction to Autodesk 3ds Max** and complete Task 1 to Task 3 in **Practice 1a: Organizing Folders and Working with the Interface**. You only have to set the user paths once.

Estimated time for completion: 15 minutes

*If a dialog box opens prompting you about a File Load: Mismatch, click **OK** to accept the default values.*

*The **NVIDIA mental ray** must be the active renderer for Lighting Analysis. It also requires mental ray materials with physically correct settings.*

1. Open **Lighting_Analysis_mental_ray_start.max**.

2. In the Enhanced Menu bar, select **Lighting Analysis> Lighting Analysis Assistant**.

3. In the Lighting Analysis Assistant, verify that the *General* tab is selected. In the Analysis and Rendering Precision rollout, in the *Validate Rendering Settings* area, note the rendering settings, as shown in Figure A–21.

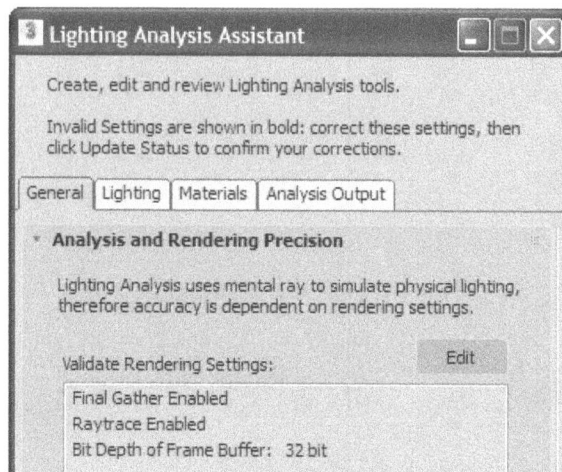

Figure A–21

4. In the Lighting Analysis Assistant, select the *Analysis Output* tab. In the Light Meters rollout, click **Create a Light Meter**. Leave the dialog box open, but move it over the doors area in the viewport so you can work in the window.

5. In the Command Panel, note that ◣ (Helpers) is automatically opened and **LightMeter** is selected. Toggle on **AutoGrid** at the top of the Object Type rollout.

6. In the viewport, note that the cursor displays a tripod. Hover the cursor over the lower left corner of the three large window objects and ensure that the Y-axis (green) is pointing up vertically and that the Z-axis (blue) is pointing outwards (towards you). Click and drag across to the diagonally opposite corner of all the three windows and release the mouse, creating a selection window., as shown in Figure A–22.

Figure A–22

7. With the selection window still selected, select the Modify panel (![icon]). Note that the **LightMeter Helper** is displayed in the Modifier Stack. In the Parameters rollout, set *Length Segs:* to **7** and *Width Segs:* to **10** and press <Enter>, as shown in Figure A–23. In the viewport, note that the segments are added to the helper window object. This increases the density of lighting analysis values. In the Display rollout, verify that **Show Viewport Text** is selected.

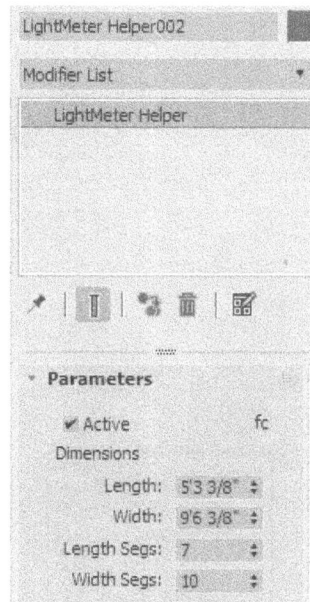

Figure A–23

8. In the Lighting Analysis Assistant, open the *Materials* tab and verify that **0 found** is displayed as *Total Objects with Invalid Materials*. This indicates that nothing needs to be corrected.

   • If you have any non-Physical materials assigned, an error displays. You can automatically assign a generic valid material to the selected objects in the scene.

   • If you click **Assign Generic Valid Material to Selected Object(s)** you lose transparency in the window glass. Reassign an Arch & Design thin glass to fix this problem.

9. Select the *Analysis Output* tab, in the Light Meters rollout, click **Calculate All Light Meters Now**. A progress bar is displayed in the Status Bar in the viewport. Once the calculations are complete, the light meter values are displayed in the viewport.

The full rollout might not be displayed. Use the

✋ *(Hand) icon to drag it up.*

10. Select the *General* tab and expand the Analysis Value Color Coding rollout. Change the value for the *Max* spinner (as shown in Figure A–24) and you should see the colors change in the viewport on the light meter. Set a max value (approximately **45 fc**) where the maximum portion displays as green, similar to that shown in Figure A–25.

   - Green indicates a good lighting level.
   - Red indicates overlit areas.
   - Blue indicates underlit areas.

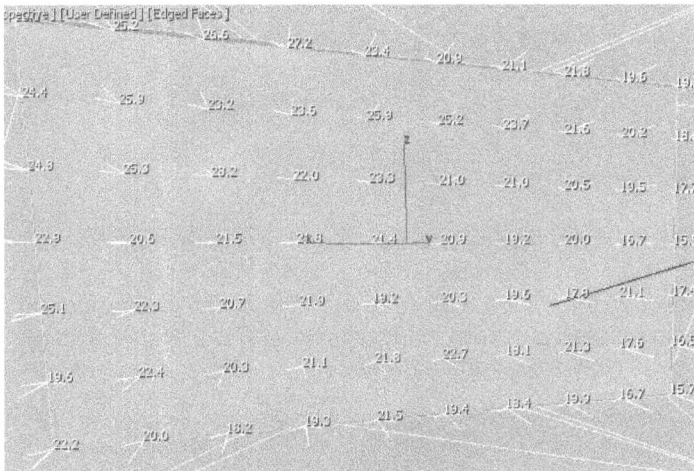

Figure A–24

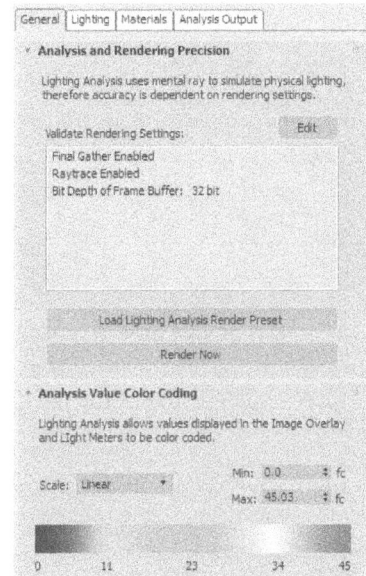

Figure A–25

11. You can add these values to the renderer output as an overlay. Select the *Analysis Output* tab, in the Image Overlay rollout, next to *Validate Image Overlay Settings,* click **Edit**.

12. The Environment and Effects dialog box opens to the *Effects* tab.

13. In the Effects rollout, click **Add...**. In the Add Effect dialog box, select **Lighting Analysis Image Overlay** to add the effect to the overlay and click **OK**.

14. In the *Parameters* area, note the Display Options settings. The first two options enable you to display the numbers over the whole image or only over the light meter object.

15. Set the options as shown in Figure A–26 (**Show Numbers On Entire Image (Screen Grid)** cleared and the remaining selected). Close the Environment and Effects dialog box.

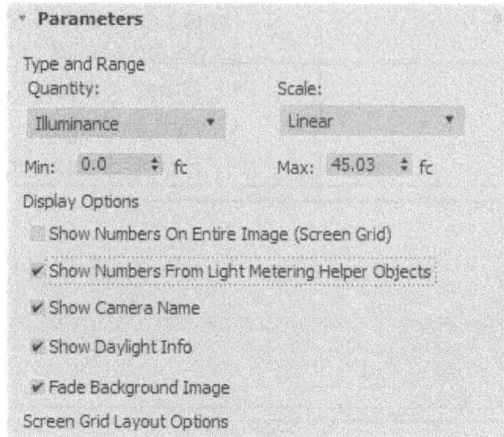

Figure A–26

16. Render the scene by clicking . It will take some time to complete the rendering process. In the Rendered Frame Window, the Image overlay is displayed when the rendering is complete, as shown in Figure A–27. A Lighting Analysis Data dialog box opens as well.

Figure A–27

17. Close the Lighting Analysis Data dialog box. In the Rendered Frame Window, save the rendered image as **LightingAnalysis.jpg**.

18. Save the scene file as **MyLightingAnalysis.max**.

A.6 Creating Hierarchies

Autodesk 3ds Max Hierarchies are collections of objects linked together with parent/child relationships. When used, transforms applied to a parent are automatically passed to its children. Connecting multiple objects in a hierarchical chain can enable sophisticated animations such as the motion of jointed robotic arms.

Most modifiers (such as Substitute) must be applied to the objects in the hierarchy rather than the parent.

In the case of the hierarchy file link options, incoming AutoCAD blocks are brought in as multiple objects so that they can maintain multiple material assignments from AutoCAD. They display together with a Block/Style Parent object, enabling you to transform the block as a unit by selecting the parent. The parent object itself does not have any geometry and does not render.

Practice A3

Create Hierarchies

Practice Objective

• Create hierarchical relationships between objects.

Estimated time for completion: 10 minutes

In many animations you will want to create hierarchical relationships so that objects move together when moved. Once you have linkages, you can animate them using forward kinematics in which you move the parent and rotate the children.

You must set the paths to locate the External files and Xrefs used in the practice. If you have not done this already, return to **Chapter 1: Introduction to Autodesk 3ds Max** and complete Task 1 to Task 3 in **Practice 1a: Organizing Folders and Working with the Interface**. You only have to set the user paths once.

*If a dialog box opens prompting you about a File Load: Mismatch, click **OK** to accept the default values.*

1. Open **Lamp Start Linking.max**. This is a model of a desk lamp, as shown in Figure A–28.

Figure A–28

2. In the Scene Explorer, use ■ (Display None) and

   ● (Display Geometry) and note the six geometry objects in the scene. The names are not indented, indicating that there are no linkages.

3. In the viewport, move the Base object that is at the bottom of the lamp. Note that it moves by itself and the other objects are unaffected. Undo the move and clear the selection.

4. In the Main Toolbar, click ✐ (Select and Link). Starting at the top, select and hold each object and drag a dotted line to its parent. You will repeat the process five times as follows:

- Select **Lampshade** and link it to **Upper Arm - Lamp**.
- Select **Upper Arm - Lamp** and link it to **Lower Arm**.
- Select **Lower Arm** and link it to **Lower Hub**.
- Select **Lower Hub** and link it to **Stand**.
- Select **Stand** and link it to **Base**.

5. In the Main Toolbar, click ▧ (Select Object) to end the linking process.

6. In the Scene Explorer, note that only **Base** is visible. Expand Base to display its dependent, **Stand**. Expand all of the children to display the dependencies, as shown in Figure A–29.

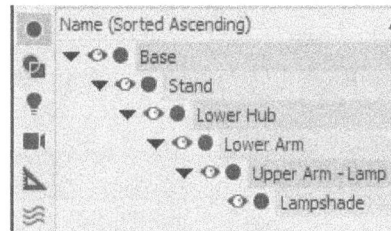

Figure A–29

7. Move the Base and note that the entire lamp moves with it. The base is the parent object and other objects are children and descendants. Undo the move.

8. Rotate the Lower Arm and note that the Upper Arm - Lamp and Lampshade, go along with the rotation. The Lower Hub, Stand, and Base are not part of the rotation. Undo the rotations.

9. Save your scene file as **MyLampStartLinking.max**.

Practice A4

Estimated time for completion: 10 minutes

Create an Assembly Animation

Practice Objective

- Create animation assembly to bring the different parts of an object together.

It is common to create an animation of a design that builds up over time. In this practice you will create an animation of the assembly of a lamp.

You must set the paths to locate the External files and Xrefs used in the practice. If you have not done this already, return to **Chapter 1: Introduction to Autodesk 3ds Max** and complete Task 1 to Task 3 in **Practice 1a: Organizing Folders and Working with the Interface**. You only have to set the user paths once.

In this kind of animation, you will add keyframes to the end of the animation and then adjust the start and end ranges for each component.

1. Open **Lamp Start Linking Animation.max**.

*If a dialog box opens prompting you about a File Load: Mismatch, click **OK** to accept the default values.*

2. In the Animation Controls, click ![icon] (Time Configuration). In the Time Configuration dialog box, in the *Animation* area, set the *End Time* to **200** and click **OK**.

3. Press <Ctrl>+<A> to select all objects in the viewport at once.

4. In the Time Slider, right-click on the **0/200** slider bar to open the Create Key dialog box. Clear **Rotation** and **Scale** leaving **Position** selected and set the *Destination Time* to **160**, as shown in Figure A–30. Click **OK**.

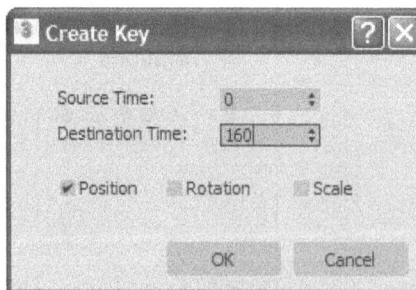

Figure A–30

- A Position key for all objects is placed at frame 160. Note that in the Track Bar, a red box is set at 160, as shown in Figure A–31.

Figure A–31

5. Click **Auto Key** to activate it (it will display in red).

If all of the objects are selected, click in empty area in the viewport to clear the selection and then select each object separately.

6. Verify that your slider bar is located at **0** (0/200). Clear the object selection, and move each individual object randomly on the screen, similar to that shown in Figure A–32. (The placement of the objects can be different to that shown in the image.)

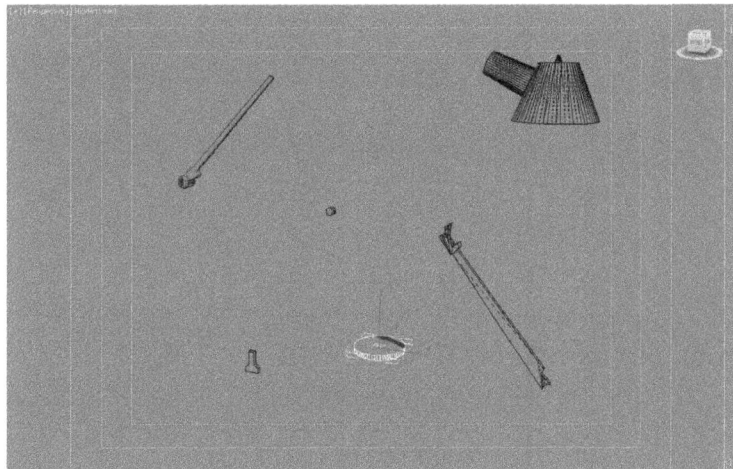

Figure A–32

7. Click ▶ (Play) and note that the components drift into their correct locations at frame 160. Stop the animation.

8. Save your scene file as **MyLampAnimation.max**.

> **Hint: Set the Selection Range**
>
> To have the components assemble one after another, using <Ctrl> select both keys in the Time Slider. Right-click and select **Configure>Show Selection Range**. A bar is added below the track bar indicating the duration of movement for the selected component. You can now move the ends of the range to control when the object starts to move and when it finishes. The shorter the line, the quicker the movement of the object.

A.7 Customizing the User Interface

The Autodesk 3ds Max software has a flexible and highly customizable user interface that can be modified using the Customize User Interface dialog box, as shown in Figure A–33. Select **Customize>Customize User Interface**.

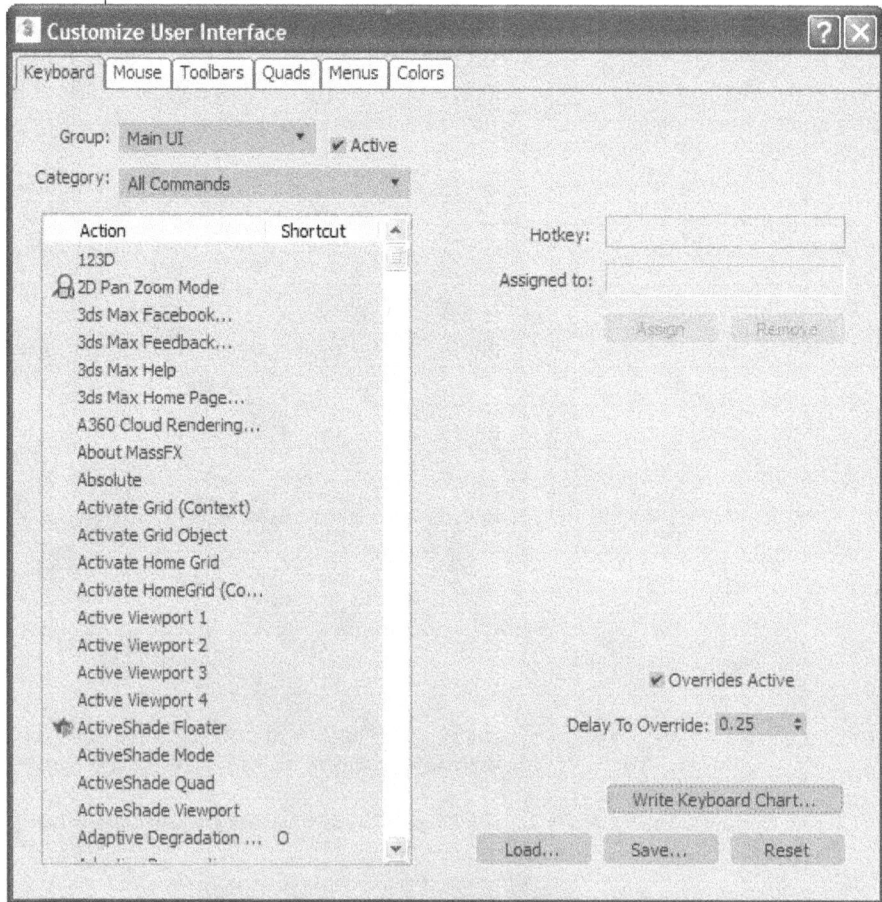

Figure A–33

- The settings located in each tab can be saved or swapped out independently with **Load...** and **Save...**.

- All of the interface settings can be loaded and saved at once using **Customize>Load/Save Custom UI Scheme**.

Keyboard tab	Enables you to assign shortcuts or hotkeys.
Write Keyboard Chart...	Can be found in the *Keyboard* tab. It enables you to save a .TXT file showing all of the current hotkeys. A hotkey is a keyboard stroke or combination assigned to launch a specific option. It is good practice to develop your own set of keyboard shortcuts to improve your productivity.
Mouse tab	Enables you to load and save the mouse settings. The mouse settings are dependent on the interaction mode set in the Preferences dialog box in which you can set the Autodesk 3ds Max mode or Autodesk Maya mode
Toolbars tab	Enables you to create custom toolbars and modify the existing one based on your requirements.
Quads tab/ *Menus* tab	Enables you to create custom Quad sets and custom menus and modify the respective existing ones.
Colors tab	Enables you to set color options for the interface elements.

- All of the keyboard shortcuts, toolbar, and menu custom settings are now saved in an upgraded file format (.KBDX for keyboard settings, .MUSX for mouse settings, .CUIX for toolbar settings, .MNUX for quad menus and menu settings, and .CLRX for color settings).

Practice A5

Customizing the User Interface

Learning Objectives

- Customize the User interface.

In this practice you learn to customize the User interface by adding different commands in the quad menu. You will then add different icons for a command to the Main Toolbar.

1. Reset the file so that you have a blank file open..

2. Select **Customize>Customize User Interface** to open the Customize User Interface dialog box.

3. Select the *Quads* tab. Click in the *Action* list and press <O>.

4. Locate **Orbit View Mode**. Click and drag it to the Quad list on the right, placing it just above **Clone**, as shown in Figure A–34. This enables you to select **Orbit View Mode** with a right-click quad menu.

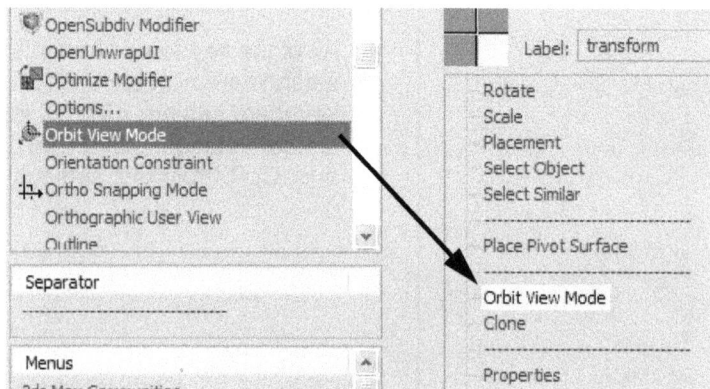

Figure A–34

5. Open the Group drop-down list and select **ViewCube**, as shown in Figure A–35.

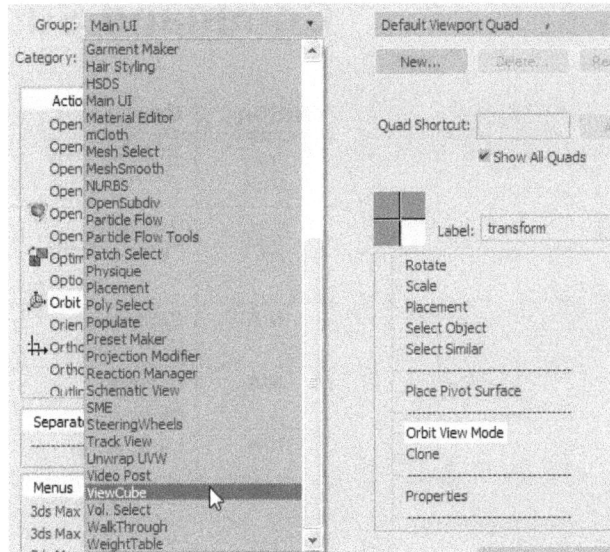

Figure A–35

*You can delete or edit the names of the listed commands by right-clicking on the command in the Action list and selecting **Delete Menu Item** or **Edit Menu item Name**.*

6. In the Action list, select **Toggle ViewCube Visibility**, drag it to the Quad list on the right, and place it just below **Orbit View Mode**, as shown in Figure A–36.

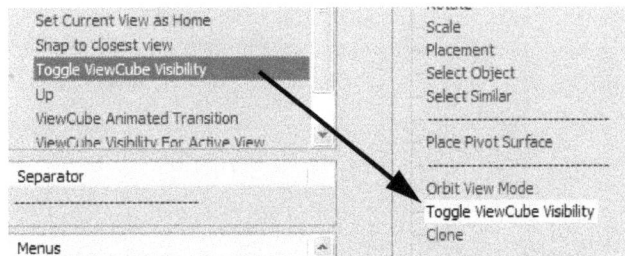

Figure A–36

7. Close the dialog box. Right-click on the viewport and select **Toggle ViewCube Visibility** to toggle it off. Note that the ViewCube is not visible anymore.

8. Select **Customize>Customize User Interface**.

9. In the dialog box, select the *Toolbars* tab. In the *Action* list, click **Ortho Snapping Mode**. Drag this entry to the Main Toolbar, and drop it before the **3D Snaps** icon, as shown in Figure A–37. The **Ortho Snap** tool is now available in the Main Toolbar. Close the dialog box.

*To delete a button from the Main Toolbar, right-click and select **Delete Button**. Some of the toggle buttons and the added buttons can be deleted.*

Figure A–37

Command Summary

Button	Command	Location
?	**3ds Max Help**	• **InfoCenter** • **Help**: Autodesk 3ds Max Help
(icon)	**Compact Material Editor**	• **Main Toolbar:** Material Editor flyout • **Rendering:** Material Editor>Compact Material Editor
N/A	**Customize User Interface**	• **Customize:** Customize User Interface
N/A	**Lighting Analysis**	• **Lighting Analysis:** Lighting Analysis Assistant
N/A	**Light Meter**	• **Command Panel:** *Create* panel> *Helpers* category • **Lighting Analysis:** Create>Light Meter

Appendix B

Optional Practices

This appendix contains additional practices that can be worked on to provide further practice using the Autodesk® 3ds Max® software.

Practice B1 | Create Additional Extrusions

Practice Objective

- Create 3D objects from 2D shapes.

You will create extrusions that define a lobby area using the **Extrude** modifier and its various options, as shown in Figure B–1.

Estimated time for completion: 20 minutes

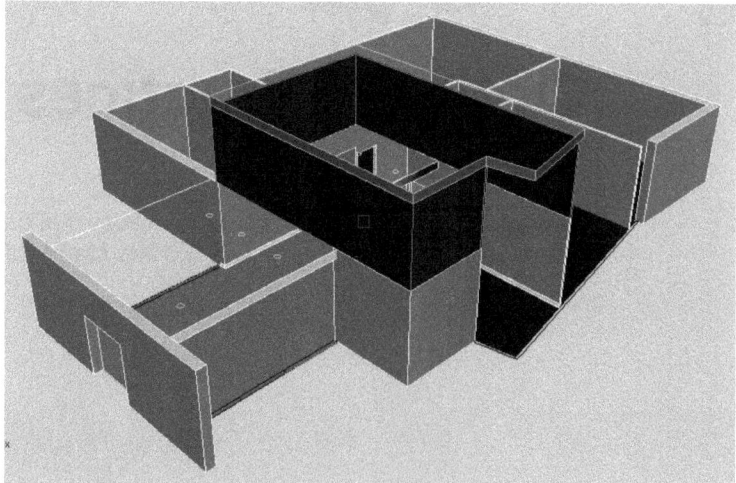

Figure B–1

1. Open **Extruded Walls with Openings.max**.

2. Select **High Quality** in the label menu.

3. Select each of the 2D shapes listed in the following table individually (use the Scene Explorer with ![icon] (Display Shapes)). Use the **Extrude** modifier (Modify panel

    (![icon])>Modifier List) on each object and extrude them as described in the table. For each object set the rest of the parameters (Select **Generate Mapping Coords.**, **Real-World Map Size** and clear **Generate Material IDs**) as shown for **Layer:VIZ-1-Ceiling**, in Figure B–2. For the objects that are required to be moved up (elevation), click

    ![icon] (Select and Move) and then, in the Status Bar, enter the Z value for elevation.

Press <Enter> after entering a value in the edit box.

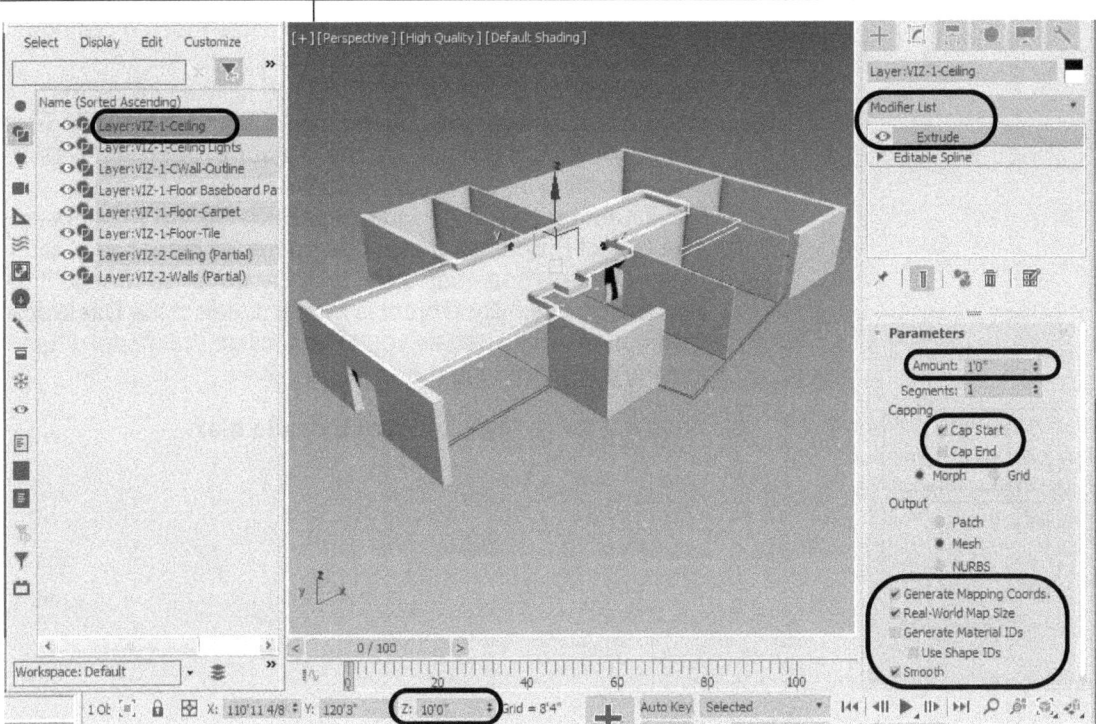

Figure B–2

Autodesk 3ds Max Shape	Extrusion Amount	Notes
Layer:VIZ-1-Ceiling	1'0"	Cap only the start (not end) Move up to elevation 10'0"
Layer:VIZ-1-Ceiling Lights	0'0"	Cap only the start (not end) Move up to elevation 9'11 7/8"
Layer:VIZ-1-Floor-Carpet	0'0"	Cap only the end (not start)
Layer:VIZ-1-Floor-Tile	0'0"	Cap only the end (not start)
Layer:VIZ-2-Ceiling (Partial)	1'0"	Cap only the start (not end) Move up to elevation 20'0"
Layer:VIZ-2-Walls (Partial)	9'0"	Cap only the end (not start) Move up to elevation 11'0"

4. When using **Cap Start** and **Cap End**, note that the ceilings are visible from the top and bottom of the model. To manipulate the display so that you can still see inside the lobby when looking down at the model but see the ceilings when looking up, you can set the **Object Properties**. Select the two ceiling layers (**Layer:VIZ-1-Ceiling** and **Layer: VIZ-2-Ceiling (Partial)**) and select **Edit>Object Properties**. The Object Properties dialog box opens. In the *General* tab, in the *Display Properties* area, click **By Layer** to change it to **By Object**. Once **By Object** is enabled, select the **Backface Cull** option. This enables you to see inside the model when looking down from the top.

You have only included the part of the second floor that connects to the lobby area.

5. Save the file as **MyAdditional Extrude.max**.

Practice B2

Making a Chair Base by Lofting Objects

Practice Objectives

Estimated time:
10 minutes

- Loft 2D shapes along a 2D path to create a 3D object and apply deformations to the shapes.

In this practice, you will create a loft object to represent the base of a chair. The extrude and sweep modifiers both use a single shape that sweeps along a path to create a 3D object. The Loft Compound Object modifier places multiple shapes along a spline path. It also gives you additional deformations to twist, tweeter, scale, and otherwise fit to shape on a graph

1. Open the file **airport_chair_startLoft.max**. The chair seat and four shapes are displayed in the viewport, as shown in Figure B–3.

Figure B–3

2. In the viewport, select the straight line shape directly under the chair. This shape is used at the path for the loft.

   - In the viewport, there are three more shapes: a **Circle**, a **Star** with three points, and a six sided **NGon**. You will blend from shape to shape along the path.

3. In the Command Panel>Create panel ($+$), click

   ⬤ (Geometry), expand the drop-down list, and select **Compound Objects**.

Hovering the cursor over a valid shape, changes it to a Get Shape cursor.

4. In the Object Type rollout, click **Loft**.

5. In the Creation Method rollout, click **Get Shape**. In the viewport, select the large circle object named **Circle01**. The circle is lofted along the selected straight line, as shown in Figure B–4.

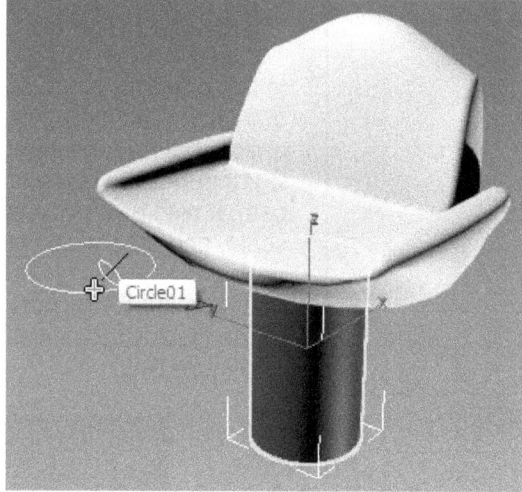

Figure B–4

6. Press <F3> to toggle to wireframe shading.

7. With the Loft object selected, in the Command Panel, select the Modify ( ). In the Path Parameters rollout, set *Path* to **40**. In the viewport, a small yellow X indicator moves up the path, as shown in Figure B–5.

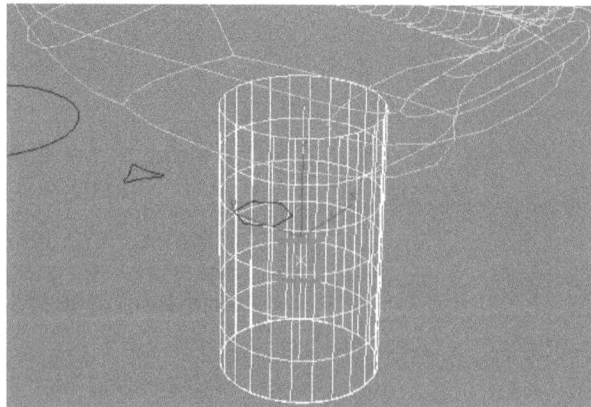

Figure B–5

*The **Zoom** and **Orbit** commands were used to display the complete loft object.*

8. In the Creation Method rollout, click **Get Shape**. In the viewport, select **NGon01** (blue **Ngon** inside the loft object). Change the *Per-view Preference* to **Default Shading**. The circular base shape now tapers to a post, as shown in Figure B–6.

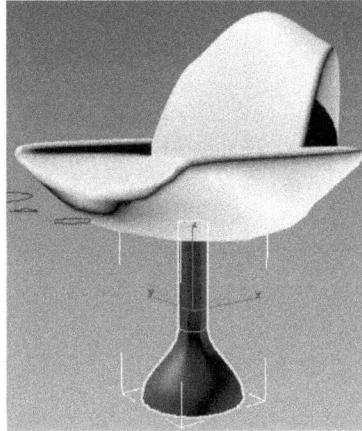

Figure B–6

9. In the Path Parameters rollout, set the *Path* value to **60**.

10. Verify that **Get Shape** is still selected (blue) otherwise select it. Select the **NGon01** again. The NGON is placed at the new location.

11. In the Path Parameters rollout, set the *Path* value to **100**. Verify that **Get Shape** is still selected and select the **Circle01**. In the viewport, note that the loft flares up before touching the seat, as shown in Figure B–7.

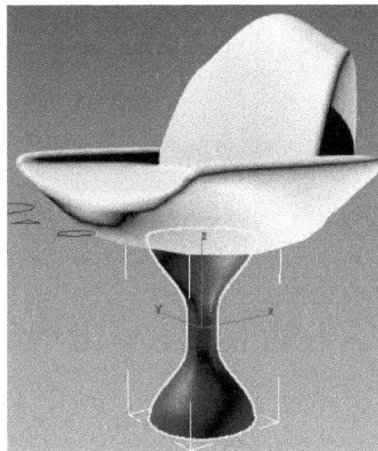

Figure B–7

12. In the Path Parameters rollout, set the *Path* value to **50**.

13. Verify that **Get Shape** is still selected (or select it) and select the **Star01** shape. Note that in the center of the loft, the geometry does not look very good. You need to add more points to the star. Click **Get Shape** again to clear its selection.

14. In the Scene Explorer, ((Display Shapes)), select **Star01**.

    In the Modify panel ( ), in the Parameters rollout, set the following values for the Star, as shown in Figure B–8. In the viewport, note that both the loft object and the star shape have been modified, as shown in Figure B–9.

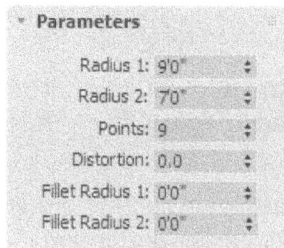

Figure B–8

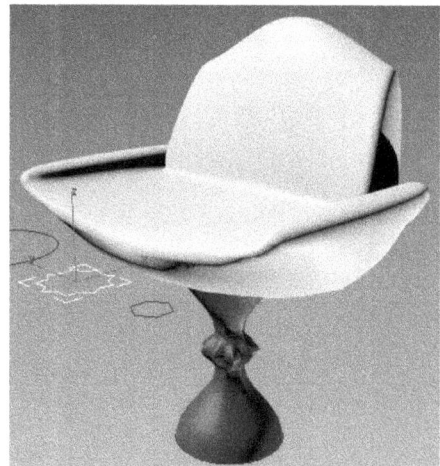

Figure B–9

15. Select the loft object and press <F4> to display in Edged Face mode, as shown in Figure B–10. Note that the mesh looks pretty dense.

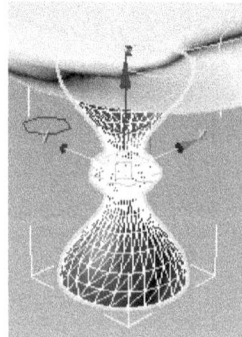

Figure B–10

16. With the base selected (Loft001), verify that the Modify panel ( ) is open in the Command Panel.

17. Expand the Skin Parameters rollout, and in the *Options* area, set the *Shape Steps* and *Path Steps* to **2**. Increase the *Path Steps* to **4** and leave the *Shape Steps as 2*, as shown in Figure B–11.

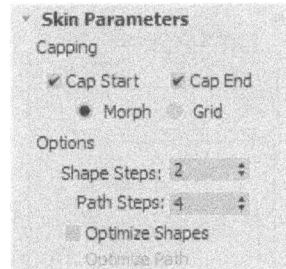

Figure B–11

18. For sculpting the final shape of the Loft object, expand the Deformations rollout and click **Scale**. The Scale Deformations graph displays.

19. In the Scale Deformations toolbar, click (Insert Corner Point). When you hover the cursor over the red line, note that it displays as a plus sign. Click on the red line under 20 to set the control point at an approximate position. In the Text edit box, at the bottom of the dialog box, enter **20** and press <Enter> (as shown in Figure B–12) to move the control point to the exact position.

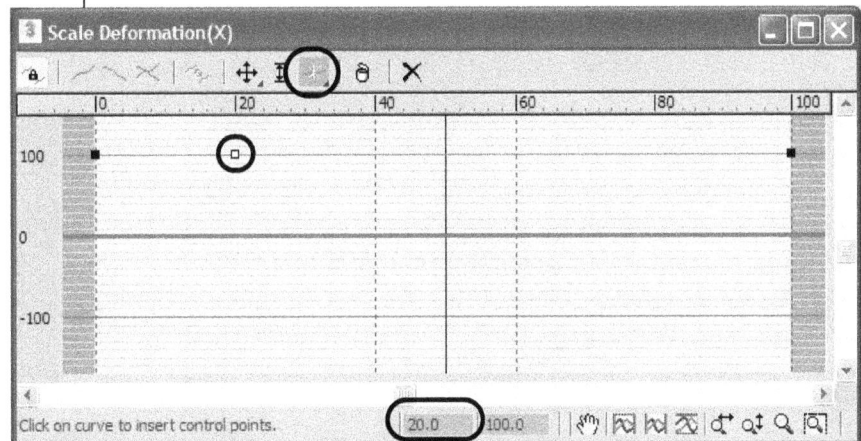

Figure B–12

20. Add new control points at **40**, **50**, and **60**.

21. In the dialog box, click ⊕ (Move Control Point) to move the points on the graph. Right-click on the points and change them to **Bezier Smooth** or **Bezier Corner**, then adjust the handles, as shown in Figure B–13. Review the object in the viewport as the points are moved and modified.

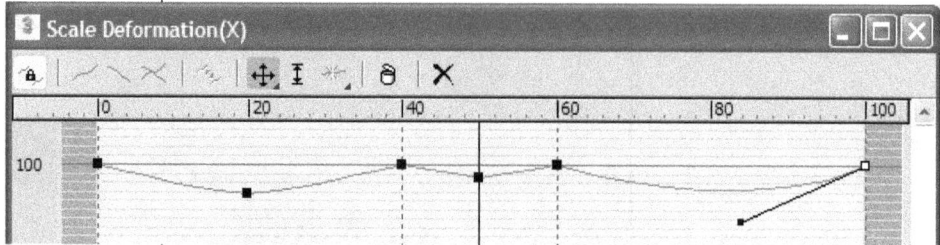

Figure B–13

22. Play with the handles and scale points while watching the interactive results in the viewport.

23. You can use other deformation tools, such as **Twist**, **Teeter**, **Bevel**, and **Fit** and note how they effect the base of the chair.

24. Save the file as **Myarmchair_withBase.max**.

Practice B3

Estimated time for completion: 10 minutes

Using the mental ray Multi/Sub-Map Shader

Practice Objectives

- Assign different colors and maps to copies of objects in a scene.
- Modify the materials and apply them.

A Multi/Sub-Map shader enables you to assign separate map files or different colors to a single material parameter (i.e., Diffuse). In this practice you will create a mental ray shader and assign a Multi/Sub-Map that assigns multiple colors to chairs in a hall.

Task 1 - Apply and Adjust the Multi/Sub-Map shader.

1. Open **Brno_Hall_Chairs.max**.
   - The scene is set up with a stage, camera, lights and a single row of six chairs that have two parts, the fabric cover and the metal frame.

2. Open the Slate Material Editor. In the Material/Map Browser, expand the *Materials>mental ray* categories. Double-click on mental ray to add it to the *View1* sheet. Double-click on the title bar heading to open the Parameter Editor.

3. In the Material Shaders rollout, in the *Basic Shaders* area, next to Surface, click **None** to open the separate Material/Map Browser.

4. In the *Maps>mental ray* categories, locate **Multi/Sub-Map** as shown in Figure B–14. Double-click on **Multi/Sub-Map**. The node displays in the *View1* sheet and is linked to the mental ray *Surface Shader* channel, as shown in Figure B–15.

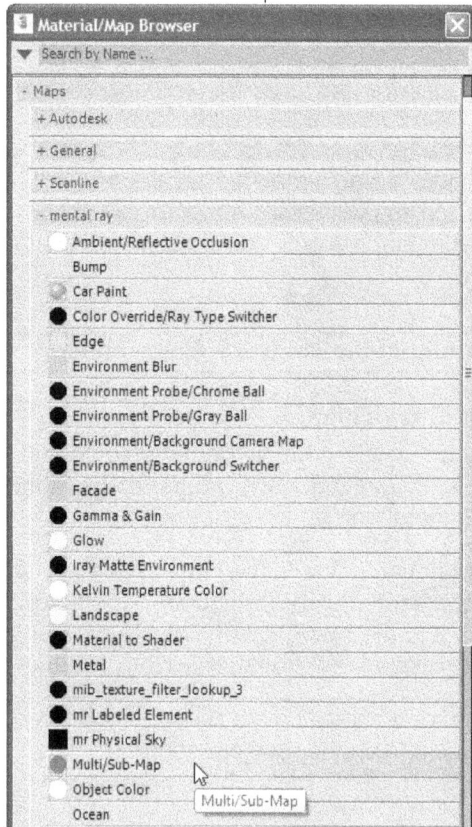

Figure B–14

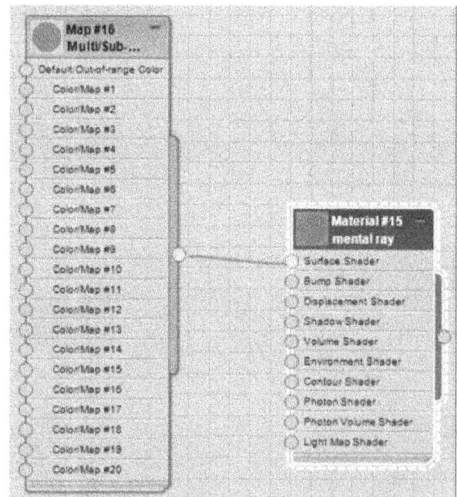

Figure B–15

5. Double-click the **Map # Multi/Sub-Map** title bar heading to open its Parameters Editor, as shown in Figure B–16. This contains a list of 20 Color/Maps each of which is assigned to a unique channel. Maps 1 to 9 display in unique colors while maps 10-20 are, by default, colored black. You will be applying these maps to objects in the scene. For any material number greater than color 20, the Default/Out-of-range Color is used.

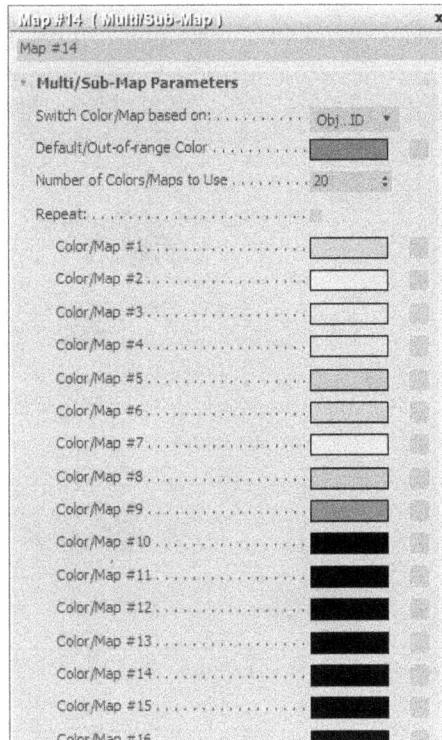

Figure B–16

6. Set *Number of Colors/Maps to Use* as **6**, as shown in Figure B–17. This identifies the first six materials as active for the shader when rendering.

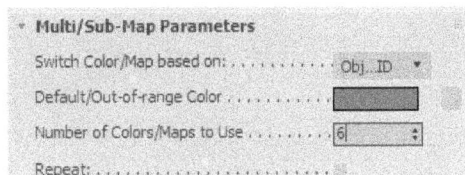

Figure B–17

Each material has a unique channel assigned to it that corresponds with its position in the list. Each of these channels has a default color that can be modified. You can assign up to 100 materials using this shader.

Task 2 - Assign Maps to Materials.

In this task you will use another mental ray shader that has already been created and assigned. The steps in the previous task were included to describe how to create a new mental ray shader.

1. In the *View1* sheet, delete both the mental ray material and its Multi/Sub-Map node.

2. In the Material/Map Browser, in the *Scene Materials* category, double-click **Chair Fabric**. In the *View1* sheet, note that this is a mental ray material and that its Multi/Sub-Map has already been created. The first six channels in the Multi/Sub-Map have been assigned to chairs 2 through 6. You will assign the material to chair 1.

3. In the **Camera01** viewport, set the *Shading Viewport* to **High Quality**.

4. In the **Camera01** viewport, select the seat back of the first chair on the left (Seat42), as shown in Figure B–18. The seat fabric and the frames are separate objects so only the seat part of the model is selected.

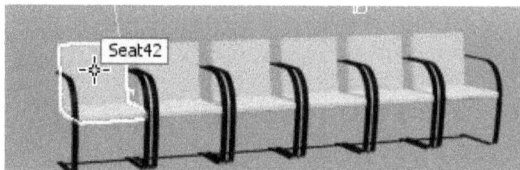

Figure B–18

5. In the Modify panel ( )>Modifier Stack, in the Editable Poly modifier of the seat, select **Polygon**. In the viewport, note that the complete seat is highlighted (red).

6. In the Polygon: Material IDs rollout, set *Set ID* as **1** and press <Enter>, as shown in Figure B–19.

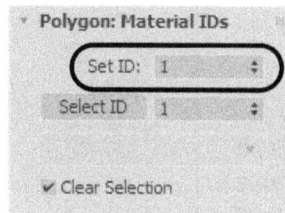

Figure B–19

7. In the *View1* sheet of Slate Material Editor, select the **Chair Fabric** mental ray node and click (Assign Material to Selection).

8. In the Command Panel>Modifier Stack, select **Editable Poly** to exit Sub-object mode.

9. For this scene, the remaining five channels were assigned separately to the remaining chairs and has already been completed. For example, seat 2 uses material channel *2* and seat 3 uses channel *3*. To review the materials that are assigned to the six channels, in the *View1* sheet, double-click on the Fabric Multi/Sub-Map node title bar heading to open the Parameter Editor, as shown in Figure B–20. Note that the **Number of Colors to Use** is set to **6** and are colored in six different colors, ranging from green to brown.

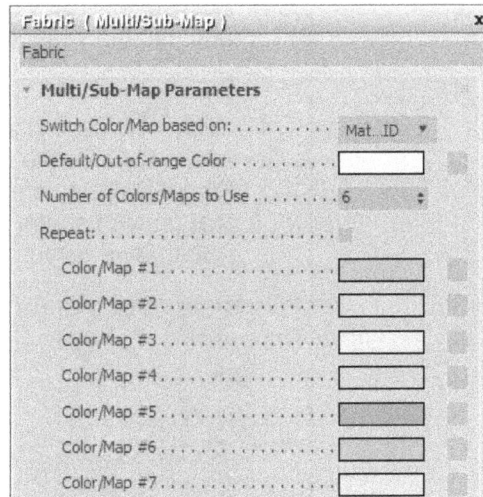

Figure B–20

10. In the viewport, select all six chair seat/backs and click

     (Assign material to Selection) to ensure that the materials are assigned.

11. Render the **Camera01** view. The six seats display with their different color materials.

Task 3 - Add Additional Seats to the Scene.

You will now populate the space with additional rows and columns of seats and adjust the **Multi/Sub-Map** parameters to make it more interesting.

1. Select **Frame42** to **Frame47** (all six frames) and **Seat42** to **Seat47** (all six seats) (Use Scene Explorer with (Display None) and (Display Geometry)).

2. In the Status Bar, click 🔒 (Selection Lock) to lock this selection, as shown in Figure B–21.

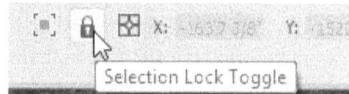

Figure B–21

3. Activate the **Top** viewport. Click 🔲 (Zoom Extents Selected) and pan the seats down.

4. Click ✛ (Select and Move). Hold <Shift> and drag the chairs towards the top of the screen (as shown in Figure B–22) to create a new (cloned) row of seats. Ensure that enough space is left between the two rows and release <Shift> and cursor.

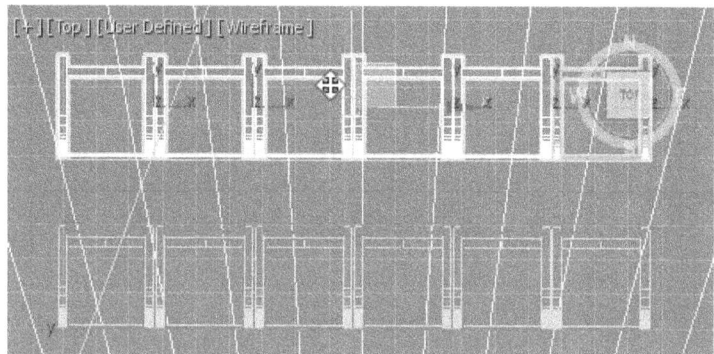

Figure B–22

5. In the Clone Options dialog box, select **Instance** and set the *Number of Copies* to **8**. Click **OK**.

6. Click ⬛ (Select Object) to exit the Move transform. You now have a total of 54 chairs in one main grouping, as shown in the Camera01 viewport in Figure B–23.

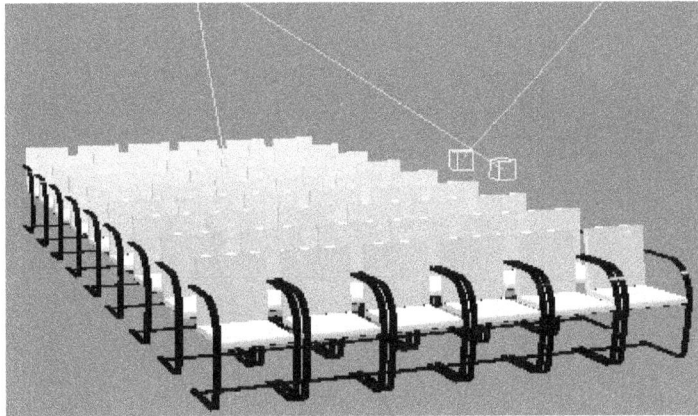

Figure B–23

7. Select all 54 chairs and their frames and lock the selection

   (🔒). Zoom out in the **Top** viewport to see all of the chairs.

   Using ✛ and <Shift>, drag all of the chairs to the left (on the X axis) to create a second group column of 54 chairs, as shown in Figure B–24. In the Clone Options dialog box, verify that **Instance** is selected and the *Number of Copies* are set to **1**. Click **OK**.

Figure B–24

8. As the group is still selected, press <Shift> and drag it to the right on the other side of the original group to create a third group column as **Instance** and set *Number of Copies* to **1**. You now have a total of 162 chairs.

9. Render the **Top** viewport, as shown in Figure B–25. Note that each group of six columns has the same regular color of chair from front to back

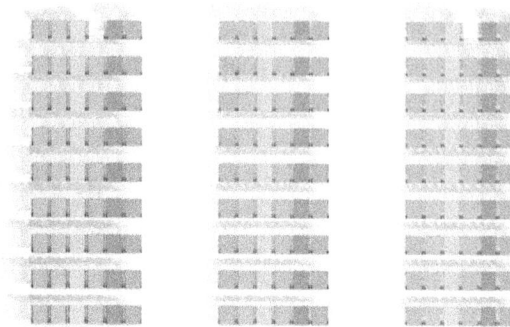

Figure B–25

You are not restricted to using solid colors with the Multi/Sub-Map shader and you can also apply maps to one or more materials. In such cases, the map replaces the color swatch.

10. In the Slate Material Editor, double-click on the Fabric Multi/Sub-Map title bar heading. In *Switch Color/Map based on* drop-down list, select **Random,** as shown in Figure B–26.

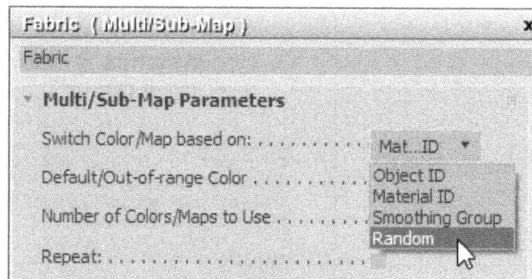

Figure B–26

11. Render the **Top** viewport, as shown in Figure B–27. Note that the uniform color by column has been replaced with a more random layout color pattern.

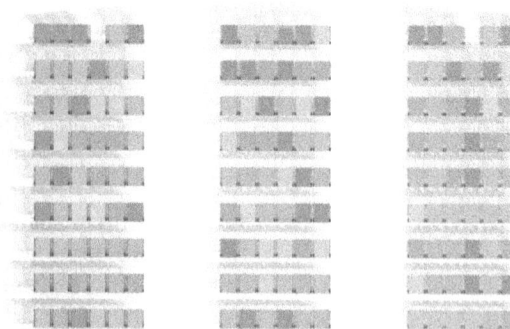

Figure B–27

Task 4 - Modify the Chair Frame Material.

The chair frames have a black glossy color applied to them but as the material is an Arch & Design type, you can change its look.

1. In the Slate Material Editor, in the Material/Map Browser, in the *Scene Materials* category, double-click on **Chair Chrome** material to add it to the *View1* sheet and open its Parameter Editor (Double-click the title bar heading).

2. In the Templates drop-down list, select **Copper**, as shown in Figure B–28.

The material has previously been assigned to the frame.

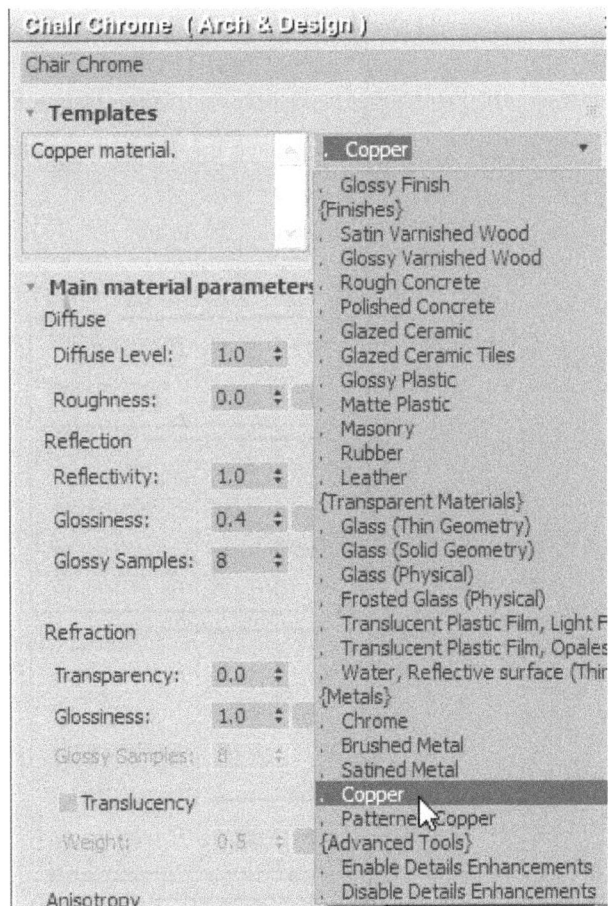

Figure B–28

3. Render the **Camera01** viewport, as shown in Figure B–29. It displays a view of your chairs with random mental ray Multi/Sub-Map material applied to the chairs.

Figure B–29

4. Save the file as **Mymentalchairs.max**.

Practice B4	# Shadow Study Animation

Practice Objective

* Animate the Daylight System to create a shadow study.

Estimated time for completion: 15 minutes

In this practice you will animate the movement of the daylight throughout a day in the exterior scene to create an animated shadow study. This study will provide an accurate representation of how daylight will cast shadows in the scene.

1. Open **Shadow Study.max**.

2. Activate the **Camera01** viewport, if not already active. This is the non-animated camera view. Change the *Shading Viewport* to **High Quality**.

3. In the Animation controls, click (Time Configuration). Verify that your default settings match the settings shown in Figure B–30. Click **OK**.

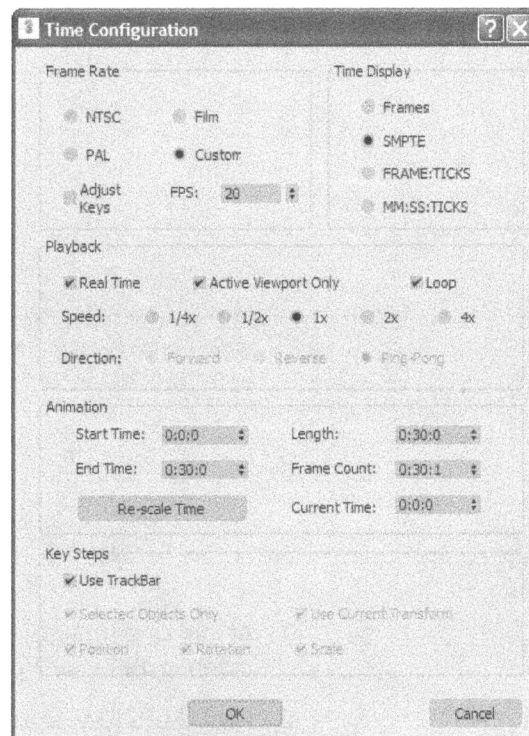

Figure B–30

4. In this shadow study you will animate the **Daylight001** object using keyframing. Select the **Daylight001** object in the **Compass001** helper object (Use the Scene Explorer,

   ▪ (Display None) and ▣ (Display Groups)). Verify that the Time Slider is located at a time of **0:0:0** (frame 0), as shown in Figure B–31.

Figure B–31

5. In the Command Panel, select the Motion panel (●). Start the shadow study animation at frame 0, representing **6:00 AM**. In the Control Parameters rollout, set the current time and date as shown in Figure B–32. Your *Azimuth* and *Altitude* values might be different.

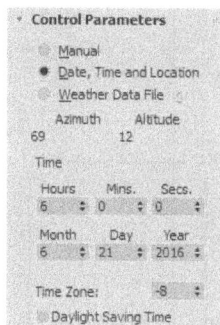

Figure B–32

6. In the Animation Controls, click **Auto Key** (displays in red). While in **Auto Key** mode, drag the time slider to the end time of **0:30:0**, as shown in Figure B–33.

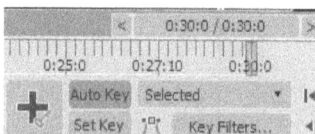

Figure B–33

7. At this time (**0:30:0**) change the sun's position to 7:00 PM by entering **19** in the *Hours* edit box in the Command Panel.

8. Click **Auto Key** again to end Auto Key mode.

9. Slide the Time Slider left and right (scrub) and in the viewports, watch the **Daylight001** object progress across the sky during the animation.

10. Open the Render Setup dialog box ((Render Setup)). In the *Common* tab, in the *Output Size* area, set *Width* to **300**. With your aspect ratio locked at 1.6, it automatically calculates the *Height* of **187**, as shown in Figure B–34.

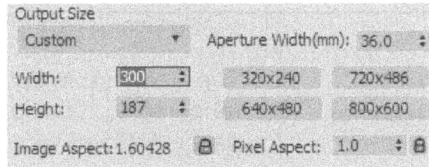

Figure B–34

11. In the *Time Output* area, set *Every Nth Frame* to **20** and verify that the **Active Time Segment** is selected, as shown in Figure B–35.

12. In the *View to Render*, verify that the current viewport is set to **Quad 4 - Camera01** and click , as shown in Figure B–35.

This enables you to always render Camera01 even if another viewport is active.

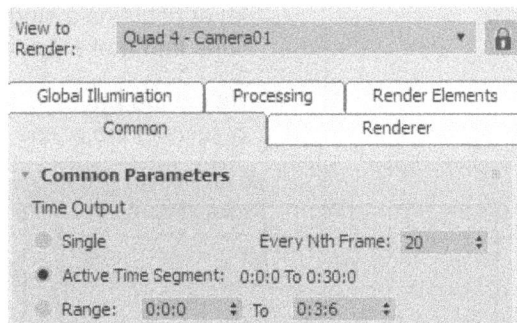

Figure B–35

13. In the *Render Output* area, click **Files...**. Render the animation to still frames named **shadow study.jpg** in the ...*renderings* folder. If prompted to specify the JPEG quality, use the highest quality **JPEG** option.

14. Click **Render** to begin animating the individual frames of the animation through the course of a day from 6.00 a.m. to 7.00 p.m. Note the change in brightness of the daylight and the movement of the shadows from one frame to another.

15. When done, use the RAM Player (**Rendering>Compare Media in RAM Player**) to combine them into a compiled animation file called **Shadow Study.mov** or **Shadow Study.avi**.

16. Save the scene file as **My Shadow Study.max**.

Practice B5

Assigning the Renderable Spline Modifier

Practice Objective

Estimated time for completion: 10 minutes

- Make the 2D lines renderable so that they are visible in the renderings.

The Renderable Spline modifier enables you to make linework renderable. In this practice, you will assign a width to the pavement markings so that they will render appropriately.

1. Open **Renderable Spline.max**.

2. Render the viewport and note that the parking lot does not display the corridor markings, parking lines, and handicap symbols.

3. Open the Layer Explorer (▣ (Layer Explorer)). Expand the layer **C-MARK-YELLOW-3D**, as shown in Figure B–36. The layer contains a single object, the combined AutoCAD 3D lines that make up the yellow pavement markings.

4. Select the **Layer:C-MARK-YELLOW-3D** object to select the objects in the scene.

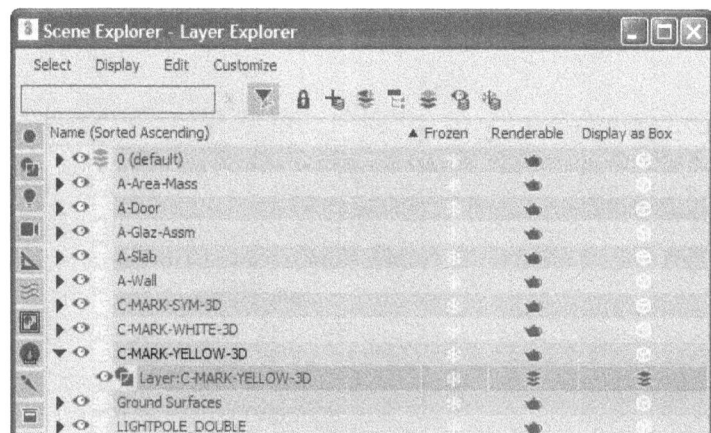

Figure B–36

5. In the Command Panel, select the *Modify* tab. In the Modifier List, select **Renderable Spline**. It is displayed in the Modifier Stack, as shown in Figure B–37.

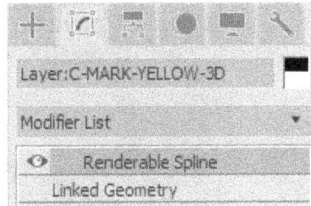

Figure B–37

6. In the Parameters rollout, select **Rectangular** and set the following, as shown in Figure B–38:
   - *Width*: **0'3"**
   - *Aspect*: **0.167**

   The *Length* automatically updates to **0'0 4/8"**. In your model, the *Length* translates into the vertical height of the pavement markings.

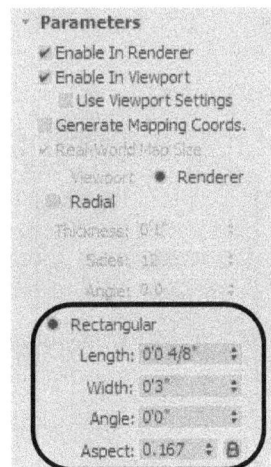

Figure B–38

7. In the Modifier Stack, right-click on **Renderable Spline** and select **Copy**.

8. In the Layer Explorer, expand **C-MARK-WHITE-3D** and select **Layer:C-MARK-WHITE-3D**. In the Modifier Stack, right-click on Linked Geometry and select **Paste** to add **Renderable Spline** with the same parameters. In the Parameters rollout, change the *Width* to **0'6"**.

9. Similar to Step 8, copy the **Renderable Spline** to **Layer:C-MARK-SYM-3D** in **C-MARK-SYM-3D**.

10. In the viewport, zoom into the parking lot area and note that the spline markings get some width, as shown in Figure B–39.

- The markings might not display entirely above the pavement due to the approximate nature of the viewport display and your computer's display driver and settings.

Figure B–39

11. Assign each of these marking layers to not cast shadows. In the Layer Explorer, select and right-click on one of these layers (not the object inside the layer) and select **Properties**. In the Layer Properties dialog box, in the *Rendering Control* area, clear the **Cast Shadows** option and click **OK**. The setting is changed for other two layers automatically.

12. Render the viewport and note the parking lines and the handicap signs are all visible in the rendering.

13. Save your work as **MyRenderable Spline.max**.

Hint: When Not to Cast Shadows

Surfaces with abrupt elevation changes require shadows to look realistic, because the raised areas of a surface need to cast shadows on themselves or other objects to look believable. To speed up rendering time, do not cast shadows on flat ground surfaces that do not have much relief for shadows. The pavement markings are meant to be completely flush with the pavement, without any appreciable height to make shadows.

Practice B6

Using Script for Converting Materials

Practice Objective

Estimated time for completion: 15 minutes

- Convert the Architectural materials to Arch & Design materials.

The conversion script of mental images, developed by Zap Anderson (http://mentalraytips.blogspot.com),converts Architectural Materials to Arch & Design materials. In this practice you will work with this script to convert the Architectural Materials to Arch & Design. You will also adjust the settings for the Arch & Design materials to achieve a realistic rendering.

1. Exit the Autodesk 3ds Max software, if you have it open.

2. Using Windows Explorer, locate the script file **Macro_mrArchMtlTools.mcr** in the ...\Scripts folder (*C:\Autodesk 3ds Max Fundamentals Practice Files\scripts*). Copy **Macro_mrArchMtlTools.mcr** and paste it into the *scripts* folder in the Autodesk 3ds Max 2017 installation directory. (Normally found in *C:\Program Files\Autodesk\3ds Max 2017\scripts.*)

3. Launch the Autodesk 3ds Max software.

4. Open **Convert_Materials_start.max**.

5. Open the Slate Material Editor and in the Material/Map Browser, in the *Scene Materials* category, note that the three **Finishes** materials are Architectural materials, as shown in Figure B–40.

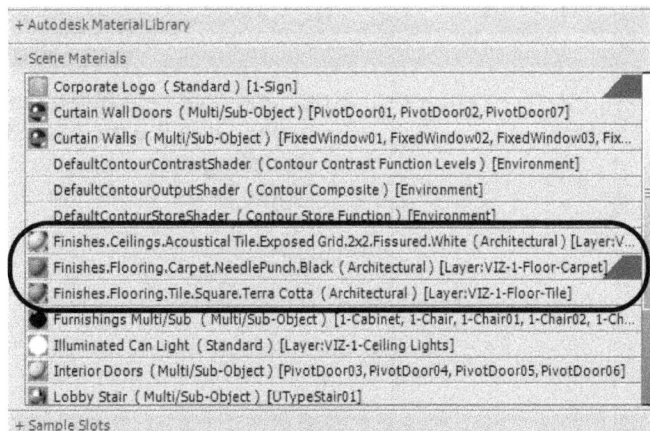

Figure B–40

*In the MAXScript rollout, use **Open Script** to open the script file.*

6. In the Command Panel, click ⚒ (Utilities) and click **MAXScript**.

7. In the MAXScript rollout, click **Run Script** and select **Macro_mrArchMtlTools.mcr** in the Autodesk 3ds Max 2017 installation directory (Program Files). Click **Open**. By running it, you retrieve it into the Autodesk 3ds Max interface.

8. Select **Customize>Customize User Interface**.

9. In the Customize User Interface dialog box, select the *Menus* tab and in the Category drop-down list, select **mental ray**. In the Action list, select **mr Arch & Design Tools**, as shown in Figure B–41.

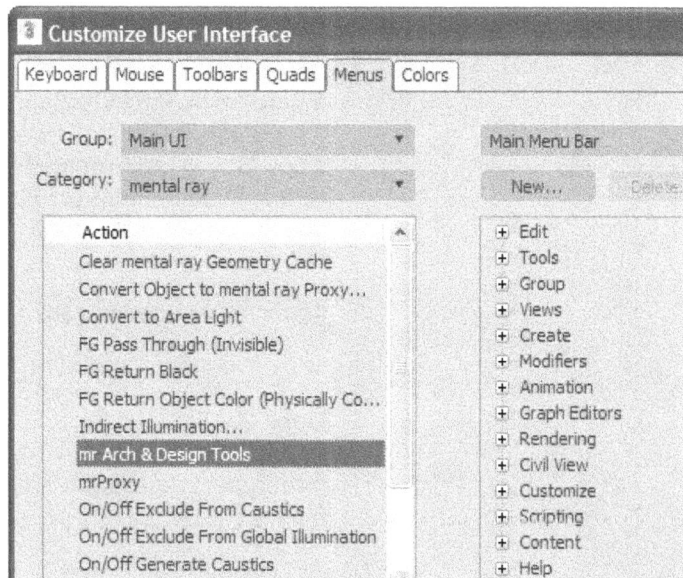

Figure B–41

10. On the right side of the dialog box, expand the **Scripting** menu. Drag the **mr Arch & Design Tools** action onto the **Scripting** menu, placing it after Run Script, as shown in Figure B–42. Close the dialog box.

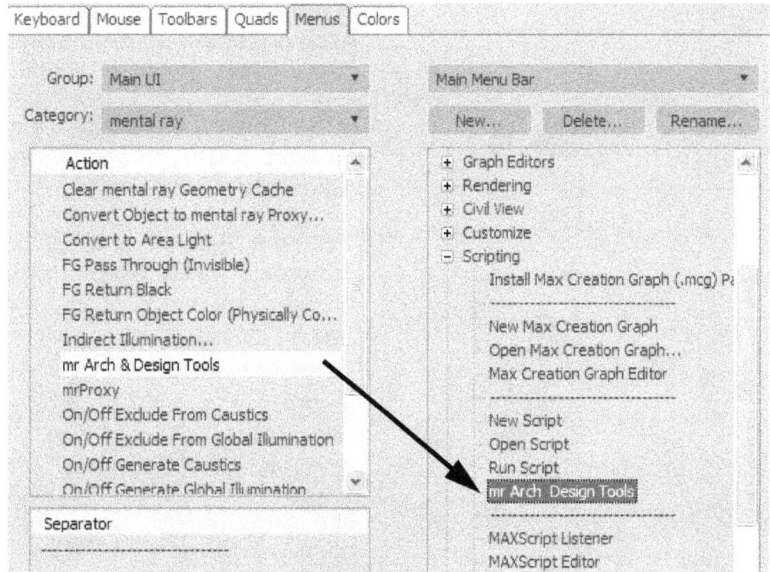

Figure B–42

11. The tool is now available from the **Scripting** menu. Select **Scripting>mr Arch Design Tools**, as shown in Figure B–43. The mrArch&Design Utilities dialog box opens, as shown in Figure B–44.

Figure B–43

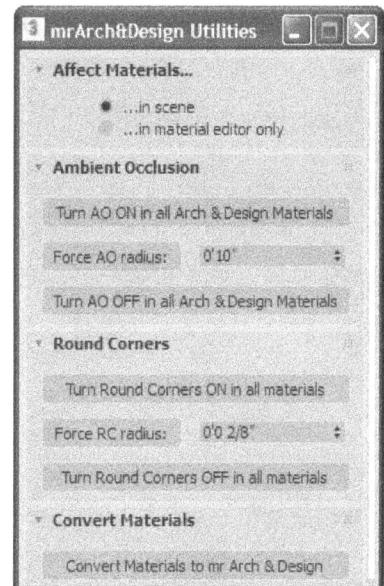

Figure B–44

12. In the Affect Materials rollout, verify that **...in scene** is selected.

13. In the Ambient Occlusion rollout, click **Turn AO ON in all Arch & Design Materials** and **Force AO radius**. This adds detail enhancement to all of the materials.

14. In the Convert Materials rollout, click **Convert Materials to mr Arch & Design** and close the mr Arch&Design Utilities dialog box.

15. Open the Slate Material Editor, and in the Material/Map Browser, in the *Scene Materials* category, note that the Architectural materials (Finishes materials) are now Arch & Design materials, as shown in Figure B–45.

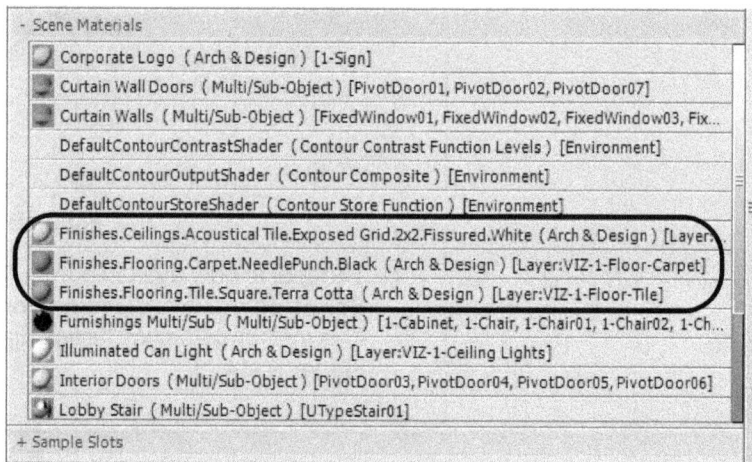

Figure B–45

Adjusting the materials is required after conversion.

16. Render the **Camera01** view, as shown in Figure B–46. Leave the Rendered Frame Window open. You will adjust the materials and lighting.

Figure B–46

Use Scene Explorer,

■ *(Display None) and*

▣ *(Display Shapes).*

17. To toggle on the Self-Illumination for the materials of the overhead lights, select the **Layer:VIZ-1-Ceiling Lights** objects. In the Slate Material Editor, in the *Scene Materials*, double-click the **Illuminated Can Light** material to place it on the *View1* sheet.

18. Open its Parameter Editor (Double-click the title bar heading). In the Self-Illumination (Glow) rollout, select **Self Illumination (Glow)**.

19. Render the **Camera01** view again.

20. In the Slate Material Editor, verify that in the *Luminance* area **Unitless** is selected. Try increasing this value and rendering until the lights in the ceiling are brighter.

21. The desk lamp material is incorrect so you will need to create a new one. In the Slate Material Editor, in the Material/Map Browser, in the *Materials>mental ray* categories, double-click on **Arch & Design** to place it on the *View1* sheet.

22. Double-click on the title bar heading of the new material to open the Parameter Editor, and do the following, as shown in Figure B–47:

    • Rename the material **Desk Lamp**.

    • In the Templates drop-down list, select **Glossy Finish.**

    • Change *Diffuse* color to **Black**.

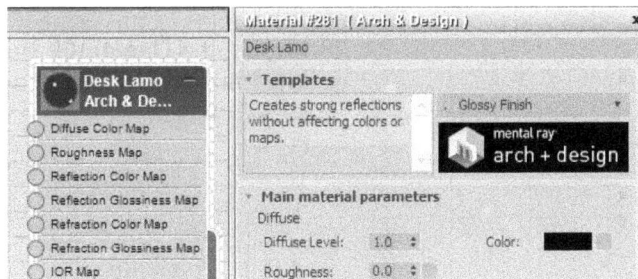

Figure B–47

23. In the viewport, select the desk lamp and in the Slate Material Editor, click ▦ (Assign Material to Selection).

24. Render the **Camera01** view again, as shown in Figure B–48.

Figure B–48

The Arch & Design materials and mrPhotographic exposure control are recommended for use with mental ray to achieve highly realistic results.

25. Open the Environment and Effects dialog box.

(**Rendering>Environment** or [icon] (Environment and Effects) in the Rendered Frame Window).

26. In the Exposure Control rollout, select **mr Photographic Exposure** control, and in the *Exposure* area, select **Exposure Value (EV)** and lower the *EV* value to **11.0**.

27. In the *Image Control* area, adjust the *Highlights (Burn)*, *Midtones*, and *Shadows* values. Increase the *Whitepoint* value to **10000**.

28. Render the **Camera01** view, as shown in Figure B–49. Note that the color is tinted and is a more yellow/sepia color, which looks warmer.

Figure B–49

29. Save your work as **MymrMaterials.max**.

Autodesk 3ds Max Certification Exam Objectives

The following table will help you to locate the exam objectives within the chapters of the *Autodesk® 3ds Max® 2017 (R1): Fundamentals* student guide to help you prepare for the Autodesk 3ds Max Certified Professional exam.

Exam Topic	Exam Objective	Student Guide	Chapter & Section(s)
Animation	Create a path animation and evaluate an object along the path	• Autodesk 3ds Max Fundamentals	• 12.2
	Identify Controller types		
	Identify playback settings	• Autodesk 3ds Max Fundamentals	• 12.1
	Locate the value of keys in the Time Slider	• Autodesk 3ds Max Fundamentals	• 12.1
	Use a Dope Sheet		
Cameras	Differentiate camera types	• Autodesk 3ds Max Fundamentals	• 11.4
	Edit FOV (Field of View)	• Autodesk 3ds Max Fundamentals	• 11.4
Data Management/Int eroperability	Differentiate common file formats and usages	• Autodesk 3ds Max Fundamentals	• 1.1 • 3.1 & 3.2
	Use the import feature to import model data	• Autodesk 3ds Max Fundamentals	• 3.1 & 3.2
Effects	Identify Space Warp types		
	Use atmosphere effects		
	Use particle systems		

Exam Topic	Exam Objective	Student Guide	Chapter & Section(s)
Lighting	Compare Attenuation and Decay	• Autodesk 3ds Max Fundamentals	• 8.2
	Identify parameters for modifying shadows	• Autodesk 3ds Max Fundamentals	• 8.4 • 9.1
	Add a volumetric effect		
Materials/ Shading	Identify Standard materials	• Autodesk 3ds Max Fundamentals	• 6.1, 6.3, & 6.4
	Use the Slate Material Editor	• Autodesk 3ds Max Fundamentals	• 6.2 & 6.5 • 7.2
Rigging	Use Character Studio for Rigging		
	Create simple Bipeds		
	Use the Skin modifier		
Modeling	Differentiate reference coordinate systems	• Autodesk 3ds Max Fundamentals	• 4.4
	Differentiate workflow	• Autodesk 3ds Max Fundamentals	• 1.2
	Identify Clone types	• Autodesk 3ds Max Fundamentals	• 4.5
	Differentiate standard versus extended primitives	• Autodesk 3ds Max Fundamentals	• 4.1
	Identify and use line tool creation methods	• Autodesk 3ds Max Fundamentals	• 5.1
	Identify Vertex types	• Autodesk 3ds Max Fundamentals	• 4.3 • 5.1
	Use object creation and modification workflows	• Autodesk 3ds Max Fundamentals	• 4.3, 4.6 • 5.2 to 5.5, 5.7
	Use polygon modeling tools	• Autodesk 3ds Max Fundamentals	• 4 6
	Use ProBoolean	• Autodesk 3ds Max Fundamentals	• 5.5
Rendering	Differentiate Renderers	• Autodesk 3ds Max Fundamentals	• 10.1 • 11.1
	Identify rendering parameters	• Autodesk 3ds Max Fundamentals	• 10.2 • 11.1 & 11.2
UI/Object Management	Describe and use object transformations	• Autodesk 3ds Max Fundamentals	• 4.2
	Identify Selection Regions and methods	• Autodesk 3ds Max Fundamentals	• 2.3
	Use Viewports	• Autodesk 3ds Max Fundamentals	• 1.8 • 2.1 & 2.2
	Set up and use Scenes	• Autodesk 3ds Max Fundamentals	• 1.8 • 2.4 • 11.3

Index

* 9 7 8 1 9 4 3 1 8 4 3 4 7 *